Under Empire

COLUMBIA STUDIES IN INTERNATIONAL AND GLOBAL HISTORY

COLUMBIA STUDIES IN INTERNATIONAL AND GLOBAL HISTORY
Cemil Aydin, Timothy Nunan, and Dominic Sachsenmaier, Series Editors

This series presents some of the finest and most innovative work coming out of the current landscapes of international and global historical scholarship. Grounded in empirical research, these titles transcend the usual area boundaries and address how history can help us understand contemporary problems, including poverty, inequality, power, political violence, and accountability beyond the nation-state. The series covers processes of flows, exchanges, and entanglements—and moments of blockage, friction, and fracture—not only between "the West" and "the Rest" but also among parts of what has variously been dubbed the "Third World" or the "Global South." Scholarship in international and global history remains indispensable for a better sense of current complex regional and global economic transformations. Such approaches are vital in understanding the making of our present world.

For a complete list of titles, see pages 465–466.

UNDER EMPIRE

Muslim Lives and Loyalties Across the
Indian Ocean World, 1775–1945

MICHAEL FRANCIS LAFFAN

COLUMBIA UNIVERSITY PRESS *NEW YORK*

Columbia University Press
Publishers Since 1893
New York   Chichester, West Sussex
cup.columbia.edu
Copyright © 2022 Columbia University Press
All rights reserved

Library of Congress Cataloging-in-Publication Data
Names: Laffan, Michael Francis, 1969- author.
Title: Under empire: Muslim lives and loyalties across the Indian Ocean world, 1775-1945 / Michael Laffan, Princeton University.
Description: New York: Columbia University Press, [2022] | Series: Columbia Studies in International and Global History | Includes bibliographical references and index.
Identifiers: LCCN 2021058052 (print) | LCCN 2021058053 (ebook) | ISBN 9780231202626 (hardback) | ISBN 9780231202633 (trade paperback) | ISBN 9780231554657 (ebook)
Subjects: LCSH: Muslims—Indian Ocean Region—History. | Muslims—Indian Ocean Region—Ethnic identity. | Muslims—Indian Ocean Region—Social conditions. | Islamic cities and towns—Indian Ocean Region—History. | Imperialism. | Indian Ocean Region—Civilization.
Classification: LCC DS339.3.M87 L34 2022 (print) | LCC DS339.3.M87 (ebook) | DDC 305.6/971054—dc23/eng/20220401
LC record available at https://lccn.loc.gov/2021058052
LC ebook record available at https://lccn.loc.gov/2021058053

Cover design: Chang Jae Lee
Cover image: Irma Stern (1894-1966), *Malay Priest, 1931*. Oil on canvas, 930 × 665 mm. Rupert Art Foundation Collection, Rupert Museum, Stellenbosch, South Africa.

Contents

Acknowledgments   vii

A Note on Transliterations, Spelling, and Dates   xi

Introduction   1

PART ONE: Western Deposits

ONE   From the Spice Islands to the Place of Sadness   25

TWO   Shaping Islam at the Cape of Good Hope   53

THREE   Sanguinary Attacks and Unruly Passions   73

FOUR   Friends Firm and Warm   94

PART TWO: Muslim Mediations

FIVE   Other Malays, Other Exiles   125

SIX   Between Shrinking Kandy and Distant Istanbul   152

SEVEN   For Queen, Country, and Caliph in Africa   178

EIGHT   Seven Pashas for Ceylon   211

CONTENTS

PART THREE: Eastern Returns

NINE   A Caliph for Greater Java   241

TEN   For Arabs, Arabic, and the Community   267

ELEVEN   Pan-Islamism, Nationalism, Pan-Asianism   296

TWELVE   Forgotten Jihad   316

Epilogue   334

Notes   339

Bibliography   419

Index   443

Acknowledgments

This book has taken a long time to come into view, but no place helped sharpen my vision as much as the Stellenbosch Institute for Advanced Studies, where I was lucky enough to join my Princeton colleague Jacob Dlamini and meet a most convivial bunch, including David Attwell, Gabeba Baderoon, Liezebé Lambrechts, Fred Khumala, Louise du Toit, David Simpson, Margaret Ferguson, Nicole Sampson, and Nelson Kasfir, among many others. I am especially grateful to the then-director, Hendrik Geyer, and excellent staff, Marie Mouton, Christoff Pauw, Gudrun Schirge, Nel-Mari Loock, and Leonard Katsokore. My time in South Africa was further enriched by many inside and outside the academy—Shafiq Morton, Yasseen Kippie, Ebrahim Rhoda, Jackie Loos, Salma Arend and family, the Rakiep clan, and the ever-generous Cathy Salter, who made her country feel so familiar in all the best ways. I also want to express my deep appreciation to the intrepid Abdud-Daiyaan or just Daiyaan Petersen, who saved me from some serious errors at the last minute, and who has collected a wealth of documentation that promises to rewrite a lot of history at the Cape, much as Shafiq's connections, determination, and generosity have really helped the story of Tuan Guru come alive for many more South Africans.

While the book crystallized in Stellenbosch, it had many other moments of inspiration and help—some whose significance I only realized very late, as with a typically learned note from my old boss George Miller sent way

ACKNOWLEDGMENTS

back in January 2013. I especially want to thank Catherine Mayeur-Jaoen and members of the École des Hautes Études en Sciences Sociales, in particular Ines Županov, Dana Rappoport, Vanina Bouté, Rémy Madinier, Elsa Clavé, Jérôme Samuel, and Paul Wormser, for conversation and care. London has its charms, too, as well as an incredibly comfortable attic in the home of Nick Duke and Karin Duke-Roedler, who took me in at a very difficult time with such grace and patience. And I could never have learned so much from the British Library without the help of Annabel Gallop—truly the most generous and warm of collaborators and an amazing authority on all things Malay and Jawi. Speaking of collaborators, I thank Andrew Peacock and İsmail Hakkı Kadı for the privilege of seeing their Brill sourcebook in press, which was crucial for chapter 10 and for helping put the late Ottoman Empire onto my conceptual map.

As always, Brill's home of Leiden played a great role for me, and more particularly a Scaliger Fellowship facilitated by Kasper van Ommen and Arnoud Vrolijk. I want to register my ongoing gratitude to the staff of the library in general over the years, as well as to Jan Just Witkam for perhaps the most amazing address in town. It was also great to deepen ties with Tom van den Berge and Marieke Bloembergen, Nira Wickramasinghe, Monique and Hendrik van Sandick, all the staff of the KITLV, and the inestimable Rosemary Robson, not to mention Jaap Plugge and Karla van der Boon in Westzaan, and, more recently, Tom Hoogervorst across the ether. Perhaps the biggest long-term debt, though, and one I can never repay, is to the late Adnan El-Mecky in Utrecht and his brother in Jakarta, Tawfik. Our meetings in Holland and Indonesia may have been brief over the years, but they gave me real glimpses into life beyond the pages of colonial reports and periodicals. I only hope that I have done justice to their father.

A flash visit to Singapore sponsored by Tim Bunnell of the Asia Research Institute was made that much flasher by the fellowship of Oona Paredes, Laavanya Kathiravelu, and Carl Hampel. I was able to present my work in Tokyo and to renew my acquaintance with Midori Kawashima due to the generosity of Masashi Haneda, as well as his colleagues and students. In Colombo I had a warm welcome from John Rogers and the staff of the American Institute for Sri Lankan Studies, not to mention those then led at the National Archives by the heroic Nadeera Rupesinghe, most especially Yurane, Sanjivini, and Nalin. I had a homecoming of sorts at Sydney, when I was a guest of the Southeast Asia Centre, thanks to Michele Ford and her dynamic

ACKNOWLEDGMENTS

corridor, especially Minh Le and Thushara Dibley, and I am further grateful to Glenda Sluga, Adrian Vickers, and Dirk Moses, recently of the University of Carolina at Chapel Hill, where he had the luck of having Cemil Aydin for a colleague. I especially want to thank Cemil, Caelyn Cobb, Susan Pensak, and Monique Briones of Columbia University Press for working so hard to extract this book from my hard drive, substituting chapters on the Cocos Islands for those on the Japanese period, and the anonymous reviewers for their advice and critiques. Emily Shelton has further worked wonders with my reversed references and parenthetic prose, and Paolo Sartori gets a special mention, too, for getting this to the finish and for workshopping the title. I also wish to thank him as editor of the *Journal of the Economic and Social History of the Orient* for permission to reuse most of my article of 2021, which now appears as chapter 12. In that vein, too, I acknowledge the Rupert Museum (represented by Eliz-Marie Schoonbee) for permission to use Irma Stern's striking painting for the cover, the British Library for the arresting visa photograph of Salih bin ʿAbdat, Shafiq Morton once again for his photographs of Tuan Guru's manuscripts, the Parliamentary Library of South Africa for its copy of George Angas's plates of 1848, the Royal Collection Trust for Sydney Hall's sketch of the arrival of the Prince of Wales at Colombo in 1877, and the family of Adnan once more for his childhood photo from Java.[1]

At Princeton I have more friends and colleagues to mention, first and foremost Erika Milam and Michael Gordin, who played such a role in the last years, but so have others, Helmut and Monika Reimitz; Rob Karl and Beth Rabbit; Tom Hare; my bemused chairs Bill Jordan, Keith Wailoo, and now Angela Creager; and new old friends hailing from Pearl Bay like Natasha Wheatley. There are also so many students past and present have taught me a lot—Nurfadzilah Yahaya, Megan Abbas, Saarah Jappie, Lindsey Stephenson, Claire Cooper, Genie Yoo, and Ahmed Almaazmi, among others, and the various crews of HIS 241, 342, and 537. Wangyal Shawa has also done a great job on the maps once again.

Lastly, I want to give thanks to Mum, Dad, my siblings and their families, Faridah, Daniel, and Vanita for their constant encouragement, patience, and love, and Judy for all the lasting memories of so many places—Asian, African, Australian, and European—that have been so interconnected for so long.

A Note on Transliterations, Spelling, and Dates

Dealing with different conventions across imperial and linguistic boundaries, I have opted for a simplified spelling of Indian Ocean vocabularies that unites speakers of Arabic and Malay who once shared the same script. For this reason, as well as general readability, I have dispensed with macrons and subscript dots favored by Arabists while retaining indications of the ʿayn (ʿ) and hamza (ʾ) for technical terms and the names of Arabic speakers. By the same token, for Malay or Indonesian, I have used a single inverted comma where either sound is commonly marked in the middle of a name or word and used more recent spelling for famous individuals—thus, Hasyim Asyʿari. I have also tended to keep Abdallah with a medial *a*, rather than Abdullah, and the double *m* in Muhammad, unless the individual commonly spelled it otherwise, as did Mohamed Hachemi. In some cases, too, I have maintained more localized voweling, though I hope that this may aid recognition and differentiation, as between Abu Bakr Effendi in South Africa, and Sultan Abu Bakar of Johor.

Dealing with Capetonian and Dutch transliteration of such names has led to particular headaches, particularly for those who are now well known, though for less famous people who appear repeatedly I have simplified. Hence Achmat van Bengalen (as he commonly appears in the literature) maintains his nonstandard spelling of Ahmad, but I use Abd al-Haris and Abd al-Hamid rather than Abdol Garies and Abdol Gamiedt, or Abd al-Wahab rather than Abdol Wahab of Cape Town.

A NOTE ON TRANSLITERATIONS, SPELLING, AND DATES

Lastly, when citing books and periodicals that are printed with dates that only appear in the Muslim lunar calendar, I give that stated date and offer a Gregorian calculation as it may not appear in any catalog as such. By contrast, if a source gives both forms, I keep the Gregorian alone.

All errors remain very much my own.

Under Empire

Introduction

The Arab with the Turkish Buttons

On November 9, 1920, Salih bin Salim bin ʿAbdat, a twenty-two-year-old resident of the lush hill town of Buitenzorg, otherwise known as Bogor, in West Java, boarded a train for the hour-and-a-half journey down to Batavia, the stifling capital of the Netherlands East Indies. It is hard to know whether he would have been confident or nervous. There is surely no record of what class of ticket he purchased, and thus whether he sat with other so-called natives or among those identified as "Foreign Orientals," occupying a carriage closer to that of the Europeans in first class with its electric fans. The humidity would have been oppressive, in any case. Sweat beaded on the brows of many passengers soon after the towering volcano Gunung Salak disappeared into the morning haze behind them.

Once at Batavia, with its canals and tramways, we do know that Salih presented himself for an interview with Josiah Crosby (1880–1958), the acting consul general for Great Britain. Already an old hand in Southeast Asia, Crosby had spent many years in Bangkok and had just been seconded from a fresh appointment to Saigon.[1] Salih hoped that Crosby would grant him a visa in order to make a much longer journey across the Indian Ocean via Colombo to Aden, at the opening of the Red Sea. From there he would sail northeast along the South Arabian coast to the port of Mukalla and then continue by camel up to the hinterland oasis corridor of Hadramawt.

Figure 0.1 Salih bin Salim bin ʿAbdat, © The British Library Board, R/20/1412/f184, IOR.

INTRODUCTION

This would not be his first journey to the striking environs of South Arabia, where patches of agriculture and mud brick compounds offered water and a modicum of cool security between desert and towering cliffs. Salih claimed a wife and residence in one such redoubt, the village of Ba Bakar. Lying at the western end of the long wadi, it was controlled from the town of Shibam by a governor appointed by Sultan Sir Ghalib b. ʿAwad al-Quʿayti (r. 1910–1922).[2] Sultan Sir Ghalib was seldom there, though. His whitewashed palace stood on the coast at Mukalla and looked away from Hadramawt toward India, and Hyderabad in particular, whence his family's wealth derived. It was by virtue of the loyal military service of his forebears to a string of fabulously wealthy nizams that they had been able to recreate a small corner of the Raj in the land of their ancestors.[3]

Ghalib's passport had been issued to Salih on August 6, 1918, perhaps soon after the young man's previous arrival in the land also of his paternal ancestors. Salih had been born in Batavia and spent his childhood both there and in Bogor, speaking Malay as well as Arabic. When dressed in the same sort of sarong worn on both sides of the Indian Ocean, he would have been hard to distinguish from many of his Indonesian relatives—Javanese and Malay, among others—but he would still have stuck out to his Arab ones as being Muwallad Jawa: Southeast Asia–born. Salih was surely not wearing a sarong the day he called on the British consul. Based on the photograph he supplied (see fig. 0.1), dressed in a modern white suit topped off by a cocked red fez with a black tassel, Salih was the epitome of the modern young Indies Arab. Such youths and their mentors were oriented to Egypt, at the moment another protectorate of the British empire, with its opportunities, its rhetoric of Muslim equality for Arab and non-Arab alike, and its booming literary and journalistic scene.[4]

Many such trouser-clad young men—and soon a number of skirted women—were graduates of the modernist Irshad School, founded at Batavia in September 1914 by an African teacher, Ahmad Surkati al-Ansari (1875–1943), and bankrolled by the local Dutch-appointed "Captain of the Arabs," ʿUmar Manqush.[5] Although Salih could not have started his schooling at the Irshad School, his father's voluble support for both men and their egalitarian movement would have seen him invest in a suite of modern languages including, at a minimum, Dutch and English, in order to negotiate business both in the Indies and en route to the hallowed homeland, or *watan*, of Hadramawt.

INTRODUCTION

The problem for Salih, however, was that his father shared something with Manqush that no money or clothing could change. As the descendant of a relatively low-born member of the larger Ba Kathir moiety—whose own sultan was landlocked in the central wadi town of Sayʾun—Salih's modern learning and his Indies wealth were seen as a threat to the elite sayyids who claimed descent from the Prophet and who, as inviolable mediators between princes, effectively controlled the valley of Hadramawt and the ways thither. To some sayyids, young Salih was barely more than a "native" (*watani*), and he should have known his place—it being one of social immobility. If they met on the streets of any major town of Java, where Arab men were vastly outnumbered by thousands of women and men of several Asian communities (Javanese, Sundanese, and Chinese, for starters), a reverent greeting and inhaling of the perfumed hand would have been due to the sayyid. Salih could never have hoped to marry one of their sequestered daughters.

Such expectations had caused Surkati, a Sudanese outsider trained in Ottoman Mecca, to establish his own school in a move that was quietly welcomed by some Dutch officials appointed to monitor their Muslim subjects. However, the political relationship between the sayyids and Great Britain had only grown during the Great War, when the Netherlands was neutral, and in opposition to the continuance of Ottoman authority over Arabia. Once the Ottomans entered the war on the side of Germany, many Irshadi Arabs and like-minded Indonesians, as they were starting to call themselves, remained sympathetic to Turkey and its sultan, whom they respected as the modern caliph of Islam. By contrast, two particularly prominent sayyids—Muhammad b. ʿAqil of Singapore and ʿAli b. Shahab of Batavia (a.k.a. Habib ʿAli Menteng)—convinced the British in both cities, and thus Aden, that fez-wearing youths like Salih were not merely Turcophiles, but pro-German enemies of the Union Jack and likely Bolsheviks.[6]

Before his interview with Salih, Crosby perused the ever lengthening list of Arabs supplied by Habib ʿAli, since updated by his visa application:

Saleh bin Salem Bin-Abdat. Born in Batavia. Address, Buitenzorg.

A reckless anti-British preacher. In conversation in the habit of condemning Great Britain and of impressing upon the Arabs (both members and non-members of the Al-Irshad Society) that the principal aim of the Society is to see the Hadramaut free from the grip of Great Britain to whom the country was sold by the Sa[yy]ids.

INTRODUCTION

> Upon being advised by certain Arabs against being to too [sic] reckless in his anti-British preaching, he replies that he has nothing to fear as he feels sure to be able to move about freely with Al-Gaity's passport which he holds. His father Salim bin Awad Bin-Abdat, resident at Buitenzorg, is one of the strongest supporters of the Al-Irshad Society and is an intimate associate of Manggesh [sic: Manqush] while he himself is highly respected by Manggesh despite his age.[7]

In his interview, Salih—whose slightly mismatched eyes subtly mirrored those of the consul—did not present in so hostile a manner. He denied "strenuously" that he was "in any way anti-British." Still, there was the slightly worrying matter of his dress. As Crosby observed, "He happened at the time to be wearing in his coat buttons the device of the star and crescent stamped upon them. I asked him why he chose to exhibit the national Turkish emblem in this manner, whereupon he professed ignorance of the fact that the device in question had any connection with Turkey at all! (The same type of button is largely stocked in the local bazaar and is much in vogue with the native public here. The possibility exists that the sale of it may in itself be a form of pro-Turkish propaganda)."[8]

While hardly likely that such sales were Turkish propaganda, Salih could not have been ignorant of the powerful symbolism of his buttons. If they didn't suggest an allegiance to Turkey, saddled with a suite of occupiers after the 1918 Armistice of Mudros, they most decidedly invoked an Islamic identity in 1920, an increasingly global one that wedded all manner of local struggles against a ubiquitous colonialism: British, Dutch, French, Italian, and American. Few places were free in Africa and Asia. Empire was the rule.

Crosby—who later embarrassed himself as the pro-Japanese consul at Bangkok in 1942—had already expressed his doubts about the biased information that he had been receiving from Bin Shahab. He decided to issue Salih with a visa because of his youth and the hearsay of the charges against him; the young Arab could travel. But he would be watched, and ultimately with reason. In 1924, his paternal kinsmen, ʿUmar and Salih b. ʿUbayd Bin ʿAbdat, would attempt to build a state of their own centered on the tiny fortified town of al-Ghurfa, which lay between Quʿayti Shibam and Kathiri Sayʾun, eventually allied by British agreement in 1937.[9] Starved of resources by the Japanese occupation of Java in 1942, the Bin ʿAbdats held on to their patch of the wadi until 1945, when Great Britain sent troops over from Hyderabad, and as yet more Indian soldiers were being mobilized to help the Dutch regain

INTRODUCTION

control of Java from nationalists who had declared independence two days after Japan's surrender.

* * *

From the extended perspective that will be explored in this book, Salih was lucky in 1920. Hadramawt was not his only option. Many hundreds of youths like him would decide that the land of their birth—almost always the birthplace of their mothers and grandmothers—was the true watan. What was different was that they had more of a choice than many. At the same moment that people like Salih opted to claim an Arabian home, thousands of other descendants from the same complex web of families were accepting that they were now "Cape Malays" or "Ceylon Malays." This all depended on the British Empire that had both claimed the Malay Peninsula, having enfolded their displaced forebears, and inherited a shared history of exilic experience, community formation, and the negotiation of (ethnoreligious) sovereignty, which forms the central theme of this book. As much African and South Asian, their stories are similarly bound up in the long and complex histories of the rival Dutch and British East India Companies and the imperial formations that succeeded them, arrogating the right to hand out passports and assigning unambiguous ethnic categories in place of pan-regional affiliations. One was Arab, but not Malay, or Malay, but not Arab—or distinctly Javanese, Moor, Egyptian, Tamil, or Omani. The list goes on.

Moreover, setting aside their differences of ethnicity, the 1920s were a time of worry about the future of all Muslims on a global stage, when many looked to Egypt and the unraveling Ottoman Empire for religious leadership and moral support. And yet they had not always looked in that direction, just as few people had previously thought to buy crescent and star buttons to demonstrate their politics. As this book will show, the modern caliphal ideal emerged out of a history of partnership with Great Britain that predated the nationalist conflicts of the twentieth century. It was also given form at a time when minority Muslims sought to demonstrate their loyalty to the empire, which succeeded the formations that had displaced their own sovereigns or sent them to the same oceanic spaces that had absorbed countless enslaved people, laborers, and soldiers in an age of global revolution and counterrevolution.

This is a book recounting many journeys—some exilic, many forced, most permanent—taking place at or between moments of global turmoil, and

INTRODUCTION

across a key space being steadily restricted or governed by Western power. It furthermore ponders the moments of outreach for patronage undertaken by the descendants of those who had made these journeys, and who often felt left behind. Like the person of Salih himself, this book joins two peoples in a historic embrace across the Indian Ocean. The first is often invoked with reference to a watan in the interior of modern Yemen that sees seasonal flooding every few years, though its most articulate representatives abroad sometimes came from a wider mix of Arabic-speaking nations, including those of the Nile and the Mediterranean. The other people is much more numerous and yet strangely elusive, reaching back to a dizzying array of tropical islands whose unity is celebrated by the modern Indonesian state even as they are marked by numerous differences.

Their situation is reminiscent of Stuart Hall's evoking of the Caribbean with its lesson for complex identity formation on a global stage.[10] They furthermore share a deep history and character with neighboring Malaysia, which today holds Chinese and Indian minorities in an anxious and not quite postcolonial assemblage.[11] To be sure, former premier Mahathir Mohamed (b. 1925), who rose to prominence in the wake of race riots in the 1960s, drew heavily on the colonial playbook for his *Malay Dilemma* of 1970. Here, the momentarily frustrated politician asserted Malay-as-Muslim primacy to the land by virtue of cultivating the first states and allowing the presence of outsiders, including the Western colonizers whose categorizations inflected who was and was not a true Malay in the first place.[12]

Mahathir himself claims both local and Indian ancestry, and his forebears would have been labeled as mixed outsiders, or Jawi Peranakan, by those same colonizers rather than the term he embraced so fully under their tutelage. To be sure, the spread of Western power in the eighteenth and nineteenth centuries saw the Dutch and the English engage with many such peoples; though observers like the former resident of Penang and lieutenant governor of British Java Thomas Stamford Raffles (1781–1826) posited an Arab genesis for all such seemingly hybrid Muslims of the Indian Ocean.[13] More modern scholars have offered narratives suffused with examples of the specific Hadrami Arab and the general Indian, sometimes pushing their importance and collective consciousness back in time.[14] This book will show, by contrast, how all of this is only a part of a more complex story. It also extends the formal bounds of geography to integrate the adjacent terrain of the Western Cape on the shores of the South Atlantic; the

Ottoman vice-regency of Egypt between the Arabian and Mediterranean Seas; and the farther reaches of Island Southeast Asia, dotted and splayed between the Arafura and South China Seas.

This is to be a succession of what I would call the undercurrents, or perhaps even understories, of Indian Ocean history, if I may do the violence of borrowing an arboreal metaphor for an aquatic space. This is not to say that our understories are all subaltern, or salvagings of unrecorded lives. Some are well known in the successor nations of empire, having unfurled beneath the canopy of high politics; sometimes they are even visible at the global level, as with the Egyptian revolution and British invasion that caused the exile of Ahmad ʿUrabi and his peers, though the ensuing years mattered more to a distinct subsection of the people around him in Ceylon than his fellow Egyptians or Malay watchers. Equally, some of the people I focus on had lives that intersected or overlapped in indirect ways: sharing roots in one land or grafting their experiences onto the boughs of others and ultimately becoming one with them.

Binding Neglected Trajectories of Global History

This book tells the story of successive imperial engagements with Muslims across the Indian Ocean from the 1770s, when Great Britain's East India Company was poised to ransack the territories of its Dutch rival from Cape Town to the Moluccas, to the 1940s, when Japan laid waste to all the claims of Western empire in Southeast Asia, most especially of Great Britain. Laying more emphasis on the framing and possibilities of Muslim lives than internal debates about doctrine and praxis, the operative thesis for much of the first two parts of this book is that an interrelated set of peoples from Southeast Asia, either subject to Dutch authority or to the consequences of Dutch actions in the eighteenth century, were objectified as potentially dangerous and fiercely loyal, both to their faith and their new and ostensibly "milder" British masters, who labeled them as "Malays" into the nineteenth century.

At the same time, I will suggest, by way of evidence from scattered petitions, newspaper articles, and court cases, that some of these same peoples were necessarily strategic in staging loyalty as a means of securing rights—first to religious practice, and ultimately to place. Sometimes that loyalty

INTRODUCTION

was staged though tamed violence, as when Prince Alfred toured the Cape in 1860 and witnessed a performance of the Califa, or *ratib*, in which devotees of Sufi mysticism pierce their bodies with awls to the beat of tambourines. At others it was marshaled against other peoples at the blurring edges of empire, or put to use within it.

Even if it is not performative, I recognize that loyalty is in itself hard to pin down or measure, especially when it is not put to the test, as it was for Maya Jasanoff's cast of individuals who were scattered by the American Revolution.[15] To be sure, loyalty need not even be singular, but concentric—to home, place, and family—and multiple, as Natalie Rothman has shown for the Ottoman and Venetian worlds of the sixteenth century, and as Pieter Judson suggests for the neighboring Habsburgs thereafter, where people of many varying cultures linked themselves to the imperial family.[16]

As we shall see, despite the increasing dominance of the Union Jack, the Indian Ocean was another sort of transimperial space where the odd uniform and foreign decoration hardly went astray. Sometimes it seemed that there was little else that Britain's sometime allies the Ottomans could offer to the peoples of the Indian Ocean arena, though we should not dismiss the rather successful outreach of that empire before the Great War that partnered with a sense either of religious insecurity or grievance in the face of new challenges from Dutch, Siamese, and British expansion.

Hence, from part 2 onward, I try to disentangle the overlapping story of how the modern caliphal image was refracted through cosmopolitan Mecca and Anglo-Ottoman Cairo, becoming part of the package of Islamic patriotism. It was furthermore generated in partnership with Indian, African, and, most especially, Arab fellow Muslims of the Indian Ocean who began engaging with the globalizing modern sphere of papers and journals—produced in Arabic script and with the full knowledge of colonial states. Hereafter, and with the collapse of the Ottoman Empire, Muslim confraternity was reformulated in the 1920s and 1930s as a strand of both distinct nationalism and wider revolutionary Afro-Asian solidarity. This was ultimately tested by Japanese occupation and readied for the postcolonial moment when figures like Nasser joined Sukarno at Bandung in 1955, offering Muslim demographic heft for what would become the Non-Aligned Movement.

Touching as it does on East Africa, Southern India, and Lanka, some of what follows will be familiar to historians of the Indian Ocean. At the same time, much of it will be alien, especially when stretching to encompass what

[9]

is today Eastern Indonesia. And if some histories of the vast waterscape have focused on the Arabian Sea at the expense of the Bay of Bengal, with Janet Abu Lughod and Abdul Sherrif previously eliding Southeast Asian and Chinese histories, there is no escaping the almost universal expansion of Western power that found its feet in the same muddy estuaries and sandy islets on the far side of India.[17] Hence the first and fifth chapters will unfold over the last decades of the eighteenth century, as the moribund Dutch East India Company (Vereenigde Oostindische Compagnie, or VOC)—once enriched by the export and inter-Asian circulation of spices and bulk crops—faded in the face of intense rivalry from the British East India Company (EIC), firmly entrenched in Bengal and abetted by a parliament and king reeling from the loss of the American colonies. The home cities of the VOC and the networks of capital they had supported were fading, too, threatened by domestic calls for reform and the weight of events in Paris. The "Batavian" uprising of 1794 and a supportive invasion orchestrated by France saw the end of the ancien régime in the Netherlands in 1795 and the venerable company founded in 1602.

With Holland in French hands, Prince William V (1748–1806) had sowed confusion in the Indian Ocean territories of the fast-dissolving VOC, which, from exile at Kew, he ordered to submit to British authority. At Cape Town in 1795, the united forces of British crown and company would best an unenthusiastic mix of Batavian loyalists and European mercenaries, followed by similar skirmishing and occupations of remaining Dutch possessions on Malabar and Coromandel, Ceylon, and then the distant Moluccas in 1801.

With the brief Peace of Amiens of 1802, the Dutch would return to the Cape before being forced out yet again in 1806 while the Napoleonic Wars swept Europe. Worse still for Dutch ambitions, the city of Batavia—their Asian capital for nearly two centuries—would fall to the British in 1811, along with surrounding territories. These were handed back in 1816 following the restoration of the Netherlands as an independent state under the House of Orange in 1813. This was all to the chagrin of the temporary master of Java, Raffles, who plotted the transformation of Singapore into a potent rival for a more clearly Netherlandic Indies from 1819, which the smaller island did become after his death through the generous application of Indian convict labor and the passing trade in cotton, opium, and tea.

The formal exchange of Cape and Ceylon was ratified at London in 1824, locking two related Dutch- and Malay-speaking assemblages in place. It also

INTRODUCTION

brought the peninsular city of Malacca into British hands, where local merchants worried that enslaved people might claim freedom under the Union Jack. Such worries were briefly placated. In lieu of Indies slaves and exiles being sent westward by the Dutch, the British crown would oversee the export of military muscle from the Malay Peninsula, as well as indentured Indian bodies to answer the needs of a colonial system. This was particularly so in Eastern and Southern Africa, though only after overseeing the binding of supposedly freed Africans into contracts that differed little from slavery. Malaya would also see ongoing imports, but more often of the criminalized Indian, making Penang an Asian analogue for the white settler colony of New South Wales.

With a new incarnation of British empire taking shape on the southern fringes of EIC domains, commissions of inquiry were established. Judicial officers were sent to Sydney in 1819, then the Cape in 1823, Mauritius in 1827, and Ceylon in 1829, to see how Britannia's dust had settled. Who was convict or slave, and who was free? What form of labor might best be used in the future? What were the habits and laws of the various peoples over whom the crown now held sway? How did Muslims, Hindus, and Buddhists swear to uphold the truth in court? Who might best translate British authority?[18]

At the same time, the Dutch did not have an easy return to Java and the surrounding islands they would annex for the metropolitan purse. After full-scale rebellion on Java led by Prince Dipanagara (1785–1855) from 1825 to 1830, and then as a more clearly Islamic insurrection on West Sumatra abated in 1837, the Netherlands Indies accelerated its own rhizomatic growth. Dutch absorption of Muslim coasts and diverse hinterlands always paled, however, in the face of the insatiable appetite of the EIC. On the subcontinent, raja after raja and sultan after sultan was subdued, forcibly allied, or incorporated to feed the military state, providing yet more push factors to a swell of laborers headed for the crown lands of Southern Africa and Ceylon, and the company ones in lower Burma and Malaya.

While much attention has focused on the final creep of the EIC across the Ganjetic Plain, culminating with the shock of 1857, the earlier annexations of Southern and Western India—snuffing out the kingdoms of Tipu Sultan of Mysore in 1799, the "Polygars" by 1805, and the Maratha Confederacy in 1819—had already fed into wider regional anxieties, including Muslim ones. This was despite the fact that some Muslim rulers, such as the Nawab of Arcot, had been complicit in the spread of the Union Jack. Similarly, the Nizam of

Hyderabad had assisted in the defeat of the French-allied state built by Hyder Ali (1722–1782), whose son Tipu had tried to enlist aid from the Ottoman sultan in the 1790s.[19] Unfortunately for Tipu, as Cemil Aydin also reminds us, the Ottomans had already made an alliance with Great Britain to expel the French army from Egypt, which they succeeded in doing in 1801.[20]

Regardless of Ottoman or Hyderabadi friendship with Great Britain, the subsequent growth of a new regime of taxation on Malabar under the Madras presidency intensified the discontent of a Muslim minority previously used to a measure of self-government when not under direct sultanic rule. Periodic insurrection and resistance ensued. After a series of revolts into the 1840s, some inspired by his father Sayyid ʿAlawi (1752–1845), the thirty-two-year-old Sayyid Fadl (1820–1901) was forced to leave Malabar for the Hijaz in 1852.[21]

Fadl's exile came at a time when the Ottoman Empire was in the process of renewing its authority over its Arabian provinces. These had been under Egyptian military occupation ever since Muhammad ʿAli Pasha (r. 1805–1848) had been tasked with uprooting the Wahhabi-Saudi alliance in 1811. The pasha's men may have gone, but there was great uncertainty in the Hijaz. Given the constant pressure exerted by Great Britain to suppress the slave trade, merchants of the Western Indian Ocean—some close to Fadl—fomented an uprising at Mecca in 1855. This was followed by the massacre of Christian consular staff at Jeddah in 1858, believed by some to be an outgrowth of India's Great Revolt of 1857 that had ended EIC rule and spurred the creation of a fully amalgamated Asian empire under Victoria.

After a season of spectacular revenge in India, some Britons imagined an incipient Muslim conspiracy with the power to carry away their gains across the oceanic arena. Officials at the more easterly stations of Penang, Malacca, and Singapore cast anxious eyes over the largely unfettered ranks of their Indian convicts, especially when they performed costumed marches at Muharram in honor of the family of the Prophet. But despite decades of anxiety about such marches and "Wahhabi" intrigues on the part of British officials in India, north and south, there had been no wider jihad in 1857. There was yet no such term for an explicitly transnational undertaking. Nor yet was there a clear commander for the enterprise. Having worked for the EIC courts as both clerk and munshi, in 1859 the widely regarded Syed Ahmad Khan (1817–1898) was at pains to emphasize the inherent loyalty of Victoria's Muslim subjects in his Urdu pamphlet *Asbab-e-Baghawat-e-Hind* (The

INTRODUCTION

Causes of the Indian Revolt)—though he also complained of the past actions of his employer, their missionary friends, and ignorance on all sides. If the British company had neglected the languages and literatures of its Indian servants, his peers were fools indeed to invest their hopes in an emasculated sultan he painted as a delusional wastrel.[22]

Rather than express support for his Mughal contemporary in 1857, the Ottoman sultan Abdulmecid had publicly backed Great Britain and sent aid to EIC victims in 1858 while his Arab domains would become a site of exile and supplication for some of the veterans of that same revolt.[23] Such even-handed generosity was due to the fact that, after several decades of revolution and military setbacks—including the loss of Greece, their Egyptian viceroy's ambitions in Syria, and the latest extension of Russian claims on their Christian subjects—the Ottomans had strengthened their practical alliance with Great Britain. This had helped Abdulmecid to victory over Russia in the Crimea in 1856 and secured promises from other European states concerning the inviolability of his territory. Still, he would soon lose much of the Caucasus to the tsar in the 1860s, setting in train a demographic shift whereby the Russian Empire would contain more Muslims than the Ottoman at the end of the century.

Effectively the last standing Sunni emperor of a multiethnic and cosmopolitan domain who counted Christians, Jews, and Druze as his subjects, Abdulmecid had nevertheless acquired a most useful partner in Victoria, who had inversely acquired Muslims, Hindus, Buddhists, and Jains. In 1867, she would array his successor, Abdulaziz (r. 1861–1876), with the Order of the Garter. Aydin notes that some Ottomans and British officials even mooted the idea of a marital alliance between Crown Prince Murad and one of Victoria's daughters.[24] While an unlikely proposition for the Muslim-curious but piously Christian Victoria, her elder sons had already met a lot of her Muslim subjects, having been packed off on tours of her Afro-Asian domains, witnessing the spectacle of Sufis on-stage at Cape Town or in the throngs at durbars in India.

The Ottomans may not have sent junior members of their royal household on such tours of the Indian Ocean, whether to Yemen or the domains of their ubiquitous aquatic ally, but they had already recognized the value of waving the flag and of having consular representation, starting with the placement of an honorary consul at Bombay in 1849 and Cape Town in the 1850s. As this book will show, such appointments began to answer long-standing calls for aid from a commander of the faithful, not necessarily to deliver believers from Christian rule, but to guarantee their proper treatment, instruction, and safe passage on the roads to Mecca. In discharging their duties, these appointees were often struck by the role played in the Indian Ocean by the sayyids in whom such hopes were additionally placed. Were not the holy cities of the Hijaz *and* the valleys of Hadramawt Ottoman?

But if imperial collaboration and saintly sanction seemed the rule by midcentury and in an era when steam, cable, and print knitted together the increasingly colonized spaces of the world, the management of the annual hajj and support for the resident scholarly communities of Arabia signaled the cohabitation of past and present. Following journeys powered, as Chris Low reminds us, by modern steam and traditional muscle alike, more and more people heard in the holy cities how their coreligionists were reduced to a servile state and juxtaposed Muslim sovereignty with the supposed freedom of religion and employment proclaimed under Victoria, Willem III, or the French and Russian empires.[25] And many watched with more than passing interest as the Dutch fought to suppress the sultanate of Aceh, in Sumatra, from 1873; as the tsar's coalition continued to gnaw at the Ottoman domains, detaching Romania, Serbia, and Montenegro in the war of 1877–1778; or when France invaded Tunis in 1881.

By then the Anglo-Ottoman alliance was growing decidedly colder. Benjamin Disraeli had thrown the new sultan Abdulhamid II (r. 1876–1909) to Alexander II by remaining neutral in 1877, and in the year when Victoria formally assumed the title of empress of India. Abdulhamid's council accordingly embraced a strategy of Islamic unity to fend off the inroads of Pan-Slavism, drawing significant donations from Indian Muslims and realizing the need to keep London neutral to sustain such contributions. Despite the ongoing efforts of Syed Ahmad Khan to rebut accusations of Muslim infidelity to a Christian ruler, and all while he collected money for Ottoman relief, some colonial servants were anything but neutral.[26] In July 1882, the outgoing governor of Bombay Presidency Sir Richard Temple (1826–1902) described Abdulhamid's strategy as a new "Pan-Islamism or Political Muhammadenism" to be watched carefully in India while Great Britain asserted Victoria's de facto rule of the greatest number of Muslims on the planet.[27]

The British imposition of a protectorate over Egypt, unfolding just as Temple sent his essays to England and done in the name of Abdulhamid's

INTRODUCTION

unpopular viceroy, Tawfiq (r. 1879–1892), guaranteed ready access to the Indian Ocean for the Union Jack thereafter. It also sped the transformation of an Asian empire into an Afro-Asian one. What had been begun from Bombay by such hands as Temple's predecessor, Henry Bartle Frere (1815–1884), would eventually be completed from London.[28] Of course there were still remnant sites of rival colonial power into the 1880s, from Portuguese Mozambique, Diu, Daman, and Goa, to French Pondicherry, and the sprawling Netherlands Indies with its capital Batavia—the "Queen City of the East," as one guidebook termed it.[29] But all these entities were relative supplicants forced to watch as British-owned ships fed the lion's share of raw products to the smokestacks of Manchester and Liverpool.

At the same time, Muslim rulers such as Sultan Barghash of Zanzibar (r. 1870–1888), Nizam Mahbub Ali Khan of Hyderabad (r. 1869–1911), and Abu Bakar of Johor (r. 1862–1893) carved out spaces for themselves in respectful British orbit. Barghash, for instance, had gone from being an exile in Frere's Bombay in the 1860s to the modernizer of his capital's port in the 1870s, to the benefit of British shipping. Similarly tied to Great Britain, Mahbub Ali Khan's ancestors had recruited Arab soldiers from Hadramawt in the wake of the 1819 defeat of the Marathas, and they had proven loyal to Great Britain in 1857. Some veterans and active officers alike returned to Arabia to found pro-British polities such as Qu'ayti Mukalla. It became a protectorate in 1888 at the expense of the Kathiri hinterland, whose similarly Hyderabadi sultan had forged a relationship with the Ottomans in 1867—back when Sultan Abdulaziz had sent steamships of his own to the Indian Ocean.

Not that all Indian Ocean sovereigns felt that they had to choose between Victoria and Abdulhamid. The khedives of Egypt remained Ottoman subjects whose lands hosted Christians and sometimes Anglophile Muslims drawn from the neighboring Levant. Barghash, too, had started a process of engaging with the Ottomans, making the hajj in 1877 and accepting a Mecidiye medal from Abdulhamid—but not his claims to overlordship.[30] Fifteen years on, Abu Bakar of Johor, enriched by the export of the natural rubber that coated the world's first web of submarine cables, would pay his respects to Abdulhamid as commander of the faithful, being similarly awarded the Mecidiye. Stopping at Cairo on the way there, Abu Bakar had also made sure to meet with Muhammad 'Abduh (1849–1905), the spokesman for a new Muslim reformism that embraced modernity and claimed to remove the needless accretions of ages past, from the Sufism of preceding generations to the pretensions of the sayyids, who demanded that their hands and hems be "kissed" by all and sundry. The almost universally colonized Muslims of the world needed reform, ʿAbduh argued, to be enacted at the level of the self and the community before being able to reclaim the reins of self-government.

The followers of thinkers like ʿAbduh and his many Indian analogues (and predecessors) would finally be forced to choose sides between imperial ideologies in the Great War once the Ottoman Shaykh al-Islam declared jihad on behalf of the empire that had joined with Germany in November 1914. This alliance—charted by the ironically named Committee for Union and Progress—and the ensuing defeat had a profound impact on the aspirations of subrulers of the Arabian Peninsula such as Sharif Husayn of Mecca and Sultan Sir Ghalib at Mukalla. Most threw their lot in with London and thus joined Aden, Bombay, and Singapore. The Kathiris of hinterland Hadramawt also turned to Great Britain as they began to look anxiously at the returnees from distant Jawa. While neutral in the war, the Dutch had allowed the growth of what some sayyids saw as an egalitarian incubus. In their view, too many émigrés, once deemed little higher in station than "tribals" in Arabia, had profited under Western empire in the verdant East, and now they were back to change their home societies with the same schools and thought that had been embraced by their "Malay" or "Jawi" cousins. Salih bin ʿAbdat, with his Turkish buttons, was one such potentially threatening product.

The two edges of the Indian Ocean must never have seemed so close, or threatening, bound by an empire without rival that suffocated the last gasps of the Ottoman Empire and yet claimed to be strictly neutral in matters of religion. For their part, the Dutch held on in the East and continued to foster reformist voices that seemed to harmonize with their own rhetoric of confessionalized equality. But if equality seemed fine in principle, growing local calls for independence would be crushed in the 1920s, especially once the Great Depression began to bite everywhere, exacerbating communal divides in Zanzibar, Colombo, and Rangoon, to give but three examples. As Asia edged toward total war in the 1930s, a new constellation of empire taking shape at Tokyo would lay claims to commonality that excluded the Westerner and the Eurasian. Its propagandists, furthermore, looked askance at Arabs as they tried to bend Muslims to their will. And just as Arabs were becoming ever more Asian outsiders on the Swahili coast, they found it harder to mix in in Indonesia unless they became Indonesian, too.

INTRODUCTION

A Much-Churned Sea

I have laid out the synoptic history above as a fragment of the larger account rendered by many before me, and not always with an eye to Islamic interactions. Over the past decades a number of scholars, including K. N. Chauduri, Sanjay Subrahmanyam, and Christopher Bayly, plotted the steady rise of the European commercial empires (Portuguese, Dutch, and British) binding the interlinked shores, dealing with contestation or accommodation by a range of actors.[31] These shores have since been revisited by another generation of writers, with some, such as Elizabeth Lambourn and Sebastian Prange, drawing on the Geniza archives and remnant inscriptions to highlight connectivities in a world "before European hegemony," to use Janet Abu Lughod's felicitous phrase, linking Aden to Mangalore through the trade in spices, metals, and textiles.[32] Whereas the former grouping of scholars have often emphasized the global economic underpinnings of Western hegemony—perhaps none more so than Bayly, who saw the period 1780–1830 as the "axial age" for the making of a modern, almost uniform, world—the newer generation (and the indefatigable Subrahmanyam) have populated Afro-Asian coasts and hinterlands with greater detail about the connected social lives, intercultural engagements, and political aspirations of their diverse peoples.[33]

Much was made possible at new nodal cities by print, as Nile Green reminds us, placing the defenders of what he calls "Customary Islam" alongside the more famous disseminators of reformism such as Syed Ahmad Khan, who hardly envisaged the idea of the independent Muslim state that would be promulgated by Muhammad Iqbal.[34] After all, and as Aydin points out, the empires of the mid-nineteenth century were all multiconfessional, regardless of whether they were ruled by queens or sultans.[35] Similarly erasing modern assumptions of a preconceived sectarian divide into the twentieth century, Sugata Bose has set Tagore's literary offerings alongside narratives of Indian soldiers in Mesopotamia and then those who wedded their struggles to Japanese propaganda.[36] Coming from the southwest of a maritime world expanded by the Portuguese incursions, Isabel Hofmeyr exposes the ambiguities of Gandhi's years in South Africa as a sometime printer and protégé of Gujarati Muslim businessmen, and at a time when Afro-Asian solidarity was an afterthought for Indian nationhood.[37]

On the other hand, over the past decades, and in densely documented and deft connectings of past and present, Ulrike Freitag and Engseng Ho have reoriented discussion of the Hadrami diaspora that preceded the European ones in Africa and Asia and was curiously late to engage with print and imagine a discrete homeland as more than a sacred setting for the visitation of entombed patriarchs.[38] Ho points to the many ways in which Hadrami migrants, almost always male, were adept at marrying into local societies and maintaining their status and distinction across the creolizing generations, sometimes mediating for empire in the outside world and at others times bringing it "home" to resolve their own political crises.[39]

Similarly, when writing with an eye to East Africa, the Gulf, and pivotal Aden from the nineteenth century, Scott Reese, Matthew Hopper, and Fahad Bishara all consider how diasporic communities—Omani, Indian, Swahili, and Somali—have made use of, or even anticipated, empire in staking claims to place, indigeneity, and authority.[40] With circulations of Islamic law now strengthened with British certification and registration, the Western Indian Ocean became a venue for the increased movement of African bodies and products whose generation depended on their labor—such as ivory, dates, pearls, and even spices like cloves, grown on island plantations where once they had been shipped westward from gardens tended by those meeting the demands of the VOC.

This circulatory world had long included the Malabar Coast and Lanka, famous for spices of their own, from cardamom and pepper on the mainland to cinnamon on the island, but less well documented in terms of their histories of labor extraction and any Muslim role in such processes. While Nira Wickramasinghe points to all manner of slaveries on Lanka, including its aftereffects within the island's Tamil-speaking Muslim community, Wilson Chacko Jacob is curiously uninterested in the aforementioned Sayyid Fadl's views of the slave trade, whose interdiction by the Ottoman state was so problematic for merchants living in the Hijaz in the 1850s.[41] After all, Fadl is better known as a lodestone for Southern Indian and Hadrami Muslims in Mecca, and then as an aspirant peacemaker on the borderlands of Hadramawt and Oman in the 1870s. Over the course of two difficult years, he tried to instantiate Ottoman rule at Dhofar, drawing on the finances of Hyderabad, like the Kathiris before him, and anticipating the more successful Quʿaytis afterward.

INTRODUCTION

As Low has pointed out, Arabia was very much on the fringe of Ottoman imperial governance at the time, and its officials worked hard under Abdulhamid to bring its various shaykhs into more conscious alignment with technological projects and a greater focus on facilitating the hajj, thereby linking up with millions of Indian and Jawi pilgrims and resident scholars.[42] There were other patriotic projects to contend with, from that of still Ottoman Egypt, whose advocates such as Mustafa Kamil (1874–1908) also drew Jawi thinkers to Cairo.[43] Yet the khedival city was very much ancillary in importance to the mass of pilgrims—whose experiences of the age of steam have been surveyed by Eric Tagliacozzo.[44] Similarly, the pilgrims now barely touched on Ceylon, once a key site of what Ronit Ricci has inscribed as one of banishment *and* belonging—where once Jawi soldiers became Malay and subject to Anglo-Mohammedan law drafted with Northern Indians in mind.[45]

Such legal requirements, made visible to the colonial eye at moments of marriage and even more so of divorce when questions of inheritance and trust arise, are the grist for Nurfadzilah Yahaya's recent work exploring Arab engagement with colonial jurisdictions and the rare appearance of daughters and wives in courtrooms.[46] It is remarkable that, in light of the long history and historiography sketched above, few scholars have taken up the questions of gender and law in the ways that Yahaya has for Southeast Asia, though the very male bias of migration and even the field into the 1990s explains this to some extent.[47] As Ho found during his fieldwork, the home worlds of most Arabs are opaque to male outsiders—though he learned a little of how women are celebrated and respected. Some wealthy women continued to subsist on rented properties on opposite sides of the ocean; others endowed schools with their passing, with an eye to preserving family as much as Islam.

In this regard, I wish to register my own discomfort. Regardless of whether they are Arab or Malay, Javanese, Indian, or African, these are not my stories. My own family history as the descendant of not always willing migrants from Ireland is closely imbricated with the dispossession of others in Australia and North America. In some cases, I am aware that my interpretation is at variance with accepted narratives and cherished dreams. In making use of colonial sources, I am conscious of the agendas underpinning the collection and storage of information, and the very heavily male biases of the narratives. Where possible I try to bring out what fragments I can of the experiences of the mothers, partners, or daughters of some of those whose lives were documented—though in the early sources I never knowingly came across a peripatetic maternal saint or many women who left more than their names in the court records or newspapers. Still, there is something to be salvaged in such mentions, whether of the manumitted Sarah van Boegis or Keijda van de Kaap in South Africa; Been and Nilofer, who coordinated petitions on behalf of their husbands on Ceylon; the patient Fatima Ba Mahmush whose eldest children were sent to Tunis; or the now forgotten Sitti Noerdjannah, who wrote articles for the propagandist press during the Japanese occupation. This was, and is, their history, too.

Chapter Outline

This book is structured in three parts, each comprising four chapters. Part 1 focuses on the alternating transition from VOC to British rule at the Cape of Good Hope, with special attention to the life and struggles of a Moluccan exile and the Afro-Asian people he inspired—enslaved and free—who were in search of princely leaders to call their own. It also historicizes the British stereotyping of Malays, as they called the Muslims of the Indies and the Cape, seemingly prone to violence and yet ideally tamable for the Union Jack, as they certainly would be on Lanka. Indeed, this book suggests that we cannot fully understand the British categorization of Malay without attention to the more westerly and once Dutch possessions in the Indian Ocean. Part 1 ends with the prospect of another empire, that of the Ottomans, that would prove particularly attractive to these Capetonian Muslims, who yet felt some affinity with the wider Jawi world whence their leaders came.

Part 2 toggles between the Cape and Ceylon and its role as a historic Muslim connector between Southeast Asia and the Middle East, most especially Egypt, occupied in 1882. Having excavated the parallel Lankan history to that of the Cape, it highlights the distant pull of Istanbul as an Islamic metropole, via a heterogenous set of displacements. These are once more like those of the Cape—including exiles, former slaves, and teachers—yet distinct in terms of the island's swiftly becoming the testing ground of Malay military loyalty in a starkly different context. Rather than constituting the leadership of the Muslim community, they were conspicuous by their numerical insignificance and their difference, given that their fellow

INTRODUCTION

Muslim "Moors" emphasized ancestral linkages to Arabia that few of them claimed, preferring to remember their officer forebears as princes of Java and Makassar. Minor as they were, these figures were the loyal base on which to claim a share of religious independence and recognition by the empire.

Having probed both Western extensions of a Malay world, as some now see it, the third and final part of the book brings us back to the wider Jawi homelands in the age of high imperialism to see how the popularization of the Ottoman caliphal ideal played out into World War I, and with very different results depending on which empire held sway. In this part, switching between Dutch Java and British Malaya and tracking individuals like Salih bin ʿAbdat or the Tunisian printer Mohamed Hachemi, we also see how the category of Arabness, once hard to separate from notions of descent from the Prophet, was exploded. At the same time, notions of Jawi identity coalesced anew under Dutch rule as Indonesian-ness—distinct from almost-British Malayness—and all just before the arrival of a new empire that posited the primacy of Asia over Islam, with little thought as to how to manage a world of different traditions.

PART ONE
Western Deposits

ONE

From the Spice Islands to the Place of Sadness

ON APRIL 9, 1780, watchers stationed high on the flanks of Cape Town's Signal Hill caught sight of the *Zeepart*, a vessel of 1150 tons built six years earlier in Amsterdam for the faltering United East India Company (VOC). The *Zeepart* had just made a ten-week journey from the company's capital of Batavia, over 5,180 nautical miles away, on the northwest coast of Java. Once the pride of its Asian portfolio, Batavia was by then infamous for its dank castle and fetid canals, where about a thousand company servants and their often-mixed-race families lived among over two hundred thousand people of other ethnicities. These others were often called "Orientals" (*Oosterlingen*) or "Indians" (*Indianen*) by their overlords, with little distinction, save as to whether they were enslaved or free, the former often being taken from hinterland communities, being shoeless, listless, and much abused—especially if tasked with joining the convicts to dredge the canals, stuff the old walls with unsalable spices, or labor in the shipyards. Most of the free Oosterling majority, by contrast, were Muslims, and their men would gather at mosques outside the western walls on Fridays, given long-standing laws prohibiting the intramural practice of any faith other than the Calvinism of the States General.

Now in Africa and blinking hard after the long sojourn spent largely below deck, one such Oosterling and an all-too-brief denizen of sprawling Batavia would have looked out with great apprehension at the spectacular form of Table Mountain, which loomed over the much smaller whitewashed

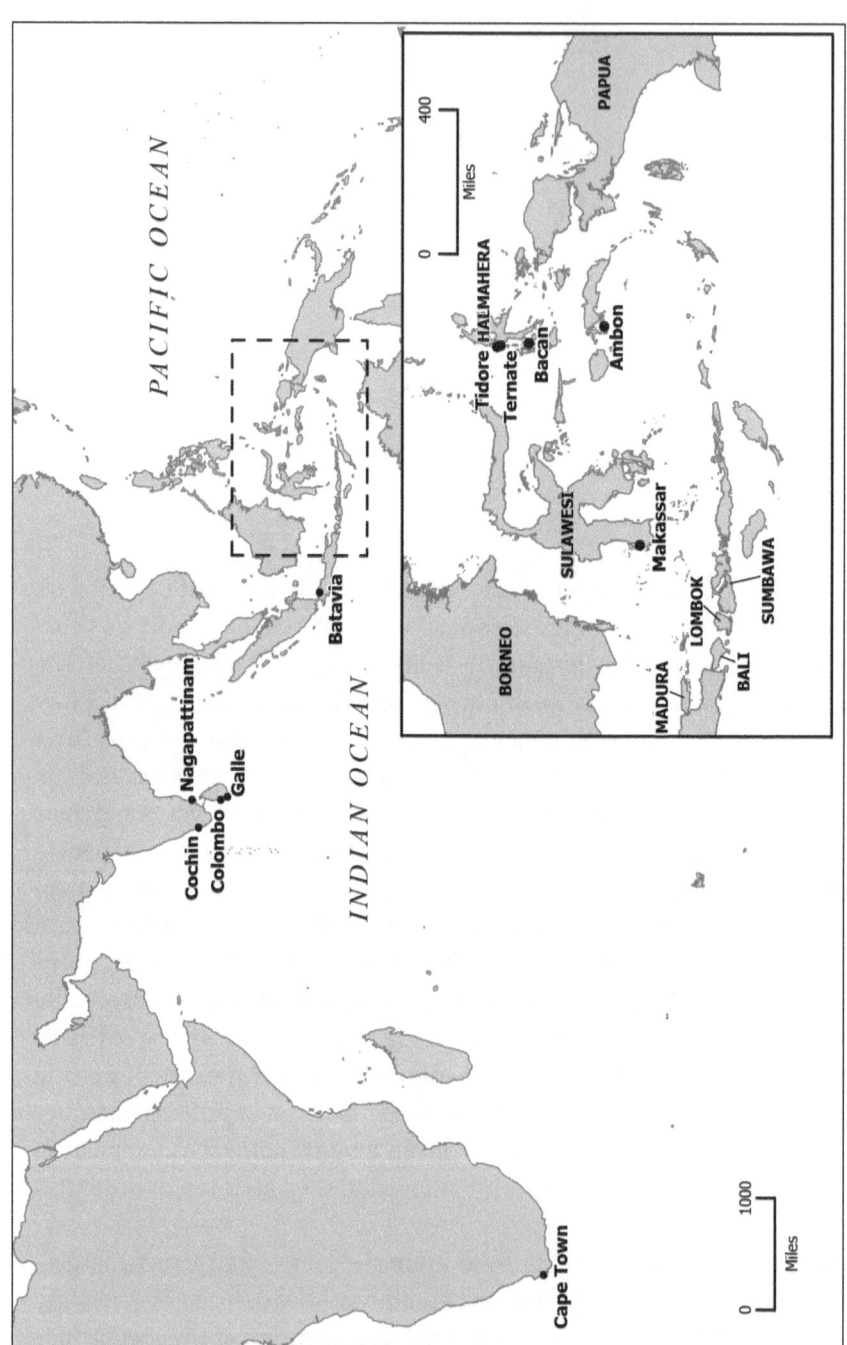

Figure 1.1 VOC possessions, 1780.

and unwalled town counting over seven thousand souls. A middle-aged man of no great height, Abdallah was no slave. He was a political prisoner who had served as both an imam and a senior counselor at the court of Tidore, located by one of the famous—and equally spectacular—clove-bedecked volcanoes of the Spice Islands. Seen from the Cape, though, both Tidore and its neighboring rival Ternate were but tiny dots mapped onto an archipelago that was found another 1,300 nautical miles further east again of distant Batavia.

To be sure, Abdallah was but an exilic speck at the southern tip of Africa, one of four new arrivals from his island home whose immediate fate was not to be placed among the squat buildings beneath Table Mountain, nor yet on one of the nearby farms whose vineyards were gaining the colony a name as something more than a provisioning station for ships entering or leaving the Indian Ocean. Rather, Abdallah would soon be placed aboard a smaller vessel and sent to languish on the flat expanses of Robben Island, some eight miles into the bay. There he would meet numerous other such castaways of the Dutch commercial empire and set to work easing the pain of separation by transcribing a Qur'an from memory. As this chapter will show, the complicated social world of Eastern Indonesia would have its representatives and analogues on the island and at the Cape, with many an exile mixing with people sent from Java, Sulawesi, and the more easterly isles. Equally it will show how Dutch rule in Africa would be disrupted by both an attempted British invasion and the desperate acts of slave and convict alike, in the midst of which Abdallah would sadly pen the pages of a manual of prayer and learning for which he would one day be famous.

Of Tombs, Blessings, and Saintly Precedent Across the Indian Ocean

IN THE NAME OF ALLAH, THE BENEVOLENT, THE MERCIFUL

Praise be to God, Lord of the Worlds, and blessings and peace be upon the noblest of messengers, our lord and master, Muhammad, and upon all his family and friends. O God, I ask You in Your great name, which is that of the Maker of Religion, ... O Lord of [the angels] Gabriel and Michael and Israfil and Azra'il and [the Prophet] Muhammad (God's peace and blessings be upon him), O Shaper of heaven and earth, O Being of majesty and honor, O God, I ask you for forgiveness and preservation from the torture of the grave and its terrors. O Best of the best and Most Generous of the generous, Lord don't leave me alone, for You are the greatest of providers.

[Written down in] the Christian land, the abode of the accursed, the place of sadness.

—From the sayings of the imam Abdallah, son of the imam and qadi Abd al-Salam

This prayer is but one of numerous texts in circulation that are attributed to the now-sainted Abdallah, better known in Malay as Tuan Guru, the "Lord Teacher," buried on the lower slopes of Signal Hill in 1807.[1] His place of interment was already prestigious at the time, being close by the much-visited grave of Sayyid ʿAlawi, or Tuan Said, an Arab exile who preceded him at Robben Island from 1744 to 1761. Both were enclosed by whitewashed stone walls that protected them from grazing animals, accessed of an evening by supplicants who entered a low gate and placed colored candles in niches at their heads in quest of blessings and intercession.

The Malay teacher and the Arab shaykh make a remarkable pairing, with their tombs perched above the city, intertwining oral histories, and the curious visitation of outsiders in search of the picturesque. The first saint, reputedly from Mocha, in Yemen, had his own experience in Java as counselor to the sultan of Mataram, in central Java, before the eruption of the cataclysmic Chinese War in 1741–1743, though that apparently counted less at the Cape over time than the fact of his descent from the Prophet.[2] Meanwhile, Tuan Guru's name is reported today more fully as Abdallah bin Qadi Abd al-Salam— that is, Abdallah, the son of the qadi Abd al-Salam. And he, too, is gaining a reputation by turns as having been the descendant of the Prophet via the long oasis valley of Hadramawt in modern-day Yemen. Indeed, my first encounter with the African legacy of Tuan Guru came at the generous hands of a descendant curious to know whether Tuan Guru and, thus, she and her children were connected to the Prophet. Already convinced of that status and his princely role at Tidore, other relatives—custodians of several of his manuscripts and treasured possessions—have engaged with distant family in the Moluccas reconstructing a genealogy that ties their forefather to the Prophet by way of the conjoined princely and saintly lines of Java and Arabia.[3]

Sayyid or not, Abdallah's words are now said to take their reciters out of depression, to bring strength and honor to those "forced to eat dirt and live in their own faeces," to ease the pain of separation, and even to fill the space left by the need for money or housing. Indeed, they are said to help achieve "anything needed in human and spiritual life."[4] Put another way, the prayer of Tuan Guru offers comfort to a people still dealing with the legacy of slavery under the VOC, the classificatory regimes of the ensuing Batavian and British Empires, the South African Union, the crippling era of apartheid, and ongoing uncertainty under the African National Congress.

Tuan Guru and Sayyid 'Alawi are not the only saints of recourse for Capetonian Muslims. The city and its surrounds are dotted with the tombs of many such exiles from the largely Muslim polities that constituted the archipelagic nation of Indonesia. The most famous of such Capetonian tombs, known by the Malay term *kramat*—which derives from the Arabic plural *karamat* and pays tribute to the "miraculous powers" of their occupants—is even older still. This one is of Shaykh Yusuf of Makassar (d. 1699), a seasoned traveler of the Indian Ocean who was doubly displaced by the Dutch. Originally from the Makassarese port town and capital of Gowa on the island of Sulawesi, Shaykh Yusuf had studied in Arabia and Syria for many years before his return to the archipelago in the 1670s and his capture in West Java a decade later.

Yusuf was first sent to Ceylon with his family and retinue in 1684 as punishment for having led the resistance to Dutch interference in the sultanate of Banten. He and his followers were not entirely isolated there, however, given that the island remained a node of the Indian Ocean Muslim networks. Most likely consigned to Colombo or Galle, Yusuf remained in communication with followers who stopped at the island en route either for the holy places of Arabia or on their way home. From 1688, moreover, he was in close contact with an Indian descendant of the Prophet called Sharif Habibullah. Having departed from Masulipatnam on the Coromandel Coast, Sharif Habibullah had toured Southern Siam and then the sultanates of Jambi and Palembang on Sumatra before going to Cirebon, Java, where he, too, was arrested and banished for fomenting unrest against a VOC client.[5]

Yusuf's Dutch captors were already concerned that he was in regular receipt of parcels on Ceylon, and that with his own epistles he might himself be causing further trouble back in Southeast Asia.[6] Such was never proven, though he clearly continued to write for a Southeast Asian audience in exile and back home, and in Arabic. As Asyumardi Azra observes, Yusuf took the opportunity to focus on pietistic works, including *al-Nafha al-saylaniyya fi al-minha al-rahmaniyya*: "The Ceylonese Scent Concerning the Merciful Gift."[7] As Yusuf made plain, this was a compilation of mystical teachings that he had transcribed to ease the new situation for himself, his peers, and their eager students.[8] Its opening already paints the picture of a small, if hierarchical, community of mystical "seekers" looking for comfort far from home:

> I have called this modest epistle and charming compilation *The Ceylonese Scent Concerning the Merciful Gift* which I have written for our group of followers and our seeker friends, and most especially for the lover of the teller of truth (*al-sadiq*) among the brethren of God [here], the sincere and simple one . . . Abi al-Siddiq Muhammad Sadiq. . . . For as we were in the land of Saylan, [also] known as the Isle of Sarandib, the destination of sinners and abode of the exile (*marma al-maʿasi wa maʾwa al-gharib*) in accordance with God's primordial decrees and eternal will. . . . One of the friends of the group, beloved of this poor and miserable creature who confesses his own ignorance and deficiency, gave permission for a certain one to read with me the Sufi epistles and their like of useful matters concerning religion and the world.[9]

While Yusuf found comfort in contact with his student company and sincere fellow mystics, his despair was laid bare in a letter he wrote to the VOC governors in late 1688 or early 1689. Its gist survives in a Dutch translation:

> To the honorable lord Joannes Camphuys, Governor General, and to the noble lords of the Council of India at Batavia, may God bless them with long lives. . . . Know that I am Sjeech Josuff, now weak and aged, being moreover so old that I am unable to stand up for a long period of time. [Know too that] I am descended from powerful and influential people—who had many under their authority—not to mention being burdened with children and grandchildren. It thus pains me greatly, being in a strange land and in such miserable circumstances, to beg for mercy: [yet] I admit to being guilty and to having done wrong, to my great regret, and I have sworn never to repeat such. Hence, I pray most earnestly for forgiveness, and that, having atoned for my misdeeds, I might return to Batavia. I warrant that such mercy and beneficence on the part of your noble lords shall be rewarded by the Most High, for while I realize that such a boon would

never be pleasurable to you, there is nobody else for me to take recourse to, or under the shadow of whose wings I might seek shelter.[10]

Rather than the mercy of return, Batavia determined in July 1693 that Yusuf was to be kept at a windswept farmstead twenty-four miles from Cape Town, well outside the Islamicate network that threaded the Indian Ocean, though he retained an impressive retinue of nearly fifty followers, family, and the enslaved. As Saarah Jappie reminds us, the decision of 1693 had been made due to pressure from the Mughal governor of Surat, who had by then brought Sharif Habibullah back to India. From Malabar, Habibullah was petitioning for the release of all the learned Muslim prisoners of the Dutch on Ceylon.[11] Thus, it was to Zandvliet, at the Western Cape of South Africa, that Yusuf would be consigned and later die in 1699, leaving behind close to thirty individuals (including fourteen family members) to be repatriated, as well as an unknown number of enslaved people initially ordered to be kept at the Cape for the company's benefit and to defray the expense of the rest.[12]

The Dutch minister François Valentijn (1666–1727), whose first venture in the East began the year after Yusuf's exile began in Ceylon, would reportedly visit Yusuf's African grave in 1705. This was en route for his second tour of the Indies, and in ignorance of the nocturnal exhumation of Yusuf's remains and their return to Sulawesi with most of his surviving followers the previous year.[13] But this is beside the larger point. The dream of a local shepherd later fixed his spiritual presence at what would become a site of Easter visitation in the nineteenth century.[14] Yusuf's grave also emerged as a foundational node in a protective ring that eventually embraced Cape Town, including the resting places of Sayyid ʿAlawi and Tuan Guru. In 1929, the imam of the Lower Chiappini Street Mosque invoked this arc when he claimed that some 260 years beforehand his ancestor Khardi Abdusalam (i.e., Tuan Guru) had told the benighted slaves of his day to be "of good heart," for one day their liberty would be restored, and their descendants would "live within a circle of kramats safe from pestilence, flood and famine."[15] The imam also told the journalist about the exploits of the adjacent Tuan Said, whose grave was a part of the same circle, though it is worth noting the precedence that Tuan Guru's name invoked.[16]

The notion of a protective ring was evidently common currency, as well. After coming across another tomb on the ridge of Signal Hill in 1934, Kathleen Jeffreys (1883–1968) was similarly eager to lay out the stories of the "tombs of the Holy Circle," which she serialized in the *Cape Naturalist*.[17] In doing so she drew freely on the documents to which she had access in her day-to-day work at the Cape Town archives. But if the famous Shaykh Yusuf was relatively well documented, the more recent points of the circle would present a greater challenge. Indeed, the identity of Tuan Guru was particularly opaque to non-Muslims in the 1930s. Jeffreys was apparently ignorant of the *Cape Times* article of 1929 that had placed his arrival around 1770, or perhaps simply that he and "Khardi Abdusalam" were one and the same. Still, there were people to ask. According to an unnamed local authority she interviewed (and whose account she admitted might be questioned):

> It is said that he was the founder of the first mosque in Cape Town, situated in Dorp Street and still in use. He came from the Dutch East Indies, but why he came to the Cape, or when, is shrouded in mystery. . . . Apparently he was a man of education and high moral character. On his arrival here he was shocked to see the low state to which the Moslem faith had sunk among his compatriots, and how neglected were education, culture and religious observance among his people. He set to work to bring about a religious revival. At the time there was no copy of the Koran at the Cape; but fortunately this pious man had memorised the sacred scriptures in his own country, and he set about transcribing them from memory, so that he would be able to impart his knowledge to the rest of the community. Many years after, when copies of the Koran were obtained from Arabia, and compared with his version, it was found that the Guru had made very few errors. Descendants of his are still living at the Cape and one of them is the Imaum (priest) of the Mosque in Dorp Street and the doyen of all the Imaums in Cape Town. He has in his possession the historic copy of the Koran made by his illustrious ancestor.[18]

Actually, the then imam of Dorp Street was not a descendant, and there is some irony to be noted in the fact that Jeffreys had been transcribing documents relating to Tuan Guru for some years, being unaware of his personal name, his association with a 1781 escapee called Abd al-Rauf, and his perceived threat to the local slave order in 1786. Doubtless Jeffreys—who would later reflect on her own Anglo-Indian ancestry—would have been intrigued to hear the stories circulating about Tuan Guru that claimed he was possessed of a call to prayer so strong it could be heard in Simon's Town, twenty-four miles to the south.[19] Others celebrated his playful ability to befuddle the colonizers, as when an arrogant Dutch farmer found his potatoes turned to stones for his high-handed treatment of the aged scholar.[20]

These stories still circulate, due in part to the publications of the Afrikaner folklorist Izak David du Plessis (1900–1981), who had a special interest in the "Malays" by virtue of his studies and a key role in the apartheid state.[21] Tuan Guru also looms large in the remarkable marriage of oral and archival history performed by Achmat Davids (d. 2012) from the 1980s. While Davids rejected the nomenclature of "Cape Malay" in favor of "Cape Muslim," he accepted some of Du Plessis's contentions about Islam in Southeast Asia. Delving among death notices, wills, and court cases once curated by Jeffreys, Davids edged closer to proving just how and when Tuan Guru had transcribed a Qur'an that was a testament to his endurance of the bleakness of Robben Island and then established a community in the new suburb around Dorp Street.

The fruits of these investigations were his seminal studies on the mosques of the Bo-Kaap and the equally famous graveyard that overlooked them, the Tana Baru, updated most recently by Shafiq Morton in his biography of Tuan Guru.[22] Like Morton, Davids had had a good relationship with Tuan Guru's descendants, most notably the tailor Nurul Erefaan Rakiep, who proudly displayed his treasured heirlooms and his most famous juridical manuscript, identified as the *Ma'rifat al-Islam wa-l-iman* (The knowledge of Islam and belief). Nurul Erefaan also showed Davids a manual of spells, a predictive die, and even a sword and shield said to have been used in the battle of Blauwberg in January 1806.[23] Indeed, Nurul Erefaan, who performed the hajj in 1971, was enchanted by his family's origin story and often engaged in conversations at the port with visiting Indonesian sailors. In 1980 the *Argus* ran a feature on him—sword and shield in hand—that he later interleaved with the pages of his own synopsis of his ancestor's life to welcome a delegation of Malaysian visitors in April 1993.[24] Also included with these documents was a statement of Tuan Guru's royal status, vouched for in June 1993 by none other than Sultan Mudaffar Sjah of Ternate (1935–2015).

While one can access this document at the Simon's Town Heritage Museum, run by the redoubtable Aunt Pattie, the objects relating to Tuan Guru's precious physical inheritance, and even a photocopy of his compilation deposited at the South African Library, are now overseen by a trust managed by Nurul Erefaan's sons. Like the trusts established to protect the kramats at Faure and Signal Hill, this ensures that Tuan Guru's legacy is made legible for respectful inquiry. In the early 2000s, both Auwais Rafudin and the late Seraj Hendricks analyzed the mystical and theological aspects of Tuan Guru's writings.[25] Yet there was then less questioning of the temporal framework laid out by Davids, who had accepted that the compendium was written on Robben Island in 1781, and little awareness of the information subsequently brought to light by the visits to Tidore made by Nurul Erefaan's son, Muttaqin Rakiep, who studied in both Mecca and Malaysia.

The few images of the manuscript in public circulation suggest that the compendium may well have been commenced on Robben Island. But even if it was completed there some years thereafter, Morton and I agree that the bulk of the writing was done in circumstances a little different to those once reported.[26] This is not to deny the suffering of Tuan Guru, or the importance and legacy of his mission. Still, it is important to reconcile what information is at hand and to better understand his work and the people around him who accepted his leadership and formed a fully conscious and assertive Muslim community that the British would call "Malay." It is one of struggle, make no mistake, but it is also one of hope and achievement, echoed time and time again. To proceed, however, we must return to the eastern reaches of archipelagic Asia in the 1770s to see where Tuan Guru came from, and why he was set to follow Shaykh Yusuf and Sayyid ʿAlawi to Africa while other close colleagues and family were kept at Batavia or Colombo.

Anglo-Dutch Rivalry and the Fate of the Moluccas

> My Father finished his Letter, charging me never to become an Ally with the Dutch, and to do all in my power to obtain an Alliance with the English.
>
> —PRINCE NUKU OF TIDORE TO ALEXANDER SHORE, 1796

In February 1801, Alexander Dalrymple (1736–1808), the Scots hydrographer and servant of the English East India Company (EIC), completed a memoir concerning the powerful Moluccan prince Kaicili Nuku (ca. 1738–1805).[27] Nuku had been raised on the volcanic island of Tidore, which, with its looming twin of Ternate, lies off the coast of the much larger body of Halmahera in what is today Eastern Indonesia. At the time of Dalrymple's writing, Nuku had bested the forces of the VOC, subsequently dissolved by the French-allied Batavian Republic (1795–1806). By 1797 he claimed mastery over most of the northern Moluccas, a major source of cloves. This victory had come after nearly two decades of conflict and was furthermore sealed by a pragmatic alliance with the British in line with the advice of his late father, the deposed Sultan Gamal al-Din (r. 1757–1778, d. 1783), which had been given in a letter smuggled from exile in Batavia sometime after 1778.

Gamal al-Din had found himself at Batavia together with another former ruler, Muhammad Sah al-Din, the erstwhile sultan of Bacan. Both had been accused of dealing with slave raiders coming from the Sulu Sultanate of what is now the Southern Philippines. Even worse in Dutch eyes at the time, Gamal al-Din had been treating with the British, who in 1773 had founded a base on the island of Balambangan, which lay in Sulu territory.[28] The Dutch had good reason to be suspicious, as the Tidorese had first decided to explore an alliance after receiving a letter from Dalrymple's friend and fellow Scot Thomas Forrest (1729–1802), who had established the Balambangan outpost at Dalrymple's suggestion. But while Nuku claimed that the Malay-speaking Forrest had made an overture to the Tidorese in 1777, Dalrymple deduced that the offer must have come when Forrest was first exploring the islands off New Guinea between 1774 and 1776.[29] It is noteworthy that Forrest did so in a Sulu-built *garay* called the *Tartar* and crewed by a mixture of people whom many Britons would call "Malays." It was furthermore piloted by the trusted Tuan Hajji Ismail, a relative of Muhammad Sah al-Din of Bacan who had previously worked for the Dutch, and who related the Muslim history of the region from its purported conversion by a sharif of Mecca, the holy city where he had himself made the pilgrimage. Certainly he gave great deference to their steersman and "kind of Musulmen priest," whom Forrest only knew as Tuan Imum.[30]

Many of the *Tartar*'s mixed crew of Malays, Visayans, and Lascars were Tuan Hajji Ismail's personal "vassals and slaves," whom he paid directly, and whose "liberties" Forrest learned to ignore.[31] There was no denying that "Ishmael Tuan Hadjee," as Forrest knew him, was a man of authority and charisma. He was extremely well connected throughout all the islands east of Sulawesi, where the interlinked sultans of the Moluccas had extensive and cascading personal networks of vassals who were required to supply tribute in the form of large, rowed vessels known as *kora-kora*—filled with warriors, forest products, and captives.

Although Forrest had passed Tidore on the way to Bacan in late 1774, contact was first initiated with a Ternaten kora-kora under Dutch flag at Dory, near present day Manokwari, on February 1.[32] The following month, Forrest was surprised at Esbe, on the island of Misool, by the arrival of another kora-kora from the Tidorese. After salutes and during their friendly discussions, the Tidorese officers now warned the EIC captain that the Dutch were searching for him. The grateful commander offered customary presents of cloth, flints, and probably compasses (of which he had many for just such a purpose). He also sent the Sultan Gamal al-Din a further "handsome present"—though Forrest later claimed that he had only ever written to formally request that Gamal al-Din's subjects might supply him with food and water.[33] The die was cast. It was also a sign of things to come at Esbe that Forrest met with the "consort" of the banished raja of "Salwatty" (Salawati), a nearby dependent of Tidore's rival Ternate, whom Forrest was told had been tricked and exiled to the Cape of Good Hope in 1770.[34]

Lacking Forrest's original letter to Tidore, one might well wonder what he had offered Gamal al-Din, for there must have been some expectation of reciprocity for their aid. Such confused dealings were a part of local diplomacy when individuals wore many hats as they traveled through islands bound by multiple and cascading sovereignties.[35] If Forrest had represented the British company state on this occasion, this was not always so unambiguously the case. His portrait for the flyleaf of the later *Voyage from Calcutta to the Mergui Archipelago* (1792) shows him in an alternate role, now decorated as an *orang kaya*, or "notable," of the Sumatran sultanate of Aceh, where he had ended his mission in 1776.[36] Beyond this, many EIC officials like Forrest and the country traders who resembled them were in the habit of making offers to such sovereigns that they disingenuously argued were not to be interpreted as alliances. Ten years on, in 1786, Calcutta would offer Tidore a company flag as a token of friendship, though not, it was emphasized, as a symbol of any formal alliance—or not then, anyway.[37] By contrast, some 1800 miles to the west, Forrest's associate Francis Light (1740–1794) would represent himself to the very Malay sultan of Kedah as an emissary of the EIC, obtaining a concession to the island of Penang that same year after implying that it would lead to British protection from the exactions of the vastly more powerful Buddhist rulers of Siam and Burma.[38]

Whereas no such formal alliance with the EIC had been on offer to Nuku's father in 1775, Sultan Gamal al-Din had decided to pursue the possibility. He first sent a ship to look for Forrest near the island of Fao, off Gebe and halfway to New Guinea. Failing to find him there, Gamal al-Din dispatched Hajji Usuf—whose title showed that he had been to Mecca like Forrest's pilot, Hajji Ismail—on a further mission to locate the Scotsman and hand him a letter proposing an alliance with Great Britain. Unluckily, that mission was intercepted by the Dutch, who determined to obtain fresh concessions from their exposed vassals. As Nuku had it, writing from his own Papuan stronghold many years later, the Dutch, with the incriminating letter in hand, had tricked his father and the crown prince into crossing to the rival shores of Ternate:

> The Dutch asked him, wherefore he had written inviting the English to an alliance with him? Showing him the Letter he had delivered in charge with Hadjee Usoffe, he answered it was very true, that they were worn out by the Tyranny of the Dutch, and wished to form an alliance with the English, of whom they had heard all that was good: That when the Dutch proposed first to him, and then to Raja Mooda [the Crown Prince], to let them return on condition that either of them would accept of being Sultan of the little Island of Teedoré alone, and that all the Rajah's of his extensive Domains should pay their Annual Tribute to their Governor at Ternaté; but both my Father and Brother rejected this with Scorn, and preferred to submit to the Sentence passed on them, of banishment and Imprisonment for Life. My Father finished his Letter, charging me never to become an Ally with the Dutch, and to do all in my power to obtain an Alliance with the English.[39]

Beyond the demotion and loss of their numerous Papuan vassals, Gamal al-Din's refusal was based on the principal that making Tidore subservient to Ternate would have upset a calibrated relationship that had existed for centuries.[40] So it was that Gamal al-Din was taken with two of his sons (the Raja Muda Kamal al-Din and his brother Zayn al-Abidin), his four chief advisors (including the future Tuan Guru), and the women of their various families into what Nuku had first imagined was a short period of exile at Batavia, where many would stay until early 1780.[41]

Nuku claimed that he had awaited his father for five years until he received the letter urging him to seek an alliance with Great Britain. Yet it was already apparent at the April 1780 installation of Gamal al-Din's successor, Sultan Patra Alam (r. 1780–1783), that there would be no return from dank Batavia.

A verbose Dutch declaration marking the occasion makes repeated reference to the former ruler of Tidore, his sons, and their advisors, accusing them of betraying the original VOC agreement of 1667 and creating a state of anarchy by working with Sulu pirates, Spaniards, and even Englishmen. Governor-general Reinier de Klerck (r. 1777–1780) therefore decided that they had forfeited all rights to Dutch "friendship," rendering their island an ally no more, but a reduced vassal.[42]

Worse still for Gamal al-Din, the VOC had already decided that his two eldest sons should be sent to Ceylon along with two sons of the sultan of Bacan. According to Ary Huysers, chief scribe to De Klerck, the elder prince—whom the Dutch believed to be behind the entire affair—had begged him to intercede from prison before he was dispatched to Ceylon, though without two of his daughters, who had shared his cell but soon died at Batavia.[43] Similarly, on January 20, 1780, the council had determined that "the Tidorese statesmen"—Gamal al-Din's nephew Qadi Abd al-Rauf, the secretary Nur Iman, our Imam Abdallah, and his scribe Badr al-Din—would be banished to the Cape of Good Hope.[44]

Java, the VOC, and the Politics of Exile

As we saw with the story of Shaykh Yusuf, there was long-standing precedent for such exilic punishment that is arguably worth exploring in more detail to understand the changes occurring in the 1770s and 1780s. Almost from its inception as a provisioning station in 1652, the African outpost of the VOC had received a stream of important figures who had crossed the Dutch or their allies in Asia—from Lanka and the Coromandel Coast, to Sumatra, Sulawesi, Timor, and the Moluccas. In the wars of succession on Java in the early 1700s, and then again as the Chinese emerged as a decisive force on that island during the tumultuous 1730s and 1740s, the sultans of Java would consign or lose family members there, with parents and children often separated between island and cape.

Such figures were a minority among many thousands of slaves and discarded servants of returning officials, whom the Dutch were also generally careful to separate from the exiles. Some, such as Prince Dipanagara of Mataram, exiled in 1723, were placed on farms at a distance from the town, together with their retainers and families. Others were confined to the castle in solitude, as with Cakraningrat IV of Madura, who had hoped to claim the throne of Mataram in the wake of the Chinese War of 1741–1743. Exiled in 1746, he would die in Africa in 1748 while his eldest sons remained on Ceylon.[45]

Another more proximate example to Tuan Guru's time who further impacted his own life was Raden Mas Kareta, sometimes called Bagus Kareta. His family story is perhaps the most extreme intergenerational example of exilic displacement in VOC history. Kareta was born at Batavia in 1733 as the son of another banished prince, Pangeran Arya Mangkunegara of Mataram, with whom he went to Ceylon in exile as an infant that year.[46] After the 1739 death of his father, Kareta was among surviving family members brought to Java in 1741—but only as far as Batavia Castle, where they were kept at VOC convenience and due to the war that had broken out with Pakubuwana II.[47] By 1750, he and at least two fellow returnee brothers were potential candidates for the throne, or deemed a risk to the state. Accused of involvement in a murder, two older brothers were sent back to Ceylon while the younger and apparently more headstrong Kareta was sentenced on March 13, 1750, to be deposited further away again at the Cape, where he arrived with a small retinue in January 1751. After some initial struggles there, he was given a monthly allowance of 5 rixdollars (or 12.5 guilders). Put in the context of the times, this was slightly more than the wage of an able seaman or lance corporal, who both earned 12 guilders per month until the 1780s.[48] Still, it is apparent that the teenaged Kareta avoided the heaviest of punishments, and that he had some resources. He is to be found in the Capetonian archives eight years later in 1759, when he manumitted a slave, Sarah van Boegis, and her young son Amsterdam, with surety supplied by himself and the burgher Frans Lens (d. 1775).[49]

There is the strong likelihood that Sarah was also his partner, known as Sara van Batavia, with whom he borrowed over 210 guilders from another burgher, Joachim Nicolaus van Dessin (d. 1761), perhaps to subsidize her freedom.[50] The Dutch-speaking Kareta was evidently well connected, or as well connected as an exile could be at the Cape. He was reputedly friendly with successive governors Rijk Tulbagh (1699–1771) and Joachim van Plettenberg (1739–1793). Tulbagh even supported Kareta's petitions for financial support in 1756 and a return to Java in 1765, and we can assume that he had some freedom in the town.[51] Kerry Ward has also suggested that Kareta was the host of religious gatherings, such as the celebration of the birth of the

Prophet witnessed at a private home in 1772 by Carl Peter Thunberg (1743-1828). At that time the naturalist Thunberg marked that the "principal man of the congregation" who had accompanied odes of praise with his violin had been "a prince of Java, who had opposed the interests of the Dutch East India Company, and had been brought from his native country to the Cape, where he live[d] at the Company's expense."[52]

Compared to the elite Dipanagara and Kareta, though, if exiles to the Cape were deemed akin to dangerous convicts, or if they broke the conditions of their confinement, they were put on Robben Island in Table Bay, where the environment stood in stark contrast to the fertile mainland. Such was the unenviable—and probably unexpected—fate of Abdallah and his Tidorese peers. Having left a typically humid Batavia on January 26, the four statesmen would have been aghast at the brisk conditions of the new home that they were assigned on April 13. This was four days after the *Zeepart* had anchored, with them being brought ashore two days later. Abdallah later claimed in his first letter to his relatives in the Indies—including his brother, the then-Kapitan Laut of Tidore—that they had then been deposited on the island "after a single day and a night," whereupon they were each given a salary of 5 riyals per month, "without any of us being forced to work doing Company business."[53] It was also in this letter that he spelled out a now forgotten pair of relationships between the exiles, describing the "secretary" Nur Iman as the scion of the Qadi Tun Abd al-Rauf, and the scribe Badr al-Din as having been a preacher (*khatib*) and his very own son (*anakku*).[54]

Robben Island, April 1780

At first glance, and given past practice, Robben Island had probably not been a part of Batavia's plan for the Tidorese. With their open-ended sentences, and the fact that they were each to be sustained by a monthly income—the same amount awarded to Kareta in 1756—these were no common criminals. Yet they were hardly well off. Given slow shifts in VOC pay, Abdallah's salary was now roughly halfway between the monthly income of a ship's boy and a regular sailor.[55] There was little to buy, anyway, beyond what food was brought from the mainland.

It is also clear that the authorities had acted without precise information. Details about the four Tidorese only came with the delayed *Vrouw Everhardina* on April 21, a week after their being put on the island.[56] But this was not a normal year for exiles. The stunning escape of Kareta—who had slipped away to Holland aboard the *Hoolwerf* in March 1778 as "Jan van Ceylon," ultimately to plead his case at Enkhuizen—had led the castle to adopt more stringent policies towards exilic arrivals.[57] Kareta was back by now, too, as Batavia still preferred to see him remain in Africa.[58] This was especially given their ongoing troubles with his influential older brother, Pangeran Mangkunagara (1726–1795). Indeed, Batavia had only just reminded the Capetonians in another letter of late October 1779 that Kareta was to be kept under close supervision lest he encounter any foreign Europeans.[59] Beyond matters of security, there was the simple matter of cost. That year the Capetonian authorities had pleaded straitened finances as a reason for not accepting further exiles on the mainland.[60]

At least it would also seem that the poorly salaried circumstances of the four Tidorese was less harsh than the misery meted out to the enslaved and runaways sent there. Nor yet was it as bad as that given to those earlier deportees, who had sometimes been condemned to life in chains. One such designee had been the descendent of the Prophet and Arab teacher Sayyid ʿAlawi. ʿAlawi had first appeared at Mataram's capital of Kartasura in the company of the repatriated family of the late Ceylonese exile Amangkurat III in 1737, though he seems to have been in Batavia prior to this. Following VOC victory over a Sino-Muslim alliance in 1743, ʿAlawi had been consigned to Robben Island in chains in 1744 before finally being sent to the mainland in 1761, at which time the remaining exiles on the island were formally separated from the general convict population.[61]

On their arrival at their section of Robben Island two decades later, the Tidorese would meet two fellow Moluccans who would have known of ʿAlawi, at least by name. One was "Minte," a Ternaten prince who had been sent to the Cape with four retainers in 1766 and then placed out on the island by March 1767.[62] The other was Eugenius Manoppo, former king of Bolaang and Mongondow, a tributary of Ternate in Northern Sulawesi. Eugenius had been sent to the Cape in 1769 with a monthly allowance of three rixdollars, much as his father, Salomon, had been dispatched there in 1750 for four years.[63] Based on a letter smuggled out from the Cape and sent to Batavia in April 1780, we know that Eugenius, who had been moved onto the island in 1773, was on the mainland at Rondebosch three days after the arrival of the *Zeepart*. The timing suggests that he had boarded the vessel that had conveyed the new arrivals to the island. After complaining of the chilly conditions of his offshore residence, where he lacked even a candle for light, Eugenius referred in closing to having just met four Ternatens and four Tidorese.[64]

While we can be sure of the identity of the Tidorese, the four other men with whom they surely found common cause were more correctly from a Ternaten archipelagic vassal called Sulabesi.[65] These were Mochadien—who bore the title of *salahakan*—and his three sons, Mustahak, Arsalna, and Martabat. They had all been sent from Batavia by order of October 3, 1775, and were now being moved onto the greater security of the island.[66] Indeed, as we shall see from later documents, the Sulabesi foursome are recorded as being from Ternate proper.

Finally, for now, we can also point to several contemporaries of Mochadien who had been sent to the Cape from West Java around the same time. These included the Bantenese notables Raden Bagus Oedien and son Raden Bagus Nassar—both banished by their own king in May 1773—as well as two men sent in July that year bearing the minor Javanese rank of *ngabehi* and seemingly having retinues of their own.[67] Equally, they may also have found common cause with the enigmatic Nur Iman (often called Noriman or Norman), a Bugis-speaking "Mohammedan priest" ordered sent from Banten in 1773, though he was sometimes designated as having a connection to Cirebon—like one of the two ngabehis.[68] Indeed, Cirebon is the reputed birthplace of Imam Abdallah's grandfather, Umar Faruq, who seems to have been among (if not the very heart of) an extended family of Javanese at Tidore who dominated its scribal culture and who had resisted Dutch demands of their sultan in the 1760s.[69]

Such a mixed grouping was quite natural in the archipelago. The revised VOC-Tidorese contract of 1780 had referred to the subjects of Patra Alam as including "Chinese, Ternatens, Bacanese, Javanese, Makassarese, Bugis, Mandarese, Ceramese, Ambonese, Bandanese, those of the coast of Celebes or Borneo, or whatever nation."[70] To be sure, Bugis and Makassarese from Sulawesi had long traded between Java, the Malay Peninsula, and the Moluccas. In the aftermath of the Dutch conquest of Shaykh Yusuf's natal kingdom of Gowa at the end of the 1660s, many Bugis were to be found in Dutch and local service alike. Similarly, students from Sulawesi had circulated between other Indonesian islands for their educations. Shaykh Yusuf had had some of his education in Banten, on Java, and Aceh, on Sumatra. In a petition of 1804, Abdallah would claim not only to be "Descendent of Princes of the Island of Great Java," but that he had been "robed in the priesthood there," which suggests some period of education in Java—perhaps in his grandfather's hometown.[71]

Whether Javanese, Bugis, or Moluccan, it was evident that the Castle of Good Hope hoped that all these exiles of 1780 would be the last such arrivals. The newly arrived Tidorese were doubly unlucky with their timing in this respect. Having heard fresh complaints from the Cape that there was no alternative secure place of banishment for local criminals, and that the island was then brimming with deportees, the Gentlemen Seventeen in Amsterdam advised their colleagues in Batavia in November 1780 that no more should be sent there.[72]

Global War, Relocation, Confusion

Kept apart from the European convicts, who were often disgraced soldiers and sailors, the mixed "Indian" assembly that Abdallah had joined would have spent long days looking across the water to the beckoning town, or at the vessels that anchored off the seal- and penguin-rich shores some seven months of the year. Such ships were seen as a source of anxiety for the castle, given that passing captains replenished their crews with any able-bodied offering they could find, and particularly those with training in the art of war.

War did come to the stumbling VOC in late 1780 as a result both of Dutch support for the fledgling Americans and EIC ambitions for dominance in Indian Ocean waters. In London, the company leadership had already plotted a grand strategy to partner with the Crown and annex Dutch possessions in Asia. In the Indies, where the number of VOC deaths was already far outpacing new arrivals, the British hoped first and foremost to capture the Moluccas and Sulawesi, where they planned to gain the aid of Bugis princes. In Southern India, they intended to woo a Dutch client, Rama Varma VIII of Cochin (d. 1790) on the southwestern Malabar Coast, and to take VOC posts (and men) on the Coromandel Coast in the east. Meanwhile, across the Palk Strait on Lanka, they hoped to strike a deal with the upland ruler of Kandy to take possession of the ports of Trincomalee and Galle. It was also clear that the Cape was key to their ambitions, being, as they would later declare with some frustration, "the Gibraltar of India."[73]

Opposing such ambitions was a grand alliance of France, Holland, and Spain. In April 1781, the Castle of Good Hope—awaiting a relief fleet from France—decided to take the precaution of clearing Robben Island, so recently stuffed with exiles.[74] Whereas an amnesty was offered to any European who would assist in the defense of the port, the Asians were taken away to a secret location.[75] As Abdallah recalled in what appears to have been his first letter home, sent after peace and regular communications were restored in 1784, this was the more northerly Saldanha Bay:

> After a year and a month, the commotion of the Anglo-Dutch War broke out, so a boat of the unbelievers, God curse them, came to take us as well as everyone else on that island. Altogether there were 170 people apart from the sergeant, corporals and soldiers. So, they took us all to the port of the Cape. After that we were divided up, with some taken ashore, some being placed in the [Slave] Lodge, and some going into the Hospital. Some of us remaining aboard were then divided up into other ships. Four [exiles] were in each ship. So Tuan Qadi [Abd al-Rauf], the Secretary [Nur Iman], Martabat [of Sulawesi] and a Javanese were in one ship. I was together with the Khatib and Scribe [Badr al-Din], al-Haku [?], and a Javanese; while the Salahakan Din was with his son, Khatib Arsalna, and the rest in a boat. So it was, [that we] were in six ships, and afterward taken in secret to a port known as Sardan Bay.[76]

Fortunately for the Dutch, the first fleet to arrive at the Cape was the French one. Commanded by Admiral Pierre André de Suffren (1729–1788), it had already skirmished off Cape Verde with a mixed force of EIC and Royal Navy ships under Commodore George Johnstone (1730–1787), who had instructions to take the city. At that time, Johnstone's masters understood Cape Town to be defended by some four hundred regular troops and eight hundred militia.[77] But EIC intelligence was also convinced that they would gain local aid, as the Dutch were said to be terrified of their "Malay" slaves in the case of any land attack.[78]

Johnstone's expedition had been deemed even more critical to London with news of losses to the Spanish at Forrest's old base of Balambangan, already taken by Sulu raiders in 1775, scotching their ambitions in the Moluccas, and then disaster at Pune, India, following Hyder Ali of Mysore's (1722–1782) invasion of Karnatika in March, strengthening his hand over Cochin.

As there was no possibility of dislodging Suffren from the Cape before sailing to India, Johnstone went fishing for prizes in Saldanha Bay, having learned of the presence there of the annual Return Fleet. Johnstone swarmed the bay with his own ships on July 21 and captured four large vessels—the *Dankbaarheid*, *Parel*, *Schoonkop*, and *Hoogcarspel*—making use of the rigging which had been stored aboard a smaller vessel, the *Zon*. A fifth target, the *Middelburg*, was scuttled by its crew following orders evidently ignored by the other captains.[79]

In his later report, Johnstone wrote of having been approached during the battle by a rowboat "filled with people in the eastern garb, making humble signs of submission." These, he said, were "the kings of Ternate and Tidore, with the princes of their respective families, whom the Dutch East India Company had long confined on Isle Robin, with different malefactors."[80] Johnstone thus knew he had two fathers and two sons from the Moluccas in whose interest it would have been to inflate their rank and position. As an unlucky and specific Abdallah later related: "We stayed [at Saldahna] three months. Then 48 English ships came, shooting, and none of the Dutch captains wanted to fight, telling everyone to flee. So we all fled. Tuan Qadi and the Secretary and the Salahakan all waited. And when the English came they joined them. So my son, the khatib and scribe, and I walked 15 days together with the rest, until we were back at Cape Town."[81]

This is not to say that the Eastern "kings" had been recognized and embraced without question. The Dutch convict lists, which belatedly noted that several of the exiles had "gone over" to the English, also mentioned the killing one of their number. More precisely, Hendrik Cloete (1725–1799) referred to three casualties among the "crew" shot by the British during the scuttling of the *Middelburg*. One had been an English prisoner of war, the other a convict, and the third a "Malay priest" from Robben Island.[82] This last man was Mochadien, the Salahakan of Sulabesi, "stadhouder" of the Sultan of Ternate.[83]

Qadi Abd al-Rauf and his son Nur Iman were also recorded as having escaped in postscripts to the same convict roll, but this must have happened well after the dust had settled and the unlucky majority had trudged back to Cape Town, for all eight Tidorese and Ternatens still appeared in summary lists of those present at the Cape well after the attack, including one signed in September 1781 by the secretary to the council, Christian Ludolph Neethling

(1717–1790), if with jumbled sentence dates.[84] By March 1783, though, it was finally clear that all four "Ternatens" were gone, and that the Tidorese had been reduced to the pairing of Imam Abdallah and Badr al-Din.[85]

Not surprisingly, Batavia was annoyed by the great uncertainty as to which Moluccan exile was where, in addition to being worried about the potential ramifications of any regal defections to the British. VOC officials soon noted the discrepancies in the summary reports sent eastward in the aftermath of the attack and demanded more accurate information.[86] In January 1783, the Capetonian authorities had only reported the death of Mochadien and the escape of his three sons.[87] Yet Batavia introduced confusions of their own. On August 19, 1783, they demanded information regarding the escape of a "Balinese" called "Abdul Raoeff."[88] This was Abd al-Rauf of Tidore, who had since been seen with the fleet of Admiral Hughes (1720–1794) when he engaged Suffren off Trincomalee in September 1783. Abd al-Rauf's escape was confirmed in a letter sent from Ceylon by the exiled Raja Muda of Tidore, Kamil al-Din, who knew that his cousin had been conveyed to Madras, where he was supported by the English.[89]

All this information was confirmed by Abdallah in what appears to have been his first letter from Cape Town, though he only learned of it after fate had visited his scribe and son. As he wrote:

> We lived in the Cape for a year and a half, when the power and will of God was visited on the khatib and scribe, who left this transient world for the eternal hereafter in the year 1198, on the nineteenth of Dhu l-Hijja, on a Tuesday morning [November 2, 1784]. Indeed, we belong to God and to Him do we return. I am now alone with Kasiang and Darwis, who are also here, and I also heard news that when the English and the Dutch made peace, the English told the people of the Cape that Tuan Qadi and his son were in Madras, receiving a salary of seven Pagodas a month.[90]

Such details were also confirmed by our original Captain Forrest. At some time in the 1790s, he told Dalrymple that he had once seen a nephew of Gamal al-Din in Madras, much as Dalrymple's researches showed that the governor-general at Calcutta had informed Nuku of the presence there of a relation in December 1785, whom he had promised to receive with kindness and send home.[91] By then, though, the war was over, his usefulness having worn out and perhaps even transformed into a liability.[92]

While Abd al-Rauf probably never made it home, he was at least spared the fate of his deposed sultan and uncle, Gamal al-Din, and that of Bacan, Muhammad Sah al-Din, whom Ari Huysers indicated as having died in misery during his own time at Batavia.[93] And even if Badr al-Din would not survive much longer at the Cape, he and his father appear to have fallen in with someone who could provide them with a modicum of protection and something of a new identity. From March 1783, VOC exile lists often placed their names immediately below that of a man whom I shall suggest was already seen as a patron to people from the Moluccas in Africa.[94] This was "Achmet, Prince of Ternate"—or, more correctly, Ahmad, the Kapitan Laut of Ternate, who had arrived on the *Abbekerk* in January 1776 together with Mochadien and his three sons.[95] Known in Ternate as "Kapitan Laut Mamat," Ahmad had been a contender for that sultanate following the death of his father, the reigning sultan Jalal al-Din, but he had been sidelined in July 1774 by the VOC's appointment of his uncle, Arun Shah. While he had been among the members of the royal house who renewed the VOC contract at the Castle of Ternate on August 16, 1774, he and his followers represented a challenge and were sent to Batavia, where they were all sentenced to transportation on October 3, 1775. Ahmad was also given an allowance of one hundred rixdollars per year to support himself and his small retinue, all payable by Arun Shah.[96]

Perhaps Abdallah gained a share of the largesse of Prince Ahmad in the absence of Mochadien and his sons, though it is clear from a later petition that Ahmad had a growing family of his own to support.[97] The Tidorese were also now housed in the infamous Slave Lodge in central Cape Town, which had been the unhealthy barracks for thousands from Asia and Africa since its inception in 1679, serving as a depot for state labor by day and as a brothel for the soldiers by night. Abdallah and Badr al-Din didn't share the same squalid spaces as the enslaved across the courtyard, being marked apart as "state prisoners," much like another Robben Islander pairing, "Callaga Berboe" (Kalaga Prabhu) and his son "Corradoe Berboe" (Koradu Prabhu), who had been dispatched from Lanka in 1775.[98]

Despite the records describing Corradoe (sometimes Choradoe) as Sinhalese, he and his father were from Kanara, on the west coast of India. Both had been sent to Ceylon and then the Cape at the behest of Rama Varma VIII of Cochin. Their crime, much to the consternation of the client king and the allied Jewish merchant community, had been colluding with two generals in the service of Hyder Ali, who had recently taken control of Mysore.[99] Hyder Ali would annex the coastal town of Trichur soon after, in 1776, and render Cochin his vassal anyway. Indeed, his expanding sultanate threatened many on the Malabar Coast, including the English, especially after his defeat of their allies at Pune and then his alliance with Admiral Suffren. If they had been plotting with Hyder Ali, one wonders if Callaga and Corradoe were themselves Muslims.[100] Muslim or not, few of the Robben Islanders were lucky enough to remain on the mainland after Johnstone's departure. Minte of Ternate and three of his surviving followers were put back on the island by April 1782.[101] By May 1783 they would be joined by the Bantenese Bagus Oedien and Bagus Nassar.[102] Almost all the other exiles would follow in time, though Abdallah was granted more time than most. He would use it.

Writing and Teaching, Returns and Remains

Abdallah, Badr al-Din, and Corradoe would remain in the Slave Lodge until at least August 1783, after which time all three disappear yet again, possibly to join Prince Ahmad at the by-then-dilapidated hospital across the canal, though there is evidence from his later petition to suggest that the Ternaten may have been in a home of his own.[103] To be sure, there is no hint that, like those exiles who lacked an allowance, either Tidorese was forced to work for the VOC. To reiterate: state prisoners like Abdallah were distinct from the dozens of enslaved people or forgotten exiles like Norman, who was occasionally in the lodge, but often tasked with working on the company farm at the Rietvlei or tending cattle in its Cape Town dairy.[104] They were also distinct from several Javanese and Bugis who had preceded them from Robben Island in occupying the cramped rooms as their guards. These included Rajab, Dul Alim, and at least one Surabrata, who were forced to emulate the late Sayyid 'Alawi and serve the fiscal as *caffers*—being the much-debased enforcers of the penal code, with the first two being employed in that capacity from February 1781.[105]

Even if their new circumstances were hardly auspicious, being housed with company slaves and many of their former fellows whose job it was to watch them, Abdallah and Badr al-Din had had some limited amount of freedom after their long walk from Saldanha Bay. While confined in the lodge at night, they would have been free during the day, and it is evident from his own hand that Abdallah began to settle into life in some way, judging by the oldest dates to appear in his famous compendium. Having laid down numerous amuletic texts and supplications, including one against "the evil of oppressors and unbelievers," he turned to transcribe works of elementary belief. These included the theological primer of Abu al-Layth al-Samarqandi (d. 983) and the *Umm al-barahin* of the North African Yusuf al-Sanusi (d. 1490), which he completed on Thursday, 12 Muharram 1196 (December 27, 1781), and thus in the lodge.[106] He also had one of his now famous Qurʾans with him, too (see fig. 1.2). In Cape Town in September 2017, his descendant Muttaqin Rakiep pointed out that this entire compendium is prefaced by a prayer recited at the completion of the recitation or transcription of the holy text.[107]

The existence of his writings implies that Abdallah was ministering to his fellow internees and perhaps some outside the walls. That he transcribed the texts of Samarqandi and Sanusi is moreover suggestive of them requiring elementary training. Still, it is important to remember that if Abdallah was teaching, then he could only have been doing so quietly. This was due

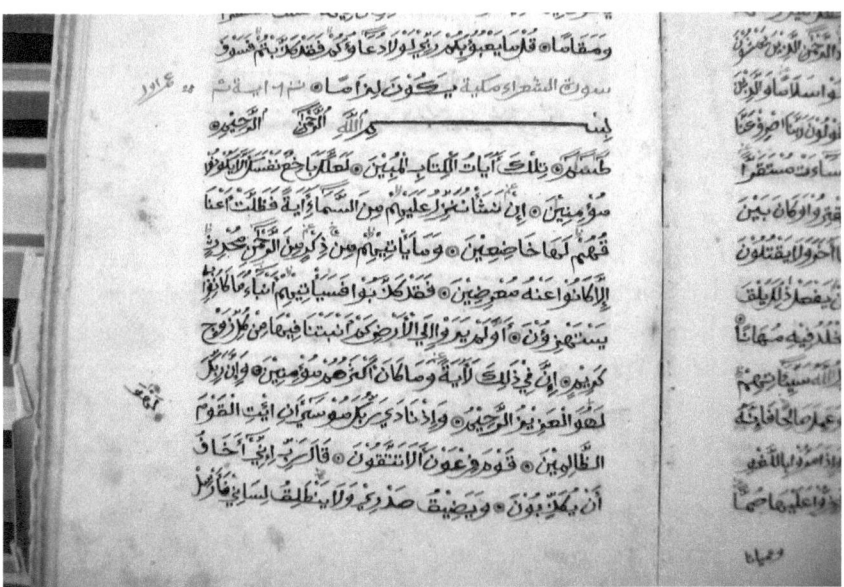

Figure 1.2 A Qurʾan of Tuan Guru, detail of Surat al-Shuʿaraʾ. © Shafiq Morton.

to a long-standing ban on the practice of their faith in the fortified cities under direct VOC authority, although, as we saw from Thunberg, Muslims had been carrying out their ritual observances and even celebrations in the homes of elite exiles for some years. We also know that in 1763 C. L. Neethling had been a member of a commission interviewing the "Mohammedan priest" Sayyid ʿAlawi after the death of his Chinese landlady in July that year.[108] It is quite possible that, during Thunberg's visit to Kareta's *mawlid* festival some nine years later, ʿAlawi had been one of "two priests distinguished by a small conical cap from the rest, who wore handkerchiefs tied round their heads."[109] Thunberg made no mention of ʿAlawi's grave when he visited what was then a Chinese burial ground on Signal Hill, though Anders Sparrman (1748–1820) referred ambiguously to a cemetery for Chinese and "free Malays" in April 1772.[110]

While we cannot ever be sure who the priests of 1772 had been, it is probable that a similarly discrete hierarchy of religious operation was in existence when Abdallah arrived at the lodge nine years on with his Qurʾan and the first pages of what would become his compendium. The community's elite violinist Kareta would remain at the Cape until early 1786, after his appeal for clemency had finally been approved by Sultan Pakubuwana III and affirmed by the VOC, though he was not a wealthy man. For if Kareta had still had money enough to manumit slaves in 1759 (Sarah van Boegis and her son Amsterdam) and again in November 1781 (Jeptha of the Cape), he needed one hundred rixdollars in February 1786 to assist the return to Java.[111]

Kareta would seemingly be in for a rude awakening on Java. Whereas his cousin, Pakubuwana III, had allowed him and his son, now Wirakusuma, to wear their wigs and coats after their arrival at the new royal capital of Surakarta in early 1787, the Crown Prince ordered that both abandon such dress and carry out lives of religious contemplation.[112] Hardly contemplative, the exilically potent Wirakusuma soon became the prince's key religious advisor, boasting a hajji among his personal retinue and being offered a set of *gamelan* instruments by a leading courtier. Indeed, the late Merle Ricklefs pointed to this moment as the first instance of the future Pakubuwana IV (r. 1788–1820) exercising the religious zeal for which he later became famous.[113]

Setting aside the prestige of an exilic return that echoed the acclaim given to the "Ceylonese" arrivals of 1737, those with long memories must have wondered if Wirakusuma had been taught in his youth by Sayyid ʿAlawi, who had been patronized by Kareta's uncle, the Susuhunan's father, Pakubuwana II.

In any case, Wirakusuma's clique worried the Dutch. They soon saw to the Africa-born teacher's arrest in April 1787, confiscating texts in his possession and sending him to Ceylon in July together with his wife, mother, five children, and stepfather.[114] The mention here of a stepfather confirms that Wirakusuma was none other than Amsterdam of the Cape, Kareta's adoptive son by his former slave Sara.

So it was that Kareta, once known as "Jan van Ceylon," would end up back in the middle of the Indian Ocean. Few faces would have been familiar to him after so long an absence. His father's grave in Colombo was empty, with the body having been repatriated to Java much as that of Shaykh Yusuf had been taken back to Sulawesi, with both endowing their former surrounds with vestigial holiness.[115]

Even without Kareta and son, a sacred geography was also emerging in the streets overlooking Cape Town. The lower slopes of Signal Hill offered an especially concentrated site of holiness around the grave of Sayyid ʿAlawi, who was never taken home.[116] To be sure, Abdallah's learning, texts, and status would have marked him out in the absence of the Arab teacher who had also been kept on Robben Island and then housed in the Slave Lodge. But if Abdallah was teaching and, in distinction to his predecessor, actively writing in the city, it remains unclear as to whether he was yet functioning as an imam at public prayer. Although he was always named as an imam by the Dutch, Abdallah only styled himself as such in his colophons from December 1785.[117] At the very least he would have acted in a discrete pastoral capacity for his fellow detainees, echoing Yusuf on Lanka and ʿAlawi before him, who had once been called in to comfort the queen of Mataram during her final illness of 1738 and who is remembered as having looked to the needs of the enslaved in the lodge in the 1760s.[118]

The most telling piece of information pointing to Abdallah's pastoral role remains his compendium, whose surviving elements were largely completed before October 1786. Based on a section within it, this is often identified as the *Maʿrifat al-islam wa-l-iman*, a compilation that is very well known across Southeast Asia. But while Abdallah's compendium contains many of the same core elements of its Jawi namesake (such as the primers of Samarqandi and Sanusi), it was very much his own in terms of the prayers and supplications he interspersed within it, including passages offering reverence for the ʿAlawi sayyids, if not necessarily the late Sayyid ʿAlawi himself.[119]

Abdallah's access to paper for his project, coupled with the fact that he decorated some of his colophons with colored inks, also indicate that he was living beyond the means of most of those consigned to the lodge. The compendium is rightly deemed a major achievement at the Cape and shows Abdallah preparing in some way to build a community in the future. But this is not to claim that he was in any way reveling in his situation among the Christians. Following his completion and translation of Muhammad b. ʿUmar al-Tilimsani's commentary on Sanusi's work, on 11 Rabiʿ I 1200 (January 12, 1786) and some 480 pages into what would ultimately become his magnum opus, he described himself in Arabic as "Abdallah the Tidorese, writing at the Cape, the place of sadness (*makan al-huzn*)."[120] There was no hyperbole in this. Doubtless still grieving for his son, and at a time when more and more newly arrived enslaved people were dying in the lodge, the accursed Christian year 1786 would bring yet more sadness.[121]

TWO

Shaping Islam at the Cape of Good Hope

> The scholars are the heirs of the prophets. The prophets do not bequeath a dinar or a dirham, rather they bequeath knowledge and whosoever takes from them has taken a profuse fortune.
>
> —TILIMSANI, *COMMENTARY ON THE* UMM AL-BARAHIN, CITED BY IMAM ABDALLAH, CAPE TOWN, 1786

BEYOND ABDALLAH'S LONGING for the family he had left behind in Asia, and now for the son he had lost in Africa, 1786 would prove one of the cruelest for the brutalized subjects of the VOC at the Cape. In October, the masters of Batavia Castle would once more decide to send two or three exiles with every homebound ship.[1] Its council did so in ignorance of critical events that were then playing out there that would take Abdallah back to Robben Island. Already stretched thin after war with Great Britain and suffering from testy relations between burghers and the French soldiers filling the town's streets and new hospital, the Castle of Good Hope was determined to enforce control over its enslaved bodies. A major test came when a party of six runaways attacked the farmstead of Sebastiaan Rothman on August 6, killing several members of his family and slaves alike.[2] The group, including Jonas van Batavia, who had been on Robben Island before the clearance of 1781, was soon apprehended and brought to the castle for interrogation, revealing a fake letter of passage forged by a schoolboy. Of greater concern, though, was a lead amulet and a document composed in an opaque language—described as Arabic but in reality Bugis. Both items were connected to Southeast Asian Islamic praxis, and the question was just who among the community could have contrived them. Fingers would be pointed at Noriman, a "priest" sent from West Java in 1773, who was by then residing in the dairy at the edge of the Company's Garden.

Figure 2.1 Jan Brandes (1743–1808), view of Cape Town, 1787. Rijksmuseum, Amsterdam.

However, prior to this determination, Capetonian society would witness a yet greater shock. This was the now infamous running amok of Surabrata, who had been sent to Robben Island from Batavia in October 1772.[3]

Surabrata had been appointed as a caffer in 1786, just as Noriman's son Kahar had been the first of twenty-four such employees listed as working in that thankless capacity in February 1783.[4] Perhaps Kahar and Surabrata had had a hand in dragging Jonas and his accomplices to the cells in late August. By then Surabrata had become utterly despondent about his own situation, learning that his request for clemency and a return to Batavia had been rejected, unlike Kareta's success earlier that year. Ordered to guard a group of French mutineers on September 25, 1786, Surabrata mortally wounded his officer and ranged about in wild anger, killing a young slave who had come to the latter's aid and several other men and then injuring many more before fleeing up the mountain.[5]

A dazed Surabrata would return to the terrified town the next morning, weapons still in hand, whereupon he was violently apprehended. Incoherent at his hastily assembled hearing by virtue of a head wound he had received, Surabrata was arraigned by the acting fiscal Gabriel Exter and quickly ordered to be broken on the wheel, with his hand cut off and his heart pulled from his chest—this being a slightly swifter punishment than that meted out at Batavia, which often saw impalings.[6] Being a sentence intended to instill fear in the other subalterns, this hardly quelled the alarm of the burghers and castle. On October 3, the governing council recommended the removal of all remaining exiles to Batavia.[7] But Batavia was never going to take back the problems that it had exported, nor was the castle of Good Hope ready to give up all its involuntary manpower in one fell swoop. Hence the men destined for Robben Island "by provision" that month in the hope of instruction from Batavia must have been seen as especially influential and dispensable. Certainly the majority were, like Abdallah, identifiable as Muslims.[8]

It may also have been convenient, given the impending destruction of the hospital where some of them may have been living at that time—for they were no longer in the lodge. It is clear from another document that Prince Ahmad was also sent out around this time, and that they would be joined in November by a shaken Noriman, who had refused to confess to assisting Jonas's party, as well as the priestly "Ingabeij van Cheribon" (d. 1817), who was actually a man from Banten whom we shall meet again in 1813.[9]

I would suggest that this was the moment when Robben Island would, in a repeat of what had occurred with the late Sayyid ʿAlawi, become the incubator for the future Muslim elite of the Cape. There was little tolerance for their faith on the mainland at this moment, and new restrictions had been instituted to curtail the movement of slaves at night.[10] Such only engendered greater subaltern rancor in the town so sleepily rendered by the Lutheran minister Jan Brandes (1743–1808) in 1787. When a British fleet bearing the first convicts for Australia passed by in October that year, many of the town's slaves were said to have tacitly approved of Surabrata's actions.[11] Some fifteen years later, John Barrow (1764–1848) would write of a time within recent memory when many had openly told mistresses in their sedan chairs that "by-and-by it will be your turn to carry us."[12]

Back on Robben Island and with evident bitterness, Abdallah put the finishing touches on his compilation, destined for a community he hoped to rejoin. On 14 Rabiʿ II 1201 (February 3, 1787), Abdallah completed a Malay epistle declaring himself in Arabic to be "the wronged imam" (al-imam al-mazlum) in addition to being "the son of the wronged qadi, our master Abd al-Salam," whose designation implies a Sufi vocation. It is further worth noting how explicitly he aligned himself on juridical and theological grounds, adding that he was "Tidorese by country, Shafi'i by juridical school, and an Ash'ari by doctrine."[13]

Given the almost hereditary attribution of being wronged, one wonders what may have befallen his father, and where indeed he had served as qadi. According to his descendants in the Moluccas, Abdallah's father had propagated Islam in the isles to the east of Tidore and is buried on Jilolo. Those same descendants are, moreover, in possession of an undated letter written by Abdallah at the Cape. Addressed to Prince Ahmad in Batavia, it raises all sorts of questions about the possibilities of movement, exilic communication, and his intentions at the time around the time of his return to the mainland in 1791:

> All praise be to the Lord of Worlds, with prayers and peace upon our master Muhammad and all his family and friends. That said, this epistle, in which are mentioned warmest greetings and regards as well as fervent prayers for [your] wellbeing, comes from a sincere heart: that being me, the lowly and mean Imam Abdallah at the land of the Cape, the abode of accursedness. Hopefully that which I have sent, whatever it may be, has arrived with your Excellency Lord Prince Ahmad, Kapitan Laut of Ternate and son of Our Master Sultan al-Muhtaj Jalal al-Din Shah, who resides in comfort in the City of Batavia at Kampung Pejaga[lan]. . . . All that said, I have laid out this white sheet of paper as a substitute for myself in doing obeisance before your lordship, begging your forgiveness. Please don't be annoyed with me given your lordship's request for a book from me, yet I am anxious and worried lest it does not arrive. Still, if Adolf Kandir can be trusted, then forgive me for asking in advance whether Encik Usuf, who is on the island of Lombok, sent a box with two letters. Did they arrive with your lordship or not? Until now I haven't heard any news let alone word [of this]. I ask your lordship most earnestly, that if your lordship has any mercy on me, then your lordship will send a man to [my kin] Abu Qasim or Sha'n with my lord instructing them to come here. I once more ask forgiveness, laying myself at your feet.[14]

Given the unusual spelling and context, there can be no doubt that the mention of Encik Usuf was to the pilgrim-emissary whom Sultan Gamal al-Din had charged with finding Captain Forrest back in 1777. More important, though, the primary addressee was the man who had shared time with

Abdallah at the Cape and on the island before being allowed to leave in 1788. Indeed, November of that year saw Prince Ahmad awaiting passage on the *Voorberg*, petitioning the castle to allow him to take his immediate dependents—consisting of seven local family members, a Bugis companion, and an enslaved Ternaten.[15] With his crown since passed to his uncle, and then a brother, the former Kapitan Laut of Ternate was evidently too risky a proposition for his home island. After arriving in February 1789, he was allowed to reside at Batavia's Kampung Pejagalan, the central part of the Moorish district of Pekojan, just west of the city center, and in easy reach of the VOC authorities behind the western wall that divided them. Still, he was evidently in close contact with the people of the Moluccas and their allies scattered in the islands to the south and east, including at Lombok, where Encik Usuf had moved.

It is also clear from Abdallah's letter that Prince Ahmad had desired a work from him. Was a section of his now famous compendium even intended for Ahmad? To be sure, Abdallah had come to know of his fellow Moluccan's circumstances by the time of his return to the mainland in July 1791, by which time the "Cirebonese" aristocrats, Oedien and Nassar, whom he had known on Robben Island, had also been granted clemency and a return to Java.[16] Had they even taken letters back themselves? With its reference to unacknowledged packages, the above letter was clearly not the only one that Abdallah had written to Ahmad in Batavia. The draft copy of another anxious missive, with several lines crossed out, remains in Cape Town today (see fig. 2.2). Datable to sometime later in 1791 or early 1792, Abdallah addresses his old patron at Kampung Pejagalan in similar ways, and from the same "place of sadness and abode of accursedness" (*makan al-huzn dar al-laʿna*), before asking for news of "the land of our mountain including Tidore and Ternate" (*tanah gunung kita pada antara Tidore dan Ternate*); though he scratched this line out which is suggestive of having received word from Batavia in the interim. And beyond the customary begging of the latter's forgiveness, he evidently intended Prince Ahmad to be the one to give his family news of his own: that he had recently married "the Servant Lady Qaʿida, the daughter of Tata Layar" (*Patik Nyai Qaʾida anak Tata Layar*).[17]

Beyond being esteemed and marriageable, it is furthermore clear that, in the absence of the noble Ahmad and the elite Bantenese, Abdallah had effectively come off Robben Island as leader of the dwindling number of elite exiles, if once more in unclear habitations. Quite unlike the scattered 1780s,

Figure 2.2 Draft letter of Tuan Guru to Prince Ahmad of Ternate, ca. 1791.
© Shafiq Morton.

however, where so many of the enslaved were kept at the back of private homes or harassed between the lodge and since-demolished hospital, that community was beginning to have a locus in a new set of streets above the town. The next time we can extract a hint of Abdallah at the Cape it is by way of his known associates in that very area, given he is said to have been active in a warehouse on Dorp Street, within easy reach of a mountain stream and the grave of Sayyid ʿAlawi.

The warehouse in question had been one of two properties bought in September 1794 by the freedman Coridon of Bengal.[18] Although on first inspection Coridon sounds a match for the Kanaran state prisoner Choradoe, based on the will he submitted together with his wife, Catharina, or "Trijn" van de Kaap, Coridon had been born enslaved on Ceylon. And while he later claimed that he had been manumitted by a certain "Salie," the evidence points back to his own wife in 1783.[19] She had some experience of her own in this regard. In 1766, Catharina—herself the daughter of Grisella, a slave in the lodge—had sought to manumit her two-year-old daughter Saartjie (d. 1847), whom we know she later brought up with Coridon.[20] Catharina furthermore inherited Coridon's property on his death in late 1797, ultimately holding it for Saartjie.[21] This is where Abdallah comes in, so to speak, for it is commonly asserted that by the time of the first British occupation of 1795–1803 he was already sharing space at the warehouse with his wife "Keijda van de Kaap" (namely Lady Qaʻida) and their young son, Abd al-Rakib.[22]

At first glance, the move to Dorp Street seems to have been arranged by Abdallah's dedicated follower Ahmad van Bengalen (ca. 1750–1843), who had married Saartjie and thus become, in the view of Achmat Davids, the senior male of the family that owned the property.[23] Whenever he arrived at Dorp Street, which lay just across today's Buitengracht Street, named for the "external ditch" that marked the edge of the city, Abdallah must surely have been relieved that he was no longer made to suffer the indignities of the lodge well below in the center of the city. This contrasted with three impoverished "Indian princes" he had known on Robben Island—Minte, Eugenius, and Noriman—who were only brought there in October 1795, two months after the British landing in August. It is also worth noting that they would share their corner of the lodge with the more recently exiled Raden Tumenggong Agie, sent from Batavia in 1789, and one Machmet. Said to be a "priest," Machmet (also written Machmut) had been sent from Ceylon in April 1793 and was reputedly born in "Mandura"—that is, Madura, a major island off the east coast of Java that supplied many men-at-arms to the VOC.[24]

We can already sense that, in marrying locally, Abdallah had abandoned any hope of return to the Indies and was fully committed to his new mission of transforming the Cape from the accursed Christian place that it still was for so many. Why else would he seek to be reunited with family members unless he knew them to be accomplished enough to lead the fledgling community in the religion of their forebears? Now that community was opening wider still to take in some of the many enslaved people who had been brought from Madagascar, Mozambique, and Zanzibar, where VOC ships had been turning more frequently since the 1770s and as the castle had tried to staunch the perilous flow of Asian bodies.[25]

The British Interregnum, 1795–1803

Cape Town got its first taste of direct British rule in September 1795. Its new master was General James Henry Craig (1748–1812), acting for the exiled

Stathouder Willem V after the declaration of the Batavian Republic at Amsterdam in January. After a confused landing and a half-hearted battle at Muizenberg in August, Governor Sluysken surrendered, and Craig's soldiers were led into the city by Captain Robert Percival (1765–1826). This was followed by the capture of the entire naval force that the Dutch had assembled to regain their colony, and in Saldanha Bay yet again. Craig was replaced in May 1797 by George Macartney (1737–1806), famous for his unsuccessful mission to the Qing court four years earlier, though Macartney retired in November 1798, to be succeeded by the unpopular Sir George Yonge (1731–1812) and then, from April 1801, by General Francis Dundas (1759–1824).

None of these short-timers necessarily sought to remake local society, even if a new barracks loomed over the parade ground, and the gibbet was used far less ghoulishly. Lady Anne Barnard (1750–1825), a cousin of Alexander Dalrymple whose husband, Andrew Barnard (d. 1807), served as colonial secretary from 1797 to 1802, painted the barracks and redundant impaling post from the roof of the castle around 1800 and made it clear that the English preferred to expedite sentences less spectacularly.[26] Yet, even as the post had become redundant and as numerous individuals petitioned to manumit their slaves, the local regime remained very much intact. Or at least the elements that had stayed loyal to the old Dutch order remained, rather than the "Jacobin" one that John Barrow alleged had caused those enslaved to mistakenly believe that their freedom was nigh.[27]

Tuan Guru's community, in sore need of space and comprised of many such unfree bodies, evidently sensed an opportunity. Long-standing VOC regulations limiting the freedom of religion were now in abeyance, and there was a chance to have their house of worship recognized. Some three decades later, Achmat van Bengalen would assert that this right had been accorded to what was then his Dorp Street address in the form of a deed, though he was unclear as to whether the physical evidence came from the time of General Craig or the later General Janssens, who oversaw the return of the Cape to Dutch hands in March 1803.[28] Indeed, despite hints of just such a document having been sent to London in 1828, the first hard evidence both of any British approval of a mosque and of the conservative local forces arrayed against it survives in the form of a petition forwarded to Governor Yonge on January 31, 1800. On this occasion, another of Tuan Guru's men—a freed slave turned wealthy fisherman called Frans van Bengalen—pitched the matter.²⁹ As Frans put it, this was a question of social improvement and the making of better subjects (rather like himself):

> The aforesaid humble Petitioners beg permission to approach your Excellency with all possible humility, and to represent to your Excellency that they labour under the greatest distress of mind by having no place of worship in which they may pay their adoration to God, conformably to the principles of their religion. They assure themselves your Excellency will admit nothing conduces so much to the good order of Society as a due observance of religious worship, and though they trust it will be allowed them that few enormities have been committed by the persons subject to your Majesty's Government who profess their faith, yet they believe their being by your Excellency's paternal indulgence furnished with the means of regular worship, that the manners and morality of their brethren will be greatly improved, and that they will thereby become more valuable members of society. They therefore implore your Excellency to grant then a little spot of unoccupied land of the dimensions of one hundred and fifty squarereoods whereon to erect at their own expense a small temple to be dedicated to the worship of Almighty God. Your Excellency knows that the form of the religion requires frequent ablutions from whence it is indispensable that their mosque should be contiguous to water. A suitable spot is situated at some distance above the premises of General Vanderleur, and they humbly conceive there will be no objections to their little temple being there placed. They throw themselves at your Excellency's feet, and beseech you to their humble and pious solicitations, and if your Excellency is pleased to give a favourable ear to their Petition they will by their conduct demonstrate they are not unworthy of your Excellency's indulgence and protection.³⁰

Frans was a wise choice of partner who was already making a name for himself. Abdallah regarded him highly. The draft of a letter later written in 1802 to Abd al-Shukur on behalf of both men and Keijda's father Tata Layar refers to Frans with the honorific *Enci'* and mentions his ownership of a boat (*peluciam*), as well as their sending gifts to Abd al-Shukur's family, among others, with Abdallah offering a bottle of rosewater and Frans a tin of honey.³¹ According to the English migrant Samuel Hudson, who knew him as "Old Frank," Frans was not merely a fisherman, but the provender of choice to the British navy on personal terms with Admiral Roger Curtis. Governor Yonge, who had arrived with Curtis in 1799, was favorably inclined to the petition. The original index of his outgoing correspondence records it as having been approved, and that he had Andrew Barnard forward it to the Burgher Senate on February 1, 1800, expressing his desire that a commission of two men be formed to look into the possibility.³² One was accordingly established that day, and on February 15 Hudson reflected that Cape Town would soon see "a temple dedicated to Allah and the Mahometan religion openly professed."³³

No such recommendation was made. Hudson later recalled that "such was the selfish prejudices of the old inhabitants" that Frans's "good intention was overruled."³⁴ Lutherans and Anglicans were strangers enough to the patricians of the castle, whose senate included such slave-holders as Abraham Fleck, H. A. Truter, and Gerhard L. Cloete (b. 1760), the owner of the land on which Shaykh Yusuf's kramat lay, not to mention Jacob G. van Rheenen (1749–1827) and Oloff M. Bergh Jr. (1763–1835), whose younger brothers had dealings with Tuan Guru.

This did not mean that Muslims feared to practice openly. Rather than confining their activities to the homes of certain Free Blacks, as Thunberg had observed in 1772, Tuan Guru's people now made their Friday prayers very publicly above Chiappini Street, using a nearby mountain stream for ablutions. Such an action was not lost on John Barrow. Writing from London after the return of the Cape to Dutch hands, Barrow recalled how, "being refused a church," the Muslims had been performing "their public service in the stone quarries at the head of the town."³⁵

For day-to-day usage the Muslims continued their activities at the Dorp Street address, known appropriately today as the Auwal Masjid (First Mosque). Here Tuan Guru continued to make use of Samarqandi's primer and Sanusi's *Umm al-barahin* to inculcate in dozens of students a proper understanding of the "qualities" (*sifat*) inherent in God and the relationship of the believer to Him. At other times, he offered his supplicants healing, drawing from his knowledge of the *Bustan al-salatin* of Nur al-Din al-Raniri (d. 1658), who had inspired a young Shaykh Yusuf to travel from Makassar to Aceh in the 1640s. He also had passages on divination to be accessed using an inscribed die that would lead the supplicant to key passages of the Qurʾan. He was, in short, their imam and leader in all things not regulated by the penal code.

If Tuan Guru was the acknowledged master teacher of the Muslims, he was hardly alone among a range of people that Arab speakers and many

Southeast Asians called "Jawa" in general. Matching some of the names mentioned in histories of the Auwal Masjid, including those encountered as petitioners during the British interregnum, Abdallah clearly had plenty of local assistance of a wider Jawi nature. Devoted servants included two men deemed worthy of succeeding him who had come off Robben Island as servants of the fiscal in 1781. They would moreover have resided in the lodge close to Prince Ahmad and Imam Abdallah after his walk from Saldanha Bay, given their employment as caffers—namely, the Buginese Rajab (d. 1805) and one Abd al-Alim (or Dul Alim, d. 1811), who seems to have come from Java.[36] As we shall see, another occupant of that unhappy rank, Sakkur van Java (Abd al-Shukur), was the likely recipient of letters from Abdallah after his apparent return to Batavia in 1802.[37]

Also remembered today are the aforementioned Frans van Bengalen, Abd al-Wasi (Abdol Wassie a.k.a. Galant van Balie), and Abd al-Malik, who do not appear to have been exiles or guards. It is clear that Frans was particularly influential before his departure from the colony in 1811, even being involved in the establishment of a second mosque in 1807. By the 1810s, moreover, Abd al-Wasi and Abd al-Malik would oversee congregations (and enslaved people) of their own. The latter, sometimes known as Abdol Malik Betawi, was additionally known as a Malay doctor in the Cape almanacs, which is suggestive of his having imbibed some of Tuan Guru's healing techniques. He now lies buried on the slopes of Table Mountain, where he is anachronistically remembered as a master of the Qadiri Sufi order who had accompanied Shaykh Yusuf in the seventeenth century. We may well wonder about the weight to give to Tuan Guru's affiliation to any form of Sufi order. If his manuals include litanies identified with those promulgated by the Qadiri tradition, there are also prayers to be associated with the 'Alawiyya, which lends weight to the idea of him feeling some sort of attraction to the presence of Sayyid 'Alawi.[38]

For many years, and certainly since the visits of curious Westerners to the Auwal Masjid in the 1920s, it seemed that the most important person to link himself to Tuan Guru and the Dorp Street congregation was his housemate Achmat van Bengalen. By his own account of 1825, Achmat had arrived at the Cape from Chinsurah around 1785 and was of "Malay" origin, which may well hint at his father having been a soldier or servant in the Dutch garrison in India.[39] However he arrived, whether as an exile or even (as was later asserted) a slave, Achmat van Bengalen was well placed in the emerging hierarchy and able to defend that place when challenged. He was married to Saartjie, who was destined to take over much of the Dorp Street property from her mother in 1809.[40] Hence, even if his name was never on any deeds, given that under the British free Blacks were no longer allowed to own property without permission of the governor, Achmat was Tuan Guru's shadow landlord much as his spiritual master avoided the colonial limelight.

There was practical sense in this. If we are to believe the observations of Robert Semple (1766–1816), "Malay" slave women were often entrusted with the running of (white) households and accounting for their contents, which implies that many must have had some facility in bookkeeping and, thus, literacy.[41] Saartjie's confident roman-script signature on Achmat's death notice of October 28, 1843, would appear as testament to this, all the more so when contrasted with the marks made by her late mother and the men around her, later imams included, who were less ready with the pen.[42]

Even if he did not own his residence and rarely appeared in the census documents, we do find Tuan Guru's name from time to time, and an evolving one at that. According to a listing from December 30, 1802, "Imam Abdul" was one of sixteen exilic convicts supporting themselves in the city, alongside such old hands as Noriman and Ingaby.[43] Whereas he would later complain that this was a period of straightened circumstances for his family, Abdallah—now known to the Dutch as "Iman Java"—had had resources and reputation enough to take out a loan on December 20, 1800, for an enslaved girl (*meid*) called Mawaa of Ternate. Signing his name in Jawi on the associated loan document as "Imam Jawa Tidore," Tuan Guru promised to pay two hundred rixdollars to her then owner, Adriaan Vincent Bergh (1765–1852), the younger brother of Olof Martini Bergh, who had been among those who had refused him the right to a mosque in February.[44]

Tuan Guru evidently required help with Keijda, as she had just delivered their second child, Abd al-Rauf. It also seems that he had also come to rely on the aforementioned fisher and businessman Frans van Bengal, and perhaps by default on Frans's deputy, Jan van Bugis (d. 1846), whose grave marker records an early life at Bone, in Sulawesi, and preferred personal identification as Muhammad bin Fadl.[45] Current histories, inflected by the claims and hostility of Achmat van Bengalen and partisans, meanwhile have it that Jan had arrived by way of Ceylon as an eastern slave in April 1789, subsequently marrying his owner, Salea van Makassar, before 1800.[46] He wouldn't emerge in the eyes of the state until well after the English had handed the Cape back to General Janssens of the Batavian Republic.

Spouses, Slaves, Soldiers, and Scribes

Before turning to the 1803 arrival of General Janssens, we must note another rare instance in which Tuan Guru registers under British eyes, but before the same Cape Dutch faces. On July 20, 1801, "Iman Abdallah" would make a will before the Leiden-trained notary J. H. Neethling (1770–1838). Neethling was the second son of the long-serving secretary to the castle, C. L. Neethling, who had once been secretary to the commission interviewing Sayyid ʿAlawi in July 1763. He had also signed the summaries mistakenly asserting that Abd al-Rauf of Tidore was still at the Cape in September 1781, and the order dispatching Abdallah to Robben Island in October 1786.⁴⁷ In J. H. Neethling's statement of 1801, meanwhile, Tuan Guru is described as a "former prince" of the domain (*landschap*) of "Tidore in Ternate" and as being eighty-nine years old, which probably reflects a sense of Hijri years. This is not to say that Abdallah necessarily thought of himself as being Ternaten, like the departed Prince Ahmad or his new meid Mawaa, even if they shared the same "mountain." Rather, the younger Neethling applied the relevant Dutch administrative category for the Moluccas used since the 1779 reduction of his homeland by Reinier de Klerck. Indeed, the castle had been recording him as a Ternaten from 1786.⁴⁸

Furthermore, Abdallah made his will together with Keijda, whose local Muslim marriage was noted for the first time by a state that didn't recognize non-Christian alliances. Both designated two children as heirs: "Abdul Rakib" (Abd al-Rakib) and the recently born "Abdul Rauf" (Abd al-Rauf), apparently named after Abdallah's escaped colleague. Abd al-Malik was named as executor. Abdallah was clearly mindful of his mortality and his legacy. Letters from this time destined for Batavia indicate the boundaries of his local family, with there being mention of two children, and his infirmity. In drafts of one missive written in late 1802 to his "older brother" (*kakanda*) Abd al-Shukur, he mentioned an injury he had suffered "when Musa was killed by his boy," which meant that he could no longer bear heavy loads. He found the recent news of the death of a daughter in the Indies, Aisha, equally hard to take, telling of "tear-filled eyes" and resignation to God. He was similarly sorrowful that he could not advise her mother, Nyai Saliha (evidently still at Batavia), how to deal with the estate of their daughter, and in accordance with the sharia, crossing line after line out in evident dissatisfaction.[49]

Dissatisfied as he was, Abdallah's legacy was now in place at the Cape, much as his reputation had been built among the community that recognized his authority and his frailty. Both factors would be remembered many years later, as we shall see, when Achmat van Bengalen's rival Jan van Bugis wrote how the newly arrived General Janssens attempted to entice the Muslim community into an embrace of the Dutch state as auxiliary soldiers. It is also a curious quirk of fate that, two months before J. H. Neethling signed off on Tuan Guru's Dutch will, his older brother in the Netherlands, H. L. Neethling (1763–1822), had made recommendations for the Batavian government recommending the recruitment of Capetonians into military service with land as a reward. He also advocated the immediate cessation of slave importation, the incremental amelioration of slavery in the settlement, the granting of land to those manumitted, and the very death of the trade itself. His was an argument for land in exchange for loyalty and ultimate freedom for all.[50]

H. L. Neethling was not the first Cape-born Dutchman to propose such measures. A servant of the ancien régime, Hendrik Swellengrebel Jr. (1734–1803) had expressed similar views from Utrecht in the early 1780s, even proposing the abolition of the Slave Lodge.[51] Neither man was liberal. H. L. Neethling opposed mixing between white and Black and the "superstition" it supposedly engendered. Nor yet were his recommendations the root cause of the formation in 1803 of two companies of "Javanese artillery" overseen by J. H. Neethling as colonial secretary.[52]

There was precedent for this elsewhere in the Dutch empire, now run by the Batavian Republic. Whereas the castle at Colombo had been eager to trade "Moorish" lascars for "Javanese" and "Malays" in the 1790s (as we shall see in chapter 5), that of Cape Town needed replacements for its Hottentot Regiment, disbanded after numerous clashes with Boers during the British interregnum.[53] This shift would mark a signal change to the possibilities for (male) Muslim engagement in the Cape colony. Three decades on, Jan van Bugis claimed that General Janssens himself had called on the Muslims to enter service with the Dutch and "exhorted" (*suruh menyuruh*) Imam

Abdallah in person, beseeching "the old priest in the mosque and wanting to give him a weapon." Old Abdallah demurred, though, stating that he was too "frail" (lemah).[54]

While the essence of this story is often accepted, its relater in the 1830s was seen with suspicion on Dorp Street.[55] No such stigma ever applied to his mentor Frans, though, who would use the gifted dagger and his part-time military position as a "field priest" as leverage for the community. In late 1804, for instance, Frans was at his master's side to engage a notary to compose a petition seeking nine years of lost income, and in a tone echoing that of Shaykh Yusuf at Ceylon over a century beforehand:

> With all possible respect, your most obedient subject Iman Abdúlla, Descendent of Princes of the Island of Great Java, and robed in the priesthood there, [acknowledges] that the Lord Governor General and Council of Netherlands India at Batavia, for reasons of state and necessity, made themselves his master and ordered that he be removed from the island of Java and sent here for some 28 years [sic] to remain kept as a Prisoner of State. That since his arrival at this corner, and until the colony fell into the hands of the English, the Supplicant was given a monthly allowance of Five Rixdollars for his maintenance; which was immediately withdrawn by the English government of this settlement, which certainly could not be without significance for the sustenance of a Prisoner of State from whom the Government could have so little to fear; for he has ever made such prudent use of this [allowance] and is now brought to the bitterest poverty, which oppresses him in his current age of ninety-one. That his hope, in this advanced age, is not to die broken down. Rather, it has always been founded on the belief that once thus colony was restored to the Batavian Republic, he would once more have a right to the allowance granted him by the High Government of the Netherlands Indies.[56]

With Jawi signatures for Abdallah and Frans (though Abdallah seems to have signed on his behalf or vice versa), this petition is remarkable for Tuan Guru's explicit claim to have been descended from Javanese princes. But while Abdallah claimed descent from Cirebonese royalty via his grandfather, that he had studied on Java, and that he was sent from Batavia, he had hardly been a lord of that island at the time of his capture. Nor yet had he felt he was Javanese when reporting the parceling up of the exiles into ships for Saldanha Bay back in 1781—if we recall that he wrote of being in a boat with other men of Maluku and a "Javanese." Now, over twenty years later, Abdallah had warmed to such a public identification; after all, local Muslim leaders like Kareta had been Javanese, if not Jawi in a broader sense, like Rajab. No wonder, then, that he had begun signing documents as "Imam Jawa Tidore."

The restored Dutch regime accepted his claims quite readily, offering immediate back payment of 105 rixdaalders and a letter guaranteeing continuance of his allowance until his death.[57] Seven months later, Frans would successfully petition the Burgher Senate for a new burial plot northwest of that already in use on the Lion's Rump.[58] This enlarged "Javanese" site would soon take some of Frans's artillerists, killed in the defense of Blauwberg in January 1806. Having just remarked on the death in the Slave Lodge of Noriman some months later, an admiring Hudson would further comment that he would often see Frans and "his boys working all the leisure he has ... erecting a rude wall round this sacred spot that the remains of his sort may not be disturbed by the cattle that are constantly grazing upon the side of the mountain."[59] Crucially, this act of building enclosed the older plot of Sayyid ʿAlawi. By his guardianship of the site, Frans had also become the effective leader of the community while Tuan Guru gave him living sanction. As Hudson noted, "Frank" oversaw "all their great feasts and holidays," adding that "their Nabhis [sic]" were generally under his direction.[60] Rather than referring to laborers or "navvies," Hudson's *Nabhi* may refer here to the ancillary Javanese title of *ngabehi*. More specifically, it could point to an exile who would come before Neethling in 1813, as we shall see in chapter 4.

We must assume at this time that an increasingly frail Abdallah made his final plans with an eye to the new Javanese plot on Signal Hill, too, having Frans offer a Jawi epitome of his will to a notary on May 2, 1807, recording Abd al-Malik and Abd al-Wasi as his original witnesses (*saksi*), with Abd al-Malik his executor.[61] Lodged with the Orphan Chamber on May 28, 1807, the Jawi will bequeaths all his property in a brief and formulaic way to his two local sons and their mother, who is dignified by the name of Nyai Arafiyya. The use of the title *nyai*, which Abdallah had already used to refer to Keijda in a letter to Prince Ahmad of Ternate, is remarkable.[62] In the Javanese milieu, the nyai is often the accomplished partner of the religious teacher, or *kyai*, and possessed of knowledge to be handed down to the women of the community. Frustratingly, we know little about Keijda/Nyai Arafiyya, who soon remarried and left their home, unlike her two sons.[63] Both would remain at Dorp Street and be informally adopted by Achmat van Bengalen and Saartjie, who continued to live together with their seven children.⁶⁴

There had been no such provision for this adoption in either will. Achmat's relationship to Tuan Guru is similarly unclear on another score. Had he, too, been bought and taught by Abdallah? As we shall see, Jan van Bugis's allies would one day imply this relationship to deny him the right to be an imam over them. Yet there is no record for now of Achmat having had this status or yet of any manumission. Rather, in Tuan Guru's Malay will the category of "slave" (*budah*) is the first form of property he leaves, followed by the metals *suasa*, gold, and silver.⁶⁵ Setting aside the slim chance of Tuan Guru having an extensive store of such precious metals as suasa—an amalgam of gold and silver that is much prized in Southeast Asia—we can recall the instances of him having bought persons. We already know of Mawaa. Then there is Damon van Bugis, who evidently passed into his household sometime after 1800, when he had been bought by Jacobus Arnoldus van Rheenen (1757–1815), the brother of yet another member of council.⁶⁶ Damon was manumitted by Abdallah's executor, Abd al-Malik, in June 1816.⁶⁷ This was probably because Abd al-Rauf was by then old enough to support himself through a trade with Abd al-Rakib, by which time both were recorded as slave holders in their own right—indeed, they would register "Mawaá" from 1810 until her death near two decades later, alongside a younger woman from Mozambique, Rachbat, and her seven children, born between 1817 and 1828.⁶⁸

There is also precedent for the purchase of people with skills to match or exceed those of Achmat. Later evidence suggests that another of Tuan Guru's enslaved or redeemed protégées was a successor imam called Sourdeen (d. 1822), whom he had trained.⁶⁹ To be sure, Abdallah was hardly the only Muslim to have slaves and to offer a path to freedom and elevation through service or conversion; such had been a practice for many years.⁷⁰ Likewise, Hudson wrote in 1806 that whenever Frans had purchased a slave, he made a deal that if they were to serve "faithfully for so many years" then they would go free, and with "sufficient money" to make themselves anew, much as he had done himself.⁷¹ Of course, Frans was doing good business with the navy as its provender of choice. One wonders, though, just how Tuan Guru had had the means to purchase or manumit people under the first British occupation, unless he was subsidized by Frans at home or from abroad by his relatives and Prince Ahmad. And did he really have reserves of gold and silver?

Such purchases also clash with Tuan Guru's complaints of impoverishment put before the Batavian authorities. There were many slaves other than those of Abdallah on Dorp Street. His landlady, Trijn, not only had slaves but housed those of a burgher neighbor, William van Oudtshoorn, for a fee.[72] Van Oudtshoorn's sixteen-year-old son had also been one of the witnesses to Tuan Guru's purchase of Mawaa.[73] Trijn's daughter Saartjie had slaves, too, and became wealthy in her own right. Having already become the formal owner of the Dorp Street property in February 1809, she then obtained an adjacent parcel of house and land from her mother in December 1811 for the sum of three thousand guilders.[74]

We must remember in all this that even as Islam commends manumission as a virtue, most Muslims—and indeed most Asians, Africans, and Europeans active in the Indian Ocean world—were members of slave-owning societies. Still, the lot of the (promised) Muslim convert was generally milder. When the Indo-Persian traveler Mirza Abu Taleb (1752–1806) stayed at the Cape in 1799, he remarked upon the comparative cruelty of Dutch masters and social mobility of pious Capetonians of African and Asian backgrounds who had purchased their freedom or been manumitted by their masters.[75] Similarly, the patronage of people, Muslim or otherwise, was seen a key marker of distinction in Southeast Asia; any self-respecting worthy should have attendants. Recall that Shaykh Yusuf had brought servants and slaves with him into exile, whom he struggled to support alongside his retainers and family, and that the peoples of the Moluccas had long competed to gain access to the populations of Papua as they were themselves raided from Sulu.

The acceptability and ubiquity of slavery was reinforced both in traditional Islamic law, which affirms the condition, and Muslim historiography, which valorizes (former) slaves who defended the public order. The first muezzin of the prophet's community was a manumitted Ethiopian called Bilal, whose name Capetonian imams would invoke as a rank for mosque functionaries into the following century. Equally, the texts they knew, such as that of Tilimsani, encouraged the just treatment of the enslaved, though a commentary, well known across the Muslim world, also claimed that the recitation of the prayer of a companion of the Prophet, ʿUkasha, would ensure the restoration of a runaway. In fact, this prayer and its benefit are both cited in a volume that was on display at the Heritage Museum at Simon's Town in 2013, and in a hand resembling that of Tuan Guru.[76]

Close comparison with elements of a different volume once owned by the family of Achmat van Bengalen shows that it is unlikely that Tuan Guru was the writer in question, however, and raises the possibility of an emulator who even may have acted as his scribe. To start with, it is beyond doubt that Tuan Guru was the transcriber of the first, and subtly different, element of this compilation.[77] Written on paper watermarked around 1794, Abdallah's neat vertical strokes of the *Umm al-barahin* of Sanusi are unmistakable, as are his cursive Jawi glosses.[78] The volume also includes various prayers in another hand, with some intended to be uttered for the dead born either in or out of wedlock, which must have been of particular concern at the Cape. This second hand is moreover identical to the scribe of the prayer of ʿUkasha and written, most tellingly, on paper watermarked the year after Abdallah's final passage up Signal Hill.[79]

Ends and Beginnings

> Muhammad is the messenger of God, and those who are with him are stronger than the unbelievers.
>
> —TUAN GURU, CA. 1805, CITING QURAN 48.29

Surrounded by the men of his community, one of them—perhaps our mystery scribe—would have whispered reminders into Abdallah's ear of what answers to give when the angels of the grave came to interrogate him, and before being ultimately brought into the Divine Presence on the Day of Judgment, with the place of sorrow left far behind. However he was known, whether as Imam Abdallah, Tuan Guru, or even Imam Jawa, by 1807 this scholar from Tidore had left a legacy among a section of Capetonian Society that could not be ignored. It would continue to expand up the new streets of Signal Hill as much toward his grave now as that of the earlier ʿAlawi, whose memory he would occlude.

As we shall see in chapter 4, Abdallah was invoked in the claims of many imams to come who could proudly identify with his presence and family, signified most powerfully by access to "his" texts. The explicitly Shafiʿi treatises he transcribed would be copied and shared while his handwriting would inform many short tracts that aimed to give students easily memorized principles to invoke in their daily life and to hand on to their families. Despite their sometimes-woeful circumstances, they could take comfort in the fact that God was the Omnipresent, All-Preceding, and Sustaining Lord. As one imam later claimed in 1825, he and his colleagues would teach those in bondage that, while their bodies were in slavery, their souls were free. Tuan Guru's apparent successor at Dorp Street, Imam Achmat, meanwhile affirmed that while women could come to the mosque if they chose, all male believers were expected to attend, to observe the rules prescribed by law, to make their wives and children conform to those laws, and to be aware that "their duty in the world" consisted in their "paying respect to authority" and "performing the work of their employers."[80]

The major issue that would bedevil the community in years to come, though, would be the looming matter of precedence. As I shall suggest, Capetonian Muslims, emerging from the experiences of slavery and exile that had shaped their world in the eighteenth century, would have to reconcile two models of authority. Was religious leadership vested in the sons and grandsons of an exiled "Javanese" prince from the Moluccas? Or was it defined by consensus, a dash of military training, and consequent recognition by the new imperial state that saw them as "Malay?" Or could it be a mix of these things? Before turning to such questions, though, we must explore just what their new overlords thought of their imperial charges across the Indian Ocean.

THREE

Sanguinary Attacks and Unruly Passions

ON JANUARY 4, 1806, a British fleet under Vice Admiral Home Popham (1762–1820) sailed into Table Bay, destined to unload troops commanded by Lieutenant General David Baird (1757–1829), the victor against Tipu Sultan at Seringapatam in 1799. General Jan Willem Janssens (1762–1838), the representative of the Batavian Republic in Africa, mobilized his own forces, which included European auxiliaries and members of the recently created "Javanese Artillery." Battle would be joined below Blauwberg Hill four days later, with a result echoing the stuttering combat that had occurred almost a decade earlier before the walls of Colombo Castle. While many of the Europeans fled, the British watched in admiration as the local artillery stood their ground and continued to fire despite mounting losses. Among the steadfast were many whose names would long be remembered at the Cape, including their chaplain Frans van Bengalen, the bombardier Jan van Bugis, and Mamat van de Kaap. And regardless of the diverse origins hinted at in the names they used with their Dutch neighbors, they would be labeled by their sometime admirers and future occupiers as one people: Malay.

A Newly Configured World, and New Opportunities

In the previous two chapters, I sketched three decades of the life of Tuan Guru against the shifting tides of Dutch and English control at the Cape, linked in turn to changes of authority sweeping the southern coasts of the Indian Ocean. In his last years, Imam Abdallah adopted a mediated attitude to the local authorities he could scarcely trust, opting to practice his faith, but not to register directly in their eyes until compelled by financial worry, whereupon he invoked a conjoined scholarly and princely tie to Java. In some ways he was taking steps toward affirming his Islamic authority in a land with neither a sultan nor the attendant possibility of having a Muslim judge or qadi. The latter position is usually predicated on the existence of a Muslim ruler, according to most schools of Sunni law, though Shafi'i scholars such as Zayn al-Din of Malabar (1531–1583) worked on the assumption—based on the long history of autonomous Muslim communities of Southern India—that qadis and imams could be appointed by their constituents.[1]

For some of Tuan Guru's avowedly Shafi'i followers at the Cape, it became clear that their activities could only gain in strength by virtue of official, albeit non-Muslim, recognition. Such must have been clear to Frans van Bengalen, who broke with the Dorp Street community when it—or perhaps just Achmat van Bengalen—refused his nominee for imam. On November 20, 1807, the veteran of Blauwberg joined with that unwelcome cleric, the chandler Jan van Bugis (known to his intimates as Muhammad bin Fadl), to finalize the purchase of a house on Long Street, with an eye to establishing a mosque of their own.[2] They also brought along other men of their regiment, among them the locally born Mamat van de Kaap (d. 1864), who eventually served as imam after the death of Jan four decades later in 1846.[3] The first such officer at Long Street was a brother-in-law of Achmat van Bengalen called Abdol Gamiedt (Abd al-Hamid). He only acted as imam for a year, though, before returning to Dorp Street and then setting out on the hajj, reportedly never to return—though the *African Court Calendar* mentions a fisherman priest of that name living on nearby Loop Street between 1811 and 1814.[4]

With hindsight, a visit to the Hijaz was hardly to be recommended at the time, given the occupation of the holy cities by the Saudi-Wahhabi alliance. A frustrated or returning Abd al-Hamid might well have told his countrymen about this in 1811, the year in which Egyptian soldiers of the Ottoman sultan succeeded in ejecting their Najdi opponents. Frans, meanwhile, had taken over as imam on Long Street before his final departure for Java at the end of the year, at which point the mosque became firmly associated with its remaining owner, Jan. Consequently, the establishment even took his name among Capetonian Muslims, if we are to judge by the will of his second wife, Sameda (d. 1860).[5]

The Long Street branch of Tuan Guru's larger endeavor was but one fragment of "Malay" activity that would profit from a relationship with the British over the course of the nineteenth century. Later evidence suggests that Jan was soon attached to the hybrid courts of Cape Town, overseeing the oaths of his coreligionists as an official Malay interlocutor. But even if religious freedom, belatedly promulgated by the Batavian state in 1804, had been affirmed by what would become a more permanent British regime from 1806, Cape Town was hardly a city of equals. The authorities had ignored H. L. Neethling's advice regarding abolition in 1801. And, despite Great Britain's incremental measures to oppose its trade at sea from 1807, slavery and its analogues would remain firmly entrenched into the 1830s, with the absorption of thousands of "prize Africans" taken from hostile European ships or Arab dhows off the coast of East Africa and pressed into fourteen-year apprenticeships that scarcely differed from slavery in practice. New challenges would emerge in this environment for an expanding community that both resisted the taint of slavery and yet profited from its continuance, and all under the panethnic rubric that placed them at the top of the subaltern hierarchy. To be Malay was no mean thing.

From the 1820s, the partisans of Dorp Street would also set themselves more forcefully against those of Long Street, though theirs were hardly the only religious leaders at the time. As Shamil Jeppie has shown, an expanded patchwork of local imams only grew once freedom came in 1834.[6] Some of these new imams asserted a link back to Tuan Guru, either through the consensus of their congregations and the transmission of his texts, or via claims of a form of kingship vested in a line that stretched back to the Moluccas and (Greater) Java. As we shall see in chapter 4, these battles would be reconfigured with the rise of a new order of wealthy hajjis. But, before considering the implications of their rise, we should first see in this chapter what the British had assumed of their new subjects and the imagined commonalities linking others at Ceylon (discussed in chapter 5), and their ancestral homelands in Southeast Asia, taking the first steps toward the idea of a martial race created by the intersection of Islam and European governance.

Seeing Malays Before Manumission

Even at a distance his upright form, his nervous make, his free step, announces the Malay, or native of the Island of Java, the king of slaves. As he approaches, mark his long, coal black hair which hangs half down his back, his yellow complexion, his glancing and jealous eye, which looks askance upon slavery. He knows well that from his class are formed the house-painters, the musicians, the ingenious workmen of the Cape. He is proud of this distinction, and glories in the name of Malay.

—Robert Semple, 1803

Despite the seeming novelty of such caricatures as that drawn by Robert Semple for Cape Town in 1800, the wider "Malay" peoples were hardly strangers to the British.[7] Having established factories at Banten and Makassar in the early seventeenth century and then maintaining a more enduring presence on Sumatra at Bengkulu (Bencoolen) from 1685, some servants of the EIC probably felt that they had a good idea about who the generally coastal or maritime Muslims of Southeast Asia were. Such ideas were only reinforced with the momentary acquisition of fresh territory at Balambangan, off Borneo, in 1773, and more especially at the enduring redoubt of Penang, off the Malay Peninsula, in 1786.

As we saw in the waters around Ternate, Bacan, and New Guinea, the EIC had long competed with the VOC for influence among these peoples. Prior to the middle of the eighteenth century, the English company had usually been bested by its Netherlandic rival, being dislodged from West Java and losing out in the spice race in the Moluccas. Confined to their unpromising patch of Sumatra, the EIC would focus its efforts on India, where the Dutch presence was less extensive, ultimately gaining more territory at the expense of the Nawab of Bengal (and France) in the 1750s. The two companies clashed there, too. In 1759, the VOC sent a force—including several hundred European and Asian soldiers from Java—to reinforce their bases at Chinsurah in support of the new nawab, Mir Ja'far (d. 1765), who wished to be rid of Robert Clive. However, in an all-too-common occurrence, the ill-prepared VOC forces were defeated in several engagements and their actions disavowed by the States General.[8]

With British ascendance in Bengal in the 1760s, the Dutch would go from once potent regional rivals to weakened bystanders, affected as much by the ravages of disease as war. The death rates were extreme for clerks at Batavia across the decades after 1730, and 1775 alone saw 70 percent of the soldiers brought from Europe expire within one year of landing.[9] Worse still, the company was bankrupt after so many wars for influence in Java. The desperate directors sought a loan from the States General in 1780 in order to continue their operations, though the Fourth Anglo-Dutch War put paid to any hope of recovery. It was in some respects a preamble to the revolutionary conflicts to come, when the VOC would suffer final losses of forts and men in Africa and India and on Lanka.

It was also during this period that the Dutch and the British began to form different views as to who the Malays were, with the new hegemons of the Asian seas expanding the definition of what made them identifiable as such, despite the published caveats of one leading expert in the admiralty (discussed below). While Dutch works had mentioned Malay people from the time of Jan Huyghen van Linschoten (1563–1611), they had tended to confine them to the western reaches of the archipelago and in relation to the city of Malacca.[10] This is not so strange, considering the strong pull of that city in canonical texts like the *Sulalat al-Salatin*—later known as the *Sejarah Melayu*, or *Malay Annals*—whose genealogical claims no good Malay king could do without.

These claims were first summarized for the Dutch by the preacher Petrus van der Vorm (1664–1731), who advocated the study of the *Sejarah Melayu* to understand the Malays and the fall of their most famous city-state to the Portuguese in 1511.[11] Yet neither Van der Vorm nor his contemporary François Valentijn dwelt on defining the Malay peoples. Both saw Malayness as a regrettably Islamicate linguistic culture of the western half of the archipelago to be adapted for the inculcation of their own religion, and most often in its eastern reaches among the peoples of Ambon and the Moluccas, where their primary business lay beyond Java.

We have already seen how the summary convict lists of Cape Town often referred to prisoners from South and Southeast Asia collectively as "Indians," though "Easterner" (Oosterling) was common, too. Despite being used in VOC census data, especially after an influx into Batavia from the straits in the late 1770s, the term "Malay" seldom featured in published Dutch writings as an ethnic category, being relatively insignificant as far as the VOC was concerned.[12] In 1789, for instance, Ary Huysers cited data for 1778 from the capital where he had once served that counted some 800 European men in a city counting over 110,000 males, almost all Oosterlingen. The largest groups of such Easterners were reportedly mixed Christians and manumitted slaves (10,455 all together), the Balinese (13,073), Chinese (23,309), and the Javanese majority (33,408). All lived alongside 20,072 enslaved people often taken from the east, and many other smaller eastern groups such as free Makassarese (1,983) and Bugis (3,707), who outnumbered the newcomer western Malays as well, then standing at 1,852.[13]

The appellation "Malay" is also rare, and thus even more striking, in the influential writings of the naval officer Jan Splinter Stavorinus (1739–1788). Stavorinus visited the Cape, Bengal, and the East Indies over two tours, the first between 1768 and 1771, during which time he encountered the *Endeavour* of Captain James Cook (1728–1779) at Batavia. Observing the declining fortunes of his employer, more particularly on the second set of voyages from 1774 to 1778, Stavorinus had sometimes written about Oosterlingen, except when referring to Moors of Surat, Chinese, Javanese, and people of Sulawesi more specifically—as when remarking, for instance, on the apparent proclivity of enslaved Makassarese and Bugis to run amok at Batavia of an evening.[14] It was also on his second tour that he had something to add of Malays at Makassar itself, where many were quartered as outsiders on an island so famous for its own warrior people: "Apart from Europeans, the Company has a great number of Malays in service in times of war. These people, who in the sixteenth century overran the Malay coast from *Djohor*, *Patani* and other such places, are now settled here in a sort of separate town, apart from the Bugis, which they call *Campo Maleyo*. They are under a Captain or chief, chosen by the ministers of the Company, to which they are inseparably attached, and for which they have rendered great service on land and at sea."[15]

As we shall see in chapter 5, other exceptions that prove the Dutch rule may be found at Colombo from 1760, but then with greater clarity from 1785. By 1792 there were, moreover, three explicitly "Malay" battalions active on the island. But rather than being from the peninsula, their members were, conversely, drawn both from the island's diverse ranks and across the entire archipelago. A notable complement had only recently been recruited from Madura, or at least from among Madurese employed at Makassar. Similarly, the British who took those battalions on after 1796 had already begun to cast Malayness as an agglomeration of characteristics applicable to many peoples from across the region, though such notions had long been contested by an experienced savant, and by then first secretary of the admiralty, William Marsden (1754–1836).

Marsden had served the EIC at Bengkulu's Fort Marlborough from 1771. Inspired by the exploits of Cook in the Pacific, he returned to London in 1779 and soon joined Thomas Forrest and Alexander Dalrymple in the circle patronized by Cook's famous passenger Joseph Banks (1743–1820).[16] Marsden's own scholarly claim to fame was his 1783 *History of Sumatra*. This text, soon revised in 1784, was marked for its attention to the Malays alongside Bataks, Acehnese, Rejangese, and Lampungese. But while Marsden was well acquainted with pious members of the Sumatran court of Palembang—just as Dalrymple and Forrest had enjoyed a close acquaintance with the Muslims of Sulu who were said to been converted by way of Malacca—he saw the Malays as untrue to their origins, which he placed in the Minangkabau highlands by virtue of his own reading of the *Sejarah Melayu*.[17] Claiming to avoid the "too facile" division of "Mahometan" coast and "Pagan" hinterland "usually made by the writers of voyages," or else the indiscriminate application

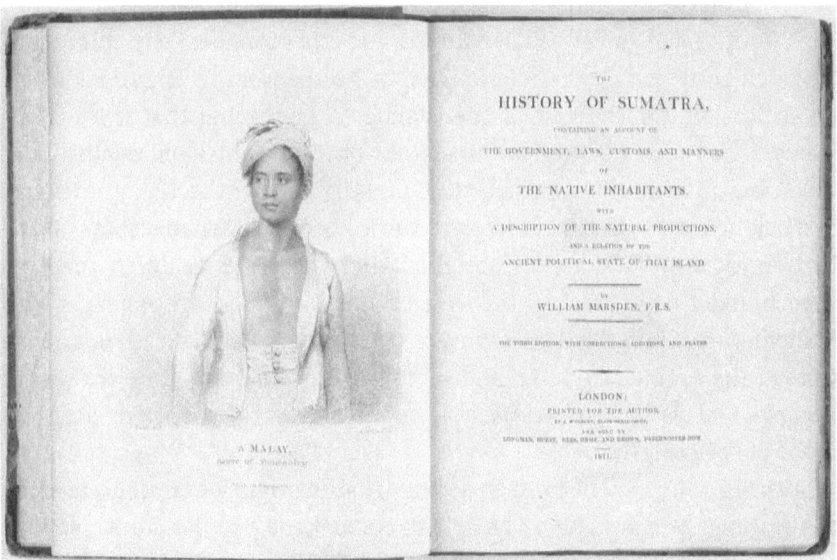

Figure 3.1 *History of Sumatra* by William Marsden, edition of 1811. Heritage Auctions, HA.com.

of "Malay" for all the broader archipelago's peoples, Marsden first proposed to steer "a middle course" in "distinguishing the variety, almost endless, of petty sovereignties and nations," found on Sumatra, many of which he claimed were indistinguishable "in person or manners from their neighbors."[18] He also announced in a footnote that the Malays, "now so called," were "in comparison to the internal Sumatrans, but as a people of yesterday." And although they had "spread their language and manners far and wide, since the founding of Malacca in the thirteenth century," they were "considered as intruders only, among the aboriginal people of the eastern islands."[19]

Addressing the origins of the Malay language, Marsden had originally celebrated it in 1783 as "the Italian of the East."[20] In so doing he echoed Van Linschoten, who had praised its capacious and melodic borrowing that "took all the best words from other tongues," as well as the more recent assessment of Pierre Poivre, who declared it the "softest" language in Asia somehow spoken by "the most treacherous and ferocious people on the face of the globe."[21] Certainly there seemed something inherently contradictory about the Malays, and the purist Marsden bemoaned the "encroachments" of Arabic in their language; by 1784, he averred that it was a dialect both "much corrupted, or refined by a mixture of other tongues."[22] In this regard Marsden returned to the relationship of its speakers to Islam, and their identification "by the rest of the islanders," conceding that if the word "Malay" had once denoted an inhabitant of the neighboring peninsula, it was "now understood to mean a Mussulman, speaking the Malay language, and belonging, by descent at least, to the kingdom of Menangcabow." As he further sighed, "It must be observed that the term *Malay*, in common speech, like that of *Moor* on the west of India, is almost synonymous with Mahometan. When the Sumatrans, or natives of the eastern islands, learn to read the Arabic character, and submit to circumcision, they are said to become Malays (*munjaddee Malayo*). But this is not a proper or accurate mode of speaking."[23]

Although Marsden insisted on a Minangkabau origin for an accurate mode of speaking, he would never be able to combat the popular equivalence of Malayness with archipelagic Islam, and an Islam of *written* texts, at that.[24] For now the adoption of religion and language was enough to trump the new European obsession with blood, and there were other cultural practices, sometimes adopted or performed as a part of their faith, for Westerners to note and fear—though these paled in comparison to that of amok.

Treating Amok with the Superior Mildness of British Rule

> Previous to the English arriving at Ceylon the Dutch, by mean and cowardly insinuations, unworthy of a civilized nation, worked up their passions and minds against us to a state of desperation, which led them to attempt those cowardly acts of assassination for which the Malays are so much and so justly abhorred. How dearly have the Dutch now paid for their conduct! All confidence between a Dutchman and a Malay is lost, wherever the English have appeared.
>
> —ROBERT PERCIVAL, 1804

If Marsden disapproved of the chosen faith of the growing body of Malay speakers, and thus Malays beyond the heartlands of Sumatra and the Peninsula, he did at least attempt to explode one myth about their wider world. This concerned the linkage commonly asserted between the general habit of opium smoking, often observed among the Bugis and Makassarese soldiers who served in garrison towns, and the "cowardly acts" for which Captain Percival would later claim that the Malays were "so much and so justly abhorred."[25]

In his history, Marsden had dismissed as "idle notions" the idea that the consumption of opium led to "the furious quarrels, desperate assassinations, and sanguinary attacks" so often related by "travelers addicted to the marvelous." He preferred to place the cause of the "desperate acts of indiscriminate murder, called by us *mucks*" in their "unruly passions."[26] Such passions—the supposedly momentary inverse of a generally passive disposition and fatal resignation—were most often inflamed by ill treatment.[27] To make his point, Marsden offered the tragic story of a slave from Nias treated by his Portuguese mistress "with extreme severity, for a trifling offence":

> [He] vowed he would have revenge if she attempted to strike him again; and ran down the steps of the house, with a knife in each hand it was said. She cried out, *mongamo*! The civil guard was called, who having the power in these cases, of exercising summary justice, fired half a dozen rounds, into an outhouse, where

[81]

the unfortunate wretch had sheltered himself, on their approach; and from whence he was at length dragged, covered with wounds. Many other *mucks* might perhaps be found, upon scrutiny, of the nature of the foregoing, where a man of strong feelings was driven, by excess of injury, to domestic rebellion.[28]

This seemed commonplace. Of his journey off New Guinea, Forrest had already written that the bondsmen of Raja Salawati had been prepared to *mengamo* before his arrest by the Dutch in 1770.[29] But while Marsden conceded that Malays might "fortify themselves with a few whiffs of opium" prior to battle, he judged them more guilty of "stupidity than frenzy." He also felt that British rule was a natural antidote to such passions, claiming in a much-repeated passage that at Batavia, "where the assassins ... when taken alive, are broken on the wheel, with every aggravation of punishment that the most rigorous justice can inflict, the *mucks* yet happen in great frequency; whilst at Bencoolen, where they are executed in the most simple and expeditious manner, the offence is extremely rare."[30]

Not only were such offences rare, but "piratical adventures" had supposedly ceased on the west coast of Sumatra in the British orbit, and employment had become a given to the Malays as guards of "smaller English settlements," alongside a scattering of Bugis and Makassarese. Actually, it seems that "Malays" had become the trusted intermediaries for all British affairs on Sumatra in ways that anticipated a later dependence on "Sikhs" throughout the empire: "Europeans, attended by Malays only, are continually travelling through the country. They are the only persons employed in carrying treasure to distant places; in the capacity of secretaries for the country correspondence; as civil officers, in seizing delinquents, among the planters, and elsewhere; and as masters and supercargoes of the *tombongans, praws*, and other small coasting vessels. So great is the effect which habit has upon a national character esteemed the most treacherous and sanguinary."[31]

Marsden's lesson stuck for a time. In 1798, on the heels of the first British occupations of Cape and Ceylon, Samuel Wilcocke (1766–1833) translated the late Stavorinus, whose accounts of Batavia had described the nocturnal appearance of mucks—or *amokspuwers*, as he had called them in Dutch—among the Makassarese and Bugis slaves. Having detailed the appalling punishment so often meted out to treacherous Oosterlingen, including a stoic Makassarese whose death he witnessed in 1769, Stavorinus had then recounted how, acting under the influence of opium or through "other means," instances of amok were frequent during his time in the capital. He further described their rare apprehension alive by means of long forked poles, and their subsequent breakings on the wheel after desultory hearings.[32] Noting Stavorinus's caveat about opium, Wilcocke made sure to temper his translation with an instructive footnote drawn from Marsden and Cook's purported mention of an instance at Batavia—where a free subject had run amok with his "brain fired more by the maddening fury of jealousy, than by any adventitious intoxication."[33]

Wilcocke was similarly convinced of the superiority and moderation of British rule. Although he had spent most of his youth in the Netherlands and was acquainted with the Stavorinus family from his time in Middelburg, Wilcocke had little time for the people whose country he had been forced to flee with the French invasion of 1794.[34] He also used Stavorinus's passing mention of the governing Gentlemen Seventeen to append a note on "the tyranny of the Dutch Company over the native princes," embellishing Huysers on the tragic fate of the exiled kings of Tidore and Bacan with another nod to Marsden.[35] But this did not mean that Wilcocke valorized their native subjects. He accepted the apparent irony of the universal employment of slaves drawn, according to Stavorinus, from "a treacherous race of men unrestrained by any moral principles from the perpetration of the greatest crimes," though this was in harmony with Marsden's remarks about the seeming irony of the peaceful employment of Malays as free agents under the milder British.[36]

And well employed they would be on Lanka. As we shall see in more detail in chapter 5, after the British took Colombo in February 1796, governor Frederick North (1798–1805) saw to it that the trained Malay soldiers in VOC service were offered a role under the British, led in some cases by French prisoners of war.[37] Even the most cursory examination of their ranks shows just how heterogeneous such troops were, coming as they did from the same more easterly mix of Dutch-ruled places and experiences of bondage we have seen at Cape Town. For instance, the muster roles for December 1803 present a broad range of names pointing to the archipelago, though now inflected by Anglo-Indian pronunciation and orthography, as may be seen with Captains Dole Samat (Abd al-Samad), Vera Bengala (Wira Manggala), Gonavajoyah (Gunawijaya), and Vera Wangxa (Wira Wangsa).[38]

Writing of the events of 1796, Percival (whose observations I will also return to) cast the Malays as "the only troops which either kept up discipline, or displayed any sort of bravery in the field."[39] A veteran of the Cape, Lanka, and then the Poligar campaign in Southern India, Percival would issue his *Account of the Island of Ceylon* in 1803 and describe the soldiers he had seen at some length.[40] Having clearly read his Marsden, Percival spoke with the added authority of his military experience, painting "this race ... known to Europeans chiefly by the accounts of its barbarous ferocity" as having been moderated by birth and upbringing in colonial possessions and thus rendered "less cruel and vindictive" than their fellows in Malacca and "other native possessions."[41]

Natural ferocity still had its uses. Percival delighted in describing the fear that these same men inspired, writing that they were "brave ferocious and desperate to the last degree on any occasion that blood is to be shed; cruel and vengeful in their wrath, beyond what human nature can almost be thought capable of," and "looked upon with horror by the effeminate and timid Indians." Percival further claimed that he had "often had occasion to observe these sentiments, in the natives of Ceylon who start affrighted on accidentally meeting a Malay soldier," with the latter garbed in their European uniforms but with *krisses* ever at their sides. In battle they would "throw down their muskets and bayonet" and rush upon the enemy with these more familiar weapons to "carry terror and destruction wherever they come."[42]

Proud they were to do so, as Ronit Ricci reminds us.[43] Two generations on, Baba Ounous Saldin (1832–1906), a respected and avowedly Malay descendant of their diverse ranks, would chronicle the exploits of his "Jawa" forebears at Panchalankurichi, India, in 1800:

> At that time the English took them / Five hundred Jawa with their leaders
> Sumenep and Mandura were the names of their lands / Big and strong, brave of heart
> This was the first time that the Jawa were taken / By the English to attack a country
> From Semarang, Bugis, and Batavia / Palembang, Surabaya, Bogor, and Singasari
> Every leader was an aristocrat / A strong commander and the son of a prince
> Princes with brave hearts / Their skins could withstand bullets and blades
> They were sent to Cochin / Willing to attack Panjanang Kurci.[44]

Then, on 10 Muharram, the anniversary of ʿAshura, they put their "mustached and hateful" enemy to the mortal test:

The soldiers advanced, wishing to attack / The Jawa were at the front
The enemy, too, appeared bravely / The cannon fired without cease
All the while the enemy attacked and attacked / The muskets fired in frenzy
The enemy stood the length of the battlefield / A brave enemy, but disordered
Laksana Singa wanted to pounce[45] / His pistol thrown aside, his keris drawn
The cannon gave the signal / The Jawa set to stabbing
Amazing to see in battle / Their enemy perished enraged
See the king of a distraught people! / The Jawa were as lions![46]

Proud as lions, to be sure, Percival attributed the much-vaunted Malay "phrenzy" in battle to both a "natural savage cruelty" *and* the religion of which Marsden so clearly disapproved. But if Percival admiringly noted their pious attendance of their "temples and mosques dedicated to their saints and their dead," he still hoped for the spread of Christianity among them.[47] Contrary to Marsden, too, he delighted in outlining the attacks by which a slighted individual would supposedly take an appropriately large dose of drugs, draw his conveniently poisoned kris, and run into the street stabbing all and sundry "crying aloud, *amok, amok.*"[48] Returning to the Marsdenian line, though, Percival blamed the birth of many such a muck on a "cruel, capricious and insulting" Dutch regime, to be contrasted with the "superior mildness of the English government."[49]

Capetonian Analogues

Percival followed his Ceylonese effort with his *Account of the Cape of Good Hope* of 1804, in which he once more hearkened back to the Malay thirst for revenge and violence with examples of near misses in his own life—one involving a poisoned kris in Kerala.[50] Yet Percival remained clearly enamored of the men with whom he had served for nearly four years, claiming that their "contempt of their former masters, and their admiration of the valour of our troops," had served to render the Malays "our most sincere friends . . . now formed into a steady and well-disciplined regiment."[51]

Such imagery of tamable violence had already bled into other English accounts of Isle and Cape alike, where the heterogenous people increasingly labeled Malays without distinction would be cast as clever but insolent servants of the Dutch capable of industrious freedom under the British. John Barrow—who would serve under Marsden at the admiralty from 1804 to 1807—was perhaps most responsible for promulgating this image in his *Account of Travels into the Interior of Southern Africa*. His first volume of 1801, which described journeys made in 1797-1798, was mined heavily by Percival, just as Barrow had relied on Marsden.

In general, Barrow had concentrated on the contentious relations between Boers, "Hottentots" (Khoisan), and circumcised "Kaffer" (Xhosa) tribesmen he thought descended from Bedouin, just as Percival had it that the Sinhalese had originally spoken Arabic.[52] Barrow also made some space for discussing the sober Malay subalterns of town and farm. Remarking that there was "no part of the world, out of Europe, where the introduction of slavery was less necessary," Barrow reflected gladly that the executioners now had much less work under the British and were no longer able to earn extra money by smashing limbs on the wheel.[53] He also declared that the Malays were the "most active and docile" of the enslaved, but still "the most dangerous." Although "faithful, honest and industrious," they were so "impatient of injury, and so capricious, that the slightest provocation [would] sometimes drive them into fits of phrenzy, during the continuance of which it would be unsafe to come within their reach."[54]

Barrow followed this line three years later in his second volume, in which he revisited such stereotypes for a terrain so regrettably returned to the Dutch by the Peace of Amiens:

> Is it not then a most unaccountable circumstance, that the Dutch should have given the preference to a race of men, of talents much inferior, and whose temper, always capricious, becomes on slight provocation cruel and revengeful?—I mean the Malay slaves. The negroes of Mosambique and of Madagascar ... soon become cunning and dishonest by intercourse with their elder brethren. In full possession of all the vices that must infallibly result from the condition of slavery, there is yet no part of the world where the domestic slaves of every description are so well treated, and so much trusted, as at the Cape of Good Hope. They are better clothed, better fed, and infinitely more comfortable that any of the

peasantry of Europe. Yet such are the bad effects, which the condition of slavery produces on the mind, that they are incapable of feeling the least spark of gratitude for good and gentle usage, whilst under the severe hand of a rigid and cruel master, they become the best of slaves. It is an axiom or self-evident truth, that such are and always will be the consequences of degrading man to the lowest of all conditions, that of being made the property of man.[55]

Perhaps Barrow's opinions on Malay nature were influenced more by his Dutch relations than his new boss Marsden. His travels into the interior had been led by William Somerville (1771–1860) and his father-in-law, Petrus Johannes Truter (1747–1825), the son of yet another member of the Burgher Council who denied Tuan Guru a mosque in 1800.

Setting aside his ambivalent taste for emancipation and Boer farmers, Barrow's second volume was an argument for the retaking of the Cape to foil the French, "those assiduous disturbers of the human race," who remained a threat to their Ottoman allies in the Mediterranean as much as they lurked in India and Burma.[56] Recalling Lord Macartney's view that the Cape formed "the *physical guarantee* of the British territories in India," and the earlier plans of the EIC hatched in 1780, Barrow claimed that the almost Jacobin Tipu had fallen at Mysore and the French had been stopped at Egypt with the injection of fresh troops brought from Africa.[57] If Great Britain would only recommit, the Cape would be an "easy conquest."[58]

Such a conquest would also arrest the ongoing outflow of settlers to "Manilla, Batavia, Prince of Wales' Island (Penang), and other parts of the Eastern World" that affected his calculation of the balance of the enslaved to remaining Christians.[59] Beyond the fact of continued British governance on Ceylon, Barrow had Percival in mind when offering his recommendations for the retention of the Cape, given that the officer had made a similar case in his own essay. Barrow and Percival also shared in their distaste for the rural Boers, whom they portrayed as corpulent, drunken, and violent, seeing the land's other inhabitants as a potential resource for empire that might be best put to work unshackled.

The ills of slavery were meanwhile outlined in perhaps the strangest depiction of the Cape and its subaltern peoples. In 1803, Robert Semple contrived a dreamy account in which he toured the streets and beaches of Cape Town, opining that the "long-haired" Malay or Javanese was the "king of the slaves" before trotting out standard vignettes of opium-maddened mucks with surprising access to daggers and indifference to the horrors of judicial executions:

> He exacts some deference from his master; his gestures, his speech, sometimes slow and sedate, at others rapid and violent, seem to say, "I know I am your slave, but be cautious how you use your power." A reproach stings and irritates him; a blow wounds his proud heart; he hoards it up in his remembrance, and broods upon his revenge. Time passes on, the master forgets that he has given the blow, but the Malay never. At length the bad part of his character is cruelly displayed: he intoxicates himself with opium and the madness of revenge, he rushes upon his unguarded master with his *kris* or crooked Malay dagger, and stabs him once, twice, ten times. The unfortunate wife and children are not safe if they cross his way, he sallies out into the street, and running madly along, sacrifices all he meets, till overpowered by numbers he is brought to suffer the punishment of his crime. Follow him to the place of execution. Some days are past, and the intoxication of opium is over, but do you observe his countenance in the least changed by fear or remorse? Not at all. He is bound to the wheel—the executioner breaks all his limbs one after the other—but not a tear, not a groan escapes him—at length nature is exhausted—perhaps he breathes the name of Hali his Prophet, and expires with the consolation of having had his revenge.[60]

Much of this was plain wrong, but it was commonplace. Semple's contemporary Hudson jotted very similar remarks in his diary circa 1807 about the "treacherous, shrewd, deceitful race," claiming that with each with his "*crese* and his drugs" might "pass over an injury for a time, but let the years roll on . . . and they will watch the unguarded moment to revenge it." No wonder he constantly lauded the qualities of "his" somehow "affectionate" Mozambiquans.[61]

Semple and Hudson showed a friendlier touch when dealing with Malay funerals, as did an anonymous officer present for the occupation of 1795-1803, whose less-affected missives were published in 1806. These included an extended discourse on the evils of slavery, and remarks about the proclivity of "revengeful" Malays toward gambling and cockfights, which were subject to police harassment.[62] The officer also offered remarks on an aged healer—most likely the exile Noriman, who died within months of the Battle of Blauwberg, where Frans's men distinguished themselves by remaining at their posts. Such service marked them for recognition, but not the formal recruitment obtained by the fully trained subalterns of Ceylon. British medals were hung next to their orange sashes, taking the first step toward the construction of the image of the loyal Malay of the Cape. As Hudson remarked, "The Dutch when they armed the Malays made Frank a Captain but from him, the English had nothing to fear."[63]

It is hard to know what an ailing Tuan Guru would have made of all this, or his likely recategorization as a "Malay priest" by the British, with whom his sultan had so fatally tried to correspond three decades earlier. Perhaps he once more feared the loss of his pension. Abdallah of Tidore would die in May 1807, and Frans would take himself off to Long Street by November, either because he had failed to obtain the support of the congregation or was so well positioned with the returned British. Even with such backing, the military chaplain would have already felt that he needed something more to justify his aspirations for authority among the community. According to Hudson once again, Frans had sought passage to Arabia, checking with ships bound for India in 1806.[64]

As noted above regarding the possible return of Abd al-Hamid, Frans eventually opted for some place like home, sailing for Java in late 1811 after selling his share of the Long Street property (and its remaining debt) to Jan van Bugis.[65] He also gifted Jan an unnamed slave who was perhaps the chandler's future wife, Sameda. One also wonders whether Frans had been planning the trip eastward once he had heard that Java had been placed under the control of General Janssens in May, or if word of that general's second surrender to the British that September had created a greater sense of opportunity for the man so well known to the Royal Navy.

Reannexation of the Cape spurred metropolitan interest once more. Barrow's *Travels* were reissued, with the reconquered Cape affirmed as the physical guarantee for India. His one-time master Marsden released a third, and much enlarged, edition of his *History* in 1811, now opting to use the phrase "Malayan Archipelago" in place of his previous "Indian Archipelago" and including several plates, most notably the depiction of "a Malay native of Bencoolen" by Thomas Heaphy (1775–1835; see fig. 3.1).[66] Not to be left out, John Stockdale stitched together a tome that he hoped might attract the notice of the *Edinburgh Review*.[67] The key to Stockdale's success was the splicing of Stavorinus's gory detail with the freshly published account of a French engineer, Charles François Tombe.[68] In so doing, Stockdale asserted

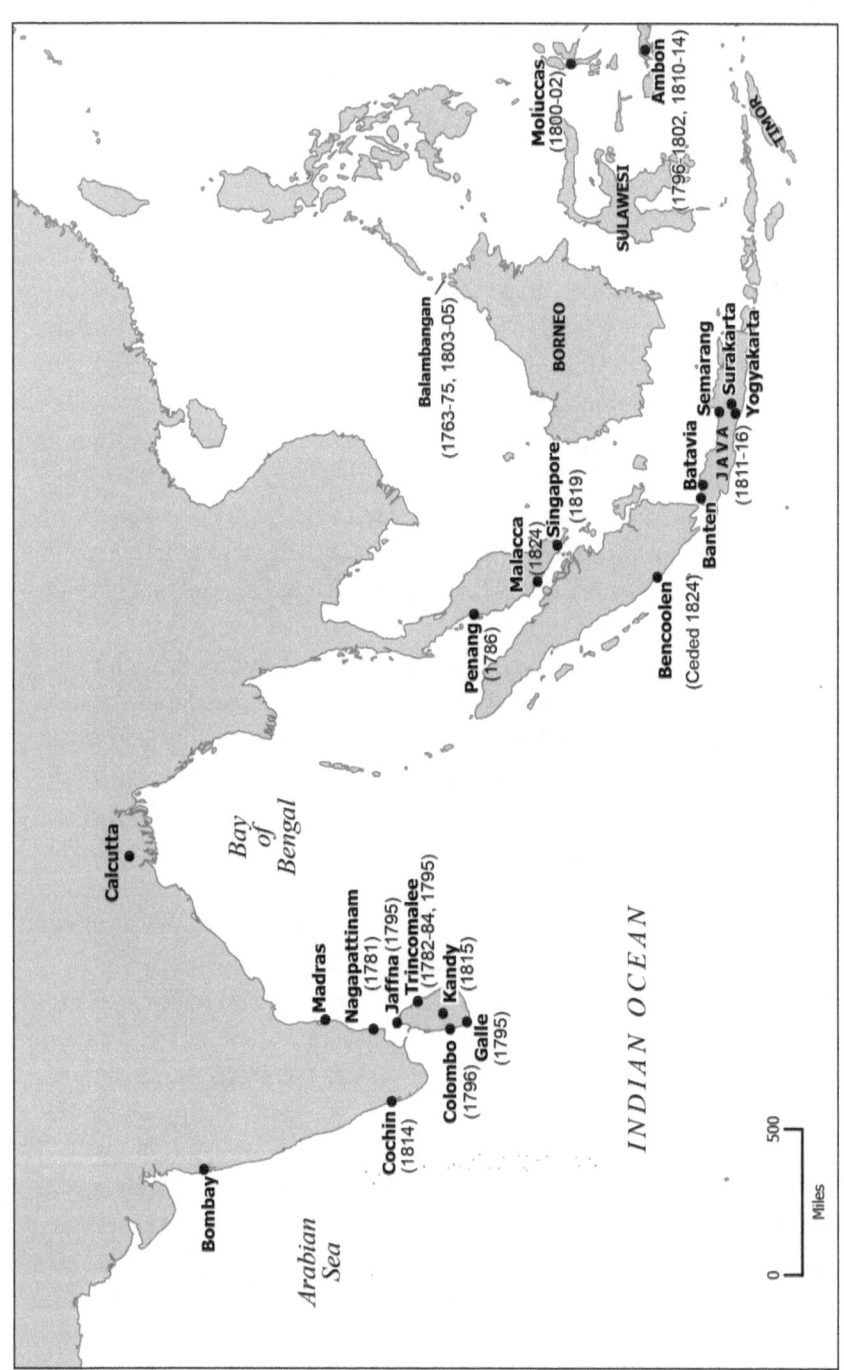

Figure 3.2 British bases and acquisitions.

the amateur's capacious vision of Malayness by offering a sweeping travelogue stocked once more with opium-addled mucks and general observations of "Malay" villages at Batavia and its harbor of Tanjung Priok, where one found the "Kramates" or entombed "Malay priests" who had been to Mecca—though the saint in question was actually an Arab.[69]

Tombe had also recounted a tour of Balambangan, East Java, whence Tuan Guru's successor Sourdeen claimed an origin, and visits to petty courts like Besuki, where Bordeaux wine was said to be quaffed by European, Chinese, and Malay soldiers alike.[70] At Pasuruan, Tombe observed that a Dutch worthy had a household of thirty "Malay" slaves brought from Bali and Makassar, some of whom he employed as musicians.[71] Like the popular Percival and sensationalist Semple, coastal Javanese and Malay were as one for Tombe and Stockdale. Exceptions could also prove the rule. When recounting the murder of the king of Banten by an enraged relative, Tombe added that the assassin surrendered to the Dutch resident for execution rather than "running about to attack whoever was near him or in his way, as the Malays generally do."[72]

Having defeated Franco-Dutch forces in the west of Java, the British found that the courts of the island's traditional center and Palembang on neighboring Sumatra were not prepared to exchange one European for another. Arriving from Penang, where he had been since 1805, the newly appointed lieutenant governor, Thomas Stamford Raffles (1781–1826), faced staunch resistance. He sacked the court of Yogyakarta in 1812 in one punitive raid, carrying off a body of texts and sowing the seeds of religious exasperation that would germinate in the Java War of 1825–1830.[73] Such consequences would be faced by the Dutch, and well after Raffles and colleagues had revived their scholarly inquiries into the history of the archipelago.

Raffles was soon frustrated by the agreement that saw the Cape and Ceylon retained but Java returned after all of his efforts to acquire it for empire. Transferred to dismal Bencoolen in 1816, he would offer his tribute to Marsden and the prince regent in the form of *The History of Java*. Just as Barrow had pleaded to keep the Cape in 1804, this monumental work of 1817 was a call to retain that island.[74] Unlike Barrow, who had envisaged a settler colony with some subaltern assistance, Raffles imagined a land under British empire cultivated by its own people, whose commitment to Islam he then belittled when compared with their mercantile, if not piratical, "Maláyu" and "Búgis" cousins.[75] Raffles's notes on the Malays of Sumatra

[91]

meanwhile conformed to his patron's views, whereby the "Mahometan institutions had considerably obliterated their ancient character."[76] To be sure, Marsden had not been so discerning about the Islam practiced by the Malays either, despite his exposure to their texts. In his revised *History* of 1811, he still claimed to be unsure as to whether they were Sunni or Shi'i, given the frequent mention within their pages of 'Ali (a simple question would have done the trick), but he felt that they were decidedly less bigoted and observant than "western Mahomedans."[77]

Perhaps the ultimate Rafflesian word came with his 1818 essay "On the Maláyu Nation," appearing in the months before he moved to establish a lasting British entrepôt at Singapore. Now Raffles affirmed the Malays as "one people, speaking one language ... and preserving their character and customs in all the maritime states lying between the *Súlu* seas, and the Southern Ocean, and bounded longitudinally by *Sumatra*, and the western side of *Papua* or *New Guinea*."[78] He had also come to see them more explicitly as a people created rather than debased, and by a specifically Arab genesis that made them cousins to other Indian Ocean Muslims like the Moors, or the interrelated Jawi Peranakan of the Straits, who straddled South and Southeast Asia. One such exemplar was the young Munshi Abdullah (1896–1845), the part- Tamilian and part-Arab Malay whom Raffles had hired as a scribe at Malacca in 1810. Channeling Marsden, again though, he declared that

> the most obvious and natural theory on the origin of the *Malays* is, that they did not exist as a separate and distinct nation until the arrival of the *Arabians* in the Eastern Seas. At the present day they seem to differ from the more original nations from which they sprung, in about the same degree as the *Chuliahs* of *Kilíng* differ from the *Tamul* and *Telinga* nations, on the *Coramandel* coast, or the *Mapíllas* of *Malabar* differ from the *Nairs*, both which people appear, in like manner with the *Malays*, to have been gradually formed as nations, and separated from their original stock by the admixture of *Arabian* blood, and introduction of the *Arabic* language and *Moslem* religion.[79]

Whether Raffles would have applied the same definition to the Malays of Cape Town is moot, though his *History* would serve its officials when they turned their gaze eastward to understand their Muslim subalterns in future years.

SANGUINARY ATTACKS AND UNRULY PASSIONS

Just as Marsden had also equivocated on the religiosity and even the sect of the Malays, one of Raffles's appointees at Singapore, John Crawfurd (1783–1868), painted the Javanese as superficial Muslims in his *History of the Indian Archipelago* of 1820. Evidently Crawfurd remained convinced of Indic influence. Writing of the ceremonies to commemorate the birth of the Prophet, including the courtly processions with their giant cones of saffron-infused rice, Crawfurd saw but the leavings of the religions that he had known from his time on the subcontinent.[80] Had he been at the courts of Banten or Cirebon for the celebrations of the birthday of the first caliph, Abu Bakr (d. 634), he would have been more bemused again to witness the *debus*, a ritual that originated with the Rifaʿiyya Sufi order that saw devotees pierce their bodies with blades or awls of various sizes to the beat of drums and tambourines. Although this practice was well known in India and regarded in the archipelago as a very Arab one—an observation translated by Marsden in his last publication concerning the Indies—we shall see how it would take root at the Cape as the quintessence of subaltern Muslim and, in British eyes, Malay alterity.[81] Indeed, it is with one such instance that we shall return to Africa in 1813.

FOUR

Friends Firm and Warm

> There is something in the Malayan character which is congenial to British minds, and which leaves an impression, very opposite to that which a much longer intercourse has given of the more subdued and cultivated races of Hindostan.
>
> —THOMAS STAMFORD RAFFLES, 1820

> Of all the colonies belonging to England, there is not one where ... an experiment of emancipation could be so safely made as at the Cape of Good Hope.
>
> —WILLIAM WILBERFORCE BIRD, 1823

IN THE PREVIOUS chapter, we saw how the British vision of the "Malay" that formed across the Indian Ocean—especially after the capture of VOC territories west of their homelands—was of a proud people whose men were capable of extreme violence. At the same time, it was felt that they were tameable if treated "mildly," and justly usable as subjects of British interests. Cape Town was important as a proving ground for this hypothesis: there, once-enslaved men were donning uniforms and adapting concepts of martial loyalty already demonstrated on Ceylon with deeper training, settling down with women admired for their flexibility and managerial skill. As this chapter will show, it was not merely the (male) proclivity to run amok that some believed needed taming. With increasing connections up the African coast to Mecca, more and more returned pilgrims began to join the authorities in questioning the legitimacy of religious rituals that would entertain or shock audiences well into the reign of Queen Victoria, all while cadres of veterans and imams regimented their mosques in quest of recognition by her appointees. In short, the community sought respectability in the eyes of its temporal masters and guidance from a spiritual patron with more than local prestige. That guidance would come in time from the caliphate, but first there was the Califa to deal with.

Griep of Mozambique and Nabe of Banten

In the decade before Raffles and Crawfurd could paint their pictures of the once Indianized archipelago and peoples since united by Islam, the Capetonian authorities would deal with a local manifestation of faith that they deemed pure superstition. On September 2, 1813, J. H. Neethling, now serving as a fiscal to British masters, would recommend the sentencing of Griep of Mozambique for a fatal accident that had occurred on the night of August 16.[1] The incident had occurred during a performance known locally as the "Califa" at the house of Hammat van Macassar, which lay at Diep Rivier, just south of Cape Town. Hammat, who had been born on Sulawesi and was by then a relatively wealthy farmer of seventy years of age, had arranged for the performance at the request of his children. With its drumming and mortifications, this was intended as the culmination of the celebrations for his daughter's birthday. Having been contracted to perform for the event, the twenty-one-year-old fisherman Rafiek had brought with him the requisite awls, swords, embroidered silks, and tambourines, which he had originally purchased from a local "Moor" who had also instructed him in the practice.[2]

Neethling's summary named the Moor in question as Albaatje. While hard to identify ("the Pasha?"), his ethnic designation suggests the engagement of South Asian Muslims in Capetonian Islam, given that the Dutch generally used the term "Moor" for such Muslims who often claimed Arab ancestors. It is also possible that a local Arab was indicated, as the term enfolded ever increasing numbers of those people venturing into the Dutch spaces of the oceanic arena and assuming positions of authority at Colombo or Batavia. For instance, Ary Huysers had written of 966 Moorish men residing at Batavia in 1778 without any separate number for Arabs, who would emerge from and ultimately displace that census category in the 1820s.[3]

According to the collected testimonies of 1813, after two sets of performers had used their awls to make shallow piercings of their cheeks and tongues to the beat of the tambourines, an overly enthusiastic Griep had pushed a sword into the abdomen of the much younger Abdol Zaghie as he lay shirtless on the ground. Despite quick stitches and fervent prayers, the youth died a couple of hours later. Hammat, who claimed to have been asleep at the time, alerted the veldcornet of Constantia the next morning and informed him that the twelve-year-old had stabbed himself during the performance.[4] The day after that, the police surgeon, a German migrant called Ludwig Godlieb Biccard (1775–1822), determined otherwise.[5] Several men were brought in for questioning, including the host of the gathering and his locally born son Abdol Garies; the similarly local Azor, Chiri, Rafiek, and Awaladien; and the prime suspects, Griep and Edries. Also called in was a much older fisherman called Nabe, who, like Hammat, reckoned his age to be about seventy, and who may have been the troupe's leader—though this was never determined by, nor of interest to, the commissioners.[6]

While there were occasional differences in their testimonies—such as whether Azor had participated in the piercing or merely played the tambourine—most confirmed the scenario where an overly eager Griep had mistakenly wounded his young friend. Indeed, the thirty-year-old African laborer told his interrogator, landdrost Johannes Zorn, that the various men were hardly enemies but treated each other "like brothers." Showing his wounds from previous encounters, he nonetheless declared that it had been an accident he could never have imagined.[7]

Others had imagined it. Awaladien, a twenty-six-year-old fisherman, said that they would normally only penetrate the flesh to the depth of "half a thumb."[8] Nabe went even further, declaring that he was never injured, and that "the children" were only ever wounded through "stupidity."[9] Nabe, exiled to the Cape as Ingabeij van Cheribon in July 1773, actually claimed an origin at Banten and would have known this all too well.[10] Both Cirebon and Banten were famous for the same ritual, and the signature on Nabe's testimony is a rare exemplar of Javanese script in the Capetonian archives. It seems, though, that Nabe's experience rather than his reputation or any apparent learning carried weight with the burgher jury. Its president, Neethling, seized upon Nabe's characterization of the youthful stupidity of the act, noting that all agreed that the so-called play was more appropriate for "blood thirsty cannibals than members of a civilized society."[11] As such, the patrician court—whose members included Petrus Johannes Truter, his nephew Johannes A. Truter (1763–1845), and the manager of Groot Constantia, Hendrik Cloete Jr. (1758–1818)—decided to make an example of Griep, sentencing him to three years on Robben Island in irons.[12] Landdrost Zorn had also demanded that his fellow dancers be made to witness the passing of sentence at the execution ground together with Hammat, proposing that the host be fined twenty-five rixdollars for hosting an illegal gathering involving the use of deadly weapons.[13]

The participants found it strange that anybody was supposed to obtain permission for such a gathering. When Zorn had asked Rafiek whether he felt he should be punished for having performed "so violent and dangerous" an act, the fisherman offered that the fault was certainly not his, but, rather, his grandfather's—assumedly for his having been sent there in the first place and having brought the practice with him. He also opined that at the Cape there was no point asking about a performance that was considered domestic business instilling "common knowledge for us all."[14] Awaladien meanwhile stated that they performed the ritual frequently, lacking any other form of entertainment.[15]

While Griep was out on the island receiving his colonial requital for practicing such knowledge, Great Britain would claim full possession of the Western Cape in 1815. Soon enough British eyes were cast toward the eastern coast, which was felt to be ripe for further settlement, regardless of the objections of the Xhosa, who had long moved their herds along its rivers. The question remained as to what to do with all the people already within British boundaries, including the remaining "Hottentots" on the fringes of various farmsteads and towns. More particularly, the British were concerned with the numerous slaves, prize Africans, and free Blacks whose labors were crucial to vineyards such as Cloete's Groot Constantia, as well as the transportation and construction industries.

The missionaries were already at loggerheads with the farmers, who feared the loss of wine-averse workers who might turn Christian, or of perhaps too-educated people who might claim some form of equality. Whereas missionaries were starting to attract subaltern children to their school benches, they made little headway with their souls, so they began to inspect the facilities of their adversaries. On February 11, 1814, John Campbell of the London Missionary Society visited Dorp Street and watched as a corpulent "priest" (perhaps Achmat van Bengalen) led a service, ascending and descending the pulpit with a staff, known in Malay as a *tongkat*.

> The place was small—the floor was covered with green baze, on which sat a hundred men, chiefly slaves, Malays, and Madagascars. All of them wore clean white

robes, made in the fashion of shirts, and white pantaloons, with white cotton cloths spread before them, on which they prostrated themselves. They sat in rows, extending from one side of the room to the other. There were six priests, wearing elegant turbans. A chair, having three steps up to it, stood at the east end of the place, which has a canopy supported by posts . . . one of the priests covered his head and face with a white veil, holding in his hand a long black staff with a silver head, and advanced in front of the chair. When the other [priest] had chaunted a little, he mounted a step, making a dead halt; after a second chaunting he mounted the second step, and in the same way the third, when he sat down upon the chair. . . . The people were frequently during this form, prostrating themselves in their ranks as regularly as soldiers exercising.[16]

It was not just missionaries who were troubled by the increasing ranks of Islam forming as they surveyed the field. One hardly disinterested observer was William Wilberforce Bird (1758-1836). The former member for Coventry had arrived at the colony in January 1808 and was appointed as comptroller of customs in 1810. Together with the notorious collector, Charles Blair, Bird exercised power of allocation over many of the Africans taken from Indian Ocean vessels and bound in contacts not much differing from slavery, generally passing into the hands of well-connected Anglo arrivals (who also made use of poor Scots and indentured Irish). Bird was also a sometime confidante to Charles Somerset, the autocratic governor from 1814 to 1826 who was accused of overseeing the entire corrupt arrangement at a celebrated court case in 1824.[17]

Eager to see the colony transformed with the formal dissolution of many of its burgher institutions, but fully aware of the resistance it might engender given the ties between Somerset and the Dutch elite, Bird did not add his name to his survey, *State of the Cape of Good Hope in 1822*, though it was an open secret. Appearing in London in 1823, Bird's work was edited by the Sanskritist Henry Thomas Colebrooke (1765-1837), who had owned property at the Cape from 1815, including a farm close to the city called Zonnebloem.[18] Having emerged as a leading voice for the many new Anglophone settlers at the Cape, which drew more India hands, Colebrooke had just returned to London and established the Royal Asiatic Society. But if the society was concerned with "the encouragement of science, literature and the arts in connection with India and other countries eastward of the Cape of Good Hope," Bird's text took aim at many aspects of local Dutch society at that very spot, including his worried reaction to the rise of Islam—though probably more because it was eating into the workforce that he controlled than out of a desire for its Christianization.[19]

Much of Bird's data came directly from Barrow, whose work was something of a bible for the colonists arriving in 1820.[20] Unlike Barrow, who had married into the Truter family of magistrates in 1799, Bird would express his astonishment at the juridical arrangements in the colony. He seemed particularly perturbed by the cozy situation in court, where the Leiden-trained fiscal Daniel Denyssen (1774-1855) sat beside the judge, Johannes Truter, Barrow's father-in-law and a previous fiscal himself.[21] Bird was doubly impressed that Denyssen inspired universal fear among the slaves. This was only exacerbated by the excesses of his rough and ready police force. Once armed with swords, but then equipped with staves "in consequence of some outrageous acts," Bird deemed its officers "the refuse of the Cape population, drunken, worthless, and inhuman, [and] frequently selected from the convicts banned to Robben Island."[22]

One wonders if Griep had been forced to serve Denyssen in such a capacity once he rejoined the Malay circles of which he was clearly a part. Despite his criticism of the police, Bird was no advocate of the Muslims they harassed, whom he estimated amounted to some three thousand devotees making use of various "rooms and halls . . . and occasionally the stone quarries near the town." Reluctantly acknowledging that "Mahometanism" was making "great progress amongst the lower orders at the Cape," Bird confessed that "where there is the greatest zeal, there will be the most effect."[23] Pace Barrow, Bird's "lower orders" ignored a swathe of indentured Europeans and consisted of three sorts—Mozambiquan, "Africander," and Malay—with the last cast as the dominant mischief-making class of

> coachmen, tailors, painters, shoemakers, carpenters and fishermen. In fact they are usually engaged in every thing where what is called cleverness is required. The females are house-servants. This class of slaves requires the unremitted vigilance of the police; for a theft, or indeed mischief of any kind, is rarely perpetrated without the participation, if not by the contrivance, of a Malay. Many Malays, by the oeconomy of that money which they have these means of procuring, manage so as to purchase their freedom, and the number of free Malays is very considerable. The majority of them keep small subterranean stores throughout the town, in which iniquity, in all its shapes, is hatched into action.[24]

Colebrooke did not quibble with the alleged criminality of the Malays, or the issue of slave-holding. He had owned slaves himself during his brief time at the Cape and was surely the recipient of prize bodies from Bird as well.[25] He did, however, endeavor to contextualize the tendency toward conversion in an extensive endnote:

> Muhammedanism is said to be gaining ground at the Cape: that is to say, more converts among negroes, and blacks of every description, are made from Paganism to Muselman, than to the Christian religion: notwithstanding the zealous exertions of pious missionaries. One cause of this perversion is asserted to be a marked disinclination of slave-owners to allow their slaves to be baptized; arising from some erroneous notions, or overcharged apprehensions, of the rights of which a baptized slave acquires. Slaves certainly are impressed with the idea, that such a disinclination subsists; and it is not an unfrequent answer of a slave, when asked his motives for turning *Muselman*, that "some religion he must have, and he is not allowed to turn Christian."[26]

Colebrooke further bewailed the fact that the missionaries were late to a game being won by Muslims with far less effort and envisaged a future in which the colonists would find themselves outnumbered by this rival faith. At least the Malays seemed shorn of any proclivity toward running amok, much as Bird had ignored their ecstatic rituals.

While it was true that Muslim numbers were increasing, so too were those of poor white migrants headed to the eastern frontier to take land from African pastoralists. It was also increasingly hard to say that there was but one Malay or Muslim community in Cape Town. As we shall see, the later Commission of Eastern Inquiry was but dimly unaware of the rivalry between Dorp and Long Streets, or of how any of the several smaller prayer rooms were outgrowths of either establishment or wholly independent. At the level of the law, we do know that Jan van Bugis—now styling himself as Imam Hasan Allah or Asnoun—was the government's man, overseeing the oaths of Malay witnesses in court and perhaps attending to the prisoners in the local gaol. Yet differences existed, to be tested with reference to a widening Muslim world.

While Arab traders from Zanzibar had been present at the Cape at times, a new source of global connection came in late 1820 with the arrival of a party of eight men from the island of Nzwani (often called Anjouan or

Johanna), in the Comoro archipelago. Their journey had hardly been direct. Led by a prince whom the missionary John Campbell simply called "Anza," the group had been shipwrecked in the Gulf after performing the hajj and was rescued by an Arab vessel and taken all the way to its destination of Penang.[27] The EIC then paid for his party's repatriation via the Cape on the *Minstrel* in November 1820, as their home island had often provided shelter to its sailors, including in the wake of Johnstone's attack of 1781. It surely helped that the English-speaking prince had been known in Madras ten years before.[28]

During their nearly six months at the Cape, the Anjouanese engaged in friendly debates with the missionaries who accompanied them home in May 1821.[29] According to John Schofield Mayson in an address given in 1855, these same "distinguished Arabs" had found a particularly warm welcome among the Malays of the Cape, "whom they further instructed in the faith and practice of Islam," and with whom they had "since corresponded, sending them also supplies of the Koran and other books."[30] Unfortunately, there is little memory of such visits today, or of whose particular company the Nzwana notables kept. Even if Mayson was specific about the years of their visitation, his informants were more likely recalling the 1833 sojourn of the displaced Sultan 'Abdallah II (r. 1821–36), who encouraged a local tailor called Carel to go on the hajj while he waited for British aid to recover his kingdom from a Malagasy prince.[31]

The Commission of Inquiry

By the time that Bird's account appeared in 1823, Parliament had begun to dispatch commissions of inquiry to Great Britain's southern acquisitions. First conducted at New South Wales from 1819, these were replicated at the Crown possessions of Cape Town, Mauritius, and Ceylon. The glacial force behind the first two inquiries was judge John Thomas Bigge (1780–1843), empowered to solicit evidence from every level of society. In Sydney, Bigge crossed swords with the much-lower-paid Lachlan Macquarie—a Scots veteran of Ceylon and Egypt—as he sought to determine the efficacy and economy of convict punishment in that settlement, recommending more of the latter, and far less ostentation.[32] Bigge was then ordered to proceed to Cape Town in 1823, where he was joined by H. T. Colebrooke's cousin, William

MacBean George Colebrooke (1787–1870). This much younger Colebrooke had also served on Ceylon, and then with the expedition to Java, including Raffles's sack of Yogyakarta. He rose to the post of acting deputy quartermaster general on that island in 1813 and was a founding member of the Royal Asiatic Society at London ten years later.[33]

Bigge and the younger Colebrooke—joined by a third commissioner, William Blair, in 1825—were assisted at Cape Town by a secretary, John Gregory (1795–1853).[34] As their inquiries proceeded in 1824, they were mindful of the scandal over the allocation of prize Africans, of missionary complaints about the increasing numbers of slave converts to Islam, and whispers of financial inducements being offered to that end.[35] Certainly the commissioners were interested in the unfree laborers of the Cape, collecting voluminous data from owners in a much larger area than that considered by Bird. In his report, Bigge tried to be even handed when dealing with both an institution he felt should be abolished, and the reputations of certain individuals he did not wish to tarnish openly.[36] He finished his report on the question of the slaves in 1828, conceding "the powerful attraction presented ... by the principles of the Mahomedan faith" and adding that "it was strongly believed that the manifest preference" that they showed for it was "regarded with indifference" by masters who had no desire to create Christian workers. This was in sharp contrast to "the zeal and activity of the Malay priests," who were "amply rewarded by the increased number as well as by the constancy of their followers."[37]

Much as his lines smacked of the elder Colebrooke, it is worth noting that Bigge was seldom relaying Muslim speech directly. His report on Muslim institutions derived from Gregory's conversations with local Muslim "priests" as 1824 became 1825. Yet, rather than interview the very known quantity of Jan van Bugis, occasional functionary of the fiscal's office, Gregory first spoke with a certain Muding, sometimes known as Meeding, and, eventually, at his death in 1878, as Imam Hadjee Medien or Imam Hadjee Mogadien. Described by Gregory as a "Javanese or Malay Priest," though in 1836 he would only claim the status of "onder priester," Muding said he was the son of a slave brought from Balambangan at the age of sixteen. At some point his father had been acquired by an old "Malay" priest (i.e., Tuan Guru), who had bought, taught, and manumitted him at his death, whereafter he served as imam at his mosque.[38]

Muding's father, named on his death certificate as Salomon, can be identified as a shopkeeper and imam called Sourdeen who had died in 1822. Salomon/Sourdeen had indeed been one of Abdallah's loyal followers, and he had trained his son to such a level that, aside from working as a priest and carpenter, as his daughter recalled when she lodged a death notice in November 1878, Muding also served as interpreter to the Supreme Court, which his son noted in his own belated lodging of September 1884.[39]

In 1824, such work was yet to come. Muding was evidently at some distance from Dorp Street and Imam Achmat when he explained that there were two main mosques in the city, as well as five subordinate ones. The priests, he said, generally received no income beyond their trades, whether as hewers of wood like himself or retailers of foodstuffs and other merchandise. However, on the two special feast days of the year, they oversaw a general collection to cover the costs of feeding all the participants, and he implied that that would be the case at a forthcoming "tambaroo"—perhaps referring to a performance of the ratib with its drums and tambourines.

As for the slave members, Muding remarked that they were taught to believe that their souls were free, and they were to "look up to God" to make them free" at their deaths—for in this life all were taught that "their duty in the world" consisted in "paying respect to authority, performing the work of their employers" and abstaining from alcohol or theft.[40] The famously dour Gregory was further curious about absences from the mosque or the abrogation of Islamic law, at which point Muding volunteered that refractory members could be liable to flogging or excommunication, which may well have been the sort of treatment meted out by Jan van Bugis, who was certainly committed to discipline.[41]

Many of Gregory's other questions pertained to marriage and the potential separation of slave couples through their sale—not to mention the unfortunate equation of so many dissolute kerchief wearers with pious Muslims. Regarding Muslim marriages, which were not recognized by the state, Muding indicated that polygamy was rare, with two wives being the upper limit embraced by those of the "priests" who had been in Mecca. This was even more pertinent since it had been "Arab" priests who imposed the limit in the first place.[42]

Such references to hajjis and Arab leaders are intriguing, especially given that scholars often claim that Prince Abdallah's advisee Carel returned from

Mecca as the first Capetonian hajji in the 1830s. Yet we may recall that Abd al-Hamid had attempted the journey in the difficult year of 1809, perhaps returning by 1811, and that between 1823 and 1828 Cape Town directories referred to a tailor living at 39 Dorp Street called "Hadje" or "Hatje" van de Kaap.[43] While it is possible that the name could be merely that, rather than any reference to the hajj, that this latter man is not claimed as a local is perhaps bound up with Muding's reference to the presence of Arab priests. Setting aside the memories of the long-dead Sayyid ʿAlawi, there are strong possibilities for these figures. The first is a contemporary of Tuan Guru called Shaykh ʿAbdallah. According to Mirza Abu Taleb, who stayed at the Cape for a few weeks in 1799, this ʿAbdallah was the son of a Meccan trader who had settled at the Cape prior to the British annexation and had married the daughter of a local Malay.[44] A decade later, between 1811 and 1820, the *African Court Calendar* listed an "Achmet of Arabia" (his son?) as a "Malay priest" active on Vredenburg Street.[45]

It is further possible that this Achmet is identical with a subsequently recorded "Hadje" who would have reached a Hijaz more securely under Egyptian control in 1821–1822, returning by 1823 as the pilgrim tailor of 39 Dorp Street.[46] A decade after Gregory's departure, there was a similarly named schoolmaster and tailor operating a few doors away at 27 Dorp Street, while the original address had since been occupied by another "Malay priest" called Abdolrapiek—perhaps the fisherman who had obtained his awls and fabrics from the mysterious Moor pasha in 1813.[47]

All of this aside, the question of manumission on the demise of a Muslim owner had intrigued Gregory in 1824. Three days after speaking with Muding, he secured a report from the slave registry documenting the holdings of a few Muslim owners—Abdul Jappar (Abd al-Jabbar), Abdul Malek (Abd al-Malik), and Secour—indicating that this practice was not universally followed. Some slaves were required to produce the funds for their purchase while, in the unhappy case of Phillida, others were passed on to their descendants.[48]

These were but a sampling. While dominated by Europeans (including the fiscal Denyssen and the absentee Colebrooke), an incomplete list of slave owners at the Cape up to 1826 included many Muslims. Imam Achmat and Jan van Bugis are perhaps the most prominent, though there are several other people who have appeared in this book so far. For instance, there were the just-mentioned Abdul Jappar, Tuan Guru's witnesses Abd al-Malik and Abd al-Wasi, his indirect patron Catharina van de Kaap, and his sons Abd al-Rakib and Abd al-Rauf. Also listed are Hammat van Macassar, whose ratib had gone so badly wrong in 1813, and "the estate of the late Iman Abdoela" by which their fellow fisherman Damon van Bugis had been freed in June 1816.[49]

There was no doubt that ever more slaves were gravitating to Islam. According to a return obtained for 1825 printed at the end of Imam Achmat's statement, an incredible 490 free Blacks and slave children were attending the school of a Muslim teacher.[50] While it has long been thought that the school was of Achmat van Bengalen, the commission's notes suggest that it was of "Dollee Mansoer," who appears in the slave-owning lists as the locally born Dolie van de Kaap, and in the *African Court Calender* as first a gingerbread maker and then a priest from 1825.[51] Regardless of Mansoer's apparent success (or someone's accounting error), the looming presence in Cape Town was that of the largest mosque. Hence, when Gregory decided to reach out to its "High Priest" on January 10, 1825, he learned that the aged fishmonger had come to his position with the passing of his predecessor (Sourdeen) in 1822. Achmat van Bengalen also declared that this predecessor had been the one who first obtained permission from General Craig for their mosque to function, arguing that the "obstruction of the free exercise of religion" had been "prejudicial to the conduct of the lower classes."[52]

This claim sounds very much like the petition presented by Frans van Bengalen to George Yonge in 1800, though there is much bleeding of information in the printed version of the interview, which is indicative either of Gregory not quite understanding his interlocutor in 1825, or of the typesetter not knowing what to make of his handwriting in 1835. For instance, there is a garbled reference to the fiscals having raided the mosque in search of stolen goods and confiscating their papers, whereupon the word "Denaus" is given.[53] This must have been a reference to Denyssen, whose overweening presence in court had so offended Bird.[54]

Achmat was more forthcoming on the division between his mosque and that of Jan, whom he said was not acknowledged by his followers, just as many other priests were deemed unauthorized. He also confirmed the general picture that slave and free were treated as equals in faith, that no true Muslim would sell a slave against their will, and that the imams subsisted from their own trades rather than through subscriptions—though he denied that they were empowered to apply any sanction beyond expulsion. He was also quite explicit that his establishment was the largest in Cape Town.

All this information was duly gathered up by the commissioners and fed into their reports, most notably that upon "Slaves and the State of Slavery at the Cape of Good Hope," which is worth quoting at length:

> As the influence of the Mahomedan Priests over the Slave Population was a subject that had been frequently noticed, returns were obtained from them of the Slaves who attend the Mosques and who are recognized as Mahomedans, and some explanation was offered by the Chief Priests, of the Principles by which their authority over their followers is regulated.... To be admitted to the Mahomedan Faith Infants must be brought to the Mosque seven days after their birth and are then named by the Priest; they are afterwards taught the precepts of the Koran and they learn to read and write Arabic.—Many also are sent to the European free schools where they are taught to read and write the Dutch language, but it does not appear that the instruction which they receive at these schools has any influence upon their faith.—As it is contrary to the Precepts of the Koran that a Slave should be a Mahomedan, the Priests endeavour to make the Slaves believe that although their bodies are held in Slavery, yet that their souls are free, and that they must trust in God to make them free when they die.—It is also contrary to the Mahomedan Law, that those who follow it should sell their slaves, and if a Mahomedan buys a slave of a Christian, and the Slave becomes a convert to the faith of his new owner he is entitled to be considered as an equal in his family and cannot afterwards be sold, and at his Masters [sic] Death, both himself and his Children are enfranchised: at the same time the Slave is allowed to earn the means of redeeming his Freedom, or if he wishes to be sold or to separate from his Master, he is allowed to find a Purchaser.—Although the abstinence and sobriety which the Mahomedan Law enjoins is found to be favourable to the Morals of the Slaves who yield obedience to it, yet the Influence of the Malay Priests over the Slaves, is said to be used in encouraging the latter to acts of dishonesty and Plunder, the fruits of which are either divided with the Priests or applied to the support of their Mosques and the celebration of their festivals.—In the reports upon the Criminal Law and Police notice was taken of the heavy suspicions to which the Free people and Slaves Professing the Mahomedan Faith had long been liable and the Peculiar interference of the Police Officers to which they were subject.—In the course of their examination upon these points (2 No. 13) the Priests asserted, that many persons who have been apprehended and prosecuted for crimes have been taken by the Police for Mahomedans, although they possessed no other title to be so considered that

that of wearing the Mahomedan handkerchief, and had never been admitted to the Mosques or had been expelled as unworthy members; and they solemnly declared, that their true followers contribute nothing for the private use of their Priests, who derive their subsistence from the pursuit of various Trades and occupations; ... Polygamy amongst the Mahomedans at the Cape has according to the Practice observed by the present Priests, been limited by the authority of their Predecessors who were Arabs, to two wives, and it is only allowed when the husband can afford a separate establishment.—The number of persons at Cape Town who were so situated was not considered to exceed 20.[55]

While the report was never published, coming well after its recommendations had been implemented, the paraphrased statements of Muding and Achmat were offered as inclusions among papers on the "Condition and Treatment of the Native Inhabitants," which circulated in Parliament in 1835. Sadly misplaced, however, like several of the original documents taken by Bigge and sent from Mauritius in early December 1828, was a certificate once in Achmat's possession respecting the establishment of his "church."[56]

It is worth reiterating here that even if some shadow remained in terms of perceived criminality, the image of inherent Malay violence had been dispelled. No wonder, given so many positive testimonies about their being the most temperate "mechanics" whom it was customary to supply with tea.[57] Although Truter and Denyssen were not named, Bigge took the question of police harassment seriously. A bare three weeks after the last tranche of supporting documents was shipped from Mauritius, George Greig's *South African Commercial Advertiser* paid tribute to the Malays as victims of overzealous magistrates liable to their homes being searched by the police. Now it pronounced them to be "an industrious and peaceable class of inhabitants. ... Many of them are men of the most estimable character, inoffensive in their demeanour and humane and generous in their dispositions. And the whole class may be considered as a most valuable addition—the fruit of the late ordinance—to our effective and improving population."[58]

The ordinance in question was No. 50 of July 3, 1828, which gave non-Europeans freedom of movement. This and the right to own property (granted in 1830) fed into the final process of emancipation proclaimed in 1834.[59] But even if the process of manumission dragged into the late 1830s while a renewed apprenticeship scheme continued to provide unfree labor to the city, Cape Town would witness a fresh proliferation of imams and ever greater pressure among them for establishing some form of hierarchy.[60] This last fact is demonstrated by the increasingly bureaucratic terms they adopted. Most mosques had a complement of officials bearing such titles as "priester" (priest), "onder priester" (deacon), "merbout" (sexton), "koster" (undertaker), "katib" (clerk), "modin," and "bilal" (muezzin). But while there was no hard and fast distinction between such occupations, there was another title whose usage would soon raise hackles in an increasingly competitive religious economy.[61]

The Prince of Bo-Kaap

Bigge's belated report was not the only printed document that circulated with the name of Achmat van Bengalen in the mid-1830s. On February 13, 1836, the *South African Commercial Advertiser* published a letter that had been written five days earlier by an outraged Jan van Bugis. Signing himself as Asnoun—a contraction of his preferred ecclesiastical title, Imam Hasan Allah—he issued a Dutch address to his "beloved countrymen and fellow Mohammedans" stating that, "having seen and read a printed document in which Achmat presents himself as being a Priest appointed by the late Prince Abdoela ... I, as the oldest Priest, ... declare that there was never a Prince Abdoela at the Cape of Good Hope, but rather an Iman Abdoela, or High Priest. As the oldest teacher of the Mohammedan language [i.e., Arabic], who taught Achmat, which I can prove, I express my gratitude to the Government and to all the Officials for so many years of favour."[62]

It is unclear just which instance had so riled Jan van Bugis. Achmat had previously declared himself to be a "High Priest" to Gregory, and he further arrogated that title to himself in a death notice for Abd al-Rakib that was published in the same paper in February 1834.[63] In any case, Jan's complaint invited a collective response from Dorp Street and a potted history of the transition of 1807. It is remarkable that it was offered in the form of an English petition to an unnamed patron, suggesting that the intended audience was the new governor, General Benjamin D'Urban (1777–1849). Writing furiously on the day Jan's letter appeared, Achmat declared in his own missive, published on the 24th, that before the death of Emaum Abdulla, he sent for me and said, that he was sure that after his death the people would make another Church, but he said, I must not mind it, all those who wished to leave me I must let them go, and those who would remain I could keep. Again Emaum Abdullah said, "Remember, that John of Bonghis [sic] can never, as long as he lives, take my place, and whoever gives him my place must answer for it on the day of judgement, and not to me. I have made the Church with a hope that it may remain as long as the world stands." Emaum Abdulla then gave me the rules and laws of our Religion, ... and then recommended to my care and protection his two Sons, that I must act towards them as a father, and teach them all things necessary; that when they arrived at such years, and were capable, they might take his place. This I also promised, and I have always taken trouble with them more so than my own sons, as can be plainly seen.

But there was more:

After the death of Prince Abdulla, came old France [sic] the Field Priester and said he would place John of Bongris [sic] in the place of the deceased. I told him so, it was impossible for us to do it, at which he said he would leave me. I answered him, very well; do as you think proper. One of the witnesses present at this time was Abdolwasy ... then Clerk, or what we call Belull. Shortly after, old France and John of Bongris bought a house and made a Church of it. My brother-in-law Abdolgamit became Priester there, and John of Bougris his under Priester. Scarce a year had passed when Abdolgamit again returned to my Church, because they did not use him well. He also brought his scholars with him to me. Old France would have returned with Abdolgamit, but was ashamed, and went back to Batavia, so that John of Bongris was left with his Church and a small community, and that is the reason he calls himself the highest Priest.[64]

It is evident that Achmat was either reacting to an earlier copy of the letter, or unable to read the newspaper. Jan's letter had been printed with the support of two others: Achmat's rival (Dolie) "Manzur" and Tuan Guru's witness, Abd al-Wasi, whom Achmat had expected to back him.[65] It must have been a yet heavier blow to learn that Abd al-Wasi had declared that while Achmat might be fit for his own community, he could not be so for theirs on grounds of his insufficient knowledge. Not that his missive would have entirely pleased Jan. Referring to their late master as "Prince Abdoela" and thus assigning him the title that Jan denied, Abd al-Wasi had asked how the elders could not have known of such events when they transpired.[66]

Then again, Achmat did find signed support from eight such men, in addition to testimonies from Achtardeen (d. 1845), Hagi (a.k.a. Ahagé), Abdolbazier (Abd al-Basir), and Abdolbarick (Abd al-Bari), with the last recalling his days as a "scholar of Prince Emaum Abdulla."[67] The most powerful letter, though, came from the surviving son of Tuan Guru. "Prince Abdul-Roove" announced his right to "stand at the head of all" and recalled Achmat's steadfast support of him and his late brother, and his desire to follow him until he came of age (forty) and knew enough of the rules and regulations laid out in the books of his father. While breathing a united spirit of support for Achmat and his history, it is notable that all the letters betrayed an anxiety that the "laws and regulations" of their mosque were under attack. It is furthermore notable that, with their language of service and gratitude, they emphasized their loyalty to the British government.[68]

The response of Achmat and his partisans was repeated in Dutch on February 27.[69] By this time D'Urban had already received a Malay-language memorial submitted on Jan's behalf, together with a petition supportive of his status as "Mohammedan High Priest." As the expansive petition related, "In 1798 upon the arrival of Sir Francis Dundas the Mahommedan High Priest Abdoulla appointed the Memorialist together with Rajep as Priest, and ever since that time the Memorialist has performed his functions as such." As it continued:

> That upon the arrival in this Colony of Jan Willem Janssens in 1803 all the Mahommedan inhabitants were called upon to enter into military service and the Memorialist was appointed a Bombadier in the Malay artillery under the command of Major Kuchler.
>
> General Janssens at that time sent the High Priest Abdoela a present of a dagger by Major Kuchler with an invitation to enter the service but Abdoela being too old and weak declined it, and recommended that the dagger should be presented to Old Frans whom he had appointed in his stead as a High Priest whenever the corps should enter into an engagement; I then also upon application received permission to hold a church every Friday.
>
> In the year 1811 when Old France left this Colony for Batavia he resigned the Office of High Priest in the Memorialist's favor, in the presence of the whole

Mahommedan Community, *so that he is now the High Priest having regularly been appointed thereto with the consent of the whole community which is acknowledged by the priests Abdol Wassie and Abdol Mansoer* [emphasis mine].

That Achmat of Cape Town has endeavoured to persuade the inhabitants of this Colony that he is the High and oldest Priest, having been thereto appointed by Prince Abdoula. But in the first place Abdoula was an Imam or High-Priest and not a Prince, and in the second place never appointed him as an Imam or high Priest but only as a Priest, the Memorialist having previously given him the necessary instruction to perform for his office.[70]

Much as Jan would have hoped, his Malay source document was entrusted to his old boss, J. H. Neethling, who oversaw its transliteration by four of Jan's peers (including Muding), providing his own translation and testimony on the matter. There are curious variations in detail throughout. While the Jawi text makes no mention of Major Kuchler, speaking of the direct presentation of a weapon (*senjata*) to Tuan Guru, its translators turned that weapon into a kris, which Neethling rendered as a sword in his draft, before shrinking it to a dagger in his report.[71]

In his response, penned with J. A. Truter, Neethling, who acknowledged having overseen the formation of "the Malays and Freeblacks into a Corps of Artillery" as colonial secretary in 1803 and who had a property on Long Street not so far from Jan, claimed to remember this all very clearly.[72] Hearkening back to his earlier role as deputy fiscal from 1792 and having later considered cases concerning the Malays and other free Blacks as a magistrate (as we saw with Griep), Neethling remarked that he had "known no other Priests than one Nabe who since died, Frans who left the Colony, and the said Jan van Boegies, who were acting in that capacity without however being acknowledged by the Dutch Government." Moreover, he claimed that neither Achmat nor any other priests had been known. His memory jogged by the transcription he oversaw, Neethling confirmed that Frans had been made the "Chaplain" of the artillery, and that he had been personally "decorated by General Janssens with a dagger and sash which, on his departure from the Colony, he handed over to Jan van Boegies."[73]

Truter saw fit to add that, during his presidency of the Court of Justice between 1812 and 1827, Jan had "constantly been considered the competent Mahomedan Priest, to administer the required Oaths to the witnesses professing the Mahommedan faith," adding that their own investigations had informed them that Achmat had been a slave at the time when he and Abd al-Wasi were being instructed by Jan. Unsurprisingly, Neethling closed with the observation that he "perfectly" recollected that Janssens had granted permission to Jan and Frans to purchase a house "for the express purpose of being used as a church for the Mahomedan people, at a time when Achmat was not known. And this was the first instant of a Mahomedan Church being by Government admitted as such."[74]

Lacking the documents taken from Dorp Street, it is hard to contest their claim. We should well doubt it, though. Janssens was no longer governor when the Long Street property became a mosque. Even allowing for the onset of age, it is curious that Neethling—who had actually been appointed in 1793 and who had signed the will of "Iman Abdullah" in 1800—claimed not to have known any other imams than Jan, Frans, and Nabe. Equally strange is the assertion that Achmat was not known, as he had been sought out by Gregory in 1825. Evidently neither Truter nor Neethling questioned Jan's history too closely. While Jan claimed a 1786 arrival at the Cape, the naval officer and ship he mentioned match records for 1789, much as his naming of the fiscal as (Gabriel) Exter suggests that he had been under his jurisdiction at the time.[75]

D'Urban evidently let the matter drop, and the papers fell silent. But the matter of precedence was not resolved. Achmat's next gambit was to reach even further into the Capetonian Muslim past, petitioning the following governor, George Napier (1784–1855), to grant him the role of protector and renovator of the kramat of Shaykh Yusuf, presenting it in late 1837 as an alternate site of pilgrimage to Mecca. But while Napier made no motion in his favor, he also took no issue with Achmat's terming himself in the petition as "High Priest of the Mahommedans of this Colony."[76] It was this title he bore on his death certificate of October 1843.[77] Dorp Street's authority was momentarily confirmed, if in the unsteady hands of his successor and creditor Abd al-Bari.[78] Indeed, rather than remain, Achmat's own sons would move to found a new mosque around the corner on Buitengracht Street, taking their adoptive and talismanic princely brother Abd al-Rauf as their imam.

While Achmat and his community were still engaged in asserting some form of authority at the Cape to rival that of Jan, who died in 1846, it is worth remembering how all the letter writers and petitioners expressed their loyalty to their "king" in England even as they reached back to Batavian history to validate their claims. In court in 1842, for instance, Magmoud, an elder of the mosque of Imam Samoudien (Sami al-Din, 1800–1869) claimed that his adoptive father, Noriman, had been a good servant of General Janssens, and that the English had granted his family a space for their graves above the Bo-Kaap.[79] But it was not enough to be linked to the state, past or present, to assert precedence; nor yet could one claim to have been among Tuan Guru's intimates. Samoudien knew this well, departing for Arabia in the mid-1840s and returning to join Carel as one of its most prominent local-born hajjis.

Pilgrims and Volunteers

It is striking today that no successful pilgrimages are remembered before the 1837 return of Carel. Taking the name Hajji Gazanodien (Hasan al-Din) Abdallah thereafter, but being more commonly known as Carel Pelgrim, he became a celebrity among Muslims and missionaries alike until his death in 1863. Despite never formally founding his own mosque or school, George Angas's famous depiction of circa 1848 shows him as a kindly teacher instructing young students in reading. Another shows the bearded figure at prayer beside the pulpit, with prayer beads strewn at his feet and incense burning in a brazier nearby. This image had a counterpart in his unveiled second wife, Nazea, dressed in her day clothes of a voluminous dress topped with an Indian shawl. She further stands before the Lion's Rump, with the growing suburb of Bo Kaap below and the walled garden of Sayyid 'Alawi or Tuan Guru laid out a little above and to the right (see fig. 4.1).[80]

While it seems unlikely that Carel was the first Capetonian pilgrim, indeed the later Abu Bakr Effendi was told in 1863 that the first returnees had come back some fifty years earlier and been disturbed by the hereditary arrangements of many mosques, Mayson was probably correct in stating that he was one of only four such men active in the city in 1854, alongside Samoudien, Medien (Muding), and Omar (Imam Haji, d. 1860).[81] Shamil Jeppie argues that such prominence affirmed a distinction between imams in terms of knowledge. With their celebrity and sartorial choices that echoed the restored Ottoman order after 1840, these figures became patrons to their fellow Muslims and another stumbling block to the missionaries. This is not to say that they were united. Samoudien's supporters had sued those of Carel

WESTERN DEPOSITS

Figure 4.1 George Angas (1822–1866), *Karel, a Malay Priest, and His Wife Nazea*, 1849.

in 1842 in regard to the erection of further walls above the once "Javanese" cemetery, stressing their ties to the long-dead Noriman.[82] Another strong candidate for precedence over Carel was the already noted "Imam Hajji," whom Davids says had been a student of Tuan Guru and an assistant to Achmat van Bengalen.[83] Identifiable as Ahagé of Walendorp—listed in the *African Court Calendar* of 1829 and a supporter of Achmat in the princely dispute of 1836—he would found his own congregation on the corner of Chiappini Street and Hillegar Lane after Achmat's death in 1843. His success would be tied up with that of another figure and future pilgrim, Abdol Wahab (Abd al-Wahab, d. 1872), a son of Abd al-Basir who had also backed Achmat in 1836.

But while both were tied to the lineage of Achmat van Bengalen, their prominence would be affirmed by repeating the techniques of Frans and Jan, aligning themselves to the state through military service. The challenge this time was not to repel a European attacker, but to participate in the ongoing invasion of Xhosa and Zulu (Hlubi) lands. While some Malay men were perhaps convinced to join in 1846 by a young Petrus Emanuel de Roubaix (1828–1897), then serving as an unpaid scrivener in the office of the clerk of the peace, others volunteered for what would be known as the War of the Axe.[84] Achmat's youngest son, Sadick, and his then follower Abd al-Wahab served as chaplains on that campaign with the hope of greater recognition for their congregations. This was duly given to the latter in the form of a larger parcel of land on Chiappini Street that would see the establishment of a new mosque in 1850. Sometimes called the Victoria Mosque in honor of the imperial sovereign, it would supplant those of Dorp and Long Streets.[85]

Although the War of the Axe was never a triumph of interfaith relations, it would be remembered as a key moment. Many of those sent to the Eastern Cape became disgruntled when they learned that their families were not receiving the support promised them. They were soon demobilized, making a striking entrance into Cape Town Harbour in 1847—or at least this was the image presented by Thomas Baines that now hangs in the Castle of Good Hope, showing a throng of conical-hatted soldiers massed in several longboats with a green banner that united the Union Jack and the Muslim Profession of Faith with three crescents.[86]

Islam and its symbols were to remain a marked feature of the town. Its adherents, now numbering around one-third of the population of around twenty-two thousand, absorbed the attention of the Mancunian cotton merchant John Schofield Mayson during his visit in 1854. In an address delivered to the Manchester Statistical Society in February 1855, Mayson drew a broad history from Raffles and his successors before offering positive observations of the Malays of Cape Town and their new communal mosque, describing a prosperous society of artisans led by Abd al-Rauf and the four hajjis. While he resorted to stereotypes—quoting Alfred Cole's cynical remarks on the "jugglery" of a ratib in the 1840s and claiming to have witnessed an instance of drug-infused frenzy at Rondebosch—Mayson concluded that the Malay's "Mahometanism, so closely associated with his nationality," deserved "calm consideration."[87] After all, the virtues of the Malays were "numerous":

> Perhaps none of these are more striking than their cleanliness, their devotion to each other, their bravery, and their fidelity to the government under which they live. Constant in distress, they allow no hindrance to obstruct the mutual discharge of the smallest office of kindness. To their old masters they were

valued servants, and to the British, who freed them, in 1834, from the inhuman bond of slavery, they have often proved themselves, as at the conquest of the Cape in 1795, and in the Kaffir war of 1847, friends firm and warm.[88]

Calling for Christian "candour and kindness" to undo the convergence of Islam and bondage, Mayson believed that such friendship had only been magnified by Great Britain's alliance with the Ottomans in the Crimea, with British swords "drawn in defence of a Moslem monarchy, of common rights and a common independence."[89]

Apparently some of Great Britain's African opponents, hearing rumors of that conflict and having seen Muslims ranged against them, had vainly hoped for the arrival of Russian allies from late 1854 once they heard of the Crimean demise of General Cathcart, their old enemy.[90] It is also clear that some of the hajjis who welcomed Mayson in Cape Town saw the British as a natural recourse in times of trouble, being the most effective masters of the routes that they travelled to the Holy Places. In September 1856, for instance, and thus eight months before the great uprising that would derail Muslim fortunes and reshape British attitudes on the subcontinent, Samoudien sent a worried petition to the local colonial secretary, Rawson W. Rawson (1812–1899), seeking information about his two sons, Abdullah and Cassiem (Qasim), both of whom had gone to Arabia in 1851 to emulate their father. The last news of them came in a letter sent from Jeddah at the end of that year. At the time, their host reported that they were planning to travel to Zanzibar to collect money and letters, and that he had advised them to consider studying there (where so many Hadrami and Comorian Arabs were making their mark under Omani patrons).[91] While the outcome of this story is unknown, the British were prepared to entertain such requests, given their firm belief that subjects like Samoudien were so loyal. The good pilgrim Samoudien and his peers had just proven it with reference to the latest scandal over the Califa.

For Queen and Califa

Whereas the Malays were increasingly seen as worthy subjects, missionaries continued to worry about their more spectacular entertainments. In 1835 the American George Champion (1810–1841) had happened upon "the confused noise of singing" and "the beating of drums" emanating from a house in Cape Town, writing that what he saw of a ratib was emblematic of the increasing power of this "religion of the false prophet," whose dancing priests appeared to him as devils incarnate.[92] On the other hand, a cynical Alfred Cole mocked a performance he saw a decade later as being nothing but fakery geared to obtain money as cheeks were pierced and daggers dangled from sides.[93] It was also the latter that Mayson would reference in his address of 1855, and at a time when other similarly gory performances—such as "hook swinging" in India—were being critiqued by missionary-inflected accounts across Africa and Asia.[94]

As with these other sites of ecstatic performance under colonial eyes that impacted new religious movements, such images would impact those whom we might label Muslim reformers, especially if they could claim to have experienced daily life in the holy cities of the Ottoman Empire. Just such a scenario played out ten months after Mayson gave his Mancunian address. When, in December 1855, European residents complained to Petrus de Roubaix, then voluntary acting judge and superintendent of police residing at 36 Long Street, about the rowdy and exuberant performance of the Califa at the nearby house of "Jawakel," he forbade them to continue. This earned the appreciation of several local Westerners, including one of his enduring supporters, Dr. F. L. C. Biccard (d. 1884), whose father had examined Abdol Zaghie four decades earlier.[95]

While designed to celebrate De Roubaix, source documents published by J. S. De Lima in 1857 show that some Muslims worried about their freedom of practice and petitioned governor George Grey. But while they fretted lest the Califa be permanently banned, the three adult sons of Imam Achmat ("High Priest" Mochamat, and his priestly brethren Gamiem and Sadick)—with their letters rendered by De Roubaix in his additional capacity as "sworn translator to the High Court"—were also conscious of the excessive manner by which it was often being celebrated. They were thus open to its limitation outside the customary date commemorating the death of the first caliph, Abu Bakr.[96]

However, there were others again who favored its complete abrogation. Most notable were those who had performed the hajj. Their ranks included Medien (our Muding of old), now a fully fledged imam and occasional High Court translator in his own right. He declared that, with his education at Mecca, he could not (or perhaps no longer) deem the Califa to be a part of his religion. While he conceded that it could perhaps be allowed for the celebration of the Prophet's immediate successor, he had apparently warned his own congregation against it. Medien had support from fellow pilgrims Carel and Samoudien, who also found it a discredit to their religion and community. There were joined by the imams Raban (son of the late Imam Hajji Omar) and Abd al-Wahab, both yet to make the hajj.[97]

Perhaps the most powerful voice of opposition to the Califa came from a man never to make the pilgrimage, but whom Mayson understood to be the paramount imam at the Cape. This was Abd al-Rauf, now head of the mosque on Buitengracht Street, just around the corner from that established by his father. He also lined up with Raban and Abd al-Wahab rather than his stepbrothers to fully condemn the "discreditable" way that the Califa was played. In his own letter he advised that the ritual tended to "bring our religion into disrepute" and was "the cause that many of the Malays become bad characters," eroding "the good feeling . . . subsisting for so many years, between us and the white population."[98]

Few establishment voices supported what they saw as the dance of undistinguished divines. It is also evident that De Roubaix had earned sufficient capital with the Muslim elite, enfranchised since the provision of a representative council in 1853. This had first accrued after his interventions during the conscriptions of 1846. Hence his decision to enforce a partial ban was largely respected, as much as some would seek him out for aid as when, in 1857, an imam sought De Roubaix's arbitration to resolve a dispute about burial.[99] In the wake of the Califa dispute, Imam Achmat's sons presented him with a silver inkstand by way of thanks for his impartiality, just as several other imams presented themselves before Governor Grey for cordial meetings underlining their loyalty to Victoria's government, which they knew to be in alliance with Istanbul.

The sons of Achmat also proposed that the documents of the entire affair would be presented "to Her Majesty's Government in England, who recently stood so closely connected with Turkey . . . with a request that Her Majesty will forward the Documents of the Califa matter, and expressions of approbation of the measures devised to the Chief Authorities in Turkey."[100] In July 1857 they further had a letter published in the *Cape Argus* expressive of their steadfast loyalty.[101] Such would have been all the more valued in light of the news of the violence that had been sweeping Northern India since May. As Maximilien Kollisch would later condescend of the Malays—paraphrasing De Roubaix on "the advantages of British rule under which they so happily live[d]"—a "Revolt of Islam" was "likely to remain a myth" at the Cape.[102]

Such loyalty was on full display in late July 1860 to mark the visit of Victoria's sixteen-year-old second son, Alfred, who had been dispatched on tour as a crewman aboard HMS *Euralyus*. After being met at the docks of Simon's Bay by crowds of Muslims, the midshipman prince rode through triumphal arches to a thoroughly dressed Cape Town, where he met with a deputation of Malays at a reception at Government House. Abd al-Wahab, representing what was now seen as "the chief Mahommedan Mosque" of the city, delivered him the text of an Arabic address wishing him "joy and prosperity, and the blessings of God" in the name of "all other priests and elders, and pilgrims." Another imam then assured him of their "devoted loyalty and affection" to his mother, "under whose beneficent rule" they enjoyed "such freedom and prosperity."[103]

While we might imagine that one of the sons of Achmat was the second imam, the *Manchester Guardian* offered a slightly different version of events, reporting Alfred meeting the second Malay delegation on August 5 at Graham's Town, where many—including a son of Nabe—had remained after the War of the Axe, and noting a long exchange at a levee there with a Malay doctor, Isaak Jukkie (d. 1891).[104] This seems to overlap with an account of the entire tour commissioned by Saul Solomon (1817–1892), the progressive parliamentarian and founder of the *Cape Argus*, which had a Mr. Pearson reading an address from the loyal Malays of Algoa Bay.[105] The volume, replete with photographs, paraphrased Mayson on the emergence of the Cape Malays as a loyal and industrious class ever eager to meet "the Son of the Queen who freed them."[106]

As the *Cape Argus* had already approvingly noted, no section of the community had expressed more enthusiasm for Alfred's arrival. One old woman had walked into the Government House reception in the hope of seeing him, informing the flustered ushers that he was as much her prince as theirs. An indulgent Grey waved her in.[107] Thomas Baines moreover depicted Malays raising their conical hats when Alfred inaugurated a new breakwater at Cape Town Harbour, and Solomon spoke at his departure of a rowboat bedecked with the "Malay colours" (probably the green banner of their unit of 1847), full of "loyal followers of Mahomet." Steered by their "priest," they nimbly circled the *Euryalus* "like a duck upon the crest of the waves" and cheered their (British) prince as it bore him away.[108]

With all this enthusiasm, then, it is ironic that at a great fair held in the botanic gardens in the days before his departure, some two hundred

Muslims had mounted a stage and given a performance of the Califa, adding a potentially scandalous spectacle to the visit. As Solomon had it:

> Though not strictly prescribed in the Koran, it is one of the most favorite rites of the Moslem faith, and serves its devotees instead of still more mischievous and offensive forms of fanatical excitement. It is usually performed in the darkness of the residences of the leading Malays of the town, and is supposed, by the ordeals through which its "experts" must pass, to test their faith, and contribute as effectually to their spiritual welfare as its hideous noise and tumult prove as unceasing nuisance to all who may unhappily chance to come within earshot of it. On this occasion, however, the managers of the Fête determined that is should be exhibited to the Prince as a characteristic feature of South African life, in one of the most interesting of its multifarious varieties—which might compare in barbaric picturesqueness with the war-dances of Basutoland or Natal. The principal Malays themselves, priests and laymen, were delighted at the opportunity thus offered them of displaying their loyalty, which is as thoroughly earnest and sincere as any other section of the community.[109]

The account then drew from the *Advertiser and Mail*, detailing the modified dress of the participants, whose loose linen robes, sashes and "Turkish caps" had supposedly replaced their customary "semi-nudity":

> At a given signal they commence with a slow, monotonous chaunt of some verses from the Koran, accompanied by a wild clashing of cymbals and fretting of parchment. The high priest rises from his seat behind the flags, crescents, and incense burners at the head of the platform, and walks all around the line of musicians, touching each instrument and muttering some words. Having returned to his seat, a number of athletes (armed with falchions held at the point and hilt and with pairs of long stilettoes having large globular heads, with light bronze chains attached to them) step forward and repeat the action of the priest. They all now go through a variety of slow movements; and keeping time to the music and rattling their chains, these nimble youths alternately advance and retire, bowing their heads before the shrine, genuflexing [sic] to the priest and tossing their arms aloft. Soon the music grows faster and faster, and so do their movements; at length they all get into full swing, and perfect frenzy seems to possess them. They dance like maniacs. No pause, no rest, no breathing intervals are allowed them. The music and the singing and wailing get faster and faster. The

perspiration runs off them in streams. They stab and slash themselves, and press their keen edged weapons against their sodoriferous breasts and necks and waists, until one grows faint with the fear of blood spurting out as a consequence.... Moving scarcely an eyelid, one sees these gleaming swords and glittering steel flashing and circling in the air, and yet never any one is wounded, terrified, or stained with blood. Faces hitherto sluggish and apathetic are now lighted up with a glow of ecstasy which is positively awful. The fury of fanaticism seems kindled in each lurid eye.[110]

There was even more to come. The correspondent went on at similar length to detail the ensuing dances with flames and the piercing of cheeks and eyelids, all "to the evident discomfiture of the Prince ... more shocked than interested" by the "utter recklessness and needless torture," though it was also noted that "very few accidents have ever been known to have occurred amongst them."[111] Abdol Zaghie and Griep had been forgotten. There was no threat of injury or amok, merely the spectacle of tamed loyalty.

While it is unclear if the command performance of the Califa ever came to the ears of the Ottoman sultan, his caliphate would be invoked in that city in short order. Certainly, there were increasing signs of Ottoman correspondence at the distant docks of South Africa, which were to be made safer by Grey's new breakwater, inaugurated by Alfred. In 1860, Sultan Abdulmecid's officials saw to it that De Roubaix would receive a jeweled Parisian snuffbox for his efforts, and in December 1861 Mochamat Achmat and his party would gather to honor Abdulaziz on his ascension as sultan.[112] Much was expected from both sides. And much had happened across the Indian Ocean world to raise such expectations, which compels us to travel eastward, and well back in time again: from the East Indies to once Dutch Ceylon.

PART TWO
Muslim Mediations

FIVE

Other Malays, Other Exiles

SOMETIME BETWEEN LATE May and September 1791, while Tuan Guru readjusted to life on the African mainland, one of the many sails skirting the Indian Ocean would latch onto the southwest monsoon and deposit an aged but exercised scholar at Penang, on the Malay Peninsula, completing the long journey from his usual home in Arabia. The passenger was the already famous ʿAbd al-Samad of Palembang, reputedly born in 1704. His works were often requested by the sultans of Sumatra and the Peninsula, and his word was similarly esteemed at the courts of Java. During the months and years when Tuan Guru was first consigned to Robben Island and the cramped quarters of the Slave Lodge, where he laid out his manual, ʿAbd al-Samad had been active in Taʾif and Mecca working on a text of his own, the *Sayr al-salikin*, an abridged translation of al-Ghazali's *Bidayat al-hidaya*.[1] ʿAbd al-Samad would not linger in the now British port after his arrival, surely with some of his texts in hand. Hardly enamored of the Christians who frequented the seas and his natal region, his mission was directed at restoring the sultanate of Pattani, recently despoiled by troops sent by Bangkok. Reportedly gathering an army of some four hundred pilgrims from neighboring Kedah, which had itself been disciplined by the Siamese in the past, he marched off with them to face the Buddhist enemy in early 1792, never to return.

One did not have to sail so far eastward from Mecca to face a Buddhist opponent at that time. Burma and Lanka, too, had Muslim minorities and challenging rulers of their own who sometimes involved them in their conflicts. Furthermore, at the opening of that same (admittedly Christian) year, one Jurang Pati would sign himself and a party of fellow subjects of the Panembahan of Madura into VOC service. Later remembered by family members as a descendant of Pangeran Pali of Bangkalan, Jurang Pati and his men were sent to Ceylon to be deployed as members of a new "Second Battalion of Malays."[2] Once there, the Madurese-turned-Malays might have expected to face the Buddhists of the upland Kingdom of Kandy as often as any European rival of their Dutch employers.[3] Five years later, though, and after much-praised valor outside the walls of Colombo, they would retrieve their surrendered krisses from British chests, exchanging battered blue uniforms for oversized red coats manufactured in London. And they, too, would transcend the infamy of amok to be channeled into battle against Buddhist and Hindu alike, as when they were dispatched to attack the fortress of Panchalankurichi in Southern India in 1801.

Malays Between Madras and Bangkok

In the last chapter we saw how, by the middle of the nineteenth century, some of the increasingly confident Muslims of Cape Town had made the hajj, connecting with the terrain, prestige, and orthodoxy of the Ottoman Empire while proclaiming their loyalty to its newfound British allies, and to the family of Queen Victoria above all. I shall return to examine that relationship more closely in chapter 7, exploring a time when the Capetonians would be seen as a very useful object of concern in Istanbul. For just as the people of the Cape would become a better-known quantity at Mecca in the decade that saw the opening of the Suez Canal, and then targets of Ottoman enthusiasm during the reigns of Abdulaziz and Abdulhamid II, the story of "Pan-Islamism" as it relates to the interconnected South and Southeast Asian peoples is much broader and deeper. This has been shown powerfully by İsmail Hakkı Kadı and Andrew Peacock, whose excavation of the Ottoman archives brings the question of a Buddhist other into the story.[4] It is also, as John Slight suggests, a more collaborative story than the one I have previously sketched, especially when viewed from an Anglo-Indian rather than a Netherlando-Javanese angle.[5] As we shall see, British Ceylon—with a majoritarian other of its own—complicates this even further, emerging from its older history of Dutch entanglement, to which we must perforce turn below before returning to the Cape and the broader Indies being made more Dutch after the opening of the Suez Canal.

There is no doubt that the Dutch would become extremely anxious about the potential for Ottoman interference in the many territories they were amalgamating as their India at the end of the nineteenth century, and in the wake of losing so much global trade to their Atlantic rivals. By contrast, the British were often more pragmatic about Istanbul, paying lip service on the subcontinent and in their consulates to their effective position as patrons of the largest concentration of Muslims in the world, dispatching members of the royal family to visit on occasion, as the Prince of Wales would do in 1875-1876.[6] Moreover, given the choreography of EIC conquest spreading across the Gangetic Plain from Bengal, the British understanding of Islamic law would be dominated by a northern Indian interpretation of orthodoxy making explicit recourse to works of the Hanafi juridical school, or *madhhab*.[7]

Despite their differences in nuance and interpretation of Sunni law, the madhhabs were seldom a barrier between believers in the modern period. While also overwhelmingly Hanafi in orientation, the Ottomans recognized four major Sunni juridical traditions. Here they emulated their Mamluk predecessors in Egypt, whose responsibility for the protection of the Holy Places they had assumed in 1517, bolstering their claim to the caliphate when it mattered thereafter. Whether on the coasts of Africa and Southern Arabia, or yet from the Red Sea to the Strait of Malacca, many a Shafi'i Muslim would look to the Hanafi Ottoman Sultan by the last third of the nineteenth century to protect their spiritual interests—if not their material ones—as they ventured on the hajj and out of range of the Dutch and British Empires. The twinned Ibadi states of Muscat and Zanzibar, separated with British blessing in 1861, were a rare exception in this regard, though their substantial bodies of Shafi'i subjects were also invested in Ottoman Mecca by way of ancestral scholarly networks linked to the valleys of Hadramawt.

Although the Ottoman state hosted and supported scholars from around the world, the rich courts of Asia often supplied the more immediate needs of the ulama and their retainers living and working near the sacred precincts. Such patronage, which could include the provision of housing, had long created distinctions between respective communities. Yet they could be transcended. One Jawi pensioner of Arab background who had inspired broader regional support at the end of the eighteenth century was the aforementioned ʿAbd al-Samad. Born in Sumatra and educated on the Malay Peninsula in what was then the Siamese dependency of Kedah, he is remembered today in part for the letters he wrote from Mecca in 1772 recommending two fellow scholars to the princes of Surakarta—including Mas Kareta's brother Mangkunegara—offering formulaic praise for their struggle against unbelievers and a banner.[8]

It was once suggested that ʿAbd al-Samad was a client of Sultan Ahmad Najm al-Din of Palembang (r. 1757–1776).[9] By the mid-1780s, though, he must have depended on the largesse of Tengku Lamidin of Pattani on the Malay Peninsula. ʿAbd al-Samad was evidently so dependent on that prince that when he learned that the king of Siam had despoiled Pattani in 1788 and deprived him of what Francis Light termed "his accustomed receipts," he sailed to Penang to gain aid from neighboring Kedah. Its sultan, Abdallah Mukarram Shah (r. 1776–1797), did not offer an army, as such, though ʿAbd al-Samad was able to assemble "four hundred Hadjees" for a jihad, which was put down with customary brutality by mid-1792.[10]

Although we should be suspicious of claims of there being so many hajjis among the volunteers, ʿAbd al-Samad's recruitment had been assisted at Penang because Siam also loomed large over Muslim Kedah. Francis Light, who reported ʿAbd al-Samad's jihad, had been able to gain the concession of the island of Penang in 1786 by giving Sultan Abdallah to understand that he would gain a powerful ally in Calcutta. Indeed, Abdallah and his predecessor had been trying to establish just such a relationship for over a decade, first sending an emissary to Light when he was at Aceh in 1771. Abdallah ultimately realized that the EIC would be of little help to Kedah against Bangkok. He doubtless dreaded the ramifications of his failure to send tribute to the Siamese in 1787–1788, in addition to allowing the Europeans to construct fortifications. The fortuitous arrival of a fleet of raiders from Sulu in late 1790 provided him with the manpower to attempt to eject the British from Penang, which he sorely needed as a defensive redoubt, but without success, and he was forced to terms in August 1791.[11]

The rulers of Bangkok would continue to demand tribute from many of the Malay kings of the south like Sultan Abdallah in the form of golden ornaments and, far more valuably, men to prosecute campaigns against any other sovereign who defied them. Often they would demand people for use against their major Burmese rivals, who were well aware of the position of the Malays of Kedah in relation to the EIC at Calcutta, and, further, of the challenges faced by their Buddhist coreligionists of Kandy.[12] In 1808–1810, for instance, Sultan Abdallah's son and successor, Ahmad Taj al-Din (r. 1803–1821), was compelled to assist Siam's generals in disciplining Pattani and then to remove a Burmese force from the island of Phuket. While both acts were memorialized by Ahmad Taj al-Din's courtiers as evidence of duty and loyalty, this did not mean that they liked it. The men of Kedah had dragged their feet against their fellow Muslims at Pattani and needed to prove themselves loyal against the mainly Buddhist Burmese. As the secretary to the commanding officer recalled of the latter campaign, "Although [Ava and Siam] were indeed of a religion different to ours, we had to go through with it, in the interests of the realm," later adding that had "things not turned out as they had, the Siamese might well have invaded us."[13] Such arguments had not convinced one religious leader, Tengku Idris, who withdrew from the campaign after pointing out that the shared Buddhism of the Burmese and the Tai meant that any assistance rendered would be sinful.[14] Nor yet could Sultan Ahmad have accepted the British favoring Bangkok's claims over his own people while encouraging the migration of more and more Chinese to what they called Prince of Wales Island. Muslim Penang was lost.

As John Barrow complained from the Cape, Penang and Prince of Wales Island had become a draw for European migrants out of Southern Africa as well. They were also the object of visitation by members of neighboring Malay states interested in a relationship of their own with Great Britain, even via the company that represented its empire so ambiguously. In August 1819, the *Prince of Wales Island Gazette* reported the arrival of sixty-seven members of the more southerly court of Selangor.[15] It is somewhat surprising, then, that the Anjouanese we met at the Cape deserved no such mention the following year, when the EIC decided to pay for their repatriation on the *Minstrel*, which left Penang for Cape Town in early December 1820.

The denizens of Prince of Wales Island would hear a lot of Cape Colony in 1820, first being advised in June that its gates had been flung open for aspirant migrants (and from Scotland in particular) to make the Cape "one of the most populous of our colonies."[16] On July 1, the *Gazette* published selections from the late Semple, whose *Walks and Sketches* was deemed to offer a "peculiarly valuable" and faithful description of the city and its peoples.[17] Some of those peoples described by Semple were not so different, as we shall see, from the men of Kedah who were then being recruited at Penang for deployment on Ceylon, or those of their ranks who were occasionally reported in the colonial press as having deserted to the hinterland Kandyan "rebels" of that island after 1815.[18]

Then again, Semple's description of so many Malay, Mozambiquan, and even "Malabar" slaves at the Cape would have been read rather differently on the more clearly Malay coast of the Indian Ocean. The December 1819 announcement that slaves at Dutch Malacca would be incrementally emancipated evidently troubled owners at more northerly and British Penang.[19] Rumors of the English having similar plans under the incoming governor had already circulated for some months. In March, twelve men described as the "principals among the Arabs, Malays, Chuliahs and other Mahommedan Inhabitants" had submitted a worried petition stressing that, even if its southerly trade had been banned, slavery was an established right in Muslim societies that had been accordingly recognized by the previous governor. They claimed to be "much distressed" that their properties were making recourse to the British magistrates to gain their freedom without proof of manumission, or marrying without their permission.[20] In August, company officials, who opined that slavery had many advantages to servants and masters alike and responded that their Muslim subjects at Penang were unnecessarily alarmed, requested approval for new laws that they felt conformed as much to British jurisprudence as "the peculiar habits of the people."[21]

Although the EIC could claim to protect the rights of Muslim owners and (somehow) their slaves, Great Britain would lend no such favors to any Malay vassal who resisted Bangkok. In 1821, the Siamese subdued Kedah for failure to provide tribute in anticipation of a Burmese invasion, forcing Ahmad Taj al-Din to flee to Penang along with many thousands of refugees. While sympathetic, the British did nothing to aid them.[22] Hence the embittered sultan began to look for another patron across the seas. In 1824, his exiled court sent a rather extraordinary Arabic letter westward in the hope of gaining help from a more distant patron:

> In the name of God the merciful the compassionate; . . . [to] the king of Arabs and non-Arabs, bearer of the banner of most noble glory, sultan of Islam and the Muslims, leader of the ghazis and those who wage holy war, helper of the nation of Muhammad, suppressor of rebels, king of the two lands and the two seas, servant of the two holy shrines, aider of the sharia, lord of all creation, . . . the sultan of all sultans may God protect him and keep him and aid him and destroy anyone who

opposes him, resists him or betrays him.... we had heard of your Hashemite zeal for the rest of the land of Islam.... I was the sultan of one of the lands of Jawa peoples, which is beneath the equator [sic], called Kedah, which has belonged to us since ancient times. We have there 15 ancestors, all of them sultans there. We inform you of this only because of our long association with you, for in our beginnings, our lands were only conquered and became part of the land of Islam because of your exalted zeal. Last year [sic] we went out to take care of a village in our land, and there approached us the unbelieving Magian king—they burn their dead—and by trickery and betrayal he entered my land of Kedah, claiming he was merely passing by, looking for provisions. When he did not find me, he attacked the land and occupied it, killing four of my ministers, my brother, the senior officials of my state, and some of the ʿAlawi sayyids. They took my son captive after he was wounded in battle, my sister, my brothers' sons, two small daughters and a son of the sayyids—who are descendants of the Prophet. After that he headed to the village in which I was resident; a messenger reached me before he did, but I did not have the means to fight in the place I was in, so I fled along with those children and dependents with me, to an island called Pulau Pinan[g], which previously belonged to us but was in ruins; the British leased it from my father and made it flourish. I am now resident there, waiting for relief from God, his Prophet and from you, for, sire, your ships, [sent] by Muhammad ʿAli Pasha, governor of Egypt, reach the aforesaid island every year. O God, sire, help, help with your Muhammadan zeal and Hashemite aid to save the land of the Muslims and your monotheist brothers and the descendants of the Prophet of God, peace and blessings be upon him. May God increase you in honour and aid you with his soldiers, and may you remain the refuge and goal for every weighty matter which is referred to your Exalted State; and may your manifest force and your protected sultanate be increased by God in honour and may He support them till the day of resurrection.[23]

İsmail Hakkı Kadı presents this letter—infused with appeals to a Hashimite lineage that the Ottomans could not actually claim—as the first attempt by a Southeast Asian polity to invest the Ottomans with caliphal authority in the nineteenth century.[24] Such recognition had been similarly embedded in letters from Malabar and Aceh in the sixteenth century, and it was revived in the appeals of the Ali Rajas of Cannanore and Tipu Sultan of Mysore in the eighteenth.[25]

Perhaps the Kedan letter had been encouraged by the missive's agent, an Arab called Sayyid ʿUthman, who had migrated with his family from

Southern India to Southeast Asia in 1811 (and thus on the heels of the battle for Phuket and Lord Minto's expedition to Java), remaining there for some years before moving to Medina.[26] On his second journey to the peninsula, in 1822, ʿUthman would have found his Jawi patron in exile and therefore been all the more eager to seek caliphal favor. The timing was bad. The Greek revolt meant that Istanbul could do little. Worse still for Kedah, the Burney Treaty of 1826 would affirm British acceptance of Siamese hegemony. Abdallah would attempt to regain his fort in 1831, dispatching a vassal referred to in EIC sources as the "notorious pirate Tunku Kudin." This earned his further removal to now British Malacca, which had been swapped with Bencoolen after the 1824 Treaty of London.[27] As many Malays would learn, London and The Hague would often agree going forward on the borders of the world and their place in it. The Europeans had also come to something of a consensus as to *who* they were as a people, and even how useful they could be to empire. Crucially, majoritarian Buddhist Ceylon had been a key site in the shaping of that consensus.

The Malays of a Once Dutch Ceylon

Despite never being answered, we should return to the 1824 appeal to Istanbul to note that a ship of Sultan Mahmud II's Egyptian governor, Muhammad ʿAli Pasha (r. 1805–1848), was its likely vehicle. The pasha's increasingly assertive domain arguably offered a modicum of hope to Muslims of the Indian Ocean arena, if not to restore the rapidly changing political order, then to grant petitioners prestige and status. During the tumultuous Java War of 1825–1830, occasioned by the uprising of Prince Dipanagara of Yogyakarta (1785–1855), some Jawi actors took the name of Egyptian figures, including that of Muhammad ʿAli, and the Ottoman military ranks they held as they raised the banner of rebellion and nearly dislodged the Dutch from their island so briefly ruled by the British.[28]

As we shall see for Lanka, only fifteen years later, some Europeans could ironically play a role in assisting Indian Ocean Muslims attempting to contact the Egyptian state, having cast their eyes over communities on the island to discern how they should best be governed. Before we get to that moment, it is important to remember that there had been another powerful actor and patron to Muslims on Lanka before the final conquest of 1815.

OTHER MALAYS, OTHER EXILES

Just as its rulers shared the faith of Siam and Ava, the landlocked kingdom of Kandy also functioned as a sometime patron to Muslim traders and emissaries, and very much like Ava again. Certainly, Kandy was an eager employer of Southeast Asians as soldiers, whom the Sinhalese majority generally called Ja Minissu (People of Java), and who fitted in a world with the same horizons stretching from the Red Sea to the Strait of Malacca. Such traces remain, too, in the place names of the island, such as Colombo's Jawatta Road, named for the "Garden of the Jawa" (Jawa Watte) since the early nineteenth century at the latest.[29]

I have touched on Ceylon on several occasions thus far, at times accompanying proponents of a supposedly "mild and tolerant" British empire. Percival cast the partnership between Briton and "Malay" as a successful one at both the Cape and on the island. But much is occluded by this vision, which does not consider significant differences at the two former sites of VOC exile. It also ignores the fact that on Ceylon the renamed Malays were not merely a small minority among Muslims when contrasted with their generally Tamil-speaking fellow believers (at roughly 5 percent), but that the Muslims were themselves an acephalous minority compared with Tamil-speaking Hindus and majoritarian Sinhalese-speaking Buddhists (at 5 percent yet again).

As in the East Indies, the Dutch had gained their dominant position on Lanka's coasts by defeating and absorbing their Portuguese rivals. First based at Galle from 1640, the VOC would relocate their administrative hub northeast to Colombo in 1656, though the more southerly town and its superior harbor would act as an occasional point of transfer between Batavia and Cape Town (most ships ran straight between the two). While small in comparison to the eastern capital, and with its mercantilist agents focused on overseeing the extraction of cinnamon by the Sinhalese peasantry, Colombo and its satellites—such as Galle and Jaffna, as well as Cochin on the subcontinent—also absorbed a significant number of enslaved people and convicts beyond the exiles whom we have already met.[30]

Whereas some exiles had been placed around the island previously, most of the elite Southeast Asians seem to have been in the vicinity of the capital by the middle of the eighteenth century. In July 1743, Colombo Castle had decided that locally born children of "Javanese and other Easterner convicts" should be put into active service and placed under the authority of the chiefs of the Moors until such time as they emerged as a discrete community.[31] The children of persons of high rank among them—described as *pangerangs* and *patis*—and most especially those who had already served in recent Dutch actions against the ruler of Travancore, were to be incorporated as soldiers. Had he attained his maturity in Lanka, rather than being returned to Batavia in 1741, such may have been the career of the Capetonian exile Kareta. In September 1743, Colombo Castle confirmed that senior exiles like the newly arrived Patti Malaijo of Ambon were excused from corvée labor (*oelijdienst*), much as "Javanese and other state prisoners" were to be allowed their liberty.[32]

As with earlier deportees to Lanka such as Shaykh Yusuf, some of the state prisoners at Colombo maintained connections with their distant families, and with greater facility than those at the Cape. No wonder, then, that one of the more common terms for exile in Javanese was synonymous with that island rather than the more distant continent.[33] And while these figures and their extended families had allowances calculated to maintain some vestige of their status, the castle had to intervene on occasion to increase their allocations of rixdollars, rice, and condiments to support them and their dependents. For instance, Tuan Guru's superior, Prince Muhammad Zayn al-Abidin, was granted a personal emolument at Ceylon that was ten times higher than the four statesmen sent to the Cape in 1780, being paid roughly the wage of a VOC captain. But while it was reported that he had nine dependents in 1786, by 1788 his retinue counted four family members and eighteen servants.[34] He also complained on that occasion that while he had been granted an increase by Colombo from fifty to fifty-nine rixdollars (along with twenty-seven parras of rice, one-third of a parra of salt, and one parra of pepper), he had originally been promised a full sixty rixdollars and a house.[35] A certain degree of envy underlay his request. His uncle Patra Alam, whom we may recall had displaced his father in 1780, had since been deposited at Ceylon for conspiring with Nuku in 1783, with the relatively healthy monthly salary of one hundred rixdollars to support twelve family members with nine servants and slaves.[36]

By comparison, the former king of Goa, Sultan Fakhr al-Din (a.k.a. Raja Oesman, d. 1795), had only been allotted sixty-eight rixdollars when he was exiled for conniving with the British in 1767. Twenty years on, he was still given the same sum to support his new wife Sitti Hapipa, five sons, two daughters, and seven servants.[37] Raja Oesman long bemoaned the amounts required to educate his children in Western ways—most born at Ceylon by Sitti Hapipa—but he was also famous for his mounting debts. These would be called in by the castle rather than being bailed out as his creditors had hoped, leading to an edict in June 1786 that nobody could lend an exile money without permission.[38]

Money was in short supply at Colombo, and for the Dutch, too. In September 1788 the governing council of policy acknowledged the poverty of "Sitia Isa" (Sitti Aisa), the ailing widow of the exiled Rato Bagoes of Banten, who was unable to support herself with her modest allowance of six rixdollars. Hence, they allowed her to return home with her eight servants.[39] They also raised the allowances of two princes of Bacan who had been exiled with those of Tidore. Prince Major Sadar Alam now had twenty-five rixdollars rather than fifteen, and his brother, Gagugu Naʿim al-Din, went from twelve to twenty. As with the case of Muhammad Zayn of Tidore, this must have proven cold comfort given the recent arrival on the *Batavia* of the former Sultan Iskandar (r. 1780–1788), who had displaced their father for eight years and now had his own living of eighty rixdollars raised to one hundred.[40] In 1792 the two princes of Bacan would write to governor-general Willem Arnold Alting (r. 1780–1797) bemoaning both Iskandar's presence and the high cost of living in Colombo. They furthermore placed themselves as his grandchildren at "the toes of his feet," hoping to be moved to Batavia at their own expense and arguing that it was just as much a place of exile for them. Batavia was also the place where they had last seen their father, Sultan Sah al-Din, whom Ary Huysers had seen immiserated and near death, and whose grave they longed to visit.[41]

Graves were one thing, houses another. We may recall that Muhammad Zayn al-Abidin had claimed he had been promised a house prior to his banishment. However, no exile got free housing at Colombo anymore, regardless of the precedent of Pangeran Arya and whatever they had been told in Batavia. Most of them rented homes or compounds in the town befitting their status. These were sometimes close to the wealthier Moors just beyond the Pettah, the eastward market zone beyond the castle toward Wolvendaal Church. Appropriately enough, this area was called Kampung Pangerang (Prince Village), though it was first settled by a settlement of demobilized and Christianized Javanese in the 1660s.[42] By contrast, the families of the subalterns in general service tended to live across the lake on a spit of land closer to the southern gate of the fort and the sea. While occasionally, and erroneously, called Slave Island by the Dutch, its occupants preferred to remember their peninsula as Kampung Kertel, using a Portuguese term (*quartel*) to refer to the barracks that developed there. Lastly, by the 1780s, most company slaves and those condemned to the public works were housed behind the walls of the castle in a depot originally built by the Portuguese as a Franciscan monastery.

The distinction between Eastern slaves, soldiers, and royal exiles was thus clear at the moment of deposition. Over time the sons of slaves and convicts might become soldiers, to mingle with fresh troops recruited in the Indies, typically from Makassar or Madura. The literate sons and grandsons of the exilic minority meanwhile served as their officers, though they were not necessarily in overall authority. In fact, 1760 saw the appointment of "Oedoemakandoe Meestriaar Aydroos Lebbe"—who claimed links to the ʿAydarus clan of Hadramawt—as "Chief of the Moors and Malays," and "Master of the pupils in the Seminary & Caffers."[43] While it is unclear whether the term Malay was used in the original 1760 document, it does start to appear in records from the mid-1780s, echoing practice at Batavia.[44] Still, the 1760 reference to a "seminary" brings yet another contrast with Cape Town into sharp relief and reminds us of Shaykh Yusuf's presence a century earlier. The Muslims of Colombo evidently had access to a religious education.[45]

This was long known to be the case in Java, where returned exiles were imbued with a pious aura, as Kareta's adoptive son so briefly found to his benefit. Ronit Ricci also reminds us how, in the *Babad Giyanti*, the wife of Sayyid ʿAlawi's former patron, Raden Ayu Juru, recalled the ministrations of two gurus during their time on Lanka between 1742 and 1758. These teachers were named as "Sayyid Musa Ngidrus" (i.e., our Aydroos Lebbe, who was evidently a sayyid) and the Javanese "Ibrahim Asmara." Their Friday gatherings attracted throngs of believers, including ship captains from Surat, Selangor, Bengal, and Hyderabad.[46]

There is little memory today of who facilitated Islamic education for the exiles and their retainers after Musa ʿAydarus and Ibrahim Asmara, or to what extent the "caffers" of 1760—remembered as Africans today—belonged to the Muslim community at large, unless, much like in Cape Town, the term was being used for the lower ranks of the police. There are indications from both the Dutch and British periods that Africans, Moors, and Malays often mingled, though being arguably a hybrid category beyond the straits, as we have seen in Cape Town, the last grouping proved particularly resilient on Lanka. It is moreover clear that the Southeast Asians of Colombo had already been deemed numerous enough to constitute a body of their own by August 1769. At this point, Tumenggong Sasranegara, the son of an exile from Mataram, was appointed their chief. While probably leaving the seminary under Moorish authority, many of the Javanese would henceforth be more narrowly defined by their military service with Sasranegara and his family. Documents from 1787 show that Sasranegara's son, Sasrawijaya, would claim his title and become head of the Javanese after him. His grandson, meanwhile, obtained a commission as an officer (at fifteen rixdollars per month), and probably felt himself to be headman-in-waiting—if alongside Southeast Asian officers arriving from elsewhere in the archipelago and forming up in new ranks beside them.[47]

The equation of Southeast Asians with military muscle had already been reinforced by an order from Batavia in 1782, under pressure due to the war with Great Britain, that obliged Colombo to employ all exiles who had not been condemned to military service.[48] This equation was affirmed after the war in June 1785, when the castle decided to reduce a "costly" regiment of free Moors to a part-time militia. It was not all about money. Citing, but not explaining, a "well-known cowardly act" committed by Moors, it was felt preferable to have "free Javanese or those of Malay origin" take their places.[49] Colombo's council of policy further decided that it needed to keep closer records of the troops and to survey the intermarried body of exiles who were then grouped into around a dozen households.[50]

Soldiering was not necessarily a path to wealth. As is already clear from the instances reported by two commissioners, by March 1788 most such exiles reported an impoverished state, which varied due to the numbers and employment of members supported. Sasrawijaya's family by then counted sixteen members, including his stepmother, mother-in-law, and his officer son. Not included, though, were six servants "slave and free," or his late father's widow, Sellia, who had her own household of four to manage, with six additional servants and slaves.[51] Such an imbalance of servers to served paled when compared with that of the sixteen-year-old grandson of a yet more exalted exile, Pangeran Adipati Mangkurat of Mataram, who reported that he was responsible for three siblings, his stepmother, grandmother, and twenty-six servants; though the commissioners remarked that two of them were more properly deemed soldiers, and thus not dependents.[52]

Given their entangled roles and prestige that was linked to the status of their home courts, it seems that these same people supported the foundation of a new mosque located closer to the military quarters than their own residences. Later known as the Wekanda Mosque (from the local place name Bai Kandi), this was founded on land endowed in December 1786 by a free Javanese called "Pandan Bali."[53] Curiously, this name would be rather close in Jawi to "Pangeran Pali," a name sometimes associated with people from Madura. Although there is little memory of its founders aside from its first imam—Saboo Latiff—or yet of any struggle for its establishment that parallels what happened in Cape Town, it would have been of interest to the passing presence of Panenga, a newly arrived "priest" mentioned in 1792 as being a relative supported by the exilic household of Raden Ariapen Panular of Madura.[54]

The only other such priestly figure to enter the surviving Dutch record from Java around this time was a generically—if inconsistently—named sayyid called Muhammad b. ʿAbdallah or ʿAbd al-Sharif of Mecca. Ordered exiled from Java, the sayyid had arrived on the *Dordrecht* in late 1787.[55] This was after being banished from Batavia due to his many followers there and at Banten, and his rhetoric that the time of the "infidel dogs" was coming to an end.[56] Sayyid Muhammad had likely gravitated to the older mosque at Maradana rather than that at the new site at Bai Kandi; after all, the Moors of the Pettah also claimed the distinction of Arab heritage. Unsurprisingly, the man whose correspondence had so frightened the Dutch at Batavia quickly angered his appointed hosts in Colombo, losing his shelter at the depot, but not his local freedom of movement. The council already felt in April 1788 that it was wiser to treat him as a regal exile rather than a criminal, granting him the relatively generous personal allowance of eight rixdollars.[57] Such largesse was granted due to the presence at Colombo of James Buchanan (d. 1793), who represented the powerful Nawab of Arcot, Muhammad ʿAli (r. 1749–1795), who had taken an interest in the sayyid's well-being—echoing the Mughal governor of Surat's intercession on behalf of Sharif Habibullah a century before. Eight months later, the well-protected Arab pressed his claims of poverty and was allotted the princely sum of one thousand rixdollars.[58] In November, Colombo was only too happy to facilitate the return of their unwanted guest to his unspecified native country.[59]

Such crossings, alliances, and patronage remind us just how diverse the Muslim community was at Colombo. It would become even more diverse with the formalization of three "Malay" battalions by 1791, subsuming Sasrawijaya (Sassaro Widjojo) as a captain of the first battalion alongside four other native captains: Singa Troena (promoted 1788), Kepping (1791), Singa Joeda (1791), and Nolland Noya (1791). All five served under Frederik Wilhelm von Driberg (1764–1807), son of the Hanoverian commander of VOC forces at Colombo, Diederich Carel von Driberg.[60] The other native captains, all given promotion dates of 1791, were Talip, Wiera Mongolo, Abitum van Fluyt, Joerang Patty (i.e., our recruit Jurang Pati), Moendoe, Mahomet Sangerang, Bonkus, and Boediman.[61] There are also later indications that members of the second battalion claimed a connection to Madura, either being born to military families there like Jurang Pati, while others were Madurese with linkages to Makassar, such as the later Captain Wira (sometimes Bira) Wangsa.[62]

Whether Javanese, Madurese, Makassarese, or Easterner in general, the Sinhalese would have seen all such Ja soldiers as dangerous tools of the Dutch often treated with favoritism. In April 1791, two Madurese serving under Jurang Pati were convicted of the theft of a bundle of fabric from a local family.[63] However, unlike another Madurese who had been convicted of theft three years earlier, they were spared their sentence of flogging and three years' hard labor in irons. Instead, they had to run the gauntlet of their unit three times before being sent as unsalaried fighters for a new battalion at Galle, where it was noted that there were "not so many Easterners," and lest it be "rendered wanting by the supply of Moorish sepoys."[64]

It is hard to know what any of the Moors made of their change of military fortune. Many of their established families had other roles on Ceylon's coasts, often mercantile or connected with the fisheries, that had no direct connection to the VOC. Some possessed of military expertise had already transferred across to the EIC in Southern India during the war of 1781–1784, or had been absorbed after the capture of bases on the Coromandel Coast like Nagapattinam.[65] With word of fresh conflict following the declaration of the Batavian Republic in 1794, and then with the VOC having already ordered that members of the Galle regiment board and protect the ships headed eastward (150 men) and westward (40 men), there were increasing signs of discontent in the ranks of those who remained.[66]

To make matters worse, in November 1795 Colombo Castle received a petition from twenty-one wives of those dispatched from Galle. While the local commandant had been able to offer the women half pay for their support, that had ceased on Batavia's instruction. As they complained—stressing that almost all of them had four, five, or even six children—each day had brought mounting poverty, and with the sale of their clothes they had perforce to stoop to begging. The petitioners claimed to "cringe at the idea" that the VOC "would intend that the women and children of soldiers, who have always served the Company so truly and faithfully ... and who yet place their lives on the line for the Company, must beg for their bread, when their husbands and fathers have so willingly accepted half pay."[67] The council recognized—much as the British would at the Cape during the War of the Axe—that immiserating the families of their eastern soldiers did them no credit. The VOC accordingly paid up, accepting that now was a time when "the largest part" of its military power rested "upon the troops of this nation" in whom they perforce had to place "utmost trust" to mount a defense.[68]

Some had already lost that trust and imagined a more stereotypical Malay with word of the loss of Trincomalee to the British in late 1795. In January 1796, the garrison commander at Kalutara pleaded to keep one of two companies scheduled to march from Galle for the defense of Colombo. Rumors already abounded that the Sinhalese were just waiting for the moment to pounce. Among them were reputedly eight or ten European deserters, "and a great body of Malays and Kaffers" who would be more than enough to make an end of the twenty remaining soldiers.[69]

The Legend of Loyalty

> From the time that He is able to hold a light Firelock, every malay Boy ought in good Policy to be enlisted in the Malay Regiment.
>
> —GOVERNOR FREDERICK NORTH, 1802

There was no massacre at Kalatura. According to Percival, the Malays and their French officers distinguished themselves in their engagements, including outside the walls of Colombo, if with wild tactics he deemed unbecoming.[70] Despite the vigor of their Easterner soldiers, the VOC would be forced to surrender their Lankan capital in February 1796, at which point the EIC set about forming some of their recent opponents into their own "Malay" ranks. The English-language terms of capitulation already named them as such and made it clear that they were to be accorded special treatment. At their Dutch commander's request, the Malays were allowed to have their swords and krisses stored in chests in order that they be returned after shipping to India and an "easy march" with their families to Madras if they did not remain under an EIC flag.⁷¹

Many did remain. With five hundred men moving from blue coats to often oversized red ones by early 1799, the newly arrived governor Frederick North looked forward to Madras sending him three hundred prisoners taken at Trincomalee to bolster their ranks.⁷² He also planned to attract to his side many more Malays whose earlier flight from Dutch ranks had put them in the countryside, where they supposedly caused "the Greatest terrors to the peasants."⁷³ As a confident North continued in his dispatch to the inaugural secretary of state for war and the colonies, Henry Dundas (1742–1811), by increasing their derisory pay, he had "no doubt" that he would be

> able to raise the number of these troops to one thousand effective men, and to get rid of the Robbers which infest the country by inducing them to inlist [sic] themselves under military discipline;... they are an active and brave troop, but require being held by a light rein; and if we should have need to furnish a supply of soldiers to His Majesty's fleet in the Red Sea, I do not know any that would be better for the Purpose. They are always ready to embark, and to go to any part of the world, and being zealous musselmans will neither offend nor be offended, with the People of that Country, but Cooperate heartily with them, against the Common Enemy of their Religion.⁷⁴

By "the Common Enemy of their Religion," North meant France, whose troops had so recently occupied Egypt under Napoleon. Two weeks later he issued a proclamation citing the "frequent atrocious acts" of the Malays and offering an amnesty for minor offences to all unenlisted men if they registered with local government officials for a passport by the end of April. Any Malay found unarmed thereafter could be liable for detention as a vagrant, while those with arms could expect expulsion from the island.⁷⁵ Exactly two years after North's proclamation, his occasional ally Dundas could only praise "the vigorous yet lenient measures adopted ... in reclaiming that Body of Men from Barbarism to good order and discipline."⁷⁶ Not only had they been joined by the captives from Madras, but the new regiment reportedly included troops taken from VOC ships off St. Helena in 1795 who had been drilled there for two years before a stint at Bencoolen.⁷⁷

Those gathered from Madras and Bencoolen probably included soldiers whose wives had petitioned in 1795. Their reunions would have made them more willing to serve their new masters, in addition to officers they had known under the Dutch, such as F. W. von Driberg, who was supposed to go on a recruiting mission to the Moluccas in August 1800, though he apparently got no further than Madras. Soon enough a colleague at Tidore, Ryan, claimed in 1802 that he had the support for such recruitment of the twice exiled "Prince Ceylon." This was Nuku's second oldest brother and unhappy renter in Colombo, Muhammad Zayn al-Abidin, returned by the Dutch in 1794, but then sent to Madras by the unimpressed English in 1799. Indeed, Ryan also returned empty handed before the return to power of the Dutch following the Peace of Amiens, surely hindered by the clumsy actions of another officer on Ternate who had threatened dire punishment to any soldier who refused to transfer to Ceylon's Malay Regiment.[78]

As time would tell, the EIC, and then the crown regime that claimed Ceylon's coasts, had already laid the foundations of what North presented as an effective force. He often referred to the Malay Regiment as his very own, drawing soldiers and their families in dribs and drabs from Penang, where they established a recruiting office in 1800. But rather than dispatching "zealous Musselmans" to the Red Sea to engage Napoleon's men, the regiment was first called to Southern India in mid-1800 for the Poligar Wars. These actions claimed the life of Ensign "Cormie Didin," whom North had promoted, and another officer now identified as having been Yusuf, the eldest son of the late Raja Oesman.[79] As North enthused in December 1801 after the taking of Panchalankurichi:

> Captain Whittlie ... has given me the most satisfactory account not only of the Gallantry of the Malays of which I never entertained the Smallest Doubt, but of their Discipline, Regularity & peaceable Behaviour, Qualities for which that nation was heretofore not so distinguished. ... the English Troops were so much pleased with their general Behaviour that they treated Them as their Brothers & divided with Them their Provisions & Water & such other Extra accommodations as are allowed to Europeans in an Indian Company. As to their Valour and Promptitude in action, it has been proved in every Engagement that has taken Place in the active Period since ... At the Storm of Panjalam Courchy, after their Gallant Commander Captain Whittlie had been dangerously wounded, They entered the Breach with the Europeans, & with Them terminated the Business, & were publickly thanked for their Behaviour by Lieutenant Colonel Agnew as soon as it was over.[80]

Marsden's advice seemed to be paying off. We have already seen that Percival, writing on the Cape, had dwelt on the capacity for British rule to cure the Malays of their alleged propensity toward running amok, if not opium—though he seems to have been echoing North's rhetoric. Percival also offered such themes in his *Account of the Island of Ceylon*, in which he remarked upon their skills as gardeners, cooks, and servants, if ones who had been poorly paid by the Dutch.[81]

Percival supplemented his account with a report of the 1800 mission to Sri Vikrama Rajasimha, King of Kandy, where translation had been performed by an unnamed "Malay Prince" and the Sinhalese lord presented with a betel dish looted from Tipu the previous year.[82] Malays were on both sides of the encounter. The mission was escorted by dozens of sepoys and Malays dragging heavy ordnance up difficult jungle paths to Kandy, where they eventually found the monarch defended by a bodyguard of his own "Malays and Malabars" whose services he was anxious to retain:

> The greatest precaution was employed by the Candians to prevent any intercourse between those of our escort, particularly the Malays and Malabars, and those in the King's service ... however, several pieces of information were procured which may be turned to advantage hereafter. Several Malays in the King's service found an opportunity of expressing their sorrow at not having it in their power to return to Colombo with their old companions. Most of those Malays had been slaves to the Dutch, and had on account of ill treatment made their escape to the Candian territories. They would have gladly returned to their former masters, and submitted to any punishment for their desertion, rather than live in continual apprehension from the caprices of a despotic and barbarous court.[83]

While General Macdowall had made no such observations in his account of the mission, or at least none that North's clerical ally James Cordiner (1775–1836) repeated in his own book of 1807, it was clear that neither side could agree to the terms of a treaty proposed by the governor of coasts claimed by both company and Kandy. These amounted to the placing of a British garrison in the vicinity of the Sinhalese capital, the crossing of Kandyan terrain to access Trincomalee, and an exclusive monopoly on the harvesting of cinnamon.[84] Although it was not proposed formally at the time, North also planned to invoke the old VOC treaty to recruit absconded soldiers, telling Lord Hobart in March 1802 that he demanded "the redemption or the

Restitution" of such Malays, under promise of a full pardon, believing that they "would flock with joy to join my Regiment of their Countrymen, were not their Wives & Families kept at Candy."[85]

Vikrama Rajasimha had no interest in English roads being cut across his territories to the port he hoped to regain. Nor yet was he inclined to release his Malays, who were useful for the pious public works he was undertaking. His immediate response to the embassy stressed the return to either side of any absconding soldiers.[86] The Malays were also key to what transpired after the hesitant British occupation of Kandy from February 1803, after which time a remnant garrison under Major Adam Davie was forced to terms on June 24. Davie abandoned the British-backed pretender to the throne the next day and was then set upon during the retreat on the 26th, in part for having spiked his guns in contravention of his agreement with the Kandyans.[87]

It was also evident that the Malay soldiers had been a prized target from the opening of the campaign, and that their serving kinsmen had tried to induce them to cross over almost as soon as they marched into Kandyan territory. With the garrison wracked by illness and heavy rains falling, some had taken the offers up from June 19, while dozens of others were subsequently absorbed as their British officers were killed.[88] Not all Malays are said to have submitted. Some were also executed by the Kandyan ruler's African soldiers. The most celebrated were two "princes," later identified as Nur al-Din and Sayf al-Din, family of the late bankrupt Raja Oesman.[89]

The story of their heroism derives from the account of the assistant Dutch surgeon to the Malay Regiment, Greeving, who escaped in August 1803. In a translated deposition lodged in 1804, he recounted how Nur al-Din had reluctantly accompanied Davie to accept terms, and what later befell him, his brother, and their servant a few weeks after the massacre:

> Captain Nouradeen and his brother were by order of the King carried away to Angarankatte: they, having arrived there, would not condescend to fall on the earth with their faces, the Adigaar would compel the two brothers thereto, but Captain Nouradeen and his brother and Lieutenant Crain Sapinanie represented to the King that he, Nouradeen, and his brother, were also descended from King's blood, and that their grandfather had also been a great King. This reply the King of Kandy did not take amiss, but requested the two brothers very friendly to enter into the service of the King and to be a head or Prince over the

Malays of Kandy, to which Captain Nouradeen replied to the King, that it would be a disgrace upon him and that he would be in no other service but would live and die in that of the English. The King, therefore, ordered Captain Nouradeen and his brother to prison: on the 17th or 18th August [1803], the King, having sent for both the brothers for the second time, asked them whether they would enter in his service or die, to which both the brothers replied firmly, they would sacrifice their lives for his great Majesty, the glorious King of Great Britain. The King of Kandy then grew very angry and let both the brothers be beheaded immediately: even the servant of Nouradeen was not spared, whom also he ordered to be beheaded. The corpses of those three persons were cast in the woods.[90]

At the time of the first Malay audience, Greeving had been in hiding, while at the time of the second he was kept away from the court in an outbuilding unless required to fan the dessave of Welpene. Indeed, not all his observations proved accurate, including that Davie had died the morning after he visited him.[91] It rather seems that much of his information was infused with the reports of his former Malay colleagues and those in Kandyan service who had saved his life after finding him in hiding, and who sustained him with additional food during his captivity.[92] Evidently none of them linked the martyred princes to a soldier who had served at the head of the Kandyan ranks. This was a man whom Greeving only referred to as "a tall, fat Malay Prince," who had led a dawn attack on the garrison with numerous deserters on June 24.[93] In Cordiner's account of 1807, that prince had gained the elements of a history, incorporating Davie's mention of a relative having tried to seduce Nur al-Din to the Kandyan side in May. He also gained a name: "Sanguylo."[94]

It is not clear when exactly brother and rival prince were found to be one and the same, and thus when Sanguylo became the Sangalen of modern memory, though there had been a Mahomet Sangerang in VOC ranks in 1792. Accepting the often posited link to Raja Oesman, Ricci names this commander as Sangkilan or Karaeng Sangunglo.[95] Half-brother or not, Cordiner pillaged Greeving in a much-celebrated passage. Having refused to bow down before the king, the princes were said to have

> saluted [him] agreeably to their own rank and usage, telling him that they inherited royal blood, and that their grandfather had been an independent monarch.

Their conversation did not displease the King: he spoke kindly to them, requested them to enter into his service, and to take command of all the Malays. Nouradeen replied, that he could not accept of his Majesty's offer, without entailing upon himself everlasting disgrace; that he had already sworn allegiance to the King of England, and that he would live and die in his service. The two brothers were then ordered into confinement, where they remained until nearly the middle of the month of August, when the King of Candy sent for them again, and asked them whether they chose to suffer death, or to serve him? They both answered, that they were ready to sacrifice their lives in the service of the illustrious King of England. The Candian Potentate turned his face from them in a rage, and ordered them to be immediately executed . . . and left as prey to wild beasts.[96]

While just as prone to plagiarism as Percival, Cordiner's rhetoric of Malay loyalty was similarly derived from the revived personal enthusiasm of North, and the "regret and indignation" he had reported that the princes of Colombo had expressed to him upon hearing that "any of their countrymen had deserted."[97] They would have been understandably defensive. North had heard that his force had been lost due to the defections of his Malay soldiers, and he had fretted that he might lose the rest of them to the offerings of the Kandyans.[98] But, sympathizing for the fears of some kept prisoner, North returned to his original position and reached out to their families to offer support. He would have felt even more justified when he had a version of Greeving's account by late August, after which time, perhaps tellingly, he forgave Sitti Hapipa's debts that related to her sons.[99]

It was naturally in the interest of the many Malay soldiers who managed to free themselves of the Kandyans after "feigning," in Cordiner's words, "to assist them in their various attacks," to offer tales of princely virtue in exchange for pardon and reenlistment.[100] Greeving's tale may also have been incidental to further accounts of the fate of Major Davie given in March 1805 by a subsequent escapee, described by North as a "native Priest to the Malay Regiment, a man of good morals, and much esteemed by his Countrymen."[101] Evidently North paid little heed to the assertions of two captured spies, who had claimed that the Kandyans had encouraged their Malays to infiltrate British ranks after a failed attempt to take the port of Batticaloa.[102]

It is telling that neither spy made mention of Malay heroism, but rather of their absorption following the killing of the Europeans. Cordiner was at least aware of the limitations of his account, remarking that as no *English* officer present at the siege had related its causes, "a more circumstantial and authentic detail of the transactions" was "rather to be wished for than expected."[103] And even as he raised his eyebrows to the "superstitious" Malay avoidance of looting Buddhist temples, Cordiner would present the Malays as ideal tropical warriors.[104] They were, in his view, "an uncommonly hardy race," suited to all sorts of privation, and needing but one "luxury": opium, which served "the same purpose to a Malay, as drams to an European, or spices to natives of other descriptions."[105] North had certainly put the same stock in their value, establishing settlements of demobilized soldiers within reach of the towns of Colombo and Trincomalee. Henceforth, his island was painted as a redoubt of unflinchingly loyal Malays amid a sea of squabbling natives.

Of Lebbies, Moors, and Sepoys

While overseeing the birth of the legend of the loyal Malay, North also had evolving ideas as to who his "Musselman" subjects were more generally. In his first report to the EIC directors he had cast the "Lebbies" as the first class of Muslims on the island. While he believed them to be of African origin—lumping them together with neighbors whose numbers he would augment with enslaved men from Goa and Mozambique—he cast them as "an Industrious and respectable class of Inhabitants" who had been unfairly taxed by the Dutch. When Colombo was threatened by the Kandyans in 1803, he even repealed the reduced taxes entirely "to employ many of them with Pikes and Firelocks, for Patroles, which They agreed to with alacrity."[106]

Yet the Moors also presented North with problems, often pressing their legal suits for his personal resolution at a time when many Dutch magistrates refused to serve their British overlords. Such approaches stemmed from the absence of any clear judicial authority established to deal with matters of Islamic law beyond a dated Dutch translation of a manual on marriage, divorce, and inheritance. Known as the *Freijer Compendium* or *Code*, it had been commissioned by governor Iman Willem Falck (r. 1765–1785), who oversaw the appointment of Sasranegara in 1769, and was derived from the opinions of Muslims officials on the island from which he came: Java.[107] Many a magistrate would later complain that it was rather unsatisfactory. And while Ceylon would, much like the Cape, continue to be governed with modified Dutch Roman law when Europeans and Christians were involved into the 1820s, its jurists were often at a loss as to what to do when matters of Muslim personal law came before them.

North had already made a proposal for Muslim legislation in his first letter of 1799. After dispensing with the poll tax of twelve rixdollars levied on Moors "from motives of kindness and justice perhaps, rather than of Policy," he claimed to have

> an idea of drawing from these people nearly the same revenue to the Public; and at the same time of procuring for them the Comforts of a correct and respectable government; by bringing into the Island a mufti to be consulted by me on all points of musselman law; and half a dozen Cazies, as Judges in the different parts of the Island, where there are now many Moorish inhabitants collected under Chiefs whose want of knowledge, manners, morality and Religion under them is a disgrace to the Government which employs them and a scourge to the people subjected to them, the expence of this Establishment will be more than defrayed, by a contribution of the musulmans, smaller than that levied in the Dutch time. . . . These Lebbies form the greatest number of small Capitalists, and active merchants in the country. They are industrious and apparently peaceable; and if they sometimes have disputes among themselves, it is not Extraordinary, as there is not one of Common knowledge of their law who can decide them.[108]

According to Viscount Valentia, North appointed one of the (he believed African) "Lebbies" as mufti, though he was dismissed for having accepted bribes.[109] Again, in January 1800, North proposed the creation of a "well regulated Medrisse or school," complaining that

> the decent Education of Mahommedans is much to be wished, for the gross Ignorance of the Professors of that Religion on this Island in matters of their own Law is the source of constant Tumult, & Dispute amongst Them. Whether I shall ever be able to induce Them to set aside Funds for the Establishment & Support of such an Institution & for the proper maintenance of Kaziss for the Decision of Disputes amongst Themselves is what I can not yet answer for. The Introduction of the Tax of Two & a Half per cent on movables for that Purpose called Zakât, may perhaps be attempted with Success, but I will not attempt it.[110]

North found little support, despite deeming such importation of qadis and encouragement of Muslim knowledge crucial to his work and pointing to (mostly Shafiʻi) Egypt and Southern India as potential sources in his private correspondence.[111] North indicated his frustration in December 1801 by observing that as all "Musselmans" were "bound to make the Koran their Rule of civil Life," any form of toleration that "subjected them to another law" was perforce incomplete. He moreover reiterated his complaint that it was a "regular & indeed a laborious Part" of his duty "to hear & Judge in Person the Principal Disputes of men of that Religion, according to their own tenets."[112] A year later he even promised "shortly to regulate in a more satisfactory manner the interior discipline of the Mohammedans, & the observance of their law."[113]

Nothing ever came of this, most especially after the disaster at Kandy was followed by the lingering uncertainty about the fate of Major Davie. With North's replacement by the intemperate general Thomas Maitland (1760–1824) in July 1805, the annexation of Kandy and the creation of a hybrid judiciary were put on hold. Almost immediately on his arrival, Maitland lamented what he saw as the excessive expenses on public services and any expansion of a bloated judiciary. Maitland was inclined to renew all taxes on "foreign" Muslims and had a marked preference for African soldiers to be purchased, even if there was soon to be a ban on the trade in slaves. It was also clear that Maitland had a particular hatred of his predecessor's pet regiment. Citing a letter from the captive Davie, Maitland placed the blame for the debacle of 1803 squarely on its shoulders:

> If the Sepoy Regiment is of no use, it is at least inoffensive; the Malay Regiment on the contrary, is not only useless but extremely dangerous, and has embarrassed me more than any one Thing since I assumed the Reins of Government here. In my Letter under Date Nov. 22nd 1805, I stated that I had managed . . . to open a Correspondence with the unfortunate Major Davie . . . You will however perceive that in his first Letters, he . . . attributes the massacre of Candy entirely to the Malays, which was indeed, I am sorry to say, thoroughly known and believed here at the time. The Malay Regiment present is generally composed of the same Individuals, who then composed it; and what is in a Military Point of View, the most astonishing and absurd Line of Conduct I have ever heard of during the Course of my small Experience, the Government in this Island thought fit, instead of punishing these Perpetrators in Truth of the Massacre to give to every one of them when they got tired of the Candians and came back into their own Country, the whole Arrears of Pay due from the Hour they joined

the Enemy and murdered our own People, under the Plea that they had returned from Desertion. I leave it to Your Lordship to decide what beneficial service to His Majesty's Government can be expected, from a Corps that has so conducted itself, and been so treated. It is in Truth neither more or less than rewarding Treachery and fostering Treason. But it is not only in the Corps itself, but with a large Class of People, that this Line of Conduct has had Influence, viz. The whole of the Malays in the Island. On my arrival here I found two Companies of Invalid Malays, upon the Island Establishment, totally useless, extremely expensive and perfectly unserviceable. Your Lordship may easily conceive that I was naturally anxious to get rid of them, and I stated My Intention so to do in my Dispatch dated 19th Oct. 1805. The Fact is, however, they are still a Burthen, and an insufferable Burthen to the Island, but as they are all connected with the Men of the Malay Regiment, who are generally Relations, I could not carry this into Effect, without creating great Disgust, Dissatisfaction and Desertion in the Malay Corps; but should we get Peace, I am most anxious that the whole of the Establishment should be done away and that some regular System should be introduced to render them if not useful, at least, not dangerous.[114]

Peace would not come for another decade, and by conquest at that. And while Maitland hoped to replace Malays with Mozambiquans, one group of their relatives was at least exportable. Despite war with France and the allied Batavian Republic having been quickly renewed after the Peace of Amiens, Maitland arranged for the repatriation of the remaining Dutch servants and their families, along with 381 exiles. Having written to Batavia to complain of the "very large" sum of money "disbursed for their maintenance and comfort" and adding threats to cut off their allowances by the end of January 1806, two ships arrived off Colombo in October to convey the Dutch officials to Batavia, with a third taking their unhappy pensioners to Ambon in 1807.[115]

Those sent in 1807 should have included Pangeran Mas Adipati Mangkurat and Sitti Hapipa. Both had written to Batavia complaining of their miserable states in December 1806 and January 1807, with the former also writing on behalf of many of his relatives and fellow exiles about the extreme exigency (*mudarat*) of their situations.[116] Certainly, the Lankan letters now preserved in Leiden referred to the mudarat that their writers faced, and by the time of the exiles' departure for further captivity, the Dutch officer sent to accompany them observed how many had been reduced to the direst circumstances, being unable to clothe their children.[117]

Also included among the petitioners to Batavia was a self-deprecating Raden Tumenggong Wirakusuma. This was none other than the Capetonian son of Mas Kareta, whose religious influence at Surakarta had seen him dispatched to his father's first exilic home in 1787. Reduced to poverty, he appealed to Batavia to save him from divine fate and British neglect in Ceylon, "the abode of error" (*dar al-dalala*). Wirakusuma claimed that, after his loyal defense of the company's interest as an officer and then his being taken to Madras for three years before being returned and poorly paid by the English, he was then languishing in Colombo with his five children and new wife.[118]

Had he ever worn it, Wirakusuma's red coat would have been a poor fit indeed, and Maitland would hardly count on his loyalty.[119] Much of Maitland's hostility toward such "Malays" stemmed from his abhorrence of what might be called martial Mohammedans, heightened by the Vellore mutiny in India in July 1806. Never one for brevity, Maitland sent Lord Minto fifty pages on the subject in September, declaring that it was "not in the Nature or Feeling of a Mahomedan to hang up his sword, and sit quietly down to Cultivate the Land."[120] As if to prove his ill feelings about Muslim soldiers, an express post from Trincomalee on the last day of February 1807 brought news of violence between Indian Gun Lascars and Malays. This had broken out during a festival—the martyrdom of Caliph ʿUthman had been commemorated three days earlier—and had led to nearly fifty casualties, including the deaths of seven or eight Malays.[121]

If Maitland regretted the loss of any men in official dispatches, he was far less guarded with the former undersecretary of state for war and the colonies, George Shee (1758–1825), deeming the dispute "of no consequence or significance of any kind further than the loss of a few lives" and adding that if they were "to lose a few more of the Malays it would be of no great consequence."[122] As I shall show in the next chapter, however, Maitland's days were numbered, and North's regiment would only affirm its place on the island, gaining in strength with the addition of bodies from briefly British Java (1811–1816), newly annexed Kandy (from 1815), and the not-so-distant Malay peninsula. This would make the military Muslims ever more Malay alongside the more populous Moorish traders and jurists. However, unlike at the Cape, it was the latter who served as interpreters of Islam for British courts that had to come to terms with their oceanic subjects and their form of law that privileged the rulings of Imam Shafiʿi, just as Tuan Guru had at the Cape.

SIX

Between Shrinking Kandy and Distant Istanbul

IN EARLY 1812, Captain Assana, the former commander of Vikrama Rajasimha's Jawi troops, traveled to the eastern seaboard of Ceylon seeking news of the captive Major Davie. Assana's mission for his new British employers was managed by Simon Sawers (1780–1849), who had arrived in 1805 in the retinue of his countryman Thomas Maitland. In stark contrast to the irritable new governor, Sawers would prove himself a popular ally of Muslims on the island. He was destined to convey a petition of those of Galle to the reigning lord of Egypt seeking scholars and aid—just as North had anticipated in his correspondence when pondering the future of Muslim education and administration on the island. But that was nearly three decades into the future, and well after Assana's cohort of Kandyan troops had merged with those of perhaps the most famous of the island's regiments, serving in uniforms of one kind or another while wondering where they might direct their gaze in quest of Muslim learning and patronage.

Moorish Codes, Malay Recruits, and the Fall of Kandy

The previous chapter explored the origins of the Jawi community of Lanka, its heavily Javanese exilic component, and the crucial—and disproportionately Madurese—military body that would be labeled "Malay." Already trained to a much greater degree than those of the Cape, such soldiers were gladly absorbed by British company and crown and then deployed against Kandy to face still other Malays, some of whom they had known in Dutch service. While not to immediate success, the first steps had been taken in reimagining such soldiers as the ideal tameable military servants and a cognate to the artisan reservists of the Cape, with the ranks expanded with fresh recruits from the east. Soon missing from the mix on Lanka, however, was the regal core of exiles, though, much like Cape Town, future generations would prefer to remember their officer forebears as having been princes of one Jawi land or another.

In what follows, I will first place the community in relation to their cobelievers from the vantage of British officials who struggled to imagine a role for Muslims on the islands. If the Malays had proven a nuisance to Maitland, the far larger community of Moors presented him with a much more clearly judicial challenge, first assessed by yet another Scot, Alexander Johnston (1775–1849). A much broader-minded person and another founding member of Colebrooke's Royal Asiatic Society, Johnston later admitted that he wrote his report of 1807 on the various religious traditions of Ceylon with a view to restoring what he imagined to be their historical concessions, opening the agricultural lands of the north to "the Hindu capitalists of Jaffna" and similarly "inducing Mohammedan capitalists of the coasts of Malabar, Coromandel, and Malacca, to make Ceylon, in modern times, what it was in ancient times, the great emporium of trade in India."[1]

In November 1807 he also submitted his translation of the Freijer Code in consultation with local Muslim scholars who gave him "a very favorable opinion of their intellectual and moral character."[2] According to Johnston, Governor Falck (who had exiled the Kanarans Callaga and his son Corradoe to the Cape) had supposedly found, "after much inquiry," that nobody on the island had a sound knowledge of the laws of inheritance and marriage, making people subject to the arbitrary exactions of their headmen. Falck had therefore sent to Batavia for a code, which was composed by the most learned of the "Mohammedan priests" who resided within the Indies government—assumedly the community to the west of the Utrechtse Poort. This code was accordingly drafted, returned to Colombo, and approved by all the "moorish" inhabitants of the districts. However, cautioned Johnston,

> since the conquest of these territories by the English, this code has not been made so publick, or so much attended to, as it Ought have been: the consequence of

which is, that the lower classes of mohamedans being totally ignorant of this law upon the commonest subjects, are obliged to refer, on every occasion, however trifling, to their headmen for information how to act: this gives the headmen so much influence, and is a source of so much secret emolument, fees being always taken by them for their opinion, that they are naturally enough extremely anxious to prevent Government from publishing the contents of this Code. In going round the island I perceived that almost all the headmen had a copy either in malabar or arabic of this code, but that they kept it as private as they could, evidently with the view of enhancing the value of their own opinion upon questions of mohammedan Law. I sometime ago caused some printed copies of it to be posted up in all the principal mosques in the Province of Colombo; this appears to me to be the surest way of making it generally known, and I should strongly advise a similar measure to be adopted in all the other Provinces.[3]

Johnston was unabashed in entitling his translation as a "Maurish Code," since it had been approved by nineteen of the "Marcair, Arbitrators Priests and Inhabitants," whose linkages with both coasts of Southern India were more than apparent.[4]

But if the Southeast Asian origins of the code were occluded, there was no escaping the need for Southeast Asian bodies. Maitland was forced to abandon his plans for the reduction of the Malay Regiment, with fresh saber-rattling between Colombo and Kandy in 1808, recognizing their utility for "internal though not external defence."[5] He was hardly satisfied with the military establishment on the island, telling Lord Castlereagh that it was comprised of "four distinct classes or descriptions of people, all differing in their religion, in their habits, their prejudices and their manners, all holding each other in thorough contempt and aversion, most of them disliking the country where they serve as much as they detest their brother soldiers with whom they are serving."[6]

Maitland's solution was the active recruitment of more Mozambiquans via Goa, "induced to enlist" rather than being enslaved.[7] Yet the question of slavery was a contingent one for Maitland. He soon echoed his deputy, Colonel John Wilson (1780–1856), who had the view that limited recruitment of slaves might be a means of "deviating the evil necessarily arising in Africa from the sudden stop of that revolting commerce." For there could be no doubting the "superior excellence" of Africans, of whom fifty, he claimed, "would do more against the Candians than any number of sepoys."[8]

Wilson would briefly act as governor with Maitland's recall in March 1811. While eager to gain more African soldiers, he had less disdain for the Malays. He therefore recommended the recruitment of volunteers to fill their ranks, to be led by Lieutenant Louis de Bussche, after his arrival from Cape Town in early 1812.[9] Wilson also proposed the employment of a refugee from Kandy called Captain Assana. This figure was a locally born Malay who had held the rank of *mohandiram* at Kandy. His position had been imperiled as he had been close to the recently executed *adigar* Pilimatalava (or Pilima Talawa), the former kingmaker from the 1790s who had threatened his erstwhile protégé in 1811.[10]

While never explicitly named as Captain Assana in any of Wilson's dispatches to the secretary of state, this Malay had battled his way from Kandy, together with sixty followers and their families, losing a brother en route. Wilson naturally valued his familiarity with the territories of the adversary and believed that there was "no risk whatever in employing him," for it was "impossible" that he would ever go back.[11] By January 1812 Assana and his retainers seemed well settled in British service. He proceeded on missions gathering intelligence about Davie at Batticaloa, while his wife and children were tutored at Colombo by a Moor whose brother had come down from Kandy in late 1811.[12] Assana certainly had close links with the Tamil-speaking Muslims of Lanka. His older sister was married to a Moor of Maralanda whose son also came down to Colombo in December 1811 on behalf of the family of the late Pilima Tilawa to encourage an English invasion.[13]

At Kandy, and reflecting Sinhalese nomenclature for Southeast Asians, Assana had been better known as the Ja Mohandiram. This Sinhalese title referenced the island of Java and the habit of some Muslim Southeast Asians to call themselves Jawi or Jawa. Java was evidently on some Kandyan minds in 1811, and Wilson sought to take advantage of the September conquest of that island to emphasize that France, whose agents were often rumored to be everywhere in the Indian Ocean, could no longer be a savior for the Kandyans. "Having found that the successes in Java were not sufficiently understood even in our own Districts," Wilson reported that he had "had an acco[oun]t drawn up and translated into Cinjalese not only of the conquest but the whole progress of H.M. arm[y] in exterminating the French from India. This has been published with great solemnity through the Districts & will of course reach our neighbour in a way that cannot fail to convince them [sic] that these events have actually taken place."[14]

The message that arrived was mixed. In some cases, the Kandyans regarded the British claim as pure propaganda. According to rumors collected by the chief British interpreter, John D'Oyly (1774–1824), some Sinhalese declared that the English had only gone to Batavia to demand "7000 Jawas to make War agt. Kandy," but were repulsed with the loss of 7000 of their own. If they had really taken Batavia, there seemed to be little evidence. "Where is the Rice? Where are the Jawas?" they had asked.[15] To be sure, the Kandyans still had Jawa of their own. A report from June 1812 noted that the palace housing both the king and his hostage Davie were guarded by 500 men, counting "Pattanis, Jawas, Moormen & Singhaleze."[16]

While hardly the rumored 7,000 Jawas, Lord Minto's campaign would have a tangible impact in August 1814 when De Bussche returned from a recruiting mission to Java and Eastern Indonesia—a mission remembered in the Malay community as bringing in ancestors from the breadth of the archipelago who were aided by a unit of Africans under Colonel Hardy.[17] De Bussche's haul of "412 fine young men" would be lauded by the latest governor, Robert Brownrigg (1759–1833), despite his own preference for Indian sepoys. It also dovetailed with his efforts to integrate the Moorish elite as mohandirams over the Maritime Provinces, following on from the efforts of Johnston, by now the island's chief justice, to bring them onto juries and voluntarily manumit their slaves.[18]

Brownrigg also knew when a spy had value, having had D'Oyly arrange in January 1813 for Assana's secret return to Kandy, where he maintained contact with the son of Pilima Tilawa and Moors like Saddaku and his Malay ally Sakandu. Assana was also in contact with his mother and a brother, Tamby, who remained in Kandyan military service as a lieutenant.[19] Having called on his frightened mother with Sakandu and Saddaku, Assana returned to his subsidized home and garden at Negombo in March 1813 with confirmation of the death of Davie.[20] Assana's informants were also among those responsible for a series of tales of the Kandyan king's descent into depravity.[21] While perhaps too willing to excuse an increasingly paranoid king of extreme behavior, Gananath Obeyesekere cautions us against accepting the oft-cited details of such accounts. Of infamy were the 1814 killings of the family of another treasonous adigar, Ahelepola Nilame of Saffragam (1773–1829), who was also close to Assana and whom the later chronicler Baba Ounus Saldin (1832–1906) claimed had desired both queen and throne.[22]

The king was losing support, most vitally that of this latest chief minister. He was also losing his much-vaunted Malays, some of whom he had employed in the construction of earthworks. After some absconded, they were caught and confined, as was Saddaku, who revealed his contact with Assana and the similarly defected Sakandu. The new commander of the Kandyan Malays, Kuppen, was then charged with rooting out any other possible turncoats who, in the words of Sannadi Writer, "had had relations with Colombo, who were worthless, & unworthy of Confidence, & to reserve only such as were good Men, who would not kill Animals, & who were faithful & trustworthy, for whose Conduct the Captain must answer."[23] Aside from the five deserters, Kuppen separated two more men. All had their capital sentences commuted to allow them to leave Kandy with their families to the number of eighteen people—including Sannadi Writer and Assana's brother Tamby. Such magnanimity seems to be explained by the promise made of a generous reward if any defectors would secure the head of Assana. One reportedly requested a knife from his superior, Captain Odin (Uddin, d. 1860).[24]

Marching from points around the island in late 1814, Brownrigg's combined forces—including 340 Malays under De Bussche and Assana—entered an abandoned capital in February 1815. On the 18th of that month, they captured the king, who was whisked into exile at Vellore, and set about sacking the holy city.[25] While averse to defiling Buddhist sanctuaries, De Bussche's Malays were reported as having carried out their share of violent "oppression" of the defeated.[26]

The fall of Kandy would bring yet more news of what had happened to Davie, as well as the family of Ahelapola. The most widely reprinted story was related by Jan Albertus Thoen, a Leiden-born artillerist who had survived in 1803 and assumed the role of drillmaster to the Kandyans.[27] He had also taken a Moorish wife, which suggests his own conversion to Islam. Thoen confirmed that the Kandyan soldiers had been led by a Malay called Sangalen, who had two brothers in the British ranks called Nouradin. But while he reported that Sangalen had been killed in the assault and that his brother had negotiated the surrender with Davie, Thoen said nothing about any regal Malay heroism in the face of death. It was, rather, about pragmatism. Thoen recalled how the always separate Malay ranks had their own drillmasters under two other brothers, Captain Coopen (i.e., Kuppen) and Lieutenant

Dusain. He also reported that the first man to go over to the Kandyans had been the drum major Odin. Odin, whose defecting men had been tasked with assassinating Assana the previous year, also remained alive in 1815. He was accordingly tried, though Brownrigg commuted his death sentence to transportation to New South Wales.[28]

Some stories were still harder to do away with. After skewering Percival's account of Ceylon as dated and derivative, William Gifford (1756-1826), editor of the *Quarterly Review*, recycled large sections from Cordiner in October 1815 "to convey a very general and concise outline of this new jewel added to the British crown" and to remind readers of the heroic sacrifices of the otherwise forgotten "Nouradeen" brothers. As he opined of the Malays in general:

> They are soldiers, sailors, fishermen, and artificers, many of whom were introduced by the Dutch in a state of slavery. The bad part of the character of this singular people ... has, we think, been greatly exaggerated. With the exception of Mr. Marsden, in his excellent History of Sumatra, it has been drawn, mostly by passing visitors, from a slight acquaintance with those whom vice had driven to piracy and plunder, or misfortune thrown into a state of slavery.... We can only observe ... that among the various nations who inhabit Ceylon, the Malays are the only people out of which we have been able to make good soldiers; and a more faithful, obedient, and orderly corps does not exist.[29]

Gifford offered dated and inaccurate views about the lack of any religious structures on the island, being blind to the role played by the Kandyan king as patron to the Buddhist clergy or *sangha*. With the assumption of British patronage over the chiefs, many Sinhalese—and certainly the ambitious Ahelapola—were shocked that the English did away with the monarchy itself, arrogating the right to act as protectors of the Buddhist religion.[30] Worried monks activated their networks linked to the Southeast Asian courts of Ava and Bangkok. But if ordained monks traveling in both directions had escaped notice in previous years, by July there was word of a plan hatched to bring in a new king from Burma.[31] Brownrigg accordingly instructed D'Oyly to pay attention to any monastic journeys to or from that state, for such missions had "the ready pretense of sending for Religious Books to that great Seat of Boodhoo Learning."[32]

It turned out that D'Oyly's own preceptor, Ihagama, had been charged with bringing a Southeast Asian prince back to Kandy. For our purposes, though, it is worth noting that Brownrigg raised a flag regarding one of the conspirators' allies in a later development that sought to elevate a local Kandyan:

> The Malay Mohandiram whom your Lordship will perceive to be mentioned in the Statement of Eknilegode [Nilame] and more particularly in that of the Expriest Kapuliadde is a Malay Man of some Rank who escaped from Kandy on the occasion of Pilemé Talawé Adigar being beheaded. He arrived at Colombo in General Wilson's time with a number of Followers, and has ever since been maintained by Government. In the Kandyan Expedition he acted under Captn. De Bussche and gave great satisfaction being a bold and active Man, and bred to Military Habits as far as they could exist in Kandy. Since the Acquisition of that Country his general acquaintance with Kandyans of all descriptions made him much more resorted than was agreeable to me to hear of. And wherever any thing of suspicion was mentioned with regard to the Proceedings of the Chiefs the name of this man never failed to be involved in it, so certain it is that at least he was considered as ready an effective a Partizan for any dangerous enterprize. The nature of his Communications with the Priest Ihagama being fairly established as far as such transactions usually admit of Proof I determined . . . to send him to Batavia, the native place of his family. [He] is now lodged in Military Custody at Galle with two grown Sons under a Warrant for removal. His family also is there in readiness to be sent with him.[33]

Ihagama blamed the collapse of the plot on the discovery of Assana, who had convinced him to forget his trip to Burma and to install a Kandyan prince on the throne. It was also Assana who had been caught as he tried to get his former soldiers to turn against their new masters.[34]

As far as the Malays were concerned, Assana was an outlier at this point. Writing in March 1817, De Bussche made no mention of his former subaltern as he extolled the virtues of his recruits, citing his fellow officers' Marsdenian consensus that they were a "faithful, obedient and brave race of people" who had ceased any "sudden fits of madness" or indiscriminate acts of murder once free of "cruel and barbarous" Dutch treatment. Going further than Cordiner, he remarked upon "the slaughter they occasioned" in the Java campaign. He further debunked the idea that they required opium, gladly added that they eschewed hospitals, and claimed they had "fewer prejudices" than other native troops of India—forgoing religious holidays and exchanging their rice and fish curries for the pork (!) messes of their European fellows.[35]

De Bussche's patron Brownrigg also evinced little general concern for his Malay soldiers in the turbulent months that followed, occasionally mentioning them as heroic fighters against Kandyan "rebels," or as individual deserters and murderers in the ranks of both sides.[36] De Bussche's teenaged contemporary Thomas Skinner (1804-1877) was delighted by his first command on Ceylon, whose resourceful and shoeless Malay soldiers he later commemorated as "the finest native regiment that any country ever possessed," not to mention their follower wives, whose stoicism and adaptability he similarly admired.[37] Both the Malay soldiers (who claimed the credit for seizing the king) and their Moorish coreligionists (who celebrated victory over Kandy in 1815) would remain loyal during the Uva Rebellion of 1817-1818 and the brutal repression that followed, of which they once more partook.[38]

This is not to say that all was peaceful in the subaltern ranks. The arrival of Bengali sepoys brought to cope with the Uva Rebellion led to communal rioting with the Malay garrison at Slave Island on the first day of 1819, just as Malays and Indians had fought at Trincomalee over a decade earlier. Starting with a fight between two youths from each camp and ending with the deaths of two sepoys, one of the Malay eyewitnesses, the son of a captain, penned a narrative poem casting blame on the "foreigners" whose insults had pricked the "arrogant" Malays, who then ran amok in the streets.[39]

Hussainmiya suggests that the fight and its outcome were recounted long into the nineteenth century. But while the riot found immediate mention in the *Ceylon Government Gazette* of January 2, 1819, its embarrassing eruption did not make its way into many official dispatches beyond those connected to the military courts. Local reports were soon overshadowed by plans for the impending departure of Brownrigg on February 1, and news of the death two days earlier of George III, whose official portrait he had recently hung in the audience hall at Kandy. Brownrigg had supposedly done so "to replace the blind and abject feelings of dread with which [the Sinhalese had] approached their former Kings."[40] Lanka, with its many peoples, old and new and often at odds, was under a British sovereign for the foreseeable future.

Minglings, the Enslaved, and the Prospect of Cairo

Given the appearance of yet another Asian community in the form of the Bengali sepoys, the Malays of Colombo may now have felt that they had more in common with the fellow Shafiʿi Moors across the lake. Many had and would intermarry at Colombo and Kandy and at times impress Western interlocutors like Johnston, just as they did in the Straits Settlements. At recently incorporated Singapore, for example, one learned scion of such meetings was Munshi Abdullah (1796–1854). Seen today as a member of the Peranakan community, his paternal ancestor had been an Arab resident of Nagore whose part-Tamil children had links to Malacca and the wider Jawi world.[41] Munshi Abdullah arguably changed Raffles's negative view of oceanic Muslims when he worked for him as a translator and scribe from the 1810s, before playing a role as an interpreter for Christian missionaries in the 1830s and 1840s, and in the long-term representation of Malays in British-sponsored print thereafter. This included his recollection of vengeful violence directed against Resident William Farquhar in 1823, and its immediate consequences when enraged soldiers mutilated the corpse of the assailant, the similarly mixed Sayyid Yasin. Muslim writers certainly preferred to see Yasin's actions as stemming from divine inspiration rather than amok. Indeed, the sultan had requested the sayyid's body from Raffles after its shameful exhibition, and Yasin was soon commemorated as a saint after his interment, transforming in time—like many other part-Tamil or half-Malay sojourners—into an unalloyed Arab.[42]

Equally, back on Lanka—which Abdullah skirted en route to his own death in the Hijaz in 1854—the manuscripts found in private homes today show numerous meetings of Malay, Moor, and Arab under British rule.[43] In the mid-1820s, Muhammad Balangkaya, the son of a retainer of Raja Oesman, redesigned the Moor-dominated grand mosque of the Pettah, which was visited by an approving governor Edward Barnes in 1826.[44] Still, the heart of the Malay community of the capital remained the barracks across the lake, and it beat most clearly in Friday attendance at the Wekanda Mosque, on whose grounds many of the regiment and their families were buried. The poorly named Slave Island should arguably have become even more Malay and less servile with recruitment shifting entirely to Penang after the return of Java to Dutch hands in 1816, and then with the exchange of Bencoolen for Malacca in 1824.

Such efforts did not necessarily meet with success in the still quite Jawi ranks, which now marched out in the company of "Caffree" women to serve their domestic needs rather than their own partners, as they had in India two decades earlier.⁴⁵ And while the imams of the Cape were filling their mosques with nearly free Africans or else through the politics of manumission, there were fewer such mergings on Ceylon once a separate regiment had been raised in 1811 to manage the recruits from Mozambique. Most full-time soldiers hardly had the means to afford a slave anyway, and, while it was a known practice among some of the Moorish merchants, proselytism through purchase and manumission was so slight a phenomenon on the island as to be of little concern to the administration or the missionaries.⁴⁶ Equally, the elite attitude to once bonded coreligionists was rather less than egalitarian, as Nira Wickramasinghe shows in the case of Packier Pulle Rawothan, whose servile family history prevented him from getting his son circumcised with customary celebration in 1825.⁴⁷

Soon after Rawothan had his apparently inconclusive day in court, the Malays would see their companies folded into the Ceylon Rifle Regiment by 1827, becoming an imperial charge in 1830.⁴⁸ Sent to the once more Dutch Indies in that year to repatriate time-expired troops and gather new ones for British ranks, Skinner, accustomed to acclimatized soldiers from the east of the archipelago, bemoaned the quality of men brought from Penang, claiming that the bulk of them were incorrigible pirates and robbers from Kedah. Having sent recruiting parties around the island, he rejected the "very inferior specimens" who had offered their services there, as well as a party of Bugis at Singapore, whom he deemed too short.⁴⁹ Skinner met with rejection himself on Java, for the Dutch administration felt disinclined to accept repatriated soldiers or yet to allow any fresh recruits to serve under a British flag. This was especially so as the EIC had refused to help during the revolt of Prince Dipanagara on Java, which had just been suppressed with the loss of over two hundred thousand lives.⁵⁰

In the meantime, the Royal Commission of Eastern Inquiry washed in from Mauritius. Reconfigured after Bigge's departure as the Colebrooke-Cameron Commission, it came to make its assessment of the island's affairs in 1829. Given the involvement of John Gregory, who had interviewed the "priests" of Cape Town five years earlier, one might have expected some interest in Islam. However, it seems that such was largely confined to inquiries about the arbitrary imposition of corvée labor on

Moors in the coastal districts.⁵¹ The commissioners were also interested in the use of Muslim law and Moorish interpreters in courts, which were now public. Colebrooke and Cameron gleaned this information by means of a survey sent to magistrates. With the curious exception of Colombo, most judicial officers reported the presence on staff of a salaried Moorish priest or interpreter. Although recourse was made at times to the Freijer Code, most judges pronounced it "defective" or "contradictory."⁵² The magistrates preferred to rely on their court Moors in most matters, even if they took their evidence with a grain of salt. Most of these jurists, generally burghers, had damning views of the truthfulness and promptness of "natives" and their assistants anyway. The exception was a positive Richard Malone Sneyd (1800–1861), the Irish magistrate for Galle and Matara, who said he dealt with some 400 cases each year, as well as having an active backlog of around 250 more.⁵³ Tangential evidence suggests that Moors were frequent litigants there, much as they had plagued North, and for matters touching on far more than divorce and inheritance. From April 1835, Sneyd submitted repeated complaints about the absence of a Tamil interpreter, pleading for the post to be filled with a salary that would prevent the loss of any further staff like Ismail Marcair, who had left for the greener pastures of Trincomalee.⁵⁴

Much more clearly reflective of ongoing tensions in court, though, is a petition signed by dozens of Galle's Moors in January 1839. Sent in the name of all the Muslims of the island of "Sarandeeb," it was addressed to the "King and Grand Pasha of Egypt," Muhammad ʿAli, whom they further designated as "Commander in Faith." This latter title, more often glossed as "Commander of the Faithful," was formally reserved in Egypt and Arabia for the Ottoman sultan, who ruled over both domains. There is moreover evidence that a khatib of the Wekanda Mosque had been (and perhaps still was) invoking Muhammad ʿAli's beset seigneur Mahmud II (r. 1808–1839) at Friday prayers. A marginal note in a contemporary collection of sermons lauds the latter as "the Greatest Sultan and Blessed Khaqan, Lord of the Arab and non-Arab Kings, [and] God's Caliph on Earth."⁵⁵

The title of caliph presumed protection of the Holy Places, and the petitioners from Galle understood that Mecca and Medina had been under Egyptian control for decades, having originally been reasserted in Mahmud II's name by Muhammad ʿAli's sons, Ibrahim and Tusun Pasha. There was also the sense that they would stay there. After the defeat of the Wahhabis, Ibrahim's defense of Ottoman Greece and his aggressive marches into Asia Minor had encouraged his father to seek independence, if not the empire itself, in 1838.[56]

Considering Muhammad ʿAli's contemporary claims and territory, the 1839 letter from Galle was a calculated and curiously stilted English-language petition that bears examination:

> That your majesty's very humble Memorialists, with their bended knees throwing themselves at your worthy feet; which are bright on [the] Mahometan world as the Moon with her surrounded stars, beg leave submissively to lay their grievance in the hope and unseigned expectation that Your Majesty as a Mahometan will graciously be pleased to sympathise with them and yield to their prayer for the sake of Almighty God and Saviour "Mahomet Nabee Sallallahoe Aalliyiou Sallam."
>
> That now for Some years back their body was considerably small than at present; which at this moment may be estimated at Two Millions. But in those days there were very much learned and pious men amongst them besides Priests of the different high orders. Consequently the religious ceremonies of various descriptions were performed quite sure and a perfect tranquility was evinced in their Brethren in the said Island: and that then such priests were not to be had in the Island, they were ultimately sent for, and has been provided for, from different part of the world through the Indians of the wealthy Kind of their profession, but unfortunately by a gradual reduction a complete vacation having at present to be seen of those worthy character, the unhappy Mahometan today has to suffer exceedingly, who since late are constantly to be found in English Courts being involved in law suits respecting their Religious controversies, disputes and other abuses on their faith.
>
> That the Gentleman S. E. Sawers Esq. who kindly favored Your Majesty's memorialists with his assistance of laying this before your Highness, and to whom Mahometans in general right to feel us him highly indebted for the general support which their Brethren in the Island received. He is indeed a worthy character, for many years he has filled very important Offices under Government, and perhaps not one Englishman to surpass his abilities with regard to the very particular of the place and to him Memorialists begs to refer Your Majesty for further information respecting their fate.
>
> Under these Memorialists most humbly pray Your Majesty to extend Mercy on a dying Mahometan world and Graciously be pleased to order down Priests of the Competent orders, Muftis, Cadies and others to water the Mahometan plants

in the said Island of Ceylon (Sarandeeb) which are yearly wracked very by the Foam of ignorance.[57]

No aid was forthcoming. Muhammad 'Ali most likely never laid eyes on the petition that Sawers took to Cairo.[58] We should not see any broad conspiracy at work, however, even as Lord Palmerston was working to prevent Muhammad 'Ali's rise. The wayward viceroy would lose all that he had gained with the intervention of the Great Powers in July 1839 in favor of the new sultan Abdulmecid (r. 1839–1861), followed by the 1840 Treaty of London, which facilitated the return of Ottoman troops to the Hijaz in 1841.[59]

The British had no fear of Muhammad 'Ali thereafter. Indeed, throughout his struggle to cement his family's place in (or even over) the empire, the viceroy had continued to protect the free movement of Western mail, which was first brought from Bombay to Suez by steamer from 1829, and to encourage the movement of Eastern scholars through its ports and among the columns of its most famous teaching mosque. Officials like Johnston felt it only natural that Ceylonese Muslims would seek juridical guidance from well-regarded centers abroad such as al-Azhar. We may recall, too, that the memorialist's writing to Egypt echoed North's notions as to the potential locus of juridical authority, and one even more relevant given the collapse of any Muslim power in Southern India. One wonders if the memorialists had been encouraged in this direction by Sawers himself, who had arrived on Ceylon in the year North departed the island, and who had then supervised Assana's intrigues at Batticaloa.[60]

Just as the connections, hand, and curious phrasing of the Galle petition indicate that the author had had experience of English officialdom or the courts whose proceedings had so distracted his coreligionists, his colleagues' looking to Cairo did not entail any act of disloyalty to the British throne. Like the later Capetonian outreach to Istanbul (to which I will turn in chapter 7), these were complimentary acts. Similarly, among the thousands of signatures collected to congratulate Queen Victoria on her marriage to Prince Albert in April 1840 are those of many dozens of Moors at Colombo. Although there is no page so clearly assigned to those of Galle, a signature on the first of eleven pages belonging to officials of Southern Province bears the name J. O. Marcair. Designated as the "translator Mohandiram Galle," his hand resembles that of the Cairene letter.[61]

While closer attention will be needed to confirm any overlap between petition and congratulation, many a designated court priest can be found offering his signature lauding the young queen. By contrast, and given the commonality of script, distinctly Malay names are hard to identify. Yet we should remember that, like all the other soldiers who are similarly absent in this enormous document which never made it off the island, the Malays had sworn their loyalty to Victoria. They would continue to serve where needed, with their ranks invigorated by more recent arrivals from the Straits Settlements. Despite Skinner's doubts as to the capacity of such men and the odd hiccough—as in the case of apparent mutiny of recruits at sea in 1841—the corps earned a warrant of good conduct in 1843.[62] Indeed, with pay raises offered to encourage recruitment in the back half of the 1840s, the regiment seemed on a firm footing.[63] The veteran Ounus Saldin later recalled the elation of six hundred soldiers and their families when they had word of their pay raises after their dispatch to Hong Kong in 1847.[64] But time would tell that this was the zenith of Malay soldiering. The Hong Kong deployment, with Captain Salimudin as its adjutant, saw significant losses to disease, and fewer recruits would be tempted to sail westward from Penang as well.[65] The corps would see its final significant action during the Matale rebellion of 1848, after which time even the local sons of Malay soldiers were discouraged from enlisting.

The Growing Appeal of a Muslim Empire

By the time that the Malays of Ceylon were serving at Hong Kong, Great Britain had drawn still closer to the Ottoman Empire, not only curtailing the ambitions of Muhammad ʿAli, but seeking to forestall Russian ascendance in the Eastern Mediterranean. It also appears that, in the decade before the congratulatory missives arrived from the Cape, the Ottomans had begun to see the merits of placing consular staff in the EIC ports of Bombay and Calcutta in 1849, realizing that increasing numbers of Indian Muslims were anxious about the future of the empire that protected the Hijaz.

British and French military aid during the Crimean War (1853–1856) would stymie Russian annexation for a moment as the 1856 Treaty of Paris guaranteed a measure of Ottoman territorial integrity. Such offers were hardly on the table for the heirs of Mughal India and their neighbors. The EIC had only continued its sweep through Asia after the conclusion of the Napoleonic Wars, adding larger and larger swathes of the subcontinent to its territories every year and justifying conflict elsewhere around the Indian Ocean arena. The Buddhist kingdom of Ava, which had been a major threat to Kedah and once seemed a source of succor to Kandy, lost its southern possessions from the 1820s after butting up against the EIC in Manipur.[66] In 1852 the last maritime tracts of lower Burma were swallowed as well, forcing King Mindon (r. 1853–1878) to establish his court further north at Mandalay.

This was hardly the end of EIC ambitions. As in India, yet more Burmese territory lay on the horizon. In April 1856, Major T. J. Nuthall of the Bengal Native Infantry proposed stationing a Malay corps at Pegu along the lines of the Ceylon Rifles, remarking that he would "far prefer serving with Malays than with any other Asiatics, not only on account of the prestige which they appear to have established, but because they can live on the produce of the Country." While an official in Calcutta conceded that Malays made "excellent soldiers & sailors," he rejected Nuthall's proposal, because they asked very high wages.[67] Scarcely five months before the great uprising that would leave EIC rule in tatters, these Muslim soldiers were evidently regarded highly and knew their value.

Once thousands of sepoys did rebel across Northern India in May 1857, it was not merely the company's reputation that was at stake. With information scanty and the leadership of the rebellion vested by some in the emasculated Mughal emperor Bahadur Shah II, a panicked Great Britain made good on its Crimean investments. Sultan Abdulmecid obligingly declared jihad against the British illicit and offered funds to relieve veterans of the war to London's satisfaction.[68] The dethroned Mughal was meanwhile sent into exile in newly British Rangoon, seeding another site of holiness for oceanic Muslims with his death in 1862.[69]

The diplomatic friendship of London and Istanbul must have seemed treasonous to those who had fought in the name of Islam or else was conveniently ignored as many slipped away to Mecca and Medina in the face of British vengeance, later to found schools or compose texts in praise of the sultan on whose largesse they would rely for sustenance.[70] There was already southern precedent for this. In 1852, a prominent Arab of Malabar, Fadl b. ʿAlawi, had been forced to emigrate to the Hijaz, having refused to submit to the demands of local British magistrates and collectors suspicious that, like his father before him, the locally born sayyid was the inspiration for resistance to company rule. Indeed, with centuries of relative autonomy, local Mapilla Muslims cared little for Istanbul's partnership with London. After Sayyid Fadl departed, his followers continued a violent campaign and hoped for his return, which was blocked by the British at Aden. In September 1855 they assassinated the collector who had seen to his departure—the same year in which Arab merchants of Mecca, some well known to Fadl, revolted against Ottoman authority and its restriction of the slave trade.

Once again, in June 1858, Hadrami traders of the Hijaz, threatened by Western-backed competitors at Jeddah, and fearful of further losses to the slave trade caused by pressure on both the Ottomans and the Bu Saʿidis of Zanzibar, fomented a massacre of the diplomatic population and their perceived allies, including Greek and Armenian merchants. The violence commenced after an Indian merchant ship flying the Ottoman flag had been forced to raise the Union Jack by an intemperate acting vice-consul.[71] Rather than defend their flag and claim the ship, the Ottomans cooperated with Great Britain and France in trying and executing the perpetrators—though they never produced Sayyid Fadl, whom the British still imagined as working behind the scenes.[72]

Like the future mufti of Mecca and historian Ahmad b. Zayni Dahlan (1817–1886), Fadl's sympathies were decidedly with his fellow Hadramis in the Hijaz.[73] Fadl even wrote a treatise defending slavery as a divinely ordained state of those who served. Herein Fadl scoffed at abolitionists and pointed to Western imperial projects as being no true improvement of the human condition, citing Java as a locus of iniquitous debt bondage afflicting men and women who were technically free, but unable to ever repay their contracts.[74]

Although he was not rendered for British vengeance in 1858, Fadl had already suffered as a result of the 1855 uprising, losing his sinecure and heading to the capital to press claims of innocence and poverty. He may have hoped to warm his welcome there, seeing a compilation of his pious works to the press at Cairo in 1857 that, aside from his treatise about slavery, should have pleased Istanbul.[75] This included ruminations on matters of piety and sovereignty by ʿAbdallah al-Haddad of Tarim (d. 1720), to which Fadl appended his own short statement on the obligation to obey one's rulers, and the (surely Ottoman) sultan in particular.[76] According to ʿAlawi al-Saqqaf (d. 1916), Fadl also included a selection of fatwas provided the recently deceased ʿAbdallah al-Ahdal of Zabid (d. 1855/1856).[77] Herein al-Ahdal had affirmed the principle of jihad against a Christian occupier who oppresses Muslims. He also labeled any otherwise respectable Muslims who praised Christian justice—including ships' captains and those who neglected to mention the sultan in the Friday prayers—as partakers of unbelief. "Is there any unbelief worse than that of the Franks?" asked al-Ahdal while condemning any Muslim who counted themselves the subjects (raʿiyya) of a Christian.[78]

Evidently many Muslims *did* count themselves as the subjects of Christian Britain in Southern India, just as they did in Ceylon and the Straits of Malacca. By contrast, Great Britain's Atlantic rivals—having nothing like the same collaborative relationship with the Ottomans and many millions of Muslim subjects of their own—would become a cause of concern reaching the council rooms of Sultan Abdulmecid. The old petition of Ahmad Taj al-Din sent from Penang in 1824 may have been forgotten, but those arriving from some of the more southerly kingdoms abutting Dutch territory were not so easily ignored, especially as the increasingly colonized Jawi peoples were making their mark on restored Ottoman Mecca as exiles, pilgrims, and mystics. In 1850, for instance, one such teacher called Muhammad Salih had joined nine other Jawi shaykhs in offering a poem of gratitude to Abdulmecid's governor, Mehmed Hasib Pasha (d. 1870), for reducing the financial burdens faced by pilgrims.[79]

There was an increasingly global political backstory here too. Many of Muhammad Salih's peers were interacting with ulama hailing from India, like Fadl, or the long-since-crushed Siamese vassals of Pattani and Kedah. All this gave officials back in the Indies pause for thought as to who all these newly returned pilgrims and priests were. The Dutch had faced a steep learning curve. With their return to power on Java after 1816, the metropolitan government had set about forging a series of new relationships with indigenous rulers as they tried to jostle numerous Arab or Arab-owned vessels thronging in their ports.[80] Violence was the order of the day. As noted at the time of Skinner's recruiting visit, Java had already witnessed the cataclysmic 1825 revolt of Prince Dipanagara. Once that island was subjugated in 1830, other areas would face invasion. From Sumatra to Borneo and Sulawesi, and in a repeat of what had happened to the princes of the Moluccas in the 1770s, Malay rulers saw fresh demands for concessions and contracts designed to give Holland an edge against the inconvenient settlements of the EIC.

As the Dutch advanced up the coast of Sumatra after the Padri wars and their final conquest of the Minangkabau lands in 1837, Malay rulers put out feelers in the hope of gaining assistance from any other power. Great Britain, France, and the United States were in the mix of potential allies, as was Aceh. But Aceh, too, needed aid. In 1849, despairing after having no response from Istanbul to messages sent with western captains between 1837 and 1845, Sultan Mansur Shah (r. 1838–1870) had dispatched Muhammad Ghawth and party to Mecca bearing further gifts and a letter for the sultan of Rum.[81] Once there they gained the sympathy of Hasib Pasha, which was surely helped by the long petition of praise. Hasib Pasha then took the visitors to the capital with their letters stressing Aceh's ancestral subject status (much like the sultan of Kedah's invoking of historic Ottoman patronage) and the present hope for military assistance.

Like the emissaries of the sixteenth century, Muhammad Ghawth would endure a long wait while Istanbul's worthies pondered the history of the relationship with his people, worried that by aiding them they might tread on European, and most especially British, toes. This had only been compounded by the arrival at Mecca in 1850 of a second envoy, the Minangkabau Ismail b. Abdullah al-Khalidi, a member of the Naqshbandiyya Sufi order who had cosigned Muhammad Salih's petition of praise. Some months thereafter, Istanbul decided to send covert operatives from Yemen on fact-finding missions about these Jawa people and their "Magian" neighbors.[82] In the meantime, Mansur Shah would get a polite refusal from Istanbul in 1851, but a channel to the region had at last been opened. It was kept vital for a time by members of the Khalidi branch of the Naqshbandi order headed by Shaykh Ismail, who was emerging as a figure of some controversy in his home region, where he was known as Ismail Simabur and a proud waver of the Ottoman flag following his return.[83] Indeed, his teachings were attacked as unorthodox in Singapore by the Hadrami teacher Salim b. Sumayr.[84]

Undeterred by such questions and the lack of success, Mansur Shah would offer donations to his intended suzerain when the Crimean War broke out in 1853. Such largesse earned him the Mecidiye medal, though such a decoration must have been seen as a somewhat foreign prize from the Ottoman side, having also been offered to British and French military officers for their service, which had seemingly secured Ottoman territorial integrity. In the years to come, and when faced by entreaties from other Jawi sovereigns, the Ottomans would always prefer to offer such decorations over any concrete military aid for fear of losing their seat at the European table. Such was the result, along with permission to mention the sultan's name in Friday prayers, when Prince Raja Ali of Riau (1808–1873) sent Ismail Simabur's deputy, Ahmad b. Uthman al-Sumbawi, to Mecca to plead his own case for Ottoman subjecthood in 1856 as a foil to British ambitions.[85] Two years later, Sultan Taha Sayf al-Din of Jambi sought the privilege of an Ottoman decoration, though perhaps in light of Bin Sumayr's critiques of Ismail Simabur, he entrusted his letter to an Arab, Sayyid ʿAli b. ʿAlwi al-Jifri, setting the pattern for the future (to which I shall return in chapter 9).[86]

Consuls to the Indian Ocean

At Cape Town after 1863—as I will show in chapter 7—Petrus de Roubaix would have his own eye on the Mecidiye medal in order to bolster his position as a champion of local Muslims. Yet it is important to recognize that his elevation was only one of several Ottoman appointments made across the wider Indian Ocean arena in the 1860s through the mediation of the ambassador to London, Kostaki Musurus Pasha (Konstantinos Mousouros, 1807–1891).

In February 1864, for instance, the Duke of Newcastle would forward the Greek pasha's request that two men be named to posts in Colombo and Galle.[87] After initial confusion, governor Terence O'Brien (1830–1903) could report that one of the men was a well-respected merchant of Colombo called Hussein Lebbe Markar.[88] O'Brien had only been able to name the man because the merchant had himself written to the government agent after learning that he had not been identified due to a spelling error.[89] Hussein Lebbe had evidently been tipped off by an insider in the agency, as his prefatory language mirrored the secretary of state's request to the very word. He also reported having made application some years beforehand, "at the request of some destitute Turks who arrived in Colombo and who were hospitably treated by me and received pecuniary assistance to return to Turkey."[90]

London was duly informed, and by February 1865 Hussein would be gazetted.[91] But if one of the respected merchants of Colombo was embracing duties for the Sublime Porte, he was not necessarily publicizing any pretensions that Abdulaziz was the sultan of all Muslims. While silence is not

[171]

always good evidence, it seems that the polyglot Ounus Saldin—the pioneer of Malay publishing at Colombo—had not quite bought into the idea either, despite the Friday addresses of the Wekanda Mosque having named Abdulaziz's father as sultan of all believers when he had been a boy.

We owe much of what we know of Saldin to the researches of B. A. Hussainmiya, which have been updated by Ronit Ricci—though neither noted that Saldin's photograph, taken by the government publisher William Skeen (1847–1903) at the end of both their lives, was later made to stand for the Lankan Malays as whole (see fig. 6.1).[92] As Hussainmiya first pointed out, Saldin's newspaper of 1869, the *Alamat Langkapuri* (Lanka city news), was the first Muslim-run Jawi periodical of the nineteenth century—pipping those of the Straits Settlements run by Jawi Peranakan editors.[93]

Saldin's grandfather had been a Madurese soldier. Although Saldin implied that this ancestor, named by later scholars as Encik Pantasih, had been recruited by the British in Southeast Asia, he was more likely to have been among the VOC defenders who opted to exchange uniforms in 1796 and serve in Southern India.[94] Such probably reflected the haziness of time past more than any embarrassment. Saldin's presentation of the British arrival was vague, to be sure. In 1905 he published a long tract, the *Syair Fayd al-Abad*, in which the annexation was represented as a simple agreement between England and Holland, with "the keys handed over, hands shaken with pleasure," and some five hundred Jawa sent off to Cochin to fight at "Panchanang Kurchi."[95]

Using a more private document, Ricci learned that Saldin's grandfather, who had been among the five hundred, had taken a Moorish wife (*bini*) from or at Cochin, thus emulating officers like Captain Guna Wijaya, who married his third spouse during the campaign.[96] Like Skinner, Saldin certainly praised the valor and services of the women who accompanied the Jawa troops from Cochin, either coming willingly to India with their officer husbands, or else marching as the new partners of sergeants.[97] Given that Ounus Saldin's father Salahudin was born at Colombo in 1796, his paternal grandmother was more likely a different woman of that city. Whoever she was, Saldin only ever reported her year of death, thirty years after her son had himself joined the Malay Regiment at Trincomalee in 1811.

Ounus Saldin's father later married the daughter of a Madurese soldier-turned-clerk from Sumenep.[98] Saldin was their fourth child. Born at Colombo in 1832, he lost his mother in 1837, his grandmother in 1841, and his recently

Figure 6.1 An aged Baba Ounus Saldin, ca. 1905, from *Twentieth Century Impressions of Ceylon*.

pensioned father in July 1848. Thus, orphaned at fourteen, Ounus Saldin was taken by a serving uncle and enlisted two months later, just around the time when such enlistments were being discouraged. He was then stationed at Kandy before moving to Badulla after 1852. While Kandy had a distinct Malay community, courtesy of its detachment of the Ceylon Rifle Regiment and mosque, Badulla was more mixed. Saldin came into contact there with a Moorish Sufi teacher, pledging himself as his disciple in 1854.[99] He also took the step of buying himself out of the remaining four years of his contract to work in the construction industry.

In 1858 Saldin was back in Colombo, by then a city of seventy thousand, working as a storeman for a European firm and earning a salary well above what he might have gained had he remained in the military. While we can only speculate as to the effect that the much anticipated opening of the Suez Canal may have had on Saldin's personal ambitions, the increased steam traffic plying the waters of the Indian Ocean both before and after November 1869 would offer opportunities on several fronts. Already a man of note in Colombo, Saldin acquired a lithographic press that year, on which he produced his newspaper of four pages. This was a major development for the people of Kampung Kertel, who had already developed an interest in books sent from India, which they often perused in the garrison reading room. Early articles in the *Alamat Langkapuri* note the arrival of a new journal from Bengal and the foundation of a lending library where readers could continue to indulge their passion for news, in addition to accessing books in Malay, Arabic, Arwi, and Tamil. As was common practice, Saldin would reproduce articles concerning the comings and goings of senior officials, including their "Maharaja" Hercules Robinson (governor, 1865–1872), alongside the international news from cables reported in the English-language press with a pronounced slant toward India.

At heart, though, Saldin's concern was his Jawa/Malay people and their religious development, which was oriented further west again. Although many of the articles and letters included traditional rhyming prose, the literary diet was almost entirely drawn from the Middle East, starting with a serialization of the life of the first caliph, Abu Bakr. As with his personal collection of manuscripts initially surveyed by Hussainmiya, few Malay romances were under discussion, though they were certainly known at Kampung Kertel. Ricci points out that Saldin drew on the Indic name for the island as Langka, rather than the more commonly Muslim Sarandib associated with the story of Adam's fall, and that one contributor to the *Alamat* offered a poem that linked their isle as such the Langka of the Ramayana epic.[100]

Saldin himself often advertised strictly religious works, such as a text of prayers from Bengal, just as he welcomed the arrival of a visiting author from "abroad" (*negeri asing*) with the Hadrami name of ʿAbdallah Ba Dhib.[101] He also advertised another text in his pages, the *Anis al-muttaqin*, as offering a path to the "science of gnosis." Saldin attributed this to his local ally, Khatib ʿAbd al-Bahhar, though Ricci suggests that it was a redaction of a well-known work of ʿAbd al-Samad, who had marched to his death against the Siamese in 1792.[102] Certainly Saldin was familiar with ʿAbd al-Samad's work, which he referenced late in life when he was living at Kampung Pangerang.[103]

Saldin was also the guiding light of a new welfare association for Malays that had its inaugural meeting at the lending library on August 6, 1869, as well as the creation of an evening Qurʾan school at the barracks.[104] He made sure to publicize notable events for the Muslims of the island in total, such as the feast of ʿId al-Fitr held at Kandy's Bukumbu Mosque in June.[105] Saldin also backed a campaign against alcohol in oblique terms, printing a history of prohibition in the Ottoman Empire sent in by "a Jawi person," starting with the actions of Mehmed II (1432–1481), the conqueror of Constantinople.[106] Two weeks later, an embarrassed A. G. Cook announced that he had ceased serving palm wine in the garrison mess.[107]

Yet cracks were more than evident between Muslim communities and within that of the Jawa-Malays themselves, whose declining regiment was in the final process of dissolution. An early hint of such divisions comes in the annoyed tone of an article concerning the burial of a "foreigner" (apparently an Indian Muslim) in the grounds of the Wekanda Mosque. Its nameless functionaries had apparently been too timid to stop the ceremony, which was, in the view of the writer, contrary to the law of the sovereign.[108] Such chauvinism seems out of keeping with the cosmopolitanism of Saldin, who touted his lithographic services in Malay, Tamil, and English. His brother also advertised their import-export business in English, offering "hunting livery & Geneva Silver Watches," while Saldin sold copies of Marsden's dictionary and a Persian-Arabic glossary.

It is also clear that Malay arguments were not restricted to Colombo. Some writers complained about the conduct of mosque officials in Kandy, supposedly selling donated rice rather than gifting it to the poor. Still, the heaviest dispute of Saldin's journalistic career—and one that we shall see mirrors contemporary arguments at Cape Town—had come in regard to the appointment of a new khatib for the Wekanda Mosque in mid-1869, and thus just after the dispute over the foreign burial.[109] Following the death of the incumbent, a descendant of the first imam, Pakir Bawa Latif, a dispute arose between soldier and civilian (*preman*) members, with the latter championing Tayyiban, a gravedigger-turned-muezzin.[110] Siding with the soldiers, the *Alamat* featured letters from the partisans of the mosque of a Kadhu/Guru Ramadan in the Pettah, where the soldiers had moved to deny Tayyiban the Friday quorum of forty men stipulated by Imam Shafiʿi. One of the military faction would even chide the remnant Wekanda congregation, urging the appointment of someone who was an accomplished preacher, quoting a "Malabari" expression to make his point:

> I ask your excellency to publish this article in your paper. For I want to give advice to the gentlemen who possess it, that being: before we place the congregation behind any imams, we must first consider matters deeply, because people other than us look for an imam who is a preacher. Yet what use is it to become a preacher if one does not care for the common people and acts as a hypocrite? The act of prayer is hardly so simple, [for one] must take turns with an imam who is a Muslim and a believer who has a connection with the common people. In this sense it is worth heeding a Malabari expression:. . . [meaning] "if there is a preacher who does not follow or connect with the majority, then he is no preacher."[111]

This would only earn a cynical retort from a self-described "mendicant" (*seorang faqir*) called Abdallah. Although he agreed that many local imams were deficient in many sometimes-scandalous ways, he warned the accusers of those various imams—"our imams of Jawi birth"—that they should beware of being criticized themselves.[112]

As the dispute raged, the welfare association would be similarly drained of members, leading the military group to install themselves under Abd al-Bahhar at a small mosque on Java Lane, closer to the end of the peninsula, that had been dominated by the castle until its demolition in 1865.[113] Seven years later, and three miles in the other direction, Abd al-Bahhar joined Saldin and five fellow trustees to establish a new cemetery and mosque on Jawatte Road, adjacent to the fashionable Cinnamon Gardens.[114]

It would be nearly two decades before the Malays of Colombo reconciled, and three years after the docks would welcome a party of Ottoman-Egyptian military exiles, whose self-regarding leader, Ahmad ʿUrabi, would settle into a bungalow in Cinnamon Gardens. A curious taste of the imagined power of the Ottoman sultan over Egypt was offered in the *Alamat* three months before the opening of the Suez Canal, entitled "The Minister of Egypt." Here, the minister in question is summoned from Paris by the "Mighty Sultan Abd al-Aziz Khan," immediately forsaking the company of Emperor Napoleon III and Empress Eugénie.[115]

Although Sultan Abdulaziz was all powerful over Egypt and its "minister"—in this case ʿUrabi's more immediate master, Khedive Ismaʿil—there is no explicit mention of any such authority over Lanka's Muslims. Nor yet was there mention of such a title in the earlier article concerning Sultan Mehmed's destruction of the vineyards of Constantinople in 1453, or of any contemporary Ottoman concern for Lankan Malays supposedly buying land to cultivate grapes. As I shall demonstrate in the next chapter, precisely this interest was emerging at the Cape, where famously teetotaling Malays toiled in the vineyards around a city that had welcomed a very Ottoman arrival in 1863. Indeed, he had been given his instructions by the same ambassador who nominated Hussein Lebbe Markar as consul to Ceylon, though without any confusing spelling mistake, and with even less concern from London.

SEVEN

For Queen, Country, and Caliph in Africa

ON JANUARY 13, 1863, a steamer came into Cape Town Harbour and raised the flags of Great Britain and the Ottoman Empire from its main mast. After a forty-three-day journey from Liverpool, the vessel, once heavily laden with coal, unloaded its passengers on the long wooden jetty. Among those disembarking that day was a forty-nine-year-old teacher called Sayyid Abu Bakr Effendi (1814–1880), accompanied by his assistant, Omer Lutfi.[1] A proud descendant of the Prophet, Abu Bakr had been teaching in Ottoman Kurdistan before being tasked with correcting the faith of the Muslims of the Cape, which saw him sent first to London to consult with ambassador Musurus Pasha. After having been met by chance at the dock by a local hajji, Abdullah (d. 1877), who ensured that the Ottoman arrivals got a warm bath and the further attention of crowds of local Muslims, he was soon hailed by a younger European man and declared friend of those Muslims, Petrus de Roubaix. Now aged thirty-five, the member of the Upper House of the Cape Town Legislative Council had been apprised by Musurus Pasha of Abu Bakr's impending arrival a few weeks earlier and had brought his carriage to convey the eminent teacher to a home that had been set aside for him. They would be at odds in four short years, and some three years after De Roubaix managed to coax the post of consul and a Mecidiye medal from their then mutual patron, Sultan Abdulaziz.

Four years later, too, on July 17, 1867, that same patron would ascend to the quarterdeck of the *Victoria and Albert* off the Isle of Wight to be invested as a Knight of the Garter by the British Queen. His maternal cousin, the "shy and subdued" Khedive Isma'il of Egypt, was also on hand to translate.² The weather was less than fair as both sovereigns, the quasi-sovereign, and assorted members of their households witnessed a naval review in Abdulaziz's honor, including fifteen modern ironclads and two paddle steamers amid a flotilla of wooden vessels.³ Heavy clouds certainly adorn George Housman Thomas's canvas commemorating the occasion at which the naval might of what was now the world's most populous empire of Muslim subjects was on display for the primary—and very much landbound—claimant to their affection as commander of the faithful.⁴ While she remarked that the sultan did not have his sea legs on that day and was struck by the shortness of those of his Egyptian viceroy, Victoria—not exactly towering herself—was a little unhappy. That evening she recorded that she would have much preferred to invest her ally with the Star of India, an award created in 1861 that she felt was more suited for those who were "not Christians."⁵ Indeed, Syed Ahmed Khan would gain the Star for his loyalty in 1869. And as one commentator had reflected on the festivities of 1867, perhaps his "English people" had "come at last to regard foreigners with other feelings than contempt" and were beginning "to learn the rudiments of courtesy."⁶

Prayers for the Sultan and Cheers for the Queen

Having laid out the shifting fortunes of the Muslims of British Cape and Ceylon into the middle of the nineteenth century, this chapter goes beyond the calculated pleasantries of diplomacy to provide a background to the vicissitudes of what would be called Pan-Islamism, which has its roots as much in an Indian Ocean story of Muslim outreach as the imperatives of the Ottoman state, threatened by both Russian aggression and its inconstant friend Great Britain. As we shall see, the ambiguous domain of Egypt, long a source of learned scholars for the Indian Ocean world, became an overlapping space for the claiming of religious commonality affirmed by the caliphate and a powerful model for modern patriotic affection known in Arabic as *wataniyya*. Like Cape Town, it would also produce partnerships between Muslim communities and those Europeans who wished to speak for them in public, if with opposing views of the alliance between London and Istanbul.

Let us start with an earlier, more amenable, iteration of such mediation. Writing from Istanbul three months after Abdulaziz's meeting with Victoria, Maximilien Kollisch—a transimperial subject par excellence—implied that the innovation of celebrating the sultan's birthday at Cape Town on February 9 that year had been a result of the indefatigable efforts of consul Petrus de Roubaix.[7] But, as Peter Coates has shown, most documents relating to the sterling services given by—and even some of the sterling gifts given to—De Roubaix came from the ardent self-promoter who had just fallen from favor.[8] Today many Capetonians remember such enthusiasms as the result of the labors of Abu Bakr, the sayyid born in Shahrazur whom he was required to assist at times, if in an informal capacity. For, despite what Omer Lutfi imagined, De Roubaix wasn't yet consul in February 1863. He would depart for Europe later that year to be formally appointed in London, returning in early 1864 with his new Mecidiye medal stippled onto his portrait.[9]

Although they intersected and even cooperated, De Roubaix and Abu Bakr seem like ships in the night. While not explicitly mentioned in July 1862, when Musurus Pasha wrote to the Duke of Newcastle concerning the recurrence of a "religious dispute" in Cape Town and a request from a local priest for books "explanatory of the formula of certain religious ceremonies in use at Istanbul," such would seem to hark back to the Califa matter. Its apparent resolution in 1856 had already led to Sultan Abdulmecid sending De Roubaix a diamond-set snuffbox in 1860.[10] Musurus Pasha's letter had also come on the heels of a letter sent by the sons of Achmat van Bengalen to honor the ascension of Abdulaziz.[11] The Ottoman court now felt snuffboxes and books insufficient for their Southern African supplicants and proposed to send Abu Bakr, then teaching in Erzerum. Abu Bakr was no provincial teacher. He had previously served in the Ministry of Internal Affairs, making his mark as a committed propagandist for the caliphate in Iraq.

As one of Abu Bakr's sons once told it, his father's arrival was hardly auspicious. Having missed an audience with Victoria the day before commencing his long voyage, it was three nights before Capetonian Muslims were aware of his presence at the Royal Hotel.[12] Yet this tale, like the oft-repeated notion that Abu Bakr had been sent at Victoria's direct request, is belied by a tranche of Ottoman documents studied by Halim Gençoğlu and the short account of Omer Lutfi. Not only did De Roubaix come to meet him with his carriage, Abu Bakr would report how the amenable Capetonian had been on

Figure 7.1 The Cape Muslim community, 1863.

hand when he presented his credentials to governor P. E. Wodehouse on January 24.[13]

De Roubaix also limited the visits of numerous locals eager to meet a man some imagined to be an Ottoman pasha, rendering him a "prisoner" at his accommodation.[14] The sense of occasion surrounding Abu Bakr is communicated by a photograph of the leadership of the Capetonian Muslim community (see fig. 7.1). Often said to have been taken on the steps of the Royal Hotel, it shows over forty—nearly all men—with many dressed in Ottoman-style robes, turbans, and sashes of their own, and rather heavy clothing for a Cape Town January.[15] At one side stands the young grandson of Tuan Guru, Abd al-Rakib (d. 1924). It is unclear whether his father, Abd al-Rauf, then imam of the Shafi'i Mosque on Buitengracht Street, was there as well; if the still supportive sons of Achmat van Bengalen were just behind; or if indeed the original sash passed on to the late Jan van Bugis was to be seen on anybody's chest. Curiously absent, too, is De Roubaix, just as the stairs do not resemble those of the former hotel on Plein Street. It is even unclear today who Abu Bakr was. Most works identify a man sitting on the lowest step of the building, his features obscured by a robe and turban.[16]

While the identities in the photograph are now obscure (rather like its current location), the local imams were doubtless primed for Abu Bakr's visit. As we may recall, Mochamat Achmat had sent a letter of congratulation to Abdulaziz on his ascension, declaring on behalf of the "Musulmen" of the colony that they hoped for his kind attention and wished him a long and happy life to rule over the destinies of his "faithful subjects."[17] It is unclear whether Mochamat's congregation regarded themselves as such subjects. What is clear, though, is that Abu Bakr and the Tuan Guru clan recognized each other's importance, with Abu Bakr soon attending Abd al-Rauf on his deathbed, and reportedly filling him with joy that he could entrust his flock to him. When Tuan Guru's second African son passed a few weeks later in February 1863, Sultan Abdulaziz's emissary would preside over his funeral.[18]

Such felicitous placement generated high hopes in the Ottoman, which were clear in the letters he sent back for publication in Istanbul's *Mecmua-yı fünun*. From January 1863 summaries were offered concerning his arrival with a letter from the British Ministry of Foreign Affairs, the governor's appointing "Mösyö Robeks" as his aid, and the history and practices of the good-hearted if ignorant Muslim population, who spoke "Malay, Malibari, Hindi and Arabic."[19] Abu Bakr would also report their happy situation under the English, who had allowed them to erect minarets (yet unbuilt), and their disdain for the Dutch, who had once enslaved and repressed them.[20] In short, he felt that the agreeable partnership between the Ottoman and British Empires, coupled with his own gentle approach, would rid his new constituents of their petty disputes. These ranged from matters of succession in mosques to those of intimacy, marriage, and fasting. All such conflicts had reportedly been brought about half a century earlier by encounters with returned pilgrims, who looked askance at what they now recognised as local, if not ancestral Jawi, deviations. One such pilgrim was the convert Hajji Haron, whose adoptive daughter, Rakea, married Abu Bakr on April 8, 1863 despite their being unable to communicate without a dictionary.[21] Abu Bakr was so confident of being able to realize his mission that he contemplated undertaking another one to the surrounding African peoples and further interventions in the Comoros and Zanzibar.[22]

As may be expected, the alliance between Abu Bakr and the Tuan Guru party generated rivals. The most hostile was an initially welcoming Abd al-Wahab. Named only three years earlier during Prince Alfred's visit as the head of "the chief Mahommedan Mosque," Abd al-Wahab had recently taken control of a trust to maintain Shaykh Yusuf's grave, which had been a focus of Achmat van Bengalen's attentions in the late 1830s.[23] Evidently fearing the loss of position and many of his own students, Abd al-Wahab set his partisans against the new arrival, who had begun offering lessons at his home down on Strand Street. Confident of his official status and connection, Abu Bakr turned to Wodehouse for support in late July:

> Hadji Abdol Wahab is ignorant in the Mahomedan faith and forcing for disputes trying to make quarrels with his pupils against me. My name is used about this time. I do not know the reason, why my name is in the newspaper during this time I have been here till now, they interrupt my pupils, servant, and also my nephews in the street they cannot pass without they interfering them called them all sorts of bad language, those that belongs to his church [sic], my pupils does not answer at all bearing the kingdom [i.e., authority] in me.... I wish you to put some protection against it and forbid them no longer to go on with me in this manner... that I may go on with the mission, I am come for.[24]

Sending an answer three days later, a bemused and notoriously clumsy Wodehouse—recalled from Ceylon under a cloud after the Matale rebellion of 1848, yet destined for the governorship of Bombay in 1872—could only advise that the magistrate should "afford him protection against persons improperly molesting him."[25]

Abd al-Wahab would hardly be the Ottoman's only opponent over the coming seventeen years, being troubled in late 1864 by a Persian pretender to imperial subjecthood and the contrarian opinions of a Jawi shaykh of Mecca, as we shall see.[26] Nor yet was Abu Bakr's plea the last of his petitions in 1863. In early October he sought the right to solemnize births, deaths, and marriages of his pupils—though he evidently hoped that it might be extended to apply far more broadly so he could "have full power and authority in the Mahomedan Religion in this British Colony with the consent of his Excellency."[27] Acting like Governor D'Urban before him with regard to the dispute about Abd al-Rauf's princely status in 1836, an unenthusiastic Wodehouse demurred, hoping to stay above the many conflicts that saw Capetonian imams pitted against each other in court.

Unlike Colombo twenty years earlier, an Ottoman would be able to play a role in that arena. In 1865 Abu Bakr was called to testify on the question of the leadership of the mosque of the late Jan van Bugis, which had been before the courts since the October 1864 death of his old comrade Mamat. Whereas local imams had previously depended on the words and legacy of Tuan Guru in court, the English judges could now approve of Abu Bakar's citation of a manual in use in the Ottoman domains: the *Mishkat al-mathabit*.[28] Such usage only raised allegations of a plan to convert the Muslims of the Cape to the dominant juridical school of that empire. Indeed, it appears that Abu Bakr's rivals had been discounting his opinions as a foreign Hanafi within weeks of his arrival and were seeking help from a prominent Jawi and avowedly Shafiʿi teacher of Mecca. Writing to the *Mecmua-yı fünun* after July 1863, Abu Bakr complained that pilgrims to the holy city were returning with the pamphlets of Muhammad Salih b. ʿAli Batawi, which he said promoted teachings at variance with orthodoxy. Muhammad Salih may be identified with the Sufi teacher who signed a petition and praise poem in honor of Mehmed Hasib Pasha as the Ottoman governor of the Hijaz in 1850.[29] According to Abu Bakr, Muhammad Salih's deviance stretched to the point where he claimed that the Prophet had entrusted his community to Imam Shafiʿi alone, and that local imams held an account of the believer's sins and thus deserved their unquestioning loyalty.[30]

Abu Bakr also raised the issue of ignorant loyalty at this time when he finally wrote about the "heretical" ratib in late 1864. At this time, he claimed that the dangers of the "Rifaʿi" ritual, since restricted by the British to the birthday of ʿAbd al-Qadir Jilani, were compounded by the drunkenness of its practitioners and its forced subvention by authoritarian teachers. Rather than condemn it openly, Abu Bakr claimed once more that he preferred not to stir up anger in a town where Christians and Muslims lived in harmony. He preferred to stick to what he imagined were easily remedied matters, like what foods were licit, promising to inform the (British) authorities at a more opportune time.[31]

Some practices were clearly too popular. And there would be another hindrance to dispense with, now that De Roubaix was starting to make a nuisance of himself, hoping to add a knighthood to his Mecidiye medal. According to his publicist, Kollisch, De Roubaix had long been working for Anglo-Muslim harmony at the Cape. Not only had he resolved the Califa dispute, but he had since interceded at his own expense for displaced Muslims from "India, Zanzibar, Johanna, Batavia, and other countries."[32] One incident involved a party of Zanzibaris led by a trader called Muhammad ʿAli. After their interdiction off the Swahili coast in 1859, their wives had initially been deemed slaves and separated from them before the group was sent to work on a farm at the Cape.[33] Having seen Abu Bakr settled, and certainly having boasted of his efforts to aid the Zanzibaris, which the Ottoman duly reported in April, De Roubaix had taken himself to Istanbul as a part of his tour of Europe. He returned as honorary consul in early 1864 and only then relieved the inactive incumbent.[34] De Roubaix would also give a series of interviews with local imams in February that year, which were covered in the press, as well as offering pecuniary aid for the destitute Zanzibaris.[35]

In his self-aggrandizing interview, De Roubaix also lectured local recalcitrants for not heeding the views of Abu Bakr regarding the resolution of a dispute between two rival families, insisting that they come to an agreement on the sultan's birthday.[36] An ever more puffed up De Roubaix then visited Port Elizabeth, where he was on hand to receive a delegation of Muslims from Grahamstown. He also welcomed a party who were seeking Ottoman funds for the establishment of a new mosque, whose request he forwarded after having announced his approval of their acknowledging "the advantages derived from British rule" and declaring that the sultan himself believed them to be "fortunate in having so mild and wise a Sovereign as the universally beloved and respected Queen of England."[37] As the grateful beneficiaries allegedly replied, they had "hardly thought it possible that his Imperial Majesty would have noticed [them] in so favorable a manner ... which is a guarantee that the followers of the Prophet—although separated by so many thousands of miles are not forgotten by the head of their Church."[38]

Such claims of spiritual headship were encouraged by the Porte as a way of strengthening its position with friends and rivals alike, who either claimed to protect Muslims in India (as Britain now did) or the Christians in their own territories and the Holy Land (as Russia did). Abdulaziz's birthday was commemorated at the Cape for the first time in February 1867, with special attention devoted to the Victoria Mosque, as it was then commonly called. As the papers announced:

> Saturday [the ninth] last was quite a busy day with the Malay population of Cape Town, on the occasion of the anniversary of the birthday of the Sultan of Turkey, which was celebrated in the various Malay mosques for the first time with all due ceremony. The services, which took place at mid-day and eight o'clock in the evening, were more than ordinarily imposing, that more especially in the

chief mosque in Chiappini-street, which building was tastefully decorated with evergreens and flags of almost all nations, amongst which the British Ensign and the Banner of the Crescent were most conspicuous.[39]

In his addresses that day, De Roubaix remarked that such expressions were welcomed "by the Sovereign of the Turkish Empire, and the ministers of the Sublime Porte," who, like himself, desired that local Muslims should "estimate the advantages" derived from "the protection afforded by the wise and liberal Government of Her Majesty the Queen of England."[40] As at Ceylon, loyalty to Victoria was hardly in question. Some South African imams were evidently seeing the Porte as the natural authority for religious matters, however trivial they were deemed by the British.[41]

By August, moreover, Cape Town would have heard the news of Abdulaziz's journey to London. This must also have come in the wake of quite some surprise, however, with De Roubaix having been removed from his post a few weeks after the sultan's birthday. The already disgraced parliamentarian soon sought London's help for restitution of his Ottoman expenses, and for Kollisch to advertise his excellence at the Turkish capital, which he did in October. On the other hand, Abu Bakr's then allies, the sons of Achmet van Bengalen, met in February 1868 and praised the decision, warning that De Roubaix had handed out signet rings on his return to his partisans to facilitate the reception of their missives in Istanbul, in addition to falsely claiming that he had been empowered as "Commissioner over the Malays in general."[42]

Besides surely playing a role in De Roubaix's fall from imperial Ottoman grace and local Malay favor, Abu Bakr had already displaced him as an authority in court. While De Roubaix had once been involved as a mediator regarding the succession of the Long Street Mosque, in addition to partnering with Abu Bakr to expose a Persian pretender to Ottoman subjecthood in 1864, he was upstaged or ignored for subsequent matters.[43] It was also clear, though, that Abu Bakr's own relationship with some Capetonian Muslims was slipping. This was perhaps because of his missteps with Rakea Maker, who had accused him of cruelty during their very public divorce of 1866, which came before the courts again in 1870. He would also become estranged from the sons of Achmat van Bengalan due to his overweening influence over their adoptive nephew, Tuan Guru's grandson and heir apparent Abd al-Rakib.

Such tension was more than evident in the Buitengracht Mosque case. Originally known as the Shafiʿi Mosque when it had been under Abd al-Rauf and his stepbrothers, Abu Bakr was called in July 1873 to testify in support of Abd al-Rakib. The seventeen-year-old stood accused by his avuncular accusers of having adopted various "Hanafi" practices, including the position that one did not need forty attendees, as Imam Shafiʿi had stipulated, to form a quorum for Friday prayers.[44] While the last measure was probably adopted to deal with dwindling attendance, Abu Bakr may already have been pushing exactly this view in drafts of his *Bayan al-din* of 1869, a work in Arabic-script Afrikaans that inflamed his many opponents, who were already convinced that he intended to convert the population to Hanafism. It cannot have helped that he viewed al-Shafiʿi's position on the quorum as being "weak" (*swak*) and that he criticized the great imam for having emulated Jews and Christians in matters of ritual slaughter.[45]

In court, the plaintiffs, led by "Ahmad Sadik" (Achmat Sadick, 1813–1878), a veteran of the War of the Axe who had served as a lieutenant and field priest, alleged that their nephew had introduced "Hanafi" practices at their mosque. He neither enunciated the *basmala* at the opening of prayers, nor yet closed with the customary "Amen."[46] Perhaps the most intriguing innovation concerned Abd al-Rakib's handling of the preacher's staff, receiving it from a subsidiary when ascending the pulpit to give the Friday address rather than carrying it up, like every other imam at Cape Town.[47]

Such procedural issues seemed trivial to the presiding judges, who convened an open and very crowded court without a jury. For them the matter concerned a breach of contract, given that Achmat Sadick and party had argued that with his "election" Abd al-Rakib was obliged to maintain Shafiʿi rites in order to retain his imamate, which he had only assumed five years earlier with the death of Abd al-Rauf's nominated successor, "Ammie" (Achmat Sadick's older brother Chamiem or Hamim).[48]

The plaintiffs claimed that, before seeking their injunction, Abd al-Rakib had oscillated in his habits. He had even been subject to consultations, at which point Abu Bakr was invited to the mosque, allowing his protégé to cease his practices on the understanding that the "sin" of their omission was upon the community. Everything came to a head in June 1873, when the young imam returned from Port Elizabeth and resumed his troublesome ways, leading to a court injunction. When pushed in court to explain their opposition from juridical works, the plaintiffs got into trouble. Resting on the precedents established by Tuan Guru, they had no books with them in court and simply invoked the authority of Imam Shafi'i, whose name they said was found in the *manuscripts* they used. Nor yet were they unable to understand the English summaries of their laws. They evidently got flustered, too. Achmat Sadick fatally—and rather incomprehensibly—declared that he had no idea what "Sonna" (i.e., the *sunna*) was.[49]

Abu Bakr made a contrastingly strong impression, referring to texts and declaring (not entirely truthfully) that he had always been a Shafi'i. But he was not the only man to sway the Anglophone judges. Much was heard from a local hajji, Abdullah, whose oath was taken by Abu Bakr. Although a known confederate of the Ottoman—indeed, he had been the first person to have communicated with the teacher in Arabic on his arrival at the Cape—he served as a translator for both sides. By his own account, Abdullah had made the first of his three pilgrimages in 1859 and could reference a *printed* work that affirmed that the Hanafi rites could be followed by Shafi'is if a quorum was not met. With his own history of travel and study, Abdullah was able to debunk the whole question of how the staff was handled, claiming that there was no special law about it: "In Mecca the tonka is handed to the Imaum by the Belaal. I have seen the Shafie service in Johanna, Zanzibar, Aden, Suez, Egypt and Constantinople. In Constantinople some Shafies use the Tonka. In Aden I saw a Shafie Imaum take the tonka by himself. I was in Mecca in 1866 for a couple of days. In 1870 I was there again and remained about a year studying with the professors, who are Arabians, following the Shafie sect." Under cross-examination, Abdullah affirmed the equality of the juridical traditions in Mecca, where none were higher, and all was holy. A deflated Achmat Sadick could only protest that he had not come to talk about his faith, but about his "church."[50]

If judge James Coleman FitzPatrick (1802–1880) did not wish to decide on what was or was not proper ceremonial practice for Muslims, Daniel Denyssen's son, Petrus Johannes Denyssen (1811–1883), felt no such constraint. In ruling for the defendant, he opined:

> It cannot escape attention that while witnesses for the plaintiffs have never been out of the colony, [and] had no acknowledged authorities to refer to support their claim, the witnesses for the defence, the Effendi and Abdullah, were men who had made the Mahommedan doctrines, forms, and ceremonies their study in Mecca and elsewhere, who openly professed themselves Shafees and not

Hanafees, and who spoke with an authority which could not be ignored. I am satisfied therefore that this question affects only certain ceremonies, not the doctrines of the Mahommedan faith; that the observances of those ceremonies are unimportant and non-essential.[51]

There could be no breach of contract either. Abd al-Rakib had never been elected but had been appointed as per his late father's wishes once Achmat Sadick's brother had died.

Whereas he had declared himself a trained Shafi'i before the court, Abu Bakr continued to offend those who claimed to be guided by that approach alone. Living up to his promises to correct the culinary habits of Capetonian Muslims, Abu Bakr overrode the Shafi'i juridical opinion that the consumption of crayfish was "despised" (*makruh*), declaring it "illicit" (*haram*).[52] This was perhaps more controversial at the Cape than the matter of the quorum. Despite three Sunni madhhabs despising crustaceans by reason of their subsistence on carrion, they remained staples of Capetonian—and, indeed, oceanic—Muslim cuisine. According to Davids, Abu Bakr's ally Abdullah had even brought up the matter on one of his earlier trips to Mecca, and a petition circulated at the Cape in 1871, building yet more pressure against the Ottoman teacher and the British government that had seemingly sanctioned his arrival.[53]

Abu Bakr must have been the subject of several petitions to Istanbul as well as some debate in Mecca. It seems odd at first glance that neither De Roubaix nor his former handler, Ottoman foreign minister Ahmad Emin Aali Pasha (1815–1871), made public mention of the imam. But we must remember that their correspondence, published in 1871, was really designed to amplify the achievements of the former consul, like De Lima's earlier gleanings on the Califa dispute. The other effect of this work, like De Lima's assemblage once more (and certainly Kollisch's description), was to relegate any details of Capetonians like Abdullah who were going to Mecca in greater numbers and calling at many of East Africa's islands on the way. Not only did they continue to encounter scholars beside their favored Jawi imams like Muhammad Salih, they would also join with them to bemoan Dutch pressure on Aceh, whose emissaries once again tried to gain Ottoman protection in the 1860s (as we shall see in chapter 9).

Of course, the Ottoman schoolmaster of Cape Town did appear in local print, if in an unfavorable light. This was especially so after the breakdown of his first marriage.⁵⁴ Just as De Roubaix retreated to Europe to gain allies in 1873 (and in the same year that the Acehnese would send an Arab ambassador to Istanbul), Abu Bakr would leave in 1876 to go to Mecca and then Istanbul to get firmer support from the new sultan, Abdulhamid II, who had been aboard the *Victoria and Albert* on that dreary day in 1867. The Hamidian regime accordingly saw to the publication and wider dissemination of his *Bayan al-din* in 1877. This was arguably Abdulhamid's propaganda gift to the Cape, as well as Mozambique and Mauritius, which were deemed to fall within Abu Bakr's bailiwick. This zone might have been expected to grow still larger that year with the appointment of old India hand Henry Bartle Frere as high commissioner for Southern Africa. A veteran of 1857 and former governor of Bombay, Frere aimed to incorporate Boer, Xhosa, and Zulu people under an even greater British state—and all without waiting for London's assent.⁵⁵

Alas, there was no glittering career awaiting Abu Bakr at the Ottoman capital in 1877, which was preoccupied with war with Russia, even if the evidence indicates that he may have been expected to stay at that time. Besides, the Ottomans generally paid less direct attention to the trickle of pilgrims coming up the African coast compared with the lucrative torrent from South and Southeast Asia, where sympathies and monies could be directed to the Caucasus campaigns. Hence, the many Hadrami residents of the Ibadi Sultanate of Zanzibar played a role as facilitators for Shafi'is from the south, though an appreciative British consul felt in April 1877 that the people he had seen passing through the East African archipelago had demonstrated a greater attachment to the British Empire than the unnamed Portuguese, Omani, and Turkish ones:

> These people, the descendants of Dutch slaves, are a great industrious race, contrasting most favourably with every other class of pilgrims. In conversation they told me the trip would on the average cost each of them £100, but this sum no doubt includes the price of the presents they take back with them to their friends. The principal affect of the journey appeared to have been to increase their affection to the British Government and to contrast the liberty and justice they enjoy under British rule with the treatment they everywhere else received.⁵⁶

Such a good impression would have been confirmed by a party of thirty such deck passengers from Cape Town and Algoa Bay who arrived at "Gingerbar" that July and transferred to the *Abyssinia*. Led by several experienced imams

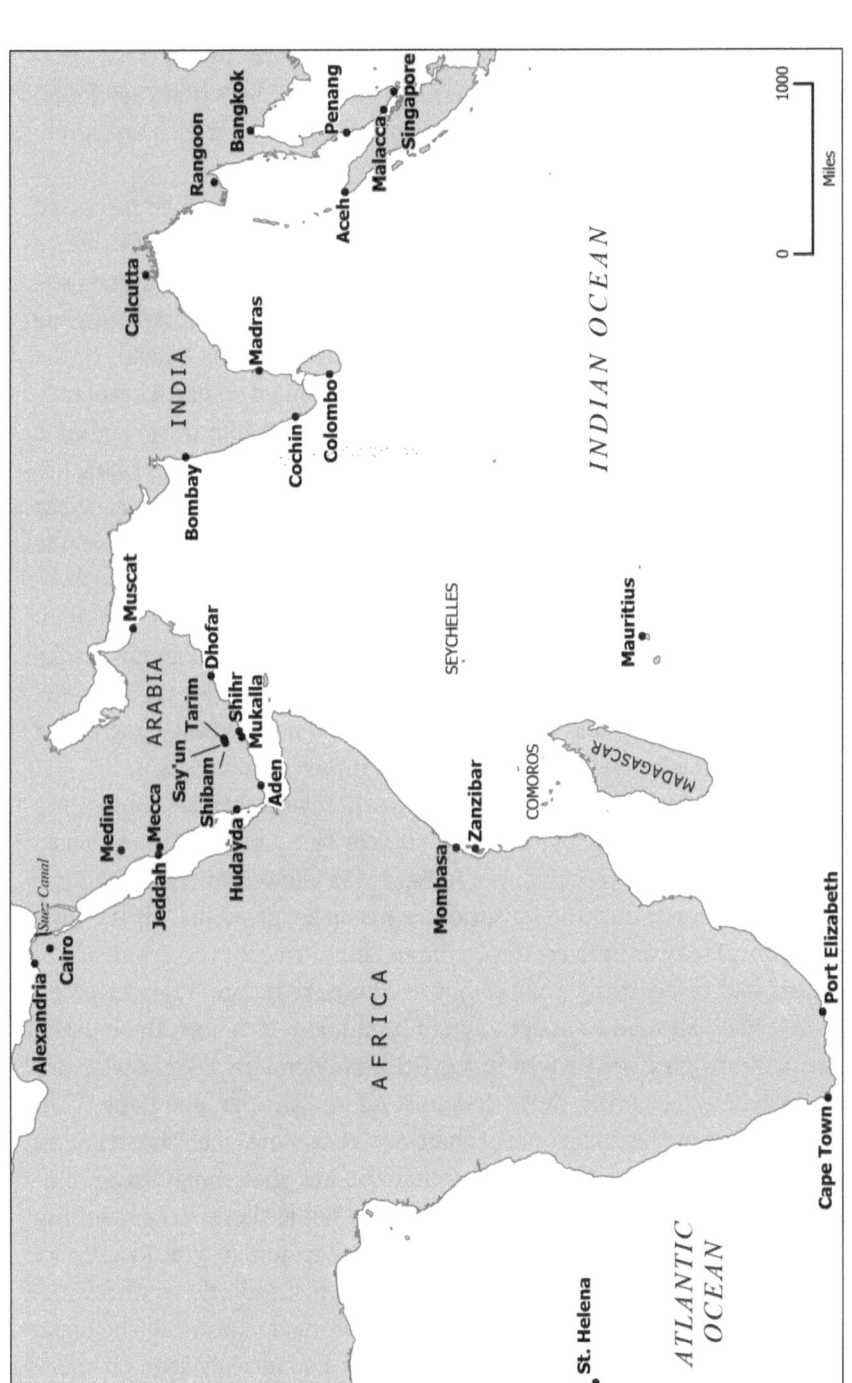

Figure 7.2 Indian Ocean 1870.

and a participant who boasted of doing so for the eighth time, it is nonetheless evident in their report to the *Cape Argus* in April 1878 that they found their money had gone a long way on a journey that was, overall, quite agreeable under British and Ottoman auspices alike.[57]

It was quite a different set of conversations for Abu Bakr when he passed southward the following month. Intercepted on his return from Cairo, where he had enrolled his son Ahmad Attaoullah at al-Azhar, and then via Hudayda, in Yemen, he would experience what Muhammad ʿAli of Zanzibar had gone through two decades before. This time the British held the "sheikh of the Musulmen community of the Cape of Good Hope" at Aden on suspicion of trafficking in arms and slaves. In particular they accused him of smuggling a young girl called Zaynab, whom he claimed to be his wife.[58] After placing her in a Catholic convent and sending his boxes on for examination at Zanzibar (where they turned out to be full of books), Abu Bakr was forced to return to Cairo to produce a certificate that proved that he had married Zaynab. There was no mystery to the document he brought back. Attested by the Ottoman-appointed (and thus Hanafi) chief qadi of Egypt, Sayyid ʿAbd al-Rahman Naqid, it confirmed that Abu Bakr, "director of religious education for the people of the Cape of Good Hope and its dependencies," had married the daughter of Muhammad Agha ibn Nal Band for a dowry of fifteen gold pounds.[59]

Once translated at Aden, this jibed with investigations confirming Zaynab's tragic parentage of a Rumelian officer held captive in Russia and a mother killed in a train accident. Abu Bakr was allowed to return to Cape Colony, though without compensation or his bride, given his "shifty" dissimulations. This was because the Ottoman Committee for the Sheltering of Refugees had respectfully pointed out to Abu Bakr in late August that he had only been allowed to adopt Zaynab in January 1878 with the express purpose of bringing her up within the Ottoman domains.[60] Whereas Cairo and Hudayda were within those domains, Aden, Zanzibar, and Cape Town were beyond them, even if some of their denizens mentioned the Ottoman Caliph at Friday prayers. It thus seems that Abu Bakr had sought to circumvent the conditions of Zaynab's adoption. And while there was something of a sliding precedent for his marriage—his first Capetonian wife, Rakea, had been fifteen, and in 1866 Abu Bakr had married his similarly youthful student Tahora Saban—this latest match was never made known at the Cape. Like his sometime aide De Roubaix, Abu Bakar had already seen far more coverage than he wanted anyway. After contracting malaria on a journey to Mozambique, the teacher would die at the Cape on June 29, 1880, declared a "Malay Priest" on his death certificate.⁶¹

Laid to rest by his loyal—if not royal—followers, family, and students, the man now credited with correcting the sartorial choices of the women of the Cape was interred halfway up the Lion's Rump. This was above the enclosure of Sayyid ʿAlawi and Tuan Guru, and a little below the unwalled monument to Noriman. While his grave was not visited by the wider community at first—for Abu Bakr merited no mention in the early lists of kramats of the holy circle around Cape Town—he had established a learned dynasty that remains in South Africa today. His school remained under his family's control, with Tahora pioneering Muslim women's education, and his students continued to adhere to his line of teaching.

With or without Abu Bakr, an Ottoman awareness had been firmly planted at the Cape by the time of his death. While not regarding themselves as the direct subjects of the sultan, or necessarily friends of his emissaries, Capetonian Muslims admired the empire and scholars supported by Abdulhamid II in much that same way that Syed Ahmad Khan did from India.⁶² By now, too, their fashions had started to tilt away from the old Malayo-Brittanic combination of conical hats for men and voluminous dresses and wooden pattens for women, shifting to the modern fezzes, suits, and veils that Syed Ahmad Khan also advocated in India. Similarly, Ottoman nomenclature would become popular for some of the most prosaic things. A Capetonian Malay cricket team bore the name "Ottoman" from 1882, just as the Malays of Ceylon had firmly invested in this very English game by 1873, transforming their parade ground into the pitch it remains today. That said, it would take a little longer for the people of Colombo to make as firm an Ottoman connection, and it would be rather confused, to say the least, by the arrival of fifty-two Egyptians in January 1883, with their seven heads accused of rebellion against Abdulhamid and his viceroy, Khedive Tawfiq. To understand why this was so, we must now divert to Cairo by way of Mecca, where Cape Malays met a Muslim world under Ottoman auspices.

Ottoman Mecca, Khedival Cairo

Ottoman Mecca was already a nexus for information in the Muslim world prior to the explosion of newsprint, and the site for the intellectual and spiritual leadership of ulama like Abu Bakr's print rival Muhammad Salih and his Naqshbandi contemporary Shaykh Ismail Simabur. But while the holy cities were Ottoman, there remained a clear sense of the importance of many other sovereigns whose influence overlapped there, usually in the form of the guesthouses they maintained and the donations they dispensed. Whereas they were subject to the Ottomans—defending the northwestern routes to the Hijaz, supplying grain to its people, and delivering the mantle for the Ka'ba each year—the governors of Egypt had also made a name for themselves on the world stage. We may recall that Muhammad 'Ali, an Albanian officer who had helped to restore the Ottoman order in Egypt after the British defeat of Napoleon's forces, had sent his son Ibrahim Pasha to crush the Wahhabis in the Hijaz in 1819 before he moved to conquer much of the Sudan and then challenge Sultan Mahmud II in Syria and Anatolia in the 1830s.

The successors of Muhammad 'Ali, especially Sa'id (r. 1854–1863) and Isma'il (r. 1863–1879), developed their domains after his death in 1849, and in ways that anticipated Japan's rise from the 1870s. Adam Mestyan points out that the Ottoman sultan Abdulaziz first experienced train travel in 1863 when touring from Alexandria to Cairo, where he visited factories and museums.[63] Having already invested in steam, print, and telegraph, Egypt was momentarily enriched by its exports of cotton, which had increased to meet European demand during the U.S. Civil War. The French-educated Isma'il—who had translated on the *Victoria and Albert* in 1867 and whose embarrassing recall from a Parisian banquet had been the subject of the *Alamat Lankapuri* in 1869—had gained recognition as a fully fledged viceroy, or khedive. After annexing Darfur in the southwest, Isma'il attempted to further enlarge his nested domain up the Nile and from the shores of the Red Sea with two disastrous expeditions against Abyssinia between 1874 and 1876, helped in part by Confederate officers.

Such developments, from the founding of the dynasty to the expeditions in Asia and Africa, were well known across the Indian Ocean. We have already seen how, in his petition of 1824 addressing Sultan Mahmud II, the exiled ruler of Kedah had made mention of the frequent arrival of vessels from Egypt. Similarly, we found the Muslims of Galle writing to his ambitious governor directly as "Commander in Faith" in January 1839 in the hope of gaining fresh scholars to replace their brethren warring in the English courts, anticipating the later Capetonian petitions that would secure the arrival of Abu Bakr. It was clear, too, that Abu Bakr saw the Azhar as a site of key importance in the 1860s and 1870s and maintained close links with its religious scholars. His first Africa-born son would study there.

Egyptian or Egyptian-educated scholars, distinguished by the appellation "Misri" or "Azhari," had long found willing followers in the Indian Ocean arena, alternately complementing or impinging on the popularity of the Hadrami sayyids. One such figure claiming the distinction was ʿAbd al-Rahman al-Misri, born in the same Sumatran town as the late ʿAbd al-Samad. Well known in Batavia by the middle of the nineteenth century, al-Misri's daughter married the locally born Sayyid ʿUthman (1822–1914), a traditionalist who had ventured to the Middle East in the 1850s, including Cairo, though he later watched with some warinesss the rise of a new reformism emanating from that city. To be sure, Egypt and its increasingly active print media would worry as many Muslims traditionalist or customary as inspire those reformist or modernist in the Indian Ocean arena by the end of the nineteenth century. But if Egypt would become a model of physical modernity under Muhammad ʿAli's successors, it is worth remembering that calls for Muslim self-strengthening and reform were often refracted through the lens of a more clearly Ottoman Hijaz and its scholars, whose students brought all manner of news from their various homelands. This might concern the struggles with the French in Algeria, the Russians in the Caucasus, and the British in India, where a Muslim press had long existed and alternately lionized or renounced reformers and revolutionaries.

As we saw in chapter 6, British pressure in Malabar had already led to the exile of Sayyid Fadl in 1852, to be followed, after the cataclysm of 1857, by a suite of northerners such as Rahmatullah Kairanawi (1819–1891). Many such outcasts were anxious for Ottoman blessing and resources. Fadl and Kairanawi gained this in part through publications invoking the sultan's beneficence as a defender of Islam. Others found it among communities who identified their struggles with their own.[64]

Restored Ottoman Mecca was also a prime location for discussions of Dutch and Siamese pressure in the more distant Jawi world, whose students gravitated to some of the Indian exiles, and to the school founded for Kayranwi's benefit at Mecca in 1874. By that time Jawi students were especially concerned about the fate of Aceh, whose Hadrami chief minister, Habib ʿAbd al-Rahman Zahir (1833–1896), was sent into exile in the Hijaz after the Dutch invasion of 1873. His presence in Arabia, his close alliance with the chief Shafiʿi imam Ahmad b. Zayni Dahlan, and his eventual appointment as head of the sayyids at Medina in 1886 would add fuel to wider sympathies for the Acehnese in the Ottoman domains, and distaste for the Dutch.

The British who encouraged Dutch aggression in Sumatra were also of rising concern on the eastern fringes of the Indian Ocean, having begun their de facto conquest of the Malay Peninsula after the signing of the Pangkor Treaty of 1874, obliging a set of states to accept British residents at their courts. They would generate Southeast Asian exiles as well, as when they dispatched Sultan Abdullah of Perak to the Seychelles. This was after the 1875 assassination of the first resident, James Birch, who had been sent to Perak from a career in Trincomalee via Singapore in 1870, to affirm the difference between prince and pirate as far as London was concerned. The Seychelles were off the well-sailed routes to Mecca. Besides, given the relatively small number of pilgrims from Perak, Sultan Abdullah never obtained the support that the more directly imperiled Acehnese would find from all manner of Southeast Asians sojourning in Mecca, echoing the exilic flow from Pattani in previous decades. The former sultan was a placid deportee anyway. He remained on good—and cricket-playing—terms with his captors until his return to more proximate banishment at Singapore in 1893 after numerous petitions to Victoria. Abdullah would even make a point of visiting England that year, rather like his erstwhile peer Abu Bakar of Johor, with his military uniform and braid intact as he emphasized his loyalty to Victoria.[65]

At first blush, the most consequential story for Indian Ocean Muslims would appear to be that of the highly publicized arrest, trial, and exiling to Ceylon of the Egyptian army officer Ahmad ʿUrabi Pasha (1841-1911) at the end of 1882. He was certainly famous in British imperial circles. Abu Bakar of Johor called upon ʿUrabi on his way to London in 1885, and Robert Aldrich has observed that his fate bears many similarities to the experience of other African and Asian sovereigns displaced in the nineteenth century.[66] On the face of it, moreover, the exile of ʿUrabi and his colleagues should have had broader ramifications for a Muslim world that he himself invoked in the revolution of 1882, as he was lionized by Azhari reformers like Muhammad ʿAbduh, not to mention a quixotic Briton of ʿAbduh's acquaintance whose connections took him in and out of imperial offices in London. The latter's enthusiastic defence of the Muslim world would similarly earn him a hopeful welcome of his own when he visited Ceylon in 1884. As such, this chapter will now divert, like both Abu Bakr Effendi and Abu Bakar of Johor, to Ottoman Egypt—the new physical guarantee for British control in India—to read events against the grain of that Briton's campaigning. Instead of the once hoped for "Priests of the Competent orders" requested from Galle in 1839, the Muslims of Colombo would welcome the households of seven demoted pashas in January 1883, no matter how much their captors tried to discourage the use of the title, and even as they celebrated the caliph in whose name they had been banished. But, to begin, we must see why they were exiled in the first place, for this history is linked to the emerging tension between a reconstituted caliphal order and an even newer Muslim nationalism vested in rethinkings of the homeland, or *watan*.

The Gadfly, the Reformer, and the Champion: The Revolution of 1882

> There is undoubtedly a strong wave of religious feeling passing over Islam and the Sultan has put himself at its head and so identified himself with the cause of orthodoxy. I do not however see in this anything more than a matter of policy. The antagonism to the Turk is too deeply rooted in the Arabian mind to allow itself to be deluded by Ottoman promises.
>
> —BLUNT TO GLADSTONE, FEBRUARY 1882

As we saw in chapter 6, the Islamic linkage with Lanka is an ancient one, symbolized by the tenth-century tombstone found by the Maradana Mosque. Such stones bear witness to the presence of emissaries of the ʿAbbasid caliphs, and the ongoing movement of peoples in a frontier space that an enthusiastic biographer of Ibn Battuta once called a "Muslim Lake."[67] We have also seen that, even in exile, Muslims from Southeast Asia could interact with "Moorish" believers on the island, some of whom stressed their Arab lineal descent, or shuttled between the courts of the subcontinent and both extremes of the Indian Ocean, where sayyid heritage was similarly esteemed.[68]

With the opening of the Suez Canal, Khedival Egypt was rendered the primary gateway to what had become a very Britannic Indian Ocean, with Lanka its pivot en route for the riches of the farther East. Many colonial officials and monied adventurers would include both Egypt and Lanka in their itineraries. So, too, would Victoria's son, Crown Prince Albert (1841–1910), who met with Khedive Isma'il at Suez on the way to India and Ceylon in 1875, together with palace favorite Bartle Frere.[69] Another such visitor to Egypt was Prince Albert's friend, the Irish landholder and Tory William Henry Gregory (1816–1892), who had welcomed him to Ceylon as its governor. Gregory had already visited Egypt and Tunis in the mid-1850s. In 1859 he published essays about these travels, expressing scant regard for Africans and Turks alike, claiming that, "as a general rule, wherever the crescent flies, insecurity, neglect and bad government destroy whatever prosperity might have prevailed."[70] He also gave an account of a dervish assembly, already a must-see for tourists in Cairo, which was entirely in keeping with contemporary critiques of the ratib in Cape Town.[71] A supporter of Greek and Bulgarian independence (as well as the American Confederacy and Irish home rule), Gregory was back in Egypt from November 1881 to April 1882. At that time, he and his wife, Augusta, played host to Wilfrid Scawen Blunt (1840–1922) and his wife, Anne Isabella King-Noel (1837–1917), after their return from Damascus to find the Ottoman province in ferment.[72] An energized Blunt wanted to be a part of the fermentation that had begun some years earlier, engaging nativists and reformers, among others, against informal European colonization and the heavy impositions of the bankrupted Isma'il and his heir, Tawfiq, who had placed some of the burden on the shoulders of the military and the scholarly classes.[73] Writing from Helwan on November 27, 1881, Gregory wrote that Blunt was "quite in the thick of it all, and entirely in the confidence of the army and the sheikhs of Azar [sic]."[74]

Similarly romantic on questions of Irish, Greek, and Arab independence, Blunt had commenced a career in the consular service serving at Constantinople from 1859. His advantageous marriage to the granddaughter of Lord Byron allowed him the independence to pursue his great love of horses, which he would import from the Wahhabi stronghold of Najd, and then anything that might undo the empire of Abdulhamid. Not that Blunt had always been an enemy of the Ottomans to the degree that Gregory claimed to abhor them. Reflecting on their honeymoon of 1869, Blunt confessed that his and his wife's

> first impression of the Turks in their true home in Asia was a most agreeable one. . . . . Our English character was a passport everywhere to their regard, for the help given them in the Crimean War was still in all men's minds and no shadow of distrust had risen up between the British and the Moslem mind. Abdul

Aziz was Sultan and our good ally, and we were credited with all the virtues Christendom could show, the English being a form of Christianity accounted Unitarian in its creed and honest in its commercial practice. We were therefore everywhere received with smiles.[75]

The world of 1881 was rather different. After the betrayal of 1877, Abdulhamid—who had also been on Victoria's yacht with his since deposed maternal uncle in 1867—was now an insistent claimant to the caliphate in the face of Russian aggression. He had antagonized much of Europe in his efforts to retain Bulgaria. Some sections of the British foreign office labored under the notion that he was promulgating global resistance to the colonial powers using his network of propagandists, such as the Malabari Sayyid Fadl and the Syrian Abu al-Huda al-Sayyadi. At Jeddah in 1881, the British consul, James W. Zohrab—whose Perso-Armenian father had been Ottoman consul general in London before Musurus Pasha in the 1840s and who had himself served as an interpreter in the Crimea—reported rumors of an alliance being encouraged by the newly reappointed sharif, 'Abd al-Muttalib (1790–1886), who had presided during the massacre of 1858.[76] Soon enough the Dutch were similarly on their guard against any letters, Arabs, or pilgrims returning to Java.[77]

Blunt, who had been on hand in Jeddah, did not believe that such schemes had any chance of success. He was far more alive to the expressions of anti-Turkish sentiment encouraged by the Anglo-American missionaries in the Levant. His path to Cairo and many of his thoughts on the caliphate had already been confirmed, if not ordained, by his wife's teacher, John Louis Sabunji (1838–1931). A former Catholic priest and sometime chemist born in Diyarbakir, Sabunji was well known for his newspaper *al-Nahla* (The bee), founded at Beirut in 1870 and relocated to London in 1877. Sabunji had been a buzzing supporter of the Ottoman cause during the Russo-Ottoman War of 1877–1878, and still hopefully pro-British, though he became disaffected by the Zulu Wars of 1879 prosecuted by Frere, and he was rounding on Abdulhamid as well.[78]

Blunt first suspected that the ex-Khedive Isma'il had been behind Sabunji's labors.[79] His more likely patron was Sultan Barghash of Zanzibar. Not only had Barghash been subject to Frere's oversight at Bombay and on trips to London, but both had also negotiated the end to the island's role in the slave trade in 1872.[80] Barghash moreover resented Abdulhamid's pretensions to a caliphate that implied supremacy over his own Omani and Ibadi dynasty.⁸¹ Sabunji first openly expressed anti-caliphal views in London in January 1881 in a pamphlet titled *al-Khilafa*. An anxious Musurus Pasha tried unsuccessfully to buy him out before Sabunji reproduced the same themes in a journal called *al-Ittihad al-ʿArabi* (The Arab union), financed by his new backer: Blunt.⁸² Briton and Levantine furthermore collaborated in March to spread a clumsy handbill, *Bayan-nama li-ummat al-Sharq*, across Asia Minor bewailing the recent wars with Russia and calling on Muslim and Christian Arabs to unite against their Turkish rulers after centuries of misrule and oppression.⁸³ There was no strong reaction.

Although Sabunji and Blunt failed to unite the Arabs against the caliph, their opinions divided some in British India, which Blunt saw as a key place from which to weaken Ottoman claims. Most Indians dismissed *al-Khilafa* as official British propaganda.⁸⁴ Indeed, there is some evidence to suggest that it and the wild rumors it engendered bolstered support for the sultan in India.⁸⁵ And while Sabunji released his first pamphlet in London, Blunt at Cairo had eagerly spelled out such ideas to his old friend Edward Hamilton (1847–1908), now private secretary to prime minister William Gladstone. It must have seemed a perfect opening. Gladstone had returned to prominence in 1876 by condemning Ottoman repression in Bulgaria and deployed anti-Turkish rhetoric for his second successful tilt at the premiership in 1880. Writing just after a failed attempt to return to central Arabia in January 1881, Blunt had boasted of the gossip he had heard at Jeddah, proposing that Hamilton's "chief" would have to "harden his heart and take the Sultan by the throat," given that Abdulhamid had been emboldened to use his claims to the caliphate as a foil to British policy, though he belittled them at the same time: "I do not, from what I could hear at Jeddah, believe that the Sultan has any special influence over the Indian Mussulmans as Caliph, or that they would pay much attention to any proclamation he might make on a Jehad. But he is certainly intriguing against us, and, if allowed to go on unchecked and apparently able to defy us, will as certainly increase his influence with them and do us a bad turn at the first opportunity."⁸⁶

Based on discussions with the Jeddan commercial agent, ʿUmar Nasif (1822–1908), Blunt had been convinced that the previous sharif of Mecca had been assassinated in 1880 at the behest of Abdulhamid because of his friendship with the English, and to make way for the "bitterly hostile" ʿAbd al-Muttalib of old.⁸⁷

The pilgrims, coming from all parts of the world, hear these things, and talk them over, and go back home impressed with the idea that the reactionary party in Islam is the strong one and European influence on the wane. It is a pity that it should be so, for a year ago the liberal party was strong at Mecca and if properly supported might have exercised a powerful influence at the present moment on the tone of Musulman thought. I hear from the Sheekhs here that they intend to fight, and if that happens you will have an opportunity. Only I should like it made distinctly known that anything we do against the Sultan should be done on political not religious grounds. A crusade, as a crusade, wd be always a little dangerous & we ought to appear as protectors not destroyers of Islam.[88]

Blunt also suggested that London make such protections plain by supporting independent Muslim princes, collecting the revenue from pious endowments in India for the sharif, "as the Sultan or the Viceroy of Egypt do," and undertaking "the proper direction of the Indian Pilgrimage," citing the Dutch as exemplary in that regard.[89]

Blunt would soon be happy enough to encourage more localized Egyptian resistance to Abdulhamid and his representative, Khedive Tawfiq. In fact, it was already underway. Forced to accept an Anglo-French commission to oversee the crushing public debt in 1876, Tawfiq's authoritarian father had tried to mobilize sentiment against the West and was retired to Istanbul at the behest of Great Britain and France in 1879. His heir experimented momentarily with constitutional reform, before similarly squeezing the population through his chief minister, Riyad Pasha, with the support of his British advisors. He was soon opposed by local elements of the armed forces, who resented his favoring of the Circassian elite and the continued reduction of native Egyptian ranks, which had swollen under his father to upward of one hundred thousand men, some of whom had served in the Sudan, Ethiopia, and then the Russo-Turkish War for little and generally late payment. By 1879 they were reduced to near twelve thousand, with no room for local officers, though figures like Ahmad 'Urabi evidently maintained influence well beyond their official rank.[90] In January 1881, 'Urabi was among three officers who presented a petition to Riyad Pasha authored by fellow colonel 'Ali Fahmi calling for an end to discrimination against Arabic-speaking officers and to dismiss the then minister of war. Arrested, they were soon released by a wavering Tawfiq when their men rioted.[91]

Tawfiq was also disliked by many local Shafi'i and Maliki scholars whom he or his father had forced abroad when unable to bend them to their wishes. Blunt's enthusiasm was only fueled by his encountering their stronger variant of what he termed "liberal" Islam, pioneered by the recently expelled Persian activist Jamal al-Din al-Afghani (1938–1997) and kept vital by the Azharite Muhammad 'Abduh. As editor of the official gazette, 'Abduh was then loosening the bonds of khedival control over the press, and he would later serve as Blunt's pathway to 'Urabi.[92]

Blunt first gained his introduction to 'Abduh by way of his tutor, Muhammad Khalil (d. 1883). In his memoirs he recalled how he was taken to the shaykh's house on January 28, 1881:

> It began for me a friendship which has lasted now for nearly a quarter of a century with one of the best & wisest and most interesting of men.... Sheykh Mohammed Abdou when I first saw him in 1881 was a man of about 35, of middle height, dark, active in his gait, of quick intelligence revealed in particularly penetrating eyes, and with a manner frank and cordial inspiring ready confidence. In dress and appearance purely Oriental, wearing the white turban & dark kaftan of the Azhar Sheykhs & knowing as yet no European language or indeed other language than his own. With him [and] with the help of Mohammed Khalil who knew a little French ... I obtained before leaving Cairo a knowledge really large of the opinions of their liberal school of Moslem thought, their fear for the present, & their hopes for the future.... Sheykh Mohammed Abdou was strong on the point that what was needed for the Mohammedan body politic was not merely reforms but a true religious reformation. On the question of the Caliphate he looked at that time, in common with most enlightened Moslems, to its reconstitution on a more spiritual basis ... The House of Othman for two hundred years had cared almost nothing for religion & beyond the right of the sword had no claim any longer to allegiance.[93]

Blunt said little of 'Abduh's public role at this point in allowing the blossoming of pro-'Urabist papers. Whereas Blunt's publicly declared position was always one of solidarity for the Muslim world, his maneuvering prior to the revolution and invasion of 1882 was as often about the Great Game, counseling Gladstone to throw the Turks to the Russians and emulate the Dutch in the management of the hajj. His "us" was still a British one. Certainly there was a disjuncture in the language of his diaries and their publication in

1907.⁹⁴ At Damascus in March 1881, Blunt had had dreams of bringing the sons of the exiled Algerian Emir ʿAbd al-Qadir (1808–1883) on side, claiming to have it in his power "to unite the most important Bedouin tribes of Syria" against the detested Ottoman centralizers.⁹⁵ Such scheming is also evident in his *Future of Islam*, serialized in the *Fortnightly Review* from July 1881, which predicted the imminent collapse of Abdulhamid's empire and the creation of a new Arab caliphate at Cairo or Mecca while declaring it imperative for Great Britain to take "Islam by the hand and encourage her boldly in the path of virtue."⁹⁶

On their return to Cairo from Syria, and some weeks after the first installment of his essays, the Blunts, the Gregories, and Sabunji watched the political battle rage between the old elite and the subaltern officers backed by the nativist intellectuals and middle class. Western bankers, and especially comptroller general Sir Auckland Colvin (1838–1908), fretted lest their loans remain unpaid. Many were eager for a solution in the same form of intervention that France had just undertaken in similarly bankrupted Tunis, declaring the Ottoman beylicate a protectorate in May and sparking Egyptian military demands to restore their ranks and boost their own defenses, which they presented to ʿUrabi.⁹⁷

That summer, the nativist faction and the talismanic ʿUrabi compelled Tawfiq to accept a more representative Egyptian parliament under Sharif Pasha (1826–1887). Restored to the premiership in September, he oversaw provincial elections in November 1881. As Juan Cole has shown, this did not dislodge the Circassian elite and their European advisors. The newest government promised to repay the nation's debts and affirmed its loyalty to the sultan—though it seems that ʿUrabi had a vision of the khedive as a mere titular representative of the latter.⁹⁸

The British press fretted all the same, marking ʿUrabi out as the rabble-rouser in chief. In late December 1881, Blunt announced that he would remain and help ʿUrabi, extolling his virtues in the *Times*. Writing to Gladstone as well, Blunt began to outline his views on the proper relationship between Istanbul and Cairo, admitting to their religious commonality but claiming pronounced resistance then being voiced at al-Azhar, where the Hanafi (and thus "conservative" and pro-Turkish) rector Muhammad al-ʿAbbasi (1803–1893) had been deposed in favor of the more "liberal" Shafiʿi Shams al-Din al-Imbabi (d. 1895).⁹⁹ Blunt was also at pains to paint ʿUrabi as no tool of Constantinople or the former khedive. He transformed the colonel who had

had but a few years of education at al-Azhar into a paragon of reason from a "tradition of Arabian thought inherited from the days when Mohammedanism was liberal" and "before Turkish ignorance limited its scope":

> He is a Sayyid of the Koreysh, a descendent in the male line of Huseyn the grandson of Mahommed,—a fact which no doubt has had its influence with his fellow soldiers. Of his own position he speaks with modesty. "I am," he says, "the representative of the army because the circumstances have made the army trust me; but the army itself is but the representative of the people, its guardian till such time as the people shall no longer need it. At present we are the sole national force standing between Egypt and its Turkish rulers who would renew at any moment were they permitted the iniquities of Ismaïl Pasha. . . . Such is Araby. I cannot understand that these are sentiments to be deplored or action to be crushed by a Liberal English Government.[100]

Yet Gladstone's government would be concerned by allegations of ʿUrabi bullying the token chamber of deputies, of his soldiers misbehaving at Alexandria, and perhaps contracting for arms from Germany. Consul general Edward Malet (1837–1908) forwarded information that painted ʿUrabi as a creature of Ismaʿil, which his childhood friend Blunt would try to counter with direct telegrams and letters to Gladstone, unaware that France and Great Britain were already resolved to intervene for the khedive.

Sharif Pasha's cabinet fell on February 1, 1882, just over a year after Blunt's meeting with ʿAbduh, leading to the ascent of the nativist Mahmud Sami al-Barudi (1839–1904) as prime minister. Barudi then appointed ʿUrabi as minister of war and promoted him to major general, a symbolic coup for the Arabophone cause, as no native Egyptian had yet made it above colonel.[101] ʿUrabi further made sure to communicate his intentions with British officials and the press via Blunt. Fully aware that his own channel to the British prime minister was unconventional, and that he had taken on the "position of unofficial interpreter of their complaints," in mid-February 1882 Blunt offered a fresh summary of what he called the National Party of Egypt and the level of support it enjoyed, claiming that it had already made "prodigious strides."[102] Blunt once more grounded the party in the "liberal and progressive" Azhar, which he claimed was "an university which has the pretension of directing the thought of the whole Mohamedan world." Allied to them was the army, "weeded of every doubtful element," and the country

Shaykhs, who still bore "the stripes of Ismail's rule upon their backs." Added to this, though, was an overwhelming support among the "artizans": "These can almost all read and write. They read the newspapers and, like the artisan class in every country, are easily fired with enthusiasm. Their ideas are rapidly assimilating themselves to those of Europeans on political matters. They attend meetings, make speeches, applaud and love noise. Araby is with them the hero of the hour, and they would join him to a man if it was a case of resisting invasion or armed intervention either from Europe or Constantinople."[103]

Ranged against them were the arriviste Syrians, the Circassian elite, and those landowners who regretted the loss of corvée and slave labor, and whom Blunt implied vested their hopes in a sultan that 'Urabi dared not oppose in public. Blunt only wished to encourage such ideas, or at least the ideas he attributed to 'Urabi. He was moreover eager to disassociate the Egyptian officers from the sultan-caliph to whom they pledged their public loyalty, claiming that, "in the eyes of the more enlightened Egyptians," the Ottoman empire and caliphate was "doomed."[104] In Blunt's view, there was not merely an opportunity for the Egyptian officers:

> Panislamic ideas find a certain sympathy at the Azhar, but it is panislamism of a very different sort from Abd el Hamid's—one which seeks to unite Mohammedans by aiding their enlightenment. I think, Sir, if you will allow me to suggest it, that you have a noble work before you in encouraging openly the liberal movement so strangely begun in this country. It will certainly spread before long to Syria and in due course of time to India and the rest of Asia, and in it lie the best chances of *our own rule and of civilization* [emphasis mine] in the Musulman East. You have but to speak now and all the Arab race will be with you. In six months it may be already too late.[105]

Much of this was fantasy. 'Urabi's "National Party"—as *al-Hizb al-Watani* was rendered—had well realized that it had to affirm the position of Abdulhamid as caliph in its manifesto of December 1881.[106] This was also a document drafted by Blunt in consultation with 'Abduh and approved by 'Urabi in retrospect.[107] Despite their doffing of fezzes, Abdulhamid was incensed that his viceroy had been so frequently disobeyed by the troublesome officer. With 'Urabi's promotion in February 1882, his key counselors Shaykh Muhammad Zafir and Ahmad Ratib Pasha still communicated Istanbul's support, claiming that the sultan valued his loyalty and urged him to be wary of any intriguers seeking to separate Egypt from the caliphate.[108]

Already on the back foot, the intriguer Blunt confided to Hamilton that it was "throwing away a great game not to go in with the liberal movement in the East," a movement, which, "if it works out in spite of us . . . will destroy us."[109] Destruction was coming, and there was little that Blunt could do, despite darting in and out of the offices on Downing Street the following month. While he thought Gladstone welcomed his "eloquent" advice, the indifferent foreign secretary Lord Granville (1815–1891) was adamant that the case was hopeless.[110] A March 14 visit to the "quite out of date" soldier-Assyriologist Sir Henry Rawlinson (1810–95) had earned both Blunts nomination to the Royal Asiatic Society and a lecture on how the Egyptians, "like all Eastern races," were meant for despotic rule.[111] The following day Blunt was pumped for information by an "amused" General Garnet Wolseley (1833–1913)—veteran of Burma, the Crimea, and India—whom the self-appointed spokesman of Egypt advised to take sixty thousand men to occupy the desert between Canal and Delta.[112]

Nor yet was there much that ʿUrabi could do, even when his own words reached the prime minister "translated" with Blunt's flourishes after being rendered by Sabunji or professor Edward Palmer of Cambridge (1840–1882).[113] As one such adapted missive read:

> To our respected, sincere and free minded friend Mr. Wilfrid Blunt . . . We can assure you that all is now tranquil. Peace reigns over the country; and we and all our patriotic brethren are with our best will defending the rights of those who dwell in our land, no matter of what nation they may be. All treaties and international obligations are fully respected; and we shall allow no one to touch them, as long as the Powers of Europe keep their engagements and friendly relations with us. . . . Our only aim is to deliver our Country from slavery, injustice and ignorance, and to raise our people to such a position as shall enable them to prevent any return of the despotism which in time past desolated Egypt.[114]

Malet had meanwhile reported that ʿUrabi had threatened the chamber of deputies and speaker Sultan Pasha. In fact, the government had to avert a countercoup in April by Circassian staff officers, who were sentenced to be exiled to the Sudan.[115] The order was commuted by the khedive on Malet's advice to a more leisurely removal to Istanbul.[116] This precipitated a major standoff with the ʿUrabists, and Blunt engineered a response from the leading nationalists to send telegrams to London affirming popular support for ʿUrabi. By mid-May they had all obliged—from ʿUrabi to ʿAbduh and Shaykh Imbabi—claiming perfect peace and tranquility.[117]

Granville was enraged, and Gladstone had long since ordered the dispatch of the naval force "to protect European property."[118] After the arrival of the Anglo-French fleet at Alexandria and its issuance of a joint note of demand on May 25, the khedive dismissed the Barudi cabinet, but he soon restored his minister of war after public outcry. Although the population backed the revolt and was prepared for war—with ʿAbduh naïvely arguing that the British were ill suited to fighting on land—Blunt was fully aware that the Egyptians would share the fate of Tunis.[119] He also wondered what part of that fate he might share and began to offer his services to mediate between London and Cairo, urging Egypt to make peace with the sultan lest he send his own troops in.

The Great Game was still very much afoot. Promising to remain in moral support, but not to fight himself, due to his ignorance and "horror of war," the self-appointed spokesman of the revolution declared that he would have "no need to repress fanaticism," claiming that he would join his "voice with Arabi's in favour of the humanist interpretation of the laws of war," for his "idea of a policy for the Egyptians" was "that they shd act by a rule diametrically opposite to the common Oriental ones. I would have them tell the truth even to their enemies; be more humane than the European soldiers, more honest than their European creditors. So only can they effect that moral reformation their religious leaders and I have in view for them."[120]

Such was not up to the Egyptian army, nor the religious leaders ventriloquized by Blunt, who dispatched Sabunji to Alexandria, where he remained from June 7 to July 10.[121] Indeed, the final act of ʿUrabi's political career was ushered in by anti-European riots in the city on June 11, which led to the deaths of 250 Egyptians and 50 Europeans. The violence provided the justification for the shelling and invasion that eventually followed on July 11, whereupon the British secured the khedive in his summer palace. Tawfiq accordingly declared ʿUrabi a rebel, so he and a rump government met at Cairo on July 29 with some 60 ulama for their Second National Congress. There ʿAbduh read out the charges of apostasy and incompetence against Tawfiq, and the assembly consequently declared his viceregency—though *not* Ottoman authority—at an end.[122] Egypt's first revolution had begun.

Juan Cole has cautioned us against seeing the action—or, yet, the revolution—as being structured in Islamic terms. Whereas the violence at Alexandria devolved into a conflict framed by Islam and Christianity, many Coptic delegates to the first nationalist meetings held in that city had preferred to see the issue as one of common patriotism in the face of intruders of any sort that still affirmed the place of the sultan. They had been accordingly mollified by ʿAbduh.[123] On the other hand, when writing to Gladstone prior to the landing—and through Sabunji and Blunt—it is undeniable that ʿUrabi had made what Europeans would henceforth call "Pan-Islamic" claims about the ramifications of the British expedition that would be further printed in the *Times*:

> England may rest assured that the first guns she fires on Egypt will absolve the Egyptians from all treaties, contracts and conventions; that the Control and debt will cease; that the property of Europeans will be confiscate; that the canals will be destroyed; the communications cut; and that use will be made of the religious zeal of Mohammedans to preach holy war in Syria and Arabia and in India. Egypt is held by Mohammedans as the key of Mecca and Medina; and all our bound by their religious law to defend these holy places and the ways leading to them. Sermons on this subject have already been preached in the mosques of Damascus; and an agreement has been come to with the religious leaders of every land throughout the Mohammedan world. I repeat it again and again that the first blow struck at Egypt by England or her allies will cause blood to flow through the breadth of Asia and of Africa, the responsibility of which will be on the head of England. . . . [But if] she prefers to . . . threaten us with her fleets and her Indian troops . . . let her not underrate . . . the patriotism of the Egyptian people. . . . We are determined to fight, to die martyrs for our country, as has been enjoined on us by Our Prophet.[124]

As Khalid Fahmy has shown, the explicit linkage of religion to the imperatives of the Egyptian army was hardly new in a force where Turkish and Circassian officers had so counterproductively derided the capacity of their "Arab" soldiers.[125] Now one of those self-declared Arabs had publicly invoked the sentiments of Muslims beyond the formal reach of their suzerain. As Blunt further editorialized in the wake of the riots, while it was possible that ʿUrabi had overestimated the implications of his call "as regards the Mohammedans of India," for Egypt itself, his was "no idle boast."[126]

By then the French had steamed off, British and Indian troops had landed, and Tawfiq had sacked ʿUrabi. Blunt, too, retreated, fearing charges of treason, while his occasional translator Palmer died playing the Arab in the Canal Zone.[127] Blunt continued to forward ʿUrabi's letters to Gladstone, but began to imply that he may have been misled, praying only that Egypt might have its freedom from Istanbul.[128] All that remained for the revolutionary government were the battles themselves. The Egyptians successfully repelled the British for several weeks at the chokepoint railway station of Kafr al-Dawwar before being attacked from the Canal Zone, with ʿUrabi captured after the final battle of al-Tall al-Kabir on September 13.

Consigned to prison with the proviso that the khedive could not execute him without London's assent, ʿUrabi and his peers were soon transformed into objects of pity. The official observer, Lieutenant Colonel Charles Wilson (1836–1905), doubted that they were guilty of anything other than revolting against the khedive and defending their own country.[129] They were also the objects of British legal interest. Blunt had dispatched two lawyers, Mark Napier and Richard Eve, to defend ʿUrabi. They were later joined by Alexander Broadley (1847–1916), who came to terms with Malet and Lord Dufferin (1826–1902), ambassador to the Sublime Porte. Dufferin proposed a deal by which the defendants would plead guilty to breaking Ottoman military law of rebellion rather than orchestrating the violence in Alexandria.[130] Broadley had also hoped to subpoena witnesses from Istanbul—including Ahmad Ratib and Muhammad Zafir—adducing evidence of ʿUrabi's claims that it was the khedive and Great Britain that wanted to separate Egypt from the caliphate.[131]

As Selim Deringil notes, both ʿUrabi and al-Barudi had indeed petitioned the sultan for recognition and aid, the first in late November 1881, and the second in the wake of the Circassian coup attempt of 1882. Both had been rebuffed.[132] Abdulhamid had not offered public support to ʿUrabi after March and refrained from sending his own troops to Egypt, partially because of already stretched resources, but also because the British refused any such cooperation.[133] Abdulhamid also had to weigh the popular domestic view that the Egyptian officers were Muslims defending their territory against Christian aggression. Still, when it came, his personal repudiation of ʿUrabi carried the sting of excommunication. In August he telegrammed that if ʿUrabi persevered he would be deemed to have "disobeyed God, His Prophet, and His Representative on Earth."[134] Besides, Abdulhamid had already washed his hands of the unruly "Arab" by allowing Great Britain to invade, hoping for a favorable restoration of Ottoman rights thereafter.

So it was that, in certain expectation of death, the leading revolutionaries—including ministers like al-Barudi and fellow officers ʿAbd al-ʿAl Hilmi and Tulba ʿIsmat—accepted Dufferin's offer to plead guilty to rebellion in exchange for exile at a place of Great Britain's choosing.[135] This would take some further weeks to organize, against the fact that Gladstone, Tawfiq, and Victoria herself had all been keen on their execution.[136] As Broadley scribbled to Montague Guest (1839–1909) in late October, on the back of a widely disseminated photograph of ʿUrabi in prison: "Then the rope was very close to his neck. English justice 'a chargé tout cela.' Now he is as good looking and interesting as ever."[137]

Ceylon was not the first choice of exile. Blunt had pushed for Aden, Malta, or Cyprus as destinations. ʿUrabi, meanwhile, was inclined toward the Cape, understanding it to be a location with Muslims enough to keep him company.[138] While Ceylon was envisaged as a temporary solution, Dufferin could content himself with the notion that exile itself would prove unbearable for the towering officer, who proudly styled himself "the Egyptian" in his correspondence.[139]

Dufferin would soon gain his cherished ambition as governor-general of India, overseeing the final enfolding of Burma in 1885, while Broadley gained his special reward in the form of a book contract and compliments from the prosecuting state.[140] For his part, Malet was instructed not to accept a decoration offered by Abdulhamid, and for Blunt there was a rather different reputational gain to be made after sinking far more money into the trial than he had anticipated. His *Future of Islam* had already seen the first of several reprints and an Urdu translation, and he would visit India the following year, to mild Muslim approval. As a relieved Hamilton noted in November 1882, Blunt would not be "be further troublesome."[141] While not quite true, the question now was how to manage the potentially turbulent exiles of two empires whose jurisdictions overlapped down the Nile, and that both now eyed the loyalties of Muslims in India and beyond.

EIGHT

Seven Pashas for Ceylon

A RELIEVED FORMER leadership of Ottoman Egypt took stock of their circumstances while Dufferin and peers debated just how many of their family and retainers might be carried away with them. Lord Kimberley of the Colonial Office had first favored Hong Kong, but by mid-December it was agreed that Ceylon was secure enough. Once there the exiles would be able to select their own accommodations, paid for by the Egyptian purse after the seizure of their properties and an attendant promise not to confiscate the substantial effects of their wives. Dufferin stressed the need for "as much indulgence as the requirements of humanity might require."[1] What followed was a period of negotiation over numbers, ultimately restricted to fifty-two souls who were gathered on the *Mareotis* at Suez on December 27, 1882, sailing down into the Red Sea and the Indian Ocean beyond.

The journey to Colombo was not the first such seaborne venture for the unofficial champion of the Egyptian revolution. ʿUrabi had been a participant in Khedive Ismaʿil's failed invasion of Abyssinia (in what is now Eritrea), where Anne Gregory claimed that he had distinguished himself by preaching to his soldiers by night.[2] This time he and his peers of varying piety were sent into exile with no clear idea as to when it might end, or if Colombo was their final destination. Grateful to have had their lives spared by the empire to which they had surrendered, they had sworn "by God who gave us the Koran" and their "personal word of honour" to "go to the place which the Government designate[d] . . . and to stay there."[3] They would keep it.

Having laid out the circumstances by which London and Istanbul merged their interests on the Nile, if to the decided advantage of the former, this chapter turns to the potentially revolutionary consequences of the exilic presence. First focusing on British anxieties about their potential for stirring up the island's Muslim communities, it tracks their relative integration while not losing sight of the disagreements that saw the famous Ahmad ʿUrabi both lauded and loathed before his eventual return to Cairo. In the process, it asks just what the Muslim community was, and where the Malays—once praised as the most loyal of imperial subjects—figured in the story. Indeed, in so doing, it will test just how far the bonds of Pan-Islamism could stretch over the decades when Victoria marked two jubilees on the throne. As I shall suggest, the impact of the Egyptians was uneven at best, and very much oriented to a westerly vision of the Muslim world that made little space for their more easterly fellow believers who seemed so resolutely allied to Britain, at least on Lanka.

The Welcome Pashas of Colombo

There is the possibility that in the event of any Mohammedan excitement . . . the prestige of Arabi's name [could] supply a leader who would at once attract the Mohammedans generally to his standard. Arabi and his associates are not isolated here either by race, creed, or language.

—James Longden, January 1883

After their sojourn aboard the *Mareotis*, treated for all intents and purposes as guests—albeit ones requiring an escort of twenty soldiers to pair with the occasional glass of champagne—the Egyptians were gratified by the large crowd that swarmed the docks to bid them welcome on the morning of January 10, two decades after the quiet arrival of Abu Bakr at the Cape.[4] According to their captain, miffed not to have been thanked by his most famous passenger, the boat bearing ʿUrabi ashore was met by a rapturous crowd eager to kiss his clothes and boots.[5] Deputized to oversee the landing, lieutenant governor John Douglas also observed how word gleaned from the Indian newspapers had ensured that a large, enthusiastic, and "almost exclusively Mohamedan" crowd had gathered at the wharf almost as soon as the

Figure 8.1 "Arabi in Exile," *Graphic*, February 1883.

Mareotis had appeared offshore. Having waited quietly overnight and as the first boats came ashore, the general order was shattered when ʿUrabi landed, "followed and cheered by a large crowd of his coreligionists who enthusiastically kissed his hand."[6]

Having arrived two days earlier to secure the rent of several mansions in Cinnamon Gardens and the much larger Lake House at Maradana, Douglas and Major Tranchell oversaw the operation to convey the "much pleased" exiles and their families to their temporary homes for the next three months. The erstwhile ministers—ʿAli Fahmi, Yaʿqub Sami, Mahmud Sami al-Barudi, and the military engineer Mahmud Fahmi—were placed with their households in large homes. ʿUrabi meanwhile shared Lake House with fellow officers Tulba ʿIsmat and ʿAbd al-ʿAl Hilmi, the erstwhile governor of Damietta. Each was furthermore supplied with furniture, a cook, a caretaker, and a female attendant, while sharing the services of a dragoman, Negib Abcarius, seconded from the consulate at Jerusalem.[7]

The exiles did not plan to rely on Abcarius forever. Some had already taken the opportunity to study English aboard the *Mareotis*, and much was made in the press of their request that their children should find places in the best schools at Colombo.[8] The papers certainly made exotic mileage of their arrival, featuring John Van Dort's sketches of the officers and their shrouded women welcomed by Douglas and the preeminent Moors, with one shaykh's hand even receiving a kiss of veneration from the former pasha (see fig. 8.1).[9] Among the Moors arrayed in their best robes was Siddi Lebbai of Kandy (Mukammatu Kacim Cittilevvai, 1838–1898), a proponent of Islamic reform allied with Syed Ahmad Khan. He was also the recent editor and publisher, since December, of the *Muslim Nesan* (Muslim friend) that featured an interview with ʿUrabi soon after his landing.[10] Siddi Lebbai's financial backer was likely there, too: A. M. Wapche Marikar (1829–1925), who had made his fortune as chief contractor for major buildings in Colombo, including the Galle Face Hotel and the town hall at the Pettah (1873). He had also been the natural choice for the Colombo Museum, perhaps the most prestigious structure erected during the tenure of William Gregory.[11] Sited at the northern edge of Cinnamon Gardens, it housed the collection of the Royal Asiatic Society, of which Gregory was a leading member. At its inauguration in January 1877, Gregory is often said to have offered to keep the museum closed on Fridays out of respect for his builder. In this regard he was rather different to his successor Longden, who on January 21, 1883, cast the Moormen as "fanatical Moslems."¹² He had also summarized Douglas's report the previous week with an implicit warning:

> Your Lordship will not fail to gather ... how warmly the Mohammedan population here sympathize with the exiles. The Musulmans of Ceylon number 197,775, of whom 32,208 are concentrated in the city and suburbs of Colombo. They are without doubt the most energetic race in the Island. It is not difficult to account for their sympathy with Arabs, for besides being united by the bond of a common religion the great majority of them are Moormen (so called) descended from an Arabian ancestry who emigrated to Ceylon from the Persian Gulf at a period long anterior to the European conquest of the Island, but who still retain many national characteristics which clearly distinguish them from the peoples round them descended from Indian ancestors.¹³

One wonders if the previous governor may have asked his Moorish builder to be among those guiding his fellow Arab's footsteps from the dock to his residence, and then at the head of the procession to the nearby Maradana Mosque on January 12. Gregory had written to others on Ceylon asking that they would be kind to ʿUrabi, recognizing that opinion was divided as to whether he was "ange ou démon."¹⁴

ʿUrabi was most decidedly an angel in the eyes of Siddi Lebai, who hosted a dinner for several of the exiles in March, when, according to one hostile listener, he lauded his guests as "patriots and true believers who were suffering cruel treatment in their country's cause at the hands of infidels" and were thus entitled to the "respect and support of all Mahomedans."¹⁵ Such rhetoric should be taken with a grain of salt. Indeed, Siddi Lebai was cast by the intelligence officers of the Thuggee Department—to whom this report ultimately went—as a bit player in global networks of rumor linked to Abdulhamid and his sayyid guests Fadl and Afghani. As the worried superintendent at distant Simla advised, the exiles seemed far too close to India, and their presence had supposedly agitated the Muslims of Colombo. Friday prayers were fuller than ever at the mosques the Egyptians attended, the *khutba* was now being delivered in Abdulhamid's name, and "the Pashas" were receiving letters of sympathy from Alleppey in Kerala and as far afield as Singapore.

> The Pashas welcome all strangers. Their common topic of conversation is naturally their country's grievances. How the Egyptian revenues were being eaten up by foreigners; how they acted throughout under orders from the Sultan. His instructions, however, were to annoy the English Government, and not to proceed to open war. But when their homes and lives were threatened, what could they do? Dervish Pasha sold his country for English gold. Egypt now belongs to England; Tunis to France; soon the Harums of Mecca and Medina will pass away to the infidel, unless Islam shows united strength. All good Mahomedans in Turkey and Egypt esteem their Indian brothers and look for their co-operation. Though themselves exiles, they are still subjects of the Sultan, and to him they look for deliverance.[16]

But there was more to signal. Lambert's informants claimed that the exiles were close to the "illiterate" Turkish consul Hussein Lebbe Markar and his nephew, M. T. Cardo, who had allegedly received instructions to treat the exiles with respect. In one especially confused report, the consul was said to have provided Istanbul with information about the island's Muslims capable of bearing arms, and to have entertained a nephew of Sayyid Fadl, Abdul Rahman Ijahad, (and?) the "Raja of Cochin," to whom he gave the credentials of a Mahomed Nur al-Din of Singapore in order that he might support him in carrying on hostilities with the Dutch in Aceh.[17]

Such reportage of Indian Ocean intrigue and anticolonial activism soon evaporated. Wapche Marikar and Siddi Lebbai—and practically all the local merchants cast by Lambert as followers of "the Moplah Priest" Fadl—were soon counted among the many loyal figures of British empire praised by Longden's kindlier successor, Arthur Hamilton-Gordon, though he would not assume office until December. This was well after the exiles had commenced a campaign to increase their allowances and had fallen out with each other. Tawfiq certainly resented having to support men he had not been allowed to hang. His administration set about stripping their estates at home while stinting on their allowances abroad. All this led the exiles to band together to protest in late May that they had not surrendered to the Egyptian government; rather, they had been doing the *British* one an earnest "service." They also complained that their "word of honour" (*kalimat sharaf*) had been given to "the English nation," and the "government" (*hukuma*) mentioned in their original Arabic undertaking had been the "British state and no other." After all, it had been the British who had made them prisoners of war, and it was by virtue of their being convinced by Dufferin of the reforms that Britain was to carry out that they had pled guilty to rebellion.[18]

Blunt saw to it that the exiles received coverage in the London papers, with the *Times* printing a translation of their declaration on June 5.[19] It was also at this time that Lord Granville got wind of perhaps too delicate treatment by Longden, having the Earl of Derby remind him that he was required to affirm that his additional residents were no longer pashas, but merely private effendis to be shown neither ill treatment nor special favor. Longden admitted that he had hosted three of the exiles at the time of his return to Colombo in May, and that his wife had entertained their partners the next day, though the men in question ('Urabi, Tulba 'Ismat, and Mahmud Sami) were merely included among a larger party of two dozen invited to combat the idea among Europeans that they were "martyrs to the cause of their country and their faith to the exclusion of more wholesome influences."[20] That said, Longden's successors would prove sympathetic and actively encouraged them to play a social role on the island, and especially among their coreligionists, who read many of the same papers and pledged themselves to the same queen.

Trouble in Exile

Blunt's earlier writings and his actions on the behalf of the exiles gained attention in Lanka via the Indian press and the local *Muslim Nesan*. When he and Lady Anne proceeded to Colombo in October 1883 together with Sabunji, whom they had collected in Cairo, they were met by a small flotilla on the 19th. Proposals for a welcoming arch at the dock had been rejected by the acting governor, so one was erected at Whist Bungalow, the new home of Mahmud Sami al-Barudi, where fireworks were let off in celebration.[21] If one were to go by official reportage and the press alike, the visit went well, aside from Blunt having a fever, later diagnosed as malaria. Not only had the exiles conveyed him to Customs House and then provided a halal dinner at Lake House (with music supplied by the police band), Siddi Lebbai offered an address on behalf of "the Moorish community" thanking Blunt for his travel and labor in the Muslim interest, adding that the fact of his Englishness had raised their already high estimation of his people, making them "still more loyal to . . . Her Majesty Queen Victoria, under whose sway we have been living as a happy and contented people." The Blunts were then acclaimed and thanked in Arabic by all seven exiles, praying that "Providence" might crown with success his efforts "to bring the truth to light, to unravel those great arcana that seem to perplex the world, and which with our names have been associated." Wilfred merely responded in "a very low" voice.[22]

The Blunts and Sabunji stayed on with al-Barudi, who arranged for a performance by the Malay Dramatic Club of Slave Island to add some local color.[23] Blunt later waxed about the time he had had at the villa, where he was restored to health, and he claimed to have found ʿUrabi happy enough at his new residence.[24] An excited ʿUrabi called on him daily, but the visit laid bare the hopelessness of Blunt's plans and the former officer's wilder dreams. Indeed, discord had emerged within their ranks during the trial and was exacerbated after their placement. A resigned Mahmud Fahmi grew closer to the local English, whose language he studied and whose histories he devoured, rather than ʿUrabi and his Moorish boosters. Within weeks of their arrival, too, ʿUrabi's Cairene cellmate, Tulba, and their housemate at Lake House, ʿAbd al-ʿAl, had already taken issue with ʿUrabi wedding the teenaged housemaid he had been assigned in the absence of his pregnant partner in Cairo. ʿUrabi meanwhile objected to Tulba's fondness for wine and suspected him of spying for the khedive. At the conclusion of their three-month rent-free period, the highborn officers made off with the lion's share of the furniture, leaving ʿUrabi to depend on the charity of the local Muslim community, who delivered with alacrity.[25]

While it is worth noting that Tulba was soon taking issue with almost all his peers and, as a result, was very much isolated from most of them, Mahmud Fahmi—a veteran of the Balkan Wars and committed rationalist—mocked the propensity for local Muslims to flock to the exiles, and to ʿUrabi in particular as some sort of holy man, something both the local police and Blunt also noticed.[26] Mahmud Fahmi even implied that ʿUrabi emphasized his Husaynid lineage to profit from the adulation of the many mosque-goers, whom he noted had an especially high regard for the sayyids, scrambling over each other to kiss his hand in scenes resembling those of "the Egyptian country jurists or the trickster masters of the Sufi orders."[27] Clearly not to Mahmud Fahmi's taste in Ceylon as much as his old bailiwick, such men were on hand in the lead-up to Blunt's visit. Again according to Fahmi, ʿUrabi had heard of Blunt's impending arrival from Sabunji and suggestions that plans were afoot for his return to Egypt, perhaps even at the head of a new government.²⁸ Blunt had held some such hopes for ʿUrabi in August, at least of an early return, if not an official post of some sort.²⁹ As recounted by an incredulous Fahmi, writing in 1891, ʿUrabi started to tell local Muslims of his possible return, which then became rumors, magnified by some "madmen," of dreams that God had ordained that he might even return to power as an Arab prince.³⁰

Such high hopes were assuredly dashed by the arrival of Sabunji the night before the febrile Blunt landed. After he set the exiles straight about the possibilities of return, they quickly fell out with each other while ʿUrabi imagined it was all a plot hatched by Tulba.³¹ Sabunji soon reported the discord among them in his London paper, *al-Nahla*, citing some of the disgruntled exiles who, Fahmi said, had written "an ugly account" to lambast ʿUrabi. After Blunt left for India, Sabunji remained for a time, as Tulba convinced most of the exiles that ʿUrabi's true aim had always been part of a well-funded plot to take the khedivate for himself. Meanwhile, Sufis from the Maghreb were said to have attended ʿUrabi's home for nightly prayers, offering litanies that supposedly proved his destiny. Having related such rumors, Mansur Fahmi scoffed at them all, recalling the ignorance of local shaykhs when they had been under his jurisdiction in the Egyptian countryside.³²

Hardly helping matters, in his correspondence with Blunt in India, Sabunji also accused the since isolated ʿUrabi of arrogance and bigamy, leading to the severing of their relationship; though Fahmi believed the cause was the matter of the 2000 rupee debt incurred by Blunt, which was levied on the needy exiles and caused many local Muslims to whom they had once turned to avoid them.³³ Equally, the strategists of London were less than pleased by Blunt's fresh wanderings once events began to take a less positive turn in the Sudan under the leadership of a martial Sufi par excellence, Muhammad Ahmad (1844–1885), the infamous "Mahdi." Back in London, Longden was attuned to rumors of Afro-Asian conspiracy, perhaps because ʿUrabi was known to one of the Mahdist generals, and Gregory proposed ʿUrabi as a worthy emissary to Khartoum.³⁴ But if ʿUrabi and allies had their views of the Mahdi (positive) and the evangelist general Gordon (decidedly negative), who were both a hot topic when Blunt visited in 1883, there was no real question of their seeking any southern alliance or rescue.³⁵ High-placed sympathy was the best tonic that they could obtain, and that was all that was to be had once a restored Blunt had steamed away to India to find that Egypt's new puppet master Lord Cromer (Evelyn Baring, 1841–1917) had ensured that he was persona non grata there for another several years.[36]

Petitioning Victoria

Almost from the moment of their arrival and parceling out into different and far smaller estates, the exiles had begun petitioning to be joined by family members or for a change of environment.[37] Some—most especially Tulba on Slave Island, supported by his wife, 'Aynifar, in Cairo—commenced long campaigns in defense of their health, and had to involve the British authorities to obtain their allowances. During Blunt's visit, the former minister of war Ya'qub Sami, also at Slave Island, bemoaned the relative expense of daily life in a city that was pricier than Cairo for his twelve dependents, and that offered rather less than might be desired to a gentleman like himself.[38]

Then there was the issue of daily harassment by local speculators and merchants convinced of riches to be had from the seven pashas.[39] On the eve of Blunt's visit, the superintendent tasked with their surveillance remarked that the exiles made far more use of the police than anyone in the city, and that funds should be requested from the Egyptian government to cover such usage.[40] His superior, George Campbell, also had a charitable view of the intentions of the exiles who, given the relatively light surveillance, could "easily have been in India or halfway to Egypt."[41] As he put it, the seven effendis, as the secretary of state had instructed them to be called, were all "intelligent purposeful men," who kept "quiet, orderly, households" and were "on friendly terms with some of the leading Burgher lawyers, and with the leading Ceylon Mahomedans—the best of whom are thrifty, prosperous, shopkeepers and small traders, all very loyal to our Government."[42]

This linkage to respectable Moorish loyalty manifested afresh when 'Urabi agreed to act as patron to Siddi Lebbai and Wapche Marikar at the time that they founded a boys' school in 1884. The school was set on land adjacent to the Maradana Mosque, though obtaining the ground had required 'Urabi's mediation between two rival parties.[43] It also seems that the government agent for the Western Provinces consulted the exiles as a group regarding the formulation of a Muslim marriage and divorce law in 1885.[44]

The practical loyalties of the exiles had barely been tested when allegations surfaced in mid-1884 about possible escapes involving hidden supplies and French steamers (and again in 1885, as some still mooted a relationship with the Mahdi).[45] Sincere to his word to remain wherever he was placed, there were few official complaints from ʿUrabi of Cinnamon Gardens—or at least few compared with ʿAli Fahmi and Tulba, who had again joined their wives to correspond with the solicitous Gregorys. Such letters had their impact. With Sir William having written to his successor Gordon, the latter would advise London that the generally impoverished exiles should be able to live as "gentlemen of moderate means ... readily performing the duties which naturally fall to them as well-educated members of the Mahommedan community."[46] It was quite clear that they were well liked by the local British, who were supposed to deny them their old titles. But even if they were still popularly known as "pashas" to local islanders, the loss of rank pained men like Yaʿqub Sami, who had to come to terms with the public shaming he had endured prior to departure, unlike ʿUrabi, who had been spared having his epaulettes ripped off in front of his regiment.[47]

In April 1885, Yaʿqub Sami also complained that the women of his household—not least his recently arrived wife—were domestic prisoners who "could not be expected to perambulate the streets and to be jostled by the motley crowds that [we]re more or less indifferent of their conduct."[48] Such complaints were moderated in time, as the independently wealthy women came to grips with their employees and environment. Some mastered Sinhalese and enjoyed the company of elite women in the city, including the wives of Inspector Campbell and Major Tranchell.[49] Mahmud Fahmi's wife deployed her French with their missionary neighbors at Mount Lavinia while her husband set to work on translations of scripture and *Rollin's Ancient History of the Egyptians*, which served him for his extensive chronicle of world history, *al-Bahr al-zakhir*, largely based on Western books and published posthumously by a forgiving Egyptian state press in 1894–1895.[50] With their statements, women like ʿAynifer gave strong evidence of their status and education as they maintained links with Lady Gregory, coordinating parallel petitions in the names of their families addressed to the woman who sat, "as a Mother, and Grand Mother," on the most important throne in the world.[51]

Although he had fallen out with Blunt, Gregory abetted his wife's efforts and found agreement from successive governors who forwarded the many petitions, growing more morose and desperate. In June 1887, Yaʿqub Sami both thanked governor Arthur Gordon for ensuring the continuance of his allowance and bemoaned his ongoing presence in such a "strange land," where "the thought that I am a rebel tortures me."[52] Writing directly to Victoria that October, he and the two Fahmis pleaded "in our names as well as the names of our wives and children" for their families' repatriation, which was allowed in December 1888.[53]

As the months and years wore on, various policemen who oversaw the exiles would decry the waste of money spent observing the day-to-day inactivity of men who could have easily fled long before, and whose health was ultimately the subject of two hostile medical reviews. Perhaps the largest drain on police time were the hucksters and day-trippers who began to incorporate a visit to Elizabeth House, the home of the leading ex-pasha. Gregory already complained that ʿUrabi was a subject of secondary entertainment (after a nearby tortoise of great age) for various visitors—a fact not lost on Fahmi, who felt that passing Australians and tourists were no real substitute for earnest local Muslims.[54] One image from the *Illustrated London News* of 1889 showed a rather poorly drawn "Arabi Pasha" receiving a deputation of well-heeled visitors.[55] In such images there is little of the belligerent colonel without rank; instead, he appears in the suit and fez of a gentleman, reportedly "always pleasant and courteous ... resigned to his loss of power."[56] Not all such visits ended well, as Albert Gleaves (1858–1937) had found when he confessed to having witnessed the events at Alexandria as an observer for the U.S. Navy.[57] Gracious defeat had its limits.

Naval Gazing and Retreat to Kandy

The relative anonymity and dispersed locations of ʿUrabi's colleagues spared them the special harassment that he endured, which was at its worst when drunken crewmen from HMS *Bacchante* pushed past his police guard and hammered on his doors in April 1887, and not for the first time. As ʿUrabi complained, he had "too trouble for the sailors who always come at my house by dranking & wishs come inside without regards our costume, they braking the doors & beating on my servant."[58] Superintendent Tranchell would soon report that every time the Bacchante comes in the sailors give provocation to Arabi Effendi, and they will not listen to anybody. On Saturday last several of them went to Arabi Effendi's residence, scaled the gate and wanted to see Arabi Effendi, with some difficulty they were induced to leave. Yesterday when I was at Arabi's gate 3 carriages with passengers came to see Arabi, I told them these being the Effendi's fasting days he does not receive visitors & so they went away. I got a Sergeant and a Constable at the gate, but a Constable in uniform will be advisable when the Steamer is in the Harbour to keep the sailors away.[59]

On further inquiry, Inspector David reported to Tranchell that the men of the *Bacchante* were especially hostile, as they had "suffered severely in the Egyptian war," adding that "all English man of war's men take a delight in going to see Arabi Effendi and by their postures, grimaces and other antics testify to their satisfaction on seeing him in exile," which was naturally "extremely distasteful to Arabi Effendi."[60] David thus proposed stationing a European sentry at ʿUrabi's gate whenever such ships were at port, given that the sailors generally "beat all the natives they come across."[61] Tranchell could only request more European manpower for such circumstances, knowing that he would not receive it.[62] Instead—and as subsequent visitors would note—ʿUrabi's "native" guardsman would be replaced by a Sikh soldier, who followed the glum and greying exile wherever he went, peering at the ground in introspection.[63]

ʿUrabi is said to have affected this same manner a few weeks later when, to the chagrin of some Western observers, he, al-Barudi, Tulba, and ʿAbd al-ʿAl left the pavilion in which they were watching a parade in honor of Victoria's Golden Jubilee (June 20, 1887) and inserted themselves between a group of Siamese monks and the rest of the Muslim community, forming what one critic termed the "skeleton" at the jubilee feast, clad as they were in "sombre black" suits topped off by their red fezzes.[64] Questioned in the follow-up to the *Bacchante* incident, Campbell could report to the colonial secretary that some exiles had indeed joined the parade, "but at a little distance, to mark their good feeling towards Her Majesty."[65] The nonmarching Fahmis and Yaʿqub Sami—who earnestly resented being lumped in with ʿUrabi, and who emphasized their agency as individual gentlemen in the pages of the *Ceylon Observer*—also paid a visit to Governor Gordon three days later to congratulate the queen. They also went to "express their heartfelt thanks for their good treatment," which only earned a mix of cheers and laughter when it was reported in the British Parliament.[66]

Five years later, John Ferguson—the fervent Baptist proprietor of the *Ceylon Observer* and a former neighbor of Mahmud Fahmi at Mount Lavinia—would repackage things rather positively. Drawing on the same coverage of the day and correcting the names of the exilic attendees, he painted a variety spectacular that surely outdid that put on for Prince Alfred at the Cape nearly three decades earlier:

> About 25,000 human beings of all classes and races, the vast majority in bright garments ... were assembled round the centre where the Governor read the Record of the Chief Events of the Fifty Years.... High festival as it was, the quiet and orderly conduct of the crowd was the subject of emphatic and approving remark.... There were numerous processions of various races and religionists, including some seventy-seven Buddhist priests in bright yellow robes.... Salutes consisting of the cracking of long Kandyan whips were sources of curiosity to newcomers, while the chanting of both Malay and Sinhalese processions to well-known popular tunes produced much amusement. One of the most striking incidents of the day was the appearance of Arabi and three of his fellow exiles—Mahmood Samy, Toulba, and Abdulal, at the head of the Muhammaden procession. Their appearance imparted an element of romance to the proceedings, reminding one of those "Arabian Nights Tales," in which the Isle of Serendib figures prominently. The most fertile of imaginations could not, some years ago, have anticipated that a contingent of Egyptian officers, exiled to Ceylon for rebellion against their own sovereign, should take a voluntary part in celebrating the Jubilee of a Queen whose army had defeated the forces which they had led in insurrection, and so rendered abortive their ambitious (or patriotic?) designs.[67]

As Ferguson continued, correcting the reportage of his own paper, both Fahmis and Yaʿqub Sami had offered an address at Queen's House in Kandy, with a view to it being put before Victoria "with heartfelt loyalty":

> No one would deny that for the period of fifty years during which Her Majesty has uninterruptedly occupied the throne, Her Majesty has been just and merciful, and the brightness of her reign has reflected all over the world, and been a source of gratitude which we always feel in our hearts, and of which we are full.... We must confess that, in our position which is known to all, the pain in

the centre of our hearts, as strangers from our country, felt, has been removed since our stay in this country, by the prompt extension to us of relief and justice, by the many acts of kindness, humanity, and generosity done to us. All these acted as a remedy which cured the pain which we felt in our hearts, making room for our peace and comfort. We have indeed, therefore, special reason to be most sincerely loyal and faithful, and to humbly yield to the feelings and inclinations of our hearts. We beg, therefore, to lay at the foot of Her Majesty's throne our unbounded heartfelt thanks, and to offer the same to your Excellency, as Her Majesty's great Representative in this country, in which we enjoy favours and overflowing justice.[68]

While one might well raise an eyebrow with the members of Parliament as to whether the supplicants really held Victoria in such high regard, it is even less clear just what feelings they harbored for Abdulhamid, or what lingering affections for his caliphate were awakened by the arrival of his warship, the *Ertugrul*. When it docked at Colombo on November 1, 1889, the wooden-hulled frigate was headed to Japan to invest the Meiji emperor with a decoration. It was also intended to bring the caliphal banner into the waters of South and Southeast Asia.

The consul was evidently gratified by the interest showed by local notables at Ceylon, who toured the vessel during the week it was in port, just as their cobelievers had flocked aboard in Bombay.[69] Such reports of elite interest also aligned with largely favorable coverage in the English papers, which spoke of the landing of several hundred men to attend mosque services, and the appearance of English- and French-speaking officers at local events.[70] After it steamed off on November 7, word arrived of an extended stay at Singapore enforced by a lack of funds and equipment, leading some to denigrate a venture that had captured the imagination of Muslims in Southeast Asia.[71] The next that any Lankan would see of the mission was some sixty survivors being repatriated on two Japanese vessels in late 1891. With its Ottoman medal delivered, the *Ertugrul* had sunk in a typhoon off the coast of Honshu.

Whereas contemporary depictions often caricatured a generic "Arabi" driving out to the port in his carriage to look out at the ships of the harbor, he must have had enough of any oceanic reminders of his separation from home.[72] In May 1890, he and ʿAli Fahmi inquired as to where they were allowed to move on the island and were reminded that they were free to move anywhere save the (more escapable) northern and eastern provinces.[73] Gregory told Blunt that he had found an unhealthy ʿUrabi when he had visited in early 1890, and both would soon urge Cromer to recommend a pardon as a consequence, with Blunt offering to keep an eye on him at his estate near Cairo.[74] Gregory's sympathy was as much for ʿUrabi's company as his health, rejecting a later suggestion of Western Australia as an alternate site of residence. "The Ceylon climate is bad enough for them," exclaimed Gregory, "but to send them to a place where they would have no mosques and no co-religionists would be a terrible punishment."[75]

Encouraged by Gregory, Blunt, and the departing Gordon, ʿUrabi had joined most of the other exiles in a renewed push for clemency on medical grounds in May 1890, though Cromer was having none of it, just as Mahmud Fahmi—writing in 1891—scoffed at the idea that Ceylon's climate was so injurious to them in the first place and avoided their contact in favor of his studies of English, Tamil, and Sinhalese.[76] The only concession allowed by a medical board in October was that some of the exiles might move locally.[77] There were, after all, no worries on security grounds. The police had reported in late September 1890 that the exiles hardly seemed busy, while those who had already moved to Kandy (Mahmud and Yaʿqub Sami, now linked by marriage) were almost never seen.[78] After visiting ʿUrabi in November 1890, a member of the Foreign Office would reflect on their assumed leader's withdrawn state, proposing that he be allowed to make a visit to Bangalore. In his view it had all the advantages that the once "great bulk of a man" could wish for, from the "ride round the oblong maidân, Polo & Golf Ground, Lawn Tennis, gymkhana clubs, Us and native clubs, Libraries, Racecourse, Mosque, Mahomedans, 2 Magistrates 3 Municipal Commissioners. Several Mahomedan shopkeepers . . ."[79] Advantages indeed. He had even forgotten the new government museum (opened in 1877), with its collection of Hoysala statuary and, oddly enough, Burmese Buddhas and Malay krisses.[80]

ʿUrabi, though, would have had little interest in such entertainments as he, too, retreated up the hills to Kandy after 1892. This may have been due to the blandishments of Thomas Lipton (1848–1931), who had used him to advertise his famous tea and even offered him a sinecure as estate manager.[81] He had also found the infamous Egyptian in generally low spirits in 1891, and, as the latter told a typically sympathetic reporter who called on him in January 1892, the days of the exiles were "drawing to a close."[82] For if he played the part of the engaged patron to the Moorish community of Colombo, accompanying peers on medical visits, or joining Siddi Lebbai and Wapche Marikar once more to establish the Muslim Educational Society in 1891, the days were drawing short. The first shock came with the death of ʿAbd al-ʿAl in March of that year. Deemed to have died naturally of a cerebral hemorrhage, the government doctors were exonerated. This must have shocked the surviving exiles, especially Tulba and his wife, whose complaints had resulted in unsatisfactory offers of relocation to the Cape, Cyprus, and then British Somaliland.[83] Writing to a solicitous Anne Blunt in October 1892, ʿUrabi claimed to desire nothing more than to die at home.[84] Still, the prematurely aged and bent officer was doubtless happy to have his case kept in the British eye, with allies placing letters in the press and questions in Parliament. Hardly in agreement with Blunt, Cromer was less than eager for his return, worrying about a potential alliance between the nationalistic new khedive, ʿAbbas Hilmi, who had taken the throne in January 1892.[85]

Probably less hard to bear for ʿUrabi was the August 1894 death of Mahmud Fahmi, who suffered a stroke in 1892, though one biographer of Fahmi, relying on ʿUrabi's papers, argues that they were reconciled in the end, despite his subject's stated desire to be left alone by his peers.[86] And yet, despite all the privations and emotional separations, ʿUrabi continued to offer positive comment on Britain and its actions in Egypt, praising Cromer for enacting reforms that he suggested he would have carried out himself had he had the chance.[87] If such comments were intended to soften the latter's attitude, they fell on deaf ears. The days would drag on. June 1897 saw yet another jubilee come and go, though without a controversy at Colombo. While some of the Kandyan exiles and their remaining wives appealed to Victoria as a mother and a grandmother, ʿUrabi was at a distance from their efforts.[88] He was also by now estranged from his first son, whom he sued in court.[89]

Victoria most likely never saw the letters of congratulation for her jubilees, nor the petitions of the Kandyan transplants, though governor West Ridgeway sympathized with them and with Tulba's self-assessment that they were no longer the military leaders they once were, but "spirit-broken old men" seeking their end in Egypt.[90] Tulba was allowed to return in January 1899 while ʿUrabi and his surviving peers—their names mixed up with some of their dead colleagues—were told not to expect this to be some form of precedent.[91] Quietly confident, ʿUrabi pledged to keep his original word of honor, hoping that English public opinion would change and allow him to return home.[92]

It was more by virtue of relative indifference that most of the remaining exiles would be returned by ʿAbbas, save Yaʿqub Sami, who would die in October. ʿUrabi would be the last to go, notified with ʿAli Fahmi of his pardon in May 1901 and deluded that Cromer had interceded on his behalf with the khedive and Edward VII. Ironically, it was more the doing of Blunt and the newly crowned sovereign, who had been aboard the unscathed *Bacchante* when it toured Egypt and Ceylon in 1881 and had been refused any role in the expedition of 1882 by his mother. He had also just visited the island again on his return from Australia in April 1901.[93] Besides, one stray old Egyptian was hardly of concern when compared with hundreds of Boer prisoners sent to Ceylon after refusing to pledge their loyalty to Great Britain.[94]

At a banquet held in ʿUrabi's honor at Colombo in September, there were speeches delivered in Tamil and Arabic, with toasts to the king, the sultan, the khedive, and the governor. One local Muslim paper extolled his behavior of "loyal obedience to the ruling power."[95] ʿUrabi reportedly thanked king and khedive, as well as the lords and officials who had aided him.[96] He also declared that his heart would always be with the Ceylonese people who had given him such a warm welcome. Absent in this speech, apparently, was any reference to the caliph who had let him down so completely in 1882. And, as with his arrival in 1883, ʿUrabi hardly stood on the jetty alone. Among the crowd of well-wishers, his much-enlarged party of twenty-nine dependents, which had swollen to include four wives and fifteen children, was over half the size of the entire party that had come with the *Mareotis* over seventeen years earlier. But in place of his Egyptian servants, he took back the two local women and their many offspring—not to mention an attitude to the British empire that would perplex his fellow Egyptians, especially those who had since claimed the mantle of al-Hizb al-Watani.[97]

Shoeless Memories of a Pasha: Between a British Maharaja and an Ottoman Sultan

> It seems as if it were but yesterday, so fast does time fly, that a good proportion of [the Ceylon police] went barefooted, whether out of personal preference, or the parsimony of a niggardly Government, I cannot vouch for; but the fact remains that such an incongruity used to cause no little merriment to the Egyptian Pashas in Ceylon.
>
> —ALI FOAD TOULBA, 1926

Figure 8.2 Sydney Prior Hall (1842–1922), the Prince of Wales arriving in Colombo, Sri Lanka, December 1, 1875, Pencil | 16.2 x 24.5 cm | RCIN 931213, Royal Collection Trust / © Her Majesty Queen Elizabeth II 2021.

Looking back to the story of the seven effendis and their families today, there seems little to remind Sri Lankans of their visit, aside from certain lore about the contributions of ʿUrabi to the loyal "Mohammedan" society with which he was encouraged to affiliate. Even if Egyptian advice had been sought for the drafting of the marriage code of 1884, the most tangible edifice attesting to their presence remains that of Zahira College, established in 1893 with ʿUrabi as its honorary patron.[98] This is recalled in the displays about the fez-wearing exiles that are housed in a large home represented as ʿUrabi's final residence at Peradeniya, though the nameplate of a much smaller address up the hill bears the cryptic name "Abdin"—referencing the palace and surrounding suburb of Cairo to which he eventually returned. But, run with the support of the Egyptian embassy, the museum is more about placing the exiles in a lineage linking the pharaohs to Nasser (Gamal ʿAbd al-Nasir, 1918–1970), whose career echoed that of ʿUrabi.

Zahira College is famous today for its many graduates, who have excelled in all fields, and in "all" of the national languages, proudly donning school uniforms and identities linking Islam to the modern Sri Lankan nation. However, there is one group also associated with Zahira College whose presence hardly seems to have figured in the Egyptians' experience, or at least that which they recorded.[99] This is even more ironic because some of them were tasked to be within earshot in the first eight years of their banishment. At least two of the exiles lived in their midst at Slave Island. Whereas they still were deemed respectable and dependable, with many maintaining their ranks in retirement, most Ceylon Malays were seldom well-to-do in the 1880s. With the 1873 disbanding of the Ceylon Rifles—and the consoling foundation of their Malay Cricket Club, with the assistance of Major Tranchell—many had turned to employment as clerks for the railways developed under their former officer Major Skinner, or as policemen caricatured by Dort as shoeless and fez-wearing, with some often struggling to obtain their pensions.[100] There was also some irony in the latter regard, given that Skinner believed in his memoirs that the provision of European boots had led to the downfall of "the finest native regiment that any country ever possessed."[101]

Either way, they were ubiquitous and trusted, if often unremarked upon. A sketch for the 1876 visit of Prince Albert Edward focuses on a Malay sentry, his back to the throngs of "Tamils" looking to greet Victoria's son (see fig. 8.2).[102] The Malays also appear as bit players in the Lankan landscape during the exiles' sojourn, as when al-Barudi hired the Malay Dramatic Club to perform for Blunt during his 1883 visit, or when Malay musicians performed popular tunes separately from the designated Muslim marchers at Victoria's Golden Jubilee four years later.[103] In 1892, a correspondent to the *Graphic* remarked that the "clean and active, but short Malays" since transferred into the auxiliary Gun Lascars alongside Hindu and Christian Tamils were by then best known for their "great display during the Hussain Houssain festival [*sic*]."[104] This was the *tabut*, popularized by sepoys during Muharram festivals at garrison towns in Bencoolen and the Straits Settlements and then continued by the mostly Indian convicts who built Singapore.[105] Focused on the parading of replica coffins of the martyred Husayn, this had caused quite a stir in the anxious 1850s and 1860s, when it was accompanied by the same sorts of piercings that one would find in Capetown's *ratib* or the spectacles of Singapore and India, where some participants dressed as tigers.[106]

This was all in significant contrast to the pride of the earlier decades of the century, when Malay soldiers had been stalwarts of empire—deployable in theory from Egypt to Burma. In his public plea for ʿUrabi in late October 1882, Gregory had still seen fit to recommend Malays as the ideal bodyguard for a khedive who could depend on neither "native" troops nor drunken Englishman.[107] Despite Gregory's calling them "brave as lions" and having the "inestimable advantage of being Mohammedans," an editor of the *Ceylon Observer* noted that the Malay Regiment had been disbanded for reasons of poor recruitment, while the *Madras Mail* resurrected allegations of opium consumption and a propensity to run amok—perhaps even to reenact the horrors of 1857.[108] Marsden, Skinner, and Saldin would have been annoyed.

By the time of ʿUrabi's arrival, then, there were no Malay princes or active officers to greet him. Nor yet was there an assembly of wealthy Malay traders to match the Moors of the Pettah. Rather, their respectable but moderately remunerated community was riven between veterans and civilians, with the former being buried off Jawatte Road, close to what would become ʿUrabi's frequently disturbed bungalow. In 1887, an Australian journalist, Julian Thomas (1843–1896), mentioned in passing how ʿUrabi's Malay sentinel had checked his papers and doubted whether the "badger" (i.e., the pasha) would see him.[109] It bears thinking, too, that it had in all likelihood been this policeman or one of his peers who had been brushed aside by the crewmen of the *Bacchante*, to be replaced by a burly "Sikh," as was increasingly standard across the empire.[110] Again, if there was a Malay who could have rubbed shoulders with the Egyptian exiles and the Moorish elite, it would have been Baba Ounus Saldin, the print modernist and pious mystic whose diary records encounters with ʿAbd al-Qadir Jilani, ʿAli, and the Prophet himself.[111] Unfortunately, he said nothing of any inspiration from a morose Egyptian officer who claimed to be the latter's descendant, and who may well have frequented very different shaykhs than him.

Saldin would eventually recommence his activities as a publisher in October 1895, having played a key role in reconciling his community in 1886. Although ʿUrabi and his remaining colleagues had since settled in Kandy, where there was also a Malay presence, it remains curious once more that neither they nor their Moorish partners were mentioned in the pages of Saldin's new Jawi venture, *Wajah Selong*, even when the question of educational reform arose. Compared with its predecessor, *Wajah Selong* offered limited reportage of local Malay issues. Rather like the *Muslim Nesan*, whose editors praised Saldin for promoting Malay unity, *Wajah Selong* operated in a broader imperial milieu.[112] It was full of articles from the English-language presses of India, most often the *Muslim Chronicle*. But while readers would learn much of the conversions of Hindus and the activities of the "Church of Islam" at Calcutta, there was little attention to Moorish concerns across the lake, nor yet of Zahira College. In fact, the first school to gain attention in its pages was that of local, "praiseworthy Sinhalese" (*bangsa Cinggala yang dipuji*), who had bought a field for a new "madrasa to provide boys and girls with a proper Buddhist education, and in the face of missionary hostility."[113] This was also seen as an inspiration for a new Malay school for the Kampung Kertel and its wayward children. As the founders declared:

> We have no pretensions of big-noting ourselves, rather we are simply filled with longing when we see children doing nothing other than running and playing in the streets of the kampungs, or gawking at gambling dens, attending places where people sing, dance, and conjure. In the end they will come of age, trying to seek a livelihood, and decorating their clothes beyond their means. Then they will fall into the evil ways of the criminal, knowing nothing of the principles and rules of religion, not knowing how to distinguish right from wrong, nor good from evil.[114]

Like the *Muslim Nesan*, Saldin's *Wajah Selong* was linked to a wider network. Within weeks he boasted a set of Jawi Peranakan agents across the Bay of Bengal.[115] Saldin also had an eye to their markets, seeking agents for his exports of gems and manufactured articles, though he may not have anticipated being asked to export his opinion on matters affecting Malays in general, as when a writer from Perak sought to understand the relative understandings of status and rank in the British and Dutch territories. "Why don't the English have the institutions of the Hollanders?" he asked:

> Every person of rank that I see on Java or Sumatra has insignia. Whether among the Dutch or the indigenous people (*bumiputranya/anak negeri*) on Java—be they the Lord Susuhunan or Bupati or Amangkunegara or of a low rank like a Wedono and the like named with a rank of importance—all have insignia of having been appointed by the Dutch Government. It is not like this in these English lands (Straits Settlements) or the Malay lands. Be they a Sultan or Raja Muda, Bendahara

or Tumenggong, Panglima or Datu, or yet anyone of rank, we cannot know what they are as they all look the same as the subject little people of the population (the Orang Preman)! What is the reason for this Mr Editor?[116]

Having recommended that the British adopt a policy of uniforms for officials so that a grateful people could know who was high and who was low, the man of Perak signed off. Saldin had some sympathy for his position. He agreed that the common people could take their example from people of rank and added that the English *did* make such distinctions, as one could see from the officers of the military.

Saldin would later celebrate the military relationship in the first pages of his *Fayd al-Abad*, noting the actions on Ceylon of the "Malays and Jawa" from peninsular Kelantan to Singasari in East Java. He had also been interested in the example of an oft-uniformed Malay prince. This was the Tumenggong turned Maharaja and finally Sultan Abu Bakar of Johor, who had just died in London in June 1895. After the repatriation of his body by British warship, his September interment was reported in some detail. So, too, was a letter from his chief minister, expressing gratitude to Enci' Abu Salih bin al-Wahid and the "fellow Malays of Colombo" (*bangsa kita Melayu yang ada dalam negeri Kolombo*) for the condolences they had conveyed with clippings from the English press of the city.[117]

Such regard for a sultan who had been raised up by his connections to colonial capital, and who claimed excellent personal relations with Victoria herself, already speaks to the type of Malay ruler that Saldin admired. Loyal to the British Empire in his uniform, well traveled and connected, Abu Bakar of Johor would also be celebrated well after his death by Muslim reformers in Singapore, who also spent much time translating the ideas of 'Abduh and praising a modern Japan, which a curious Abu Bakar had visited in 1884.[118]

Abu Bakar was furthermore to be lauded for his connection, however belated, to Abdulhamid. Indeed Abu Bakar is now said to have visited both Sultans Abdulaziz and Abdulhamid in 1876 and 1893, respectively, returning on each occasion with a Circassian concubine.[119] As time would tell, Abu Bakar was to be contrasted with his heir, Ibrahim (1873–1959), who was apparently very interested in Ahmad 'Urabi, even inviting him to visit Johor in 1899, though Abu Bakar had also called on 'Urabi when passing through Colombo in 1885, so perhaps the offer was first made on that occasion.[120] The constraints of exile meant that 'Urabi could only send his third (very

Anglophone) son, Ibrahim Bey, who enjoyed a warm welcome in Kedah and Penang.[121]

We can only wonder what Saldin would have made of Abu Bakar's visit to ʿUrabi and, later, the young sultan's invitation. Indeed, we must wonder entirely, as there is no hint of the Egyptian in his writings. The indications are that he may have been something of a problem for Saldin, much as there was only one Muslim sovereign in the West that mattered to him. It is worth noting that when an opportunistic local British official was celebrated in *Wajah Selong* for having embraced Islam, his adopted name echoed that of the sultan, to whom all should now be bound.[122] At some point since the opening of the Suez Canal, Saldin had become a committed propagandist for Abdulhamid, often declaring him to be "our lord, Commander of the Faithful, the Sultan of Turkey"—the lord ʿUrabi had renounced by rebelling against Tawfiq and pledging himself to Great Britain in exile.

Even in the shortest reports of goings on at Istanbul—from lavish receptions with the innovation of women being present in English ballgowns to the announcement of honors and awards for officials and princes—Saldin cast Abdulhamid as the paramount ruler and friend to all his subjects throughout his domains, regardless of faith.[123] This would become an increasingly difficult proposition as news filtered through the European presses of atrocities committed against Armenians in the course of 1896. Saldin held firmly to the line frequently advanced in Indian Muslim papers that Abdulhamid was a source of succor to all, distributing bibles on the Christian frontier and cheered by his invincible soldiers in the subsequent war of 1897, where Muslim soldiers could pray unharmed by a hail of "Greek" bullets.[124]

Strangely, too, there is no sense of fellowship in Saldin's paper for the aspirant Ottoman subjects of Aceh, who were still engaged in their conflict with the Netherlands. One issue merely had a brief report of an ill soldier running amok in the Dutch ranks and wounding his surprisingly forgiving commander.[125] The editors of *Muslim Nesan* seem to have had a similarly colonially inflected view of the conflict, drawing on news from Penang in 1885 to imply that the Aceh War was but child's play compared with the turmoil roiling the Sudan. It seems that Egyptian soldiers and Malay rebels were deemed no match for the more clearly "Arab" forces of the Mahdi. The latter view soon found its way back to allied Tamil papers of Singapore such as *Singai Nesan*. By comparison, the Malay-language *Jawi Peranakan* of

Singapore was either less interested in the affairs of Sudan and Egypt or less questioning of the official narrative of events as it extolled the merits of British troops.[126]

The strongest argument that can be made for the relative lack of Lankan Malay interest in the dwindling group of effendis, though, can be seen in Saldin's coverage of Egypt itself. The veiled protectorate was only ever presented as the most loyal, grateful, and active part of the Ottoman domains—whether reporting the receipt of imperial awards and medals by ʿAbbas and his officials, or their sending of silver for the Greek campaigns. Yet Cairo had changed. And if a party of Sumatran visitors who had visited that city had apparently found nothing major worth remarking on when they had made a tour of its saintly graves soon after ʿUrabi's banishment, by the time of his 1901 return new scholarly tourists were making their way from Johor and Riau to a city they associated far more intimately with ʿAbduh, who had endured his own brief exile in Europe and Lebanon before returning in 1888.[127] Some such visitors were drawn to the salon of the young nationalist protégé of ʿAbbas, Mustafa Kamil, editor of *al-Liwa'* and leader of the new *Hizb al-Watani* from its inception in 1907, but few "Malays" bothered with his much grayed forebear or what he might have said of his place of banishment.

On first inspection it is frustrating that so little is published about ʿUrabi in Lanka that goes beyond the bounds of British government files and the writings of Blunt.[128] Few of the published memoirs of the exiles make much mention of events after the trials of late 1882. Barudi preferred to concentrate on elegiac poetry, for he lost a wife and several children on Lanka (rather like the unlucky Saldin), while he cemented his reputation as the "master of sword and pen" before his return, blind, in 1899.[129] An obvious candidate is the memoir of ʿUrabi himself, started in prison, with the first part sent from Colombo in 1883, though a later version features a coda that breezes past his years of exile to reflect on the generosity of the then Duke of York, the sultan, the khedive, and his abiding love for the Egyptian people.[130] Mahmud Fahmi is the real exception, though he buried his dyspeptic account of their travails in a few pages of his *Bahr al-zakhir*, which was otherwise dedicated to explaining the achievements of (largely Western) nations that had preserved the territorial integrity of their respective homelands. Indeed, in these passages, oddly republished with ʿUrabi's cursory notes in 1976, Fahmi made plain the gullibility of ʿUrabi and the hypochondrial efforts of most of the exiles who had so strategically moved their homes close to the governor's residence in Kandy.[131]

Unaware of his own impending demise, Fahmi was certainly cynical about the estranged and supposedly sickening Tulba, writing his history and perhaps even advising on local rail and bridge projects—affirming his nickname "Engineer Pasha" in Muhammad 'Awda's short story of 1971.[132] Tulba can't have complained too loudly at home. In 1926 his son nostalgically cast Ceylon as "the Garden of Adam," a site of wondrous return and the staging ground for imperial tolerance worthy of emulation.[133] It was just this position that 'Urabi took on his return to Egypt, very much to the surprise of old allies and new watchers. In October 1901, James Rennell Rodd (1858–1941) had reported the arrival of the once towering colonel, first greeted more by curiosity than adulation. Some even hissed at him after granting an interview to the Syrian-dominated and pro-British *al-Muqattam*, with various other papers complaining, in line with Kamil, that he had "brought about the British occupation and betrayed the Moslem cause."[134] This view would later prevail, though it had had to be enforced by the new claimants to the defense of the watan, as we shall see. Rather than quickly falling into obscurity, 'Urabi received numerous visitors from the emerging middle class, accompanied by throngs when he went to prayers at the mosque of Sayyida Zaynab. As at Colombo in the early days, many commoners gathered to see him and even to touch the hem of his clothes. 'Urabi maintained the position of pious subjecthood throughout, praising the British, to the evident confusion of some. When questioned as to the position of Muslims in India, he reportedly "gave his own experiences in Ceylon, and enthused about the broad spirit of toleration which prevailed in the British Empire, and the perfect freedom enjoyed by all religions, whether Moslem, Buddhist or Christian." As a bemused Rennell Rodd went on:

> Arabi himself, although a commonplace individual of no particular gifts or powers, appears to have preserved, or perhaps rather acquired since his exile, with the middle and lower classes of Egypt, a kind of legendary reputation as the advocate of their cause and the champion of their liberties against the old oligarchy of the foreign Pashas. As such he appears to enjoy, for the present at any rate, a great popularity which has much impressed the impartial observer.
>
> These facts have not failed to attract the attention of the Palace, where the notice given to Arabi is viewed with great jealousy, especially as he now appears

in the character of the most ardent supporter of the British occupation, which has, he says, brought about all the dreams of his ambition. This jealousy reveals itself in the liberal abuse bestowed upon him by the native papers which support the Palace, and reflect the views of so-called patriots of the Mustapha Kamel type. Emissaries have been sent to the most important persons who have frequented Arabi, as well as to the Ulema of the El-Azhar University, who, strange to say, appear to have paid some attention to the former leader of rebellion, recommending that such visits should be discontinued.[135]

The nationalists sponsored by the khedive spurned the aged revolutionary as an embarrassment and played a key role in consigning him to history as a failure—indeed, as the very cause of British intervention.[136] While ʿUrabi continued to entertain Western visitors and remained on good terms with Blunt, the latter focused his attention on his sometime neighbor and critic of Kamil, Muhammad ʿAbduh, who had quietly supported ʿUrabi's return, but was soon embarrassed by his old comrade's praise of Great Britain that went far beyond his own cautiously collaborative attitude.[137] Indeed, more and more students from abroad sidestepped ʿUrabi and sought out Kamil as the (still Ottoman) advocate of the watan or ʿAbduh as the propagandist for a reformed Muslim *umma*. Elevated to the rank of grand mufti in 1899, ʿAbduh's global image was further amplified by his Syrian acolyte Muhammad Rashid Rida (1865-1935), whose journal *al-Manar* boasted readers from West Africa to Java after its establishment in 1898. Again, if there is material in its pages about issues in Southeast Asia, and a set of fatwas for Muslims in the Transvaal in 1903, there was little specifically about Ceylon and its Muslims, let alone the Malays of that island—even counting the poetry of al-Barudi.[138]

In the mid-1920s, the Anglophile and Ceylon-educated son of Tulba—who had nothing to say about ʿUrabi having been the cause of his father's exile or their poor relationship on the island—would reflect on the exemplary Malay "bobbies" of the island to which he returned as English redactor to the cabinet of King Fuʾad (r. 1917-1936):

> I wonder whether the Ceylon policeman has ever heard of that Gilberitan expression "A policeman's lot is not a happy one," and if so, whether he concurs in it. As far as appearances go it seems that he disagrees with it, else why should his offspring be ever so anxious to follow in the footsteps of their father, and to take

so enthusiastically after his vocation. The very sight of a young "Bobby" in embryo, as with cap tilted at a rakish angle, and a self-assumed martial air he struts about, causes no little amusement.... The Ceylon policeman, often a Malay, is a credit to the island. Well-built and wiry, like the neighbouring Gurkha, but trim and well-shod.[139]

In a way, one might say that the ongoing commitment to empire of these well-shod functionaries had impeded the early flow of Islamic nationalism, or at least delayed its onset among their regal kin on the Malay Peninsula. One can also only wonder just what sort of welcome ʿUrabi might have received at the Cape from the uncrowned princes of Bo-Kaap had he had the relative fortune to be sent there. For the moment, it was not yet Kamilian nationalism versed in the watan but, rather, the overarching commitments to the caliphate and religious reform for a colonized umma that would circulate between Cairo, Bombay, Colombo, Singapore, and Batavia. To examine this story as it played out in the Jawi lands, we shall now turn back to diasporic Arabs as much as to itinerant Malays and Javanese, to see that an enthusiasm for all things Ottoman could be articulated by people whose lives were never regulated by the Sublime Porte or its fractious vassals.

PART THREE
Eastern Returns

NINE

A Caliph for Greater Java

IN EARLY 1865—while Abu Bakr Effendi was getting bogged down in polemics at Cape Town and as Hussein Lebbe adjusted to his elevation at Colombo—yet another Ottoman appointee to the Indian Ocean world would descend into a waiting lighter to be taken the last mile or so to the customs station of the walled and humid town of Jeddah. The son of the late ʿUmar al-Junayd (1792–1854), who had arrived in Singapore from Palembang back in 1821, ʿAbdallah al-Junayd had followed in his father's footsteps as a trader in the Jawi lands, expanding the family's extensive portfolio of land holdings. Wealthy and respected by the British authorities, he was also a philanthropist—like his father and an equally well-known uncle back in Hadramawt.[1] In 1855, for instance, he renovated Singapore's Kampong Melaka Mosque, which ʿUmar had founded. Ten years on, the eminent mercer planned to go to Istanbul to be formally invested as the first Ottoman representative to his natal city. But first he wanted to undertake the hajj, the culminating fifth pillar of Islam.

Jeddah, then a town of twenty thousand processing an unusually large body of pious arrivals, would not then have seemed quite the perilous place it once was, at least politically. The Wahhabis and their Egyptian vanquishers may have been long gone, but only seven years earlier local merchants—many of them Hadrami—had fomented riots over increasing limitations on the slave trade. This precipitated a massacre of Western consular staff, their mediators, and Indian allies, not to mention a nascent community of Greeks and Armenians.² By 1865, however, the representatives of Great Britain and France were back in action, mainly to stamp the passports of people like ʿAbdallah and the increasing numbers of arrivals from South and Southeast Asia, but also to keep an ear out for occasional news of potential insurgents like Sayyid Fadl of Malabar, whom the British had blamed for the massacre. At the same time, other elite Arabs with strong Britannic connections, like Sayyid Muhammad al-Saqqaf (Mohamed Alsagoff, 1836–1906), also of Singapore, were expanding into the business of shipping pilgrims.³ Alsagoff's family was starting to develop a monopoly over water distribution in the Hijaz that had once been piped into the town in the 1850s after interventions by the former head of the guild of merchants, Faraj Yusr (d. 1873), an Ottoman subject of Indian origin who had operated his ships under the Union Jack and had therefore been targeted in 1858.⁴

With his passport duly stamped in British Singapore and now by the Ottoman authorities in Jeddah, Sayyid ʿAbdallah might have looked forward to finding a guide to convey him to the holy places of Mecca, which lay a further night's journey ahead by caravan. Although he had relatives in the Hijaz, he would have arranged to do this in the company of some of the Jawi people from his steamer. Such an itinerary may well have doomed him. While a brief notice in the *Law Reports* of 1865 does not record what ship he originally took, or how he died in Mecca in May, his demise coincided with that of fifteen thousand pilgrims (out of a record ninety thousand visitors) who succumbed to cholera that year.⁵ In at least one instance reported that season, the disease had been brought to Jeddah on Singaporean ships that had stopped at already-infected Mukalla. At the conclusion of the hajj, cholera would spread back to India, North Africa, and Europe at disastrous levels. Soon thereafter a new era of sanitation and control would bind the steam-powered empires—Ottoman, French, British, and Dutch—in an unhappy embrace threaded by the Suez Canal.⁶

The new era would also herald greater efforts by the avowed protectors of the holy places to live up to the hopes of the Muslims of India and the surrounding ocean. Those of "Jawa" were eventually seen as a particularly important constituency, yet they were often represented at the highest levels by the Arabs who lived among them, and more especially by those Arabs who could claim descent from the Prophet, like Sayyid ʿAbdallah. It was in many ways a time of steam and sayyids as much as steam and print.⁷ As such, this chapter will focus on the inverse story of Indian Ocean connections involving the Jawa/Malays, tracking the movements of people who identified themselves, or who were seen by others, as Arabs—and, moreover, as the faithful representatives of claims to the caliphate vested in Istanbul and proven in Mecca. It is, furthermore, the first chapter to foreground the return "home," in the final third of this book, although the actors are once again imbued with more than one sense of place, more than one idea of belonging. For many, the ideas of an Ottoman caliphate and Pan-Asianist solidarity offered intersecting rubrics under which to place discussions of nation and religion as compared with Western empire, as much of the Indies slowly became Indonesia—and as some Malays and Arabs became Indonesians, too.

The Indies and Its Arabs

By the end of the nineteenth century, large swathes of what the naturalist Alfred Russel Wallace designated as "the Malay Archipelago" in 1869, affirming Marsden's revised usage of 1811, would be subordinated to the reborn Kingdom of the Netherlands.[8] Reconstituted at the end of the Napoleonic Wars in 1813, the Dutch state had reunited with the most easterly of the VOC's former Asian possessions following Raffles's reluctant withdrawal from Java in 1816. With the ongoing rise to dominance in India of the EIC, the Dutch had rushed to establish more direct control over what they deemed their own India, albeit a second-class one, reached after passing the surrendered hubs of Cape Town and Ceylon, and often on ships that were connected to British capital. Ultimately stretching 2,200 miles eastward from what would prove to be the restive gateway province of Aceh, the Dutch well knew that most of their new subjects—and those of the many client rulers with whom they made agreements—were Muslims. They would also become aware of the need to engage more directly with these peoples, if under pressure from an intersecting mixture of missionaries, who had hoped to find fresh fields for conversion in the absence of the VOC and the revolutionary Batavians, as well as social reformers who felt it was no longer enough to merely demand ever increasing profits from an economy dominated by the sugar industry after 1830.

There were, of course, other products of the plantation sector—most notably coffee, tobacco, and indigo—in addition to the copper, tin, and coal extracted by mining. From the 1850s, many of these industries claimed spaces along coasts designated as Malay and their heterogeneous hinterlands, drawing bonded laborers from Java, the Straits Settlements, and Southern China. Such demands only increased once the Netherlands opened up its colonies to private capital in 1870, dealing a death blow to an interlocking system of agrarian dynasties and trading networks that channeled Sumatran goods into the world system. Worried Malay rajas would write to Istanbul, while millenarian movements in West Java looked to Mecca for guidance from the ulama. This was not lost on the Dutch. The increasing prominence of returned pilgrims, and ever more migrants from the reclaimed Ottoman provinces of the Hijaz, Yemen, and (most tenuously) Hadramawt would cause the authorities to establish a consulate in Jeddah in 1872 followed by an advisory post to the colonial state at Batavia.

The first formally accredited advisor on Muslim legal affairs in the Indies was the lawyer L. W. C. van den Berg (1845–1927). A translator of legal texts for colonial officials, he gained the role in 1878 and worked closely with many local Arabs, including the famous printer and polemicist Sayyid ʿUthman b. Yahya, producing a much-read report on their place in the Dutch colonies in 1886.[9] After he vacated his post in 1887 to pursue a career in Holland, Van den Berg's role slowly transformed into the Office for Native Affairs (Het Kantoor voor Inlandsche Zaken, or KIZ). It would have much to do. The twentieth century would herald what many activists called "an age in motion" (*zaman pergerakan*), based on the ubiquitous Malay verb for movement—*gerak*—when societies, schools, and newspapers became the foundational elements of a new national public sphere that was often framed with reference to Islam as a shared identity.[10]

Yet, well before that time, the functionaries of KIZ, especially those under the critical eye of its long-standing director and former sojourner in the Hijaz, Christiaan Snouck Hurgronje (1857–1936), would spill much ink seeking to counter the aspirations and rising influence of a series of Ottoman enthusiasts, many of whom came from the late ʿAbdallah Junayd's network. These Arabs, whose leaders also claimed descent from the Prophet Muhammad, had generally done well under the Union Jack. As we have already noted, Muhammad al-Saqqaf facilitated the hajj from Singapore and drew seasonal labor to a plantation of his own on nearby Kukup Island in Johor, ruled from 1862 by the upwardly mobile Tumenggong (later Maharaja) Abu Bakar, eulogized in the pages of *Wajah Selong* in 1895. But if Hadrami prestige and capital found ready purchase in the Hijaz, Straits Settlements, and Malay sultanates of the peninsula, the situation was far more constrained under the Dutch on Sumatra and Java, given their anxieties about both Islamic and British ambitions.

The Ottomans had first negotiated at The Hague in 1856–1857 to place a consul in the Dutch colonies, to no avail.[11] Rather, it was in keeping with the later moment of Capetonian and Lankan engagement with an allied British Empire that the Sublime Porte gained a representative in a region bemused Ottoman officials called "Java" or sometimes even "Hind" and, eventually, "Malayzia." In June 1864, Musurus Pasha had nominated ʿAbdallah al-Junayd as consul in Singapore. "Obedient and loyal to the Imperial Sultanate," Junayd was appointed in September once his nomination had been confirmed by the foreign secretary, Earl Russell.[12] Perhaps Russell felt he had had little choice. The Junayds had well-established bona fides with Great Britain from the days of Raffles. Before his 1854 death, ʿUmar had proposed supervising the "mosques and priests" of Singapore for the authorities.[13] Moreover, the original request for the elevation of ʿUmar's ill-fated son had been made at the suggestion of Lord Stanley (1826–1893), a former secretary of state for the colonies and son of a two-time prime minister.

Not that any of this would serve as an effective precedent for the Dutch, who would continue to resist the suggestion that there were any Ottoman protégés to be found in the islands under their jurisdiction. The first person to test such possibilities was a Dutch trader at Semarang who was already serving as consul of the Grand Duchy of Baden in 1865. Despite his claims that "the native and immigrant Muslims" with whom he interacted had often expressed "their desire for the appointment of an official by the Imperial Sultanate," nothing came of the attempt.[14]

Admittedly, little formal acknowledgment resulted from the Singaporean post either. Having apprised the Porte of ʿAbdallah's demise, his brother Junayd al-Junayd continued to occupy the position of informal advisor, as when he reported Ottoman shipping arrivals at Singapore in February 1866.[15] Still, no move was made to confirm him in the position, due to trenchant Dutch objections. To be sure, the arrivals of Ottoman vessels or even suspiciously stray Ottomans were of interest to the Dutch, given Singapore's mercantile links to Aceh. Its beleaguered sultan, Mansur Shah, was looking to Istanbul once more for help, sending another Junayd—Shaykh Muhammad b. Ahmad—to the Hijaz as his emissary in 1868. Istanbul apparently remained

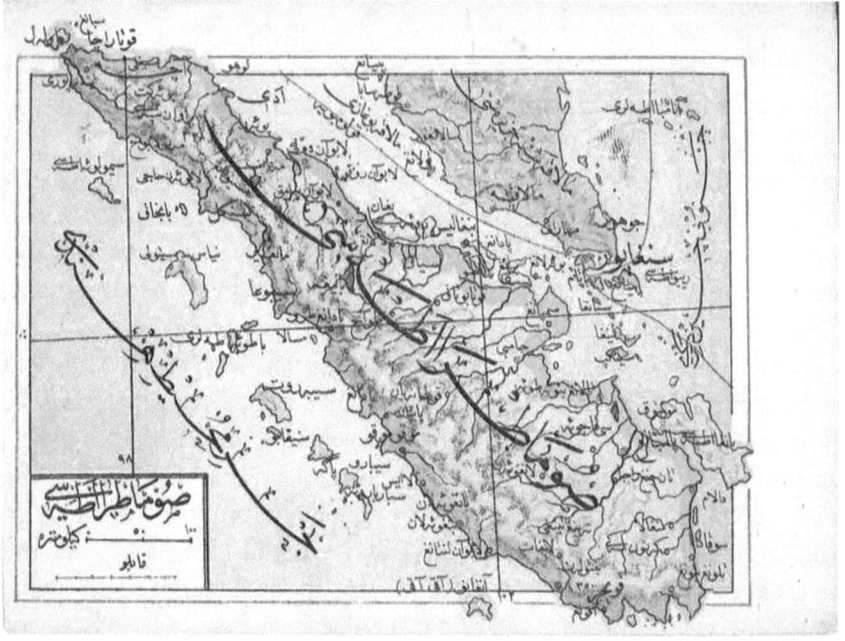

Figure 9.1 Ottoman map of Sumatra, ca. 1900. Collection of the author.

confused about his distant Jawi kingdom, ransacking their files for evidence of the tributary relationship to which the Acehnese so insistently referred.[16] In 1868 or 1869, ʿAli Junayd, who had returned to Arabia by 1863, was prevailed upon to provide information about Aceh to the Porte.[17]

Beyond engaging the Junayd clan, Sultan Mansur Shah was actively recruiting agents from among the wider network of sayyids with links to Southern India. This culminated with his promotion of the forceful Habib ʿAbd al-Rahman al-Zahir al-Saqqaf, who had moved to the region via Malabar and Hyderabad and served as advisor to the young Abu Bakar of Johor from 1862. Rising rapidly through the ranks at Aceh after 1864, the Habib—as he was better known—acted as coregent to Mansur's successor, Mahmud Shah (r. 1870–1874), who dispatched him as his emissary to the Porte in the face of Dutch threats. He was actually en route for Istanbul when the Dutch launched their invasion in March 1873.

As we have already seen with the long-forgotten message sent to Istanbul by the displaced sultan of Kedah in 1824, well-to-do Arabs like the Junayds and the Habib were obvious interlocutors for Southeast Asian rulers wishing to (re)connect with the ancient seat of Rum, as some called it, despite the empire's historic failures to aid them in ages past. When a Dutch mission had come to the Achenese capital in 1871, the Habib had donned a Turkish sword, and the Mecidiye medal that had been presented to the late Mansur Shah for his generosity in the Crimean War.[18] Perhaps the Habib felt such sartorial claims were his due and that he was already Ottoman. After all, the Porte claimed his ancestral home of Hadramawt, whose harbors functioned as a sometimes choleric gateway to Arabia. After arriving at Istanbul on an Egyptian ship in late April 1873, he spent eight fruitless months at the Ottoman capital, much as Muhammad Ghawth had in the 1850s. Having briefly excited the press, which reported the imminent dispatch of Ottoman warships, he would return to the Indian Ocean arena in 1874 with little more than a Mecidiye medal of his own.[19] Still, he tried to plead the Acehnese case, cajoling officials at Singapore and Penang in between stints in Kedah and Malabar, where he had married a woman related to Sayyid Fadl.[20]

Singapore would also become a useful outpost for waving the Ottoman banner once the opening of the Suez Canal saw a major increase in shipping via Aden, Bombay, and Colombo. Still, the cash-strapped and militarily beset Turks remained cautious. There had still been no official replacement for ʿAbdallah Junayd in April 1871, when Teuku Muhammad Arifin wrote to Istanbul requesting the post, claiming connections to once British Bencoolen and ambassadorial experience representing the sultan of Terengganu at London two years earlier.[21] He met with no success in the year that England and Holland agreed to end all pretense of recognizing Acehnese sovereignty. Finally acting on the petitions of the somewhat embarrassing Habib, whose articles about naval assistance in the Ottoman press were retracted, and numerous Acehnese at Mecca, who copied out the petition of the late Mansur Shah, Istanbul had offered to mediate in the conflict in September 1873. This was rebuffed by the Dutch with a condescending note that the relations between the Porte and Aceh were hardly vital.[22]

Despite the insults, the Ottomans would push on. Junayd al-Junayd, since linked to the returned Habib through marriage in 1874, would be formally nominated as consul to Singapore in 1882, but without success, just as the Dutch still tried to block a similar appointment in Batavia in that year.[23] It was by now nine years after the Acehnese state had fallen, initiating a guerilla conflict that would continue for three decades, and four years after the Habib and his family had been packed off to Mecca in late 1878 on a Dutch pension that limited his residence to Arabia.[24] In many ways the Habib was an analogue of his reputed kinsman by marriage Sayyid Fadl, at Dhofar when he arrived in the Hijaz. Echoing feelings at Malabar in the 1850s, too, the reduction of the Acehnese court and the dispatch of the Habib had been to the chagrin of many Arab traders at Singapore, and, more especially, their locally born sons, who had had no direct experience of Ottoman rule. Some were starting to look for Istanbul's help to solve their predicament of restricted movement in the Dutch colonies.

Yet they were not the only ones looking to the Ottomans. The impending change of Muslim century (coinciding with November 1, 1883) saw many Malays and Javanese invest in millenarian stories of an agreement hatched between the caliph and the sharif of Mecca to remove European control from their lands.[25] Moreover, given Great Britain's evident perfidy in allowing the Dutch annexation of Aceh and in abandoning Abdulhamid to the Russians, Malay and Acehnese accounts of the Russo-Turkish War of 1877–1878 understandably painted the English as an enemy or as indifferent bystanders. One popular account had General Muhammad Shamwili testing magical weapons on a "stupid" British soldier before taking them into the field against the tsar.[26] Certainly, the colonial files of the early 1880s were filled with news of wonder weapons and conspiracies that aligned with alarmist reports coming from Arabia. As we saw from Blunt's correspondence, James Zohrab at Jeddah had reported numerous Ottoman plots and intrigues. Likewise, the Dutch consul whose operation Blunt admired would deliver various unsubstantiated rumors of Pan-Islamic intrigues from his own network of informants. These included claims from the Habib himself concerning the role of a "fanatical" Mansur al-Junayd of Batavia, the shipping of weapons and Egyptian artillery experts to Aceh, and the allegation that Ahmad ʿUrabi had sent his Afghan agent to the Indies.[27]

The presence in Southeast Asia of a retired Turkish officer or two at Palembang in 1881, and then parties of Meccan shaykhs headed to Singapore and Java in 1882, led the Dutch and their local British allies to act aggressively to expel many Ottoman Arabs or deny others entry.[28] The idea of global Muslim unity (al-ittihad al-islami), so recently glossed as "Pan-Islamism," was emerging as a potential threat, and Abdulhamid was assumed to be its devious manipulator, ready to unleash jihad if his wishes were not respected.[29]

However, given that such claims were soon proven exaggerated—rumors in Egypt revolved around ʿUrabi displacing the sultan as a sort of Arab king—the Dutch were finally forced to acquiesce at last to the placement of an Ottoman consul.[30] The Hague had moreover become anxious about Istanbul's hardened resolve to deny reciprocal accreditation to its diplomats. Some of Abdulhamid's servants were now convinced that something needed to be done to counteract "the oppression of the Dutch state against the Muslims on the island of Java."[31] After the Dutch played for time by rejecting the credentials of an Arab trader from Baghdad, the Porte would insist on sending Ghalib Bey Effendi, a well-regarded clerk working in the translation office.[32]

Ottoman Consuls to Greater Java

Ghalib Bey arrived at Batavia in June 1883, five months after ʿUrabi was consigned to Colombo. Despite British apprehensions of ʿUrabi's having official Ottoman friends, Ghalib does not seem to have called on the rebel and former holder of the Mecidiye medal on his way out east. That October Ghalib was invested with a Mecidiye medal of his own to help bolster his status among the decorati.[33] He would also receive a continuous stream of Arab visitors in the tropical Dutch capital and confirm with his own eyes that many locally domiciled and officially Foreign Orientals were forced to maintain their homes in particular cantonments and to obtain travel permits for visits to other parts of the archipelago.

In his first report to Istanbul on June 25, 1883, two decades after Abu Bakr Effendi had written from the Cape, the gratified Ghalib reported how, regardless of the absence of the leading sayyids of the city (and here we can assume the nonappearance of Sayyid ʿUthman), he had been thronged by local Arabs. None was more enthusiastic than Sayyid ʿAbd al-Rahman Ba Junayd, son of the late ʿAbdallah. Following his inspection of the explicitly Arab-led mosques of Batavia, Ghalib Bey was also able to assure his masters that the caliph's name had been invoked for the first time on Friday, June 22. A meaningful connection had been made.[34]

Yet, in the same week that Ghalib Bey saw to the promulgation of Abdulhamid's name in the Arab mosques of Batavia, he also sought confirmation that the many local Hadramis were to be afforded Ottoman protection.[35] Bearing in mind the fragmented state of Hadramawt itself, Istanbul realized that it needed to reassert its relationship with the shrinking hinterland dynasty of the Kathiri sultan, Mansur b. Ghalib of Sayʾun (r. 1880–1929), who was engaged in a struggle with Quʿayti Mukalla. Then under Sultan ʿAbdallah b. ʿUmar al-Quʿayti (r. 1882–88), the once choleric port was on its way to becoming a British protectorate in 1888.

With Aden already in British hands since 1839, the Ottoman presence in Southern Arabia was shrinking. This had created the possibility of British Indian Arabs and undermined the idea of Ottoman Hadramis; hence the plaintiffs of Southeast Asia were a most useful quantity. While the Dutch would never countenance the notion that Indies-bound or resident Hadramis were Ottoman subjects, Ghalib Bey offered them passports anyway. And even if these were seldom honored at the docks, some of the Dutch evidently gave him a welcome.[36]

Ghalib was repatriated in 1886 due to his "inability to adapt to the climate of that place," though he can't have been viewed as a failure, as he was soon rewarded with the more important post of Bombay.[37] Once there he sent a long history back to Istanbul, reporting that all of the "Indian Islands" were "colonies of the Dutch state with the approval of Britain," and that its majoritarian "Javanese" were "mild-mannered" if "prone to debauchery," even as they performed their prayers regularly.[38] To Ghalib's mind, the fault for Javanese failings—including their reluctance to don the veil—was entirely Dutch. Meanwhile, the valiant resistance, aside from the Acehnese, was entirely Arab, and thus the subject of determined oppression. As Ghalib put it, the Dutch state was eager to counteract any possible sedition against them, especially on the part of religion. Since Arabs were of the same Shafiʿi disposition, he alleged that they were "not allowed onto the islands," especially if they were religious scholars, effectively dooming the local people to ignorance.[39]

While it was not true that Arabs were always excluded from the archipelago—though a party had famously been blocked at the height of the panic of 1882—it is fair to say that many urban Hadramis were starting to invest in very Ottoman hope for uplift. As Ghalib reminisced happily:

> When I arrived at my station . . . the exalted name of our lord the exalted Caliph, the most just Sultan-Protector of religion and the ever-fair King of Kings was mentioned [in the Arab mosque] with a complete desire and longing, and the Muslims present were very happy and prostrated themselves in gratitude.

During the following Friday prayers, the other mosques throughout Batavia followed suit and read the sermons in the most noble name of the most exalted Commander of the Faithful, the Caliph of God on Earth, His Majesty our most exalted Sultan. A few days later, a number of the residents of Batavia applied one after the other to the consulate, each professing their knowledge of the glory and greatness of our lord, His Majesty the Caliph of God on Earth, and requesting imperial salvation by petitioning to be granted subject status.[40]

Batavia was not the only site of Ottoman interest and rhetoric. Recall that the Arabs had not been the original supplicants to the caliphate, but rather the messengers of the imperiled princes of the Malay Peninsula and Sumatra. It is thus surprising that Ghalib was able to arrange a visit alongside the Dutch governor to the restive territory of Aceh and the Friday Mosque of Kuta Raja (built with monies raised by the Habib), where so many locals "pretended to obey the Dutch," and where the Ottoman consul once more cast himself as the harbinger of Abdulhamid's name:

> They shed tears and prayed rising their hands and their voices whilst saying "amen" when the exalted name of the Caliph was mentioned in the sermon for the first time. Thirty years ago, the Imperial Government and the Dutch state signed an agreement concerning the appointment of consuls from the Imperial Sultanate to the Dutch colonies. It was only in the year 1883 that it was deemed necessary, and a consul was appointed for the first time. Through this, the millions of Muslims residing on the Indian Islands will strengthen their connection and loyalty to the Caliph, further connecting the Muslims of this quarter of the Earth with the wider nation of Muhammad. This is one of the signs of the fruits of the reign of the World-Holder, and of the exalted success of His Imperial Majesty's deeds.[41]

Ghalib Bey's replacement was Rifki Bey, who continued to do his imperial duty and forward information on aspirant vassals, once more summarizing Aceh's history of relations with the Porte.[42] Aceh had certainly remained a contentious subject during Rifki's tenure with the arrival at Singapore in late 1889 of the *Ertugrul*. The Ottoman banner and crew made a strong impression on local Muslims, who eagerly sought tours of the vessel, just as their fellow believers had in Bombay and Colombo. Unlike at Ceylon, though, some also sought to hand over letters of grievance to captain Osman Pasha. These were primarily directed against the Netherlands, but there were also complaints against Great Britain and Siam.[43]

There were many Jawi requests for Ottoman aid, some too late for the *Ertugrul*, others interdicted. Still others expressed hope that the frigate would stop in at various ports on the way back from Japan, or even to acknowledge that they were Muslim in the first place. Abu Bakar, the Anglophile sultan of Johor once advised by the Habib, complained to Blunt at Cairo in early April 1893 that Osman Pasha had seemed unaware till the last moment that his state was even a Muslim one.[44] In this sense, history repeated itself. When she had first met Abu Bakar in 1878, Victoria had apparently thought Johor was in Ceylon, or that this independent prince came from somewhere near India.[45]

The Hague was alarmed by the prospect of an Ottoman landfall in Aceh, though the Dutch need not have worried. By this time the Ottoman ambassador to Holland was cautious about raising the hopes of the disappointed locals of the "Sunda Islands," and keen not to give any ammunition to the Western press.[46] Having exchanged medals in Japan, the vessel met with disaster off Kobe in September 1890, its surviving crew ferried westward by two Japanese vessels. Stirred by this gesture, in January 1891 Ghalib Bey suggested a change of policy to unfurl the Ottoman banner in Japan before seeking its popularization in the more southerly Indies.[47]

Truth be told, the Ottomans were now enjoying some success in inclining Jawi hearts and minds toward an affection for the sultan, if more in the Malay-speaking west of the archipelago. After meeting Blunt at Cairo, Abu Bakar of Johor met both Muhammad ʿAbduh and Sayyid Muhammad Tawfiq al-Bakri (1870–1932), the youthful Sufi ally of the new khedive, ʿAbbas II, a confirmed admirer of Japan. Both provided introductions and advice for his journey to Istanbul. At the imperial capital, Jamal al-Din al-Afghani played a role in convincing Abdulhamid to grant not only an audience fit for a sultan, as the mere "Indian rajah" so annoyingly styled himself. He was also given a lavish state dinner and a diamond-encrusted Mecidiye medal—though this must have been on offer after his claim to Ahmad Muhtar Pasha that the sultan's name was mentioned before his own in Friday prayers.[48]

The delighted Abu Bakar would return home with his medal and a concubine, Hatice Hanım (d. 1904). He would also add the crescent and star to his currency, in addition to applying the Ottoman legal code in his domains.[49] Muhammad al-Saqqaf, his traveling companion, would henceforth bear the

Mecidiye medal (second class) as acting honorary Ottoman consul at Singapore, renaming his plantation the Constantinople Estate, where he also issued new currency of his own bearing the crescent and star.⁵⁰

As Malay rulers and their Arab advisors looked to the symbolism and recognition of a distant court for support, many a pilgrim would be encouraged to think that some of the Jawi sovereigns were his representatives, being issued with Qur'ans imprinted in Malay with the Ottoman sultan's name as "king of the believers."⁵¹ Some traditional sojourners also began to look beyond the Hjiaz and more recently visited Egypt for their studies. In 1895, Sayyid ʿAbdallah al-ʿAttas of Batavia (1850–1929) took his sons and two other locally born Arab youths to Istanbul for a subsidized education, claiming insufficient funds for their support in Cairo.⁵² These "Java" boys, as the Ottomans called them, were followed in December 1898 by a number of others of similar background, including several sent by ʿAbd al-Rahman Ba Junayd, now the Dutch-sanctioned chief of the Arabs at Bogor, and his friend Abu Bakr b. Sunkar. Whereas the new Ottoman consul to Batavia, Mehmet Kamil Bey, sought to delay their departure, they left anyway, traveling via Dhofar, since enfolded by Anglo-Omani claims to the south Arabian coast.⁵³

The Meccan Shaykh, the Dutch Advisor, and the Ottoman Consul

None of this pleased Snouck, by now the advisor for native and Arab affairs. After traveling to Jeddah for research funded by the Dutch government in 1884, where he was hosted by the same consul whose intelligence gathering networks had so impressed Blunt, Snouck converted outwardly to Islam and moved to Mecca in early 1885. Once there, he circulated with the assistance of resident Jawi scholars such as Abu Bakar Djajadiningrat of Banten (d. ca. 1915) and Hasan Mustafa of Garut (1852–1930), with whom he maintained a lifelong connection, as well as Muhammad Arshad b. Alwan, who returned to West Java and rose to the well-regarded rank of chief penghulu of Serang, though not for long.

In Mecca, Snouck attended the lectures of prominent Arab professors favored by these same scholars. Sayyid Ahmad b. Zayni Dahlan was the most popular. By then the primary Shafiʿi authority and mufti of the Holy City, Dahlan depended both on the largesse of the Ottoman state and a constant stream of supplicants from throughout the Shafiʿi world. These included the wealthy arrivals from the Cape, though it is clear that Snouck—who opened his chapter on the "Jâwah" of Mecca with mention of the "Ahl Kâf" and the successes of Hanafi Pan-Islamism—had little to do with these arrivals from British territory, who were now more generally Afrikaans-speaking Muslims and who had less to do with their Southeast Asian kin.[54]

A committed Sufi and enemy of the Wahhabis, Dahlan was also a chronicler of the Holy City who made sure to devote a section to the validity of the Ottoman caliphate in his *Futuhat al-islamiyya*, published posthumously in 1893. In it he offered fulsome praise to the Sharif ʿAwn al-Rafiq and his rival, Ottoman governor Osman Nuri Pasha (1840–1898), for their reforming the rotating schedule of imams in the sacred precinct, with its throngs of pilgrims and residents.[55] Naturally there was room for Abdulhamid as "the great Sultan, the Sultan of Arab and non-Arab sultans, surpassing in learning, righteousness and honor, ennobled by good works and the Holy Sanctuary, holder of sword and pen, the shadow of God on earth and refuge of humanity … Commander of the Faithful, our Lord … the dearest adornment of the throne of kingship and the Caliphate."[56]

Admittedly, Abdulhamid's righteous reign—like that of his more immediate predecessors—had been afflicted by serious military setbacks. Dahlan cataloged Russian interference in Bosnia and Bulgaria, the French invasion of Tunis, the British annexation of Egypt, and ʿUrabi's exile.[57] At the same time he was heartened by the rise of Shaykh Muhammad Ahmad and General Digna in the Sudan, whose warriors had dealt destruction to the better-equipped British. It was this last event that caused Dahlan to offer an exposition as to whether the Sudanese mystic was, in fact, the Mahdi. He concluded that the world had yet to witness the anticipated messiah, who would surely arise in Mecca in the absence of a caliph, which of course they had in the person of Abdulhamid. This mahdi's primary role, therefore, was to resist British depredation of the Ottoman state while all Muslims should concentrate on the pious following of the sharia.[58]

Dahlan, whose networks of sayyid correspondents has been studied by Ulrike Freitag, seemed on the whole uninterested in affairs too far beyond the immediate fringes of empire, or in histories not born of Muslim conquest.[59] Hence, while there was much to be said of Syria, Andalusia, Constantinople, or India, Dahlan only mentioned the "Jawi lands" fleetingly in terms of their being occupied by "the State of Holland called Fleming" after its eighty-year fight for independence from Spain that ended in 987 AH (1587 CE).[60]

At the time of Dahlan's writing, Snouck—whom the Meccan had asked for details about such events—marked a strong sense of Jawi difference born of the experience of life in Mecca, and scorned Ottoman interest in the widely discussed events in Aceh. He also downplayed the learning and "fanatical" attitude of Sumatrans like the recently departed Minangkabau Shaykh Ismail, who we may recall had been a go-between for the Acehnese court in the 1850s, and whose Sufi teachings and Ottoman pretensions had been a cause of debate in Singapore.[61]

Snouck had had even greater cause to be an enemy of the Ottomans once he was hauled before governor Osman Nuri Pasha, accused of being a spy in Paris and Istanbul. His subsequent *Mekka*, written in anger after being forced from the Hijaz, included a long section on the Jawa community that embedded a call for a more informed handling of Muslims by the Netherlands within warnings about the dangers of millenarianism. It was also his most forceful argument for a job with the colonial service, which he obtained after a localized uprising at the town of Ciligon, in Banten, in 1888. By mid-1889, Snouck was touring Java and its religious establishments, deepening his connections with Sayyid ʿUthman and Hasan Mustafa. Neither was a great admirer of Abdulhamid or his emissaries. Snouck later tasked Hasan with serving as Chief Penghulu (and thus his eyes and ears) in Aceh after he carried out his own counterinsurgency research in the province in 1891–1892. From the mid-1890s, Snouck's role as advisor for native and Arab affairs positioned him to direct the relationship between The Hague and its growing population of Muslim subjects, who were increasingly aware of their shared colonial status and the claims of Mecca and Istanbul to their loyalties.

Yet, at the same time, Snouck, who ruled his office with an imperious hand, was often blocked by a constant stream of new officials in regional departments, and even more so by a legal bureaucracy that could stifle his recommendations. Such was the case with his Meccan friend Muhammad Arshad, who had been caught up in the wave of arrests after the Ciligon unrest. Despite Snouck's protestations in 1889 that Arshad was no supporter of such outdated notions as jihad, he was exiled to Timor, where he and his family would remain until 1919—or, at least, that is what Snouck would claim later in life, when he reflected on a Dutch system that seemed only able to see Muslims as pliant natives or threatening jihadis.[62]

None of this sympathy was apparent to the Ottoman consul Kamil, who complained about what he saw as Snouck's activities to manipulate the Muslims of the region. Equally, Kamil emerged as a bête noir for the head of KIZ, who argued that the consulate was coordinating a campaign against Holland in the Arabic presses of the Ottoman capital. Snouck took particular offence at the ways in which various poison pens were writing from Singapore and Batavia to attack his right-hand mufti, Sayyid ʿUthman.[63]

If hostile articles had previously appeared in the Turkish capital, under Kamil they took on such an edge as to break long-standing friendships between sayyids and to impugn the prestige of the Dutch state. Yet, again, not all people had access to their contents in the Indies. And despite the rhetorical affection for the many Jawi Muslims among whom they lived, most of the writings of Ottoman press and consul concerned the Arab minority. In December 1897, Kamil had told his masters that there were "almost no people knowledgeable among the locals beyond some teachers from among the Hadrami and Somali Arabs who reside[d] in first and second degree cities and towns."[64] This supposedly suited Holland, which had appointed Snouck as "chief mufti for the colonies," assigning Sayyid ʿUthman as his assistant, with "willing simpletons to act as legal interpreters and judges" in the provinces.[65] Thus, even as Kamil forwarded letters or even donations to the Ottoman war effort in Macedonia from local sultans seeking caliphal aid, like his colleague at Singapore, his efforts were still geared to a "foreign" community whose members sought higher status under the Dutch flag.

In April 1898, Kamil forwarded a large petition signed by over a hundred members of that community, claiming to speak for thirty thousand ʿAlawi sayyids in the Dutch Indies.[66] He furthermore sent on a report about those residing in Batavia, Cirebon, Semarang, and Surabaya that had been offered by four of the principal signatories and requested funds to support their mosques.[67] As he dutifully added in his report of May 17, his master Abdulhamid's name was always mentioned in the Friday prayers outside Aceh—as long as the preacher was an Arab.[68]

Technically, there should only ever have been one sermon given in any town on a Friday, regardless of the ethnicity of the congregation, though such matters were hardly settled from the Cape of Good Hope to Colombo and Kelantan. Five years earlier, in 1893, the partisans of rival mosques in Palembang had sought the guidance of separate authorities as to whose house of worship was preeminent. The older royal party appealed to Sayyid

ʿUthman in Batavia while several sayyids and hajjis sought succor from a proud Sumatran representative of caliphal authority in Ottoman Mecca.[69] This was Ahmad Khatib al-Minangkabawi, an imam behind whom many Jawi Muslims would stand as they said their prayers over 4300 miles from home. The matter had dragged on, and the Arab-pilgrim faction would take their case to Kamil, who forwarded the texts of Ahmad Khatib and Sayyid ʿUthman to Istanbul in the hope of the empire providing a resolution.[70]

Even if they weren't lining up at prayer behind Ahmad Khatib in Mecca or among those with Arab fathers standing in front of the consuls requesting passports in Batavia and Singapore, more and more Malay speakers now thought of the Ottoman sultan as a distant benefactor whose wars and projects they would support in the name of fraternal solidarity. In December 1897, various notables had proposed collecting donations to aid the orphans of martyrs of the latest "Greek" wars.[71]

As the Ottoman consul noted, such enthusiasms were recent among many local peoples to the east of Aceh. By contrast, with his analysis of Malay romances of the Russo-Turkish wars—some of which were only written in the late 1890s—Braginsky implies that such sentiments were connected to a deep literary history of using the figure of the foreign Turk for Malay self-empowerment. Yet one of the chronicles he paraphrases actually cites Middle Eastern, Indian, and European newspapers, and it must also have been inspired by local news of passing Ottoman officers like Ahmad Effendi at Penang in 1877, and two former Ottoman officers who caused a stir at Palembang in 1881.[72] Regardless of the literary tropes linking the traditions of Sumatra and Java before 1890 then, few Malays (and still fewer Javanese) would have perforce linked the Sultan Rum of Jawi lore to the more tangible and very modern master of Istanbul who was so often maligned in the European newspapers in circulation in colonial towns. Singapore's *Jawi Peranakan* (1876–1895), Batavia's *Wazir India* (1878–1879), and Colombo's *Wajah Selong* were rare Malay-language pioneers providing (and sharing) Arabic-script news of the sultan of Turkey across the Indian Ocean before 1900.[73] The Ottoman sultan was arguably more present in the Tamil language analogues of the Straits Settlements, such as the *Singai Nesan*, whose first issue of 1887 celebrated both Victoria's Golden Jubilee *and* Abdulhamid's role as patron to Muslims the world over.[74]

Regardless of the efforts of his consul that were so responsive to Arab interests in the Indies, Abdulhamid became a concrete figure for many Jawi

Muslims after their own journeying on the pilgrimage, their almost obligatory purchase of printed Qur'ans, and their encounters with the scholars and sayyids who depended on his largesse in the Holy Cities. By the 1870s there were already hundreds of such returnees in the port towns of Java and the princely states of Surakarta and Yogyakarta.[75] It thus seems strange that, in his 1897 Malay-language summary of the Macedonian and Cretan War, Ferdinand Wiggers (b. 1869), who had been translating a series of Dutch volumes on the "mysteries" of the Turkish palace since 1892, still felt the need to outline just *who* the Turks were to his local audience, as well as outlining their claims to the caliphate.[76]

Such an explanation, replete with a photograph of Abdulhamid, would hardly have pleased Snouck. He was furious about Kamil's activities across colonial borders and communal boundaries, whether in forwarding further requests for Ottoman subjecthood on behalf of Arabs at Batavia, proposing scholarships for their children, or reporting the travel plans of the displaced sultans who had once sent messages to the captain of the *Ertugrul*. Citing the awe inspired by that vessel's still remembered visit to Singapore, Kamil would declare in August 1898 that "feelings of conscientious connection to the exalted office of the Great Caliphate of the millions of Muslim people of Malaysia" had been "firmly proven."[77] Sayyid ʿUthman would also be in his glancing sights once more in September of that year, after Snouck's mufti had composed a prayer for the young Wilhelmina to be read in all the mosques of Java on her formal ascension to the Dutch throne:

> During the week-long celebrations on the occasion of Her Majesty the Queen's coronation, an order was given for the preachers to recite a prayer in the noble mosques in her name, and to erect and display the Dutch flag in the holy buildings. A discussion arose among the imams, pilgrims, and sayyids as to whether it was appropriate to put [the Dutch] flag on display, or to recite prayers in the mosque in the name of anybody except the Caliph of Islam. These discussions became an issue here and gained importance, and hostility was displayed by fixing banners at night in the streets, squares, and public places criticizing the local government's actions, whilst the Dutch-language newspapers included some heated articles with offensive language about the Arabs who were considered to be the cause of this problem, advising the government to keep a close eye on the said community. According to the newspapers, two sayyids and another one were threatened with imprisonment for three months without trial,

and with terms of hard labour. During the recitation of the prayer, all mosques were kept under surveillance by the police and military personnel, and the names of those who left the mosque before the recitation of the prayer were recorded by the police.[78]

At least that is how Kamil reported matters, though an image taken for the festivities in Surabaya would give something of a lie to this, where the Arab community assembled before a triumphal arch holding aloft both a portrait of the young queen and a banner adorned with the crescent and star, albeit buried in folds of cloth. Indeed, the Arab militia present seem almost Ottoman in their costumes of jackets and fezzes, abetted by a mock camel and elephant.[79]

This seems exceptional, though. Quite unlike the twinned fluttering of the Ottoman banner and Union Jack at the Cape in 1867, Dutch officials were increasingly instructed by Snouck to be sensitive to any symbolic presentation of the caliphate that might impinge on Dutch dignity. This was especially so when the complaints of Kamil's supplicants appeared in the pages of Arabic papers of the empire like the semiofficial Maʿlumat.[80] At Snouck's insistent prodding, Dutch diplomats had begun to put direct pressure on the Porte, which resolved to swap Kamil with a colleague serving in Liverpool (after Kamil had been refused accreditation at Singapore for daring to marry the late Sultan Abu Bakar's widow, Hatice Hanım, in late November 1898).[81] Of course the articles about Dutch oppression would still issue from Istanbul from time to time, though the Ottomans soon found that the "Java" students whom Kamil had encouraged were something of a drain on the metropolitan purse and welcomed news of the planned establishment of an Arab school in Batavia.[82]

Backed by none other than Sayyid ʿUthman, this educational effort would find expression of a form at Pekojan in 1906 under the auspices of a new sayyid-led welfare society, Jamʿiyyat Khayr (founded ca. 1901). Its members proudly lined up one year outside their headquarters on the Prophet's birthday, and under the paired Dutch tricolor and Ottoman banner once more. This was probably after Snouck had departed for Holland in 1906, replaced by successors who were far less wary of the Porte and the rhetoric that filtered into newer Jawi publications such as Singapore's al-Imam. Abdulhamid was meanwhile sidelined by the Committee for Union and Progress during Snouck's visit to Istanbul in 1908, and not as the result of any advice on his part.

A Very English Turk

If the Ottoman-Dutch relationship had been especially testy for the duration of Snouck's stewardship in Batavia, the Anglo-Ottoman one—guided by a web of well-regarded sayyids and Peranakan newspapermen—could still be relatively cordial once the Aceh question had abated. It was able to permeate Dutch borders as a result. In November 1899, the interim consul at Batavia proposed that Istanbul repeat the efforts of Kamil by sending several hundred Ottoman Qur'ans to the region for distribution by Arabs—"our only intermediaries in these quarters because of their complete obedience and submission to the Imperial Sultanate"—along with gilt editions for local "Javanese" rajas, and alphabet books, "which the Javanese Muslims continuously request."[83] Echoing John Wilson's proposal of 1812 to publish tracts in Sinhalese detailing British successes against the French, the interim Ottoman consul recommended distributing a couple of hundred Arabic histories of the successful war with Greece, though he proposed that these should be sent in anonymous wrappers and handled by Muhammad al-Saqqaf in Singapore.[84]

As with Abu Bakr Effendi at the Cape, books were not the only Ottoman import to gladden Muslim hearts beneath indulgent or perhaps narrowing British eyes. Now there would once more be a direct link between Singapore and Istanbul. November 1901 saw the arrival at Singapore of his eldest son, Ahmad Attaoullah, who in April had been granted the post of acting consul general "for his special services to education in opening the Ottoman school in Cape Town" that had "reinforced the religious sentiments of the Muslim children and ... [developed] their connection to the great Caliphate."[85] Having traveled to Cairo with his father in 1876, the twelve-year-old Ahmad Attaoullah had remained to continue his formative education in the roiling atmosphere of al-Azhar, where he graduated on January 31, 1883, a month after ʿUrabi and colleagues had been exiled. Attaoullah then returned to the Cape for further education at the Marist-run St. Aloysius School in the center of Cape Town, before completing the Western part of his education at the McLoughlin Academy on Boom Street, founded by the liberal former soldier and newspaperman Patrick McLoughlin (1835–1882). He then departed for a period of teaching at the new Ottoman School in the Kimberly from 1887, returning to Cape Town to stand for parliament in 1894 before going back to the Kimberly to serve as editor of the *Muslim Journal* (and as occasional "Ottoman" mufti). He went on to Istanbul in 1898, where he won what would be his final appointment.[86]

While the elevated position of honorary consul general was already quite a reward, Attaoullah knew how to bargain for its further gilding. He requested both a higher salary, given the great distance from the imperial capital, and a gold decoration to pin on his already Mecidiye-laden uniform.[87] He would soon have occasion to wear the silver decoration he received. On October 17, 1901, the *Ceylon Standard* reported the passing presence on the island of the newest star in the consular firmament, from a place that was more often supplying Boer prisoners.[88] What the just-departed ʿUrabi might have made of him—or he of the once Mecidiye-bedecked Egyptian who had dominated the last months of his Egyptian education—was not recorded.

Moving on to Singapore and echoing the role played by the ill-starred captain of the *Ertugrul*, the multilingual sayyid cut a popular figure, assisted by Muhammad al-Saqqaf's son Hamid Effendi after his own appointment in April 1901. Warm coverage in the *Straits Times* shows that Attaoullah patronized the Parsee Theatre and was a regular at Western galas. He also performed his Ottoman tasks with enthusiasm, being close to the royal family of Johor, who were themselves growing ever closer to the Saqqafs by marriage. Attaoullah was sure to patronize prayers for Abdulhamid when they were offered by the Meccan exile ʿAbdallah Zawawi (d. 1924), and he dutifully forwarded the distressed correspondence of (former and threatened) Jawi rulers, such as the fugitive sultan of Jambi, whom he allegedly promised two warships in 1902.[89]

Evidently such promises did not come to Snouck's ears that year, and he remarked that, while the Capetonian "Turk" was a similar creature to Kamil, he was far more circumspect.[90] It was, moreover, a loss of Pan-Islamic proportions in November 1903 when Attaoullah, dressed in his official uniform, died of his injuries after he leapt from a runaway hansom cab following the governor's birthday ball. Indeed he died on the very grounds of Government House. Carried the following day from the home of Muhammad al-Saqqaf, which had been thronged by mourners, Attaoullah's coffin, draped in his bloodied uniform and both the Ottoman and British flags, was followed to a grave in the royal cemetery of Johor by an extremely large crowd of mourners, including members of the Saqqaf, ʿAttas, and Junayd clans, as well as numerous hajjis and officers of various regiments, Asian and European.[91] Attended at his interment by the acting governor, numerous consuls, and prominent members of the Singaporean community, not to mention the sultan of Johor, he had been, in the words of one saddened correspondent, "a very English Turk," who had just given a lengthy and "eulogistic" speech on the British rule in all the colonies of the empire and who looked forward to a posting at Bombay.[92] He was arguably an anachronism—one of the last products of the alliance of the previous century, and the son of a mislabeled Iraqi sayyid and a Capetonian Muslim of Anglo-Malay birth. After Sultan Ibrahim's belatedly informing Abdulhamid of the demise of his emissary, and given Johorese and Dutch protests about the proposed return of Kamil Bey, the affairs of the consulate would pass into the hands of the Germans for a time, giving a glimpse of the future.[93]

Matters were hardly more satisfactory for the Ottomans at Batavia. Kamil's successor, Emin Bey, had barely stayed a year before being replaced by Sadiq Baligh Effendi, a Swiss-trained jurist who initially cooperated with Snouck on the question of Ottoman citizenship for Indies Arabs before being ordered replaced in 1903 for "exhibiting behavior contrary to the principles of Islam."[94] While Kamil was nominated yet again, he does not ever seem to have arrived, nor yet did Sadiq Baligh leave.[95] To be sure, Kamil's previous efforts were starting to bear prickly fruit for the Dutch. April 1904 saw the return to Java of some of the famous students, including two Junayd boys, Ahmad and Saʿid, who were dressed as modern effendis in their suits and fezzes. Although hospitably received at the dock by Sadiq Baligh and the Dutch police, other local officials (who disregarded their Ottoman passports) sought to deprive them of their headgear and uniforms, which were adjudged to have contravened local sartorial laws.[96]

Taken together, this was, as Snouck observed, a propaganda victory for Istanbul.[97] The Ottoman embassy in London further proposed that the English might once more put pressure on their Dutch cousins, but gained little. Nor yet did some of the students. The struggling ʿAli b. Sahl was repatriated from Istanbul without a degree in 1905, when the sartorial laws were repealed on Snouck's advice, though the empire still accepted a few more such "Java" pupils.[98] Of course there were symbolic successes for those who had made the long journey, even if they did not quite fit into the empire they admired and sometimes returned to. In lieu of the appointments on offer to their

Ottoman classmates in the imperial civil service school, Ahmad and Saʿid Ba Junayd applied for Mecidiye medals, which they were awarded in 1906.[99]

Another ironic nominee for that decoration in 1908 was Sayyid ʿUthman, who had been knighted in 1899 for composing the prayers for Queen Wilhelmina on her ascension—the very address that had enraged Kamil in 1898. Now Kamil's successor praised ʿUthman for his ceaseless publications condemning heretical innovations among the locals and for his steadfast loyalty to the sultan.[100] It is unlikely that ʿUthman ever received the decoration; Dutch proposals to the Ottomans to do just that in 1900 had already fallen on deaf ears.[101] Had the medal been awarded, many of the younger generation of pro-Ottoman Arabs would have fumed. In any case, it was with the Golden Lion that the ancient shaykh posed for a rare photo late in life, his eyes blind to the coming troubles when his elite peers would choose to side with Great Britain and the sharif of Mecca over Istanbul and what would remain of the caliphate after the Young Turk revolution. That linkage was increasingly the object of younger and, to their minds, far less noble affections.

A Changing World

> Some 300 years ago the Hadramis began to emigrate to Java and Sumatra with the sole idea of earning a livelihood. Among them were, and are, a certain number of the arm-bearer class, whose lack of respect and arrogance has culminated in endangering the position of all.
>
> —LEE WARNER, CAIRO, DECEMBER 1918

While far less united than their already divided coreligionists in Cape Town, by the 1910s more and more Southeast Asian pilgrims were investing in the notion that the Ottoman sultan was their spiritual protector, if a still distant one. As we have seen, Arab migrants to Southeast Asia had also been sending letters directly to the presses of Istanbul and Cairo bemoaning Dutch oppression and citing the violent excesses in Aceh in particular. And just as Ahmad Dahlan at Mecca had dedicated his world history to the Ottoman sultan in the 1880s, his Hadrami successors—Muhammad Ba Busayl (d. 1912) and ʿUmar b. Abi Bakr Ba Junayd (1853–1916)—would ensure that those sultans remained firmly in the consciousness of their Indian Ocean coreligionists.[102]

These pro-Ottoman scholars of Mecca had also been just as adept at outsourcing their imperatives to the sayyid network as the state that they served. For instance, because the multiplicity of Friday mosques remained a particularly turbulent issue at the Cape in 1913, the newly elevated ʿUmar Ba Junayd would task his Comorian follower Ahmad b. Sumayt (1861–1925) with its resolution. The latter, who had also been close to Sayyid Fadl and enjoyed a cordial relationship with the sultan of Zanzibar and his British minders, would in turn send three fellow Comorian sayyids to South Africa, among them Shaykh ʿAbdallah Ba Kathir, who had also toured Java with Bin Sumayt in the 1890s.[103]

But if steam reinforced such traditional networks of religious authority across the Indian Ocean, it had also enabled many Hadramis of less august lineage to migrate to Southeast Asia and to seek their fortunes in the ports with their clearly defined Arab enclaves. At times they claimed leadership positions of those local communities with Dutch approval. Around the time of Attaoullah's death, the Dutch appointed the wealthy ʿUmar Manqush as captain of the Arab community at Batavia.

In so doing, the Dutch were seeking to undermine the sayyid-consular nexus. At the time of the return to Batavia of the two Junayd boys, Sadiq Baligh claimed that he would certainly like to beat the "Arab dog" if he saw him.[104] Manqush was no sayyid, and he famously refused to honor the hand of any who claimed the distinction, which some asserted was their religious right. As Snouck remarked in June 1901, when recommending Manqush and responding to anonymous letters of complaint, the then deputy captain may well have been a high-handed parvenu, but his independence from his peers would work in Dutch favor.[105]

Equally, advisors like Snouck's deputy G. A. J. Hazeu respected the reformist impulses of Cairene scholars and their Singaporean emulators, whom Manqush also admired. This was especially the case when they hewed to ʿAbduh's contention that all Muslims could be equal, at least in terms of non-slave descent. An Indian Muslim, argued his spokesman Rashid Rida in 1905, was just as suitable a partner for the daughter of a sayyid living in Singapore as a descendant of the prophet.[106] Many sayyids were appalled at this assault on what they deemed the proper rules of "parity" (kafaʾa) designed to govern such alliances. They would likewise have bristled at Rida's celebratory claims in *al-Manar* in 1910, when he boasted of overseeing a global movement of reform for "Arab, Turk, Persian, Indian, Tatar, Chinese, Malay, and African," before appending "and the Hadrami among them," almost as an afterthought adjacent to the lowly Bedouin.[107]

Make no mistake, Rida's rhetoric of reform and uplift was finding non-Arab emulators. Yogyakarta's Ahmad Dahlan (1868–1923), for instance, was a rare Jawi member of Jamʿiyyat Khayr. In 1912 he founded the Muhammadiyah movement, which was geared to providing religious education, health care, and orphanages to Javanese Muslims.[108] His effort was also linked to the Sarekat Islam. This swelling mass organization designed to advance the position of indigenous traders was founded at nearby Surakarta and then led from Surabaya by R. A. Tjokroaminoto. It was initially admired by both Sayyid ʿUthman and Snouck as an opportunity for Muslims to seek economic advancement under Dutch rule.[109] But if the Jawi members of such movements often welcomed Arab finance in quest of supplanting the Chinese business owners who had outpaced them in the later years of the nineteenth century, they soon chafed at Arab leadership, which was increasingly divided between traditionalist sayyids and many less elite reformers abetted by KIZ.

In 1915, the link between colonial advisers and the Cairene faction was made yet plainer when Manqush bankrolled the expansion of al-Irshad, a new Arab educational movement that was explicitly against sayyid privilege. Its raison d'être was personified by an African, Ahmad Surkati, who was born in the Mahdist state in 1875 and who had arrived on Java in October 1911. Initially recruited from Mecca to be headmaster of Batavia's Jamʿiyyat Khayr School, Surkati—one of five Sudanese arrivals by October 1913—soon affirmed the reformist position that no Muslim was exalted by virtue of their birth, deserving neither preferential marriage nor the customary attention to their hands (*taqbil*) that was ubiquitous in local society. He parted company with Jamʿiyyat Khayr in September 1914.[110]

It is also curious to note that Snouck's Sundanese friend and advisor to KIZ, Hasan Mustafa, referred to the matter of taqbil as sharply dividing highborn sayyids from their *zanghala* fellows at Batavia in May 1916.[111] While perhaps a misspelled reference to the East African (*Zanji*) origin of Surkati—or even the town of Dongola, where Surkati had been born—this term also sounds reminiscent of the Arabo-Malay term for "Sinhalese," which perhaps made light of Moorish claims to Arab ancestry. Indeed, I have not encountered this term outside Lanka, when it featured in the pages of *Wajah Selong* with reference to Sinhalese founding schools.

Nor yet were Surkati and his fellow Sudanese the only outsiders among the usual array of Asians and Arabs. Far less noticed in the story of conflict between sayyid and less elite "shaykh," is that the Indies remained a destination for Arabic speakers from beyond Hadramawt and its hierarchical diaspora that reached into almost every Indian Ocean hinterland. Such figures often claimed connections to Cairo and the Mediterranean shores of the wider Maghreb, where new academies were producing subjects to serve in the modern schools and bureaucracies, adding European languages to the traditional suite of Islamic sciences. But if Cairo was emerging as the most prestigious of destinations for Malays and a few Javanese of reformist bent, most would still make their connection to Southeast Asia at Mecca, where the Ottomans had reformed the educational system in 1905 to create new degrees, and thus new graduates who were even more attractive to pro-Ottoman educationalists visiting from beyond the empire. Surkati had been one such awardee, and others like him gained employment on Java as the educated servants of the Hadrami majority, often seeking a voice in the nascent Arab press. Again, like Surkati, some of these outsiders were seen as the cause of the divisions, and the distancing of the sayyids from their supposedly natural places of leadership of indigenous Muslims.

In the next chapter, I shall turn at times to the activities of another such outsider and self-imposed exile, Surkati's friend and publisher, in order to interrogate their place at a time when the relationship between post-Ottoman ideal and colonial reality became particularly fraught. Still, they were only part of a larger story of familiarity and alienation among the "Jawa" or "Malayu" peoples, as they so often called them. In leafing through the pages of the Arab press of the Indies, from the opening of the Great War to the impending collapse of the Ottoman caliphate, one senses the same tensions of longing and loyalty we have seen voiced elsewhere across the Indian Ocean—though now there would be a final snapping of the frayed cord binding the British and the Ottoman empires in some semblance of friendship. English courtesy could only ever have lasted so long.

TEN

For Arabs, Arabic, and the Community

IT HAS RECENTLY been argued that 1913 was a pivotal year for Java that would see a profound change of mindset for many of its indigenous inhabitants, most especially for those who engaged directly with European mentors and overseers—some of whom were encouraging, but most decidedly hostile.[1] In July, Soewardi Soerjaningrat, the future Ki Hadjar Dewantara (1889–1959), would issue a biting pamphlet in which he dared to imagine himself as a Dutchman. Already an act of defiant appropriation, Soewardi's imagining—if just for a moment—reflected on the irony of mandated celebrations of the centenary of Netherlandic independence from Napoleonic France while the Dutch lorded it over the natives of the Indies. Initially published in Dutch, its translation into Malay would earn him arrest and banishment.[2]

Also in 1913, more and more highly educated Javanese like Soewardi, educated in Dutch but assigned low-paying jobs as medics or clerks and spoken to in Malay, would follow the well-publicized struggles of such colleagues as Prawiradinata at Pekalongan, who endured various humiliations. They would also ruminate on or emulate the transgressive acts that he had dared: addressing their masters in Dutch, sitting on chairs rather than squatting with their hands in poses of supplication, or simply dressing in the same white trousers and jackets of empire and modernity alike.[3] As the correspondent from Perak had noted to the *Wajah Selong* back in 1896, one's rank was apparent everywhere one looked in the Dutch colonies, particularly on Java. Arnout van der Meer points out that not that much had changed in the ensuing two decades. Despite a series of official proclamations, many European officials still felt it their right to speak down to their employees in low Javanese while peons held parasols of rank over their braid-encrusted shoulders.[4] Now, though, mass movements such as Sarekat Islam were forming to assert the equality of indigenes in the colonies, where one was defined by law as inferior to a European or Indo-European, or marked in the middle as Foreign Oriental, be they Chinese or Japanese, Indian, or Arab.

Speaking of Arabs, the previous year saw the relatively unheralded arrival at Batavia of a thirty-one-year-old teacher called Mohamed Hachemi. Far taller than many of his new colleagues, he, too, favored the white suits and modern ties of the educated youths of the colonized world. Yet he was considerably harder to categorize. A native of Tunisia, which had been declared a French protectorate a few months before his birth, he had come to Java from Istanbul. Having descended onto the crowded wharf of Tanjung Priok, Hachemi would have been met by the staff of his new employer: none other than Sayyid ʿAbdallah al-ʿAttas, the wealthy entrepreneur and patron of education for Arab boys in Batavia who had once sent his own sons to Cairo and Istanbul. This was Hachemi's reason for being there, and he was soon shown around the school where he was to inculcate in his new pupils a respect for learning, a love of the homeland of Hadramawt, and deep regard for the Ottoman sultan, now Mehmed V, protector of the holy cities of Mecca and Medina.

In this chapter, we shall look in on Hachemi at times to see what the British imagined of his actions on Java at a moment when they were not merely on the lookout for Ottoman and German sympathizers, but also deeply mistrustful of the official neutral Dutch state. Indeed, they were guided in many ways by their old sayyid partners, who were deeply troubled by a new breed of reformers oriented beyond Hadramawt, and all before the explosion of a new and assertive Indonesian nationalism where once there had been so many Jawa and Malays. But first we should open the story in the interlinked capitals of Singapore and Batavia, to trace the emergence of an Arab voice among those peoples.

Finding an Arab Voice Among the Jawa

As we saw with the prolonged resistance to the appointment of a consul to Batavia, the Dutch were always far more obsessed with Ottoman ambitions for the far-flung subjects of "their" India than the British were in their much larger holdings. But while Snouck was eternally annoyed by the many attempts at raising caliphal awareness that were bound up with the complaints of the Arab community and attacks on his own person, after his return to the Netherlands in 1906 less imperious successors like the Javanist Hazeu and then D. A. Rinkes (1878–1954) were more interested in the position of "natives." And they were seldom as threatened by reportage of the sultan-caliph, his fleet, or the new railway linking Damascus to Medina that garnered donations from across the Muslim world.

Such content could be found in the first reformist Muslim journal in the archipelago, Singapore's *al-Imam*. It was run by a mixture of self-identified Arab and Jawi editors—including at least one who had celebrated the opening of the Ottoman consulate in the city in 1901. This was the Minangkabau shaykh Muhammad Tahir, also known as Muhammad Tahir Jalal al-Din "al-Azhari," following his graduation from Cairo's premier institution.[5] In August 1906, Consul General Spakler at Singapore, who had once stood solemnly at the grave of Attaoullah, advised the Dutch governor-general about *al-Imam*'s appearance and its mixed editorial board, including Tahir. Also mentioned were Sayyid Shaykh al-Hadi, an Arab from Riau, and Sayyid Hasan b. ʿAlwi b. Shahab, who had "repeatedly come before the courts in Netherlands India." The publisher was of concern, too. Shaykh Muhammad Salim al-Kalali was said to be a native of Cirebon who had "played a certain role in the first years of the Aceh War," though all seemed in order and forgiven, as Sayyid ʿUthman had visited the office and approved of the enterprise.[6]

Although written in Singapore, some of *al-Imam*'s content did contain oblique critiques of colonialism, lauding the efforts of Mustafa Kamil in Egypt, or the purported advice of the late Amir of Afghanistan to his son to be cautious of the British.[7] At the same time, the late Abu Bakar of Johor was praised as a state-builder who had granted his people the boon of independence in partnership with Great Britain. At Batavia in December 1908, Hazeu would argue that *al-Imam* was merely an organ for laudable modernist ideas.[8] That month, though, and five months after the revolution that ended the absolute reign of Abdulhamid, *al-Imam* would cease publication, riven by factionalism between its Jawi editors, like Abas b. Muhammad Taha (who had stepped in for Tahir) and their Arab funders and colleagues, most especially Muhammad b. ʿAqil (1863–1931), who sought modernization and independence, but not at the cost of sayyid privilege.[9]

While part of *al-Imam*'s decline had stemmed from the journal's attacks on local Sufi practices, and just as attention had been focused on the successor Malay reformist journals, the ephemeral nature of several sayyid-run Arabic periodicals at Singapore shows that they struggled in a market where the issues of the Egyptian press jostled with more urgent local concerns and a growing fascination for Japan.[10] *Al-Imam* had been a key part of this, relaying the enthusiasms of the Japanophilic Egyptian nationalist (*and* committed Ottoman) Mustafa Kamil. But *al-Imam* was not the only conduit. The richly illustrated *Bintang Hindia* had played a major part, with its circulation reaching some twenty-seven thousand issues in late 1904, replete with photos of the Russo-Japanese War.[11] Hazeu and his new master, governor-general A. W. F. Idenberg (1909–1916), would mark the strong impact of the conflict and the common currency of slogans such as "Asia for the Asians."[12] They had paid for it, after a fashion. *Bintang Hindia* had been subsidized by the Dutch government.

This is not to say the Ottoman global did not matter. In fact, it was resonating more and more in the unsubsidized pages of many new periodicals. The Italian invasion of Libya in 1911 and then the Balkan campaigns of 1912–1913 saw the Turkish state lose the last of its African and European possessions. The empire accordingly attracted donations to the Red Crescent, its answer to the Red Cross, its global reach famously drawing the efforts of future members of the Khilafat movement in India. A branch was similarly facilitated at Batavia in late 1912 by members of the newly formed Jamʿiyyat Khayr under Abu Bakr al-ʿAttas, the son-in-law of ʿAbdallah al-ʿAttas.[13]

Snouck's colleague Hasan Mustafa had already written from Garut in January 1912 that the war in North Africa had seemed to be a very Arab concern on Java, with the latter apparently having slaughtered sheep to celebrate the (evidently false) news of Ottoman victories.[14] Even so, many non-Arabs were clearly interested in—if not worried about—the fate of the Ottomans. Raden B. Kartadiredja published a three-volume account of the Tripoli campaign, championing the Ottomans and celebrating the resistance led by the Sanusi and Idrisi Sufi orders.[15] Expressions of sympathy for Istanbul would flow into Malay successor papers to *al-Imam* like Singapore's *Neracha*, edited by Abas Taha and assisted by K. H. Anang, and *al-Munir* of Padang, under Abdullah Ahmad (1878–1933).[16] *Al-Munir* offered a striking combination of reportage valorizing the struggles of Muslims in Libya and the Balkans while reflecting on the rise of the Japanese as vanquishers of Russia. Yet it also counseled patient development under the colonial state in the face of those who condemned the wearing of Western clothing and having an infidel government. One article even cited the late Muhammad ʿAbduh, who argued that the peace and security of the country was more important than ejecting the British.[17]

Certainly, *Neracha* and *al-Munir* maintained close links with Cairo and with *al-Ittihad*, a Malay paper founded there in late 1912 by two Jawi students: Mohamad Fadloellah from Java and Ahmad Fauzi Imran of Borneo.[18] The fact remained, conversely, that there was no stable Arab paper in the Indies to editorialize on Ottoman concerns before late 1913. Readers of Arabic depended largely on journals from Cairo, Beirut, and Istanbul supplemented by gleanings from the often hostile Western press. The first truly successful Arabic-language offering of the Dutch Indies—and one that maintained a significant Malay section—was *al-Bashir*, which appeared at Palembang in December 1913 and was the voice of Muhammad b. Hashim (1883–1960), a sayyid educationalist who ran an Arabic English school in the city.[19] He also had connections to Batavia, Singapore, and Cairo, where he owned a house resorted to by members of the Jawi community seeking respite from the crowded arcades of al-Azhar. That network was more than evident in the letters of approval he received from fellow publishers such as Abas Taha.[20]

Bin Hashim was, moreover, the grandson of Sayyid ʿUthman, though for the moment he eschewed the polemics against the rising movement of the "new generation," or *kaum muda* (glossed in his paper as the *shabiba*, or "youth"), whose orientation to ʿAbduh and Rida was proving so troubling to his grandfather.[21] After all, Bin Hashim had previously corresponded with Rida, and his stated primary concern was the uplift of Arabs and, as a consequence, the broader Muslim people, including women, whose education he championed.[22] The very subtitle of *al-Bashir* said as much, proclaiming that it served "Arabs, Arabic, and the Community." There thus remained an obvious hierarchy of concerns, and, as Sumit Mandal has pointed out, not all the content was necessarily translated.[23] Some of *al-Bashir*'s Arabic articles bemoaned the fact that Arabs were being left behind by local "Malays," who were outdoing them by founding schools that taught modern languages, especially Dutch and English. "How will the Arabs rise?" asked one rhetorical book, and thus the lead article that reviewed it in January 1914.[24] One might also have asked where. Three months later, the leading Arabic article, by

ʿAbd al-Rahman b. Saqqaf, would bewail the loss of past greatness, as the Arab homelands were being divided up by foreigners.[25] This was one of the pieces that deserved no translation in *al-Bashir*. The issue's Malay section commenced with an unrelated article that ran under the classic aphorism ascribed to the Prophet: "Indeed, Muslims are brothers."[26]

Other early Malay responses from Bin Hashim dealt with questions from local readers about the obligatory mention in the Friday address of the Ottoman sultan as opposed to the local sovereign, or the necessity of the Arabic language for such addresses. For Bin Hashim, such questions were easily answered. Arabic was the language of divine revelation, the Prophet, and the sacred law; it was also a language for all Muslim peoples. He cited the example of its usage by the "non-Arabs" of Cairo, Tripoli, and Beirut, whom we should remember seldom identified with impoverished Arabia at this time.[27] The "sultan of Turkey" was to be invoked by virtue of his position as Commander of the Faithful and his protection of the holy places.[28]

It must be said that, even as his concern was for the Arabs—or, soon enough, "Hadramis above all"—Bin Hashim felt a certain discomfort with the biases inherent in questions about the legitimacy of newly forming associations in the Indies, which often had both indigenous and Arab members, not to mention the claims to respect being made by nonsayyids like ʿUmar Manqush.[29] "What is up with the Malays and Javanese who hate the sayyids?" one reader had asked in early 1914, critiquing a previous writer's claims that Arabs and Malays were not mixing in Sarekat Islam and an emerging branch of the Red Crescent. Bin Hashim was swift to editorialize that he did not really think that such was the case, and that the original author had not used the term *sayyid* when speaking of the trend toward self-segregation.[30]

The target of such animosity was the *shabiba*. Given their local parentage and nonsayyid fathers, many could feel as much Malay or Javanese. Now, with their apparent emulation of the West, donning trousers in place of sarongs and replacing turbans with fezzes or brimless black felt caps, they appeared to be forgetting that true advancement was done for the sake of properly attired people *and* the real ancestors back in Hadramawt. Regardless of his own enthusiasm for modern teaching methods, Ottoman trains, and Muslim aviators, Bin Hashim remained committed to the traditional hierarchy. In June 1914, under the headline "Don't Rush to Judgment," he justified printing a letter critical of certain sayyids in Batavia for reasons of "freedom of publication" (*hurriyyat al-nashr*). Apparently some more conservative member of Jamʿiyyat Khayr, likened in the letter to "worshippers of graves," had been hounding an unnamed teacher (the Sudanese Surkati) at their Batavian school alleging corruption, both intellectual and spiritual.[31] A few weeks later, Sayyid ʿAli b. Ahmad b. Shahab—a.k.a. Habib ʿAli Menteng (1865-1945)—would complain about the tone of the letter, though he admitted to having been a part of a group taking teachers to task. Habib ʿAli, one of Consul Kamil's four leading petitioners in 1898, further claimed that he had only ever insisted that students at the school should study "the geography of the Arabian Peninsula and learn the places of their *true* homeland" (*watanahum al-haqiqi*).[32]

This did not mean that the increasingly defined Dutch Indies and its concerns were abandoned by sayyid activists worried about the reformist tone of their imported and increasingly disaffected staffers like Surkati. Bin Hashim still cast indigenous Jawi "people of the country" (*wataniyyin*) as allies on the road to progress under a caliphal banner. He also engaged with other papers that were then concerned with the question of the defense of the colony as the Great War loomed, transforming the Japanese into a potential threat to the Dutch with their ill-prepared fleet.[33] In May 1914, *al-Bashir* ran an article on the question of colonial readiness for war taken from the Malay-language *Pancaran Warta*.[34] The fact that another article in the same issue reported the establishment of a trilingual Ottoman paper was hardly contradictory.[35] The Dutch and Ottoman Empires were not headed to war with each other.

Little did Bin Hashim know just how the German-Ottoman alliance of November would put pressure on Arab and Jawi alike, or that the Dutch would soon hesitate to allow further donations to the Red Crescent, which he had encouraged in his paper, for fear of violating their neutral status, potentially inviting British or Japanese annexation.[36] Before this happened, however, Bin Hashim's publication would be in a momentary hiatus as he moved to Batavia in October 1914 for treatment after a car accident.[37] He was also to take over teaching duties at the Jamʿiyyat Khayr School for the departed Surkati, who had since founded his al-Irshad movement in August and a school of the same name in September.

It seems that there was little overt religious reaction in the Indies after the Ottoman shaykh al-Islam issued a declaration of jihad against the colonial enemies of Germany on November 11, 1914. Bin Hashim, who relied on Reuters for most of his news, opined a month later that Turkey had joined the war in opposition to its old foe Russia, wishing victory and honor to the caliphate.[38] The following issues saw cautious editorials. Japan had been forced to come on the side of England by virtue of the pact of 1902, and, while *al-Bashir* featured photos of the Kaiser and German dreadnoughts, Bin Hashim was "not prepared to say" that the way of Turkey was exactly the way of Islam. Reflecting on the German offer of freedom to the colonized Muslim world in "India, Ceylon and the Malay Islands," he put it firmly: Germany fought for its own interests and was not really interested in the faith disparaged by its own missionaries. Still, where it went, so, too, did the leading nation of Islam.[39]

As with Blunt and Sabunji's pamphlet of 1881, there was no groundswell from an even more explicit handbill in circulation from Cairo that urged the benighted "Jawa" subjects of the Dutch to rise against their colonial overlords. Issued by the former editor of *al-Liwa*ʾ, it was only retracted in May 1915. Snouck was unsurprised that the Dutch officials at Pera whom he had long despised had failed to notice something picked up by French and British intelligence. He was even more unimpressed that the (French) language of the retraction implied that the blameless Dutch had a "correct" understanding of the rights of the caliphate.[40] Snouck's two-decade campaign against Ottoman claims had failed just as the sultanate was on its last legs. Indies Muslims of all stripes had now started to wave the caliphal banner, or variants of it, and hang pictures of the sultan on their walls. It was no longer just imperiled rajas and restricted Arabs who would seek to aid the Ottoman Empire from an Indian Ocean vantage. In 1914, the three dozen Jawi students in Cairo rallied in support of the empire in the pages of *al-Ittihad*, focusing on its older and more proximate Italian enemies.[41]

Back in Java, by May 1915 the Sarekat Islam leader Tjokroaminoto, whose organization had found a patron in Rinkes, would campaign for donations to the Red Crescent at Surabaya, expanding the reach of what had been an Arab association under Abu Bakr al-ʿAttas.[42] An awkward Rinkes had even been present in April at another Red Crescent gathering at Batavia that had called for donations. Introduced by the Turkish consul general, Reʾfat, Rinkes commended the idea and soon found monies being sent to his office.[43] This was because of his already having toured Java with Tjokroaminoto to promote Sarekat Islam in late 1913 and early 1914, and his parallel role—undertaken in partnership with Tjokroaminoto, Hasan Mustafa, and Ahmad Djajadiningrat in early 1915—in collecting funds to collect pilgrims stranded in the Hijaz by the Great War.[44] Now Sarekat Islam and the Red Crescent could raise portraits of the Ottoman sultan next to those of the Dutch queen without major hindrance, as at the Surabaya meeting, though an embarrassed Rinkes had requested that Tjokroaminoto stop the practice before Governor-General Idenberg decided to let the matter rest.[45] No wonder the Ottomans believed that their "Fleming" cousins finally had a "correct" attitude to the caliphate.

Looking for London's Arabs

Understandably far more colonial anxiety was felt on the other side of the Straits of Malacca, and by a power that now sought to interdict any traffic with the Ottoman Empire. The Ottoman declaration of war had a major effect of transforming perspectives on hostilities in the Indian Ocean, including the exploits of a raider, the SMS *Emden*, which had attacked Allied shipping between Ceylon and Penang in September and October 1914. By and large, Muslims of both territories would remain allied to the British, and the Muslim League in India also maintained its loyalty. Ottoman sympathizers like the Ali brothers and Abd al-Bari had even telegrammed the sultan in August hoping that he would either support Great Britain or remain neutral, despite the entente with Russia.[46] In Ceylon, moreover, and before the formal declaration of jihad, the *Emden* had been cheered less by Moorish stalwarts of Great Britain than rival Sinhalese nationalists, who had already moved closer to Germany.[47]

With jihad declared, though, the *Emden* story could intersect with Muslim global histories, and very soon after its sinking off the Cocos Islands by HMAS *Sydney* in November 1914.[48] While the landing party made a famous escape to neutral Sumatra and thence to fame at Istanbul and Berlin, some of the prisoners taken to Singapore helped inspire a mutiny among the Muslims of an Indian regiment—"the Loyal Fifth"—in February 1915. Rounded up with the aid of French, Russian, and Japanese sailors, the ringleaders (none of them German) were shot in batches outside Outram Road Prison.[49] While news was suppressed outside the island, ʿUmar al-Saqqaf and Muhammad b. ʿAqil coordinated delegations to quell official fears, as well as multiethnic marches to demonstrate ongoing Muslim subject support of Great Britain.[50]

By mid-1915, the Muslims of South and Southeast Asia were inhabiting what may have seemed an inverted world. Great Britain was now the declared enemy of the last Muslim empire. Holland was but a nervous bystander. As we have seen, its liberal governor-general had even allowed the activities of mass organizations with Muslim memberships who could wave Dutch and Ottoman flags together. Pragmatic loyalty to Holland and an affective relationship to Istanbul was now much less of a fraught subject for well-heeled Hadramis living in the Indies, too. Many of the restrictions of past years had been publicly eased, even as emigration and the pilgrimage had been quietly curtailed.[51] Loyalty to the Dutch wasn't a problem for the pro-caliphal Bin Hashim (at least not on the printed page), nor yet was it for ʿAbdallah al-ʿAttas, the pioneer of the Arab renaissance who had taken his sons to Istanbul in 1895, and whose son-in-law, Abu Bakr, was now head of the Red Crescent. Meanwhile, another Egyptian- and Western-educated son-in-law, Ismaʿil, was gaining attention among admiring members of KIZ. By 1919 he would take his place in the Volksraad, a token parliament established by the Dutch in May 1918.

The true turning point for many Indies Arabs, most especially for those living at the mercantile hub of Surabaya, came when Sharif Husayn of the Hijaz rebelled against the Committee for Union and Progress government in June 1916. Although he pledged his continued loyalty to Mehmed V as caliph, many sayyids in Java were perplexed, largely coming around to a more explicitly sharifan position under a since-turned Bin Hashim. Surkati's Irshadis meanwhile stayed loyal to the Ottoman sultan and his state while they maintained their commitment to local activities in education and welfare. One close friend and Anglophone teacher at the Irshad School was Mas Abdul Hamid (a.k.a. K. H. Anang). Born in Lampung to Haji Rahim of Palembang, he first translated pro-British articles after his graduation from the Raffles Institution of Singapore. By mid-1915, though, following the closure of *Neracha* and *Tunas Melayu*, for which he had been Abas Taha's subeditor, he moved to Batavia to serve as secretary to Ottoman consul Reʾfat.[52]

While the Irshadi movement gained ground in Java, where it continued to enjoy the tacit admiration of KIZ, it was the increasingly defensive sayyids who would launch the next major Arabic paper in the Indies. This was *al-Iqbal*, which appeared at Surabaya in mid-1917 under Muhammad b. Salim Baraja. Again its focus was on educational uplift, taking the same name as Bin Hashim's first school in Palembang, and lauding new schools such as the Shama'il al-Huda of Pekalongan, once again led by Bin Hashim.[53] Whereas *al-Bashir* had once asked how the Arabs in general might rise, the question was now squarely addressed to the Hadramis—both at home in the watan of Hadramawt, or abroad in the place of emigration or *mahjar* of "Java" writ large.[54]

In February 1919, and in response to Irshadi moves to open a school in Surabaya, *al-Iqbal*'s pages would feature letters from eminent conservatives. One was ʿAli al-Shibli, who bemoaned the schoolboy ignorance of local peers who, apparently with a little Ibn Taymiyya and a smattering of writings from Egypt and Sudan, claimed the rank of shaykh or *mujtahid*. Al-Shibli pointed to the example of the learned sayyids educating all in Hadramawt as a true land of milk and honey and a proper society that recognized natural differences in rank between townsman, tribesman, and slave—for slaves remained on the Arabian Peninsula. As for Java: "Are the learned equal to the unlearned? And is a European equal to a Chinese, an Arab, or a native (*watani*) under Dutch law? Of course not!"[55]

In his comments, Baraja noted that the "intruders" of al-Irshad were al-Shibli's target. Many of his peers had gone further, attacking Surkati as "the black slave," or even the "black death."[56] The specter of national and racist comparison loomed large as the war came to an end, and especially once the British began to gain ground in formerly Ottoman territories, which culminated in defeat in Syria and the contest for Anatolia. The withdrawal of Turkish forces from Mesopotamia, the Levant, and Arabia saw France and Great Britain claim protectorates over the wider Middle East under Sharifan auspices. Hardly dead as an empire, London began a process of agglomerating territories in South Arabia between Aden and Muscat. Hadramawt lay in the middle, and little could be done from Java. One January 1919 issue of *al-Iqbal* featured a lament for the "Valley of Hadramawt" issued by the Egyptian poet Hafiz Ibrahim (1871–1932).[57] "How are we to preserve our rights?" asked one of Baraja's readers the following week, given that "we Hadramis in Java know we are among the most backward people in the world."[58]

This recognition of relative weakness at "home" could still be ameliorated by a sense of pride for Arab achievements among the almost universally colonized peoples of Asia. *Al-Iqbal* serialized the history of the Dutch Indies taken entirely from Western sources. Equally, the sometimes scurrilous sense of humor of their Jawi brethren could become a call to action. In February 1918, the editors had bristled at a satirical article that had appeared in the Javanese paper *Jawi Hisworo* in which two local rustics speculated about the form of God and claimed, in manifest ignorance, that the Prophet had been fond of wine and opium, which they therefore consumed at the *slametan* ceremony.[59]

Much has been made of this scandal, which led to the creation of a protest "Army of Lord Prophet Muhammad," the Tentara Kanjeng Nabi Muhammad, claiming to defend his honor.[60] It had prominent Irshadi leadership under Salim Bin ʿAbdat of Bogor—the father of the young Salih whose quest for a visa opened this book. Salim Bin ʿAbdat was abetted by a Tunisian Ottomanist, Salih Shawashi. Yet at the same time the scandal engendered a reaction within Sarekat Islam from some Javanese who did not want to be pushed around by "foreigners" intimidating their supposedly less orthodox coreligionists. By October 1918, the army had dissolved, and almost all Arabs had withdrawn from the de facto national movement.[61]

But it was not merely the Javanese of Sarekat Islam who took public issue with Arab leadership, even from the more sympathetic Irshadi side, and at a time when Indies Arabs were wondering just who would represent them on the world stage. Less has been noted in the scholarship about the furor caused by an article by S.E. in the leading Sino-Malay journal *Sin Po* that appeared in January 1919. This mouthpiece of the supporters of Chiang Kai-shek in Java compared the arrival of the Arabs to that of the Dutch, claiming that the former had blended with the local population and threatened their long-term interests, being neither concerned with their welfare nor caring to share their resources in the form of hospitals or associations.[62] Arabs of all stripes decried such claims in the increasingly pro-sayyid *al-Iqbal*. In his own response in *Sin Po*, Ismaʿil al-ʿAttas—reacting to the claim that natives would cut off the Arabs from their associations—pointing out that while natives and Arabs shared Islam, it was a faith for all humanity and that all Foreign Orientals (*al-ajanib al-sharqiyyin*) and Chinese should be striving for equality and common purpose.[63] In March, though, he contrasted the Arabs with the Chinese in terms of their very positive desire for Dutch subjecthood, arguing that, while the Chinese were now fixated on loyalty to an alien government (that had so recently overthrown its monarchy), the Arabs were longing to see their fractured homeland gain the benefits that they enjoyed under the Dutch queen.[64]

There were many such issues that continued to unite conservatives and reformers, at least in theory. The most notable at the war's end had been the question of the caliphate. All agreed that there should be a caliph. The problem was who. Whereas "natives" and locally born Irshadis stuck with Istanbul, the sayyids more often veered toward Sharif Husayn, and in ways that finally answered Blunt and Sabunji's propaganda of 1881. Still, when *al-Iqbal* quoted the *Nieuwe Rotterdamsche Courant* to the effect that Husayn had claimed the office of "Caliph of the Hijaz" in February 1918, this had been given short shrift. More attention was given to the Ottoman appointee named in his place at Medina in 1916.[65] Such reportage evaporated in 1919 with British victory and the rightward tilt of the paper. News of the Ottoman Hijaz was then replaced by pragmatic reflections on the "mastery" of Great Britain over the waves and the Muslim world.[66]

With Sharif Husayn in their pocket as Arab king of the Hijaz, the British were on the way to weening the last sayyids of their attachment to Istanbul. There was quite some irony here. In December 1918, Captain W. H. Lee Warner of the Arab Bureau had boasted how, during the war, his office had convinced many Javanese that rumored plans for an Arab caliphate had been a German fiction that in turn had led gullible natives to think that the English and the sayyids were colluding against Islam.[67] Again, none of this was felt to conflict with the local Arab desire for a strong relationship with the Dutch state, which gave something back to a community no longer engaged in the increasingly fractious rallies of Sarekat Islam. Isma'il al-'Attas, who had criticized Dutch policies toward Arab migrants in the Volksraad, would be rewarded for his tact and loyalty with the formal announcement of the ending of restrictions on the domicile of all Foreign Orientals.[68] As of April 1919 they could reside where they chose. But if the benefit accrued to all Arabs, al-'Attas's loyalty to Queen Wilhelmina hardly pleased some of the founding writers of the Hadrami renaissance in Singapore. These included Muhammad b. 'Aqil, who had reputedly complained to the Ottoman press from Singapore in the 1890s, and, especially, Batavia's Habib 'Ali, who had sent his son to study in Istanbul after having tried to enroll him in a Dutch school, worked for the consulate as an occasional translator, and petitioned Kamil Bey in the name of all the sayyids in 1898. Both were now disquieted by the freedoms enjoyed by their opponents in the egalitarian ranks of al-Irshad, whose political maneuverings under the Dutch one correspondent to *al-Iqbal* claimed had brought nothing other than "nihilism and destruction."[69] Bin 'Aqil would go further. In August 1919 he protested to B. J. O. Schrieke (1890–1945) that the Dutch failed to realize that the sayyids had long been their true friends in the Indies, opining that the Irshadis were now nothing less than a virulent disease that threatened their beloved homeland and stable colonial rule alike.⁷⁰

This was quite a turnaround for Bin ʿAqil, once of *al-Imam* and still described by Rashid Rida as an "old friend" when recounting a meeting at Cairo in early 1914 reflective of his assumed role as spokesman for Southeast Asia.⁷¹ This had occurred when Sayyid Muhammad Wajih al-Kilani (d. 1916) had been invited to an audience with Khedive ʿAbbas while returning to Istanbul from the Philippines. Bin ʿAqil's fellow sayyid had been dispatched from the empire the previous year as the new shaykh al-Islam for the American colony in response to a petition from Moro leaders of Zamboanga in 1912. The petition had been delivered by John Finley (1854–1943), the outgoing governor of the province—distantly echoing Simon Sawers in 1839 and Petrus de Roubaix in the 1860s—though his peers and superiors were far from impressed. Soon after Kilani's arrival, the U.S. government scotched the mission that should have mirrored that of Abu Bakr at the Cape half a century before.⁷²

But that was before the war, and before Cairene reformism had become the new cholera in many sayyid eyes. Bin ʿAqil and Habib ʿAli had already done a great deal to prevent the spread of al-Irshad beyond struggling Dutch territory. For, as it had been Lee Warner's task during the war to oversee the production of propaganda declaiming Great Britain's "love for Arabs and Islam," the formerly pro-Ottoman Habib ʿAli saw Great Britain as a force to be bent toward an Arab caliphate and homeland—especially now that the rival sultans of Hadramawt had been brought to an agreement with the crucial mediation of his friend Bin ʿAqil.⁷³ Lee Warner was a willing helpmate in all this, remarking that the sayyids looked to England "with confidence to see that their hegemony in Hadramaut [was] not wholly overturned."⁷⁴ He obligingly compiled reports on the leaders of KIZ and any members of Irshadi who were to be denied entry into what was effectively British territory guarded by Sultan Sir Ghalib b. ʿAwad at Mukalla. Beyond this, Habib ʿAli had convinced the British Agency at Batavia that KIZ was a nest of German sympathizers, and that the al-Irshad movement was not only pro-German, but Bolshevik, which chimed with many other lists being drafted by Western agencies at the time.⁷⁵

All such information came together in Lee Warner's listings of the good, the bad, and the Bolshevik, disseminated from Singapore to Batavia, Aden, and Cairo. With his travels in the Middle East and "perfect knowledge of geography of Hadramawt and character of every tribe," the fifty-six-year-old Habib ʿAli was accounted Great Britain's "first and most reliable and faithful Arab in Java," ready to be deployed in Yemen.[76] The list of enemies was, by comparison, long, including Ismaʿil al-Attas, for good measure:

> Born Batavia, Address Djati, Weltevreden (Batavia). Age about 26. Educated in Egypt, England and Holland. Studied Arabic in Cairo; commerce in Birmingham; Dutch, French and German in Holland. Extensive travels Europe. Member of a certain political society in Switzerland where he was connected with a pamphleteer L. F. Hoffman in the pay of the Germans. Was also in contact with an Egyptian nationalist. In 1917 returned to Java. On way rumoured to have been examined in Singapore, consequence report re European associates. Employed Niedere & co., Batavia (pro-German firm) during 1917. Nominated member Volksraad. Disliked by the Saids on account of his adherence to Shaikh Oemar bin Yoesoef Mangoesj. Is on intimate terms with high Dutch officials. Now manager and partner of Barakah trading company. . . . Supporter of al-Irsjad . . . pro-German and frankly anti-British.

Ahmad Surkati meanwhile earned a relatively cursory attribution: he was accounted as the "most useful" right hand of Manqush. "Actively pro-German and pro-Turkish and extremely anti-British," he was said to sacrifice his "time and brains for the purpose of attacking Sa[yy]ids and of damaging British interests."[77]

A Troublesome Entry

Thus far I have outlined a story of increasing contestation between sayyids and upstart "shaykhs" still united by their regard for the position of the caliph and the claims of a homeland far distant from their usual places of residence. In 1918, Lee Warner had claimed that a troublesome minority of the subordinate warrior class had spoiled the situation for all Arabs in Java.[78] But not all Arabic speakers on Java were the consistent partisans of the traditional sayyids or the shaykhs of al-Irshad. There were enough Egyptians, Tunisians, and Sudanese in the Indies to complain to the Cairene press about their treatment at the hands of the Hadramis, whom they still looked down on at home.⁷⁹ While the example of the African scholar Ahmad Surkati has often been brought up, far less notice has been taken of his friend and publisher Muhammad b. ʿUthman al-Hashimi. Although Mohamed Hachemi (as he styled himself in roman script) had already made his presence felt at gatherings to support the Red Crescent by 1916, he came into sharp focus in the listing of hostile Arabs in 1920.

The cause for Hachemi's designation was a critical attack on Sharif Husayn in his first Indies journal, *al-Salam*. This was published at Surabaya in April 1920, ostensibly in reaction to the polarization of its Arab community. As Lee Warner inserted bitterly:

AL-HASHIMI, MOHAMAD BIN OSMAN

A native of Tunis and a French protégé. Is an able Arab journalist, who at one time did useful propaganda work for us in return for pay. Later, he became editor of Al-Irshad's journal "Assalam," which survived one issue only and contained articles directed against the British and the King of the Hedjaz. According to one authority, he stated that he had been forced to write these articles by the Al-Irshad leaders. Al-Hashimi has, however, denied this to H.M. Consul General and accepted full responsibility for the articles; he has alleged that his dismissal from the post of editor was due to his writing them. Very probably, he was threatened or bribed by Al-Irshad to assume responsibility for the articles, which are said to have displeased the moderates and have forced the heads of the Society to replace "Assalam" by another newspaper, known as "Al-Irshad," under a new editor. Al-Hashimi is now ostensibly a staunch supporter of Al-Irshad, which he declares to be an innocent and non-political organisation. He is to be regarded as a venal personage who is ready to sell his pen to whichever side will pay him most for it.⁸⁰

So, who was this "venal personage?" And why was he so angered by the actions of Sharif Husayn in the Hijaz? Assuredly, Hachemi was not the typical Arab. The similarly named Muhammad b. Hashim had hesitated to apply the designation to the people of Tripoli in 1914, and he would doubtless have felt the same ambivalence about those from neighboring Tunisia, such as Hachemi and Shawashi, who had reportedly arrived on Java from Istanbul in October 1912. As Shawashi's file noted:

Born Badja Tunis. Age about 37. Resident Sourabaya. Speaks very little French. Highly educated. A good Arabic writer and fluent speaker. Been in Constantinople before coming to Java in October 1912 to sell Turkish Government Loans. Member of the Union and Progress. Founder of Tentera Kandjeng Nabi Mohamad. Well known for his pro-Turkish and pro-German activities. Keenly interested in Islamic propaganda. On way to Java called at British India and Singapore. The man who occasionally expresses his firm belief that downfall of Turkey is the downfall of Islam.[81]

Hachemi shared many of his countryman's views, but had the added ability of French. Born in the date-rich oasis of Tozeur on July 14, 1882—just after the British bombardment of Alexandria had ceased and in what had recently moved from being an Ottoman province to a French protectorate—Hachemi's education fused traditional learning at the Grand Mosque of Zaytuna with the modern curriculum of the Khalduniyya, which opened its doors in 1896. With its classes in physics, chemistry, mathematics, history, and geography, the Franco-Beylical Khalduniyya was a peer of Cairo's Dar al-ʿUlum. It was also a perfect fit for the mischievous youngster who was already disposed toward the writings of ʿAbduh, and whose family saw the ebbing Ottoman state as their enduring patron.

Like Ibn Khaldun, Hachemi came from a scholarly family with a distant Yemeni pedigree. According to his Java-born son Kussaï (1915–2010), Hachemi also inherited an impulsive spirit and a sarcastic sense of humor from his father, Othman Belgacem Elmekki (1847–1931). Othman Belgacem had served as the qadi of Tozeur before taking a teaching post at the Grand Mosque and marrying (for the third time) into the elite Turkic Bash Hamba family.[82] Othman Belgacem often had to defend his son from this privileged position, as when he was forced to resit his final exams of 1904 for jokingly asking why nobody wanted to add music to Qur'anic recitations.[83] Father and son also had a similar understanding that the practice of Islamic law and a dislike of colonialism in no way impeded an enthusiasm for Western learning. Shaykh Othman was known for his library of classical Arabic and Western titles, as well as a fascination for Napoleon and the expedition to Egypt.[84]

In line with reformist thinking, Othman also had an aversion to the litanies and prayer beads of the region's marabouts. But while Kussaï suggested that the marabouts had earned his grandfather's ire for being favored by the French, it would appear that the opposite had been true in the 1880s, if we sample the writings on Algeria of Louis Rinn, which became a manual for surveillance.[85] Many of the marabouts owed their positions to the Bey, and one needed to be careful with both, as Hachemi would learn. After graduating, he was involved with a reformist paper, *al-Islam*, which openly questioned the role of the Sufi orders in Tunisian life. It was ordered closed after its tenth issue, in June 1908, anticipating the fate of *al-Imam* at Singapore six months later.[86]

With religion being too contentious a subject, Hachemi set his sights on politics, language, and modernization. His new vehicle in July 1908 was the satirical *Abu Qisha*, its title taken from the colloquial term for a Barbary ape.[87] Hachemi's editorials touched a raw nerve indeed when he likened his fellow Franco-Beylical subjects to sheep led to the slaughter at the annual feast of the sacrifice, though his real undoing came in January 1909, when he denounced an official of the Majer moiety for corruption. Hachemi fled to the neighboring and still Ottoman province of Tripoli and promptly restarted his activities, gaining a name for himself in Libyan national history.[88] He was then unwisely back in Tunis in 1910. Sentenced to a month in prison, he was released within a few days following his father's intercession and attempted to start yet another paper before returning to Tripoli to continue *Abu Qisha*, in time to witness the Italian invasion of September 1911. He then journeyed to the Ottoman capital in 1912, together with demobilized Ottoman officers, where he met with other Tunisian émigrés such as the journalist Taïeb ben Aïssa. It was also at Istanbul in April that he met a visitor from much further afield who would change his life.

This was Abu Bakr al-ʿAttas, the Hadramawt-born son-in-law of ʿAbdallah al-ʿAttas of Batavia.[89] This particular Abu Bakr, who moved to Johor as a child in 1888 and then to Pekalongan in 1892, was newly returned to the Ottoman capital after a venture in Iraq, where he had attempted to secure an appanage.[90] He was also tasked with finding teachers for his father-in-law's Hollandsch-Arabisch School, then under the umbrella of the Jamʿiyyat Khayr, and much as Surkati had been recruited by the same organization in Mecca the previous year.

Thus engaged, the towering Mohamed Hachemi would set sail for distant Batavia in 1912.[91] His month-long journey would take him through Anglo-Egyptian Suez. After calling at much more clearly British Aden, Colombo, and Singapore, he would encounter the capital of the tropical Netherlands. Here lay always humid Batavia, with its whitewashed buildings, red tile roofs, remnant rice paddies, and local wards clustered around their mosques. Here, too, were fancy public buildings and fashionable Western suburbs linked by tramlines and canals. His Batavia-born son would certainly recall the yellow three-car trams, with their divisions for Europeans, "foreign" Asians, and natives.[92]

Classified by the Dutch as a French subject, Hachemi was able to ride in whichever carriage he chose and to live outside official Arab quarters, though he would remain connected to the al-ʿAttas clan for the rest of his life. Soon after his arrival he married the sixteen-year-old divorcee Fatima Ba Mahmush, whose father was a close friend of ʿAbdallah al-ʿAttas, and whose mother was from Xinjiang.[93] Regardless of his own distant Yemeni heritage, and now his marriage, Hachemi was most assuredly not a member of the clan, or even the Hadrami community; even so, his printing press ultimately became a key element of its renaissance, first at Batavia and later at Solo. Marked by his preference for a suit and bowtie and, on special occasions, a fez, Hachemi was proud of his nearly natal Ottoman distinction.

Hachemi was also quick to raise the hackles of the parents whose fez-wearing children he taught in Batavia, famously encouraging the donning of shorts as opposed to the customary sarongs. Angry parents accused the al-ʿAttas School of being a venue for Christianization. Recall that many conservatives were worried by the apparent wave of Frankification sweeping their world. Not that all conservatives were distinguished by their dress— Abu Bakr al-ʿAttas was often in a suit and tie. Despite Abu Bakr's father-in-law counseling patience with the worried parents, the combative Hachemi staged a photo in which his scandalously clad charges demonstrated the martial art of *pencak silat* around 1914.[94]

Hachemi eventually fell out with Abu Bakr, if not ʿAbdallah, teaching at other institutions, doing translation work, and being active in Surabaya in early 1920. A copy of the infamous silat photo, once available for purchase from the school, bears the marks of Hachemi's anger, with the ʿAttas name scratched from the print.[95] Perhaps the first real difficulties had only come with Hachemi expressing views on the sharif that would so upset the British and their sayyid allies, though these were only announced from the other end of Java in April 1920, and in the inaugural issue of a new journal.

Hachemi deemed this venture his "return to the world of the press in the Far East," even as he adopted the voice of his employers and referred to their "blessed homeland" of Hadramawt.[96] The opening paragraphs of *al-Salam* were all about the need for the study of the past and future of the valley, and the emulation of its ("our") men of action. The most important questions for the assumed readership both in the homeland and abroad were the most existential: "Where are we? And where do we want to go?" Knowing the character of the (male) Hadrami to be one of force and action and dedication to his religion, Hachemi's opening declared that there could be "no parties or sects," but, rather, one thing: "The homeland that is calling you all." Unusually for the times, that homeland remained technically independent. It was ironic that colonized Java had become "a second homeland" of opportunity and a place from which to develop and prosper while taking lessons from the politics and Islamic questions then afflicting the Arab lands in general.[97]

All of this was well and good, if somewhat forced. Local sayyids suspected Hachemi's political sympathies, both locally and globally. And if they didn't, his out-and-out attack on "the Anglo-French" sharif on the following pages would have convinced any doubters. Hachemi excoriated Husayn as a traitor to the sultan who unjustly claimed a patchwork of kingdoms for his family in Iraq and Syria.[98] Husayn's patrons were taken aback; Hachemi's friends were aghast. The journal ostensibly intended to bridge the yawning divide between sayyid and shaykh immediately closed. Ever hopeful of pressing their advantage, the British looked to exacerbate the divide among some Irshadi members who preferred not to antagonize the keymaster of greater Yemen. As the acting consul would report from Batavia in June:

> Mohamed Al-Hashimi ... is now at Batavia and intends shortly to set up a printing business of his own. His former employers, the members of the Al-Irshad Society, are said to be endeavouring to place upon him the sole responsibility for the publication of "ASSALAM," which they allege to have been a private venture of his ... It is even reported that certain Sourabaya members of "Al-Irshad" contemplated visiting this Consulate General, in order to voice their repudiation of "ASSALAM" and all its works.
>
> I hope that it may be possible to play on Mohamed Al-Hashimi's fears by letting it be conveyed to him that promoters of "ASSALAM" are about to incriminate him in order to screen themselves. He may, perhaps, then be induced to defend himself by offering definite proofs (which he is said to possess in writing) of the complicity of "Al-Irshad" in the publication of "ASSALAM."[99]

When Crosby closed his letter, he detailed the root cause of British surprise: Hachemi was supposed to be one of *their* men: "a native of Tunis and a French protégé.... In 1918 he was employed by the French and ourselves to do propaganda work by translating various pamphlets into Arabic. I gather that he is a man who entertains no pronounced political opinions of any kind but who is willing to place his pen at the disposal of whichever side is prepared to pay him most. I understand that Mr. Lee Warner knows him. He is said to be an able journalist."[100]

Hachemi was certainly able, though hardly devoid of principles. His propaganda work had been geared to translating articles discouraging the pilgrimage in a time of war, which would have aligned with his hopes of depriving the sharif of much-needed revenues. Sayyid-informed British reports meanwhile suggested that Hachemi had become close to a wealthy Malay shoe trader who felt that the Arabs squeezed natives and took their profits away from the country. Hachemi had accordingly couched his critique as one of Arabs exploiting "the natives for their own profit," stating they "sucked in gold as their deserts did water."[101]

Whether Hachemi believed that the Hadramis he ventriloquized were the oppressors of natives is moot. He was not invested in the sayyid narrative of exceptionalism. He remained a natural partner to members of al-Irshad in Surabaya whom he had helped establish another journal in June. Titled, not so oddly, *al-Irshad*, its editors explicitly walked back the rhetoric of *al-Salam* and allied Malay journals in September while Manqush and Surkati commenced a campaign to convince the British legation that their organization was a purely religious one, hoping to regain admission to the homeland for its members.[102] They seem to have made a personal breakthrough with Crosby. As he later confessed of the relationship with Bin Shahab: "As regards the Netherlands East Indies, he and he alone holds the keys to the Hadramaut. The Sheikh party realises the position quite clearly, and one of the Al Irshad leaders remarked to me only a few days ago: 'You have a list of suspect Arabs in the Consulate-General. The list is based on information supplied by bin Shahab. Please remember that bin Shahab is our enemy and that he does not speak the truth about us.' I must confess that the above accusations distressed me not a little."[103]

List or no, the contents of *al-Irshad* had already excited Sultan Ghalib of Mukalla. He arranged with the British agency at Aden to have official condemnations of the organization published at Singapore, though Crosby preferred the letter to be published in *al-Iqbal* without Ghalib's references to "the Resident at Aden" or his "friend Britannia."[104] And even if Aden now agreed with Crosby that Irshadis such as the young Salih Bin 'Abdat could be admitted and watched, Ghalib was unconvinced. He banned *al-Irshad*, which was defunct on Java by mid-May 1921.[105]

Back at Weltevreden by the end of 1920, Hachemi had since established another Arabic paper that was much more his own. Printed in the workshop abutting his home under the trusty eye of his assistant, Mustafa, it boasted a circulation of eight hundred by October 1921.[106] This was *Burubudur*, named after the ninth-century Buddhist monument of Central Java. It was also, as the masthead declared, a periodical dealing with learning and history, of which plenty was on offer, from what Crosby admitted was a balanced account of the sayyid-shaykh dispute, to discussions of great leaders past and present, including George Washington.[107]

Hachemi admired resolute leaders, and it was clear from his paper that he could not abide the king who had betrayed his caliph. Often sourcing his material from Tunisian papers, he consistently mocked Husayn as a creature of the British.[108] He was also more than happy to expose the consulate's hostility to al-Irshad, earning him censure from the sayyids, who sent messages to Arabia. Critiques soon appeared in the pages of *al-Qibla*, the official paper of Husayn funded by Cairo's Arab Bureau.[109] Not that Hachemi was solely concerned with the failing Hashimite state. With the demise of most other Arabic periodicals in the Indies—including *al-Iqbal*—his paper became the default journal for advice in Arabic.

In August 1921, one reader asked whether it was licit to toast a young couple in the presence of Europeans, men and women alike. The question was intended as a trap, for it referred to the twinned July celebration of 'Umar Manqush having been awarded the Order of Oranje Nassau, and the wedding of his daughter Fatmah to 'Awad b. Sunkar, to which many Dutch dignitaries were invited.[110] In reply, Hachemi could only remark that his journal was not really been in the habit of issuing fatwas and proposed that readers refer to the pages of Pekalongan's *Soeloeh Hindia*, where the long-running matter of mixed marriages was covered. Alternatively, the writer might well get in touch with KIZ or refer to the works of Ahmad Surkati as *its* trusted advisor on the rights of marriage between sayyids and others. Hachemi mischievously asked who claimed that Manqush was even an Arab in the first place and openly wondered how, setting aside anxieties about socializing in mixed assemblies, the more hidebound sayyids could cope with the fact that their uncloistered local wives mixed with Chinese in the market every day.[111]

Looming Nationalism and Fears of Another Empire

Five months earlier, in March 1921, the surely weary Ottoman consul general at Batavia reflected on the almost universal state of Christian rule over Muslim subjects around the world:

> It is impossible to deny the Europeans' political skills in administering various peoples and lands. Without exception, all the European countries that have lots of Muslim subjects investigate closely every aspect of spiritual vigour, religion, convictions, emotions, desires, morals, and customs, and inform their governments extensively on the issue. On the other hand, they employ commissions and associations that consist of knowledgeable people and experts who work day and night to prepare all kinds of tricks to prevent their [Muslims'] spiritual and material progress, and to spoil their religious beliefs, convictions, and even their morals. This is because [they believe] that as long as the people remain Muslim, they cannot be loyal to a Christian government![112]

Re'fat Bey did not blame the Western advisors alone. He reserved a part of his report to critique the sayyids, whom he said had "made every effort to destroy the men of enlightened ideas with Islamic zeal."[113] Such a view was diametrically opposed to the hopes and plans of his predecessors. It was also a reversal of an early incarnation of himself, having once lauded the efforts of Bin ʿAqil at Singapore in 1908.[114] Little did Re'fat know, of course, that the religious bona fides of his own government would be declared void within a few short years, and that the last claimant to the caliphate would be denied the vestigial privileges of his office in 1924 by Mustafa Kemal, who had once defended it as a volunteer in Libya and led its forces at Gallipoli.

This move would surprise some of his admirers. Among them was Hachemi, who in November 1920 had featured the future Ataturk on the cover of *Burubudur* with as much enthusiasm as he would treat Washington the following August—though, naturally, only the Turkish figure was accompanied by the Quranic injunction that "if there are twenty among you who will patiently fight, they will defeat two hundred."[115] British watchers were unimpressed.

Whereas Hachemi's enthusiasm for Mustafa Kemal appalled some watchers in the British consulate, it hardly worried the Dutch advisers of KIZ, some of whom—such as G. F. Pijper (1893-1988)—took Arabic lessons with Surkati. Their articles were equally welcomed in the pages of Surkati's own journal, *Azzachirah al-Islamijah*, which Hachemi printed. In January 1924, the Malay edition featured a report by the former Dutch consul to Jeddah (1917-1921) and now adjunct advisor for native affairs Emile Gobée (1881-1954). Entitled simply "Islam," Gobée's essay was written as a review of the developments of the previous twenty-five years and offered a favorable perspective of the Salafi thought of Muhammad b. ʿAbd al-Wahhab and Muhammad ʿAbduh as mediated by Rashid Rida.[116] Gobée further chronicled the penetration of such reformism in Sumatra and Java, noting both the genesis of laudable organizations like Sarekat Islam and Muhammadiyah, but also the violent disputes between "old faction" and "new faction" on Sumatra, and sayyid and shaykh on Java.

Gobée was firmly of the opinion that, under the leadership of men like Surkati's ally Ahmad Dahlan, the modern Muslims of Java would outstrip the Egyptian effendis, whom he felt merely emulated the West. All the Dutch needed to do was return the favor by enabling the addition of spiritual guidance in their technical and medical schools. In this way it could combat the malodorous Communists, in addition to properly overseeing the collection of funds and establishment of mosques, while easing the burdens on the pilgrims who faced the corruption of the king of Mecca. Of course, the state should not interfere with the practice of Islam and continue to follow Snouck's advice by giving the most freedom of action to lead to the uplift of Muslims to the level of their Dutch rulers.[117]

In offering Gobée's essay as their leading article, the satisfied editors, Ahmad Surkati and ʿAbdallah Badjerei, remarked that none of this needed any comment.[118] A sampling of issues in *Azzachierah* shows wide interest in Islam as a reformist message for the world that could be sanctioned by KIZ, furthermore offering the sorts of fatwa that Hachemi eschewed in the *Burubudur*. Serialized articles discussed issues of innovation and deviation, "Buddhism and Islam," "East and West," and "The Rights of Husbands and

Wives." *Azzachierah* also published a letter about the contemporary state of Islam at the Cape of Good Hope from a Mr. Mahad, who discussed the role of many people of Southeast Asian origin—Javanese, Malay, and Bugis—who were holding fast to their faith while surrounded by "Christians and Magians." It was fortunate, observed Surkati, that they had the leadership of people like Dr. Abdullah Abdurahman (1872–1940), the first nonwhite member of Cape Town's Provincial Council and president of the South African Malay Association.[119]

Had they been aware of developments in Colombo, the editors would just as happily have reported the parallel discourse of the All-Ceylon Malay Association, formed in January 1922 under M. K. Saldin (1870–1944), the youngest son of Ounus Saldin. Inspired by the London-educated principal of Zahira College, T. B. Jayah (1890–1960) and patronized by the sultan of Johor, there was great interest in the notion of Islam's role in developing a future Ceylon. All the same, some members suggested that they should be wary of the "pitfalls of patriotism" and attuned to the dominant culture of the Island's "Lion race."[120] Istanbul and the Hijaz did not rate a mention.

It was nevertheless clear that some Ceylon Malays were reflecting on history and trying to find their place in it, whether framed as "Javanese" or Pan-Malay and stretching from the Transvaal to the Philippines with very different sources of inspiration. T. B. Jayah preferred to cite the work of theosophists and art historians like Ananda Coomeraswamy (1877–1947), who, like Hachemi, was enamored of the Borobudur, and whom he said knew "more about Malay institutions and Malay civilization than any Malay in Ceylon." On the other hand, fellow Malays such as Yahya Dane Surood (a.k.a. Poespajaya) preferred to point to the influence of ʿAbduh back in the Dutch Indies, where most of their ancestors originated, and fused the activities of the Muhammadiyah and Sarekat Islam.[121]

Although very much mistaken about the foundation of Sarekat Islam "purely on religious principles at Padang" and having extolled the virtues of Tjokroaminoto as a "national hero" exiled to Timor during the Great War (he hadn't been), Poespajaya at least had a good idea of the major Malay-language journals of the national movement. He accordingly listed Yogyakarta's *Soeara Moehammadijah*, Solo's *Medan Moeslimin* and *Islam Bergerak* (both printed by Hachemi), and Semarang's *Sinar Hindia*, with the addition of the leftist *Soeara Ra'jat*. It was also apparent that Poespajaya had read an essay by the editors of *al-Imam* in 1908 on the origins of the Malays as an inherently "pliant people."[122] This he paired with the assertions of their inherently tolerant and gentlemanly character given in a paper presented to the Royal Asiatic Society:

> For the last five centuries they have been Mohammedans of an orthodox and simple type, not fanatical as a rule, indeed rather tolerant of the alien beliefs of foreigners, they have many pleasing characteristics. A Malay of whatever class has generally speaking the instincts of a gentleman. He is sensitive himself but he respects the feelings of others. He is courteous in manner, rather reserved and shy. Towards Europeans he is almost uniformly friendly. He is now becoming acutely conscious of his shortcomings and is keenly anxious of qualifying himself by education and otherwise to take a more active part. He is getting somewhat jealous of the Chinese and Indians who have made his country a happy hunting ground for themselves, and he wants to take a hand in the game.[123]

Like the similarly pro-Johorean editors of *al-Imam*, the movers of the All-Ceylon Malay Association echoed the established British notion of the Malays. In doing so they invoked the scholarly authority of Marsden, Raffles, and Crawfurd, alongside a more recent governor of the Straits Settlements, Frank Swettenham (1850–1946).[124] While mindful of the unhappy precedent of Javanese exiles under the Dutch, Poespajaya recalled how British Ceylon had been made home to Egyptian exiles, Boer prisoners, and, lately, an "Arabian prince."[125]

But if, back on Java, Surkati and his editorial team had capacious visions of a Muslim world with elected Malay or Arab components, they could be patronizing, to say the least, of their local peers. In this regard they followed their Cairene fellows, who shook their heads at the quality of the average Jawi student at al-Azhar, by which they now decidedly meant *Javanese*, and not Malays.[126] In 1925, having outlined the responsibility of the religious to speak up to the now repressive colonial state on questions of education, Surkati declared that it was "well known" that the Jawis were "like children ... lovers of the sweet and angered by what is bitter."[127]

Such sentiments would have annoyed many locals, and there had been a lot of bitterness expressed by both sides when Surkati made his remark. As Sarekat Islam and Muhammadiyah had developed, with the former seeing gatherings of thousands in Central Java in the 1910s, it became clear that most Indonesians, as many would start to call themselves in the 1920s, preferred Arab funding to Arab leadership or assumptions thereof in relation to a future caliphate. Writing in April 1920, for instance, K. H. Anang had called in the *Islam Bergerak* for Javanese to efface the "fictitious stories" that had "taken root in the heart of our nation" regarding an Arab caliphate. He also announced that it was the duty of that paper and the allied *Medan Moeslimin* (which he edited) to guide "the Muslims of Java to the right path" and "glorify the name of Javanese Muslims in the history of Islam as well as before Muslims abroad."[128]

Given the weight of decades of Ottoman propaganda and the commonplace appearance of caliphal symbols at Sarekat Islam rallies, a significant portion of its members (and Anang to be sure) were as perturbed as Hachemi by Husayn's reported moves to claim the caliphate.[129] Such annoyance had only been magnified once he had been forced to govern the Hijaz with a harsh hand in the absence of subsidies from Istanbul. With sayyid advice, he was further hostile to the establishment of a branch of the Muhammadiyah or Sarekat Islam in the Hijaz, just as the guardians of Hadramawt kept the "Bolshevik" al-Irshad at bay.

With their many Malay- and Javanese-language periodicals, Indonesians had now become avid consumers of news about a wider Muslim world from the Balkans to India, where the Khilafat movement had taken firmer shape with assistance from Gandhi in 1920. *Islam Bergerak* and *Medan Moeslimin* played their part in raising awareness of the movement on Java with the personal support of Tjokroaminoto. But not all Indian residents in the Dutch Indies were on side; some were in the pay of the British consulate. Sent to Sarekat Islam rallies in Sumatra in late 1920, Agent "D" offered an alarmist summary of the rhetoric of Mohammed Samin, the editor of *Merdeka* and head of the Khilafat Committee for Deli.[130] In speeches purportedly given on tour up the coast of Sumatra at Tjokroaminoto's behest to "fanatic" audiences, Samin was said to have contrasted the non-cooperation movement of Gandhi and Shaukat Ali with the parlous and divided situation in the Indies, proclaiming that indigenes "ought not to follow the Arabs," who had "sold Mecca and betrayed Islam and Kaliph." Samin proclaimed that Muslims of the world were still brothers who should be invested in the reestablishment of the caliphate, and that there was a difference between the still trustworthy Arabs of Java and the treacherous Husayn and "a few other Arab

Amirs," who had been the real "offenders" and "the cause of this mischief."[131]

Samin's attack alienated many Arabs on Sumatra, who were said to have boycotted prayers at mosques in the control of Malays in favor of those they dominated. Sarekat Islam was further alleged to be using caliphal propaganda "as a very sharp weapon to awake the ignorant and poor masses who readily yield to religious pressure to do any desperate thing," including revolution, for which "Japan would secretly supply arms."[132]

Thanks in part to the evident obsession of Agent "D," the British were already concerned about furtive attempts from Japanese actors to make a play for Muslim attention.[133] In June 1921, the Batavian consulate worried about Surkati's close associate Anang, who had written anti-British articles in *Islam Bergerak*. He was also teaching Malay to the staff of the Mitsui Bishen Kaisha, as well as engaging with those of the *Jawa Nippo*, which Hachemi also printed.[134] Indeed, Hachemi's home and office were close to the many Japanese shops of Pasar Baru. The previous year Anang was assumed to be the "Kiyai Reksooepojo" who offered a Hachemi-like attack on British plans to use an Arab caliphate in *Islam Bergerak* and *Medan Moeslimin*, if with a rebuke of Tjokroaminoto for not having done enough to combat the sayyids.[135] Again in early 1922, Anang—by now living in Yogyakarta—was assumed to be behind a critique of British interference in the Hijaz and Mesopotamia.[136]

Setting aside the prescient anxiety of the British and their Indian agents, hardly comfortable with their Asian allies in the Western Pacific, Japan remained on the menu of interest for readers of reformist journals, though not necessarily as the military savior that it would pose as in the 1940s.[137] Lecturing in Arabic across Java in the 1920s, Ahmad Surkati implicitly discussed Japan when comparing the merits of Buddhism to Islam in articles that rolled off Hachemi's press in January 1924 alongside a remarkable essay by a certain "Ramsees," who praised Japan as an example for the Muslims of Java, "whether Arab, Malay, Sundanese, or Javanese." Citing an epigraph by Kipling, Ramsees declared that the best of the West was to be emulated in the Japanese manner by keeping one's culture and language. "May God bless us always!" added the editors in English.[138]

Writers like Rida and Surkati still saw Japan as an example that was simultaneously fertile ground for conversion. Already imbued with wataniyya, all that was needed was Islam. Empire had the capacity to enfold both. Samin evidently believed this into the 1930s, heading a committee to welcome the

Japanese to Sumatra in 1942, though he soon became jaded. But there were also Muslims of more Western education who became disappointed well before the arrival of any Japanese soldiers, and who worried that in appealing to an outside power in Asia, they would only gain a new exponent of imperialism. Sukarno was one.

ELEVEN

Pan-Islamism, Nationalism, Pan-Asianism

THE ARRIVAL OF British forces in France in August 1914 saw the Netherlands hindered both in Europe and Asia. Already nervous about antagonizing either of its powerful neighbors at home, the Dutch found their tropical empire under naval blockade, echoing the situation in the 1790s when VOC vessels had struggled to maintain a lifeline to the Batavian Republic. This time, though, the interisland economies were strangled by shortages of gunny for the sacking that held so many products, and the pilgrims to and resident scholars of the Hijaz became collateral by virtue of the Committee for Union and Progress alliance with Germany, despite early assurances from Great Britain that the hajj would be unhindered. Eighteen months before Sharif Husayn's defection to London, no Dutch-flagged pilgrim ships would risk the journey—indeed, the Dutch government actively discouraged the journey as both dangerous and wasteful. The Office of Native Affairs furthermore made common cause with Tjokroaminoto to gather funds for the support and negotiated repatriation for those stranded in the Hijaz. In mid-1915, four vessels were able to pick up some of the several thousand expatriates struggling to make ends meet, to the disappointment of local guides, who had expected fresh clients.[1]

Among those who made it home to Java around that time—whether on a relief vessel or by some alternate flag and route—was an awkward nineteen-year-old called Mas Mansur. He had been abroad for some five years by then.[2] Perhaps relieved, he reported to his friends how keenly he had missed the mangoes and jackfruit of his childhood home while in the holy cities and further afield in Cairo, where he had also ventured. With his broad belt girding his sarong, he must have felt a particularly odd fit in that city, where his peers favored the suits and fezzes of the rising middle class who had marched behind the funeral cortege of Mustafa Kamil in 1908. But he seems to have settled in and soon sharpened or imbibed the ideas that would define his future trajectory: of homeland and Muslim nationhood felt keenly in the presence of others, Arabs included.

Having outlined the story of outreach for Ottoman patronage often mediated by very Arab concerns, this chapter will now reinfuse the twentieth-century story with some of its Jawi actors, like Mansur, seeing how they came to construct their place in a Muslim world as Indonesian subjects. In this process, some of the same "foreign" actors will serve as windows on the makings of this subjectivity. Indeed, we shall see how their foreignness was reinscribed in new ways, causing some to turn in very different directions for inspiration and perhaps even practical aid from advocates of a reimagined Asia that overlapped with the old Pan-Islamism.

The Fantastic Kyai Hajji Mas Mansur

Mas Mansur was born in the busy port city of Surabaya, East Java, in June 1896. His father, Ahmad Marzuqi, claimed the prestigious ancestral post of khatib of the mosque of Ampel, deep in the Arab quarter of a city then counting close to 150,000 people. Ahmad Marzuqi also had familial connections to the court of Sumenep on the nearby island of Madura, where so many future Malays had once been recruited for VOC service. It was thus appropriate that Mansur was sent to study there with the eminent Khalil Bangkalan before embarking for Mecca around 1910.[3]

This was the standard trajectory for the scholarly elite of East Java. Once at Mecca, Mansur joined the vital community of Jawa students, scholars, and their families, dominated by a close-knit core of religious scholars. Their often cheek-by-jowl existence was also in evidence in mid-1912, when al-Munir's agent from Padang Panjang reported his safe arrival at Mecca with eleven colleagues and a troubling story. The anecdote concerned a fatal fire at the home of Shaykh ʿAbd al-Raʾuf Sabban, which had raged opposite the home of the Sumatran Ahmad Lampung and next to that of his fellow Jawi scholar ʿUmar Sumbawa, both of whom had been active in Mecca since the 1880s.⁴

The fires of the Hijaz were also political. It seems that the environment—under the governance of Sharif Husayn following the 1908 revolution of the Committee for Union and Progress and soon in a ferment with the forced 1909 abdication of Abdulhamid—led Mansur to Cairo in 1912 or 1913, where Shaykh Sabban had himself moved in 1910. Once there, Mansur mixed with a much smaller community of around two dozen Jawi students making their way in a confusing city that was half Ottoman and half Parisian in its architecture and aspirations. With the country still occupied by British Indian troops, Khedive Abbas now represented Abdulhamid's successor, Mehmed V, while claiming a throne of his own and an army to run the country and its southern colony, the Sudan.

The Jawi students in residence around the colonnades of the ancient university included Muhammad Fadlallah, the editor of a new Malay journal called *al-Ittihad*, or "Unity." Fadlallah—or Fadloellah, as he was often termed in roman script—was the son of a Singaporean, Muhammad Suhaymi, and he was in regular contact with the reformist movement on Sumatra. He also had close ties with several Malay students from Dutch territory like the Sumatran Abd al-Wahid Tapanuli, as well as the brothers Muhammad Basyuni (b. 1885) and Ahmad Fauzi (b. 1890), who had arrived from the court of Sambas, on Borneo, in 1910, and who assisted him with *al-Ittihad*.⁵

Mansur's Cairene venture is known because of letters written to his family appealing for support. Far from happy with this impetuous sojourn or the possibility of his frequenting teachers like Rashid Rida, Ahmad Marzuqi had cut off his son. There is quite some mystery regarding Mansur's time in Cairo, where some now believe that he spent a year living hand to mouth while studying under a "Shaykh Maskawayh."⁶ Beyond this, it is now claimed that Mansur, a keen exponent of traditional martial arts, traveled westward across the Libyan desert to an oasis madrasa called Shinggit (Shinqit?), where he received training in horse riding and marksmanship at the hands of a Sufi master called Sidi ʿAbdallah.⁷ While there is little doubt—despite his absence in lists kept by the Dutch legation—that Mansur slipped from Mecca to Cairo to keep company with the dozen or so Jawi students who attended Rashid Rida's new preparatory school on Roda Island (founded in 1911), the stories of training in Libya (?) derive from confused reportage of the Cairene press, for there does not ever seem to have been such a Sufi among the pro-Ottoman ranks of the Sanusiyya.[8]

To be sure, the nationalist press of the day was focused on the Italian and Balkan wars against the empire to which Egypt officially belonged, just as it had been taken with the exploits of Russia's Asian enemy at Port Arthur and in the Strait of Tsushima. Perhaps the most convincing evidence for Mansur's Cairene adventure was his imbibing of the discourse of Egyptian nationalism within the context of an Ottoman empire, especially that preached by the late Japanophile Kamil, who had been patronized by Khedive ʿAbbas.[9] Kamil may have died young in 1908, but his ideas about the importance of the Egyptian watan under the protective benevolence of the caliphate touched many in the Indies, and not just among the Arab diaspora and their occasional Sudanese teachers. To see the impact of such thinking, one only needs to look at the names of the several organizations and papers that Mansur would establish after his return to Java while serving as a bridge between Cairo-oriented reformers and Meccan traditionalists. In Surabaya, Mansur joined the circle of the noted traditionalist Wahab Hasbullah to found a salon, Taswir al-Afkar, which produced its own journal in Javanese from 1919.[10] Beyond this, Mansur was engaged with several educational ventures linked to the Muhammadiyah movement that paid direct homage to Egyptian nationalist thinking, including Nahdat al-Watan (Rise of the Homeland), Khitab al-Watan (Speeches of the Homeland), Ahl al-Watan (People of the Homeland), Faruʿ al-Watan (Branches of the Homeland), and Hidayat al-Watan (Guidance of the Homeland).[11]

Evidently Mansur played a role in pushing modern Arab—and thus Islamic—notions of the homeland directly into the Surabayan bloodstream, where, as chapter 10 has shown, it was projected back to the other side of the Indian Ocean by both conservative sayyids and their Irshadi rivals. By the same token, it was clearly embraced locally by activists in search of a name for their own country that transcended the bounds of Java. For it was at Surabaya that Tjokroaminoto had both a home and (briefly) a son-in-law in the young Sukarno.

It was also only natural that Mansur would be drawn to both Tjokroaminoto's Sarekat Islam movement and Ahmad Dahlan's Muhammadiyah. The latter, which Mansur joined in 1921, claimed his primary loyalty the following year, when Snouck's former protégé Agus Salim (1884–1954) instituted a policy of single loyalty for Sarekat Islam aimed at purging that movement of Communist elements and rival leaders.[12] It was also in 1922 that Salim and Mansur would attend a meeting at Cirebon aimed in part at defending the caliphate that both had experienced, the former as a trusted employee of the Dutch consulate in Jeddah from 1906 to 1911 and the latter as a student sojourner. Given the small staff of that agency, it was quite possible that the Sumatran had stamped the young Javanese's passport at some point, though neither ever spoke of such a connection that marked them both as subjects of the Dutch Indies in the still Ottoman holy land.

An End to Sultanate and Caliphate

On August 10, 1920, the Ottomans signed the Treaty of Sevres with the Allied Powers, ceding large tracts of Asia Minor and accepting the placement of armies of occupation in parts of Anatolia. Pro-caliphate Muslims the world over were both anxious and galvanized. In India, the Ali brothers and Gandhi saw each other as useful political partners, and the Khilafat movement soon facilitated the emergence of the non-cooperation movement. Whereas neither leadership espoused violence, and the Muslim League maintained its stance of loyalty to the British state, the Southern Malabari branches of the movement harnessed their own long history of frustration and broke into open rebellion in August 1921.

The uprising, labeled the Moplah revolt by the British, was put down in 1922, soon filling the infamous prison of the Andaman Islands with a new cadre of national heroes to link to the legend of 1857. By 1922, the consensus of the Khilafat movement was being replaced by anxieties about the deliberately Turkish rather than Pan-Islamic course plotted by Mustafa Kemal. Such worries also pervaded Islamic discourse in the Dutch Indies, although, in the absence of British censorship, a great many were still inclined to see the future Ataturk as an analogue to Saladin and a hero of the Muslim world, as we saw in the pages of Hachemi's paper.[13]

Leaving aside the fact of a riven Arab community and local British suspicions of Japanese funding underpinning calls for a revived caliphate, many Jawi reformers and traditionalists were united by what were seen as very British threats to the caliphate, joining at Cirebon on the last day of October 1922 for the inaugural Indies Islam Congress (Kongres Al-Islam Hindia).[14]

Tjokroaminoto may have presided, but it was directed for all intents and purposes by Salim, with the support of Muhammadiyah and al-Irshad. A more traditionalist outlook was meanwhile represented by Abdul Wahab Hasbullah of Surabaya and Kyai Asnawi of Kudus. Both were members of Taswir al-Afkar like its cofounder, Mas Mansur, who was also present.[15]

The event played out before a large audience also gathered in anticipation of the Prophet's birthday celebrations. The traditionalists evidently made sufficient impact on the discussions when, on the second day, proceedings broke down as they attacked Surkati for claiming the right to interpret the sources of Islam. Surkati defended himself in an Arabic address translated by Salim in which he affirmed a commitment to the Sunni juridical schools and a desire to change only the form of Islamic instruction.[16]

The next day saw extended discussion and argument about the education of children while adhering to the government's regulations for the registration of schools, the consistent ill treatment of pilgrims by the guides in Mecca, and the uplift of Muslim women in the Indies. All of this pushed the caliphate question into the background. In retrospect their timing as regards discussion of that office could not have been less fortunate. November 1 saw the Turkish Grand National Assembly dissolve the office of sultan, and thus the empire, though news was yet to make it to Cirebon. Despite Hachemi having overseen a disappointing collection for the Red Crescent on the first evening, Salim had gone so far as to send a congratulatory telegram to "Le Grand Moustapha kemal et héros conquérants Patrio-Nationaux," for his defense of the Dar al-Islam.[17]

With the caliphate already an unsteady proposition in 1922, a Cirebonese delegate's suggestion that the Dutch should request the Ottomans to appoint a shaykh al-Islam for an Indies-wide council of ulama would be moot.[18] Salim still tried to put on a brave face. At a Sarekat Islam meeting at Madiun in February 1923, he pushed a resolution applauding Ankara's separating state and caliphate, while the former consular secretary Anang echoed the Khilafat movement's ongoing support of Kemal and celebrated him as "the sword of Islam and renovator of the caliphate."[19] The final erasure of that lingering office the following March, and then King Husayn's claim of the rank two months before the second Indies Islam Congress of May 1924, found Salim floundering and suggesting that a solution had to be found for all Muslims.

Just as Hachemi detested the sharif for his betrayal of the empire, Salim had been unimpressed by his administration when he had worked at Jeddah.

Husayn's pretensions were soon dealt a mortal blow in September 1924 with the victory of the Saudis over the town of Ta'if, leading to his forced abdication under pressure from the merchants of Jeddah on October 3. Mecca would fall ten days later, with Jeddah and Medina to follow in December 1925. The defeat of the Hashimites of the Hijaz left two rival sovereigns to claim the mantle of the Prophet on either side of the Red Sea. Both had British support, whether in the case of the unpopular King Faruq of Egypt, elevated to that post in Khedive Abbas's absence at Istanbul in 1914, or Ibn Sa'ud, whose polity lacked much of the technical expertise that would be required to establish a modern state. Indeed, that would often come from now independent Egypt or still British India.[20]

Many Indonesian Muslims reacted with horror to news of the Saudi regime's abolition of the posts of the four imams, of their enforcement of Wahhabi interpretations of Islamic law, and of their cracking down on Sufi activities. But there were also apologists. An Arab journalist based at Buitenzorg, Muhammad al-Fattah al-Makki, switched from supporting the Ottoman caliph to singing the praises of the Saudis in the pages of his bilingual paper, *al-Wifaq*. Perhaps this was only natural for a man who, aside from being known as "the Meccan," sometimes went by the sobriquet Najdi—referring to the Arabian region whence the Wahhabis had sprung. His comparatively fancy paper, printed by Weltevreden's G. Kolff, only went from strength to strength, and boasted a Malay edition (*al-Wivac*), just as *al-Bashir* once had and Surkati's *Zachierah* still did.

Such views engendered no great love from the embattled sayyids. Muhammad al-Fattah was assaulted twice by the partisans of the rival *Hadramawt* of Muhammad b. Hashim and 'Aydarus al-Mashhur. The first attack occurred when he visited Surabaya at the height of the Meccan crisis in October 1925. He was promptly set upon again as he was released from a two-week stay in the hospital.[21] Al-Fattah also had a poisonous relationship with Hachemi, who had launched attacks on his "infidel and debauched" paper in 1924, bemoaning his linguistic abilities and complaining of the "Meccan" hatred of the Turks.[22]

Although rivals, Hachemi and al-Fattah maintained similar views of the sharif and the need for Jawi uplift, just as they shared connections with Surkati and publishers in Egypt whom 'Ali Shahab and Lee Warner had deemed so seditious.[23] Both Hachemi and al-Fattah furthermore communicated with Tantawi Jawhari (1862–1940) of the Dar al-'Ulum, whose addresses to the

Muslim world al-Fattah serialized. Tantawi was instrumental in setting up an association to assist Jawi students in Cairo in 1925 at the suggestion of the aged Hasan al-ʿAttas (1832–1932), a sayyid once patronized by Abu Bakar of Johor.[24]

Compared to Hachemi, though, al-Fattah could at times be more openly critical of the "noble Dutch state" to which he had reported allegations of sayyid plots on Surkati's life. Tantawi was also assumed to have relayed Fattah's coverage of Dutch hinderance of religious practice in Java in the Egyptian papers in late 1925. This report was blamed in part for the Surabayan assault, and an attempt by some sayyids to have him expelled from the Indies.[25] Indeed, the worst fears of the sayyids would have been realized once Western reportage of Wahhabi outrages in Medina was denied by Fattah.[26] With their steadfast loyalty to the Hashimites and their de facto support of Great Britain—now wheeling behind Ibn Saʿud—the sayyids of Java had lost the last vestiges of leadership in the discourse of affiliation to the caliphate among the Jawa of Indonesia. Still, they retained their influence in what was to become Malaysia. Such would become clear after both the Egyptians and the Saudis advertised conferences to resolve the question of the caliphate in 1926. Seizing the moment, the modernists of Sarekat Islam and Muhammadiyah dispatched Tjokroaminoto, Mas Mansur, and Sumatra's Haji Rasul to represent the Indonesian case to the Muslim world. This infuriated Abdul Wahab Hasbullah and Hasyim Asy'ari, who had dim views of Tjokroaminoto's religious knowledge. One Egyptian delegate to the unproductive meetings, Shaykh Muhammad al-Zawahiri, had a similarly negative view of the Indonesians present—of Haji Rasul and Mas Mansur at Cairo, who were joined by Tjokroaminoto in Mecca—whom, he alleged, sat quietly while all around debated.[27]

It is unclear whether Zawahiri also had in mind the Irshadi delegate to Mecca, ʿUmar b. Sulayman Naji, when he leveled his charge.[28] Not that the Jawis—especially those who now identified as Indonesians in distinction to equally proud Malays or Arabs—remained quiet any longer when their own image was at stake, as Bin Hashim found when he offered a guest lecture on the history of Java at Cairo in 1926.[29] By contrast, his fellow sayyids Hasan and Abu Bakr al-ʿAttas could still represent the sultan of Johor at Cairo, while none other than Muhammad b. ʿAqil—with his nephew and sons in tow—was said to stand for Singapore and the "Malayan lands" in totality.[30] It was to these lands that the sayyids would turn for aid for struggling

Hadramawt and its threatened rulers in 1927, culminating in the founding the ʿAlawi Bond (al-Rabita al-ʿAlawiyya) in 1928. This was facilitated by the former editor of Husayn's British-funded organ *al-Qibla*, Shaykh Tayyib al-Sasi.[31] Now, though, the British of Java had a weather eye on him after receiving intelligence from their trusted interlocutor: Ahmad Surkati.[32] The fickle empire had flipped again.

Silent or strident, what the increasingly distinct Malays and Indonesians also witnessed at Cairo and Mecca in 1926, like many other delegates from almost universally colonized Muslim countries, was chaos. Neither claimant to the office would gain the ratification that they sought, and the many different visions of the caliphate proved unworkable. In Egypt, Rashid Rida had already posited that the caliph should preside over something akin to a commonwealth of Muslim states rather than a unitary empire, dropping out of the Cairo meeting before it was abandoned. While he previously had hopes for Imam Yahya of Yemen, Ibn Saʿud fitted the bill closely enough.[33] He may not have been a descendent of the Prophet, but he held Mecca, and thus the responsibility for the protection of all who sought the holy places. He also knew where his allies lay abroad, with a much less worried British agency at Batavia remarking that the new king of the Hijaz and Najd had sent robes of honor to Surkati and Manqush.[34] So it was that Rida, Surkati, and many of their Jawi students fell more closely into Ibn Saʿud's orbit, hardening the Salafi interpretation of reformism with Wahhabism, with its profound implications for the future of the Muslim world.

That world must have seemed all the stranger in Mecca in 1927 when, in the aftermath of failed Communist uprisings in West Java and West Sumatra, the Dutch consul who had seen Bin Hashim heckled by Indonesian students in Cairo observed suspiciously high numbers of "quasi-pilgrims" fleeing to the Hijaz, though he welcomed a visit from the spritely and urbane Salim in place of the ageing and uncomfortable Tjokroaminoto of the previous year.[35] Not that any of this would have pleased Hachemi as he withdrew from Java in mid-October that same year.[36] His caliphate was at an end. Now it would be about deciding how Muslim nations, clamoring for independence, would relate to each other in the future. There would be no more caliphs for the Indian Ocean arena in the twentieth century—not for African, not for Arab, not for Jawi, and certainly not for "the Hadramis among them." What remained was a largely British Indian Ocean with scattered French,

Portuguese, and Dutch coasts, and a whole new cast of nationalist movements seeking the loyalties of Muslims and non-Muslims alike.

So it was that Hachemi paused printing for the pergerakan to make his return to Tunis. He had already sent his four eldest children to Suez on the *Tjiremai* in April 1924 carrying dated Ottoman passports and accompanied by his sister-in-law Sa'diya and her husband, 'Ali al-'Attas.[37] Hachemi might have imagined that Java, with its fractious and resolutely foreign Arab supremacists, would be a thing of his past. His family had other ideas. So did many Indonesians, who were now decidedly neither Arabs nor Malays at home or in Cairo, given that they had a named watan of their own.

To Tunisia and Back to Indonesia in Turmoil

The collapse of the political world in which Hachemi had once been so prominent seems to have spelled the end of his own journal by the middle of 1925. His son Adnan later believed that the end had come following a complaint from the sultan of Mukalla, though this may be a conflation of the fate of *al-Irshad*.[38] It cannot have helped to see his rival al-Fattah garner more readers and funding for his bilingual paper in his old stomping ground of Weltevreden.

The last print venture with which Hachemi was associated in the Indies was the apolitical *al-Ma'arif*, founded after his return in 1928 as the voice of Surkati's brother, Muhammad Abu Fadl al-Ansari.[39] Crosby was unconcerned. In April that year, the consul who had removed the barriers to Irshadi travel reflected on British rapprochement with the Dutch and the once more changed state of the Muslim world:

> It will perhaps not be out of place if I record here my impression of the Syed-Sheikh controversy as it affects ourselves in the Netherlands East Indies. As I see it, the Syeds, being partisans of the ex-King Hussein of Mecca, were almost universally pro-Ally and pro-British throughout the war. The Shaikhs on the other hand, as enemies of the Syeds—and not so much, I think, because they were fundamentally inimical to the British—sided with the Turks and Germans and were in consequence often a thorn in our side. With the conclusion of the peace, however, and the deposition of King Hussein, a fresh set of circumstances came into being. The Sheikh party here—composed of Hadramis almost to a man—had

no longer anything to hope by opposing us; on the contrary, it was to their advantage to be on good terms with us as protectors of the Hadramaut. Four or five years ago they accordingly made overtures to this Consulate-General ... [and] we have had no difficulty whatsoever with the Shaikhs, nor have any rumours reached me of their working against us. ... I must confess that my sympathies will be largely with the Shaikhs, who ... represent the forces of progress as opposed to rigid conservatism. Whatever may be the primitive conditions still obtaining in such a backward land as the Hadramaut, it is in my opinion unreasonable to expect any Arab of the Sheikh class, in this much more highly developed Dutch colony, to bow any longer to customs which would make him kiss the hand of every Syed with whom he may speak in the street, and which debar him as an inferior being from ever contracting a marriage with a woman of Syed descent. I have mentioned that the Sheikh community in the Netherlands Indies is numerous and influential; I may add that some of its more wealthy members possess considerable weight with the Dutch authorities, who are disposed upon the whole to side with them rather than their rivals, the Syeds.[40]

There was little room in this Manichaean scheme for Hachemi. He was out of the Indies once more at the time Crosby wrote. Being the Tunisian who peppered his language with French, Hachemi had ever been the conspicuous outsider with his own sense of homeland, savoring memories of fields of lavender as opposed to the honey and lamb of Hadramawt or the curries, fish, and rice of Java.[41] He also hoped such sensations would inhere in his children. Some time after the birth of Adnan in early 1924, Fatima Ba Mahmush contracted smallpox and was incapacitated in Batavia. It was for this reason that her four eldest children—Kussaï, Wassila, Hatim, and Sundus—had been dispatched to their grandfather's household in Tunis while their father relocated his operations to Solo. Once there, Hachemi had continued to operate his press catering to a crucial sector of the Muslim nationalist movement and the allied Irshadi cause.

With the frequent journeying between Batavia and Solo, Hachemi had also done as most merchants did to remain respectable in Arab eyes, by marrying the twenty-three-year-old Latifa, a daughter of the Bahfein branch of the al-ʿAttas clan. According to family members, he did so with the encouragement of Fatima, whose youngest son, Adnan, would always know the younger woman as "mother"; indeed, his older brother Kussaï, who spent much of the rest of his life in Tunisia, later recalled his mother's apparently "tranquil immobility" at Batavia.⁴² And, just as political matters had soured in 1926, relations were apparently not good with Hachemi's new in-laws. Perhaps afflicted by homesickness as much as political vexation, the imposing Tunisian returned to North Africa with his new family in mid-October 1927. This was quite to the surprise of his elder children, who were reunited with Adnan and met their new sister, Sukeina. Another brother, Tawfik, soon appeared in Tunis.

Back at home for a moment, Hachemi met once more with the journalist comrades of his youth and brief exile in Istanbul, writing articles for the local press concerning an Arab scouting movement of a place he called "Sunda" rather than Indonesia, as so many of its activists were starting to call it.⁴³ He returned to the still Dutch Indies briefly but was soon back again. His connections were furthermore kept vital via al-Azhar, where, due to his association with his publisher friend ʿAbd al-ʿAziz al-Halabi and Tantawi Jawhari's Committee for the Education of the East, he traveled to secure admission for students who accompanied him from Java.⁴⁴

Latifa was not at all happy to be left in Tunis and campaigned for a return to Java. She and Hachemi would leave his first four children with their grandfather once more. At some time in 1929, their steamer docked at Tanjung Priok, where the returning Junayd schoolboys had once been harassed for their Ottoman uniforms in 1904, and where the almost Ottoman Hachemi had bidden farewell to his children with their defunct passports in 1924. The moment of return was hardly auspicious. Hachemi's family disembarked in a troubled colony sliding into an economic downturn. A conservative regime backed by the plantation sector instigated intense censorship and sidelined the pro-Islamic advisors of old. The prewar regional status quo was seemingly returning as well, with the neighboring British in Singapore, Malaya, and India thickening connections with fellow French, Dutch, and now American colonialists, all worried by the rise of labor union agitation on their various plantations.⁴⁵

Indonesian calls for independence had become increasingly strident, to be sure, dropping any superfluous pretense of loyalty. After Communist risings in Java and Sumatra saw thousands flee for the Hijaz in 1927, the Partai Nasional Indonesia (PNI) emerged as the new force of the pergerakan. The young Sukarno stood out. Indeed, no antagonist of the Dutch was more commanding than the eloquent graduate of Bandung's Technical School. Born at Surabaya in 1901 to a Balinese mother and a Javanese teacher of the lower *priyayi* class, his formal start in life came through networks of Dutch education while he lodged with Tjokroaminoto in high school. He was gladly radicalized as a young student leader at Bandung's school for engineers, where he studied from 1921 to 1924 and founded the Algemeene Studieclub. He then moved to Batavia to practice as an architect, though he remained linked to the Bandung students who created the PNI in 1927.

Batavia was the staging ground for the Youth Congress of October 1928, at which the various delegates of a plethora of student organizations pledged themselves in closing (and without Sukarno) to a unitary homeland, a single people, and the commitment to realize one national language. Malay was to become Indonesian, and it was instantiated in an anthem: Indonesia Raya. With his many essays and connections to the pergerakan of old, not to mention his fluency in European languages, Sukarno was a natural leader of this enterprise. Also, unlike the internationalist leftist leaders of the past, many now languishing in prison or destined for exile, his history and activities had unfolded entirely in the domestic sphere.[46]

In crafting his vision of Indonesian nationalism, Sukarno saw the movement's best chances for realization in terms of a broader "Eastern" unity and resistance to colonialism, reorienting and expanding the Islamicate vision of his former mentor and father-in-law.[47] Responding to an article by Agus Salim in the Sarekat Islam journal *Fadjar Asia* (Asian dawn) in August 1928, Sukarno valorized an inherently "Eastern nationalism" to be contrasted with its Western variant. Where Salim worried about nationalism as a pseudoreligious force that had caused people to sacrifice each other at the altar of the homeland—giving very Western examples, from the French Revolution to the fascist militias in Italy—Sukarno preferred to offer cosmopolitan Eastern variants, drawing on the (now irenic) writings of the Bengali nationalists Bipin Chandra Pal and C. R. Das. This was a nationalism that was not based on calls to an ancient people, but that was welcoming of all. It was of a continent whose inhabitants had perforce to unify under oppression to truly serve each other and the world, if with admittedly Islamic inspiration at times.

> We, the people of the Indonesian national movement, do not merely feel that we have become the slaves or servants of the land for which we have shed our blood. Rather we feel that we have become the slaves and servants of Asia, the slaves and servants of all suffering peoples, the slaves and servants of the world. . . .

Again: our nationalism, that of the Indonesian national people, is no different from that of the Muslim champion, Mustafa Kamil, who said that "love for the homeland is the most beautiful sentiment to ennoble the soul"; it is no different from the nationalism of Amanullah Khan, the Muslim champion and king of Afghanistan, who calls himself the servant of his homeland; it is no different from the nationalism of the Muslim champion Arabi Pasha, who declared "with Egypt to Heaven and with Egypt to Hell"; it is no different from the nationalism of Mahatma Gandhi, who teaches that his nationalism is the same as the "feeling of humanity."[48]

Sukarno was also inclined to invoke Sun Yat-sen in addition to Indian and Muslim thinkers in his speeches to rapt audiences. However, in a political environment dominated by the planters, there was no longer any space for such opinions. In a curiously inverted mirroring of French Vietnam, where the Communist movement was seen as a continuation of the decapitated nationalist one, the PNI stood accused of being the continuation of the since-banned Partai Komunis Indonesia (PKI). So it was that Sukarno found himself in the dock in 1930, accused of press offences and advocating for the fall of the government.

The eager voice of the nation saw the opportunity for what it was. In his lengthy defense oration, which first saw publication while he was imprisoned in 1931, Sukarno offered a sweeping indictment of Dutch colonial policy over the preceding centuries. It was nothing other than an attack on the entire global enterprise of colonialism, drawing on the words of Western scholars themselves, switching from Malay to Dutch and German or English sources to propound the virtues of Indonesian nationalism as a natural mass movement born of suffering and the realization of that suffering.[49] Sukarno's many Western sources included a suite of Dutch economists and sociologists, with plenty of grist taken from the Marxist theorist Karl Kautsky (1854–1938). He also made use of Lothrop Stoddard's 1921 *New World of Islam* when valorizing Mustafa Kamil's efforts in Egypt, as well as Snouck's reflections on the extractive past of the VOC and the tone-deafness of the regimes to follow vis-à-vis the Muslims of his homeland.[50]

In Sukarno's summary view, the West (Great Britain, first and foremost) had created what he would one day term a "life-line of imperialism," running from Gibraltar and Suez to his beloved homeland.[51] Yet Sukarno, like many an Indian thinker and Tan Malaka before him, recognized that the "lust" of imperialism and the attendant race for colonies was not an exclusively Western desire.[52] Recapitulating elements of his addresses from an article of 1928—indeed, his oration was the accumulation of many essays in *Suluh Indonesia Muda*—he announced in court that Japan's claim of being the "champion of Asia's suppressed peoples" was nothing but "a fraud, a lie, an empty illusion of conservative nationalists." He went on: "[Japan] too will participate in the materialism of voracious imperialism. It will itself become the evil force threatening China's welfare. It too will later join with American and British imperialists in a horrendous struggle, endangering the peace and safety of countries over all the Pacific Ocean, and it will *itself* be one of the materialists that will one day cross swords in a Pacific War."[53] In this respect, Sukarno offered a prescient vision of Japan that echoed that of suspicious Indian writers. It was also in contrast to the hopeful imaginings of many an activist tied to Cairene discourse, where the "Muslim champion" Kamil had once linked the opening of the canal to the rise of Japan and speculated on the natural pull of Tokyo for the Muslims of India and the Indies.[54] Such worries would also occur to many secular nationalists in the 1930s, as they undertook visits northward while Sukarno was in prison, and as Japanese military figures looked west and south.[55]

Sukarno deftly spun the claims and histories of activists like al-Afghani and Shaukat Ali into an affective nationalism under the rubric of Pan-Asianism and generally had little to say about his own beliefs or the defunct Ottoman caliphate.[56] Inasmuch as he tried to downplay the divisions between Islamist and nationalist, he was keen to inspire hope, too. In his defense oration, Sukarno glossed Snouck's characterization of the "abominable acts" (*gruwelen*) of Muslims as more valorous "rebellions" (*pemberontakan*) and excised the Dutch scholar's concluding assertion that any such millenarian resistance of the rural kyais was futile in the face of overwhelming colonial power.[57]

It would seem from tangential references in his correspondence that Snouck's original statement about futile millenarianism reflected his own sometimes depressed state. It had certainly been prompted by memories of Muhammad Arshad of Banten, who had been caught up in the panic of 1888 and exiled at Kupang until 1919, after which time he returned to Mecca.[58] By contrast, and with much more evidence, Sukarno was sentenced to four years in prison, where he later claimed to have turned to the Qur'an for solace during four months of solitary confinement.⁵⁹ This inner turn was not obvious following his early release on the last day of 1931. Hardly willing to give up a struggle, which he modeled on Gandhi's non-cooperation movement, Sukarno valorized his own imagined common man "Marhaen" (and, later, woman "Marhaeni"), after whom he named his own form of politics pitted against modern imperialism as capitalism, Dutch, British, or Japanese, all while stressing an irenic past bequeathed by "Hindustan."

Never shy of giving offence, both to the Dutch and his fellow nationalists, the self-declared (and at times self-sketched) *radikal* would be sentenced again in 1933, this time to exile on the island of Flores.⁶⁰ He and his young family remained on the southeastern fringes of the archipelago for five years, largely in isolation from his fellow nationalists, despite the domestic nature of his internment. Had Holland still possessed Lanka or the Cape he surely would been sent westward, rather than east. At least religion remained an uncensored domain. For this moment fostered his reengagement with an Islamic movement avoiding party politics and attendant repression. In late 1934 he commenced correspondence with Ahmad Hassan (1887–1958), the leader of an explicitly pan-regional reformist movement, Persatuan Islam, which had also taken root in Bandung in 1923. At first Sukarno requested primers and guidance from the Islamist, who was Singapore-born and part-Tamil. But in time Sukarno actively debated with him concerning the path taken by Turkey's Mustafa Kemal in separating religion and state, a path that he would advocate ever more clearly in time, following the latter's line that true reform had to be disengaged from instrumentalist politics.⁶¹

Sukarno's newfound interest in reformism was made more apparent once he was transferred to Bengkulu in 1938. There, he took on a role teaching at the local Muhammadiyah school. He also engaged with Mas Mansur, now the movement's chairman, on the question of segregation of the sexes, emulating Agus Salim and respectfully countering that partitions should be seen as a way of subordinating rather than respecting women.⁶² He also offered articles on Kemalism that once more spoke of renovation through the separation of state and religion. Such only incurred the ire of prominent Islamists like Mohammad Natsir (1908–1993), who saw the Turkish leader as nothing other than "a dictator, a *führer*, a *duce*."⁶³ In time, Natsir and many like him would have the same view of Sukarno, as he suppressed Islamic politics in the 1950s and 1960s.⁶⁴

A World Reconfigured

While Sukarno started to publicly address his Islamic identity in the 1930s, some Indies Arabs turned to a shared Indonesia as their notional homeland. On August 1, 1934, the twenty-six-year-old journalist ʿAbd al-Rahman Baswedan (1908–1986), the son of two locally born "Arabs" of Ampel and educated at schools run by both Bin Hashim and Surkati, analyzed the fraught relationship newcomers and locals for a new Chinese-run daily, *Mata-Hari*.[65] His article, "The Locally Born Arabs and Their Full-Blood Counterparts," offered anecdotes about the scorn of the proud arrivals for the Peranakan or Muwallad, who had no concept of the harsh environment of Hadramawt and could merge with the indigenous population if they but adopted the sarongs, headscarves, and striped jackets of their Javanese fellows—as indeed Baswedan had done for a photo in his own collection, which inspired his essay.[66] Baswedan also wrote how that day in Malang in 1933, spent at the home of a Javanese friend from the Jong Islamieten Bond, had made him feel suddenly closer to his mother as an Indonesian of Javanese heritage (Indonesier Djawa). He also reflected on the differences in upbringing between the toughened *totok* who had to struggle and return home with whatever he could glean from the Indies, while the locally born Peranakan had experienced nothing but ease and anticipated dying where they had been born. Be that as it may, it was time, Baswedan implied when talking of how so many had become effectively like West Javanese, Central Javanese, or, yet, East Javanese, for the majority of some seventy thousand Arabs then living in the archipelago to "adapt" to Indonesia as their true home. In so doing, they should also push against the dismissive bravado of newcomers or, indeed, the assertions of Habib ʿAli Menteng, who had once lectured his Irshadi opponents on proper devotion to the true watan on the other side of the ocean, though Baswedan ended his article in the hope that, just as distinctions between pure-born and local were easing in the Indies by virtue of education, Hadramawt, too, might one day gain the benefits that people enjoyed in Indonesia.

As Huub de Jonge tells it, the revolution in Baswedan's mindset had come about through his close engagement with Mas Mansur, who supervised his interactions with the Muhammadiyah in East Java, and then his work with Agus Salim and the Jong Islamieten Bond, where he gained a stronger sense of the increasingly negative view of Arabs in Indonesia. From 1932, his role as a journalist for the *Sin Tit Po*, edited by Liem Koen Hian, had convinced him of the importance of a pan-Asian assemblage of Indonesian nationalism—a view shared by the future editors of *Mata-Hari*. He began to circulate among its leaders, from the strident Tjokroaminoto to the more cautious Salim, while imbibing the writings of Sukarno, who had been so active in appealing to the achievements of Middle Eastern "champions of Islam."[67] Like Sukarno, Baswedan was a fan of Mustafa Kemal, much to Ahmad Hassan's disapproval, and he continued to stay abreast of developments in the Middle East—interpreting its papers for the local milieu while drawing more and more Indies Arabs, sayyids included, into a remarkable coalition of support for nationalist anticolonialism.[68]

Once again, though, there were other Arab experiences in the Indies that seemingly unfolded in ignorance of the politics that had engulfed their parents. Writing from Holland in his retirement, Adnan El-Mecky invoked such a childhood, having investigated the person of his father in a series of short stories. His prose—part fiction, part fact—reveals much of the texture of daily life just outside the Arab quarter of Solo in the 1930s. It also contains frequent allusions to Hachemi's longing for his own Mediterranean homeland, rather than the dusty Indian Ocean ports and desert hinterland prized by neighbors who missed having daggers at their sides. As Adnan noted in one story, there were few local Arabs that his father felt completely easy with, even as they all knew each other in their small ward of the royal city.[69]

Having returned from Tunis, Hachemi was still eager to escape, or at least have his younger children escape, the bickering between sayyid and shaykh. Hence, he opted to send them to Catholic schools after they had left his own primary school.[70] Among the most cherished of the late Adnan's family photos is one of him with his father, younger brother, and his schoolmates on an excursion to the aerodrome around 1933, ranged before one of the state-of-the-art Fokkers used by the KLM (fig. 11.1).[71] The days of sail and steam were starting to ebb.

Meanwhile, some of Hachemi's in-laws were meanwhile to be found on the Dutch side of the barricades. Husain, the multilingual younger brother of his first wife, Fatima, was employed by KIZ, rewarded with a job for his knowledge of colonial history, including the exploits of VOC governor Jan Coen (1587–1629).[72] To be sure, history was being related to the present on a Pan-Asianist spectrum by people able to move between linguistic worlds among the ʿAttas family. Another member, the well-connected Ismaʿil,

Figure 11.1 Hachemi (l.) and school group including sons Adnan and Tawfik, ca. 1933.

offered corrective essays to Amir Shakib Arslan regarding the history of the Dutch Indies in response to the latter's footnotes for an Arabic edition of Stoddard's *New World of Islam*, which had first appeared in Cairo in 1925.[73] Similarly, when, in late 1930, Muhammad Basyuni would ask his old teacher Rashid Rida just why the Japanese (and others) had succeeded when compared with the Muslims in general, Rida outsourced the question to Arslan, who in 1932 produced his *Limadha taʾakhkhara al-Muslimun?* (Why have Muslims declined?).[74] And, aside from incorporating Ismaʿil al-ʿAttas's notes on the Indies, Arslan further expounded on the virtues of the Japanese in his 1934 revision and expansion of Stoddard's text.[75]

Japan had hardly been forgotten by the Muslim figures with whom Hachemi had associated at one remove from the members of KIZ. Quite the contrary: Surkati was one of several prominent figures who would travel to Tokyo in 1934 to attend a gathering of Muslims involved with the propagation of their faith under Abdurresid Ibrahim (1857–1944). More specifically, it seems he was invited to help inaugurate a new school for Tatar students in residence there, bringing the story of Pan-Islamism full circle from the Crimea and the Caucasus in the previous century. Also worth noting for our purposes was the presence that day of leading propagandists professor Toyama Mitsuru and Okawa Shumei, flanking General Senjuro Hayashi (1876–1943). Long interested in Pan-Asianist rhetoric and expansion, all three had an interest in Islam as a civilizational matrix on which to graft Japanese power.[76]

Five years later, in September 1939, the newly constituted Greater Japan Muslim League (Dai-Nippon Kaikyo Kyokai), patronized by Senjuro Hayashi now as both former prime minister (1937) and "father of Japanese Islam," invited Muslims from around the world to an exhibition at Tokyo and Osaka that November. Already primed by their journalistic connections with Japanese Muslims—in 1935 Mas Mansur had cited the construction of the Kobe Mosque and publication of Osaka's *Mukhbir al-Islam* as signs of a new Muslim age—this was attended by delegates from the similarly new Indonesian Muslim body that Mansur had helped found.[77] This was the Supreme Council of Indonesian Islam, or Majlisul Islamil A'laa Indonesia (MIAI).[78] It would be represented in Japan by a mixture of reformist and traditionalist delegates.[79]

This is not to say that such visits made Surkati or the MIAI uncritical boosters for Tokyo. After the war, Surkati's former student Pijper informed the former internee Harry Benda (1919–1971) that the delegation had been skeptical of their hosts, though they may well have been cautious in conversation with an official of KIZ about any fallout from events they had attended where their banned red-and-white flag was hoisted aloft and their similarly proscribed anthem, "Indonesia Raya," played.[80] That caution would also have been maintained at times from March 1942, and by some of the people whose thinking and reformism had chimed with that of the Dutch advisors.

In this chapter I have laid out the trajectories of the inspired young traveler Mas Mansur, a rather ambivalent and exilic Hachemi, and the entirely domestic Sukarno, to think about the overlapping claims of Islam, nationalism, and Pan-Asianism in the face of tightening colonial surveillance with a restored Anglo-Dutch entente. Certainly, the last two organizing principles would be key to the claims of the Japanese occupiers from 1942, though, as we will see, Islam was by no means off the table: both as a unifier and provider of resistance to the plans of empire, no matter how well laid. Indeed, they were barely laid at all by an imperial army that was entirely surprised by its successes among a people now committed to the idea of being Indonesian, Arabs included.

TWELVE

Forgotten Jihad

AT SOLO IN early 1942, the teenaged Adnan El-Mecky was ordered to learn Japanese.¹ The demand had not come from the new occupiers of almost all Southeast Asia. Rather, it had been the edict of his autocratic father, whom he later depicted hunched over his radio of an evening, listening to the Arabic broadcasts from Cairo, London, Paris, and Berlin, deeply worried by the changing times even as he had long wished to be rid of the Dutch in Java and the French in Tunisia.² A week after the landings on March 1, Mohamed Hachemi came home with a book in Malay that claimed to be able to equip its reader with Japanese in a month. Ordered to cut his hair short like a Japanese soldier, Adnan was told to be ready for an examination in four weeks.³

It seems that the demand to learn Japanese almost in an instant—and, worse in his teenaged mind, to adopt so brutal a haircut—was the cause for Adnan's flight to his uncle ʿAli al-ʿAttas in Batavia, now renamed Jakarta, where he enrolled in a new high school before finding work in his uncle's office. He also felt something of a traitor to his Dutch school friends from Solo. No enthusiast for the new occupiers, Adnan was obliged to learn their language anyway. After a few months in a city, he received word on July 15 that his father had died of a stroke at a hospital in Solo, having just turned sixty. Racing home on the express train, Adnan arrived just in time for the funeral. As he later recalled, an acrid smell hung over the family courtyard. Hachemi had not wanted his documents full of "priceless information" falling into the hands of his rivals; thus they had been dutifully incinerated by

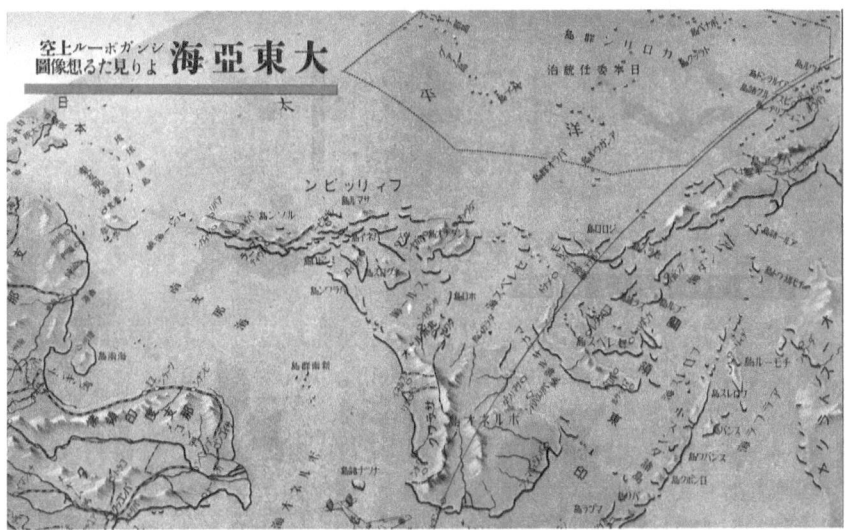

Figure 12.1 Propaganda map of East Asian Islands, 1943. Collection of the author.

his second wife, Latifa.⁴ A cynic might imagine that, aside from correspondence with fellow journalists in Cairo and Tripoli, or his print-ready history of Hadramawt, those papers may have included older and more furtive correspondence with the British and French. He had evidently not wanted his family troubled after his death, though he would earn a short obituary in the official newspaper of the occupation, *Asia Raya* (Greater Asia).⁵

The combative Tunisian had made many enemies in his sixty years. And, as he had watched caliphate and community disintegrate, he had become more of a cultural Muslim than the political activist of old. His decision to send his children to Catholic schools must have added to the rumor mill, which at one point averred that he was not even circumcised—a story Adnan decided to correct most pointedly at Friday prayers. Adnan even thought that his father was no longer a firm believer in his final years in Solo despite reacting with fury when he learned that his son had regularly added ham to his favored lunch of noodles.

Whereas postwar hagiographies usually claim that, before his death on September 6 the following year, Hachemi's old friend Surkati had refused to collaborate with the occupiers—at least regarding education—footage from October 1942 shows him at public prayer beside Abdul Muniam Inada. Also known as Hosokawa Susumu, Inada was a member of the Dai-Nippon Kaikyo Kyokai and a key figure in the Japanese administration on Java.[6] Rather more unlikely is footage from September 1944, which shows someone identified as Surkati speaking in appreciation of Japanese premier Koiso's decision to grant Indonesians independence "at some future date."[7] Such promises had been implicitly made before the war at the meetings of November 1939, back when there were fewer people who realistically imagined Mecca and Tokyo as Kamilian analogues. The late Raden Soetomo (1888–1938) had once written of Tokyo as an intellectual Mecca of the future (and exile in Papua as preferable to the hajj), while Sanusi Pané (1905–1968), a prominent future collaborator, was primed to imagine familial and greater Malay imaginings linking Japan and Indonesia.[8]

But if all now agreed on the bounds of Indonesia, the praise of inherent Easternness worried some Muslim observers of the man whom Harry Benda cast as perhaps the most enthusiastic of all collaborators in the first half of the brief and crucial rule of the Rising Sun. Benda opened his classic account of the occupation with a call he made in October 1944.[9] This caller was Mas Mansur, to whom I have already alluded in relation to the MIAI, and to whom I shall turn for the remainder of this chapter, since talking of figures like Pané takes us away from the original body of Cairene-oriented enthusiasts for Japan and proponents of homeland in a clearly Muslim context. For a significant time, Mas Mansur was the best embodiment of that continuing enthusiasm and the compatibility of both.

As outlined in the previous chapter, Mansur represented Muhammadiyah at the Al-Islam Congress convened at Cirebon in 1922. He stood for the movement once again at Cairo and Mecca in 1926, after he and Tjokroaminoto traveled to the Middle East to represent Indonesia in discussions to find a new caliph, if to little tangible result other than to emphasize a divide with traditionalist Muslims, who soon founded their own network, Nahdlatul Ulama, under the patronage of Abdul Wahab Hasbullah and Hasyim Asy'ari.[10]

In the wake of the withdrawal of Muslim political organizations or their eclipse by the PNI and its successors, Mas Mansur was to be at the forefront of attempts to create a rapprochement between Cairene reformists and traditionalist Muslims, ultimately as the national chairman of Muhammadiyah. His attempts at mediation were given voice with the resurrection of the Al-Islam Conferences and the foundation, in 1937, of the MIAI. This was joined by Salim's shrinking Partai Sarekat Islam Indonesia (PSII) in 1939, the year that saw the uncomfortable delegation to Tokyo.

Many took note of Mansur's prominence, including Salim's former masters, who reportedly offered Mansur a handsome salary to serve as an advisor or else to preside over an Islamic high court established in 1939.[11] Had Mansur accepted the former job, this would have also been in a capacity like that of Hachemi's brother-in-law, who was by then serving under the first Indonesian to graduate from Leiden University, Hoesein Djajadiningrat (1886–1960). Mansur apparently refused such offers, pledging himself fully to the reforms of Muhammadiyah and the maxim that the best of scholars are those who avoid princes—for a time at least.

This is not to say that Mansur was universally admired. In 1941, Ahmad Hassan's journal *al-Lisaan* reported a discussion that Mansur had had at his house in Yogyakarta in 1940 in which he reportedly claimed that Islam was not sufficient of itself to bring Indonesians together to achieve their independence. What they needed, he is said to have opined, was to activate the one thing that really bound them together: Easternness (*ketimuran*).[12] Even if this was disputed by his dedicated followers in Muhammadiyah, if there were any Japanese ears close by at the time, this may well have sounded a tune that they liked. And even if they weren't listening on that occasion, they would have been aware of Mansur as a prominent figure who could unite Asian traditionalists and reformists and perhaps even neutralize them in the process.

Japan Meets Indonesian Islam

For hundreds of years the peoples of Asia have been under the influence and power of Western imperialism. . . . for hundreds of years the peoples of Asia have lived in misery amidst the natural wealth of their homelands, watching the riches of Asia being stripped . . . But God is truly Just! To the north across the blue seas there lies a group of islands that Almighty God saved from the cruelty of imperialism. Dai Nippon is the name of that group of islands, and it is Dai Nippon that God has ordained to save the other peoples of Asia.

—Mas Mansur, February 2603

Thus proclaimed Mas Mansur in the pages of *Djawa Baroe* in February 1943 following an offering by Ki Hadjar Dewantara.[13] Writing after the war, Harry Benda certainly noted Mas Mansur's prominence under the military authorities of Japan's Sixteenth Army, who, following some weeks of uncertainty, had swept Dutch officials, and then himself as an anomalous Czech Jew, into internment camps.[14] Mansur's voice was often broadcast on the radio alongside that of Agus Salim, whose Friday addresses were a staple of the times. Transcripts of these addresses in *Asia Raya*—issued on a press linked to S. A. Sayyid ʿAli al-ʿAttas, who had proposed its title (Great Asia)—lend weight to Benda's assertion of Mansur's prominence, and his brief outshining of Salim.[15] Such authority was later bolstered by his overlapping role as managing editor of a more avowedly religious periodical, the *Soeara MIAI* (The Voice of the MIAI, est. January 1943), and his appearance in the curated pages of the previously mentioned *Djawa Baroe*, a photo magazine drawing on the staff of *Asia Raya* and the *Jawa Shimbun*.

Much of this had come about because of Mansur's links to the MIAI of old. It was also by virtue of his being selected by Colonel Horie Yozo—the new master of KIZ, renamed Shumubu—to accompany him on a study tour of Java from May 1942 with Wondoamiseno of the PSII. This had been fortuitous for Mansur because, as Benda points out, he had been sidelined by the MIAI leadership that had first engaged with the Japanese. Yet it was natural, given his history with the idea of a potentially Muslim Japan, of suturing Muslim divides and reaching across to nationalist friends like Sukarno, who had been similarly absent for the first phase of the occupation due to his imprisonment in Sumatra. Indeed, within a year of the landing of the Sixteenth Army, Mansur would become perhaps the most visible Islamic figure for Indonesians exposed to mass media and film, at a time when Japan still seemed in control of the former Dutch empire in Asia. Mansur's visibility had been made more memorable from late 1942 by virtue of his being one blade of the Empat Serangkai (Four-Leafed Clover) of national leaders. Often seen standing alongside Sukarno and Hatta, whom the Japanese had also released from captivity, or yet Ki Hadjar Dewantara, who in 1913 had asked how an Indonesian could place himself in the shoes of a Dutchman, Mansur's nationalist credentials were affirmed while he afforded his colleagues and Japan religious validation. In March 1943, for instance, he joined Ki Hadjar and Hatta to listen to Sukarno inaugurate the Poetera movement while wearing

Figure 12.2 Mas Mansur, Ki Hadjar Dewantara, and Mohamed Hatta listen to an address by Sukarno, *Djawa Baroe*, March 15, 1943.

the black felt hats that signified their religion, and with (Japanese) Chrysanthemum decorations pinned to their jackets (see fig. 12.2).

Such religious validation was supposed to be shored up with the compulsory mass training of rural teachers or kyais affiliated with the pesantren networks of Hasyim Asy'ari's Nadlatul Ulama (NU), following their identification as a key resource for an invader that had previously been far more interested in the oil, rubber, and tin of the archipelago earmarked for permanent absorption. As Nakano Satoshi and others have shown, there was little by way of clear or consistent planning for Java beyond the extraction of its resources with the hope of extricating Japan from China.[16] Jeremy Yellen has further made a compelling case for the highly contingent nature of Japanese expansion in Southeast Asia. The rhetoric of freedom, the purpose of the Greater East Asian Co-Prosperity Sphere, and the rights to be accorded its various peoples were all varied in tension with "collaborative nationalists" of the region as conditions of total war began to bite hard on a project born of unexpected and unsustainable victories.[17]

In this sense, the expectations of Indonesian collaborative nationalists like Mansur either vastly exceeded what was on offer or were constrained by pragmatic calculations about what could be achieved. What Islam had, however, was mass. As we have seen, Mansur came from the ranks of the traditional kyais, with whom he maintained a lasting relationship, most notably the Hasyim clan of NU. Equally, his Cairene credentials readily grafted onto nationalist concerns, as much as many Javanese Muslims accepted that what Japan called their "sacred" fight with "England and America" was in quest of Indonesian freedom, not necessarily the continued dominance of their "older brothers." While they could not push back in the ways that Ba Maw and Laurel did in technically independent Burma and the Philippines, Indonesian leaders, too, could engage with Japanese propaganda for their own ends. Certainly, the most useful rhetoric that the Japanese proclaimed from the outset was that they were only there to assist in the defense of the Indonesian homeland, since this concept was not banned in Java, even if its explicit name was still suppressed in Tokyo as late as November 1943, when Tojo hosted the Greater East Asia Conference.[18]

This commitment and its inherently Islamic tinge had already been made clear at an assemblage of several thousand Jakartans to bear witness to a united Muslim leadership assemble under Colonel Horie on September 4, 1942. Yet, after this, as Benda noted, the PSII saw no further role in negotiations, and the headquarters of the MIAI moved to Surabaya under Wondoamiseno, where they concentrated on consolidating finances with a view to shaping a national Muslim future.[19]

But while the MIAI was to all intents and purposes defunct by late 1942, during which time the Japanese pondered what composite form to give the many competing voices of Indonesian Islam, it would keep a nominal presence in the pages of the *Soeara MIAI*. This fortnightly journal first appeared in January 1943 advertising the advice of the military government, the responses and reflections of Mansur (who had just become the vice-chairman of MIAI), and even the "fatwas" of the non-Muslim Colonel Horie.[20] Frequent contributors included R. H. M. Adnan, who offered aphoristic thanks that Japan would respect loyal public officials and the religion of innocent people, and Sitti Noerdjannah (b. 1917), a teacher at Jakarta's al-Irshad School and head of the women's branch of the MIAI, who provided articles on the role of women in the state and for the homeland in regard to the precepts of Islam.[21] Another notable contributor was A. R. Baswedan, the journalist who had declared that Arabs should declare their primary loyalty to Indonesia, their place of birth, rather than some distant oasis.[22] This line was earnestly pushed in the pages of *Asia Raya*, which took the trouble to point out in September 1943 that "Arabs" like the Bajasut brothers of Tuban wanted it put on record that their homeland was Indonesia, and it was for Indonesia, and not Hadramawt or any other Arab country, that they wanted to go and fight "England and America."[23] The Japanese were suspicious of a community that had linked its fortunes to the expansion of British power in Arabia, though they were naturally interested in Arab funds. Indeed, Baswedan and his fellow Muwallad A. S. Sjahab, a board member of the Red Crescent, would soon be soliciting donations for the creation of a "patriotic army" through the Badan Pembantoe Prajoerit (Soldiers' Aid Body).[24]

Of course, the allied parts of the Muslim world could still be imagined, though the focus was inexorably on the historical wrongs committed against the Ottoman state (betrayed by the sayyids) and now the actions of Jewish settlers in once Ottoman Palestine. Embracing their Axis alliance, Harsono Tjokroaminoto and Oemar Said dealt in anti-Semitic tropes, ascribing such views to Sukarno. By contrast, another Muwallad, M. H. Alhabsji, offered a more measured article on the fate of Palestine.[25] Then again, many of the features tried to stay away from overtly racist politics. Salim's Friday addresses concentrated on early Muslim history to celebrate events such as the Prophet's birthday, while Mansur's writings—or at least those attributed to him—were more vaguely about theology and spiritual guidance. Japan was never far from view, however, with depictions of the Tokyo Mosque and the Imperial Diet sometimes gracing the cover of the *Soeara MIAI* in exchange for an Indo-Saracenic confection of a mosque at the foot of a volcano and graced by palm trees. In June 1943, yet another Muwallad, Asa Bafagih (1915–1978), offered an article on Japan and its prowess in celebration of the 1905 victory over Russia, referring directly to Kamil's *Rising Sun* and Arslan's annotations on the *New World of Islam*.[26]

At the same time, the writings of 1943 papered over the often embarrassing difficulties in apprehending Muslim sensitivities. Despite Colonel Horie having frequently appeared with Japanese converts like Inada, who assisted at Shumubu until his mid-1943 replacement by Muhammad Suzuki Tsuyoshi, there had been numerous problems in shaping the alliance with local Muslims. After their arrival, even if they celebrated the idea of Indonesia on Javanese soil, the military had taken a leaf straight out of the Dutch playbook and banned all political discussions and displays of the sort that had taken place at the Tokyo exhibition three years earlier; there could be no Indonesian flags nor a national anthem. Similarly, the Shumubu announced that mosques were placed under the authority of the Sixth Army and the use of Arabic script banned. This order was only rescinded in 1943, after around one thousand kyais had undergone education sessions about Japan and its enlightened tolerance of local "culture," provided there was no opposition.

Even so, it had proven effectively impossible to police Islam, especially at a distance from Batavia. Famously impossible to enforce was the much-hated daily ritual of bowing toward the emperor in Tokyo, known as Saikeirei. Some ulama, like the reformist Haji Rasul on Sumatra, refused to perform the ritual, in contrast to his opportunistic Java-based son, Hamka. Among traditionalists, the elderly Hasyim Asy'ari had been detained in April 1942 for refusing to perform the act, with some alleging he was tortured.[27] He was only released in mid-August following the interventions of Ono Nobuji (Abdul Hamid Ono), a local Japanese convert and recruit to army intelligence, which finally boasted a special section on Islam from November, a full nine months after landing. Tokyo could never supplant Mecca in a religious sense. Information had to be gathered. Compromise had to be made.

The administration of the first commander, General Imamura Hitoshi, had already recognized the fact that, as in Burma and the Philippines, Japanese soldiers—many of whom had seen brutal training and action in China—needed to be educated to refrain from slapping locals, or demanding that the lowest sentry be greeted by a bow. At one point the authorities even dropped leaflets to their own troops urging them to abstain from all such behavior deemed offensive to Buddhists and Muslims alike, whether in profaning temples and mosques with their boots, beating religious figures, being drunk, or using expressions from the Qurʾan.[28]

Especially galling for many Indonesians, as the war went on, was the treatment of local women, which often occasioned fights. Then there was the matter of the so-called voluntary laborers (*romusha*). Urged to enlist by the Empat Serangkai after April 1943, the majority were treated as little more than slaves, subject to exacting military discipline both on Java and then abroad, including on the Thai-Burma Railway, where many would lose their lives alongside Allied prisoners of war. Yet it was the very possibility of uniformed discipline coupled with the promise not to be deployed beyond Indonesia that won Japan its most earnest collaborators until parlous conditions saw Tokyo eyeing withdrawal and surrender.

Following the formation of auxiliary units known as Heiho in late 1942—composed at first of drivers and domestic staff—Japanese officers and Javanese nationalists were eager to create a national defense force in ways that had long been denied by the Dutch, the first out of concern for a lack of defensive manpower, and the second in the hope of gaining weapons and training. Even if the resultant body known as the Pembela Tanah Air (PETA), or "Defenders of the Homeland," was not as explicitly Islamic as the smaller Hizboellah militia that formed ranks beside it in November 1944, enough ink and celluloid was devoted to stressing its religious justification in the last quarter of 1943 to make that distinction arbitrary.

The first formal step in the creation of PETA was taken on September 7, 1943, by Sukarno's codefendant of 1930, Raden Gatot Mangkupraja (1898–1968), when he proposed the foundation of an indigenous defense force. Two days later, T. M. Moesa Machfoeld marshaled Muslim sentiment in *Asia Raya*, citing the Qur'anic injunction—"Fight in God's cause against those who wage war against you, but do not commit aggression" (Qur'an 2:190)—to justify the creation of an inherently defensive volunteer *ksatria* force that would go beyond the mere words of Gandhi, Nehru, and Tilak and do justice to the efforts of Subhas Chandra Bose in India.[29] Similarly, in the lead-up to sessions of the Central Advisory Council that had replaced the Volksraad, prominent Muslim delegates expressed the desire that the Indonesian Muslim community should build an active defense force for Java and engage on the battlefield.[30]

This was all tied into a petition presented to the office of supreme military commander by Mas Mansur together with nine other religious leaders on September 13. Observing the fact that the population of Java was essentially Muslim, and that, to expand on Sukarno's defense oration, it had suffered 350 years of Dutch colonialism *and* Christianization, Mansur and peers expressed thanks to God and the Japanese army. Citing the burden of reciprocity, and in anticipation of charting their own destinies at the end of the war, they sought permission to establish a militia to defend Java and guard the prosperity of Greater East Asia. After all, they had been primed both by bitter colonial experience and the teachings of Islam to "destroy America-England."[31]

Similar enthusiasm was reported as stemming from R. Wali Al Fatah in Yogyakarta, Hamka, and—in less explicitly Muslim fashion—Agus Salim, who reiterated his prewar requests under the Dutch for the establishment of a force as a prerequisite of national existence.[32] Consensus was presented across the spectrum, with other sectors of the community and selected women advocating for the force. In one long article, M. A. Salmoen mocked England's alleged religious neutrality, reminding readers of Richard the Lionheart's enmity for Saladin: "India, the Ottoman Empire, Yemen, Palestine, Egypt and other Muslim states" had all "born witness to England's attitude to Islam ... Let us not [therefore] shy away from Jihad!" After all, "what death could be sweeter than dying in the defense of religion and homeland? ... [For] if a native militia had been forced upon us by the Dutch, today it is the reverse: Dai Nippon has given us the hope of a shining future!"[33]

In his own parallel request for the (re)establishment of the Muhammadiyah movement, R. Moh. Syafi'i of Kebumen tied his petition to the establishment of a defense force based on a Muslim core.[34] The leadership of NU also sanctioned Mas Mansur's efforts, with Hasyim Asy'ari and his son, Wahid Hasyim, both approving of the initiative. Their ally Abdul Wahab Hasbullah furthermore obliged Muslims to advance to the front to defend any land for which they were responsible, citing the example of the Prophet's valiant wife 'A'isha.[35]

Concessions

Even with such stage-managed unanimity, it is important to note that the Japanese had made a timely concession to Muslims, which must have been calculated to improve the chances of recruitment. With the appointment of Hoesein Djajadiningrat as head of Shumubu on October 1, thus becoming the first Indonesian to lead the Office for Native Affairs since its inception, and with Mansur an official adviser, taking the post he had reportedly refused under the Dutch, the military administration removed the obligation to bow toward Tokyo.[36]

With so many of their Muslims in unbowed ranks, then, the military authorities announced the formal creation of PETA with some confidence on October 4, 1943, boasting that fifty thousand Indonesians had been mobilized "to destroy the Allies."[37] The time had come at last for Indonesia's Muslims to spill their own blood in gratitude for the efforts of Great Japan. The pages of *Asia Raya* not only praised the financial contributions of certain Arabs but drew attention to the many kyais who were joining its ranks as officers. Even the flag of the PETA embedded Islam in a way that the (still banned) Indonesian flag never had. Thirty-eight years after the defeat of the tsar, crescent and star arose alongside a radiant sun.

All of this was given added force with a radio address given by Mansur on October 13, 1943:

> After centuries of slavery, the tears and groans of the Muslim community (*ummat*) in Asia have been replaced by the cries and jubilation of sacrifice in quest of final victory. Will our nation simply watch on? Clapping our hands in anticipation of a gift? "Allah will not change the fate of a people before they change it themselves!" [Qur'an 13:11]. So I say: "JIHAD! JIHAD! JIHAD! (War). That is what is fitting these days! That is what is in keeping with our cherished aspirations! To sacrifice [one's] life: flesh and blood, that is what is appropriate and in keeping with our aspirations to free Asia from the demons and devils of the accursed Allies, and to free us from slavery. It cannot be done with mere words, orders or advice, but rather with actions, the sacrifice of our life, flesh and blood. That is the intent of JIHAD in the Quran and God's orders to His community.... O people of Indonesia! Bear in mind as well the shining age that your nation shall obtain, and trust that there is no such thing as meaningless sacrifice! Live in honor or die in struggle!"[38]

While this was one of the last times Mansur specifically invoked jihad for Japan—and in a speech that was *not* relayed in the pages of his own *Soeara MIAI*—this was hardly the end of the propaganda onslaught in quest of Muslim justification for total mobilization. The next issue of *Asia Raya* reported that women, too, were joining the ranks, perhaps mindful of Abdul Wahab Hasbullah's lauding of 'A'isha.[39] On October 16, Kiai Ageng Soerjomentaram of Solo spoke with admiration of how Japanese women—so frequently featured in the pages of *Djawa Baroe*—played a role in the war effort, which was, after all, "sacred" (*suci*).⁴⁰ In November, Soekardjo Wirjopranoto, who had just returned from Tokyo as a member of Sukarno and Hatta's delegation of observers, lectured a gathering of "wives," Arab and Chinese included, on the exemplary service of Japanese women, before pointing to Indonesia's own history of powerful Muslim women, such as the daughters of Sultan Agung (r. 1613–1645).⁴¹

As can be seen from the variant terminologies, the language of sacred war, whether jihad, *perang sabil*, or even *perang suci*, crossed cultural lines. Propagandists were willing to fuse Muslim martial prowess with older Indic notions of the virtuous warrior Rama. In February 1943, Baswedan had already likened the Samurai tradition of Bushido to that of the Indic Ksatria in the pages of *Soeara MIAI*, all under the headline "Hopes of the Government in the Kyais."⁴² Eight months later, several such ulama from Kediri engaged in training courses at Jakarta declared that the Qur'an and Hadith made enlistment in PETA a religious obligation. This was reported in *Asia Raya* with the headline "Ksatria Blood Still Flows in the Bodies of Indonesian Youth."⁴³

Similar themes were pursued into November, linking Islamic scripture to national and knightly struggle, albeit for a nation whose independence was only vaguely supported by Tokyo.⁴⁴ The emphasis for now on was preparation. Article after article spoke of the love of homeland empowering trainees, whether as officers or soldiers under Japanese direction, in newish green uniforms, and with full stomachs. One account even described night training after a "complete" meal of rice with beef, tomatoes, beans, and all the trimmings.⁴⁵ The trouble would be, of course, that fewer such meals were available into 1944, by which time PETA had been fully established, with sixty-nine battalions across Java and Sumatra.⁴⁶

A year before the foundation of the ancillary Hizboellah militia in November 1944, it seems that there were still enough Indonesians—many of nonsayyid Arab background—prepared to link Islam to their own war of liberation under (hopefully temporary) Japanese leadership. To be sure, they did the bulk of the writing for a propaganda magazine, if under relatively light and trusting supervision. There were also many obvious Muslims to be seen in pages of *Djawa Baroe*, and shorts-wearing officers of PETA were on film drilling their bamboo-wielding charges in lieu of rifles, for there were only ever about twenty thousand rifles for fifty-seven thousand men.

Moreover, the ranks of Hasyim Asy'ari's Masjoemi—a strategic merging of the forces of Muhammadiyah and NU formed on November 22, 1943—had a hybrid leadership in the form of his son Wahid Hasyim and Mansur, who still served as the managing editor of the anachronistically named *Soeara MIAI* (the MIAI had been dissolved on October 24). As Mansur declaimed on radio, Masjoemi's primary role was to strengthen "the unity of all Islamic organizations ... while aiding Dai Nippon in the interests of Greater East Asia."[47] His journal had offered hopeful commentary on its role beside PETA after repeating the formal announcement of the formation of the force in mid-October, though, curiously, without his call for a jihad that had been so prominent in *Asia Raya*.

An Army Without a State, Muslim or Otherwise

The galling fact remained that Indonesia had most assuredly not been offered formal independence by Tojo. This was in marked distinction to the unplanned addition of Burma and the unprofitable Philippines, whose leaders had convened at Tokyo on November 6, 1943, for the Greater East Asia Conference.[48] There was a glimmer of progress for Indonesians when, a few days later, Sukarno and Hatta were brought to Japan as part of a larger delegation for a two-week tour and presented with medals. Mansur was not invited. And if the MIAI had also been sidelined as the peak Muslim body for Muslims in favor of the Masjoemi that month, there was the illusion of continuity as its journal became—at least in name—Mansur's vehicle.

Reading its pages, one may well wonder if Mansur's jihad declaration was less than heartfelt, and where he even was. It is striking how infrequently Mansur wrote for his own journal. Some of his friends and followers later commented that, while he was an inspiring speaker, he was not actually a good writer, or yet interested in writing, with many of his works being produced by those under him.[49] The few columns ascribed to him after his declaration of jihad offered aphorism and guidance, but little anchored in the politics of the day. In November 1943, for instance, he was apparently busy urging farmers to raise their hoes and increase food production.[50] In January 1944, in a journal since renamed the "Voice of Indonesian Muslims" (*Soeara Muslimin Indonesia*), he offered more general reflections on the meaning of the declaration of faith.[51] Then, in the special on sacrifice of February, he offered more general "support" to readers alongside one Rapy's musings on the homeland.⁵²

Mansur's support article was republished by his followers in 1968 as one of his selected readings, based on the misapprehension that it had been written in response to the September 1944 decision to grant Indonesia independence.⁵³ Rather, the one article that I have located after that decision was published in the fourth issue of *Indonesia Merdeka*, in June 1945, still linking Indonesia's national struggle to notions of Greater Asia, though now in the context of independence that was to be declared at any moment. By that time much had happened: Masjoemi had gained its own paramilitary, the Hizboellah, in December 1944, and elements of PETA had rebelled against their Japanese commanders at Serang in Banten in February 1945.⁵⁴

In fact, Hasyim Asy'ari, who clearly had more influence on Masjoemi than Mansur, had also been named as the new head of Shumubu in August 1944. With his own community arguably in the driving seat, there was little argument in public about the nuances of reformist or traditionalist Islam as the Japanese now began disarming the men they had once trained, aiming to strip some 35 percent of the nearly twenty thousand rifles in Indonesian hands. Steel was for the home islands; Indonesia was to defend itself with bamboo. Now the Japanese turned to symbolic acts of patronage. Indonesian flags could be waved and the anthem sung, and there was even the founding of an Islamic university in Jakarta. If Benda felt such offerings tokenistic, it is worth reiterating that there was no necessary distinction between the patriotic and the Islamic, at least for the partisans of the latter. Such a dichotomy was only to emerge when battle was joined with the British and Dutch, with some weapons prised from the hands of their trainers to augment the now iconic bamboo spears.

As Soebagijo once noted, Mansur's name was mentioned less and less frequently over the course of 1945, with the piece in *Indonesian Merdeka* an obvious exception.⁵⁵ Mansur played no role in the June debates about the place of Islam in the future state, though he was still formally listed in July as one of eighty members of the larger committee intended to determine the basis of the still undeclared nation.⁵⁶ Yet his behavior had evidently been erratic, worrying his friends before the final events described by Soebagio. Most agree that Mansur was on the verge of a breakdown. Some have claimed that this was in reaction to the harsh treatment of Hasyim Asy'ari, though his arrest and alleged torture early in the occupation had not stopped his subsequent collaboration and even his elevation to the headship of Shumubu.

Something had clearly snapped by July 1945. While hardly the key figure he had been in 1944, Mansur was still on hand on July 29, 1945, when various dignitaries convened at Jakarta's new Balai Muslimin (Hall of Muslims)—another gift from the Japanese on Jl. Kramat Raya—to celebrate the founding of a Muslim university, Sekolah Tinggi Islam. Earlier in the month Sukarno had inaugurated the venture with what must have seemed the hollow cry of "Dai Nippon Banzai, Indonesia Merdeka, and Allahu Akbar." Now, Mansur was slated to offer a prayer after opening speeches from Abdulkahar Muzakkar, Wahid Hasyim, and Sukarno.

Standing mutely on stage for some time, Mansur sat down for a moment and stared into space. Once the lute orchestra took its cue to defuse the tension, he rose and began performing the martial exercises for which he was famous. Faced with the indecorous spectacle of a scholar acting like a *ksatria*, or perhaps even a *wayang* actor on the verge of running amok, both music and Mansur were stopped. Confined to his home thereafter, he would play no further role in the fading Japanese occupation. According to Baswedan, Mansur remained in a state of meditation, heartened by Sufi litanies.[57] This was hardly the stuff of a reformist playlist, and much more in keeping with the world of the pesantren and imaginings of the oasis of Shinggit.

In Mansur's absence, the *Soeara Moeslimin* would stay its own course, becoming more and more assertive and ultimately welcoming independence once it was declared by Sukarno on August 17, 1945, two days after Japan's surrender and agreement that it should maintain security for arriving British forces and the returning Dutch. One of the last articles published in late 1945 was an address broadcast on Radio Australia by Moechtar Loethfie, a former internee, first in Papua and then Australia, which was where Sukarno was supposed to have been sent in 1942.[58] By then, though, Australian officers would help run war crimes trials, pursuing Japanese and Koreans who had mistreated Allied soldiers and European civilians, but generally leaving Indonesian collaborators untouched. Mansur was an exception.

In the early days of the Allied occupation of Java, largely carried out by troops from still British India, Mansur had been back home in the front line city of Surabaya, issuing Friday addresses decrying the treachery of elite Arabs and Indians while making plans to retreat to Aceh.[59] Reflecting his comparative ascent and enduring Muslim authority among the nationalists, it was Hasyim Asy'ari who, at Sukarno's request, issued the now famous Jihad Resolution of October 22, 1945, obliging holy war for the defense of "the religion and sovereignty of the Indonesian republic."[60] Issued nineteen days before the Battle of Surabaya peaked between nationalist youths (*pemuda*) and heavily armed British troops, it is this speech, and not Mansur's earlier call, that is remembered in Indonesia today. Mansur had already been taken into custody and released to give addresses on radio urging the pemuda to lay down their makeshift weapons. Evidently not trusted, Mansur was taken into custody again by the Dutch administration, where he died in hospital on April 24, 1946.

Although he was eulogized at the time as "a father, an advisor and a leader" by the republic's General Sudirman (1916–1950), there was little specifically Islamic in the stress that he laid on the loss to the nation.[61] Yet this should not lead us to divorce Islam from the nationalist cause. Sudirman had been a fellow founder of Mansur's Hizb al-Watan and an ultimately rebellious PETA officer turning star and crescent against rising sun. Meanwhile, the students who had remained in Cairo during the war made sure to use Mansur's death to derive maximal attention to their efforts among members of the newly forming Arab League.[62]

A Mission to Cairo, a Student for Holland

Although the partisans of Hizboellah and Masjoemi were not folded into Sudirman's forces, they would play a role in fighting to remove the returning Dutch by 1949, and with the same geographic Indonesia in mind.[63] After all, Japan's occupation had made the first declaration of a nationalist jihad possible, and the heightened separation between Islam and nation only came after the deaths of Mansur and Asy'ari, with the latter dying on July 25, 1947, upon hearing the news that Dutch troops were winning a battle in Malang.

Indonesian Islam and nationhood may be seen as having a simultaneous breakup born of a changing relationship with the Middle East during the ensuing war for independence (1945–1949). Kevin Fogg has drawn attention to the importance of international Islamic networks for the foreign policy of the revolutionary government at Yogyakarta, beset by Dutch and British forces and intent on being heard in whatever international forum it could gain an ear.⁶⁴ The death of Mas Mansur touched many still active in Cairo, where he had ventured in his youth with Libya in mind and where he returned to make a pitch for a renewed caliphate in 1926. Indonesian student activities furthermore intersected with those of ʿAbd al-Rahman Hasan ʿAzzam (1893–1976), the first secretary-general of the Arab League, who ensured that the Indonesian case was on Arab minds after the recognition of Libya, whose struggle ʿAzzam had joined on the Ottoman side and as a partisan of Sayyid Idris of the Sanusiyya before his retreat to Egypt. In fact, ʿAzzam was largely abetted by a Tunisian lawyer then active in the city, Habib Bourguiba (1903–2000), who had spent the war in exile in France, and who was known to the older children of Hachemi—especially Hatim (d. 2003), who emerged as a well-regarded artist.

Indeed, the visit to Yogyakarta in March 1947 of a fact-finding delegation from the Arab League enabled an informal Indonesian one to circumvent a Dutch blockade and attend the Asian Relations Conference convened by Nehru at Delhi. The junior foreign minister, Agus Salim, and his colleague Baswedan traveled on to Egypt, where they secured recognition of their republic by the member states of the Arab League, starting with their Egyptian hosts on June 10, 1947. Indonesia had been recognized at last, and by largely Muslim nations first.

Yet this would be the high-water mark of Arab concern, with the struggle for Palestine displacing perhaps the most distant of Muslim worries, and Indonesian leaders finding greater traction and sympathy with the countries of the Central and Eastern Indian Ocean. Ceylon would prove an eloquent advocate at the UN, and Nehru would push hard for Sukarno, having once called on British Indian troops to foreswear the fight at Surabaya. With the growing international tide turning in Indonesia's favor against the Dutch, especially once America weighed in, there is meanwhile a sense of irony in the fact that Adnan El-Mecky, the son of a shape-shifting Tunisian printer to a colonized Muslim world, decided to take up the opportunity of a scholarship in the Netherlands. Rather than board the Fokker he and his classmates he had once admired as children, he traveled on a new Lockheed Constellation, hopping from city to city and ultimately beyond the world of his father.

Epilogue

As I survey this Hall and the distinguished guests gathered here, my heart is filled with emotion. This is the first intercontinental conference of colored peoples in the history of mankind. I am proud that my country is your host, and happy that you were able to accept the invitation extended by the five sponsoring countries. But I also cannot restrain feelings of sadness when I recall the tribulations through which many of our peoples so recently passed. Tribulations which exacted a heavy toll on life, in material things and in things of the spirit.

—Sukarno, Bandung, 1955

AT BANDUNG ON April 15, 1955, Sukarno might have been forgiven for thinking himself the anointed spokesman of the freed world. There he stood, as host and representative of the Colombo Powers—Ceylon, Indonesia, Burma, India, and Pakistan—addressing the assembled heads of newly independent states of Asia and, to a much smaller degree, Africa.[1] Also present were observers from the global media, a Chinese delegation under Zhou Enlai, and anxious Japanese on the sideline. Speaking in clear but hesitant English, there was little of the fire of Sukarno's customary addresses in Indonesian, or what would come when he railed against the "neocolonial" construction of neighboring Malaysia after 1957, and in a year when he would abrogate the constitution.

This was yet to come to pass, however, and, in acknowledging the suffering and ongoing struggle of many millions that was merely shifting in form in 1955, there remained a passion and a learned eloquence that the African American writer Richard Wright (1908–1960) certainly noted. Sukarno conjured up a future that could ostensibly invert centuries of colonialism—not by colonizing in turn, but by being the better part of humanity.[2] This was the Sukarno of 1930, reflecting more explicitly on the great tie that had bound them all, and after the Pacific war that he had anticipated:

> How terrifically dynamic is our time! I recall that several years ago I made a public statement on imperialism, which I called the "Lifeline of Imperialism." This line runs from the Strait of Gibraltar through the Mediterranean, Suez Canal, Red Sea, Indian Ocean, South China Sea and the Sea of Japan. For most of that enormous distance, territories on both sides of this lifeline were colonies, the peoples were unfree and their futures were mortgaged to an alien system. Along that lifeline was pumped the life blood of colonialism.[3]

Colonialism was hardly dead in Africa, and a fresh storm was about to sweep Indochina. What the assembled peoples needed, therefore, was unity in their diversity, to emulate the national mottos of the United States and Indonesia alike:

> Small and great nations are represented here, with people professing almost every religion under the sun—Buddhism, Islam, Christianity, Shintoism and others. We encounter here almost every political faith—democracy, monarchism, theocracy, with innumerable variants. And practically every economic doctrine has its representative in this Hall—marhaenism, socialism, capitalism, communism—in all their manifold variations and combinations. But what harm is there in diversity, when there is unity in desire? It is a Brotherhood Conference, not an Islamic nor a Christian nor a Buddhist Conference. It is not a meeting of Malayans nor of Arabs nor one of Indo Aryan Stock.[4]

Although he offered a generous reflection on the (masculine) cosmopolitan makeup of the assembly in its faith and politics, Islam remained very much in question in Sukarno's domestic and ever more paternalistic vision—one asserted in the face of an insurgency in the surrounding hills led by guerillas with whom he had once shared a patron in Tokyo.[5] Yet his rivals' claims were arguably part of a reaction to the steady secularization of the paths taken by their political forebears in the 1920s, and to Sukarno's ultimate advantage.

When seen from the vantage of this book and the heroic Muslims he had once invoked—both because he genuinely admired them and saw the pragmatic advantage of bringing their constituents on board—the staging of Bandung was not just the belated bequest of Tagore put in motion by the

Colombo Powers to help soothe relations between India and China. It was also a congested waypoint for a great many Muslims seeking to navigate the looming instantiations of global empire standing offshore, with the potential to overwhelm them all yet again.

Neither Sukarno's cultural and hardly pious Muslim heritage nor his call to the cosmopolitan were shared by all the delegates or their successors. Burma's premier U Nu (1907–1995), who rejected Nasser and Sukarno's efforts to condemn Israel at the meeting, patronized his own form of "worldmaking" that year with the Sixth Buddhist Council, held at Rangoon to commemorate the 2500th anniversary of the Buddha's attaining Nirvana.[6] Soon after making Buddhism the state religion, U Nu would be removed in 1962 by his once obliging general, Ne Win (1911–2002). On similarly Buddhist Ceylon, meanwhile, prime minister Sir John Kotelawala's successor of 1956, S. W. R. D. Bandaranaike, soon disenfranchised Tamil speakers, and thus the island's Hindus. Assassinated in 1959, his widow, Sirimavo Bandaranaike (1916–2000), would take up his office and linguistic cudgel to disastrous effect.

Right-wing elements of the Brazilian press would later dismiss the idea of any place for their own Catholic regime in subsequent meetings of the Non-Aligned Movement at Belgrade in 1961, casting the bloc's members as members of an alien "Indo-Arabic World."[7] One could have also been forgiven for such an assertion outside the precursor venue in 1955, when Nasser, sometimes accompanied by Prince Faysal of Saudi Arabia, had often been the most loudly cheered on the daily "freedom walks" as the participants strode from their hotels to the meeting hall.[8] After all, the former kingdom of Egypt—independent since 1922—had been the first state to recognize Indonesia's own declaration in 1947 after the visit to Cairo that had included the passportless Agus Salim and Baswedan: perfect exemplars of the partnership that this book has explored, and that Sukarno downplayed in 1955. It further seems that Nasser inspired many in the same way that the similarly uniformed Sukarno did with his own trademark sunglasses. Fifteen months after bewitching the crowds at Bandung, a much-emboldened Nasser would nationalize the Suez Canal in July 1956, precipitating invasion and embarrassment for Great Britain and France that was in stark contrast to the events of 1882. This colonel and his revolutionary government would not share the fate of Ahmad ʿUrabi, whom Sukarno had lauded during his own exile, and whom Nasser and Egyptian historiography had rehabilitated as a national, rather than Islamic, hero by 1952.[9]

EPILOGUE

Nasser and Sukarno also welcomed similarly grandiose visions of regional nationhood in the United Arab Republic (joining Egypt, Syria, and North Yemen) and Maphilindo (projected as taking in Indonesia, Malaysia, and the Philippines), the latter having been anticipated by Tan Malaka. At the same time, the postcolonial moment was an uneven one for the Muslim communities still bound by the oldest incarnation of the lifeline of imperialism. South Yemen, only assembled as a country by virtue of the Ingrams Peace of 1937, would remain a colony until 1967, emulating many successor states in terms of the inherent incompatibility of its constituent parts. Ceylon, independent from 1948, would increasingly divide over questions of Sinhalese hegemony and Tamil rights while Malays would enjoy guaranteed seats in parliament denied to their demographically more significant coreligionists, often bound to upcountry Tamils by language alone. In South Africa, meanwhile, the elections of 1948 brought white nationalists to power and hardened old British boundaries into new, seemingly ageless Dutch ones under apartheid. Three decades after Salih bin ʿAbdat had had to negotiate the boundaries of Arabness and native belonging in Java, the Malays of the Cape found themselves both awkwardly celebrated by Afrikaner nationalists and yet lumped together with Indians in the invidious middle category of "coloured," sometimes collaborating with the apartheid state to construct or restore mosques and graves on Robben Island, sometimes resisting it as whole suburbs were razed in the name of racial purity. The Bo-Kaap was meanwhile museumized, its saints protected by the community from development by outsiders, and its traditions, most especially the ratib, now imagined as survivals of ancient Balinese culture.

Seen from the vantage of 1955 as a hopeful instant of postcolonial thinking—a fact recognized by the half-Balinese Sukarno—this book has argued for the importance of recognizing not one but two imperial lifelines that were effectively braided together after 1869. The first was unspooled by the ships of the avaricious companies of old in the eighteenth century, the second dug, dredged, and laid by their metropolitan inheritors in the nineteenth. Colonies are hardly the afterthoughts of commerce, but malice aforethought.

How Islam is further wound into all this is less a single strand to be teased out and stretched, to test its relative resistance or compliance in any one place, but, rather, a tangled culmination, to be further appreciated, of many more quotidian stories about the texture of daily life maintained by individuals beyond the archive of imperial knowledge. To this end, any worldly authority—however marshaled, sustained, or trumpeted—was so often immaterial. I therefore hope that this book has offered a new spatial and temporal canvas on which to place them, for there were many others besides the wistful Tuan Guru and his exercised Meccan contemporary ʿAbd al-Samad, the wily Captain Assana and innovative Baba Ounus Saldin on Lanka, the sometimes-bemused Ahmad Surkati and contentious Mohamed Hachemi on Java, or the troubled Kyai Hajji Mas Mansur and his sometimes eloquent ally in power, if not always faith, Sukarno.

Notes

Acknowledgments

1. "The Forgotten Jihad Under Japan: Muslim Reformism and the Promise of Indonesian Independence," *Journal of the Economic and Social History of the Orient* 64, nos. 1–2 (2021): 125–61.

Introduction

1. Justin Corfield, *Historical Dictionary of Ho Chi Minh City* (London: Anthem, 2014), 76–77.
2. The village in the environs of Qatn was founded by members of the Ba Bakr clan, who had been expelled by the Kathiris of Sayʾun in 1867. See ʿAbd al-Rahman b. ʿUbayd Allah al-Saqqaf, *Muʿjam buldan Hadramawt al-musamma Idam al-qawt fi dhikr buldan Hadramawt* (Sanʿaʾ: Maktabat al-Irshad, 2002), 245–46. With thanks to Muhammad Gerhoum and Dan Varisco.
3. Engseng Ho, *The Graves of Tarim: Genealogy and Mobility Across the Indian Ocean* (Berkeley: University of California Press, 2006), 257. Sir Ghalib's son and successor, ʿUmar, seldom left Hyderabad. G. Rex Smith, " 'Ingrams Peace,' Ḥaḍramawt, 1937–40: Some Contemporary Documents," *Journal of the Royal Asiatic Society* 12, no. 1 (2002): 1–30, 7.
4. Natalie Mobini-Kesheh, *The Hadrami Awakening: Community and Identity in the Netherlands East Indies, 1900–1942* (Ithaca, NY: Southeast Asian Program, 1999); see also Arnout van der Meer, *Performing Power: Cultural Hegemony, Race, and Resistance in Colonial Indonesia* (Ithaca, NY: Cornell University Press, 2021).

5. Mobini-Kesheh, *Hadrami Awakening*, 52–90; on the captaincy, see Sumit Mandal, *Becoming Arab: Creole Histories and Modern Identity in a Malay World* (Cambridge: Cambridge University Press, 2018), 86–87, 90–94.
6. Ho, *Graves of Tarim*, 271–76; Nurfadzilah Yahaya, *Fluid Jurisdictions: Colonial Law and Arabs in Southeast Asia* (Ithaca, NY: Cornell University Press, 2020), 122–41.
7. Crosby to Political Resident Aden, Batavia, November 9, 1920, R/20/A/1412, India Office Records and Private Papers (IOR), British Library (BL).
8. Crosby to Aden, November 9, 1920.
9. Linda Boxberger, *On the Edge of Empire: Hadhramawt, Emigration, and the Indian Ocean, 1880s–1930s* (Albany: State University of New York Press, 2002), 220–25.
10. Stuart Hall, "Negotiating Caribbean Identities," *New Left Review* no. 209 (1995): 3–14.
11. For but the Malayan fragment of this *longue durée* history, see Leonard Andaya, *Leaves of the Same Tree: Trade and Ethnicity in the Straits of Melaka* (Singapore: National University of Singapore Press, 2010); and Joel Kahn, *Other Malays: Nationalism and Cosmopolitanism in the Modern Malay World* (Singapore: National University of Singapore Press, 2006).
12. Mahathir Bin Mohamad, *The Malay Dilemma* (Singapore: Donald Moore for Asia Pacific, 1970).
13. Thomas Stamford Raffles, "On the Maláyu Nation, with a Translation of Its Maritime Institutions," *Asiatick Researches* 12 (1818): 102–58, 103.
14. See the lyrical accounts of Ho, *Graves of Tarim*; and Sugata Bose, *A Hundred Horizons: The Indian Ocean in the Age of Global Empire* (Cambridge, MA: Harvard University Press, 2006).
15. Maya Jasanoff, *Liberty's Exiles: American Loyalists in a Revolutionary World* (New York: Vintage, 2012).
16. Natalie Rothman, *Brokering Empire: Trans-Imperial Subjects Between Venice and Istanbul* (Ithaca, NY: Cornell University Press, 2012); Pieter M. Judson, *The Habsburg Empire: A New History* (Cambridge, MA: Belknap Press of Harvard University Press, 2016).
17. Janet L. Abu-Lughod, *Before European Hegemony: The World System A.D. 1250–1350* (New York: Oxford University Press, 1989); Abdul Sheriff, *Dhow Cultures of the Indian Ocean, Cosmopolitanism, Commerce, and Islam* (New York: Columbia University Press, 2010).
18. The Commissions of Eastern Inquiry are the subject of an Australian Research Council collaboration, "Inquiring into Empire: Remaking the British World After 1815," involving Lisa Ford (University of New South Wales); Kirsten McKenzie (Sydney University); David Roberts (University of New England); Zoë Laidlaw (Melbourne University); and Stephen Doherty (University of New South Wales). For the period, see also Sujit Sivasundaram, *Waves Across the South: A New History of Revolution and Empire* (London: William Collins, 2020).
19. Madawi al-Rasheed, Carool Kersten, and Marat Shterin, "The Caliphate: Nostalgic Memory and Contemporary Visions," in *Demystifying the Caliphate: Historical Memory and Contemporary Contexts*, ed. Madawi al-Rasheed, Carool Kersten and Marat Shterin (London: Hurst, 2013), 1–30, 10.

INTRODUCTION

20. Cemil Aydın, *The Idea of the Muslim World: A Global Intellectual History* (Cambridge, MA: Harvard University Press, 2017), 14–15.
21. Stephen Frederic Dale, *Islamic Society on the South Asian Frontier: The Mappilas of Malabar, 1498-1922* (Oxford: Clarendon, 1980); see also David Arnold, "Islam, the Mappilas, and Peasant Revolt in Malabar," *Journal of Peasant Studies* 9, no. 4 (1982): 255–65.
22. Syed Ahmed Khan, *The Causes of the Indian Revolt*, intro. Francis Robinson (New York: Oxford University Press, 2000).
23. Gail Minault, *The Khilafat Movement: Religious Symbolism and Political Mobilization in India* (New York: Columbia University Press, 1982), 6; Azmi Özcan, *Pan-Islamism: Indian Muslims, the Ottomans, and Britain, 1877-1924* (Leiden: Brill, 1997), 16–18.
24. Aydın, *Idea of a Muslim World*, 41.
25. Michael Christopher Low, *Imperial Mecca: Ottoman Arabia and the Indian Ocean Hajj* (New York: Columbia University Press, 2020), 249–53. See also the inescapable C. Snouck Hurgronje, *Mekka in the Latter Part of the Nineteenth Century: Daily Life, Customs, and Learning of the Moslems of the East Indian Archipelago*, trans. J. H. Monahan (Leiden: Brill, 1931).
26. Minault, *Khilafat Movement*, 5n18; Syed Tanvir Wasti, "Sir Syed Ahmad Khan and the Turks," *Middle Eastern Studies* 46 no. 4 (2010): 529–42.
27. Richard Temple, *Oriental Experience: A Selection of Essays and Addresses Delivered on Various Occasions* (London: J. Murray, 1883), 312–36. The first appearance of the term in English derived from a Prussian source in relation to the suicide of Abdulaziz and the mobilization of "Pan-Islamism" against Pan-Slavism. "The Eastern Question," *Times of London*, June 5, 1876. For one early mention in India, see the *Pioneer*, December 19, 1881.
28. A supporter of Syed Ahmad Khan in India, Frere oversaw the end of Zanzibar's role in the slave trade under Sultan Barghash in 1872, took the Prince of Wales on a tour of Egypt in 1875, and precipitated the first Boer and Zulu wars in 1879.
29. G. G. van der Kop, *Batavia, Queen City of the East* (Batavia: Kolff, 1925).
30. Aydın, *Idea of a Muslim World*, 46–47, 91.
31. Ashin Das Gupta, *Indian Merchants and the Decline of Surat: c. 1700-1750* (Wiesbaden: Franz Steiner Verlag, 1979); K. N. Chaudhuri, *Trade and Civilisation in the Indian Ocean: An Economic History from the Rise of Islam to 1750* (Cambridge: Cambridge University Press, 1985) and *The Trading World of Asia and the English East India Company: 1660-1760* (Cambridge: Cambridge University Press, 1978); Michael Pearson, *The Portuguese in India* (Cambridge: Cambridge University Press, 1987); Sanjay Subrahmanyam, *The Political Economy of Commerce: Southern India, 1500-1650* (Cambridge University Press, 1990) and *The Portuguese Empire in Asia, 1500-1700* (London: Longman, 1992); and Christopher Bayly, *Imperial Meridian* (London: Longman, 1993) and *The Birth of the Modern World, 1780-1914* (Oxford: Blackwell, 2004).
32. Elizabeth Lambourn, *Abraham's Luggage: A Social Life of Things in the Medieval Indian Ocean World* (Cambridge: Cambridge University Press, 2018); Sebastian Prange, *Monsoon Islam: Trade and Faith on the Medieval Malabar Coast* (Cambridge: Cambridge University Press, 2018).

INTRODUCTION

33. Notable examples include, for the early modern era, Nancy Um, *The Merchant Houses of Mocha: Trade and Architecture in an Indian Ocean Port* (Seattle: University of Washington Press, 2009); Robert Travers, "The Connected Worlds of Haji Mustapha (c. 1730–91): A Eurasian Cosmopolitan in Eighteenth-Century Bengal," *Indian Economic & Social History Review* 52, no. 2 (2015): 297–333; and Jos J. L. Gommans and Jacques Leider, eds., *The Maritime Frontier of Burma: Exploring Political, Cultural, and Commercial Interaction in the Indian Ocean World, 1200–1800* (Leiden: KITLV Press, 2002). In this regard, too, one cannot miss Subrahmanyam's essays formulated in response to the claims of Southeast Asianists. See Sanjay Subrahmanyam, "Connected Histories: Notes Towards a Reconfiguration of Early Modern Eurasia," *Modern Asian Studies* 31, no. 3 (1997): 735–62; and *Explorations in Connected History*, 2 vols. (New Delhi: Oxford University Press, 2005).
34. On "Customary Islam," see Nile Green, *Bombay Islam: The Religious Economy of the West Indian Ocean, 1840–1915* (Cambridge: Cambridge University Press, 2011).
35. Aydin, *Idea of the Muslim World*.
36. Bose, *Hundred Horizons*.
37. Isabel Hofmeyr, *Gandhi's Printing Press: Experiments in Slow Reading* (Cambridge, MA: Harvard University Press, 2013).
38. Ulrike Frietag, *Indian Ocean Migrants and State Formation in Hadhramaut: Reforming the Homeland* (Boston: Brill, 2003); Ho, *Graves of Tarim*.
39. Ho, *Graves of Tarim*, especially 195–320.
40. Scott Reese, *Imperial Muslims: Islam, Community, and Authority in the Indian Ocean, 1839–1937* (Edinburgh: Edinburgh University Press, 2018); Matthew Hopper, *Slaves of One Master: Globalization and Slavery in Arabia in the Age of Empire* (New Haven, CT: Yale University Press, 2015); and Fahad Bishara, *A Sea of Debt: Law and Economic Life in the Western Indian Ocean, 1780–1950* (Cambridge: Cambridge University Press, 2017).
41. Nira Wickramasinghe, *Slave in a Palanquin: Colonial Servitude and Resistance in Sri Lanka* (New York: Columbia University Press, 2020); Wilson Chacko Jacob, *For God or Empire: Sayyid Fadl and the Indian Ocean World* (Stanford, CA: Stanford University Press, 2020).
42. Low, *Imperial Mecca*.
43. Adam Mestyan, *Arab Patriotism: The Ideology and Culture of Power in Late Ottoman Egypt* (Princeton, NJ: Princeton University Press, 2020).
44. Eric Tagliacozzo, *The Longest Journey: Southeast Asians and the Pilgrimage to Mecca* (Oxford: Oxford University Press, 2013).
45. Ronit Ricci, *Banishment and Belonging: Exile and Diaspora in Sarandib, Lanka, and Ceylon* (Cambridge: Cambridge University Press, 2019).
46. Yahaya, *Fluid Jurisdictions*.
47. There are, of course, exceptions. See Ulrike Freitag and Hanne Schönig, "Wise Men Control Wasteful Women: Documents on Customs and Traditions in the Kathīrī State Archives, Sayʾūn," *New Arabian Studies* 5 (2000): 67–96; and Mikhail Rodionov and Hanne Schönig, *The Hadramawt Documents, 1904–51: Family Life and Social Customs Under the Last Sultans* (Wurzburg: Ergon, 2011).

1. From the Spice Islands to the Place of Sadness

1. This quote comes from the pages of a modern book of which I have seen isolated pages. I suspect that it is sourced from an amuletic manual in the possession of Asiya Abderoof. With thanks to Salma Arend.
2. Michael Francis Laffan, "The Sayyid in the Slippers: An Indian Ocean Itinerary and Visions of Arab Sainthood, 1737–1929," *Archipel* 86 (2013): 191–227.
3. Shafiq Morton, *From the Spice Islands to Cape Town: The Life and Times of Tuan Guru* (Cape Town: Awqaf SA, 2018), 125–34.
4. See note 1, this chapter.
5. See Saarah Jappie, "Between Makassars: Site, Story, and the Transoceanic Afterlives of Shaykh Yusuf of Makassar" (PhD diss., Princeton University, January 2018), 49; see also James Armstrong, "A Footnote on Shaykh Yusuf," *Bulletin of the National Library of South Africa* 74, no. 1 (2020): 9–14.
6. K. M. Jeffreys, "The Malay Tombs of the Holy Circle: The Kramat at Zandvliet, Faure," *Cape Naturalist* 1, no. 6 (1939): 195–99.
7. For a discussion, see Azyumardi Azra, *The Origins of Islamic Reformism in Southeast Asia: Networks of Malay-Indonesian and Middle Eastern 'Ulama' in the Seventeenth and Eighteenth Centuries* (Leiden: KITLV, 2004), 98–99; and Ronit Ricci, *Banishment and Belonging: Exile and Diaspora in Sarandib, Lanka, and Ceylon* (Cambridge: Cambridge University Press, 2019), 134–35.
8. For a later copy of this text, evidently executed in Java, see Or. A 101, Perpustakaan Nasional Republik Indonesia (PNRI). With many thanks to Mahmood Kooria, who brought this to my attention, and to Saarah Jappie for further clarification.
9. Or. A 101, 1–2, PNRI. See also Ricci, *Banishment and Belonging*, 134.
10. "Translaat van een maleysche brieff door sjeech Josuff Tadja... ontfangen den 19de February 1689," inventaris nummer 1456, ff. 2176–77, 1.04.02 (VOC), Nationaal Archief (NA), The Hague. With thanks to Saarah Jappie. Translation mine.
11. Jappie, "Between Makassars," 49. For more details on their connections, see Armstrong, "Footnote."
12. Extract from the resolutions of the Castle at Batavia, October 30, 1699, in H. V. C. Leibbrandt, *Precis of the Archives of the Cape of Good Hope: Letters Received, 1695–1708* (Cape Town: W. A. Richards & Sons, 1896), 215.
13. François Valentijn, *Oud en Nieuw Oost-Indiën*, 8 vols. (Dordrecht: J. van Braam, 1724–26), 5:123. With thanks to Jim Armstrong.
14. Jappie, "Between Makassars," 66–69.
15. "A Circle of Islam," *Cape Times*, November 30, 1929; see also I. D. du Plessis, *The Cape Malays* (Cape Town: Maskew Miller, [1944]), 33–35. According to Daiyyan Petersen (personal communication, August 1, 2021), the imam of the Lower Chiappini Street Mosque was then Noore Hassiem Sahibo, who was the son of Tuan Guru's great-granddaughter Salama Rakiep.
16. "Circle of Islam."

[343]

1. FROM THE SPICE ISLANDS TO THE PLACE OF SADNESS

17. K. M. Jeffreys, "The Malay Tombs of the Holy Circle: The Tombs of Signal Hill Ridge," *Cape Naturalist* 1, no. 1 (1934): 15–17.
18. K. M. Jeffreys, "The Malay Tombs of the Holy Circle: The Tombs of Signal Hill Cemetery," *Cape Naturalist* 1, no. 2 (1935): 40–43.
19. On Jeffreys, see Meg Samuelson, "Re-imagining South Africa via a Passage to India: M. K. Jeffreys's Archive of the Indian Ocean World," *Social Dynamics* 33, no. 2 (2007): 61–85; and Samuelson, "Orienting the Cape: A 'White' Woman Writing Islam in South Africa," *Social Dynamics* 37, no. 3 (2011): 363–78.
20. For the miracle of the stones, see Du Plessis, *Cape Malays*, 35; and Achmat Davids, *The History of the Tana Baru: The Case for the Preservation of the Muslim Cemetery at the Top of Longmarket Street* (Cape Town: Committee for the Preservation of the Tana Baru, 1985), 47.
21. On the Afrikaner folklorist, see Shamil Jeppie, "Re-classifications: Coloured, Malay, Muslim," in *Coloured by History, Shaped by Place: New Perspectives on Coloured Identities in Cape Town*, ed. Zimitri Erasmus (Cape Town: Kwela, 2001), 80–96.
22. Achmat Davids, *The Mosques of Bo-Kaap: A Social History of Islam at the Cape* (Athlone: South African Institute of Arabic and Islamic Research, 1980); Davids, *History of the Tana Baru*. See also Morton, *From the Spice Islands*.
23. Davids, *Mosques*, 19, 99; *History*, 43. These objects were once more displayed for the visit of the Sultan of Tidore in 2017.
24. "Sultan's Descendant," *Argus*, March 20, 1980; Al-Haj Nur-el-Erefaan Rakiep, "Tuan Guru (Prince Abdullah bin Qadi Abdus-Salam): Qadi of the Cape, ca. 1770s—1807(?)," 1993, typescript held at Simon's Town Heritage Museum, copy in possession of the author. Both the sword and the shield were also on display in Amsterdam in 2017. See Martine Gosselink, Maria Holtrop, and Robert Ross, eds., *Goede Hoop: Zuid-Afrika en Nederland vanaf 1600* (Amsterdam: Rijksmuseum/Van Tilt, 2017), 140.
25. "The Compendium of Tuan Guru: Translation and Contextualisation (A Research File)," Universities of the Western Cape and Cape Town, 2004; *The ʿAqidah of Tuan Guru* (Cape Town: Samandar, 2004); Seraj Hendricks, "Taṣawwuf (Ṣūfism): Its Role and Impact on the Culture of Cape Islām" (master's thesis, University of South Africa, 2005), esp. 231–43.
26. Compare Gosselink, Holtrop, and Ross, eds., *Goede Hoop*, 142–43.
27. Alexander Dalrymple, "Memoir Concerning Kecheel Nookoo Sultan of Teedoré," L/PS/19/14, 1–5, India Office Records and Private Papers (IOR), British Library (BL).
28. For an overview of this history, see Muridan Widjojo, *The Revolt of Prince Nuku: Cross-Cultural Alliance-Making in Maluku, c. 1780-1810* (Leiden: Brill, 2009).
29. Dalrymple, "Memoir," 2.
30. Thomas Forrest, *A Voyage to New Guinea and the Moluccas, from Balambangan: Including an Account of Magindano, Sooloo, and Other Islands... Performed in the Tartar Galley, Belonging to the Honourable East India Company, During the Years 1774, 1775, and 1776* (London: G. Scott, 1779), 8, 15.
31. Forrest, *Voyage to New Guinea*, 8–9.
32. Forrest, 101.
33. Forrest, 145–47; see also Dalrymple, "Memoir," 3.

34. Forrest, 147–48. I have been unable to locate this figure, who does not appear to have been sent to Robben Island, but, rather, the Papuan Cape of Good Hope near Dory. Then again, a summary report of the 1769 exiling of the "King of Boelang and Magondo" appends mention of a Ternaten vassal, the former Kapitan Laut of "Tenabo" and son of the minor king of "Saijlalo" and "Padje." *Realia: Register op de Generale resolutiën van het kasteel Batavia, 1632-1805*, 3 vols. (Leiden: G. Kolff, 1882-16), 3:282. In 1771 there is a petition at the African Cape from the aged "Padje," now identified as ex-Kapitan Laut of "Tiboro," who had been exiled in October 1769. See H. C. V. Leibbrandt, ed., *Precis of the Archives of the Cape of Good Hope: Requesten (Memorials) 1715-1806*, 5 vols. (Cape Town: Cape Times, 1905-1989), 3:906. From yet another angle, it is claimed in Maluku that the Raja Salawati was a cousin of Tuan Guru, and that he had been instrumental in mobilizing a jihad in the Papuan islands. See Bunyamin Marasebessy and Moh. Amin Faroek, *Tuan Guru Imam Abdullah bin Qadhi Abdussalam: Perlawanan Terhadap Imperialisme Belanda dan Pengasingan di Cape Town* (Jakarta: Abdi Karyatama, 2005).
35. Lauren Benton, Adam Clulow, and Bain Attwood, eds., *Protection and Empire: A Global History* (Cambridge: Cambridge University Press, 2017).
36. On this, see Annabel Teh Gallop, "A Golden Sword for a Diamond Sword: Two Malay Letters from Raffles to Aceh, 1811," in *Qasidah Tinta: Sebuah Festschrift Untuk Prof. Emeritus Dr. Ahmat Adam*, ed. Lai Yew Meng, Saidatul Nornis Haji Mahali, Mohd. Sohaimi Esa, and G. Anantha Raman (Kinabalu: Pusat Penataran Ilmu dan Bahasa/Universiti Malaysia Sabah, 2013), 27–60, 33.
37. Edmonstone to Sultan of Tidore, Calcutta, January 16, 1796 [sic], F/4/9, no. 715, IOR, BL.
38. It should be noted that his predecessor had attempted to get EIC aid against the Siamese. See Wazir Jahan Karim, "The 'Discovery' of Penang Island at Tanjong Tokong Before 1785: Bapu Alaidin Meera Hussein Lebai and Captain Francis Light," *Journal of the Malaysian Branch of the Royal Asiatic Society* 86, no. 1 (2013): 1–29, 7.
39. Dalrymple, "Memoir," citing letter of Nuku to Alexander Shore, received 1796, L/PS/19/14, 5, IOR, BL.
40. On the notion of balance in the archipelago, see Leonard Andaya, *The World of Maluku: Eastern Indonesia in the Early Modern Period* (Honolulu: University of Hawaii Press, 1993), 219–20. Note that Andaya dates the arrest to 1779 and gives the sultan's name as Jamal al-Din, a more standard form in Arabic.
41. According to Ary Huysers, a witness to Gamal al-Din's arrival at Batavia, this was in 1778, with the crown prince exiled to Ceylon shortly thereafter. Ariën Huysers, *Beknopte beschryving der Oostindische etablissementen verzeld van eenige bylagen, uit egte berigten te zaamen gesteld*, 2nd ed. (Amsterdam: Jan Roos, 1792), 36–37n. See also J. S. Stavorinus, *Voyages to the East Indies*, ed. and trans. Samuel Hull Wilcocke, 3 vols. (London: G .G. & J. Robinson, 1798), 1:277–78. Dalrymple's narrative lines up with the account offered by the Tidorese embassy to Calcutta in December 1795, which he also referenced. See the translation of the letter contained in F/4/9/715, IOR, BL.
42. F. W. Stapel, ed., *Corpus Diplomaticum Neerlando-Indicum* (The Hague: Martinus Nijhoff, 1955), 433–53.

1. FROM THE SPICE ISLANDS TO THE PLACE OF SADNESS

43. Huysers claimed that the "power-hungry" prince had begged him to intervene with his master, offering him various islands and even the "beautiful princesses" to gain his freedom. Huysers, *Beknopte beschryving*, 36–37n.
44. Batavia to Joachim van Plettenberg, January 20, 1780, C 549, 25–27, Western Cape Archives and Records Service (WCARS), Cape Town.
45. 1743 saw a distressed Dipanagara seeking a return to Java with his wife, son, and four grandsons. See Leibbrandt, *Requesten*, vol. 1, 374. For details on the effects of the late Cakraningrat, see Jean Gelman Taylor, "Belongings and Belonging: Indonesian Histories of Inventories from the Cape of Good Hope," in *Exile in Colonial Asia: Kings, Convicts, Commemoration*, ed. Ronit Ricci (Honolulu: University of Hawaii Press, 2016), 165–92, 180–81.
46. On Pangeran Arya, see Ricci, *Banishment*, 79–85, 93–95. On the separation of exiles at Lanka, see also 5, 49–56, and 85n31.
47. He was lodged in a former house of a sergeant major by the Ruby Bastion. See P. A. Leupe, "Raden Mas Kareta in 1778," *Bijdragen tot de Taal-, Land- en Volkenkunde van Nederlandsch-Indië* 5 (1856): 441–48. For Kareta's own account as it percolated back to the Cape, see Kathleen M. Jeffreys, ed., *Kaapse Archiefstukken*, 7 vols. (Cape Town: Cape Times, 1926–1938), vol. 1 [1778], 490–94.
48. J. R. Bruijn, F. S. Gaastra, I. Schöffer, and E. S. van Eyck van Heslinga, eds., *Dutch-Asiatic Shipping in the 17th and 18th Centuries*, 3 vols. (The Hague: Nijhoff, 1979), 1:210–11.
49. Leibbrandt, *Requesten*, 3:966; for Lens's death, see 2:690.
50. Debts owed to estate of Joachim Nicolaus van Dessin, 1761, MOOC, 8/10.76, WCARS. The text refers to the "remaining debt" owed by Radin Mascar and Sara van Batavia. See also Taylor, "Belongings," 179.
51. Minutes, Raad van Politiek (Council of Policy), Castle of Good Hope, September 11, 1756, C 134; minutes, Raad van Politiek, Castle of Good Hope, January 29, 1765, C 143, WCARS. See also Taylor, "Belongings," 179–80.
52. Kerry Ward, *Networks of Empire: Forced Migration in the Dutch East India Company* (Cambridge: Cambridge University Press, 2009), 227ff.; Carl Peter Thunberg, *Travels at the Cape of Good Hope, 1772-1775: Based on the English Edition London, 1793-1795* (Cape Town: Van Riebeeck Society, 1986), 48.
53. See draft of a letter from Abdallah to Kaicil Muhammad, Tun Kaicil Ali al-Asghar, Tun Putri Jaliha, Aynan, Mariam, Jubuki, "as well as all the male children and nephews as well as all the female children and nieces, as well as all the grandchildren, all of them together, friends, and family," ca. 1784, Asiya Abderoof Collection, Woodstock, Cape Town. With thanks to Shafiq Morton, who located and photographed the document among several others. See also his *From the Spice Islands*, 63–64.
54. Letter to Kaicil Muhammad et al., ca. 1784. For the dates of their arrival as per the convict roster, see Rapport van de gecondemneerdens van 't Robben Eijland, April 15, 1780, CJ 3189, 204, WCARS; see also Jeffreys, ed., *Kaapse Archiefstukken*, vol. 3 [1780], 213–14.
55. Bruijn, *Dutch-Asiatic Shipping*, 1:212.
56. Jeffreys, ed., *Kaapse Archiefstukken*, vol. 3 [1780], 422–23.

1. FROM THE SPICE ISLANDS TO THE PLACE OF SADNESS

57. Jeffreys, ed., *Kaapse Archiefstukken*, vol.1 [1778], 284, 387, 490–94; vol. 2 [1779], 222. See also Bruijn, *Dutch Asiatic Shipping*, 3:506–7, Voyage 8001.3.
58. Jeffreys, ed., *Kaapse Archiefstukken*, vol. 2 [1779], 41–43, 233–36. As already noted, an inventory surveyed by Taylor suggests that Kareta's wife in 1761 was one Sara van Batavia, which is indicative of her having been a former slave if not Sarah van Boegis. Taylor, "Belongings," 179.
59. Jeffreys, ed., *Kaapse Archiefstukken*, vol. 3 [1780], 188.
60. Jeffreys, ed., *Kaapse Archiefstukken*, vol. 2 [1779], 43.
61. On ʿAlawi, see Laffan, "Sayyid in the Slippers."
62. His four Ternaten retainers were then named as Joeloe, Jande, Doeloe and Madieg. Rolle van de gecondemneertens op 't Robben Eijland, April 15, 1767, CJ 3189, 80–82, WCARS. In March 1783, Minte was mistakenly listed as a "priest." See Lyst van zodanige bannelingen als hun alhier aan Cabo de Goede Hoop bevinden, met aanwysing van den tyd huns banissements, March 21, 1783, CJ 2568, 141–47, WCARS.
63. *Realia*, 1:86; 3:282.
64. Jeffreys, ed., *Kaapse Archiefstukken*, vol. 6 [1782, pt. 2], 19–20. Governor Plettenberg seems to have had some sympathy for Manoppo, whose allowance he raised very modestly while reflecting on the difficult times and urging restraint. See *Kaapse Archiefstukken*, vol. 6 [1782, pt. 2], 387–88.
65. I am grateful to Jim Armstrong for pointing out that "Xullabessij" referred to Sula and not Sulawesi. Jim Armstrong, personal communication, April 17, 2020.
66. For first notation of their presence beside the Tidorese, if not clarity over their location, see Lyst van zodanige Indiaansche bannelingen, als hun alhier aan Cabo de Goede Hoop bevinden, met aanwijsing van den tijd huns banissements, September 15, 1781, CJ 2568, 132, WCARS. I am grateful to Jim Armstrong again for identifying the Ternaten title. See "Salahukum," in *VOC-Glossarium: Verklaringen van termen, verzameld uit de Rijks Geschiedkundige Publicatiën die betrekking hebben op de Verenigde Oost-indische Compagnie* (The Hague: Instituut voor Nederlandse Geschiedenis, 2000), 100.
67. For the two princely "rebellious" radens ordered exiled by the Bantenese king, and then the "Ingabeijs Cheribon en Doeta Laijana [read Laxana], C.S.," see *Realia*, 1:99 (May 25 and July 19, 1773). See also the Capetonian lists noting the January 19, 1774, arrival at the island of "Ratoe Bagus Oedien" and "Ratoe Bagus Nassar," sent from Batavia for life on May 25, 1773: Rolle van de gecondemneerden op 't Robben Eijland, April 16, 1774, CJ 3189, 141, WCARS.
68. For previous speculation on Norman, who arrived on December 9, 1774, and who I now realize had more of a connection to Banten, rather than his namesake of Cirebon; see Michael Francis Laffan, "From Javanese Court to African Grave: How Noriman Became Tuan Skapie, 1717–1806," *Journal of Indian Ocean World History*, 1 (2017): 38–59.
69. Copies of Capetonian genealogies show Umar Faruq as a direct lineal ancestor, which is also comparable to documentation published in Indonesia. With thanks to Salma Arend and family, as well as that of the Rakieps, in the hope that I have got things right. Personal communications, Cape Town, July 30 and

1. FROM THE SPICE ISLANDS TO THE PLACE OF SADNESS

September 16, 2017. See also Morton, *From the Spice Islands*, 125–34. On the Javanese faction at Tidore, see Andaya, *World of Maluku*, 216–17.
70. For the contract of 1780, see Stapel, ed., *Corpus Diplomaticum*, 446.
71. Petition of Imam Abdulla, December 4, 1804, and extract of December 19, 1804, no. 14, BR 348, 60–64, WCARS.
72. Jeffreys, ed., *Kaapse Archiefstukken*, vol. 4 [1781], 301–2; vol. 5 [1782, pt. 1], 456.
73. Minutes of the Secret Committee, April 10, 1778–February 23, 1782, L/PS/1/4, esp. 213–17, IOR, BL; and minutes of the Secret Committee, May 22, 1780–February 23, 1782, L/PS/1/5, IOR, BL.
74. Resolution of Monday, April 2, 1781, Raad van Politiek, Castle of Good Hope, C 159, 205–33, WCARS.
75. Jeffreys, ed., *Kaapse Archiefstukken*, vol. 4 [1781], 43.
76. Draft of letter to Kaicil Muhammad et al., ca. 1784.
77. Information relative to the Cape supplied by Colonel Richard Matthews, January 1, 1781, L/PS/1/5, 77–81, IOR, BL.
78. L/PS/1/5, 91–92, IOR, BL.
79. *New Annual Register, Or General Repository of History* 2 (October 1781): 90.
80. See Johnston's dispatch on the encounter made aboard the *Romney* as reported in the *New Annual Register*, 89–90. With thanks to Shafiq Morton.
81. Letter to Kaicil Muhammad et al., ca. 1784.
82. *Briefwisseling van Hendrik Swellengrebel Jr oor Kaapse Sake, 1778–1792* (Cape Town: Van Riebeeck-Vereeniging, 1982), 370–71.
83. *Briefwisseling van Hendrik Swellengrebel*, 370; Loopende bandieten rolle deeser voegen geformeert met den jaaren 1761, CJ 3188, 524–64, WCARS.
84. Loopende bandieten rolle, 561–62, WCARS. Note that the online transcription of Estate Papers at the Cape of Good Hope (TEPC) (http://databases.tanap.net/vocrecords, accessed December 22, 2021) incorrectly has all four Tidorese having escaped based on a post-factum annotation. For the declaration of September, see Lyst van zodanige Indiaansche bannelingen, September 15, 1781, CJ 2568, 132–33, WCARS. Batavia would cease sending any exiles to the Cape in favor of Ceylon, where in March 1782 the income of eight other Tidorese held on that island (including the princes) was raised by half. See *Realia*, 1:87.
85. Lyst van zodanige bannelingen als hun alhier aan Cabo de Goede Hoop bevinden, met aanwysing van den tyd huns bannissements, March 21, 1783, CJ 2568, 141–47, WCARS.
86. Jeffreys, ed., *Kaapse Archiefstukken*, vol. 5 [1782, pt. 1], 278; vol. 7 [1783, pt. 1), 51, 354. This was not the first time Batavia had complained about the Cape's record-keeping, having sent an order for more accurate listings in February 1777, and then for those whose time was expired in October 1778. See *Realia*, 1:87, 1:212.
87. Jeffreys, ed., *Kaapse Archiefstukken*, vol. 7 [1783, pt. 1], 435–36; see also Loopende bandieten rolle deeser voegen geformeert met den jaaren 1761, CJ 3188, 524–64, WCARS.
88. Jeffreys misread this as "Abd al-Radeff"; Jeffreys, ed., *Kaapse Archiefstukken*, vol. 7 [1783, pt. 1], 421.
89. Jeffreys.

1. FROM THE SPICE ISLANDS TO THE PLACE OF SADNESS

90. Letter to Kaicil Muhammad et al., ca. 1784. Kasiang and Darwis would appear to have been Tidorese exiles, or perhaps servants from a previous retinue.
91. Dalrymple, "Memoir," L/PS/19/14, 4n, IOR, BL; see also Edmonstone to Sultan of Tidore, Calcutta, December 20, 1785, cited in EIC political no. 112, 1796/97, F/4/9, no. 715, IOR, BL.
92. It had been in response to Nuku's request for arms and company flags for his ships and ports, and gratitude for his assistance of company lascars marooned off New Guinea, that the governor offered an EIC flag for the sultan's private use at the palace. See James Frushard (?) to Edmonstone, Bencoolen (?), December 7, 1785; and Edmonstone to Sultan of Tidore, Calcutta, January 16, 1796 [sic], F/4/9, no. 715, IOR, BL.
93. Stavorinus, *Voyages to the East Indies*, 1:277-78n.
94. Lyst van zodanige bannelingen, March 21, 1783, CJ 2568, 141-47, WCARS; Jeffreys, ed., *Kaapse Archiefstukken*, vol. 7 [1783, pt. 1], 435-36.
95. Leijst der Indiaansche bannelingen, die hun alhier aan Cabo de Goede Hoop bevinden en voor hoe langen tijd, zy gebannen zyn, April 10, 1778, CJ 2568, 62-71, WCARS. The *Abbekerk* arrived at the Cape on January 4, 1776. See Bruijn, *Dutch-Asiatic Shipping*, vol. 3, 498-99, Voyage 7950.1.
96. On the sentencing of his retinue, see Jeffreys, ed., *Kaapse Archiefstukken*, vol. 7 [1783, pt. 1], 435-36; Stapel, ed., *Corpus Diplomaticum*, 384-87; and *Realia*, 3:283.
97. Petition of November 25, 1788, in Leibbrandt, *Requesten*, 1:30.
98. Rapport van de gecondemneerdens van t: Robben Eijland, April 1, 1782, CJ 3189, 228-31, WCARS. This is also the last reference to Badr al-Din and Callaga Berboe in VOC sources. Callaga and his son Corradoe had arrived at Ceylon with the *Zuijdbeveland* on April 6, 1775. See Rolle van de gecondemneerden op 't Robben Eijland, May 8, 1775, CJ 3189, 153; and A. Moens to Iman Falck, Cochin, December 14, 1774, CJ 2568, 23-26, WCARS.
99. Moens to Falck, December 14, 1774, CJ 2568, 23-26, WCARS.
100. For the original request from the Dutch resident of Cochin to Governor Falck at Ceylon to exile both men, see Moens to Falck, December 14, 1774. Hyder Ali's successor Tipu Sultan, would ally with France (and thus the Netherlands) in the 1780s. It must have felt ironic to those who knew Callaga and Corradoe when Tipu would send Muslim emissaries to France via Cape Town in 1788. The Mysorean delegation were briefly guests of Hendrik Cloete at Groot Constantia, where the presence of a Muslim cleric was noted. *Briefwisseling van Hendrik Swellengrebel*, 399, 403.
101. Rapport van de gecondemneerdens van t: Robben Eijland, April 1, 1782, CJ 3189, 228-31, WCARS.
102. The two Bantenese are noted in one undated list as remaining in the lodge from 1782; however, this is contradicted by the Robben Island records, which have both returned there from mid-1783 and remaining until November 1789. See Loopende bandieten rolle deeser voegen geformeert met den jaaren 1761, CJ 3188, 524-64; and Rapport van de gecondemneerdens op 't Robben Eijland, August 30, 1783, CJ 3189, 243-45, 392-94, WCARS.
103. Rapport van de gecondemneerdens op 't Robben Eijland, August 30, 1783, CJ 3189, 243-45, WCARS. The use of the old hospital (demolished ca. 1790) as

1. FROM THE SPICE ISLANDS TO THE PLACE OF SADNESS

overflow accommodation was pointed out by Ebrahim Salie, who has excavated an impressive amount of material from the archives of the Western Cape. E. Salie, personal communication, Timbuktu Books, Cape Town, October 7, 2017.

104. For more on Norman, see Laffan, "From Javanese Court."
105. Lyst van zodanige bannelingen, March 21, 1783, and folios to Notitie van sodanige Chineesen en bandieten als er alhier bij de generaale monsterrolle in 's E: Comp:s Slaven Logie bekentstaan, March 28, 1789, CJ 2568, 141–47, 148, 198–99, WCARS. In 1798 the office of the fiscal consisted of a principal and a deputy, a clerk, two bailiffs, two jailors, eight constables, and nineteen "blacks and Malays." John Barrow, *An Account of Travels into the Interior of Southern Africa, in the Years 1797 and 1798*, 2 vols. (London: Johnson, [1801–1804] 1968), 2:423. For discussion of the caffers, see Ward, *Networks of Empire*, 264–69.
106. "Text in Arabic with Interlinear Melayu 613 pp (bound)," 128, N. E. Rakiep Collection [Tuan Guru's Arabic Compendium], MSB 683, National Library of South Africa (NLSA), Cape Town. I have seen internal colophons of this text by way of another photocopy of the compendium kept by Nurul Erefaan's sons, which I mapped onto the summary and partial translations made by Rafudeen. It is possible that the original is not paginated in the same way, based on the scan used for the Rijksmuseum exhibition of 2017. See also Auwais Rafudeen, "The Compendium of Tuan Guru: Translation and Contextualisation (A Research File)," Universities of the Western Cape and Cape Town, 2004; *The 'Aqidah of Tuan Guru* (Cape Town: Samandar, 2004); and Gosselink, Holtrop, and Ross, eds., *Goede Hoop*, 142–43.
107. Muttaqin Rakiep, personal communication, Cape Town, September 16, 2017.
108. Annotatie Boek van Justitieele Visitatien gedaan soo aan verdrinkelingen door sware quetsuuren schielijk overleedene als andere verongelukte lichaamen, 1757–1766, July 9, 1763, CJ 3173, 128–31, WCARS.
109. Thunberg, *Travels*, 47–48.
110. Thunberg, 49. Andrew Sparrman, *A Voyage to the Cape of Good Hope Towards the Antarctic Polar Circle and Round the World: but Chiefly into the Country of the Hottentots and Caffres, from the Year 1772, to 1776*, 2 vols. (London: Johnson, 1971), 1:12.
111. Leibbrandt, *Requesten*, 2:789; 3:966 and 3:980. An erstwhile follower, the free Javanese Rombian also appealed in 1785 for transportation on the *Voorschoten* with his freed wife, Candasa of Java, and their two children. *Requesten*, 3:985.
112. M. C. Ricklefs, *Jogjakarta Under Sultan Mangkubumi, 1749-1792: A History of the Division of Java* (London: Oxford University Press, 1974), 270, 287–88.
113. M. C. Ricklefs, *Soul Catcher: Java's Fiery Prince Mangkunagara I, 1726-95* (Honolulu: University of Hawaii Press, 2018), 285–89.
114. For mention of Wirakusuma and family's departure from Batavia on the *Maria*, see *Realia*, 1:87.
115. On the burial and exhumation of Pangeran Arya, see Ricci, *Banishment*, 93–94. See also Leupe, "Raden Mas Kareta in 1778," 448, citing documents claiming that Pangeran Arya was temporarily placed on Edam Island in November 1741.
116. A preparatory sketch made by the cleric Jan Brandes in 1786 or 1787 appears to show 'Alawi's tomb on the slopes of the Lion's Rump. See NG-1985-7-1-43, Rijksmuseum.

117. See colophon dated Thursday, 25 Safar 1200 (December 27, 1785), Tuan Guru's Arabic Compendium, MSB 683, 458, NLSA.
118. Laffan, "Sayyid in the Slippers," 200, 219. As we shall see in chapter 5, such care was similarly offered to ʿAlawi's followers exiled to Ceylon in the 1740s.
119. Tuan Guru's Arabic Compendium, MSB 683, 67–69, NLSA. Such an identification was also made by both Rafudeen ("Compendium," 46) and Hendricks ("Taṣawwuf," 234–40).
120. Tuan Guru's Arabic Compendium, MSB 683, 481, NLSA.
121. On the mortality of enslaved Africans in August 1786, see Leibbrandt, *Requesten*, 3:1333.

2. Shaping Islam at the Cape of Good Hope

Epigraph: Tuan Guru's Arabic Compendium, MSB 683, National Library of South Africa (NLSA), Cape Town, as cited by Auwais Rafudeen, *The ʿAqidah of Tuan Guru* (Cape Town: Samandar, 2004), 60.

1. *Realia: Register op de Generale resolutiën van het kasteel Batavia, 1632-1805*, 3 vols. (Leiden: G. Kolff, 1882–1886), 1:87.
2. See Nigel Worden and Gerald Groenewald, eds., *Trials of Slavery: Selected Documents Concerning Slaves from the Criminal Records of the Council of Justice at the Cape of Good Hope, 1705-1794* (Cape Town: Van Riebeeck Society for the Publication of South African Historical Documents, 2005), 537–56.
3. Lyst van zodanige Indiaansche bannelingen, als hun alhier aan Cabo de Goede Hoop bevinden, met aanwijsing van den tijd huns bannissements, September 15, 1781, CJ 2568, 129, Western Cape Archives and Records Service, (WCARS), Cape Town.
4. The listing of February 1783 mentions one Surabrata as being given general work like Norman and Ingabij and places him in that capacity for some years, which suggests that there were two people of that name. See Notitie van soodanige bandieten als 'er in deese maand Februarij 1783 in waaren weesen werden bevonden, met aanwijsinge waar deselve zijn dienst doende, February 24, 1783, CJ 2568, 138–39, WCARS.
5. Edna Bradlow, "Mental Illness or a Form of Resistance? The Case of Soera Brotto," *African Historical Review* 23, no.1 (1991): 4–16; see also Kerry Ward, *Networks of Empire: Forced Migration in the Dutch East India Company* (Cambridge: Cambridge University Press, 2009), 266–67.
6. Bradlow, "Mental Illness," 12. In the hue and cry of September 26, Surabrata had been declared the "dishumanized creature," and one hundred rixdollars was offered for his apprehension. See H. C. V. Leibbrandt, ed., *Precis of the Archives of the Cape of Good Hope: Requesten (Memorials) 1715-1806*, 5 vols. (Cape Town: Cape Times, 1905–1989), 1:20–21. For the brutal treatment of so-called *amokspuwers* at Batavia, see J. H. Stavorinus, *Reize van Zeeland over de Kaap de Goede Hoop, naar*

2. SHAPING ISLAM AT THE CAPE OF GOOD HOPE

Batavia, Bantam, Bengalen, enz. gedaan in de jaaren MDCCLXVIII tot MDCCLXXI, 2 vols. (Leiden: A. & J. Honkoop, 1793), 1:234–37.
7. Bradlow, "Mental Illness," 55.
8. Those removed were recorded as including Catip of Ternate, Goang from Cirebon, Omar from Ambon, Sakkodien and Modin from Java, August "from Bougis," the two "Cirebonese" princes (who had only just come off the island the previous year), and Imam Abdallah. See Rapport van de gecondemneerdens op het Robben Eijland, ultimo April 1789, CJ 3188, 580–82, nos. 73–78 and 95–99, WCARS. As mentioned in note 4 above, a Surabrata is listed here too, more likely a laborer found in the lists from February 1783. In November it was also proposed to substitute European employees or African slaves for some of the less trusted Asian members of the ranks. Bradlow, "Mental Illness," 15.
9. Rapport van de gecondemneerdens op het Robben Eijland, December 31, 1786, CJ 3189, 271–73, WCARS.
10. For restrictions, see Bradlow, "Mental Illness," 10–11.
11. Bradlow, 4.
12. John Barrow, *An Account of Travels into the Interior of Southern Africa, in the Years 1797 and 1798*, 2 vols. (London: Johnson, [1801–1804] 1968), 2:109. On Barrow, see Nigel Penn, "Mapping the Cape: John Barrow and the First British Occupation of the Colony, 1795–1803," *Pretexts* 4 no. 2 (1993): 20–43.
13. Tuan Guru's Arabic Compendium, MSB 683, 599–600, as reproduced in Davids, *History of the Tana Baru*, 43. Interestingly, the Robben Island records started to refer to him as a Ternaten from this time. See Rapport van de gecondemneerdens op het Robben Eijland, December 31, 1786, CJ 3189, 273ff., WCARS.
14. Bunyamin Marasebessy and Moh. Amin Faroek, *Tuan Guru Imam Abdullah bin Qadhi Abdussalam: Perlawanan Terhadap Imperialisme Belanda dan Pengasingan di Cape Town* (Jakarta: Abdi Karyatama, 2005), after page 120. Both Abu Qasim and Sha'n are remembered as his sons in Indonesia, though Abdallah was specific in his letter about the events of 1781 that Abu Qasim was a nephew by an addressee sister, Aynan. See draft of letter to Kaicil Muhammad, Tun Kaicil Ali al-Asghar, Tun Putri Jaliha, Aynan, Mariam, Jubuki, "as well as all the male children and nephews as well as all the female children and nieces, as well as all the grandchildren, all of them together, friends and family," ca. 1784, Asiya Abderoof Collection, Cape Town.
15. The last reference to him as an exile would appear to be in 1788: Rapport van de gecondemneerden op het Robben Eijland, August 31, 1788, CJ 3189, 280–82, WCARS. Those mentioned in the petition of November that year were his wife, Constantia of the Cape, with her similarly locally born mother, Dina; her Batavian grandmother Filida; their four children (Selasa, Fatima, Camies, and Abdullah); the freewoman Cita van Boughies; and the enslaved Jounga van Ternate. See petition no. 157 of 1788, in Leibbrandt, *Requesten*, 1:30. After departing the Cape on December 1, 1788, the family arrived at Batavia on February 10, 1789. See J. R. Bruijn, F. S. Gaastra, I. Schöffer, and E. S. van Eyck van Heslinga, eds., *Dutch-Asiatic Shipping in the 17th and 18th Centuries*, 3 vols. (The Hague: Nijhoff, 1979), 2:736–37, Voyage 4614.6.
16. Extract Bataviaasche Missive de dato 26 October 1790, C 989, 110–11, WCARS.

2. SHAPING ISLAM AT THE CAPE OF GOOD HOPE

17. Draft letter of Tuan Guru to Prince Ahmad, ca. 1791, Asiya Abderoof Collection, Cape Town. See fig. 2.2. With thanks to Shafiq Morton once again. Tata Layar has been identified by Daiyaan Petersen as one "Layer van Baly," who lodged a will in 1791 in which he named his eldest child as "Cayda." See Will of Layer van Baly, July, 20, 1791, CJ 2646, 53, WCARS.
18. Erf [Plot] 2839, Transfer Deed 201, September 26, 1794, Cape Town Deeds Office.
19. Frank Bradlow and Margaret Cairns, *Early Cape Muslims: A Study of Their Mosques, Genealogy and Origins* (Cape Town: Balkema, 1978), 61-62. Leibbrandt's summaries (*Requesten*, 1:275) suggest that Catharina of the Cape manumitted Coridon of Ceylon in 1783.
20. Leibbrandt, 1:263.
21. Erf 2839, Transfer Deed 27, February 3, 1809, Cape Town Deeds Office.
22. Abd al-Rakib is commonly given a birth year of 1793, though backdating his age reported in the *South African Commercial Advertizer* for February 13, 1836, gives mid-1791. It is likely that the reporter was giving his age in Hijri rather than Gregorian years, a practice that might explain the often exceptional lifespans of Capetonian Muslims.
23. Davids, *Mosques of Bo-Kaap*, 100; Bradlow and Cairns, *Early Cape Muslims*, 66–67.
24. Lyst der bannelingen van Cabo de Goede Hoop, n.d., CJ 3188, 587–89, WCARS. While he seems a match for Achmat van Bengalen, Machmet is more likely to have been an imam known at Ceylon as "Panenga," and linked to an exilic family from Madura. See Raad van Politiek, Colombo, August 15, 1792, 1/219, Sri Lankan National Archives (SLNA), Colombo. See also chapter 5, page 138.
25. For slaving negotiations with Zanzibar and competition with the Sultan of Muscat, see Kathleen M. Jeffreys, ed., *Kaapse Archiefstukken* (Cape Town: Cape Times, 1926–1938), vol. 1 [1778], 140–42. Few of those put in the Slave Lodge would survive. See *Kaapse Archiefstukken*, vol. 1 [1778], 149–50, 160–61, 170–71, and 178–79. The resumption of slave transportation in 1785 saw similar losses. See Leibbrandt, *Requesten*, 2:794; and Patrick Harries, "Middle Passages of the Southwest Indian Ocean: A Century of Forced Migration from Africa to the Cape of Good Hope," *Journal of African History* 55, no. 2 (2014): 173–90.
26. Anne Lindsay Barnard, *Lady Anne Barnard's Watercolours and Sketches: Glimpses of the Cape of Good Hope* (Simon's Town: Fernwood, 2009), esp. 7–11, 24–25, 38.
27. Barrow, *Account of Travels*, 2:147. On the revolutionary spirit among the *trekboers*, see Sujit Sivasundaram, *Waves Across the South: A New History of Revolution and Empire* (London: William Collins, 2020), 87–92.
28. "Evidence of Two Mahometan Priests, Muding and Imaum Achmat," in *Papers Relative to the Condition and Treatment of the Native Inhabitants of Southern Africa, Within the Colony of the Cape of the Good Hope: Parliamentary Papers* (London: House of Commons, March 1835), annex no. 30, 207–10.
29. Frans might be identified as a slave boy claimed by Reijnier Lafebre in 1755, though the generic name does not inspire confidence. See inventory of August 19, 1755, MOOC 8/9.6, WCARS.
30. Petition of Frans van Bengalen, BO 154, 17, WCARS.
31. Drafts of letter to Abd al-Shukur, 17 Jumada II 1217 (October 14, 1802), Asiya Abderoof Collection, Cape Town. Indeed, Abdallah had already referred to

2. SHAPING ISLAM AT THE CAPE OF GOOD HOPE

"Encik Frans" in a brief marginal note on his first draft to family back in 1784, seeking financial aid for (his son?) Sha'n, though it is unclear when he was making use of the paper for scrap at the time. It is also curious that he vocalized the Malay, but not the Arabic. See top left of draft of letter to Kaicil Muhammad et al., ca. 1784.

32. Index of outgoing correspondence noting letter of Barnard to resident and members of the Burgher Senate, Castle of Good Hope, February 1, 1800, BO 155, 44, A, WCARS; Resolution Book January 1800–December 1801, BR 9, 21–23, WCARS.
33. Samuel Hudson, "Memorandums & Occurrences," February 15, 1800. This and Hudson's larger text relating to Frans in Hudson's diary (ACC 602, 8&9, book no. 11, WCARS), were transcribed for publication with the Van Riebeeck Society by the late Rob Shell, though his death in 2015 and the transformation of the society put an end to the project, available in draft on CD-ROM. See Hudson's "Essay on Slaves at the Cape," in *Out of Livery: The Papers of Samuel Eusebius Hudson, 1764–1828*, ed. Rob Shell, Edward Hudson, and Raymond Hudson (n.p., n.d.), n.p.
34. See Hudson diary, WCARS.
35. Barrow, *Account of Travels*, 2:141, 427.
36. A "Retjap" or "Redjab van Bougis" had been exiled from Batavia in November 1772 and served in the Slave Lodge from February 1781. He was last noted in the convict lists of June 1788 while a will was lodged in his name in 1805. Naam rolle van sodaniege bandieten jongens als er voor jegenswoordig bij 't E: Comp:e slaven rolle bekend staan, CJ 3189, 181–85; Notitie van alle soodanige bandieten jongens en meijden, als 'er van tyd tot tyd in 's E: Comp:s Slaven Logie zijn gebannen, February 5, 1781, CJ 2568, 122–24; will of Redjab van Bougies, filed 1805, MOOC 7/1/50, 113, WCARS (with thanks to Daiyaan Petersen). Abd al-Alim had meanwhile been sent from Java in March 1774 as a "useless and damaging subject." He was similarly employed from February 1781 until at least 1789. Lyst van zodanige bannelingen, etc., CJ 2568, 141–47, 148, 198–99, WCARS.
37. Drafts of letters to Abd al-Shukur, 17 Jumada II 1217 (Thursday, October 14, 1802), Asiya Abderoof Collection, Cape Town.
38. Auwais Rafudeen, "The Compendium of Tuan Guru: Translation and Contextualisation (A Research File)," Universities of the Western Cape and Cape Town, 2004, 46; Seraj Hendricks, "Taṣawwuf (Ṣūfism): Its Role and Impact on the Culture of Cape Islām" (master's thesis, University of South Africa, 2005), 234–40.
39. "Evidence of Two Mahometan Priests," 209.
40. See Erf 2839, Transfer Deed 27, February 3, 1809, Cape Town Deeds Office.
41. Robert Semple, *Walks and Sketches at the Cape of Good Hope*, ed. F. R. Bradlow (Cape Town: Balkema, [1803] 1968, 52.
42. For Saartjie's roman script mark on Achmat's notice, see MOOC 6/9/31, 6387, WCARS. For its reproduction and the Jawi of Achmat, see Bradlow and Cairns, *Early Cape Muslims*, 3–4. By contrast, in December 1811, Trijn had signed the deed of her newly purchased property adjacent to the mosque over to Saartjie with a simple cross. See Erf 7840, formerly 5021, Transfer Deed 113, December 6, 1811, Cape Town Deeds Office.

2. SHAPING ISLAM AT THE CAPE OF GOOD HOPE

43. Lists of government slaves, convicts, and invalids and their stations, 1789 and 1802, SO 7/34, WCARS.
44. Deed of transfer for Adriaan Vincent Bergh giving Mawaa van Ternate to Iman Java, December 20, 1800, NCD 1/41, no. 742.1, WCARS; pledge of 200RD to Adriaan Vincent Bergh for purchase of Mawaa van Ternate, December 20, 1800, NCD 1/27, no. 734.0, WCARS.
45. I am indebted to Daiyaan Petersen for details about the grave marker, which stands in the Tana Baru cemetery, and indeed for many recent discoveries and corrections. As is common, the Hijri date on the stone does not align with the Gregorian one given on the death certificate, being adrift in this case by about a year.
46. By his own account, Jan had arrived with a Captain Laurits on the *Batavier* in 1786, though this and all the other names he gave, including that of Gabriel Exter (Adjunct Fiscal, 1785–1790), line up with a 1789 arrival of that vessel documented by Bruijn and colleagues. See the Jawi text *Ini surat menyatakan* in CO 3984, 32, WCARS; see also Bruijn, *Dutch-Asiatic Shipping*, 3:544–45, Voyage 8240.1.
47. On the Neethlings, see E. M. Neethling and L. C. P. Neethling, *Die Neethlings in Suid-Afrika* (Pretoria: Raad vir Geesteswetenskaplike Navorsing, 1979), esp. 9–27.
48. See, for examples, Rapport van de gecondemneerdens op het Robben Eijland, CJ 3189, 273, 276, 285, WCARS.
49. Drafts of letters to Abd al-Shukur, 17 Jumada II 1217 (October 14, 1802), Asiya Abderoof Collection, Cape Town. Daiyaan Petersen (personal communication, September 6, 2021) has proposed that Abd al-Shukur may have been Sukkur van Java, though he remained on the list of caffers until December 1802.
50. Memorie van H. L. Neethling over de Kaap de Goede Hoop, May 17, 1801, 1.04.17, 970, Nationaal Archief (NA), The Hague.
51. *Briefwisseling van Hendrik Swellengrebel*, 350–51, 366.
52. R. C. H. Shell, "The March of the Mardijkers: The Toleration of Islam in the Cape Colony," *Kronos* 22 (1995): 3–20.
53. Barrow, *Account of Travels*, 2:406, referring to a pamphlet on the matter by Janssens.
54. Jan van Bugis, *Ini surat menyatakan*, CO 3984, 32, WCARS.
55. "Malay Priesthood," *South African Commercial Advertizer*, February 24, 1836.
56. Petition of Imam Abdulla, December 4, 1804, notary G. Goetz, extract of December 19, 1804, no. 14, BR 348, 60–64, WCARS.
57. BR 59, 50–52, WCARS.
58. Petition of the "Javanese priest" Frans van Bengal, for a new burial ground, July 20, 1805, granted October 2, 1805, RDG 2, 132, 149–150, WCARS.
59. Hudson diary, WCARS.
60. Hudson diary.
61. See Dutch will of Tuan Guru of 1801 and copy of a Jawi version lodged May 2, 1807, MOOC 7/1/53, 66 and 66 1/2, WCARS.
62. Draft of letter of Tuan Guru to Prince Ahmad, ca. 1792, Asiya Abderoof Collection, Cape Town.
63. According to the census of December 1807 (J 41, 173, WCARS), she had moved to the home of Jacob van de Kaap. With thanks to Daiyaan Petersen, personal communication, August 6, 2021.

2. SHAPING ISLAM AT THE CAPE OF GOOD HOPE

64. Achmat's surviving children by Saartjie were listed in her will as Someela, Nuraan, Mochammat, Hammien, Sadiek, Gemra, and Rasieda; see MOOC 6/9/31, 6387, WCARS; and Bradlow and Cairns, *Early Cape Muslim*, 78–79.
65. This was standard. The first "property" to be dealt with by his father-in-law, Layer, had been an enslaved female, Rampie van Goenoeng Taloe (in West Java), who was to be manumitted on his death. Interestingly, the standard Dutch coda also noted that any slave who had converted to Christianity could not be sold on. Will of Layer van Baly, July, 20, 1791, CJ 2646, 53, WCARS.
66. The same notary who attested to the sale of Mawaa recorded that of Damon to Van Rheenen, ten days later, and for four times the price. See sale of Damon, December 30, 1800, NCD 1/41, no. 748, WCARS.
67. Memorial of the free Black Abdol Malik, June 19, 1816, CO 3905, 209, WCARS. This manumission had not been stipulated in the variants of Tuan Guru's will lodged with the Orphan Chamber.
68. Slave registry documents refer to Mawaa's ongoing servitude and then her death at some time before 1830, aged fifty-five: Register of guardianship with minors under Abdul Malek, ca. 1835, SO 20,15, WCARS. In 1830, Abd al-Rakib paid a fine for not having reported her death and that of three of Rachbat's children: see CO 3949, 55, WCARS. With thanks to Shafiq Morton and Daiyaan Petersen.
69. "Evidence of Two Mahometan Priests." The order of imams at the Auwal Mosque was reconstructed by Achmat Davids (*Mosques of Bo-Kaap*) based on letters sent to the *South African Commercial Advertiser* in 1836. These are also taken up in chapter 4.
70. In 1777, for instance, Candasa of Batavia had purchased Katjong of Bougies from Juliana of Malacca with the express plan of manumitting him after five years of service and, we can assume, conversion—though marriage ensued as well, with "Catjo" of Boegis and Candasa petitioning to leave for Batavia with their two children in 1784. Leibbrandt, *Requesten*, 1:274, 278.
71. Hudson diary, WCARS. Jan van Bugis is said to have been a great exponent of enlarging his community by just such means into the 1820s. Davids, *Mosques of Bo-Kaap*, 118.
72. Bradlow and Cairns, *Early Cape Muslims*, 63.
73. See the signature of William Ferdinand van Reede van Oudtshoorn Jr. (1784–1839) attesting to Tuan Guru's pledge of 200RD to Adriaan Vincent Bergh for purchase of Mawaa van Ternate, December 20, 1800, NCD 1/27, 734.0, WCARS; and for the deed of transfer of the same date, NCD 1/41, no. 742.1, WCARS.
74. Her mother had only just bought the latter parcel, Walendorp no. 20, from the municipal council on June 28, 1806. Erven 2839 and 5021 (later 7840), Cape Town Deeds Office; see also Bradlow and Cairns, *Early Cape Muslims*, 63.
75. Mirza Abu Taleb, *Westward Bound: Travels of Mirza Abu Taleb*, ed. Mushirul Hasan, trans. Charles Stewart (New Delhi: Oxford University Press, 2005), 25–27.
76. Manuscript once owned by Muhammad Hanif with original owner's name occluded, loaned to Simon's Town Heritage Museum in 2013 by Zakareya Davis, current location unknown. Digital photographs in possession of author. With thanks to Aunt Patty.

77. Manuscript once owned by descendants of Achmat van Bengalen via his son Hamim, current location unknown. Digital photographs in possession of author.
78. The pages written by Abdallah are on paper bearing the "Britannia" watermark that matches samples from 1794.
79. While Genie Yoo has pointed out to me that such dates are not always to be trusted, with some producers dating their paper in advance, it seems unlikely that the quires of "S. Wish & Patch 1808" found their way to Tuan Guru before his passing.
80. Amuletic text, Asiya Abderoof Collection, Cape Town. Photocopy in possession of the author.

3. Sanguinary Attacks and Unruly Passions

1. Zayn al-Din had advocated such a view in his *Fath al-muʿin*, which circulated widely in Southeast Asia; I thank Saumyashree Ghosh for drawing this to my attention. On the *Fath al-muʿin*, see Mahmood Kooriadathodi, "Cosmopolis of Law: Islamic legal Ideas and Texts Across the Indian Ocean and Eastern Mediterranean Worlds" (PhD diss., Leiden University, 2016).
2. Following a 25 percent deposit on October 16, 8000 of the remaining balance of the purchase price of 14,000 guilders took the form of a loan to be repaid to the widow Roux at 6 percent per annum, backdated to July. Erf [Plot] 3464, Transfer Deed 165, November 20, 1807, Cape Town Deeds Office. Now called the Palm Tree Mosque, it is found at 185 Long Street.
3. "Death of a Centenarian," *South African Commercial Advertiser* [1864], reproduced in *The Cape Malays: An Essay by a Cape Colonist* [by Eric Aspeling] (Cape Town: W. A. Richards & Sons, 1883), 16–17; Achmat Davids, *The Mosques of Bo-Kaap: A Social History of Islam at the Cape* (Athlone: South African Institute of Arabic and Islamic Research, 1980), 119–20.
4. Davids, *Mosques*, 114–17, 210–13; "Malay Priesthood," *South African Commercial Advertizer*, February 24, 1836; Mogamat Hoosain Ebrahim, *The Cape Hajj Tradition Past & Present* (Cape Town: Mogamat Hoosain Ibrahim & International Peace University, South Africa, 2009), 17. For the *African Court Calendar* reference, I rely on Rob Shell's unpublished "Prosopography of Cape Imams," also cited by Shamil Jeppie in his "Leadership and Loyalties: The Imams of Nineteenth-Century Colonial Cape Town, South Africa," *Journal of Religion in Africa* 26, no. 2 (1996): 139–162.
5. Will of "Samida van de Kaap," filed October 2, 1860, MOOC 7/1/251, 72, Western Cape Archives and Records Service (WCARS), Cape Town.
6. Jeppie, "Leadership and Loyalties."
7. Robert Semple, *Walks and Sketches at the Cape of Good Hope*, ed. F. R. Bradlow (Cape Town: Balkema, [1803] 1968), 47–48.
8. J. S. Stavorinus, *Voyages to the East Indies*, trans. Samuel Hull Wilcocke, 3 vols. (London: G. G. & J. Robinson, 1798), 1:501–2n. There is also the briefest of

3. SANGUINARY ATTACKS AND UNRULY PASSIONS

mentions from Batavia of the expedition for June 1, 1759 in *Realia: Register op de Generale resolutiën van het kasteel Batavia, 1632-1805*, 3 vols. (Leiden: G. Kolff, 1882–1816), 1:139.

9. On the mortality rate of 1775 and further disaster in 1782, see Femme Gaastra, "Soldiers and Merchants: Aspects of Migration from Europe to Asia in the Dutch East India Company in the Eighteenth Century," in *Migration, Trade, and Slavery in an Expanding World: Essays in Honour of Pieter Emmer*, ed. Wim Kloster (Leiden: Brill, 2009), 99–118, 104–8. For the overall decline, due in part to fish farming, see P. H. van der Brug, "Malaria in Batavia in the 18th Century," *Tropical Medicine and International Health* 2, no. 9 (1997): 892–902. With thanks to Genie Yoo.

10. Van Linschoten emphasized the courteousness and accretive nature of their language often given to ballads and amorous poetry. See *The Voyage of John Huyghen Van Linschoten to the East Indies: From the Old English Translation of 1598*, ed. Arthur Coke Burnell, 2 vols. (Abingdon: Routledge, 2016), 1:104–6. See also his passing remark on the Javanese declaring them of "a verie fretfull and obstinate Nature, of colour much like the Malayers, brown, and not much unlike the men of Brasilia" (114).

11. R. Roolvink, "The Variant Versions of the Malay Annals," in *Sĕjarah Mĕlayu or Malay Annals*, ed. C. C. Brown (Kuala Lumpur: Oxford University Press, 1970), xv–xxvii; see also Liaw Yock Fang, *A History of Classical Malay Literature*, trans. Razif Bahari and Harry Aveling (Singapore: ISEAS & Yayasan Obor Indonesia, 2013), 350–66.

12. On census usage and understandings of "Malay" at Batavia, see Remco Raben, "Batavia and Colombo: The Ethnic and Spatial Order of Two Colonial Cities, 1600–1800" (PhD diss, Leiden University, 1996), 84–88, 97.

13. Ariën Huysers, *Beknopte beschryving der Oostindische etablissementen verzeld van eenige bylagen, uit egte berigten te zaamen gesteld*, 2nd ed. (Amsterdam: Jan Roos, 1792), 3–4.

14. J. H. Stavorinus, *Reize van Zeeland over de Kaap de Goede Hoop, naar Batavia, Bantam, Bengalen, enz. gedaan in de jaaren MDCCLXVIII tot MDCCLXXI*, 2 vols. (Leiden: A. & J. Honkoop, 1793), 2:236–37.

15. J. H. Stavorinus, *Reize van Zeeland over de Kaap de Goede Hoop, en Batavia, naar Semarang, Macasser, Amboina, Suratte, enz. gedaan in de jaaren MDCCLXXIV tot MDCCLXXVIII, enz.*, 2 vols. (Leiden: A. & J. Honkoop, 1797–1798), 1:219–20. Wilcocke (*Voyages*, 2:282) was faithful on this point of translation, though he often made people more Malay, as when he stocked the abortive Dutch mission to Chinsurah with 1,100 "European and Malay troops" and added the mention of a Malay and Bugis kampong to an earlier passage on Makassar. See Stavorinus, *Voyages*, 1:502n and 2:187. Wilcocke later had twenty-eight "Moors of Surat" serving alongside twenty-five Malay or "country soldiers" aboard Stavorinus's ship on his August 1776 journey from Batavia to Surat, though the original Dutch spoke of a complement of twenty-five Moors and twenty-five "native or Buginese." It also mentioned ten Bantenese pilgrims, one of whom later fell overboard in a storm. See Stavorinus, *Reize*, 1797, 2:323; and *Voyages*, 3:202, 207.

3. SANGUINARY ATTACKS AND UNRULY PASSIONS

16. Andrew S. Cook, "Marsden, William (1754–1836), Orientalist and Numismatist," *Oxford Dictionary of National Biography*, accessed January 16, 2022, https://doi-org.ezproxy.princeton.edu/10.1093/ref:odnb/18102.
17. For evidence of his connections to Palembang, see MS 12225, School of Oriental and African Studies, containing texts copied for Susuhunan Ahmad in 1775.
18. William Marsden, *The History of Sumatra: Containing an Account of the Government, Laws, Customs, and Manners of the Native Inhabitants*, 2nd ed. (London: Thomas Payne & Son, 1784), 34.
19. Marsden, *History of Sumatra*, 2nd ed., 35n.
20. Marsden, *History of Sumatra*, 1st ed., 161.
21. *Voyage of John Huyghen Van Linschoten*, 106n1; Pierre Le Poivre, *Travels of a Philosopher: or, Observations on the Manners and Arts of Various Nations in Africa and Asia* (Glasgow: Robert Urie, 1770), 74.
22. Marsden, *History of Sumatra*, 1st ed., 161–63; see also 2nd ed., 36.
23. Marsden, *History of Sumatra*, 2nd ed., 36.
24. Marsden, 250.
25. Robert Percival, *An Account of the Cape of Good Hope: Containing an Historical View of Its Original Settlement by the Dutch, Its Capture by the British in 1795, and the Different Policy Pursued There by the Dutch and British Governments* (London: C. & R. Baldwin, 1804), 249.
26. Marsden, *History of Sumatra*, 2nd ed., 239.
27. On their supposedly "desultory" courage and resignation, see Marsden, *History of Sumatra*, 2nd ed., 170–71.
28. Marsden, 239–40.
29. Thomas Forrest, *A Voyage to New Guinea and the Moluccas, from Balambangan: Including an Account of Magindano, Sooloo, and Other Islands . . . Performed in the Tartar Galley, Belonging to the Honourable East India Company, During the Years 1774, 1775, and 1776* (London: G. Scott, 1779), 147–48.
30. Marsden, *History of Sumatra*, 2nd ed., 240.
31. Marsden, 241.
32. Stavorinus, *Reize*, 1793, 1:234–37; *Voyages*, 1:288–94.
33. Stavorinus, *Voyages*, 1:292–94. I could not verify this claim from published extracts of Cook's journal.
34. Carl F. Klinck, "Wilcocke, Samuel Hull," *Dictionary of Canadian Biography*, accessed January 16, 2022, http://www.biographi.ca/en/bio/wilcocke_samuel_hull_6E.html.
35. Huysers recalled the miserable end of one of the exiles at the age of seventy-two before his departure from Batavia. This was most likely Muhammad Sah al-Din of Bacan, in whose mouth Wilcocke placed a variation of the words of a condemned Batavian described by Marsden. See Stavorinus, *Voyages*, 1:277–78n; and Huysers, *Beknopte beschryving*, 36–37n.
36. The original Dutch of Stavorinus gave that the people of the Indies were "eene verraaderlijke natie, die door geene zedelijke beginsels wordt terug gehouden om de grootste misdaaden te plegen." Stavorinus, *Reize*, 1793, 1:236; *Voyages*, 1:291. Dutch opinion of their European recruits was not much higher. See Gaastra, "Soldiers and Merchants," 105.

3. SANGUINARY ATTACKS AND UNRULY PASSIONS

37. On the recruitment of French prisoners as officers, see Fort George, April 28, 1802, Military, Madras dispatches, October 2, 1801 to September 8, 1802, 418, E/4/889, India Office Records and Private Papers (IOR), British Library (BL).
38. Malay Regiment and invalids, 1802–1803, Ceylon, WO 12/10853, National Archives (TNA), Kew. A Wira Manggala was already to be found as an officer in the "Second Batallion of Malays" at Ceylon from 1791; see *Naam-boek van de wel edele heeren van der hoge Indiasche regering zoo tot, als buiten, Batavia: mitsgaders van de politike bedienden . . . zoo als dezelve onder ultimo december . . . alhier in weezen zyn bevonden*, vol. 4 (Batavia: Pieter van van Geemen, 1791), 95. Apparently of Makassarese background, Wira Wangsa was recruited at Madura. See Ronit Ricci, *Banishment and Belonging: Exile and Diaspora in Sarandib, Lanka, and Ceylon* (Cambridge: Cambridge University Press, 2019), 207.
39. Percival, *Island of Ceylon*, 161.
40. Percival, 146–66. On Percival, see C. R. Beazley, revised by Robert Gates, "Percival, Robert (1765–1826)," *Dictionary of National Biography*, accessed January 16, 2022, https://doi-org.ezproxy.princeton.edu/10.1093/ref:odnb/21919.
41. Percival, *Island of Ceylon*, 146–47.
42. Percival, 155.
43. Ricci, *Banishment*, 181ff.
44. Baba Ounous Saldin, *Syair Fayd al-abad: Artinya kediamannya berbagai pengetahuan* (Colombo: Alamat Langkapuri, Dhu l-Hijja, 1322), 6.
45. An evident play on the officer's name, Laksana Singa may be identified as Captain Singha Laxana, promoted by the English in 1801. See E. Reimers, "The Malays of Colombo," in *Jubilee Book of the Colombo Malay Cricket Club*, 158–59 (Colombo: Ceylon Malay Cricket Club, 1924); B. A. Hussainmiya, *Orang Rejimen: The Malays of the Ceylon Rifle Regiment* (Bangi: Penerbit University Kebangsaan Malaysia, 1990), 157. His descendants remain in Sri Lanka today, having allowed some of their manuscripts to be digitized for the British Library's Endangered Archives Programme, see EAP609/24, Rajioon Singalaxana Collection, BL, https://doi.org/10.15130/EAP609 (accessed January 16, 2022).
46. Saldin, *Syair Fayd al-abad*, 7. The final assault actually occurred some two weeks before, on May 25, 1800. Compare Robert Caldwell, *A Political and General History of the District of Tinnevelly, in the Presidency of Madras, from the Earliest Period to Its Cession to the English Government in A.D. 1801* (Tirunelveli: Government Press, 1881), 203.
47. Percival, *Island of Ceylon*, 153.
48. Percival, 158. The notion that Indonesian weapons—and those from Sulawesi in particular—were poisoned had a long heritage. See Daniel Carey, "The Political Economy of Poison: The Kingdom of Makassar and the Early Royal Society," *Renaissance Studies* 17, no. 3 (2003): 517–43.
49. Percival, *Island of Ceylon*, 159–60.
50. Percival, *Cape of Good Hope*, 288–91.
51. Percival, *Island of Ceylon*, 95–96.
52. John Barrow, *An Account of Travels into the Interior of Southern Africa, in the Years 1797 and 1798*, 2 vols. (London: Johnson, [1801–1804] 1968), 1:212; Percival, 186. See also John Rogers, "Colonial Perceptions of Ethnicity and Culture in Early

3. SANGUINARY ATTACKS AND UNRULY PASSIONS

Nineteenth-Century Sri Lanka," in *Society and Ideology: Essays in South Asian History Presented to Professor K. A. Ballhatchet*, ed. Peter Robb, K. N. Chaudhuri, and Avril Powell (New York: Oxford University Press, 1993), 97–109, 107.
53. Barrow, *Travels into the Interior*, 1:45–46.
54. Barrow, 46.
55. Barrow, 108.
56. Barrow, *Travels into the Interior*, 2:145, 202.
57. Barrow, 11, 150–68, 179–80, emphasis original. Claims that Tipu was a Jacobin were EIC propaganda, though there had been a Jacobin Club at his capital. See Sujit Sivasundram, *Waves Across the South: A New History of Revolution and Empire* (London: William Collins, 2020), 104–9.
58. Barrow, *Travels into the Interior*, 2:220.
59. Barrow, 342, 431.
60. Robert Semple, *Walks and Sketches at the Cape of Good Hope*, ed. F. R. Bradlow (Cape Town: Balkema, [1803] 1968), 48–49.
61. Hudson diary, A 602, 8&9, book no. 11, WCARS. Hudson claimed that in his time at the Cape (from 1796), Malays had "been the perpetrators of all the murders & cruelties committed," and that one had previously been responsible for an infamous muck in the 1790s, which was surely a reference to that of Surabrata in 1786.
62. *Gleanings in Africa: Exhibiting a Faithful and Correct View of the Manners and Customs of the Inhabitants of the Cape of Good Hope* (London: Albion, 1806), 245–47.
63. Hudson diary, WCARS.
64. Hudson Diary.
65. The sale was on October 20. Approved by the Castle two days later, Frans had received a quarter of his money by the 24th. See C. Bird, "Reply to the Memorial of Jan of Batavia," Castle of Good Hope, October 22, 1811, and receipt for 25 percent of 7000 guilders, October 24, 1811. Both under Erf 3464, Transfer Deed 225, October 25, 1811, Cape Town Deeds Office.
66. Marsden, *History of Sumatra*, 3rd ed., 2.
67. J. J. Stockdale, *Sketches, Civil and Military, of the Island of Java and Its Immediate Dependencies*, 2nd ed. (London: J. J. Stockdale, [1811] 1812).
68. *Voyage aux Indes Orientales*, 3 vols. (Paris: Arthus Bertrand, 1810).
69. Stockdale, *Sketches*, 307. The tomb is that of Husayn al-ʿAydarus (d. 1756) at Luar Batang.
70. Stockdale, 375.
71. Stockdale, 376–77.
72. Stockdale, 348.
73. Peter Carey, *The Power of Prophecy: Prince Dipanagara and the End of an Old Order in Java, 1785–1855* (Leiden: KITLV, 2008).
74. Thomas Stamford Raffles, *The History of Java*, 2 vols. (London: Black, Parbury & Allen, 1817).
75. Raffles claimed the Javanese to be "little acquainted" with Islam's doctrines and "the least bigoted of its followers." Raffles, *History of Java*, 2:2. For his equation of Islam and Malays with piracy, see Sivasundaram, *Waves Across the South*, 232, citing his report written after the landing at Batavia.

3. SANGUINARY ATTACKS AND UNRULY PASSIONS

76. Raffles, *History of Java*, 1:57.
77. Marsden, *History of Sumatra*, 4th ed., 346.
78. Thomas Stamford Raffles, "On the Maláyu Nation, with a Translation of its Maritime Institutions," *Asiatick Researches* 12 (1818): 102–58, 103.
79. Raffles, "On the Maláyu Nation," 127.
80. John Crawfurd, *History of the Indian Archipelago: Containing an Account of the Manners, Arts, Languages, Religions, Institutions, and Commerce of Its Inhabitants*, 3 vols. (Edinburgh: Constable, 1820), 2:259–71.
81. For an eighteenth-century Lampungese view of debus at Banten, see W. Marsden, trans., *Memoirs of a Malayan Family, Written by Themselves, Translated from the Original* (London: Murray, 1830), 35–36.

4. Friends Firm and Warm

Epigraphs: Thomas Stamford Raffles, "Introduction," in *Malay Annals: Translated from the Malay Language, by John Leyden* (London: Longman, 1821), xv; W. W. Bird, *State of the Cape of Good Hope in 1822* (Cape Town: C. Struik, [1823] 1966), 68.

1. J. H. Neethling, summary of investigation and proceedings against Griep van Mozambique, September 2, 1813, CJ 546, 4–19, Western Cape Archives and Records Service (WCARS), Cape Town. See also Robert Ross, *Status and Respectability in the Cape Colony, 1750-1870: A Tragedy of Manners* (Cambridge: Cambridge University Press, 2004), 138–42.
2. Neethling, summary, items 23 and 24, CJ 546, 6, WCARS; see also Johannes Zorn, interrogation of Rafiek, August 24, 1813, CJ 546, 52-55, WCARS. Rafiek signed his name as Rafit (رفت) in Jawi, suggesting a pronunciation more like Rafiʾ, and thus closer to the name of the saint al-Rafiʿi, whose alleged exercises they practiced.
3. Ariën Huysers, *Beknopte beschryving der Oostindische etablissementen verzeld van eenige bylagen, uit egte berigten te zaamen gesteld*, 2nd ed. (Amsterdam: Jan Roos, 1792), 3–4. On the shift, see Sumit K. Mandal, *Becoming Arab: Creole Histories and Modern Identity in the Malay World* (Cambridge: Cambridge University Press, 2018), 89.
4. L. Colijn to Zorn, Constantia, August 17, 1813, CJ 546, 20, WCARS.
5. Copy of report of L. G. Biccard, August 18, 1813, CJ 546, 21–22, WCARS.
6. Manuscript evidence in private collections indicates that Nabe was regarded by his descendants as a master of the ratib, and indeed that he was a practitioner of the Rifaʿi order, to which Tuan Guru's former khatib, the late "Sayyid Rajab," is said to have subscribed. Given his later attribution as a sayyid, had Rajab even been the "Moor" in question? With thanks, once more, to Daiyaan Petersen, for explaining the history of the Rifaʿi lineage of Nabe, now firmly present in the Eastern Cape.
7. Zorn, interrogation of Griep, August 24, 1813, CJ 546, 64–69, WCARS.

4. FRIENDS FIRM AND WARM

8. Zorn, interrogation of Awaladyn [sic], August 28, 1813, CJ 546, 56–59, WCARS.
9. Zorn, interrogation of Nabé van Banten, August 24, 1813, CJ 546, 40–43, WCARS.
10. For his original sentence or transportation date, see Leijst der Indiaansche bannelingen, April 10, 1778, CJ 2568, 65, WCARS. The census of 1807 meanwhile gives an origin at Semarang. See J 41, WCARS. With thanks to Daiyaan Petersen.
11. Neethling, Summary, September 2, 1813, CJ 546, 11, WCARS.
12. Johannes Zorn, recommended sentence of Griep (in Dutch and English), September 2, 1813, CJ 805, no. 37, WCARS.
13. Neethling, summary, September 2, 1813, CJ 546, 18–19, WCARS.
14. "Neen, dit is mijn grootvader's Schuld, want aan de Kaap, vraagt dus geene, daar 't spel aan huis geschied om kennische voor ons allen." Zorn, interrogation of Rafiek, August 24, 1813, CJ 546, 53–54, WCARS.
15. "Wij spelen het altijd zo, als wij hebben geen ander plaizier." Zorn, interrogation of Rafiek, 58.
16. John Campbell, *Travels in South Africa: Undertaken at the Request of the Missionary Society* (London: Black & Parry, 1815), 494–95.
17. Kirsten Mackenzie, *Imperial Underworld: An Escaped Convict and the Transformation of the British Colonial Order* (Cambridge: Cambridge University Press, 2015), esp. 103–58.
18. Colebrooke had properties in Hottentots Holland (Somerset), at Saldanha Bay, and on the Berg River. See Rosane and Ludo Rocher, *The Making of Western Indology: Henry Thomas Colebrooke and the East India Company* (London: Royal Asiatic Society Books/Routledge, 2011), 156–59. For slave memories linking Colebrooke to Zonnebloem—later owned by a notorious user of indentured labor, and then the site of George Grey's Kafir College—see Alan Mountain, *An Unsung Heritage: Perspectives on Slavery* (Cape Town: David Philip, 2004), 78.
19. For the first statement of intent to form the society made at Colebrooke's house, and with glancing reference to the Cape, see minutes of proceedings of the Royal Asiatic Society, January 9, 1823, https://royalasiaticsociety.org/the-founding-of-the-ras/.
20. Nigel Penn, "Mapping the Cape: John Barrow and the First British Occupation of the Colony, 1795–1803," *Pretexts* 4, no. 2 (1993): 20–43, 37.
21. Bird, *State of the Cape*, 17. Bird would find himself on their side under Somerset during the trial of 1824, though the much-scarred Denyssen would henceforth cleave to an Afrikaner identity. McKenzie, *Imperial Underworld*, 151–53.
22. Bird, 19.
23. Bird, 68.
24. Bird, 73.
25. On his slave-owning, see Index to the Names of Slave Proprietors at the Cape of Good Hope to the 31st December 1826, SO 7/34, 31, WCARS.
26. Colebrooke, annotation to Bird, *State of the Cape*, 349n.
27. John Campbell also describes some members of the English-speaking party in his *Voyages to and from the Cape of Good Hope: With an Account of a Journey into the Interior of South Africa* (Philadelphia: Presbyterian Board of Publication, 1840), 244–46.

4. FRIENDS FIRM AND WARM

28. James Holman (1786–1857) referred in 1835 to Commodore Johnson [sic] having received a warm welcome there for some three weeks in 1781. See James Holman, *A Voyage Around the World*, 4 vols. (London: Smith, Elder & Cornhill, 1834–1835), 3:11n. For the arrival of and assistance to the party at Penang, see Prince of Wales Island Public Department, November 30, 1820, F/4/663/18450; and Straits Settlements: dispatches to Prince of Wales Island, July 17, 1822–December 31, 1824, G/34/193, 125–26, India Office Records and Private Papers (IOR), British Library (BL). The EIC had only recently supplied the sultan with weaponry in gratitude for the assistance he had so often rendered. It had also previously assisted a beleaguered relative (the same "prince?") in 1808, and then his attendant "Admiral Rodney" for debts incurred at Madras. See Allowance of 30 rupees "per diem" granted to the Prince of Johanna and his attendant during their stay in Madras, 1808, F/4/277/6179; and Madras government grant the sum of 150 pagodas to Admiral Rodney, 1810, F/4/616/15319, IOR, BL. Another of the prince's attendants was referred to as Lord Nelson. See Campbell, *Voyages*, 246.
29. *Missionary Register*, January 1823, 21. See also Gwynn Campbell, *David Griffiths and the Missionary "History of Madagascar"* (Leiden: Brill, 2012), 606.
30. John Schofield Mayson, *The Malays of Capetown* (Manchester: Galt, 1861), 12.
31. Jackie Loos, *Echoes of Slavery: Voices from South Africa's Past* (Cape Town: David Phillips, 2004), 129–37.
32. Also a veteran of Ceylon, where he had overseen the Dutch surrender at Galle, Macquarie long rued the financial consequences of being too late for the spoils of the Battle of the Nile in 1798. See John Ritchie, *Lachlan Macquarie: A Biography* (Melbourne: Melbourne University Press, 1986).
33. J. Doyle, "Memorandum of Captain Colebrookes Service on Java," Colonial Office Files (CO) 48/101, 159, National Archives (TNA), Kew.
34. R. L. Wettenhall, "Gregory, John (1795–1853)," *Australian Dictionary of Biography*, accessed January 17, 2022, https://adb.anu.edu.au/biography/gregory-john-2123.
35. See Journal of Proceedings of the Commission of Enquiry at Capetown, Commenced July 28, 1823, CO 414/1, 170, TNA, referring to a "statement made by 'John Chance' upon the subject of Church money demanded from the Malays for their freedom."
36. For remarks concerning the suppression of some names in reports on the treatment of "Hottentots, Bossemen, Caffres, Prize Negroes, and Slaves," see Colebrooke and Blair to R. W. Hay, Mauritius, December 6, 1828, CO 48/160, 103r–104v, TNA. Colebrooke and Blair had also complained that the commission's investigations were hampered by not having copies of material submitted to Parliament about the slave trade and negotiations with foreign powers. See Colebrooke and Blair to Hay, Cape Town, August 14, 1826, CO 48/101, 170r–171r, TNA.
37. Bigge and Colebrooke, "Report upon the Slaves and the State of Slavery at the Cape of Good Hope," under cover of John Thomas Bigge to R. W. Hay, Mount Street [London], April 5, 1831, CO 48/160, 234–294v, 268v, TNA; see also George

4. FRIENDS FIRM AND WARM

McCall Theal, *Records of the Cape Colony*, 36 vols. (Cape Town: 1897–1905), 35:352–79, 366.
38. "Evidence of Two Mahometan Priests, *Muding* and *Imaum* Achmat," in *Papers Relative to the Condition and Treatment of the Native Inhabitants of Southern Africa, Within the Colony of the Cape of the Good Hope: Parliamentary Papers* (London: House of Commons, March 1835), annex no. 30, 207–10, 207.
39. Compare: death notice of Imam Hadjie Medien, filed by his daughter Pamela on November 27, 1878, MOOC 6/9/166, no. 6090/78, WCARS; and death notice of Hadji Mogedien alias Medien, filed by his son Hadji Slemman, September 1, 1884, MOOC 6/9/212, no. 9067/84, WCARS. Sister and brother, neither literate, also differed on when their father had died by almost a month.
40. "Evidence of Two Mahometan Priests," 207.
41. Remarkably, at the time of writing, a tranche of documents has come to light detailing Jan's tithe books and membership of the Long Street Mosque for the early part of the nineteenth century that will require analysis, being written in both Bugis and Jawi. With thanks to Daiyaan Petersen, who has shown me digital images.
42. "Evidence of Two Mahometan Priests," 208.
43. See entries in the *African Court Calendar*, 1823–1826, and the *South African Almanack and Directory*, 1827–1828. This information and much of what follows is derived from an unpublished database of the late Rob Shell, "Prosopography of Cape Imams." I am especially grateful to Sandy Shell for having pursued these references and confirmed them.
44. Mirza Abu Taleb, *Westward Bound: Travels of Mirza Abu Taleb*, intro. and ed. Mushirul Hasan, trans. Charles Stewart (New Delhi: Oxford University Press, 2005), 27.
45. Shell, "Prosopography."
46. Shell, citing the *African Court Calendar*, 1823–1826, and the *South African Almanack and Directory*, 1827–1828.
47. Shell, citing the *South African Almanack and Directory*, 1834; see also the *Cape of Good Hope Almanack* 1835 and the *Cape of Good Hope Annual Register*, 1838.
48. "Evidence of Two Mahometan Priests," 208–9.
49. Index to the names of slave proprietors at the Cape of Good Hope, December 31, 1826, SO 7/34, WCARS; memorial of the free Black Abdol Malik, June 19, 1816, CO 3905, 209, WCARS.
50. "Evidence of Two Mahometan Priests," 210.
51. Register of documents in the Office of the Commissioners of Inquiry Relating to the Colony of the Cape of Good Hope, CO 414/1, 220, TNA. See also index to the names of slave proprietors, SO 7/34, WCARS; and Shell, "Prosopography."
52. "Evidence of Two Mahometan Priests," 209–10.
53. "Evidence of Two Mahometan Priests," 209.
54. On Denyssen, see Mackenzie, *Imperial Underworld*, 44–45.
55. Bigge and Colebrooke, "Report upon the Slaves and the State of Slavery at the Cape of Good Hope," CO 48/160, 270r–274v, TNA; Theal, *Records of the Cape Colony*, vol. 35, 367–69.

56. For which, see reference to a "certificate of the Mahomettan Priest 'Imam Agmat' respecting the establishment of his church in the Colony," *Journal of Proceedings of the Commission of Enquiry at Capetown, Commenced July 28, 1823*, CO 414/1, 170, TNA.
57. For one such reference, see the testimony of William Mackrite, a former resident of the Cape, given at Mauritius, January 15, 1827, CO 48/121, 69–70, TNA.
58. "Editorial," *South African Commercial Advertiser*, December 27, 1828.
59. For an image by George Duff of the tenth anniversary of this event, see R. C. H. Shell, "The March of the Mardijkers: The Toleration of Islam in the Cape Colony," *Kronos* 22 (1995): 3–20.
60. On the ongoing capture of East Africans destined for the Cape, see Matthew Hopper, *Slaves of One Master: Globalization and Slavery in Arabia in the Age of Empire* (New Haven, CT: Yale University Press, 2015), 162–64, 171.
61. For the notion of religious economy, see Nile Green, *Bombay Islam: The Religious Economy of the West Indian Ocean, 1840-1915* (Cambridge: Cambridge University Press, 2011).
62. Letter of Asnoun, February 8, 1836, *South African Commercial Advertiser*, February 13, 1836.
63. Death notice for "Prince Abdol-Rakiep," *South African Commercial Advertiser*, February 25, 1834. Achmat also announced that he was executor for the son of "the late Prince Abdullah of Tedouri," after his death on the February 21 at the reported age of forty-two years and eight months. With thanks to Amanda Lanzillo.
64. "Malay Priesthood," *South African Commercial Advertiser*, February 24, 1836.
65. Statements of "Abdol Wassie" and "Manzur," *South African Commercial Advertiser*, February 13, 1836.
66. Statement of "Abdol Wassie," *South African Commercial Advertiser*, February 13, 1836.
67. "Malay Priesthood." Based on a listing in the *African Court Calendar* for 1829, there were eighteen active Malay priests. They included Achterdeen, residing on Loop Street, Ahagé, then in Walendorp, and a different hajji than the tailor Hadje of Dorp Street. Sandy Shell, personal communication, April 3, 2018.
68. "Malay Priesthood."
69. "Maleische Priesterschap," *South African Commercial Advertiser*, February 27, 1836.
70. "Memorial of Asnoen, Commonly Called Jan van Boughies," February 15, 1836, CO 3984, 32, WCARS.
71. Jan van Bugis, *Ini surat menyatakan*, CO 3984, 32, WCARS.
72. Trüter and Neething to J. Bell, March 4, 1836, CO 3984, 32, WCARS. For mention of Neethling's Long Street home, see Adolphe Linder, *The Swiss at the Cape of Good Hope* (Basel: Basler Afrika Bibliographien, 1997), 207.
73. Trüter and Neething to J. Bell.
74. Trüter and Neething to J. Bell.
75. Van Bugis, *Ini surat menyatakan*.
76. "Memorial of Imaum Achmet, High Priest of the Mahommedans of This Colony," n.d., CO 3996, 21–25, WCARS. With thanks to Saarah Jappie. For the enduring

4. FRIENDS FIRM AND WARM

fascination with Shaykh Yusuf, see her "Between Makassars: Site, Story, and the Transoceanic Afterlives of Shaykh Yusuf of Makassar" (PhD diss., Princeton University, January 2018).

77. Death notice of "Imaun Achmet," died October 9, filed October 14, 1843, MOOC 6/9/31, no. 6387, WCARS.
78. Frank R. Bradlow and Margaret Cairns, *The Early Cape Muslims: A Study of their Mosques, Genealogy and Origins* (Cape Town: Balkema, 1978), 67, 69.
79. Achmat Davids, *The Mosques of Bo-Kaap: A Social History of Islam at the Cape* (Athlone: South African Institute of Arabic and Islamic Research, 1980), 228–29, reproducing *De Verzamelaar*, June 21, 1842. While Samoudien's name was assumedly derived from the Arabic Shami^c al-Din, his signature is a struggling Sha^{c}m a[l-]Di[n]. See Samoudien to Rawson W. Rawson, Cape Town, September 22, 1856, CO 4087, no. 144, WCARS.
80. George Angas, *Malay School: Boys Learning to Read the Koran*, ca. 1848. Parliament of the Republic of South Africa, reference 18507; and *Karel, a Malay Priest, and His Wife Nazea*, ca. 1849. Parliament of the Republic of South Africa, reference 6620. Both plates are taken from his *Kafirs Illustrated* (London: 1849). With thanks to Lila Komnick. See also Jackie Loos, *Echoes of Slavery: Voices from South Africa's Past* (Claremont: David Philip, 2004), 129–37.
81. *Mecmua-yı Fünun*, Ramadan 1279 (January 1863); Mayson, *Malays of Capetown*, 16–17. Another since deceased pilgrim was Mogamat Taiyer of Dorp Street (d. 1843), the son of Tata Layer, and thus Tuan Guru's brother-in-law. See death notice of Mogamat Taiyer, MOOC 6/9/31, 6490, WCARS.
82. Loos, *Echoes*, 131–33.
83. Achmat Davids, *The History of the Tana Baru: The Case for the Preservation of the Muslim Cemetery at the Top of Longmarket Street* (Cape Town: Committee for the Preservation of the Tana Baru, 1985), 21–22.
84. For admiring hints about De Roubaix's role, see J. S. de Lima, *The Califa Question: Documents Connected with This Matter* (Cape Town: Van de Sandt de Villiers, 1857), vii.
85. On Achmat Sadick as "Lieutenant and Priest of the Malays," see Bradlow and Cairns, *Early Cape Muslims*, 75; for the Victoria Mosque, see Davids, *Mosques of Bo-Kaap*, 138–47.
86. John Thomas Baines, *The "Conch" in Table Bay Landing Muslim Volunteers and Burghers on Their Return from the War of the Axe*, 1847, CD57, William Fehr Collection, Castle of Good Hope. Yet another set of images, dated Cape Town, May 21, 1846, includes a preparatory sketch for the same, as well as battle scenes, with a turbaned "lieutenant and priest of the Malays" (Achmat Sadick?), bearing a rifle and clattering off on his wooden pattens. See Marius and Joy Diemont, *The Brenthurst Baines: A Selection of the Works of Thomas Baines in the Oppenheimer Collection, Johannesburg, etc.* (Johannesburg: Brenthurst, 1975), 41.
87. For a description of the ratib and claims of an instance of amok, see Mayson, *Malays of Capetown*, 19–21, 27; and Alfred W. Cole, *The Cape and Kafirs: Notes of Five Years' Residence in South Africa* (London: Richard Bentley, 1852), 44–46.
88. Mayson, 30–31.
89. Mayson, 31.

4. FRIENDS FIRM AND WARM

90. J. B. Peires, *The Dead Will Arise: Nongqawuse and the Great Xhosa Cattle-Killing Movement of 1856-57* (Bloomington: Indiana University Press, 1989), 72.
91. Samoudien to Rawson W. Rawson, Cape Town, September 22, 1856, CO 4087, no. 144, WCARS. One brother had planned to return to the Cape to study while the other had wanted to do the same in Jeddah.
92. G. Champion, *Journal of an American Missionary in the Cape Colony: 1835*, ed. Alan R. Booth (Cape Town: South African Library, 1968), 20.
93. Cole, *Cape and Kafirs*, 44–46.
94. Mayson, *Malays of Capetown*, 19–21. On the campaign against Hindu devotional practices, see Geoffey Oddie, "The Western-Educated Elites and Popular Religion: The Debate over the Hook-Swinging Issue in Bengal and Madras, c. 1830-1894," in *Society and Ideology: Essays in South Asian History Presented to Professor K. A. Ballhatchet*, ed. Peter Robb, K. N. Chaudhuri, and Avril Powell (New York: Oxford University Press, 1993), 177–95.
95. De Lima, *Califa Question*, 9. Jawakel is, I suspect, a mistaken print reference to Twakal, the fifth of seven children born into slavery in 1824 to the Mozambiquan woman Rachbat. A dependent of Tuan Guru's trust, she and her surviving children were manumitted in March 1834. See Register of guardianship with minors under Abdul Malek, ca. 1835, SO 20, 15, WCARS. With thanks to Daiyaan Petersen.
96. De Lima, *Califa Question*, 2–3.
97. De Lima, 3–8.
98. De Lima, 8.
99. Memorial of Malay Priests in Cape Town, requesting that De Roubaix be appointed arbiter of burial ground, 1857, CO 4096, 880, WCARS.
100. De Lima, *Califa Question*, 22. This proposal was also tabled in parliament and approved in June 1857.
101. De Lima, 26–27.
102. Maximilien Kollisch, *The Mussulman Population at the Cape of Good Hope* (Constantinople: Levant Herald, 1867), 22.
103. Mayson, *Malays of Capetown*, 34–35, citing the *Cape Argus*, August 1860.
104. "Prince Alfred at the Cape," *Manchester Guardian*, September 27, 1860.
105. Saul Solomon, *The Progress of His Royal Highness, Prince Alfred Ernest Albert, Through the Cape Colony, British Kaffraria, the Orange Free State, and Port Natal, in the Year 1860* (Cape Town: Saul Solomon, 1861), 32. Solomon had his start in printing with George Greig, who sold him his share of the business in 1847.
106. Solomon, *Progress of His Royal Highness*, 15.
107. Mayson, *Malays of Capetown*, 34–35. For reportage of this incident and the notion of loyal belonging placed in the mouths of Malay and African women offering their children to the young prince, see *Progress*, 5 and 15–16.
108. *Progress*, 115, 118, 138.
109. *Progress*, 107.
110. *Progress*, 108.
111. *Progress*, 109.
112. Abdulmecid's gift of 1860 was a replacement for an earlier golden snuffbox lost en route to the Cape. Kollisch, *Mussulman Population*, 5–6. For the letter, see

Mochamet Achmet to the Sultan of Turkey, Cape Town, December 21, 1861, reproduced in Halim Gençoğlu, "Abu Bakr Effendi: A Report on the Activities and Challenges of an Ottoman Muslim Theologian in the Cape of Good Hope" (master's thesis, University of Cape Town, 2013), 143.

5. Other Malays, Other Exiles

1. For a manuscript version, see Or. 15646, British Library (BL).
2. See "Surat dari Negeri Kandi," *Wajah Selong*, April 25, 1897; and Ronit Ricci, *Banishment and Belonging: Exile and Diaspora in Sarandib, Lanka, and Ceylon* (Cambridge: Cambridge University Press, 2019), 207.
3. For his placement at Colombo, see *Naam-boek van de wel edele heeren der hoge Indiasche regering zoo tot, als buiten, Batavia*, vol. 4 (Batavia: Pieter van van Geemen, 1791), 95–96.
4. See İsmail Hakkı Kadı, "The Ottomans and Southeast Asia Prior to the Hamidian Era: A Critique of Colonial Perceptions of Ottoman-Southeast Asian Interaction," in *From Anatolia to Aceh: Ottomans, Turks, and Southeast Asia*, ed. A. C. S. Peacock and Annabel Teh Gallop (Oxford: Oxford University Press/British Academy, 2015), 149–74; and İsmail Hakkı Kadı and A. C. S. Peacock, *Ottoman-Southeast Asian Relations: Sources from the Ottoman Archives*, 2 vols. (Leiden: Brill, 2020), hereafter *OSEAR*.
5. John Slight, *The British Empire and the Hajj, 1865–1956* (Cambridge, MA: Harvard University Press, 2015).
6. See also Cemil Aydin, *The Idea of the Muslim World: A Global Intellectual History* (Cambridge, MA: Harvard University Press, 2017), 65–98.
7. Nurfadzilah Yahaya, *Fluid Jurisdictions: Colonial Law and Arabs in Southeast Asia* (Ithaca, NY: Cornell University Press, 2020), 40–44.
8. Intercepted by the Dutch following the death of their hajji owner, the letters and banner were destroyed. See M. C. Ricklefs, *Jogjakarta Under Sultan Mangkubumi 1749–1792: A History of the Division of Java* (Oxford: Oxford University Press, 1974), 134, 150–54; and G. W. J. Drewes, "Further Data Concerning 'Abd al-Samad al-Palimbani," *BKI* 132, nos. 2–3 (1976): 267–92.
9. Drewes, "Further Data," 274.
10. Francis Light, July 30, 1792, quoted in Francis R. Bradley, *Forging Islamic Power and Place: The Legacy of Shaykh Dā'ūd bin 'Abd Allāh al-Fatānī in Mecca and Southeast Asia* (Honolulu: University of Hawai'i Press, 2016), 49–50.
11. For the history of negotiations with the EIC and its ambiguous agents, see R. Bonney, *Kedah, 1771–1821: The Search for Security and Independence* (Kuala Lumpur: Oxford University Press, 1971); and Muhammad Hajji Salih, ed., *Early History of Penang* (Pulau Pinang: Penerbit Universiti Sains Malaysia, 2015).
12. The Burmese sovereigns often gave the British who accessed their courts a frosty reception as they relied on Persian as a language of mediation and high culture into the 1820s. See, for example, Michael Symes, *An Account of an Embassy to the Kingdom of Ava, Sent by the Governor-General of India, in the Year*

5. OTHER MALAYS, OTHER EXILES

1795 (London: W. Bulmer, 1800); Arash Kazeni, *The City and the Wilderness: Indo-Persian Encounters in Southeast Asia* (Oakland: University of California Press, 2020); and Henry Gouger, *A Personal Narrative of Two Years' Imprisonment in Burma*, 2nd ed. (London: J. Murray, 1862). With thanks to Michael Mandelkorn.
13. Cyril Skinner, ed., *The Battle for Junk Ceylon: The Syair Sultan Maulana* (Dordrecht: Foris, 1985), 157, 253.
14. Skinner, ed., *Battle for Junk Ceylon*, 157.
15. "Shipping News," *Prince of Wales Island Gazette*, August 21, 1819. With thanks to Geoff Wade and Marcus Langdon, personal communication, June 21, 2018.
16. "Emigration to the Cape," *Prince of Wales Island Gazette*, June 28, 1820. The arrivals of 1820 would figure in Capetonian society and the struggles for authority thereafter. See Kirstin McKenzie, *Imperial Underworld: An Escaped Convict and the Transformation of the British Colonial Order* (Cambridge: Cambridge University Press, 2015).
17. "British Settlers at the Cape," *Prince of Wales Island Gazette*, July 1, 1820. By contrast, in London the previous year Barrow had ensured copious quotation of his *Travels*. Nigel Penn, "Mapping the Cape: John Barrow and the First British Occupation of the Colony, 1795–1803," *Pretexts* 4, no. 2 (1993): 20–43, 37.
18. "Ceylon Gazette," *Prince of Wales Island Gazette*, July 8, 1820.
19. Governor Timmerman Thyssen first proposed that the children of slaves born on or after December 6 would have their freedom, bringing "eternal honor on Malacca." See "Malacca," *Prince of Wales Island Gazette*, May 20, 1820.
20. Prince of Wales Island Public Department, November 30, 1820, F/4/663/18439, 5–9, India Office Records and Private Papers (IOR), BL.
21. Prince of Wales Island Public Department, November 30, 1820, F/4/663/18439, 2–3, IOR, BL.
22. Bradley, *Forging Islamic Power*, 53–54.
23. BOA HAT 785/36657, National Archives, Republic of Turkey, as translated and presented in *OSEAR*, 1:76–78.
24. Kadı, "Ottomans and Southeast Asia," 155.
25. Sebastian Prange, *Monsoon Islam: Trade and Faith on the Medieval Malabar Coast* (Cambridge: Cambridge University Press, 2018).
26. *OSEAR*, 1:80–81.
27. F/4/1309/52133, IOR, BL.
28. Dipanagara styled himself as the more metropolitan Abdulhamid. See Peter Carey, *The Power of Prophecy: Prince Dipanagara and the End of the Old Order in Java* (Leiden: KITLV, 2008), 153, 623, 648–49.
29. Ricci, *Banishment*, 247. A deed to the cemetery and associated mosque indicates that the "Jawa Garden" was known as such by 1809. "Java Lane 1876 Deed [sic]," EAP609/3/1, BL.
30. Remco Raben, "Batavia and Colombo: The Ethnic and Spatial Order of Two Colonial Cities, 1600–1800" (PhD diss., Leiden University, 1996).
31. Minutes, Raad van Politiek, July 6, 1743, 176v, 1/87, Sri Lankan National Archives (SLNA), Colombo.
32. Minutes, Raad van Politiek, September 30, 1743, 156v, 1/88, SLNA.

5. OTHER MALAYS, OTHER EXILES

33. Ricci, *Banishment*, 76–77.
34. Minutes, Raad van Politiek, June 21, 1786, 1/193, SLNA; Raad van Politiek, March 8, 1788 (no. 4), 1/200, SLNA. By 1790, his request for a return to the Indies or an increase in allowance was rejected on the grounds that he could make ends meet if he reduced the number of servants. See Raad van Politiek, January 9, 1790, 1/208, SLNA.
35. List of Javanese state exiles, March 8, 1788 (no. 4), 1/200, SLNA. It doubtless stung, too, that his older brother had been returned and enthroned in 1784.
36. List of Javanese state exiles, March 8, 1788 (no. 11), 1/200, SLNA.
37. List of Javanese state exiles, March 8, 1788 (no. 3), 1/200, SLNA.
38. Minutes, Raad van Politiek, June 21, 1786, 1/193, SLNA.
39. Minutes, Raad van Politiek, September 5, 1788, 1/203, SLNA.
40. Minutes, Raad van Politiek, September 5, 1788.
41. Cod.Or. 2241 Ia (11), Leiden University Library; J. S. Stavorinus, *Voyages to the East Indies*, trans. Samuel Hull Wilcocke, 3 vols. (London: G. G. & J. Robinson, 1798), 1:278n.
42. E. Reimers, "The Malays of Colombo," in *Jubilee Book of the Colombo Malay Cricket Club* (Colombo: Malay Cricket Club of Colombo, 1924), 158.
43. I base this on a twentieth-century index of VOC documents. See X/3/20, SLNA.
44. On a deceased enslaved man of Batavia remembered as Okon van Malaijoe, see minutes, Raad van Politiek, January 7, 1786, 1/193, SLNA. For passing mention of a "Malijdsche" sergeant in the 1790s, see the case of Linban and Tangin, February 12–May 23, 1791, 1/4722, 1–3, SLNA. For the case of a "captured Malay" thief, see the case of Tjardick of Batavia/Soerabaja, March 1795, 1/4745, SLNA.
45. It was also in marked contrast to the situation at Colombo in the first decades of Dutch rule, that saw edicts against the public gatherings of "yogis" and "Moorish mendicants." See *Memoirs of Ryckloff van Goens Delivered to His Successors Jacob Hustaart on December 26, 1663 and Ryckloff van Goens the Younger on April 12, 1675*, trans. E. Reimers (Colombo: Ceylon Government, 1932), 25.
46. Ricci, *Banishment*, 107–9. See also Hussainmiya drawing on communications with M. C. Ricklefs in 1976, in B. A. Hussainmiya, *Orang Rejimen: The Malays of the Ceylon Rifle Regiment* (Bangi: Penerbit University Kebangsaan Malaysia, 1990), 43.
47. List of Javanese state exiles, Raad van Politiek, March 8, 1788 (no. 6), 1/200, SLNA.
48. For the Batavian order, see *Realia: Register op de Generale resolutiën van het kasteel Batavia, 1632-1805*, 3 vols. (Leiden: G. Kolff, 1882–1886), 1:87.
49. Minutes, Raad van Politiek, June 24, 1785, 1/191, SLNA.
50. Minutes, Raad van Politiek, June 21, 1786, 1/193, SLNA.
51. Nor yet did it include a son who had been brought up by the late widow of Ranka Marta Widjojo of Surabaya. List of Javanese state exiles, March 8, 1788 (nos. 1, 6, and 18), 1/200, SLNA.
52. List of Javanese state exiles, March 8, 1788 (no. 17), 1/200, SLNA.
53. C. H. Mantara, "The Malays of Ceylon," in *Jubilee Book of the Colombo Malay Cricket Club* (Colombo: Malay Cricket Club of Colombo, 1924), 167; Hussainmiya, *Orang Rejimen*, 48–49, citing Murad Jayah, "Deed of the Gift of Wekanda Mosque," *Bulletin Ceylon Malay Research Organization* 2 (1969): 8.

5. OTHER MALAYS, OTHER EXILES

54. Minutes, Raad van Politiek, August 15, 1792, 1/219, SLNA. No more is heard of Panenga, who arrived with the *Draak*, which had left Batavia in mid-July 1791 and sailed on to the Cape on November 16. J. R. Bruijn, F. S. Gaastra, I. Schöffer, and E. S. van Eyck van Heslinga, eds., *Dutch-Asiatic Shipping in the 17th and 18th Centuries*, 3 vols. (The Hague: Nijhoff, 1979), 3:558–59, Voyage 8323.3.
55. Minutes, Raad van Politiek, April 3, 1788, 1/200, SLNA. Bruijn et al. (*Dutch-Asiatic Shipping*, 2:722–23; 3:540–41) have an arrival for the *Dordrecht* at Batavia on June 7, 1787 (Voyage 4533.3) and departure from Ceylon on January 17, 1788 (Voyage 8209.3).
56. Johan Karel Jakob de Jonge, Marinus Lodewijk van Deventer, Leonard Wilhelm Gijsbert de Roo, Pieter Anton Tiele, and Jan Ernst Heeres, eds., *De Opkomst Van Het Nederlandsch Gezag in Oost Indie*, 18 vols. (The Hague: Nijhoff, 1862–1909), 12:128–29n1.
57. Minutes, Raad van Politiek, April 3, 1788, 1/200, SLNA.
58. Minutes, Raad van Politiek, September 5, 1788, 1/203, SLNA.
59. Minutes, Raad van Politiek, November 11, 1788, 1/204, SLNA.
60. *Naam-boek*, 92, 95–96.
61. *Naam-boek*, 95–96.
62. One finds from a Kandyan family wedding announcement of April 1897 that the descendants of Jurang Pati specifically identified as being from Sumenep, though a document taken down after the wedding traces a lineage back to Bangkalan. Just as confusingly, the two texts alternately place Wira Wangsa as being of Sumenep recruited at Makassar or as a man of Makassarese background who had lived in Madura. See "Surat dari negeri Kandy," *Wajah Selong*, April 25, 1897; and Ricci, *Banishment*, 207–9.
63. Case of Linban and Tangin, 1/4722, SLNA.
64. Case of Linban and Tangin, extrakt missive de dato 23 May 1791 van Kolombo na Gale, 1/4722, 22r, SLNA.
65. See, for example, the 1791 testimony of the soldier Zyedoe Mira Lebbe concerning his late son Mahamadoe Mira Lebbe, who had gone over to the English at Coromandel. Minutes, Raad van Politiek, 1/4613, 147v, SLNA.
66. Some refused their commands and the punishments meted out by their officers. Minutes, Raad van Politiek, December 18, 1795, 1/232, SLNA.
67. Petition of Been et al., Raad van Politiek, November 24, 1795, 1/232, 225v–27r, SLNA; Ricci, *Banishment and Belonging*, 184.
68. Petition of Been et al., SLNA.
69. J. H. Rudolph, Kaltere, January 31, 1796, 1/4758, 1r–2r, SLNA.
70. Robert Percival, *An Account of the Island of Ceylon, Containing Its History, Geography, Natural History, with the Manners and Customs of Its Various Inhabitants: to Which Is Added, The Journal of an Embassy to the Court of Candy* (London: C. & R. Baldwin, 1803), 91–93. For specifics, see Hussainmiya, *Orang*, 57.
71. G. C. Mendis, ed., *The Colebrooke-Cameron Papers (Documents on British Colonial Policy in Ceylon, 1796–1833)*, 2 vols. (Oxford: Oxford University Press, 1956), 2:62–64.
72. North to Court of Directors, Colombo, February 26, 1799, 5/1, 28r, SLNA. The prisoners were sent in 1801; see governor-general at Fort George, June 10, 1801,

5. OTHER MALAYS, OTHER EXILES

E/4/888, 109, IOR, BL. For complaints of oversized uniforms cut in London, see North to Hobart, March 16, 1802, 5/1, 218 r-v, SLNA.
73. North to Court of Directors, Colombo, February 26, 1799, 5/1, 28r, SLNA.
74. North to Court of Directors, SLNA.
75. *A Collection of Legislative Acts of the Ceylon Government from 1796*, vol. 1 (Colombo: William Skeen, 1853), 5.
76. Instructions from Dundas to North, London, March 13, 1801, 4/1, 1r–55v, 40v–41v, SLNA. For their relationship and an overview of North's administration, see Alicia Schrikker, *Dutch and British Colonial Intervention in Sri Lanka, 1780-1815: Expansion and Reform* (Leiden: Brill, 2007), 142–59.
77. Thomas Henry Brooke, *A History of the Island of St. Helena, from Its Discovery by the Portuguese to the Year 1806* (London: Black, Parbury & Allen, 1808), 291–92; see also Hussainmiya, *Orang Rejimen*, 65.
78. For details, see Hussainmiyya, 65–67, 6n54.
79. Hussainmiyya, 69.
80. North to Court of Directors, December 15, 1801, 5/1, 189v–90r, SLNA.
81. Percival, *Island of Ceylon*, 120.
82. Percival, 383, 384.
83. Percival, 410.
84. James Cordiner, *A Description of Ceylon: Containing an Account of the Country, Inhabitants and Natural Productions with Narratives of a Tour Round the Island in 1800, the Campaign in Candy in 1803, and a Journey to Ramisseram in 1804*, 2 vols. (London: Longman, 1807), 2:316–18.
85. North to Hobart, March 16, 1802, 5/1, 221v–222r, SLNA.
86. Cordiner, *Description of Ceylon*, 2:319.
87. V. M. Methley, ed., "Greeving's Diary," *Journal of the Ceylon Branch of the Royal Asiatic Society* 26, no. 71, pts. 3–4 (1918): 166–80. On the issue of spiked guns, see testimony of Naik Gopal Naik in "Interrogation of Two Kandian spies, arrested at Jaffnapatnam 29 June 1804, by Captain John Sewell," Colombo, July 9, 1804, 7/44, 122–25, SLNA.
88. Methley, "Greeving's Diary," 166–72; see also testimony of Naik Gopal Naik, 7/44, 123ff., SLNA; Cordiner, *Description of Ceylon*, 2: 202–4; and Henry Marshall, *Ceylon: A General Description of the Island and Its Inhabitants* (London: William Allen, 1847), 85–111.
89. The princes are discussed in Ricci, *Banishment*, 199–203. For the first explicit mention by name in a Malay context, albeit by a Sinhalese admirer, see F. E. Gooneratne, "The History of the Malays of Ceylon," in *Jubilee Book of the Colombo Malay Cricket Club* (Colombo: Ceylon Malay Cricket Club, 1924), 160–66. By contrast, in 1905, Saldin only referred to two steadfast men (*si Jawa memberi sudi*) imprisoned by the king and later killed and fed to wild animals like the white officers before them. See Baba Ounous Saldin, *Syair Fayd al-Abad: Artinya kediamannya berbagai pengetahuan* (Colombo: Alamat Langkapuri, AH 1322), 11–12.
90. Methley, "Greeving's Diary," 173–74.
91. Methley, 176.

5. OTHER MALAYS, OTHER EXILES

92. Methley, 174–76. Greeving's initial saviors had served with the Dutch in 1792.
93. Methley, 168.
94. Cordiner, *Description of Ceylon*, 2:202, 208.
95. Ricci, *Banishment*, 199. Saldin (*Syair Fayd al-Abad*, 11–12) meanwhile wrote of a Laksana Kubuh as having been the key Malay commander on the Kandyan side.
96. Cordiner, *Description of Ceylon*, 2:217–18.
97. Cordiner, 220. North's vision of Malays loyal to the last was also channeled into Valentia's narrative of 1811, which was informed by Stavorinus on many points. See George Viscount Valentia, *Voyages and Travels to India, Ceylon, the Red Sea, Abyssinia, and Egypt in the Years 1802-1806*, 4 vols. (London: Rivington, 1811), 1:258–59.
98. The initial sources of news of the massacre came from two survivors: a lascar called Milihanage Johannes and Mohamed Gani, a Malay servant to Ensign Robert Barry who had killed the Kandyan Malay captain. See V. M. Methley, "The Ceylon Expedition of 1803," *Transactions of the Royal Society* 1 (1918): 92–118, 116. For North's concerns, see Hussainmiya, *Orang Rejimen*, 67.
99. Hussainmiya, 72, 77n68. The translation of Greeving's narrative of events from June 19 to August 27, 1803, was formally deposed on May 11, 1804. Cordiner mistakenly placed his escape as having been in September 1804: "Greeving's Diary," 166; Cordiner, *Description of Ceylon*, vol. 2, 214.
100. Cordiner, 220.
101. North to Camden, March 6, 1805, 5/2, 155r, SLNA. There is the possibility that this was a Shattari shaykh of Javano-Makassarese origin called Sulaiman ibn Abd al-Jalil, whose lineage was connected to the Batavian lines of Mas Haji Abdullah of Matraman. See elements of his Malay Compendium, now in Dehiwala, EAP609/1/9, BL, https://eap.bl.uk/archive-file/EAP609-1-9 (accessed January 18, 2022). By contrast, Marshall (*Ceylon*, 99) assumed that Cordiner's source had been the servant Mohamed Gani.
102. Testimony of Permaul Mootia Naik, under cover of governor's diary, July 9, 1804, 7/44, 116, SLNA. Some Malays and gun lascars had returned to British ranks, even as others continued to seduce their kin or lead Kandyan operations. See Arthur Johnston, *Narrative of the Operations of a Detachment in an Expedition to Candy, in the Island of Ceylon, in the Year 1804* (London: C. & R. Baldwin, 1810), 63, 77–78.
103. Cordiner, *Description of Ceylon*, 2:220.
104. Cordiner, 252. There seemed no such restraint for the men of Kedah in 1809, who complained that the Siamese were far more efficient looters than soldiers. Skinner, *Battle for Junk Ceylon*, 217.
105. Cordiner, *Description of Ceylon*, 2:276.
106. North to Hobart, April 20, 1803, 5/2, 89v, SLNA.
107. See J. A. van der Chijs, ed., *Nederlandsch-Indisch Plakaatboek:1602-1811*, 17 vols. (Batavia: Landsdrukkerij, 1885–1900), 7:1755–64. I am grateful to Mahmood Kooria for the identification. A compendium of civil laws for Muslims had already been commissioned for printing at Batavia in March of 1760. See *Realia*, 2:176. There is also the strong possibility it had been drafted with the Coromandel Moors

of that city in mind, given that they maintained a mosque beyond the Utrechtse Poort by the 1740s under "Iman Sadacke lebe." See *Realia*, 2:243.
108. North to directors, February 26, 1799, 5/1, 27r–27v, SLNA.
109. Valentia, *Voyages*, 1:259.
110. North to directors, January 30, 1800, 5/1, 89v, SLNA.
111. Tambyah Nadaraja, *The Legal System of Ceylon in Its Historical Setting* (Leiden: Brill, 1972), 192n21.
112. North to directors, December 15, 1801, 5/1, 173r–173v, SLNA.
113. North to directors, September 10, 1802, 5/1, 243r, SLNA.
114. Maitland to Camden, February 18, 1805, 5/75, 230–32, SLNA.
115. Governor's diary, October 27, 1806, including copy of Maitland to Wiese and Council, Colombo, November 26, 1805, 2/2, 50–56, SLNA.
116. Cod.Or. 2241 I (23 and 25), Leiden University Library (LUB). For an analysis of Sitti Hapipa's letter (no. 25), see Suryadi, "Sepucuk Surat dari Seorang Bangsawan Gowa di Tanah Pembuangan (Ceylon)," *Wacana* 10, no. 2 (2008): 213–44.
117. Alicia Schrikker, "Caught Between Empires: VOC Families in Sri Lanka After the British Take-over, 1806–1808," *Annales de démographie historique* 122, no. 2 (2011): 127–47.
118. Cod.Or. 2241 I (24), LUB. I have found no reference to Wirakusuma as an officer in the *Naam-boek*, nor was he among the exiles surveyed at Colombo in 1787 and 1788. Wirakusuma's self-deprecating, almost obligatory, language as the governor-general's "grandson" (*cucunda*) had also been used in 1792 by the exiled princes of Bacan. See Cod.Or. 2241 Ia 11 (no. 71), LUB.
119. A 1906 compilation of texts suggests that the Kareta family remained and that descendants married into a Moorish family. See Ricci, *Banishment*, 136n27, referring to Arabu-Tamil Compendium, dated AH 1324, EAP609/10/1, BL.
120. Maitland to Minto, September 21, 1806, 5/76, 101–51, 118, SNLA.
121. Maitland to Windham, separate dispatch of February 28, 1807, 5/78, 24–25, SNLA.
122. Maitland to Shee, Mount Lavinia, May 7, 1807, 5/78, 65–66, SNLA.

6. Between Shrinking Kandy and Distant Istanbul

1. Alexander Johnston, "A Cufic Inscription Found in Ceylon," and "A Letter to the Secretary Relating to the Preceding Inscription," *Transactions of the Royal Asiatic Society* 1 (1827): 545–48 and 537†–58†.
2. *Special Laws Concerning Maurs or Mahomedans*, printed text included under cover of Maitland to Castelreagh, December 1, 1807, 5/79, 301–9, Sri Lankan National Archives (SLNA), Colombo; Johnston, "Letter to the Secretary," 538†.
3. Johnstone's [sic] report of November 1807 on the customary laws of the various districts of the island, under cover of Maitland to Castelreagh, December 1, 1807, 5/79, 51, SLNA.
4. Johnstone's report, 309, SLNA. In 1814 Johnston placed Kayalpattinam on the Coromandel Coast as the primary source of authority and Quranic

6. BETWEEN SHRINKING KANDY AND DISTANT ISTANBUL

commentaries. See Tambyah Nadaraja, *The Legal System of Ceylon in Its Historical Setting* (Leiden: Brill, 1972), 204n96.
5. Maitland to Castlereagh, separate dispatch of March 10, 1808, 5/80, 164, SLNA.
6. Maitland to Castlereagh, August 20, 1808, 5/81, 167, SLNA.
7. Maitland to Castlereagh, August 20, 1808, 183–85, SLNA.
8. Maitland to Cooke, September 4, 1808, 5/82, 97, SLNA.
9. Of unclear—and probably not British—background, De Bussche was then sent to Java in 1813 to recruit more such "Malays." See L. De Bussche, *Letters on Ceylon: Particularly Relative to the Kingdom of Kandy* (London: J. J. Stockdale, 1817), 97, 129–32.
10. Marshall claimed that the Malay mohandiram had been commander of the royal guard; see Henry Marshall, *Ceylon: A General Description of the Island and Its Inhabitants* (London: William Allen, 1847), 133–34. Codrington was further of the view that he had been personally involved in an attempted assassination of the king at the order of the demoted Pilima Talawa. H. W. Codrington, intro. and ed., "Diary of Mr. John D'Oyly," *Journal of the Ceylon Branch of the Royal Asiatic Society* 25 no. 69 (1917): vii, 166. On Talawa, see also Alicia Schrikker, *Dutch and British Colonial Intervention in Sri Lanka, 1780-1815: Expansion and Reform.* (Leiden: Brill, 2007), 123–35, 199–204, 209–10.
11. Wilson to Earl of Liverpool, July 15, 1811, 5/5, 176, SLNA.
12. "Diary of Mr. John D'Oyly," 75. The same brother brought back correspondence between Davie and Jan Thoen, a Dutch artillerist in Kandyan service (78).
13. "Diary of Mr. John D'Oyly," 68.
14. Wilson to Earl of Liverpool, February 26, 1812, 5/5, 227–28, SLNA.
15. "Diary of Mr. John D'Oyly," 80.
16. "Diary of Mr. John D'Oyly," 121. The reference to Pattanis is suggestive of other routes of recruitment at Kandy.
17. Baba Ounous Saldin, *Syair Fayd al-abad: Artinya kediamannya berbagai pengetahuan* (Colombo: Alamat Langkapuri, AH 1322), 13.
18. Brownrigg to Bathurst, August 17, 1814, 5/7, 108-9, SLNA. On sepoys, see Brownrigg to Bathurst, January 25, 1813, 5/6, 236–37, SLNA. On early emancipation under Johnston and the systematic appointment of formerly slave-owning Moors as officials, see Nira Wickramasinghe, *Slave in a Palanquin: Colonial Servitude and Resistance in Sri Lanka* (New York: Columbia University Press, 2020), 107, 156–67, 163–69.
19. Assana had been working for D'Oyly on such missions from December 1911. See "Diary of Mr. John D'Oyly," 66, 106, 136. For ongoing connections and the mission of 1813, see 130–31, 160–67. His mother and brother are mentioned on 167.
20. The latter had been rumored since October 1812, when Assana was thought to be hatching a plot for his escape: "Diary of Mr. John D'Oyly," 167; Brownrigg to Bathurst, March 15, 1813, 5/6, 285–86, SLNA.
21. Brownrigg to Bathurst, March 15, 1813, 5/6, 285, SLNA.
22. Gananath Obeyesekere, *The Doomed King: A Requiem for Sri Vikrama Rajasinha* (Colombo: Sailfish, 2017), 176–77; Saldin, *Fayd al-Abad*, 13. See also Robert Aldrich, *Banished Potentates: Dethroning and Exiling Indigenous Monarchs Under British and*

6. BETWEEN SHRINKING KANDY AND DISTANT ISTANBUL

French Colonial Rule, 1815-1955 (Manchester: Manchester University Press, 2018), 32-74.
23. "Diary of Mr. D'Oyly," 175-76.
24. "Diary of Mr. D'Oyly," 175-77.
25. Robert Aldrich, "Out of Ceylon: The Exile of the Last King of Kandy," in *Exile in Colonial Asia: Kings, Convicts, Commemoration*, ed. Ronit Ricci (Honolulu: University of Hawaii Press, 2016), 48-70.
26. Brownrigg to Bathurst, July 20, 1816, 5/8, 117, SLNA.
27. For an initial synopsis, see Brownrigg to Bathurst, February 25, 1815, 5/8, 14-15, SLNA. See also "The Narrative of John Albertus Thoen," *Gentleman's Magazine* 87, pt. 2 (1817): 21-24, 119-22. Thoen, mentioned frequently in D'Oyly's diary, was later assigned to the ordinance stores: "Diary of Mr. D'Oyly," 46, 78, 103, 117, 135, 147; De Bussche, *Letters*, 63.
28. Mocked by Marshall (*Ceylon*, 101) as a "half-caste" drummer, he is now remembered as the first "Sri Lankan" in Australia. See Paul Thomas, "Oodeen, a Malay Interpreter on Australia's Frontier Lands," *Indonesia and the Malay World* 40, 117 (2012): 122-42.
29. "An Account of the Island of Ceylon . . . etc.," *Quarterly Review* 14, no. 27 (October 1815): 1-38, 22-23.
30. For Ahelapola's hopes, see Sujit Sivasundaram, *Waves Across the South: A New History of Revolution and Empire* (London: William Collins, 2020), 226-27.
31. For the monastic journeys and subsequent plot, see also Sivasundaram, *Waves*, 221-22, 228-29.
32. Brownrigg to Bathurst, November 5, 1816, 5/102, 8, SLNA.
33. Brownrigg to Bathurst, November 5, 1816, 10-11. Assana never returned to Batavia. His grandson even ended up as a head jailer at Galle in the 1860s. See F. E. Gooneratne, "History of the Malays of Ceylon," in *Jubilee Book of the Colombo Malay Cricket Club* (Colombo: Malay Cricket Club of Colombo, 1924), 165.
34. Substance of Information Communicated by Kapooliyadde Poonshi Rala, in Presence of Mahawellatenne and Ekneligoda Nilame, Colombo, September 9-10, 1816, Colonial Office Files (CO) 54/61, National Archives (TNA), Kew. Transcribed in Ramesh Somasunderum, "British Infiltration of Ceylon (Sri Lanka) in the Nineteenth Century: A Study of the D'Oyly Papers Between 1805 and 1818" (PhD diss., University of Western Australia, 2008), 351-56. See also James Holman, *A Voyage Around the World*, 4 vols. (London: Smith, Elder & Cornhill, 1834-35), 3:145-46.
35. De Bussche, *Letters*, 130-32.
36. For loyal Malays resisting rebel attempts at recruitment in 1818, see Brownrigg to Bathurst, July 24, 1818, 5/9, 466-67, SLNA. For reports of a murder and the swift execution of the Malay assailants, see Brownrigg to Bathurst, August 2, 1819, 5/10, 127, SLNA.
37. Thomas Skinner, *Fifty Years in Ceylon: An Autobiography, 1818-1868*, ed. Annie Skinner (London: W. H. Allen, 1891), 13, 20-21.
38. De Bussche (*Letters*, 51) made special reference to the decorations laid out by the Moormen goldsmiths in 1815.

39. B. A. Hussainmiya, *Lost Cousins: The Malays of Sri Lanka* (Bangi: Universitas Kebangsaan Malaysia, 1987), 104–52; Ricci, *Banishment*, 193–97.
40. Brownrigg to Bathurst, January 9, 1819, 5/10, 25, SLNA.
41. For a synopsis of his connections, see Sunil S. Amrith, "Islam's Eastern Frontiers: Tamil, Chinese, and Malay Worlds," in *Oceanic Islam: Muslim Universalism and European Imperialism*, ed. Sugata Bose and Ayesha Jalal (New Delhi: Bloomsbury India, 2020), 61–62.
42. Teren Sevea, "Keramats Running Amuck: Islamic Parahistories of Travel, Belonging, Crimes, and Madness," in *Belonging Across the Bay of Bengal: Religious Rites, Colonial Migrations, National Rights*, ed. Michael Francis Laffan (London: Bloomsbury Academic, 2017), 57–71, esp. 57–59; Kelvin Lawrence, "Greed, Guns, and Gore: Historicising Early British Colonial Singapore Through Recent Developments in the Historiography of Munsyi Abdullah," *Journal of Southeast Asian Studies* 50, no. 4 (2020): 507–20.
43. Abdullah did not land at Lanka, but his ship took on provisions off Galle and entertained a bearded "Abyssinian" in sight of Adam's peak, where the African promised to recite the opening verse of the Qurʾan for any who purchased supplies or offered a donation. Munshi Abdullah, *Kisah Pĕlayaran Abdullah ka-Kĕlantan dan ka-Judah*, intro. and ed. Kassim Ahmad, 5th ed. (Kuala Lumpur: Oxford University Press, 1968), 130–31. For examples of the many Lankan manuscripts gathered in projects coordinated by Ronit Ricci, see EAP 450 and 609, British Library (BL).
44. Hussainmiyya (*Orang Rejimen*, 80), citing Muhammad Nuhman, "A Brief History of the Colombo Grand Mosque," an account given by an old boy of Hameedia Boys' English School in 1905 and presented to the Colombo Grand Mosque Committee of Management in 1959. See also B. D. K. Saldin, *Orang Melayu Sri Lanka Dan Bahasanya* (Colombo: Sridevi, 1996), 17.
45. The 1828 schedule of the Ceylon Rifle Establishment notes the employment of fifty such women; see WO 43/492, TNA.
46. Wickramasinghe, *Slave in a Palanquin*, 85–86. That September Brownrigg would forward Johnston's proposal for the voluntary surrender of titles to enslaved children born after the Prince Regent's birthday. Brownrigg to Bathurst, September 16, 1816, 5/8, SLNA.
47. Wickramasinghe, *Slave in a Palanquin*, 160–88.
48. Schedule of the Fixed Establishment of the Ceylon Rifle Regiment for the year 1828, WO 43/492, TNA.
49. Skinner, *Fifty Years*, 103–4, 114.
50. Skinner, 128–30.
51. Report of Colebrooke upon the Compulsory Services, London, March, 1832, in *The Colebrooke-Cameron Papers (Documents on British Colonial Policy in Ceylon, 1796–1833)*, ed. G. C. Mendis, 2 vols. (Oxford: Oxford University Press, 1956), 1:202–8. For an account of the treatment of corvée laborers and slaves whose services had been purchased by the colonial state in the 1820s, see Wickramasinghe, *Slave in a Palanquin*, 126–59.
52. Colebrooke Commission, E/19, 1830, questions and answers re: provincial courts, native laws, procedures, etc., 19/66, 40v–41r, 43r, SLNA.

6. BETWEEN SHRINKING KANDY AND DISTANT ISTANBUL

53. Colebrooke Commission, 19/66, 101v–102r, SLNA. For mentions of case load, see 127v–128r. Sneyd's predecessor, H. Pennell, who had moved to Colombo in January 1829 after nine years at Matara, was comparatively curt on the question of indigenous punctuality and truth: "They are not." he replied. See 101v.
54. R. M. Sneyd to general secretary, April 24–October 8, 1835, 6/1376, SLNA. It was only in October that he was allowed to hire Mianigma Markar Apona Markar.
55. Khotba Book, EAP609/9/1, image 223, BL, https://eap.bl.uk/archive-file/EAP609 -9-1 (accessed January 23, 2022).
56. For the rise of Muhammad 'Ali and his military state, see Khaled Fahmy, *All the Pasha's Men: Mehmed Ali, His Army, and the Making of Modern Egypt* (Cambridge: Cambridge University Press, 1997), esp. chap. 1.
57. Petition of the Mohamedans of Ceylon to the Viceroy of Egypt Asking That a High Priest Be Appointed for Their Religious Welfare, Porte de Galle, January 8, 1839, Foreign Office Files (FO) 926/9, TNA.
58. Sawers's unpublished manuscript was a major source for Marshall's *General Description* of 1846. His son, Alexander Sibbald Sawers (b. Ceylon, 1814), died at Cairo in 1868.
59. Fahmy, *All the Pasha's Men*, 278–305.
60. Having served as acting collector after arriving with Maitland in 1805, his appointment as collector for Batticaloa is noted in general dispatch of January 25, 1810, 5/5, 55, SLNA. For his contact with Assana in 1812, see "Diary of John D'Oyly," 83, 88. Sawers became revenue commissioner for Kandy in 1816 and then judicial commissioner in 1826 before departing for Scotland in 1827, where he was provost of Dunbar from 1833 to 1837. He returned to Ceylon for a visit in 1838 and then went back via Egypt in January 1839.
61. "Monster Petition," 6/1438, SLNA.
62. "Mutiny of Recruits," *Scotsman*, September 11, 1841. See also "Trial of Captain Batta," *Examiner*, October 9, 1841.
63. Pay increased to encourage recruitment, 1845–1849, WO 43/492, TNA.
64. Saldin, *Syair Fayd al-Abad*, 16.
65. Saldin, 14–17. Salimudin was a copyist of several manuscripts in the garrison and a probable witness for Saldin. See Ricci, *Banishment*, 188–91.
66. For recent treatment of this conflict, see Sivasundaram, *Waves*, 206–14.
67. Further report from the officer commanding the Pegu Light Infantry Battalion relating to the Malay recruits, under India Military, December 3, 1856, E/4/840, 780–82, India Office Records and Private Papers (IOR), BL.
68. Gail Minault, *The Khilafat Movement: Religious Symbolism and Political Mobilization in India* (New York: Columbia University Press, 1982), 6; Azmi Özcan, *Pan-Islamism: Indian Muslims, the Ottomans, and Britain, 1877–1924* (Leiden: Brill, 1997), 16–18.
69. For the context and impact of Bahadur's exile and death, see Sana Aiyer, "Revolutionaries, Maulvis, Swamis, and Monks: Burma's Khilafat Moment," in *Oceanic Islam: Muslim Universalism and European Imperialism*, ed. Sugata Bose and Ayesha Jalal (New Delhi: Bloomsbury India, 2020), 143–93.
70. Özcan, *Pan-Islamism*, 18–19; Seema Alavi, *Muslim Cosmopolitanism in the Age of Empire* (Cambridge, MA: Harvard University Press, 2015).

6. BETWEEN SHRINKING KANDY AND DISTANT ISTANBUL

71. William Ochsenwald, *Religion, Society, and the State in Arabia: The Hijaz Under Ottoman Control, 1840-1908* (Columbus: Ohio State University Press, 1984), 143-51. The complex narrative is outlined in Michael Christopher Low, *Imperial Mecca: Ottoman Arabia and the Indian Ocean Hajj* (New York: Columbia University Press, 2020), 53-61.
72. Wilson Jacko Jacob, *For God or Empire: Sayyid Fadl and the Indian Ocean World* (Stanford, CA: Stanford University Press, 2019).
73. On Dahlan's sympathies, see Ulrike Freitag, *Indian Ocean Migrants and State Formation in Hadhramaut: Reforming the Homeland* (Leiden: Brill, 2003), 203-4.
74. Fadl b. ʿAlawi Mawla al-Dawila Ba ʿAlawi, *Majmuʿ thalath rasaʾil ʿilmiyya*, ed. Anwar b. ʿAbdallah Salim Ba ʿUmar (Kuwayt: Dar al-Diya,' 2018), 197-213.
75. Jacob, *For God or Empire*, 61.
76. Fadl, *Majmuʿ*, 161-90.
77. Anwar b. ʿAbdallah Salim, in Fadl, *Majmuʿ*, 161n. By contrast, Abdul Sathar holds that the fatwas were given by Sayyid ʿAlawi in response to a local question at the time of a rebellion in 1842. See K. K. Muhammad Abdul Sathar, *Mappila Leader in Exile: A Political Biography of Syed Fażl Pookoya Tangal* (Calicut: Other Books, 2012), 44-45. With thanks to Saumyashree Ghosh.
78. Fadl, *Majmuʿ*, 170.
79. İsmail Hakkı Kadı and A. C. S. Peacock, eds., *Ottoman-Southeast Asian Relations: Sources from the Ottoman Archives*, 2 vols. (Leiden: Brill, 2020), 2:661-6; hereafter *OSEAR*. It is possible that Muhammad Salih was the Acehnese Shattari Muhammad Salih al-Baghdadi (d. 1855). See Oman Fathurahman, *Shaṭṭārīyah Silsilah in Aceh, Java, and the Lanao Area of Mindanao* (Tokyo: Research Institute for Languages and Cultures of Asia and Africa, Tokyo University of Foreign Studies, 2016).
80. Mandal points out that Arab-owned shipping remained competitive into the 1850s, owning some 50 percent of the tonnage on Java alone. Sumit K. Mandal, *Becoming Arab: Creole Histories and Modern Identity in the Malay World* (Cambridge: Cambridge University Press, 2018), 48-49.
81. For his embassy, see *OSEAR*, 1:81-106.
82. *OSEAR*, 1:107-42; for mention of "Magians," see 129.
83. B. Schrieke, "Bijdrage tot de bibliographie van de huidige godsdienstige beweging ter Sumatra's Westkust," *TBG* 59 (1919-21): 249-325, 263, 266.
84. Michael Francis Laffan, *The Makings of Indonesian Islam: Orientalism and the Narration of a Sufi Past* (Princeton, NJ: Princeton University Press, 2011), 53-54.
85. *OSEAR*, 1:142-53.
86. *OSEAR*, 1:153-56.
87. Duke of Newcastle to Terence O'Brien, February 26, 1864, 4/82, SLNA.
88. O'Brien to secretary of state, June 7, 1864, 5/51, SLNA; government agent to colonial secretary, May 28, 1864, 6/2828, SLNA.
89. The reading of Abi ابي is an understandable error for Lebbai لبي.
90. Husseen Lebbe Markar to government agent for Western Provinces WP, May 28, 1864, 6/2828, SLNA.
91. Dispatch from the secretary of state, February 7, 1865, 4/86, SLNA.
92. B. A. Hussainmiya, "Baba Ounus Saldin: An Account of a Malay Literary Savant of Sri Lanka (b. 1832-d. 1906)," *JMBRAS* 64, no. 2 (1991): 103-34; Ricci, *Banishment*,

6. BETWEEN SHRINKING KANDY AND DISTANT ISTANBUL

219–46. For images of Saldin, see figure 6.1 and Arnold Wright, *Twentieth Century Impressions of Ceylon: Its History, People, Commerce, Industries, and Resources* (London: Lloyd's Greater Britain Publishing, 1907), 318, 330. A variant and one of a much younger Saldin are also in the Palinda Steven de Silva collection.

93. Unless otherwise stated, biographical details are drawn from Hussainmiya, "Baba Ounus Saldin." For an overview of his *Alamat* and its significance, see Ronit Ricci, "The Malay World, Expanded, the World's First Malay Newspaper, Colombo, 1869," *Indonesia and the Malay World* 41, no. 120 (2013): 168–82. See also Sunil S. Amrith, "Tamil Diasporas Across the Bay of Bengal," *American Historical Review* 114, no. 3 (2009): 547–72, 557.
94. The muster rolls of 1803 mention a private in the fourth company called Passasee; see WO12/10853, TNA. Given the tendency among Ceylon Malays for the Arabic letter *sin* to be written as a *shin*, the original فسي, could easily be read as Pantasi فنتسي by later readers.
95. Saldin, *Fayd al-Abad*, 5–6.
96. Ricci, *Banishment*, 232, and 233n28. Guna Wijaya is listed as a captain in the muster roll of 1803. WO 12/10853, TNA.
97. Saldin, *Fayd al-Abad*, 10.
98. Hussainmiya, *Orang Rejimen*, 114. This was most likely sergeant major "Boreham" (Burhan), who was already serving in 1803, see muster roll, 1803, WO 12/10853, TNA. He retired as an adjutant in 1832.
99. Hussainmiya claims that he was a Qadiri, Lebbai Nainar Marikar ibn Ahmad Lebbai, though Ricci names him as (his brother?) the Shattari Luwana Marikkaiyar ibn Ahmad Labbai, who died in 1881. See Ricci, *Banishment*, 236.
100. Ricci, 171–74.
101. *Alamat Langkapuri*, June 13, 1869.
102. *Alamat Langkapuri*, August 17, 1869; see also Ricci, "Malay World," 177.
103. Saldin, *Fayd al-Abad*, 39, citing a hadith found in the *Sayr al-salikin*.
104. On the association and school, see *Alamat Langkapuri*, June 27, 1869; for more on the night school, see *Alamat Langkapuri*, August 8, 1869.
105. *Alamat Langkapuri*, June 11, 1869; there was also mention later of a fund for Malays in Kandy. See *Alamat Langkapuri*, August 22, 1869.
106. "Bab al-khamir wa faʿilahu wa nasirahu haram," *Alamat Langkapuri*, July 25, 1869.
107. *Alamat Langkapuri*, August 8, 1869.
108. "Mayit Orang Asing," *Alamat Langkapuri*, June 11, 1869. The page is reproduced in Ricci, *Banishment*, 173.
109. For the Kandy Mosque dispute, see letter of Samʿun bin Muhammad, dated July 15, 1869, in *Alamat Langkapuri*, July 25, 1869.
110. Hussainmiya, *Orang Rejimen*, 127–33.
111. *Alamat Langkapuri*, July 25, 1869.
112. "Abdullah, Kampung Kertel, August 7, 1869," *Alamat Langkapuri*, August 8, 1869.
113. Hussainmiya, *Orang Rejimen*, 128.
114. The trustees were named as "Mahometan priest" Abdul Bahar, Subedar adjutant Jumat, Ahamit Veera, Ahamat Jaldeen, Baba Deen Bahoram and Ahamet Sabar—all of Slave Island, along with Baba Ounous Saldin of Kehelewatte. See title deed of Masjidul Jamiah Jawatta Malay burial ground, deed no. 4209,

December 22, 1876, EAP609/3/1, BL, https://eap.bl.uk/archive-file/EAP609-3-1 (accessed January 18, 2022).
115. "Wazir Mesir," *Alamat Langkapuri*, August 22, 1869.

7. For Queen, Country, and Caliph in Africa

1. Unless otherwise noted, biographical information concerning Abu Bakr is derived from Halim Gençoğlu, "Abu Bakr Effendi: A Report on the Activities and Challenges of an Ottoman Muslim Theologian in the Cape of Good Hope" (master's thesis, University of Cape Town, 2013). For an account of the journey from Liverpool to the Cape and their arrival there, see Omer Lutfi Effendi, *A Travelogue of My Journey to the Cape of Good Hope* (Cape Town: El-Khaleel, 1991), 11–14. Lutfi later left for Egypt in 1866.
2. Queen Victoria's journals, July 17, 1867, Princess Beatrice's copies, vol. 56, 183–86, Royal Collection Trust (RCIN), http://qvj.chadwyck.com.ezproxy.princeton.edu/home.do (accessed January 25, 2022).
3. Such was noted by way of comparison three decades later: "Naval Review at Spithead," *Sunday Times*, June 27, 1897.
4. George Housman Thomas (1824–1868), *The Investiture of Sultan Abdülaziz I with the Order of the Garter, 17 July 1867*, drawn 1867, RCIN 450804.
5. Queen Victoria's journals, vol. 56, 186. Conversely, and perhaps perversely, that year she made William Muir (1819–1905), the Christian polemicist and historian of Islam, a Knight Commander of the Star of India.
6. The Rambler, "The End of the Fetes," *Sunday Times*, July 28, 1867.
7. Maximilien Kollisch, *The Mussulman Population at the Cape of Good Hope* (Constantinople: Levant Herald, 1867), 29. A Moravian Jew naturalized as a British subject in 1858, Kollisch then worked for the Parisian *Revue de deux mondes*. Later sources suggest he took German nationality and founded the *Economista d'Italia* at Rome in 1868, dying at Florence in 1872.
8. Peter Ralph Coates, "P. E. De Roubaix's Delusions," *Quarterly Bulletin of the National Library of South Africa* 64, no. 1 (2010): 31–48; and no. 2 (2010) 86–104.
9. Portraits of Petrus de Roubaix, AG 2324 and 3845, Western Cape Archives and Records Service (WCARS), Cape Town, reproduced in Coates, "De Roubaix's Delusions," 88.
10. Newcastle to Wodehouse, July 31, 1862, GH 1/291 (1862), 112–18, WCARS; J. S. de Lima, *The Califa Question: Documents Connected with this Matter* (Cape Town: Van de Sandt de Villiers, 1857). The snuffbox would be produced many times in De Roubaix's political career to support his claims of being wealthy enough to hold a seat in parliament. Coates, "De Roubaix's Delusions," 87.
11. Mochamet Achmet to the Sultan of Turkey, Cape Town, December 21, 1861, reproduced in Gençoğlu, "Abu Bakr Effendi," 143.
12. Adrianus van Selms, "Introduction," in *The Religious Duties of Islam as Taught and Explained by Abu Bakr Effendi*, ed. Mia Brandel Syrier (Leiden: Brill, 1960), viii; see also Martin van Bruinessen, "A Nineteenth-Century Ottoman Kurdish

7. FOR QUEEN, COUNTRY, AND CALIPH IN AFRICA

Scholar in South Africa: Abu Bakr Efendi," in *Mullas, Sufis, and Heretics: The Role of Religion in Kurdish Society*, ed. Martin van Bruinessen (Istanbul: Isis, 2000), 133–41.

13. Letter of Abu Bakr Effendi, *Mecmua-yı Fünun*, Ramadan 1279 (January 1863). Gençoğlu ("Abu Bakr Effendi," 54) cites a letter sent by Musurus Pasha to De Roubaix regarding Abu Bakr on November 25, 1862. Omer Lutfi's account has it that Abu Bakr had piously refused the offer of "Ruben" to be taken to town in a carriage when so many cobelievers were walking. See Omer Lutfi, *Travelogue*, 14. I must add that I have been guided on the content of the *Mecmua* by Gençoğlu and have had the passages checked by Duygu Coşkuntuna, to whom I am most grateful.
14. Letter of Abu Bakr Effendi, *Mecmua-yı Fünun*, Ramadan 1279 (January 1863.)
15. As far as I am aware, the first reproduction of this photo, previously kept by what was the South African Cultural History Museum, was by Davids in 1985. See Achmat Davids, *The History of the Tana Baru: The Case for the Preservation of the Muslim Cemetery at the Top of Longmarket Street*. (Cape Town: Committee for the Preservation of the Tana Baru, 1985), 55.
16. Later family pictures kept by a daughter who went to live in Istanbul would suggest he is in the middle of the gathering. "From Cape Town to Erzurum: Grandchildren of Ottoman Scholar in Search for His Legacy," *Daily Sabah*, April 12, 2017, https://www.dailysabah.com/feature/2017/04/13/from-cape-town-to-erzurum-grandchildren-of-ottoman-scholar-in-search-for-his-legacy.
17. Mochamet Achmet to the Sultan of Turkey, Cape Town, December 21, 1861, reproduced in Gençoğlu, "Abu Bakr Effendi," 143.
18. *De Zuid Afrikaan*, February 19, 1863, reproduced in Fahmi Gamieldien, *The History of the Claremont Main Road Mosque, Its People, and Their Contribution to Islam in South Africa* (Cape Town: Claremont Main Road Mosque, 2004), 32.
19. Letter of Abu Bakr Effendi, *Mecmua-yı Fünun*, Ramadan 1279 (February–March 1863); and Dhu l-Qaʿda 1279 (April–May 1863).
20. Letter of Abu Bakr Effendi, *Mecmua-yı Fünun*, Shawwal 1279 (March–April 1863).
21. Gençoğlu, "Abu Bakr Effendi," 31.
22. Letter of Abu Bakr Effendi, *Mecmua-yı Fünun*, Dhu l-Qaʿda 1279 (April–May 1863). Further musings on the Comoros are to be found in *Mecmua-yı Fünun* 3, nos. 25–26, n.d. [likely November 1864].
23. John Schofield Mayson, *The Malays of Capetown* (Manchester: Galt, 1861), 34. For the early history of the Abdol Wahab trust, see Saarah Jappie, "Between Macassars: Site, Story, and the Transoceanic Afterlives of Shaykh Yusuf of Makassar," PhD diss., Princeton University, January 2018.
24. Abu Bakr to Wodehouse, July 28, 1863, CO 4129, E6, WCARS.
25. Penciled note of Wodehouse on letter cited above, CO 4129, E6, WCARS.
26. Letter of Abu Bakr Effendi, *Mecmua-yı Fünun* n.d. (November 1864). I date this issue after October because of Abu Bakar's passing reference to what can only be the demise of Mamat van de Kaap and the dispute over the Long Street Mosque.
27. Abu Bakr Effendi to Wodehouse, October 5, 1863, answered October 9, 1863, CO 4129, E7, WCARS.

7. FOR QUEEN, COUNTRY, AND CALIPH IN AFRICA

28. Achmat Davids, *The Mosques of Bo-Kaap: A Social History of Islam at the Cape* (Athlone: South African Institute of Arabic and Islamic Research, 1980), 54.
29. This is despite the Muhammad Salih of the petition identifying as the son of "Muhammad Murid al-Rawi," which sounds more poetic than patronymic. See İsmail Hakkı Kadı and A. C. S. Peacock, eds., *Ottoman-Southeast Asian Relations: Sources from the Ottoman Archives*, 2 vols. (Leiden: Brill, 2020), 2:661–65; hereafter *OSEAR*. Given the lack of a press in the Hijaz, the mention of pamphlets is suggestive of Muhammad Salih having brought them from Singapore or commissioned them from Bombay or Cairo.
30. Letter of Abu Bakr Effendi, *Mecmua-yı Fünun* 3, nos. 25–26, November 1864. Such a view is backed up by the recent discovery of letters to Capetonian imams pleading for their intercession. These letters, held in the roof of the Chiappini Street Mosque, await further analysis. With thanks to Daiyaan Petersen, who is in possession of digital images.
31. Letter of Abu Bakr Effendi, *Mecmua-yı Fünun* 3, nos. 25–26, November 1864.
32. Kollisch, *Mussulman Population*, 29.
33. Kollisch, 12–13; [De Roubaix], *Correspondence Passed Between His Highness Aali Pacha, Minister of Foreign Affairs, of the Sublime Porte, and the Honorable P. E. De Roubaix, Esq., Consul General of the Sublime Porte, Cape of Good Hope* (Cape Town: J. H. Hofmeijr, 1871), 5. The sufferings of the party of 1859 were referred to by Abu Bakr in his third letter to Istanbul, where he characterized them as having been sharecroppers headed for Africa. Letter of Abu Bakr Effendi, *Mecmua-yı Fünun*, April–May 1863. See also Matthew S. Hopper, *Slaves of One Master: Globalization and Slavery in Arabia in the Age of Empire* (New Haven, CT: Yale University Press, 2015), 162–64. Also found in the roof of the Chiappini Street Mosque is an Arabic letter from that party, though details differ. Addressed to a Shaykh Muhammad ʿArab and dated 13 Muharram 1277 (August 2, 1860), it is from eighteen destitute sailors and eight women, who describe being interdicted when traveling from Kilwa to Zanzibar on a vessel belonging to Sultan Majid and being unable to communicate locally (at their unspecified location). Hence they asked the shaykh to speak to the "English" known to him. With thanks to Daiyaan Petersen, who is in possession of images of the letter.
34. This was William Greig, brother of the former publisher of the *South African Commercial Advertizer*, who had held the post since 1852.
35. De Roubaix secured their return by 1866, as well as facilitated a mission to the Porte of more displaced royals from Anjouan. Kollisch, *Mussulman Population*, 12–13.
36. "The Turkish Consul-General and the Malays," *Cape Argus*, February 20, 1864.
37. Kollisch, *Mussulman Population*, 17
38. Kollisch, 10–11. Details about the aid are found in *Correspondence*, 4.
39. Kollisch, 31, 33.
40. Kollisch, 17.
41. Wodehouse to Duke of Buckingham, concerning the request of Hassan al-Din alias Jonathan, May 27, 1867, no. 49, GH 23/30, 231, WCARS.
42. Imam Muhammad Amin b. Imam Ahmad et al. to Musurus Pasha, Cape Town, February 1868, HR SFR 3 136/28, BOA, National Archives, Republic of Turkey.

43. On the Persian pretender, see Letter of Abu Bakr Effendi, *Mecmua-yı Fünun* 3, ca. November 1864. Typically favorable reportage of De Roubaix's role in the Long Street dispute is cited in Kollisch, *Mussulman Population*, 14.
44. *Ahmad Sadik et al. v. Abdol Ragieb*, Illiqid Cases 1873, CSC 2/1/1/156, no. 37, WCARS; see also Davids, *Mosques of Bo-Kaap*, 131-38.
45. These views were clear in his published edition of 1877. See Brandel Syrier, *Religious Duties*, 100-101, 152-53; and A. van Selms, *Abu Bakar se 'Uiteensetting van die godsdiens:' 'n Arabie-Afrikaanse Teks uit die Jaar 1869* (Amsterdam: North-Holland, 1979), 118-19, 178-79.
46. While Bradlow and Cairns identified him as an imam of the Auwal Masjid, Davids argues that he must have moved to the Buitengracht camp with the death of his father and the ascent on Dorp Street of Abd al-Bari. Frank R. Bradlow and Margaret Cairns, *The Early Cape Muslims: A Study of their Mosques, Genealogy, and Origins* (Cape Town: Balkema, 1978), 75; Davids, *Mosques*, 108ff.
47. *Ahmad Sadik et al. v. Abdol Ragieb*, Illiqid Cases 1873, CSC 2/1/1/156, no. 37, WCARS.
48. Bradlow and Cairns (*Early Cape Muslims*, 74) identify him as a different Achmat Gamien or Hamien (d. 1867); however, context confirms that he was the son of Achmat van Bengalen.
49. This was all the stranger given that Achmat Sadick had previously disseminated texts, including copies of al-Tilimsani, in his contests with Abu Bakr and local missionaries. See Achmat Davids, "Imam Achmat Sadik Achmat (1813-1879): Imam, Soldier, Politician and Educator," in *Pages from Cape Muslim History*, 2nd ed., ed. Yusuf da Costa and Achmat Davids (Gatesville: Naqshbandi-Muhammadi South Africa, 2005), 71-79, 75.
50. *Ahmad Sadik et al. v. Abdol Ragieb*, Illiqid Cases 1873, CSC 2/1/1/156, no. 37, WCARS. According to the report of a returned group of pilgrims published in the *Cape Argus* in 1878, Abdullah drowned at Quielimane in Mozambique in 1877 while on yet another hajj with two of his sons. See Du Plessis, *The Cape Malays* (Cape Town: Maskew Miller, 1944), 19.
51. *Ahmad Sadik et al. v. Abdol Ragieb*, Illiqid Cases 1873, CSC 2/1/1/156, no. 37, WCARS.
52. Brandel Syrier, *Religious Duties*, 156; Van Selms, *Abu Bakar*, 185.
53. Achmat Davids, "The Origins of the Hanafi-Shafi'i Dispute and the Impact of Abu Bakr Effendi (1835-1880)," in Da Costa and Davids, eds., *Pages from Cape Muslim History*, 81-102, 97-98; and Davids, *Mosques*, 54, citing *Ahmad Sadik v. Abdol Ragiep*, though I could not find reference to the petition in these documents.
54. "The Effendi Case," *Cape Argus*, January 18, 1870; "Achmat Sadik and Others vs. Abdul Gamiet," *Cape Argus*, August 28, 1873; "The Muhammedan Case," *Cape Argus*, September 2, 1873. On the travails of Abu Bakr, see also the articles of Jackie Loos in the *Cape Argus*, March 3, 2000, August 29, 2001, August 31, 2005, and September 28, 2005.
55. Frank Emery, "South Africa's Best Friend:' Sir Bartle Frere at the Cape, 1877-80," *Theoria*, no. 63 (October 1984): 25-35.
56. John Kirk, Zanzibar, April 16, 1877, GH 1/366, 1877, 68-73, WCARS.
57. Du Plessis, *Cape Malays*, 18-23.

58. Political Department, Bombay Castle, no. 5177 and enclosures, November 14, 1878, R/20/A/508, 141–205, India Office Records and Private Papers (IOR), British Library (BL). I am grateful to Matt Hopper for having shared these documents.
59. He had further done so before five witnesses who affirmed that the marriage was licit while Zaynab had no guardian, thus empowering Abu Bakr to take her for himself. Political Department, Bombay Castle, November 14, 1878, 165, BL.
60. Political Department, Bombay Castle, November 14, 1878, 163, BL.
61. For a reproduction of his death notice, see Gençoğlu, "Abu Bakr Effendi," 133.
62. Syed Tanvir Wasti, "Sir Syed Ahmad Khan and the Turks," *Middle Eastern Studies* 46, no. 4 (2010): 529–42.
63. Adam Mestyan, *Arab Patriotism: The Ideology and Culture of Power in Late Ottoman Egypt* (Princeton, NJ: Princeton University Press, 2020), 19.
64. One such figure was a Shaykh Ibrahim, who headed a Sufi community in Upper Egypt before returning to India sometime before 1865. See Juan Cole, *Colonialism and Revolution in the Middle East: Social and Cultural Origins of Egypt's ʿUrabi Movement* (Princeton, NJ: Princeton University Press, 1993), 196.
65. Robert Aldrich, *Banished Potentates: Dethroning and Exiling Indigenous Monarchs Under British and French Colonial Rule, 1815-1955* (Manchester: Manchester University Press, 2018), 105–10.
66. Aldrich, *Banished Potentates*, 6.
67. Ross Dunn, *The Adventures of Ibn Battuta: A Muslim Traveler of the 14th Century*, 3rd ed. (Berkeley: University of California Press, 2012), 110. Dunn repurposed a phrase used by Henri Pirenne, who referred to the Eastern Mediterannean as such in his *Mohammed and Charlemagne* of 1935.
68. Dennis B. McGilvray, "Arabs, Moors, and Muslims: Sri Lankan Muslim Ethnicity in Regional Perspective," *Contributions to Indian Sociology* 32, no. 2 (1998): 433–83.
69. William Howard Russell, *The Prince of Wales' Tour: A Diary in India; with Some Account of the Visits of His Royal Highness to the Courts of Greece, Egypt, Spain, and Portugal* (New York: R. Worthington, 1878).
70. William Gregory, *Egypt in 1855 and 1856; Tunis in 1857 and 1858*, 2 vols. (London: John Russell Smith, 1859), 1:295.
71. Gregory, *Egypt in 1855*, 1:96–101.
72. Michael Berdine, *The Accidental Tourist, Wilfrid Scawen Blunt, and the British Invasion of Egypt in 1882* (New York: Routledge, 2005).
73. For the structural causes and agents of the Egyptian revolution, see Cole, *Colonialism and Revolution*, 1993.
74. William Gregory, *Sir William Gregory, K.C.M.G., Formerly Member of Parliament and Sometime Governor of Ceylon: An Autobiography*, ed. Augusta Gregory (London: John Murray, 1894), 375.
75. "Alms to Oblivion Egypt[ian Memoirs]," pt. 5 (Proteus), 13–14, MS 313–1975, Blunt Papers, Fitzwilliam Museum (FW), Cambridge.
76. On Zohrab and his letters, see John Slight, *The British Empire and the Hajj, 1865-1956* (Cambridge, MA: Harvard University Press, 2015), 96–98, 119; and Seema Alavi, *Muslim Cosmopolitanism in the Age of Empire* (Cambridge, MA: Harvard University Press, 2015), 125–26, 141–43.

7. FOR QUEEN, COUNTRY, AND CALIPH IN AFRICA

77. Michael Francis Laffan, " 'A Watchful Eye': The Meccan Plot of 1881 and Changing Dutch Perceptions of Islam in Indonesia," *Archipel* 63, no. 1 (2002): 79–108.
78. L. Zolondek, "Sabunji in England, 1876–91: His Role in Arabic Journalism," *Middle Eastern Studies* 14, no. 1 (1978): 102–15; Rogier Visser, "Identities in Early Arabic Journalism: The Case of Louis Ṣābūnjī" (PhD diss., University of Amsterdam, 2014); compare Martin Kramer, "Pen and Purse: Ṣābūnjī and Blunt," in *The Islamic World: From Classical to Modern Times*, ed. C. E. Bosworth, Charles Issawi, Roger Savory, and A. L. Udovitch (Princeton, NJ: Darwin, 1989), 771–80.
79. W. S. Blunt, *Secret History of the English Occupation of Egypt: Being a Personal Narrative of Events*, 2nd ed. (London: T. Fisher Unwin, 1907), 86–87.
80. On Barghash and Frere in London in 1875, see the observations of Barghash's exiled sister in Emily Ruete, *An Arabian Princess Between Two Worlds: Memoirs, Letters Home, Sequels to the Memoirs, Syrian Customs and Usages*, ed. E. van Donzel (Brill: Leiden, 1993), 40–41, 376ff.
81. Abdulhamid had awarded Ismaʿil's friend Barghash the Mecidiye when he made the hajj in 1877, but the latter resented any suggestion that he was an Ottoman vassal. See Aydin, *Idea of the Muslim World*, 91; Zolondek, "Sabunji in England," 106; and Jeremy Prestholdt, "From Zanzibar to Beirut: Sayyide Salme and the Tensions of Cosmopolitanism," in *Global Muslims in the Age of Steam and Print*, ed. James Gelvin and Nile Green (Berkeley: University of California Press, 2014), 204–26, 209.
82. Azmi Özcan, "The Press and Anglo-Ottoman Relations, 1876–1909," *Middle Eastern Studies*, 29 no. 1 (1993): 111–17, 114.
83. Visser, "Identities," 106. A copy, issued on March 19, 1881, and in the name of the "Society for the Preservation of the Rights of Arabs," is found in the papers of Snouck Hurgronje, Or. 7111, Leiden University Library.
84. Özcan, "Press and Relations," 113; Azmi Özcan, *Pan-Islamism: Indian Muslims, the Ottomans, and Britain, 1877–1924* (Leiden: Brill, 1997), 120.
85. See the 1883 remarks of Jamal al-Din al-Afghani as reported by Blunt in his *India Under Ripon* (London: Unwin, 1909), 21. With thanks to Poorvi Bellur.
86. Blunt to Hamilton, Cairo, January 15, 1881, ADD MS 48,619, vol. 27, 2, Hamilton Papers, BL.
87. On Nasif as an eyewitness to the assassination of Sharif ʿAwn al-Husayn on March 14, 1880, see "Alms to Oblivion," vol. 1, 197, MS 21–1975, Blunt Papers, FW; and Wilfred Scawen Blunt, *The Future of Islam*, ed. Riad Nourallah (London: RoutledgeCurzon, 2002), 127.
88. Blunt to Hamilton, Cairo, January 15, 1881, ADD MS 48,619, 2, BL.
89. Blunt to Hamilton, Cairo, January 15, 1881, 2, BL.
90. Cole, *Colonialism and Revolution*, 218.
91. Cole, *Colonialism and Revolution*, 220, 235.
92. Blunt had also had encounters in London with the Armenian convert and Persian diplomat Mirza Malkam Khan (1834–1908). For more on ʿAbduh in the context of the times, see Cole, *Colonialism and Revolution*.
93. "Alms to Oblivion," MS 324–1975, 192–96, Blunt Papers, FW. Blunt later confessed that he had very nearly been converted by ʿAbduh, if only at a "rational" level,

7. FOR QUEEN, COUNTRY, AND CALIPH IN AFRICA

claiming he would never submit to the idea of an afterlife or the inconvenience of praying. "Alms to Oblivion," pt. 6 (Gods and False Gods), 11–15.
94. Blunt, *Secret History*.
95. Blunt to Hamilton, Damascus, March 23, 1881, Document 3, ADD MS 48,619, BL.
96. Blunt, *Future of Islam*, 174.
97. Cole, *Colonialism and Revolution*, 220.
98. Cole, 237.
99. Blunt to Gladstone, Cairo, December 21, 1881, ADD MS 48,619, 8r–10v, BL. The Hanafis maintained an outsized presence at al-Azhar and tended to lend their support to the Turkish ascendancy. See Cole, 36–38, 241. Cromer (*Modern Egypt*, 2:174) later noted that al-ʿAbbassi had been exiled to the Sudan by Khedive ʿAbbas I (r. 1848–1854) for refusing to grant him the sultanic privilege of ratifying death sentences.
100. Blunt to Gladstone, Cairo, December 21, 1881, BL.
101. Cole, *Colonialism and Revolution*, 237.
102. Blunt to Gladstone, Cairo, February 16, 1882, ADD MS 44,110, 3ff, BL.
103. Blunt to Gladstone, Cairo, February 16, 1882, 6r, BL.
104. Blunt to Gladstone, Cairo, February 16, 1882, 7v, BL.
105. Blunt to Gladstone, Cairo, February 16, 1882, 7v–8r, BL.
106. On the concept of *wataniyya* in Ottoman Egypt, see Mestyan, *Arab Patriotism*.
107. "Program of the National Party of Egypt," December 18, 1881, MS ADD 48,619, 12rff, BL; Berdine, *Accidental Tourist*, 256n100.
108. Blunt, *Secret History*, 256–61; John S. Galbraith, "The Trial of Arabi Pasha," *Journal of Imperial and Commonwealth History* 7, no. 3 (1979): 274–92, 284–85. See also "An Interview with Arabi Pasha," *Times of India*, October 20, 1887. or Abdulhamid's consistently negative views of ʿUrabi, whom his emissary proposed to lure to Istanbul with the promise of a medal in June 1882, see Selim Deringil, "The Ottoman Response to the Egyptian Crisis of 1881–82," *Middle Eastern Studies* 24, no. 1 (January 1988): 3–24.
109. Blunt to Hamilton, Hotel du Nil, Cairo, February 20, 1882, ADD MS 44,110, 10r–11r, BL.
110. "Alms to Oblivion," pt. 6, chap. 7 (The Wind and the Whirlwind), 2, 7, 23–24, Blunt Papers, FW.
111. "Alms to Oblivion," 13. See also *Secret History*, 226.
112. "Alms to Oblivion," 19. See also *Secret History*, 227.
113. A visitor to ʿUrabi in exile reported that he had gained his first introduction to the then colonel at Cairo in 1882 through Blunt's Armenian interpreter. See "Interview with Arabi Pasha."
114. ʿUrabi to Blunt, Cairo, April 1, 1882, under cover of Blunt to Gladstone, April 22, 1882, ADD MS 44,110, BL.
115. On the plot, see Berdine, *Accidental Tourist*, 155–80.
116. Cole, *Colonialism and Revolution*, 238.
117. Blunt to Gladstone, Crabbet Park, May 17, 1882, ADD MS 44,110, 30–40, BL.
118. "Alms to Oblivion," 56–60, Blunt Papers, FW.
119. Cole, *Colonialism and Revolution*, 244; Alms to Oblivion, MS 325–1975, p. 66.

120. Blunt to Hamilton, London, May 29, 1882, ADD MS 48,619, 20–22, BL; see also Blunt, *Secret History*, 290–92.
121. Blunt, 299.
122. Cole, *Colonialism and Revolution*, 245–47.
123. Cole, *Colonialism and Revolution*, 247.
124. ʻUrabi to Gladstone, Alexandria, 2 July 1882, ADD MS 44,110, 52–53, BL. ʻUrabi would later deny authorship of the letter after his capture. See E. Malet to Earl Granville, Cairo, September 27, 1882, in *Further Correspondence Respecting the Affairs of Egypt, Egypt. No. 1 (1883)* (London: Harrison & Sons, 1883), 29.
125. Fahmy, *All the Pasha's Men*, 252–53.
126. Blunt to Gladstone, July 16, 1882, 50–51, BL.
127. Blunt, *Secret History*, 400–10; see also "The Late E. H. Palmer: II. The Story of His Death," *Academy*, May 12, 1883, 329–30.
128. Blunt to Hamilton, Crabbet Park, July 27, 1882, ADD MS 48,619, 32–33, BL. Hamilton had already deemed Blunt misled in late May. See Berdine, *Accidental Tourist*, 188.
129. Galbraith, "Trial of Arabi Pasha," 277; memorandum of charges from Lieutenant Colonel C. W. Wilson, under cover of Malet to Granville, October 22, 1882, in *Further Correspondence*, 45.
130. Galbraith, "Trial of Arabi Pasha;" see also "Correspondence Between Khedive and Arabi," *Chicago Daily Tribune*, October 13, 1882.
131. Telegrams between Arabi and the Porte, in *Further Correspondence*, 71–72.
132. Deringil, "Ottoman Response," 5.
133. "Arabi Pasha and Islam," *Washington Post*, August 15, 1882; Queen Victoria's journals, August 28, 1882, Princess Beatrice's copies, vol. 77, 112, http://qvj.chadwyck.com.ezproxy.princeton.edu/home.do (accessed January 25, 2022).
134. Telegrams between Arabi and the Porte, in *Further Correspondence*, 71–72.
135. Napier later reported to Blunt that he had removed mention of the word "British" from the draft plea at the request of Nicholson. *Correspondence Respecting the Egyptian Exiles in Ceylon, Egypt. No. 8 (1883)* (London: Harrison & Sons, 1883), 2.
136. Galbraith, "Trial of Arabi Pasha," 274–92.
137. Broadly to Guest, Cairo, October 27, 1882, ADD MS 7936, BL. Emphasis original.
138. Blunt, *Secret History*, 472–73.
139. On Ceylon as a momentary destination, see Her Majesty's Government to Dufferin, draft telegram no. 19, December 8, 1882, Foreign Office Files, 78/4267, TNA.
140. A. M. Broadley, *How We Defended Arábi and His Friends: A Story of Egypt and the Egyptians* (London: Chapman & Hall, 1884); *Further Correspondence*, 154.
141. Note on Blunt to Hamilton, Crabbet Park, November 1, 1882, ADD MS 48,619, 38, BL.

8. Seven Pashas for Ceylon

1. Dufferin to Granville, Cairo, December 18, 1882, Foreign Office Files (FO) 78/4267, National Archives (TNA), Kew.
2. Anne Gregory, *Arabi and His Household* (London: Kegan Paul, Trench, 1882), 6.

8. SEVEN PASHAS FOR CEYLON

3. Enclosing Doc. Signed by Arabi and the Other Principal Chiefs, January 17, 1883, 4/158, item 32, Sri Lankan National Archives (SLNA), Colombo. The language of the Foreign Office translation has the exiles swearing "by God *and* the Koran." Compare Dufferin to Longden, Cairo, December 30, 1882, under cover of Herbert, February 21, 1883, FO 78/4267, TNA.
4. Mahumd Fahmi, *al-Bahr al-zakhir fi tarikh al-ʿalam wa akhbar al-awaʾil wa al-awakhir*, 4 vols. (Cairo: al-Matbaʿa al-Amiriyya, 1312), 1:234.
5. "Arabi as a Sailor," *New York Times*, March 5, 1883.
6. Report by Lieutenant Governor Douglas, January 11, 1883, FO 78/4267, TNA.
7. Report by Lieutenant Governor Douglas. On the Abcarius family and their move to Cairo, see Judith Cecily Laffan, "Negotiating Empires: 'British' Dragomans and Changing Identity in the 19th-Century Levant" (PhD diss., University of Queensland, 2011), 228–29.
8. Fahmi, *al-Bahr al-zakhir*, 1:234. Such enthusiasm was still remarked on in the months to come. See "Arabi Pasha Learning English," *New York Times*, January 7, 1884.
9. *Graphic*, February 24, 1883, reproduced in R. K. de Silva, *19th-Century Newspaper Engravings of Ceylon—Sri Lanka: Accompanied by Original Texts with Notes and Comments* (London: Serendib, 1998), 232–33.
10. Torsten Tschacher, "Circulating Islam: Understanding Convergence and Divergence in the Islamic Traditions of Maʿbar and Nusantara," in *Islamic Connections: Studies of South and Southeast Asia*, ed. R. Michael Feener and Terenjit Sevea (Singapore: Institute of Southeast Asian Studies, 2009), 48–67, 60.
11. Anoma Pieres, *Architecture and Nationalism in Sri Lanka: The Trouser Under the Cloth* (Routledge, 2017), 88.
12. Longden to the Earl of Derby, Kandy, January 21, 1883, FO 78/4267, TNA.
13. Longden to Derby, January 13, 1883, FO 78/4267, TNA. Emphasis original.
14. William Gregory, *Sir William Gregory, K.C.M.G., Formerly Member of Parliament and Sometime Governor of Ceylon: An Autobiography*, ed. Augusta Gregory (London: John Murray, 1894), 384.
15. Memo by J. Lambert, Simla, April 18, 1883, Simla 5, Foreign Department, Secret—E, Pros. October 1883, Nos. 66–73, Egyptian Exiles in Ceylon, National Archives of India. With thanks to Roy Bar Sadeh.
16. Memo by J. Lambert, April 18, 1883, National Archives of India.
17. Memo by J. Lambert.
18. Declaration under cover of H. Labouchere to Lord Edmund FitzMaurice, June 3, [1883], FO 78/4267, TNA.
19. *Correspondence Respecting the Egyptian Exiles in Ceylon, No. 8 (1883)* (London: Harrison & Sons, 1883), 1; Blunt to Labouchere, Crabbet Park, June 8, 1883, FO 78/4267, TNA.
20. Longden to the Earl of Derby, Colombo, July 6, 1883, FO 78/4267, TNA.
21. Lieutenant Governor Douglas to Lord Derby, October 11, 1883, FO 78/4267, TNA. See also Wilfrid Scawen Blunt, *India Under Ripon: A Private Diary* (London: T. Fisher, 1909), 19–20; and Fahmi, *al-Bahr al-zakhir*, 1:235.
22. "Mr. Wilfred Blunt in Ceylon," *Times of India*, November 6, 1883. See also A. C. Dep, *A History of Ceylon Police: Vol. 2 (1866-1913)* (n.p., 1969), 146; Rosemary Archer

8. SEVEN PASHAS FOR CEYLON

and James Fleming, eds., *Lady Anne Blunt: Journals and Correspondence, 1878-1917* (Cheltenham: Alexander Heriot, 1986), 157.
23. "Mr. Wilfred Blunt in Ceylon," *Times of India*, November 6, 1883.
24. Blunt, *India Under Ripon*, 26; John Douglas to the Earl of Derby, Colombo, November 29, 1883, FO 78/4267, TNA.
25. The anecdote about wine appears in Lambert's Simla report, cited above in note 16. Otherwise, see Fahmi, *al-Bahr al-zakhir*, 1:235; and Dep, *Ceylon Police*, 147.
26. Fahmi, 234-35; Dep, 147; Blunt, *India Under Ripon*, 23.
27. Fahmi, 1:235. A solicitous ʿUrabi subscribed to some form of Sufism and offered a charm he habitually wore to Blunt when convalescing. See Blunt, 22.
28. Fahmi, 1:236.
29. Wifrid Blunt, *Gordon at Khartoum: Being a Personal Narrative of Events, in Continuation of "A Secret History of the English Occupation of Egypt"* (London: S. Swift, 1911), 7, 40-42, 76-77. Blunt would still ponder such possibilities in 1889, just as he continued to press for the return of the exiles, ʿUrabi in particular, after he reconciled with Cromer. See Wilfred Scawen Blunt, *My Diaries: Being a Personal Narrative of Events, 1888-1914*, 2 vols. (New York: Alfred A. Knopf, 1923), 1:16.
30. Fahmi, *al-Bahr al-zakhir*, 1:235-36.
31. Fahmi, 236. As Blunt (*India Under Ripon*, 19) had it, Sabunji had sped ashore "like the raven from the Ark" and not returned. According to Zolondek ("Sabunji in England," 109), ʿUrabi had already been convinced of Sabunji's treachery to himself and Blunt by September.
32. Fahmi, 1:236. Copies of *al-Nahla* are missing after 1880. Blunt and Sabunji reconciled in the 1900s after Sabunji had served as translator to Abdulhamid. See Blunt, *Secret History*, 299.
33. Kramer, "Pen and Purse," 778; Fahmi, *al-Bahr al-zakhir*, 1:236.
34. On ʿUrabi's connection to General ʿUthman Digna (1840-1926), see Torsten Tschacher, " 'Walls of Illusion': Information Generation in Colonial Singapore and the Reporting of the Mahdi-Rebellion in Sudan, 1887-1890," in *Singapore in Global History*, ed. Derek Heng and Muhd Khairudin Aljunied (Amsterdam: Amsterdam University Press, 2011), 67-88, 74. Gregory would announce his view publicly in the wake of the death of General Gordon. See "Egypt and the Soudan," *Nineteenth Century*, March 1885, 434, 436.
35. Blunt, *Gordon at Khartoum*, 76-78.
36. Blunt would decry the "blunderheaded" decision from Bombay. Blunt to Hamilton, January 30 1884, ADD MS 48,619, 40, British Library (BL).
37. See, for instance, petition of Abd al-ʿAl and Tulba ʿIsmat, June 1883, FO 78/4267, TNA.
38. Sami also worried that ʿUrabi thought he had more money than he did. Petition of Yaʿqub Sami, Slave Island, October 31, 1883, FO 78/4267, TNA.
39. Viyaya Samaweera, "Arabi Pasha in Ceylon, 1883-1901," *Islamic Culture* 50, no. 4 (1976): 219-27, 223, citing *Times of Ceylon*, January 23, 1883; Gregory, *Autobiography*, 392-93.
40. W. S. Le Fenore to inspector general, Colombo, October 17, 1883, under cover of memo of inspector general of police, December 3, 1883, FO 78/4268, TNA. For contemporary hints of a less flattering assessment of Campbell's efforts, see

8. SEVEN PASHAS FOR CEYLON

Arthur C. Dep, *The Egyptian Exiles in Ceylon (Sri Lanka), 1883-1901* (Colombo: Arabi Pasha Centenary Celebrations Committee of the All Ceylon Muslim League, 1983), 32.

41. Memo of inspector general of police to colonial secretary, Colombo, December 3, 1883, FO 78/4268, TNA.
42. Memo of inspector general of police to colonial secretary.
43. Samaweera, "Arabi Pasha in Ceylon," 226.
44. Samaweera, 227, citing H. M. Z. Farouque, "Muslim Law in Ceylon: An Historical Outline," *Muslim Marriage and Divorce Law Reports*, vol. 4 (1972): 1-28. The agent at the time was F. R. Saunders (1838-1910).
45. Gordon to Derby, Nuwara Eliya, April 11-12, 1885, FO 78/4268, TNA. On March 28 ʿUrabi had written to the press strenuously denying having broken his word by commenting on politics, let alone Sudanese politics. *Ceylon Observer*, March 31, 1885.
46. Fahmi to Gregory, Colombo, March 24, 1883; Gregory to Derby, Coole, May 30, 1884; Tulba ʿIsmat to Gregory, Colombo, April 4, 1884; and Gordon to Derby, Kandy, May 19, 1884, FO 78/4268, TNA.
47. Yaʿqub Sami to E. Stanhope, principal secretary of state for the colonies, Colombo, December 1886, FO 78/4268, TNA. See also Galbraith, "Trial of Arabi Pasha," 287.
48. Yaʿqub Sami to the Earl of Derby, Colombo, April 16, 1885, FO 78/4268, TNA. Like ʿUrabi's wife, Sami's partner had not come on the *Mareotis*. She was also adjudged wealthy enough to make her own steam. See Dufferin to "Bertie," August 25, 1883, FO 78/4267, TNA.
49. The 1885 death of Campbell's wife also led to the exiles offering their condolences. See Dep, *Egyptian Exiles*, 19.
50. John Ferguson, *Mohammedanism in Ceylon: Moormen, Malay, Afghan, and Bengali Mohammedans* (Colombo: Observer, 1897), 12-13. For one vision of Fahmi's place in Egyptian historiography, see Yoav Di-Capua, *Gatekeepers of the Arab Past: Historians and History Writing in Twentieth-Century Egypt* (Berkeley: University of California Press, 2009), 44-45.
51. See, for example, their petition of May 20, 1897 to mark her jubilee: FO 78/5176, TNA.
52. Yaʿqub Sami to Gordon, Nuwara Eliya, June 6, 1887, FO 78/4268, TNA.
53. Sami, ʿAli Fahmi, and Mahmud Fahmi to Gordon, Colombo, September 15, 1887, FO 78/4268, TNA.
54. Fahmi, *al-Bahr al-zakhir*, 1:236.
55. Samaweera, "Arabi Pasha in Ceylon," 223n10; "A Day at Colombo," *Illustrated London News*, November 16, 1889, reproduced in De Silva, *Newspaper Engravings*, 258-59.
56. "Day at Colombo."
57. Albert Gleaves, *The Admiral: The Memoirs of Albert Gleaves, Admiral, USN* (Pasadena: Hope, 1985), 50.
58. ʿUrabi, Cinnamon Gardens, Colombo, June 4, 1887, under cover of Campbell, inspector general of police, to colonial secretary, Colombo, July 26, 1887, 6/7784, SLNA; see also Dep, *Egyptian Exiles*, 17.

8. SEVEN PASHAS FOR CEYLON

59. E. J. Tranchell, June 8–9, 1887, under report 8654, 6/7784, SLNA.
60. Inspector David, as quoted by Tranchell, July 13, 1887, under report 8654, 6/7784, SLNA. The *Bacchante* had been used for the royal tour of Princes George and Albert from 1879 to 1882, including to Ceylon and Egypt, though they were long gone by the time that Alexandria was set ablaze. It seems hard to fathom what the crew had endured, unless they had been aboard other ships or ashore during the invasion.
61. Tranchell, July 13, 1887, SLNA.
62. Tranchell.
63. "An Interview with Arabi Pasha," *Times of India*, October 20, 1887.
64. "Jubilee Celebration in Colombo," *Overland Ceylon Observer*, June 29, 1887. With thanks to Shamara Wettimuny.
65. Campbell to colonial secretary, Colombo, August 20, 1887, under report 8654, 6/7784, SLNA.
66. "The Egyptian Exiles' Procession," *Overland Ceylon Observer*, June 29, 1887; "Imperial Parliament Yesterday," *Manchester Guardian*, August 17, 1887.
67. Ferguson, *Ceylon in 1893*, 188–89.
68. Ferguson, 189–91.
69. İsmail Hakkı Göksoy, "Acehnese Appeals for Ottoman Protection in the Late Nineteenth Century," in *From Anatolia to Aceh: Ottomans, Turks, and Southeast Asia*, ed. A. C. S. Peacock and Annabel Teh Gallop (Oxford: British Academy, 2015), 175–97, 179. A translation of the brief report of Hussein Lebbe Markar is held in the Turkish National Archives: Y.A. HUS 232/66. With thanks to İsmail Hakkı Kadı, Duygu Coşkuntuna, and Şükrü Hanioğlu. Omer Lufti reported similar excitement caused by the arrival of an Ottoman Egyptian warship, the *Ibrahim*, at the Cape around 1865, though more research needs to be done in this to corroborate his intriguing account of marines handing out pencils and fezzes. See Omer Lutfi Effendi, *A Travelogue of My Journey to the Cape of Good Hope* (Cape Town: El-Khaleel, 1991), 28.
70. See, for instance, "The Turkish Man-Of-War Ertugroul," *Overland Ceylon Observer*, November 4, 1889.
71. "A Bankrupt Man-of-War," *Overland Ceylon Observer*, January 13, 1890; Barbara Andaya, "From Rūm to Tokyo: The Search for Anticolonial Allies by the Rulers of Riau, 1899–1914," *Indonesia* 24 (1977): 123–56; Göksoy, "Acehnese Appeals," 179–82.
72. "H.M.S. *Agamemnon* in Colombo Harbour," *Graphic*, October 17, 1885, reproduced in De Silva, *Newspaper Engravings*, 266–67.
73. Police File 5757, 6/8856, SLNA.
74. Blunt to Baring, May 17, 1890, MS 1-1975, 155, Blunt Papers, Fitzwilliam Museum (FW), Cambridge. In April, Gregory was reported as having a "specially interested" conversation with the exiled "pashas" ʿUrabi, Tulba, and ʿAli Fahmi when they joined his farewell reception at the Colombo Museum. See "Sir William Gregory's Leavetaking at the Museum," *Ceylon Observer*, April 14, 1890.
75. "Arabi and the Egyptian Exiles," *Ceylon Observer*, May 14, 1891.
76. Gordon to Knutsford, Colombo, and enclosures, May 22, 1890, FO 78/4589, TNA. See also copy in MS 48-1975, Blunt Papers, FW. The petition was originally

8. SEVEN PASHAS FOR CEYLON

mooted when the exiles (except for ʿAbd al-Al) had an interview with the newly arrived governor Havelock. See "The Egyptian Exiles," *Ceylon Observer*, May 30, 1890. For a cynical view of the claims and Gregory's difficulties with Cromer, see Fahmi, *al-Bahr al-zakhir*, 1:235–36.

77. Proceedings of the Board of Medical Officers, October 4, 1890, FO 78/4589, TNA.
78. Ellis to private secretary, September 26, 1890, FO 78/4589, TNA. Mahmud had married a daughter of Yaʿqub; see Fahmi, *al-Bahr al-zakhir*, 1:235.
79. Hugh Ledward to Colonial Office, Bangalore, December 3, 1890, FO 78/4589, TNA.
80. I was surprised to see so many such weapons on display during a visit in December 2019.
81. On Lipton, see the similarly dodgy James Mackay, *Sir Thomas Lipton: The Man Who Invented Himself* (New York: Random House, 2012), 136–38, 150. See also Fahmi, *al-Bahr al-zakhir*, 1:236–37.
82. Mackay, *Sir Thomas Lipton*, 137–38; "An Interesting Chat with Arabi Pasha," *Pall Mall Gazette*, January 27, 1892.
83. See, for instance, Dr. Rockwood, colonial surgeon, Colombo, March 28, 1891, FO 78/4589, TNA.
84. Arabi (the Husayni the Egyptian) to Lady Blunt, October 8, 1892, FO 78/4589, TNA.
85. Cromer, "The Ceylon Exiles," confidential, December 2, 1892, FO 78/4589, TNA.
86. Samir Muhammad Taha, *Mahmud Fahmi Pasha: Raʾis ʿumum arkan harb al-jaysh al-Misri qabil al-ihtilal al-Baritani sanat 1882* (Cairo: Maktabat Saʿid Raʿfat, 1984), 91.
87. "Arabi Pasha Interviewed," *Times of India*, March 28, 1893.
88. Petitions of Mahmud Sami, Yaʿqub Sami and Tulba ʿIsmat and "Dilruba, Inifer, and Amina" et al., Kandy, May 1899, FO 78/5176, TNA.
89. Dep, *Egyptian Exiles*, 22–23.
90. Petition of Tulba ʿIsmat to J. West Ridgeway, October 8, 1898, FO 78/5176, TNA.
91. H. White for colonial secretary to ʿUrabi, "Mahmood Femy Effendy," "Ali Femy Effendi," and "Yacoob Femy Effendi," Colombo, January 31, 1899, FO 78/5176, TNA.
92. ʿUrabi to private secretary of the governor, January 2 [sic] 1899, FO 78/5176, TNA.
93. Berdine, *Accidental Tourist*, 281n65. See also Mackay, *Sir Thomas Lipton*, 138, misrepresenting the Earl of Cromer (Evelyn Baring), *Modern Egypt*, 2 vols. (London: Macmillan, 1908), 1:323–37.
94. Richard Leslie Brohier, "The Boer Prisoner-of-War in Ceylon (1900–1902)," *Journal of the Dutch Burgher Union of Ceylon* 36, no. 8 (1946): 68–92. These were later outnumbered by those sent to India. See Isabel Hofmeyr, "South Africa's Indian Ocean: Boer Prisoners of War in India," *Social Dynamics: A Journal of African Studies* 38, no. 3 (2012): 363–80.
95. Quote from *Ceylon Mohamedan*, cited in Samaweera, "Arabi Pasha in Ceylon," 227; see also "Arabi Pasha's Farewell," *Times of India*, September 23, 1901.
96. It was agreed not to forward ʿUrabi's letter of thanks to the king. Lucas to Marquess of Landsdowne, May 29, 1901, FO 78/5176, TNA.
97. Cromer to Marquis of Landsdowne, Cairo, July 4, 1901, FO 78/5176, TNA; Dep, *Egyptian Exiles*, 21.
98. Dep, *Egyptian Exiles*, 21.

8. SEVEN PASHAS FOR CEYLON

99. A future Principal of Zahira, T. B. Jayah, was a member of the Malay community, rising to prominence in the 1920s. See chapter 10, page 291.
100. For typical instances, see no. 376, re: "pension for Doll Ganny" (1882), 4/157, SLNA; and no. 227, Colombo, May 6, 1890, re: "application for a post with the police for the son of Lieutenant Colonel Meaden, late of the Ceylon Rifles," 6/8856, SNLA. Incidentally, Meaden had been a cofounder of the Malay Cricket Club.
101. Skinner, *Fifty Years in Ceylon*, 13.
102. Sydney Prior Hall (1842–1922), the Prince of Wales arriving in Colombo, Sri Lanka, December 1, 1875, 931213, Royal Collection Trust (RCIN).
103. Blunt could only note of the Malays that they were a small community of former soldiers who mixed with the "Brahminical Tamils." Blunt, *India Under Ripon*, 23.
104. "Our Colonial Defences," *Graphic*, July 3, 1887, as reproduced in De Silva, *Newspaper Engravings*, 119.
105. R. Michael Feener, "Tabut: Muharram Observances in the History of Bengkulu," *Studia Islamika* 6, no. 2 (1999): 87–130; Clare Anderson, "History in and of a Penal Colony in the Bay of Bengal: Two Convict Mazars in the Andaman Islands," in *Belonging Across the Bay of Bengal: Religious Rites, Colonial Migrations, National Rights*, ed. Michael Francis Laffan (New York: Bloomsbury Academic, 2017), 193–206, 195–96.
106. David Lunn and Julia Byl, " 'One Story Ends and Another Begins': Reading the Syair Tabut of Encik Ali," *Indonesia and the Malay World* 45, no. 133 (2017): 391–420; Julia Byl, Raja Halid, Raja Iskandar, David Lunn, and Jenny McCallum, "The Syair Tabut of Encik Ali: A Malay Account of Muharram at Singapore, 1864," *Indonesia and the Malay World* 45, no. 133 (2017): 421–38.
107. "A Plea for Araby," *Times of India*, October 28, 1882.
108. "Sir Wm. Gregory and the *London Times* on Arabi," *Weekly Ceylon Observer*, October 21, 1882; "Sir William Gregory on Arabi Pasha," *Madras Mail*, November 2, 1882.
109. John Ferguson, *Ceylon in the "Jubilee Year"* (Colombo: J. Haddon, 1887), 359. The equation of Pasha and "badger" was not so strange, given evidence from the *Wajah Selong*, where the word "pasha" was consistently spelled "batsha." See "Akhbar telegram," *Wajah Selong*, October 18, 1895. We may also recall from chapter 4 how Rafiek of Cape Town claimed to have been instructed by a man called "Albaatje."
110. Thomas Metcalf, *Imperial Connections: India in the Indian Ocean Arena, 1860–1920* (Berkeley: University of California Press, 2007), 102–35.
111. Ricci, *Banishment*, 234–36.
112. B. A. Hussainmiya, "Baba Ounus Saldin: An Account of a Malay Literary Savant of Sri Lanka (b. 1832–d. 1906)," *JMBRAS* 64, no. 2 (1991): 103–34, 115.
113. *Wajah Selong*, October 18, 1895.
114. "Wajah Selong" [Editorial], *Wajah Selong*, November 24, 1895.
115. Named were: Ahmad Hajji Hashim in Singapore; Muhammad bin Shahab al-Din ibn Tambi Qasim at Malacca; and Hajji Abd al-Qadir bin Hajji Muhammad Salih at Penang.

8. SEVEN PASHAS FOR CEYLON

116. "Surat dari Tanah Melayu 'Perak,' " *Wajah Selong*, January 17, 1896.
117. "Wajah Selong" [Editorial], *Wajah Selong*, October 13, 1895.
118. Mohamed Salleh bin Perang in *Reputations Live On: An Early Malay Autobiography*, ed. Amin Sweeney (Berkeley: University of California Press, 1980); "An Exposition Concerning the Malays," in *Modernist Islam: A Sourcebook*, ed. Charles Kurzman (Oxford: Oxford University Press, 2002), 339–43.
119. H. Taner Seben, *The First Turkish Representatives in Singapore and Consul General Ahmed Ataullah Efendi* (Singapore: Republic of Turkey Embassy, 2015), 19–20.
120. "His Highness the Maharaja of Johore," *Ceylon Observer*, March 31, 1885.
121. Dep, *Egyptian Exiles*, 22. Ibrahim's tour of Siam, Johor, and Japan was curtailed by a fall from a horse at Singapore: see, for instance, "Arabi Pasha's Son," *Ceylon Observer*, May 25, 1899.
122. "Alamat yang khair," *Wajah Selong*, September 29, 1895; Michael Powell, "Fragile Identities: The Colonial Consequences of CJR Le Mesurier in Ceylon," *Journal of Colonialism & Colonial History* 11, no. 1 (2010): n.p. Cecil Le Mesurier (1855–1923) recast himself during the Great War as a founding editor of an anti-German paper in Perth, the *All-British*.
123. See, for instance, "Akhbar di negeri Stambul," *Wajah Selong*, September 29, 1895; and "Hidayah dari Sultan," *Wajah Selong*, April 12, 1896.
124. "Sembahyang dalam peperangan," *Wajah Selong*, September 16, 1897.
125. "Di dalam negeri Aceh," *Wajah Selong*, October 29, 1897.
126. Tschacher, "Walls of Illusion," 80–83.
127. For the laconic account of the Sumatran pilgrims, see Min Makkah ila Mesir, manuscript held by the Surau Sheikh Abdurrahman, Kecematan Akabiluru, Kabupaten Lima Puluh Kota, Western Sumatra, EAP205/3/2, BL, https://eap.bl.uk/archive-file/EAP205-3-2 (accessed January 21, 2022).
128. See, for instance, Latifa Muhammad Salim, ʿUrabi wa rifaquhu fi jannat Adam, 1883-1901 (Cairo: Maktabat al-Anjalu al-Misriyya, 1987); Ahmad ʿAbd al-Majid al-Fiqi, *Qissat Ahmad ʿUrabi* (Cairo: al-Dar al-Qawmiyya, 1966); and [Ahmad ʿUrabi] *Mudhakkirat al-zaʿim Ahmad ʿUrabi* (Cairo: Dar al-Maʿarif, 1983), esp. 59–61.
129. On al-Barudi, see Terri Deyoung, *Mahmud Sami al-Barudi: Reconfiguring Society and the Self* (Syracuse, NY: Syracuse University Press, 2015).
130. G. Schofield, "Notes and Communications," *Bulletin of the School of Oriental and African Studies, University of London* 24, no. 1 (1961): 139–41. He may also have offered it after requests from the War Office for his side of the story. See requests of H. G. Deedes, January 29, 1883 and secretary of state, February 21, 1883, 4/158, SLNA. See also ʿUrabi Pasha, *Mudhakkirat al-zaʿim*.
131. Fahmi, *al-Bahr al-zakhir*, 1:236–37; see also *Mudhakkirat Mahmud Basha Fahmi: Wazir ashghal al-thawra al-ʿUrabiyya al-munaffi wa-l-mutawaffi bi-Saylan* (Cairo: al-Shinnawi, 1976), 99.
132. Muhammad ʿAwda, *Sabʿat bashawat wa suwar ukhra* (Cairo: Ruz al-Yusuf, 1971), 17–28, 23. In keeping with the time of writing, ʿAwda had the pashas rebelling not against the khedive or the sultan, but the British invaders.
133. Toulba, *Ceylon*.
134. Rennell Rodd to the Marquess of Landsdowne, Cairo, October 1, 1901, FO 78/5176, TNA.

135. Rennell Rodd to the Marquess of Landsdowne.
136. "Arabi Pasha in Cairo," *Times of India*, November 2, 1901; Di-Capua, *Gatekeepers of the Arab Past*, 172–74.
137. Blunt, *My Diaries*, 2:12–13, 15.
138. An exception would appear to be brief correspondence of 1910 concerning Sufi practices on the island: "Tariqat al-Shadhiliyya," *al-Manar* 13 (1910): 104. With thanks to Roy Bar Sadeh.
139. Toulba, *Ceylon*, 108. ʿUrabi only features in the book as the centerpiece of a much-reprinted image of the exiles taken from Ferguson's *Ceylon Illustrated*. See Toulba, *Ceylon*, facing 224.

9. A Caliph for Greater Java

1. On ʿUmar and his brother Ahmad, a restorer of mosques and graves in Tarim, see Engseng Ho, *The Graves of Tarim: Genealogy and Mobility Across the Indian Ocean* (Berkeley: University of California Press, 2006), 69–70, 80–83.
2. For an authoritative history of Jeddah, see Ulrike Freitag, *A History of Jeddah: The Gate to Mecca in the Nineteenth and Twentieth Centuries* (Cambridge: Cambridge University Press, 2020). On the 1858 massacre, see William Ochsenwald, *Religion, Society, and the State in Arabia: The Hijaz Under Ottoman Control, 1840-1908* (Columbus: Ohio State University Press, 1984), 143–51. Regarding its momentary attribution to Sayyid Fadl, see also Wilson Jacko Jacob, *For God or Empire: Sayyid Fadl and the Indian Ocean World* (Stanford, CA: Stanford University Press, 2019), 103–5.
3. In 1872 Alsagoff would commission the SS *Jeddah* from a Scottish firm, which steamed into infamy when its cargo of returned pilgrims was abandoned by its European crew and his nephew ʿUmar in 1880. Alsagoff and family were not troubled and maintained great wealth in the Hijaz. See Michael Christopher Low, *Imperial Mecca: Ottoman Arabia and the Indian Ocean Hajj* (New York: Columbia University Press, 2020), 189–90, 228–29, 239.
4. On Yusr, see Freitag, *History of Jeddah*, 61–62, 126–27, 164.
5. J. W. Norton-Kyshe, *Cases Heard and Determined, 1808-90*, 4 vols. (Singapore: Singapore & Straits Printing Office, 1885–1890), 1:439.
6. William, Roff, "Sanitation and Security: The Imperial Powers and the Nineteenth Century Hajj," *Arabian Studies* 6 (1982): 143–60; Low, *Imperial Mecca*, 117–66; John Slight, *The British Empire and the Hajj, 1865-1956* (Cambridge, MA: Harvard University Press, 2015).
7. See James L. Gelvin and Nile Green, eds., *Global Muslims in the Age of Steam and Print* (Berkeley: University of California Press, 2013).
8. Alfred Russel Wallace, *The Malay Archipelago: The Land of the Orang-Utan, and the Bird of Paradise* (London: Macmillan, 1869).
9. Lodewijk Willem Christiaan van den Berg, *Le Hadhramout et les colonies arabes dans l'archipel Indien* (Batavia: Impr. du gouvernement, 1886). His French rendering of the *Minhaj al-talibin* had already been recommended to the Ceylonese

government in 1883. Almarie Rumsey, March 10, 1883, under cover of Derby to Longden, March 31, 1883, 4/158, Sri Lankan National Archives (SLNA), Colombo.
10. Takashi Shiraishi, *An Age in Motion: Popular Radicalism in Java, 1912-1926* (Ithaca, NY: Cornell University Press, 1990).
11. İsmail Hakkı Kadı and A. C. S. Peacock, eds., *Ottoman-Southeast Asian Relations: Sources from the Ottoman Archives*, 2 vols. (Leiden: Brill, 2020), 1:419–21; hereafter *OSEAR*.
12. *OSEAR*, 1:422–23; see also H. Taner Seben, *The First Turkish Representatives in Singapore and Consul General Ahmed Ataullah Efendi* (Singapore: Republic of Turkey Embassy, 2015), 8.
13. Nurfadzilah Yahaya, *Fluid Jurisdictions: Colonial Law and Arabs in Southeast Asia* (Ithaca, NY: Cornell University Press, 2020), 35.
14. *OSEAR*, 1:423–25. The trader was Martin Hymans.
15. *OSEAR*, 1:426–27.
16. *OSEAR*, 1:170–76.
17. *OSEAR*, 1:168–70.
18. Anthony Reid, "Habib Abdur-Rahman az-Zahir (1833–1896)," *Indonesia* 13 (1972): 39.
19. İsmail Hakkı Göksoy, "Acehnese Appeals for Ottoman Protection in the Late Nineteenth Century," in *From Anatolia to Aceh: Ottomans, Turks, and Southeast Asia*, ed. A. C. S. Peacock and Annabel Teh Gallop (Oxford: British Academy, 2015), 175–97, 176–77.
20. Reid, "Habib Abdur-Rahman." See also Francis Loch to C. Gonne, Aden, January 3, 1879, Foreign Office Files (FO) 78/3615, National Archives (TNA), Kew. With thanks to Saumyashree Ghosh.
21. *OSEAR*, 1:427–29. On Arifin, a spy in the pay of the Dutch consul at Singapore, see Anthony Reid, *An Indonesian Frontier: Acehnese and Other Histories of Sumatra* (Leiden: KITLV, 2005), 262–65.
22. *OSEAR*, 1:195–240. See also Jan Schmidt, *Through the Legation Window: Four Essays on Dutch, Dutch-Indian, and Ottoman History* (Istanbul: Neerlands Historisch-Archaologisch Instituut, 1992), 60–61.
23. *OSEAR*, 1:430–32.
24. Reid, "Habib Abdur-Rahman," 44.
25. Michael Francis Laffan, "'A Watchful Eye': The Meccan Plot of 1881 and Changing Dutch Perceptions of Islam in Indonesia," *Archipel* 63, no. 1 (2002): 79–108.
26. Known to many in Medina, Shamwili was a nephew of the more famous Imam Shamil. See Vladimir Braginsky, *The Turkic-Turkish Theme in Traditional Malay Literature: Imagining the Other to Empower the Self* (Leiden: Brill, 2015), 174–79.
27. Schmidt, *Legation Window*, 74–75.
28. Laffan, "Watchful Eye," 92–94.
29. "The Eastern Question," *Times of London*, June 5, 1876.
30. For the rumors of ʿUrabi as a Mahdi-like figure, see Juan Cole, *Colonialism and Revolution in the Middle East: Social and Cultural Origins of Egypt's ʿUrabi Movement* (Princeton, NJ: Princeton University Press, 1993), 262–63.
31. *OSEAR*, 1:433.
32. *OSEAR*, 1:432–34.

9. A CALIPH FOR GREATER JAVA

33. *OSEAR*, 1:436–37.
34. *OSEAR*, 2:769–71.
35. *OSEAR*, 2:772–73.
36. By his own account, Ghalib obtained much of his information on the Indies from a civil servant from the Ministry of War, J. E. de Sturler, who was offered a Mecidiye medal in 1885. *OSEAR*, 1:470–74.
37. *OSEAR*, 1:438–39.
38. *OSEAR*, 1:476–86
39. *OSEAR*, 1:485.
40. *OSEAR*, 1:485.
41. *OSEAR*, 1:486.
42. *OSEAR*, 1:488–89.
43. *OSEAR*, 1:243–64; Göksoy, "Acehnese Appeals," 179–81.
44. Wilfred Scawen Blunt, *My Diaries: Being a Personal Narrative of Events, 1888-1914*, 2 vols. (New York: Knopf, 1923), 1:96.
45. There is the chance that the interpolation "(Ceylon)" was an edit by her daughter Beatrice. See Queen Victoria's journals, July 12, 1878, Princess Beatrice's copies, vol. 69, 22–23, http://qvj.chadwyck.com.ezproxy.princeton.edu/home.do (accessed January 25, 2022).
46. *OSEAR*, 2:580–83; Göksoy, "Acehnese Appeals," 181.
47. *OSEAR*, 2:585–90.
48. Blunt, *My Diaries*, 1:96; *OSEAR*, 1:363–67.
49. Iza Hussin, "Textual Trajectories: Re-reading the Constitution and Majalah in 1890s Johor," *Indonesia and the Malay World* 41, no. 120 (2013): 255–72. On Hatice Hanım, see Seben, *First Turkish Representatives*, 19.
50. Seben, 11.
51. E. Gobée and C. Adriaanse, eds., *Ambtelijke adviezen van C. Snouck Hurgronje, 1889-1936*, 3 vols. (The Hague: Nijhoff, 1957–1965), 2:1646; hereafter *AA*.
52. *OSEAR*, 2:707–10. There were six ʿAttas boys in Istanbul that year, with two each at the Imperial School, the Orphans' School, and the School of Civil Services.
53. *OSEAR*, 2:714–23. On Dhofar and the efforts of Sayyid Fadl, see S. Tufan Buzpinar, "Abdülhamid II and Sayyid Fadl Pasha of Hadramawt: An Arab Dignitary's Ambitions (1876–1900)," *Journal of Ottoman Studies* 13 (1993): 227–39. See also Seema Alavi, *Muslim Cosmopolitanism in the Age of Empire* (Cambridge, MA: Harvard University Press, 2015), 126–27, 155–56.
54. C. Snouck Hurgronje, *Mekka in the Latter Part of the 19th Century: Daily Life, Customs, and Learning of the Moslems of the East-Indian Archipelago*, trans. J. H. Monahan (Leiden: Brill, 1931), 231–33.
55. Ahmad b. Zayni Dahlan, *al-Futuhat al-Islamiyya baʿda mudiyy al-futuhat al-nabawiyya* (Cairo: al-Halabi, 1968), 2:147.
56. Dahlan, *Futuhat*, 2:290.
57. On Egypt, see Dahlan, 2:292–93.
58. Dahlan, 2:293–309; Heather J. Sharkey, "Aḥmad Zaynī Daḥlān's *al-Futuḥāt al-Islāmiyya*: A Contemporary View of the Sudanese Mahdi," *Sudanic Africa* 5 (1994): 67–75.

9. A CALIPH FOR GREATER JAVA

59. For Dahlan's epistolature and the role of Ahmad b. Hasan al-ʿAttas in shaping his history of the sayyids and the Mahdi, see Ulrike Freitag, *Indian Ocean Migrants and State Formation in Hadhramaut: Reforming the Homeland* (Leiden: Brill, 2003), 201–8.
60. Dahlan, *Futuhat*, 1:315.
61. Michael Francis Laffan, *The Makings of Indonesian Islam: Orientalism and the Narration of a Sufi Past* (Princeton, NJ: Princeton University Press, 2011), 53–54.
62. C. Snouck Hurgronje, "Vergeten jubilé's," in A. J. Wensinck, ed., *Verspreide geschriften van C. Snouck Hurgronje*, 6 vols. (Leiden: Brill, 1923–1924), vol. 4, part 2, 415–36.
63. *AA*, 2:1615–28.
64. *OSEAR*, 2:512–19.
65. *OSEAR*, 2:519.
66. *OSEAR*, 2:805–12.
67. The four principal signatories were Husayn b. Muhsin al-ʿAttas, ʿAli b. Shihab, Taha b. Ahmad al-Haddad, and ʿAbd al-Qadir b. Husayn al-ʿAydarus. *OSEAR*, 2:813–18.
68. *OSEAR*, 2:600–601.
69. Laffan, *Makings of Indonesian Islam*, 162–64.
70. *OSEAR*, 2:605–6.
71. *OSEAR*, 2:598–99.
72. Braginsky, *Turkic-Turkish Theme*, 163, 167, 173–74.
73. *Wazir India*, August 29, 1878, with news of Aceh and names of the newly appointed ministers of Abdulhamid's government; and October 3, 1878, on Egyptian aid for the Ottomans against Russia. Aceh, Habib Zahir, and Japan were also frequently brought up during its brief existence. See Ahmat Adam, *The Vernacular Press and the Emergence of Modern Indonesian Consciousness* (Ithaca, NY: Cornell University Press, 1995), 40–41.
74. Sunil S. Amrith, "Islam's Eastern Frontiers: Tamil, Chinese, and Malay Worlds," in *Oceanic Islam: Muslim Universalism and European Imperialism*, ed. Sugata Bose and Ayesha Jalal (New Delhi: Bloomsbury India, 2020), 55–76, 66.
75. M. C. Ricklefs, *Polarising Javanese Society: Islamic and Other Visions, c. 1830–1930* (Singapore: NUS Press, 2007), 64.
76. F. Wiggers, *Toerki dan Joenani (Griekenland)* (Batavia: Albrecht, 1897). On Wiggers, see also Chiara Formichi, "Indonesian Readings of Turkish History," in *From Anatolia to Aceh: Ottomans, Turks and Southeast Asia*, ed. A. C. S. Peacock and Annabel Teh Gallop (Oxford: British Academy, 2015), 241–59, 243–44.
77. *OSEAR*, 1:372–73.
78. *OSEAR*, 2:532–33. On Sayyid ʿUthman and his prayers, see Nico Kaptein, *Islam, Colonialism and the Modern Age in the Netherlands East Indies: A Biography of Sayyid ʿUthman (1822–1914)* (Leiden: Brill, 2014), 144–51.
79. "Photografisch Atelier [Ohannes] Kurkdjian, De Arabische gemeenschap voor een erepoort bij een moskee in Soerabaja ter gelegenheid van de inhuldiging van Wilhelmina" (From the studio of Ohannes Kurkdjian, the Arab community before a gate of honour beside a mosque in Surabaya on the occasion of the inauguration of Wilhelmina). TM-60003143, NV, Collectie

9. A CALIPH FOR GREATER JAVA

Nationaal Museum van Wereldculturen, https://data.collectienederland.nl/search/?q=TM-60003143 (accessed January 26, 2022). For a reproduction of this image taken in August 1898, see Yahaya, *Fluid Jurisdictions*, jacket and 102.
80. Such reportage was duly summarized by Snouck in his letters to the governor-general. See *AA*, 2:1619–40.
81. Anthony Reid, *The Ottomans in Southeast Asia*, Asia Research Institute Working Paper Series, no. 36 (Singapore: ARI, 2005), 14; Seben, *First Turkish Representatives*, 19. Kamil Efendi had still not departed from Batavia in December 1898. *OSEAR*, 2:607.
82. On the experiences of the students, see Schmidt, *Legation Window*, 91–102. See also *OSEAR*, 2:820–21.
83. *OSEAR*, 2:614–17. Such efforts had been anticipated in Sumatra by a European merchant in 1890, who imported six hundred Ottoman Qurʾans. *OSEAR*, 2:590–92.
84. *OSEAR*, 2:615.
85. *OSEAR*, 1:445–47.
86. Seben, *First Turkish Representatives*, 13–14.
87. *OSEAR*, 1:447–49; Seben, 12–14.
88. "The Turkish Consul-General to Singapore at Colombo," *Singapore Free Press and Mercantile Advertiser*, October 31, 1901. For more documentation on Attaoullah's appointment, see Seben.
89. Braginsky, *Turkic-Turkish Theme*, 133, citing Locher, 119–21, 234–35.
90. *AA*, 2:1719.
91. Seben, *First Turkish Representatives*, 16–18; for contemporary descriptions and admiration, see also "Death of the Turkish Consul," *Straits Times*, November 10, 1903; and November 11, 1903; and "Funeral of the Hon. Attouallah Bey," *Singapore Free Press and Mercantile Advertiser*, November 11, 1903.
92. "Deaths," *Straits Times*, November 10, 1903.
93. "Funeral of the Hon. Attouallah Bey."
94. *AA*, 2:1719–25; *OSEAR*, 1:450–51.
95. *OSEAR*, 1:451–53.
96. Schmidt, *Legation Window*, 99–100.
97. *AA*, 2:1737–41.
98. On ʿAli b. Sahl, see *OSEAR*, 2:740–41.
99. *OSEAR*, 2:743–74, 747.
100. *OSEAR*, 2:626–27.
101. Kaptein, *Islam, Colonialism, and the Modern Age*, 159–60.
102. Anne K. Bang, *Islamic Sufi Networks in the Western Indian Ocean (c. 1880-1940): Ripples of Reform* (Leiden: Brill, 2014).
103. Achmat Davids, *The Mosques of Bo-Kaap: A Social History of Islam at the Cape* (Athlone: South African Institute of Arabic and Islamic Research, 1980), 56; Bang, *Sufi Networks*, 99.
104. Schmidt, *Legation Window*, 99.
105. *AA*, 2:1557.
106. For discussion of *kafaʾa* in the Indies, see Ho, *Graves of Tarim*, 173–87.

9. A CALIPH FOR GREATER JAVA

107. "Fatihat al-sana al-thalithata ʿashar," *al-Manar*, April 10, 1910.
108. Mandal notes that he and Hasan Djajadiningrat were members by 1910. Sumit K. Mandal, *Becoming Arab: Creole Histories and Modern Identity in the Malay World* (Cambridge: Cambridge University Press, 2018), 168. According to Bin Hashim, Dahlan stood down in February 1915 to concentrate on his work in education. *al-Bashir* 2, no. 22, April 1915.
109. Kaptein, *Islam and Colonialism*, 237–49.
110. On Surkati, see Natalie Mobini-Kesheh, *The Hadrami Awakening: Community and Identity in the Netherlands East Indies, 1900-1942* (Ithaca, NY: SEAP, 1999): 54–55; Ahmed Ibrahim Abu Shouk, "An Arabic Manuscript on the Life and Career of Ahmad Muhammad Sûrkatî and his Irshâdî Disciples in Java," in *Transcending Borders: Arabs, Politics, Trade, and Islam in Southeast Asia*, ed. Huub de Jonge and Nico Kaptein (Leiden: KITLV, 2002), 203–17.
111. Jajang A. Rohmana, *Informan Sunda Masa Kolonial: Surat-Surat Haji Hasan Mustapa untuk C. Snouck Hurgronje dalam Kurun 1894-1923* (Yogyakarta: Octopus, 2018), 208; see also Julian Millie, ed., *Hasan Mustapa: Ethnicity and Islam in Indonesia* (Clayton: Monash University Press, 2017).

10. For Arabs, Arabic, and the Community

1. Bart Luttikhuis and Arnout van der Meer, "1913 in Indonesian History: Demanding Equality, Changing Mentality," *TRaNS: Trans-Regional and -National Studies of Southeast Asia* 8, no. 2 (2020): 115–33.
2. For recent treatment of this moment, see Tim Harper, *Underground Asia: Global Revolutionaries and the Assault on Empire* (Cambridge, MA: Belknap Press of Harvard University Press, 2021), 155–56.
3. Luttikhuis and van der Meer, "1913 in Indonesian History."
4. Arnout van der Meer, *Performing Power: Cultural Hegemony, Identity, and Resistance in Colonial Indonesia* (Ithaca, NY: Cornell University Press, 2021), 77–110.
5. "A Turkish Ceremony," *Straits Times*, November 18, 1901.
6. Spakler to governor general, Singapore, August 9, 1906, A 190, 451, 2.05.03, Nationaal Archief (NA), The Hague.
7. On the late amir of Afghanistan, Abd al-Rahman Khan (d. 1901), see "Nasihat al-Amir Abdul Rahim yaitu Raja Afghanistan kepada anaknya al-Amir Habib al-Khan," *al-Imam*, December 1907.
8. Hazeu to governor general, Batavia, December 16, 1908, A 190, 455, 2.05.03, NA.
9. Michael Francis Laffan, *The Makings of Indonesian Islam: Orientalism and the Narration of a Sufi Past* (Princeton, NJ: Princeton University Press, 2011), 183–88.
10. Laffan, *Makings of Indonesian Islam*, 187–88.
11. Harry Poeze, "Early Indonesian Emancipation: Abdul Rivai, Van Heutsz, and the Bintang Hindia," *BKI* 145, no. 1 (1989): 87–106.
12. S. L. van der Wal, ed., *De Opkomst van de Nationalistische Beweging in Nederlands-Indie: Een Bronnenpublikatie* (Groningen: J. B. Wolters, 1967), 44, 158, 229, 242, 488.

10. FOR ARABS, ARABIC, AND THE COMMUNITY

13. "al-Hilal al-ahmar," *al-Munir*, December 10, 1912; Sumit Mandal, "Forging a Modern Arab Identity in Java in the Early Twentieth Century," in *Transcending Borders: Arabs, Politics, Trade, and Islam in Southeast Asia*, ed. Huub de Jonge and Nico Kaptein (Leiden: KITLV, 2002), 163–84, 168–69; Kees van Dijk, *The Netherlands Indies and the Great War, 1914-1918* (Leiden: KITLV, 2007), 295–96. For Abu Bakr and the Red Crescent, see "al-Sayyid Abu Bakr b. ʿAbdallah al-ʿAttas," *Burubudur*, February 20, 1922.
14. Jajang A. Rohmana, *Informan Sunda Masa Kolonial: Surat-Surat Haji Hasan Mustapa untuk C. Snouck Hurgronje dalam Kurun 1894-1923* (Yogyakarta: Octopus, 2018), 106–7. For early mention of donations to the Red Crescent to aid the Balkans, see report of D. A. Rinkes for May 1913 in Van der Wal, *Opkomst*, 189.
15. Chiara Formichi, "Indonesian Readings of Turkish History," in *From Anatolia to Aceh: Ottomans, Turks, and Southeast Asia*, ed. A. C. S. Peacock and Annabel Teh Gallop (Oxford: British Academy, 2015), 241–59, 244.
16. On *Neracha*, see William R. Roff, *Bibiography of Malay and Arabic Periodicals* (London: Oxford University Press, 1972), 33.
17. "Dari sejuz' ke sejuz'," *al-Munir*, April 8, 1913.
18. Mandal, "Forging a Modern Arab Identity," 169; "Al-Ittihad," *al-Munir*, January 9, 1913. Ahmad Fauzi Maharaja (b. 1890) was from Sambas, arriving in Cairo in 1910 with his relative Muhammad Basyuni (b. 1885). Lyst der Nederl: Indische onderdanen, May 1913, A 190, 451, 2.05.03, NA. Fadhloelah's presence is harder to discern in the Dutch lists, though he may be identified with the Banjarnegaran representative of Sarekat Islam in 1924.
19. Van der Wal, *Opkomst*, 384–85. Plans for his school, al-Iqbal, were first advertised in *al-Imam* in 1907. See "Peraturan madrasa," *al-Imam*, November 7, 1907.
20. "al-Tarhib bi'l-Bashir," *al-Bashir*, January 5, 1914.
21. Nico Kaptein, *Islam, Colonialism, and the Modern Age in the Netherlands East Indies: A Biography of Sayyid ʿUthman, 1822-1914* (Leiden: Brill, 2014), 161–89.
22. For correspondence with Rida, see "Halat al-muslimin fi Jawah wa al-islah," *al-Manar*, 29 Shawwal 1329 (October 22, 1911). Bin Hashim claimed ninety women subscribers by January 1915. Natalie Mobini-Kesheh, "The Arab Periodicals of the Netherlands East Indies, 1914–1942," *BKI* 152, no. 2 (1996): 236–56, 244.
23. Mandal, "Forging a Modern Arab Identity," 174.
24. "Kayfa yanhada al-ʿArab?," *al-Bashir*, January 19, 1914.
25. "Halat al-ʿArab al-hadira," *al-Bashir*, April 7, 1914.
26. "Innama al-muslimun ikhwa," *al-Bashir*, April 7, 1914. With thanks to Tom Hoogervorst for so kindly checking.
27. "al-Lugha al-ʿarabiyya," *al-Bashir*, January 5, 1914.
28. "Surabaya," *al-Bashir*, February 2, 1914.
29. "Nahnu Hadramiyyin qabla kull shay,'" *al-Bashir*, April 1915; see also article of same title in *al-Iqbal*, April 17, 1919.
30. "Menjawab karangan tidak mau campur," *al-Bashir*, January 5, 1914.
31. "La tastaʿjalu bi-l-hukm," *al-Bashir*, June 1, 1914.
32. ʿAli b. Shihab, "Ma sabab hadha al-siyal?," *al-Bashir*, July 20, 1914.

33. Van Dijk, *Indies and Great War*, 73–124. See also Heather Streets-Salter, *World War One in Southeast Asia: Colonialism and Anticolonialism in an Era of Global Conflict* (Cambridge: Cambridge University Press, 2021).
34. "Qawi [sic] al-difaʿ ʿan al-Hind al-Hulandiyya wa ziyataduha," *al-Bashir*, May 18, 1914.
35. "Majalla jadida," *al-Bashir*, May 18, 1914.
36. *al-Bashir*, April 1915; Van de Wal, *Opkomst*, 400n1, 439. For an earlier instance of campaigning, see "al-Hilal al-ahmar," *al-Bashir*, January 29, 1915. In once-neutral British India, the Ali brothers had been fined for supporting the Ottoman cause in the Balkans in early 1913. Gail Minault, *The Khilafat Movement: Religious Symbolism and Political Mobilization in India* (New York: Columbia University Press, 1982), 24.
37. Van de Wal, *Opkomst*, 385.
38. "Takhlis asbab al-harb," *al-Bashir*, December 18, 1914.
39. "al-ʿAlam al-islami izaʾa al-harb al-hadira," *al-Bashir*, January 29, 1915.
40. Snouck believed that his correspondence with German Orientalists had led to the retraction. See E. Gobée and C. Adriaanse, eds., *Ambtelijke adviezen van C. Snouck Hurgronje 1889-1936*, 3 vols. (The Hague: Nijhoff, 1957–1965), 2:1352–54; Jan Schmidt, *Through the Legation Window: Four Essays on Dutch, Dutch-Indian, and Ottoman History* (Istanbul: Nederlands Historisch-Archaeologisch Instituut, 1992), 133–39.
41. Snouck Hurgronje to secretary general, Department of Colonies, January 25, 1915, A 190, 451, 2.05.03, NA.
42. Van de Wal, *Opkomst*, 400, 439; Van Dijk, *Netherlands Indies and the Great War*, 295–96.
43. Van Dijk, 315.
44. For the committee to raise money to collect the pilgrims and propaganda to warn others away from the Hijaz, see Van Dijk, 300–301. For the initially supportive relationship of Rinkes and Sarekat Islam, see Van der Meer, *Performing Power*, 123.
45. Van de Wal, *Opkomst*, 439n1.
46. Minault, *Khilafat Movement*, 37, 51.
47. A. P. Kannangara, "The Riots of 1915 in Sri Lanka: A Study," *Past and Present* 102 (1984): 130–65.
48. It also made some in the Indies more aware of Muslims on the Cocos Islands. "Poeloe Kokos atau Keeling," *al-Bashir*, January 29, 1915.
49. Tim Harper, "Singapore, 1915, and the Birth of the Asian Underground," *Modern Asian Studies* 47, no. 6 (2013): 1782–811. See also his *Underground Asia*, 241–54; Streets-Salter, *World War One in Southeast Asia*, 17–87.
50. Nurfadzilah Yahaya, *Fluid Jurisdictions: Colonial Law and Arabs in Southeast Asia* (Ithaca, NY: Cornell University Press, 2020), 127–28.
51. Huub de Jonge, "Dutch Colonial Policy Pertaining to Hadhrami Immigrants," in *Hadhrami Traders, Scholars, and Statesmen in the Indian Ocean, 1750s-1960s*, ed. Ulrike Freitag and William G. Clarence-Smith (Leiden: Brill, 1997), 94–111.
52. For a jaundiced postwar assessment of the "venal" Anang that echoed that of Hachemi the previous year, see F. G. Gorton to Marquess Curzon of Kedleston, Batavia, February 10, 1922, and dispatch G.34 of June 22, 1921, R/20/A/1409, India

10. FOR ARABS, ARABIC, AND THE COMMUNITY

Office Records and Private Papers (IOR), British Library (BL). See also Mohamad Redzuan Othman, "The Ottoman's [sic] War with the Europeans: A Paradigm Shift in the Development of Malay Political Thought," *Jebat* 23 (1995): 89–96.

53. See, for instance, "al-Maqsud al-jalil," *al-Iqbal*, February 12, 1918.
54. "Kayfa yanhadu al-ʿArab?," *al-Bashir*, January 19, 1914; "Kayfa yanhadu al-Hadramiyyun?," *al-Iqbal*, July 21, 1919.
55. See ʿAli al-Shibli, "Laysa fi al-dunya gharib," *al-Iqbal*, February 8, 1919. Two weeks later the paper would publish on the debate between al-Shibli and Surkati: "al-Mujadala bayna al-shaykh al-Shibli wa al-shaykh al-Surkati," *al-Iqbal*, February 22, 1919.
56. Natalie Mobini-Kesheh, *The Hadrami Awakening: Community and Identity in the Netherlands East Indies, 1900-1942* (Ithaca, NY: SEAP, 1999), 96, 98.
57. "Damʿa min Wadi al-Nil," *al-Iqbal*, January 16, 1919.
58. al-Mustaʿan, "Kayfa nahfuzu huquqana?," *al-Iqbal*, January 25, 1919.
59. The offending Malay passages were reproduced under the continuation of the article "Bayna arbaʿina milyun muslim," *al-Iqbal*, February 12, 1918.
60. See, for instance, Takashi Shiraishi, *An Age in Motion: Popular Radicalism in Java, 1912-1926* (Ithaca, NY: Cornell University Press, 1990), 106–7; and Mobini-Kesheh, *Hadrami Awakening*, 46–47. As Schrieke noted, similar things had been published in the *Wedosanjoto* in 1914, and under the same editor, Martodarsono. B. Schrieke. "Bijdrage tot de bibliographie van de huidige godsdienstige beweging ter Sumatra's Westkust," *TBG* 59 (1919–21): 249–325, 288.
61. Mobini-Kesheh, *Hadrami Awakening*, 47.
62. "al-ʿArab wa al-wataniyyun," *al-Iqbal*, April [sic; February] 1, 1919.
63. "al-ʿArab wa al-wataniyyun," *al-Iqbal*, February 15, 1919.
64. "Masʾalat al-raʿiyya wa al-tabiʿa liʾl-Hulanda: Nederlandsch-Onderdaanschap," *al-Iqbal*, March 8, 1919.
65. This was ʿAli Haydar Pasha (1866–1935). See " ʿAli Haydar Basha wa al-madina al-munawwara," *al-Iqbal*, February 23, 1918.
66. "Siyadat Inkiltara," *al-Iqbal*, August 13, 1919.
67. Lee Warner to S. Gasalee, Cairo, December 3, 1918,R/20/A/1409, IOR, BL. Similar rumors had floated around India. Minault, *Khilafat Movement*, 22.
68. "Akhbar mukhtalifa: al-balagh al-rasmi," *al-Iqbal*, April 5, 1919.
69. Salim Faraj, "Ila l-mashaʾikh al-Irshadiyyin," *al-Iqbal*, April 26, 1919. On Bin Shahab and his son, see Freitag, *Indian Ocean Migrants*, 210–11. For mention of ʿAli having served as translator to the Ottoman consulate in Batavia in 1898, see İsmail Hakkı Göksoy, "Acehnese Appeals for Ottoman Protection in the Late Nineteenth Century," in *From Anatolia to Aceh: Ottomans, Turks and Southeast Asia*, ed. C. S. Peacock and Annabel Teh Gallop (Oxford: British Academy, 2015), 175–97, 189.
70. Laffan, *Makings of Indonesian Islam*, 214–16.
71. Muhammad Rashid Rida, *Tarikh al-ustadh al-imam al-shaykh Muhammad ʿAbduh* (Cairo: al-Dar al-Fadila, 2007), 600. See also page 1058 for an early attestation from Singapore of Bin ʿAqil's regard for ʿAbduh as "renewer of the century."
72. For the mission and its aftereffects, see Kawashima Midori, "The 'White Man's Burden' and the Islamic Movement in the Philippines," in İsmail Hakkı Kadı and

10. FOR ARABS, ARABIC, AND THE COMMUNITY

A. C. S. Peacock, eds., *Ottoman-Southeast Asian Relations: Sources from the Ottoman Archives*, 2 vols. (Leiden: Brill, 2020), 2:877–929, 930–57; see also Oliver Charbonneau, *Civilizational Imperatives: Americans, Moros, and the Colonial World* (Ithaca, NY: Cornell University Press, 2020), 194–97.

73. On Bin ʿAqil's earlier movements, see Sultan Sir Ghalib bin Awad to Saiyid Hussain bin Sheikh Mola Chela, Mokalla, November 29, 1918, R/20/A/1409, IOR, BL. For the later announcement and treaty, see *al-Iqbal*, July 19, 1919.
74. Lee Warner to S. Gasalee, Cairo, December 3, 1918, R/20/A/1409, IOR, BL.
75. See, more generally, Tim Harper, *Underground Asia*, 317ff.
76. Index of Arabs in the Netherlands East Indies, under cover of Lee Warner to S. Gasalee, Cairo, December 3, 1918, R/20/A/1409, IOR, BL.
77. Index of Arabs; see also Yahaya, *Fluid Jurisdictions*, 130–41.
78. Lee Warner to S. Gasalee, Cairo, December 3, 1918, R/20/A/1409, IOR, BL.
79. Dunn to political resident of Aden, Batavia, May 8, 1920, enclosing report on the Alexandrian paper *al-Ahali*, November 27, 1919, R/20/A/1409, IOR, BL.
80. Index of Arabs. Note that this entry (unnumbered) was appended in December 1920. See also, in same file, J. Crosby to Curzon, Batavia, December 8, 1920.
81. Index of Arabs, no. 238, Shawashi, Said Mohamad Saleh, BL.
82. Kussaï was also the source for the biographical details in Arnold H. Green, *The Tunisian Ulama, 1873-1915* (Leiden: Brill, 1978), 258–59. His memoir, and the writings of his younger brother, Adnan, serve as my main sources for the life of Hachemi. See Kussaï Elmekki, *Évocations: Écrits Autobiographiques, Mémoires, Lettres, Poésies; Établis, et Présentés par Rabâa ben Achour* (Carthage: Cartaginoiseries, 2011); Adnan El-Mecky, *De Schoolfoto (Een tijdsbeeld)* (Beek: n.p., 1988); Adnan El-Mecky, *Vergeten Namen* (Rotterdam: n.p., n.d.).
83. Elmekki, *Évocations*, 45–46; for a variant of the story, see the article that appeared in Tunis to mark his centenary: "Aboe Guecha," *L'Action*, November 15, 1982.
84. Elmekki, 71.
85. Elmekki, 70; Louis Rinn, *Marabouts et Khouan: étude sur l'Islam en Algérie* (Alger: A. Jourdan, 1884); George R. Trumbull, "French Colonial Knowledge of Maraboutism," in *Islam and the European Empires*, ed. David Motadel (Oxford: Oxford University Press, 2014), 269–86.
86. Elmekki, *Évocations*, 46.
87. *Abu Qisha*, July 13, 1908.
88. Elmekki, *Évocations*, 46–47. Hachemi's Libyan efforts were the subject of ʿAli Mustafa Mistrati's *Combat d'un journaliste: Abouguécha à Tripoli / Kifah sahafi: ʿard wa dirasa tahliliyya li-jaridat Abi Qisha sanat 1908-1911* (Beirut: Dar al-Ghandur, 1961).
89. Elmekki, 48; "al-Sayyid Abu Bakr b. ʿAbdallah al-ʿAttas," *Burubudur*, February 20, 1922.
90. According to Hachemi, Abu Bakr had ventured to Istanbul in 1911, having been in Cairo studying from 1909, when Saʿd Zaghlul had protested the unregulated numbers of foreign student visitors. Following his first journey to Istanbul, Abu Bakr went back to Java by way of Baghdad, Basra, and India, returning to Turkey in April 1912. See "al-Sayyid Abu Bakr b. ʿAbdallah al-ʿAttas." With thanks to Ismail Fajrie Alatas.

10. FOR ARABS, ARABIC, AND THE COMMUNITY

91. El-Mecky, *Schoolfoto*, 12. to Mobini-Kesheh, *Arab Awakening*, 54–55, who placed his arrival in 1910.
92. Elmekki, *Évocations*, 31.
93. Fatima's parental match had been arranged in Mecca. See Elmekki, 61–65. The Ba Mahmush clan were not Hadramis, but subjects of the sultan of Kishn and Soqotra. A. H. E. Mosse, *An Account of the Arab Tribes in the Vicinity of Aden* (Bombay: Government Central, 1909).
94. The image in question was the starting point for Adnan's first mediation on his father's life. Among those posing with fist outstretched was the young ʿAli al-ʿAttas, a protégé and future brother-in-law of Hachemi who married Saʿdiya, the younger sister of Fatima Ba Mahmush. See El-Mecky, *Schoolfoto*, 20; Elmekki, *Évocations*, 50.
95. El-Mecky, *Schoolfoto*.
96. "Fatihat al-jarida," *al-Salam*, 11 Shaʿban 1338 / April 29, 1920. A copy is found in R/20/A/1409, IOR, BL. The Hachemi and al-ʿAttas families remained in close contact into the 1930s. Husayn b. Abu Bakr would also marry Hachemi's daughter Sundus.
97. "Fatihat al-jarida," *al-Salam*, 11 Shaʿban 1338 / April 29, 1920.
98. "Sharif Makka I," *al-Salam*, 11 Shaʿban 1338 / April 29, 1920.
99. J. Crosby to political resident at Aden, Batavia, June 29, 1920; forwards copy of secret letter no. 86 to Earl Curzon, same date, R/20/A/1409, IOR, BL.
100. Crosby to political resident, June 29, 1920.
101. Crosby to Curzon, Batavia, December 8, 1920; and Gorton to Curzon, Batavia, June 24, 1921, R/20/A/1409, IOR, BL.
102. Crosby, very secret report of September 27, 1920, and enclosures, R/20/A/1414, IOR, BL.
103. Crosby to Curzon, Batavia, September 27, 1920, L/PS/10/630, IOR, BL.
104. Ghalib Awad al-Qaʿayti to James Stewart, Aden, April 12, 1920; and Crosby to Stewart, Batavia, July 6, 1920, R/20/A/1409, IOR, BL.
105. Mobini-Kesheh, "Arab Periodicals," 249.
106. Mobini-Kesheh, 244.
107. On Hachemi's view "without the least prejudice to either party" found in the first issue of November 5, 1920, see Crosby to Curzon, December 8, 1920, R/20/A/1409, IOR, BL. In his memoirs, Kussaï recalled the energy of its creation, of gleaming machinery and reams of paper transformed amid boxes and inks, despite the frequent interruptions of the children. Elmekki, *Évocations*, 41.
108. See, for instance, "Sharif Makka," *Burubudur*, August 10, 1921.
109. Crosby at Batavia, forwarding a petition to King Husayn from twenty-two sayyids of Java, R/20/A/1409, IOR, BL. Familiar signatories to the petition, signed at Batavia and published in *al-Qibla*, included ʿAli b. Ahmad b. Shahab (no. 1); Yahya b. ʿUthman b. Abdallah b. ʿAgil b. Yahya (no. 5); Muhammad b. ʿAgil b. ʿUthman b. ʿAbdallah b. Yahya (no. 14); and Muhammad b. Hashim b. Tahir (no. 22). A copy and summary, dated October 21, 1920, was forwarded to the Adeni consulate at the request of ʿAli b. Ahmad b. Shahab.
110. Bin Sunkar was a brother of the Irshadi representative for Pekalongan and reputed cofounder of Hachemi's press. An invitation sent to Snouck is to be found

10. FOR ARABS, ARABIC, AND THE COMMUNITY

in V4518, LUB. For mention of ʿAli b. ʿAwad b. Sunkar, see Crosby to Curzon, December 8, 1920, R/20/A/1409, IOR, BL.
111. "Suʾal," *Burubudur*, August 10, 1921. The following February, Hachemi could still report subscriptions from the rivals Muhammad b. ʿAqil and ʿAwad b. Sunkar, as well as the Jeddah consul, Dr. Schrieke, and the Office of Native Affairs. "Maʿlumat," *Burubudur*, February 20, 1922.
112. *OSEAR*, 2:658.
113. *OSEAR*, 2:658–59.
114. His journey from Cairo to Singapore was described by India's *al-Riyad*, summarized in Cairo's *al-Muʾayyad*, and finally translated in *al-Imam*: "Suara dari India," *al-Imam*, February 4, 1908.
115. See cover of *Burubudur*, November 20, 1920. For English complaints about this featuring of the "notorious Turkish Nationalist leader," see Crosby to Curzon, December 8, 1920, R/20/A/1409, IOR, BL. For the later depiction of the American leader, see "Hawla al-musabaqa: Jurj Washinton Muharrir Amrika," *Burubudur*, August 10, 1921.
116. "Islam," *Azzachierah al-Islamijah*, Jumada al-awwal 1342 / January 1924.
117. "Islam."
118. "Islam."
119. "Islam di Akrika Selatan," *Azzachirah al-Islamijah*, Jumada al-awwal 1342 / January 1924.
120. Tee Tee, "The Malayan Character and Civilization," in *Jubilee Book of the Colombo Malay Cricket Club* (Colombo: Malay Cricket Club of Colombo, 1924), 172–75.
121. "All-Ceylon Malay Association," in *Jubilee Book*, 178–82; Yahya Dane Surood (Poespajaya), "The Malayan Race and Malays of Ceylon," in *Jubilee Book*, 168–72.
122. See "An Exposition Concerning the Malays," in *Modernist Islam; A Sourcebook*, ed. Charles Kurzman (Oxford: Oxford University Press, 2002), 339–43.
123. Poespajaya, "Malayan Race and Malays," 170.
124. "All-Ceylon Malay Association," 180.
125. Poespajaya, "Malayan Race and Malays," 171. This last reference was to a former Ottoman dignitary and Iraq's first minister of the interior, Talib al-Naqib of Basra (1862–1929), expelled by Gertrude Bell in April 1921 after opposing the imposition of the Hashimite Faysal as king of Iraq.
126. Michael Francis Laffan, "Another Andalusia: Images of Colonial Southeast Asia in Arabic Newspapers," *Journal of Asian Studies* 66, no. 3 (2007): 689–722.
127. "Tanbih al-hukuma wa rijalihi," *al-Wifaq*, November 26, 1925. Surkati was playing on the prophetic injunction "Speak the truth even if it is bitter for you." He was also reacting to the imprisonment of Haji Abd al-Wahab of Deli for his attempt to open a Muslim school without a license and lamenting the departure of, and lack of governmental attention to, experts like Hazeu and Gobée.
128. W. N. Dunn to Curzon, May 18, 1920, enclosing translation of *Islam Bergerak*, April 10, 1920, R/20/A/1409, IOR, BL.
129. For Hazeu's remarks on the use of quasi-Ottoman symbols on flags and Sarekat Islam membership cards, see Van der Wal, *Opkomst*, 429.

130. On Samin, who was forced to curtail his activities in 1921 and moved to Penang in the 1930s, see Anthony Reid, *The Blood of the People: Revolution and the End of Traditional Rule in Northern Sumatra* (Singapore: NUS Press, 2014), 90. Regarding the opaque "D," see also Yahaya, *Fluid Jurisdictions*, 137. A plausible candidate is Mathura Das, mentioned in Streets-Salter, *World War One*, 133.
131. Report of "D," in Crosby to Curzon, October 14, 1920, R/20/A/1411, IOR, BL.
132. Report of "D."
133. Political and Secret Department, Dutch East Indies Affairs, 1916–18, first reports of "D," enclosed in W. R. D. Beckett to Balfour, September 6, 1917, L/PS/10/629, IOR, BL. Another early suspect was a Mr. Hatane, who attempted to disseminate a newspaper in Batavia in 1920 under the title of the *Islamic Fraternity*, though it folded for want of official patronage. C. Eliot at Tokyo, June 26, 1920, Colonial Office Files, 273/505, 74–75, National Archives, Kew.
134. Gorton to Curzon, Batavia, February 10, 1922, and June 22, 1921, R/20/A/1409, IOR, BL.
135. Dunn to Curzon, May 18, 1920, BL.
136. Gorton to Curzon, February 10, 1922, including translation from *Islam Bergerak* 3, January 20, 1922, "The Uncrowned King of Arabia: Colonel Lawrence" with a photo "reproduced by kind permission of director of Boro-Budur," BL.
137. In November 1920, Crosby had written about the favorable impression made by the Japanese navy at Medan. See Crosby to Curzon, November 11, 1920, L/PS/10/630, IOR, BL.
138. "Timoer dan Barat," *Azzachirah al-Islamijah*, Jumada al-Awwal 1342 / December 1923.

11. Pan-Islamism, Nationalism, Pan-Asianism

1. Kees van Dijk, *The Netherlands Indies and the Great War, 1914-1918* (Leiden: KITLV, 2007), 299–304.
2. According to information evidently supplied by Mansur to the Japanese in 1943, he had spent three and half years in Mecca and one and a half in Cairo. See *Orang Indonesia jang Terkemoeka di Djawa* (Jakarta: Gunseikanbu, 2604), 475.
3. For glowing accounts of Mansur's life in Indonesian, see Amir Hamzah Wirjosukarto, ed., *Rangkaian Mutu-Manikam: Kumpulan Buah Pikiran Budiman Kjahi Hadji Mas Mansur, 1896-1946* (Surabaja: Al-Ichsan, [1968]), introduction; Sutrisno Kutoyo, *Kyai Haji Mas Mansur* (Jakarta: Proyek Inventarisasi dan Dokumentasi Sejarah Nasional Indonesia, 1981); Soebagijo I.N., *K. H. Mas Mansur: Pembaharu Islam di Indonesia* (Jakarta: Gunung Agung, 1982); and Darul Aqsha, *K. H. Mas Mansur (1896-1946): Perjuangan dan Pemikiran* (Jakarta: Erlangga, 2005). The dates of his sojourn remain uncertain.
4. The fire killed five women, and the ruins collapsed the next day, causing a further fatality. See [Hajji Daud], "Perkhabaran Makka," *al-Munir*, August 28, 1912. For the mention of Ahmad Lampung and Umar Sumbawa in the 1880s,

11. PAN-ISLAMISM, NATIONALISM, PAN-ASIANISM

see C. Snouck Hurgronje, "Jâwah Ulama in Mekka in the Late Nineteenth Century," in *Readings on Islam in Southeast Asia*, ed. Ahmad Ibrahim, Sharon Siddique, and Yasmin Hussain (Singapore: Institute of Southeast Asian Studies, 1985), 70–79.

5. Information about *al-Ittihad* derives from reportage in Sumatra. "Al-Ittihad," *al-Munir*, January 9, 1913. Basyuni was a source for Mansur's student Soebagijo alongside A. R. Baswedan, Surono Wirohardjono, and Yusuf Abdullah Puar.
6. Mansur's biographers apparently misunderstood his claims to have been an autodidact who studied the words of the eleventh-century philosopher Abu ʿAli Ahmad Miskawayh. See also *Orang Indonesia*, 475.
7. Or at least that is what is asserted in the quasi-official history of Sutrisno, *Kyai Haji Mas Mansur*, 18–19.
8. Mansur's account, which he evidently adapted from an Arabic original, was featured in the *Almanak Muhammadijah* of 1348 AH (1929/1930). See Wirjosukarto, ed., *Rangkaian Mutu-Manikam*, 153–56. Moeljadi, as quoted by Soebagijo (*K. H. Mas Mansur*, 8), recalls Mansur's writing about the village of Sanggit as a producer of scholars, but does not place him there. In any case, Shinqit is usually associated with Mauritania.
9. On Kamil, see Adam Mestyan, *Arab Patriotism: The Ideology and Culture of Power in Late Ottoman Egypt* (Princeton, NJ: Princeton University Press, 2020), esp. 292–302; for his Japanophilia, see Ulrich Brandenburg, "Imagining an Islamic Japan: Pan-Asianism's Encounter with Muslim Mission," *Japan Forum* 32, no. 2 (2020): 161–84.
10. See Javanese-language prospectus of a new periodical concerned with religious matters, entitled Soeara "Taswir Al-afkar," Collectie Hazeu, D H 1083-132, Leiden University Library.
11. https://id.wikipedia.org/wiki/Mas_Mansoer (accessed March 28, 2020).
12. For a complex account of the interwoven histories of cosmopolitan and nationalist agitations in the early twentieth century, see Tim Harper, *Underground Asia: Global Revolutionaries and the Assault on Empire* (Cambridge, MA: Belknap Press of Harvard University Press, 2021).
13. This discourse has been explored by Chiara Formichi. See her "Mustafa Kemal's Abrogation of the Ottoman Caliphate and Its Impact on the Indonesian Nationalist Movement," in *Demystifying the Caliphate: Historical Memory and Contemporary Contexts*, ed. Madawi al-Rasheed, Carool Kersten, and Marat Shterin (London: Hurst, 2013), 95–116; and "Indonesian Readings of Turkish History," in *From Anatolia to Aceh: Ottomans, Turks and Southeast Asia*, ed. A. C. S. Peacock and Annabel Teh Gallop (Oxford: British Academy, 2015), 241–59.
14. Martin van Bruinessen, "Muslims of the Dutch East Indies and the Caliphate Question," *Studia Islamika* 2, no. 3 (1995): 115–40.
15. The preparatory committee was led by Abdul Wahab of Taswir al-Afkar, Fakhrudin of Muhammadiyah, Muhammad Fadloellah of Sarekat Islam Banjarnegara, and Bratanata of Sarekat Islam Cirebon. Listening attentively was Hoesein Djajadiningrat, the adjunct advisor for native affairs, whose report serves as my primary source: "Verslag van het Eerste Al-Islam Congres." Collectie R. A. Kern, KITLV3 D H 797–290 mf, Leiden University Library.
16. Djajadiningrat, "Verslag," 8–9.

11. PAN-ISLAMISM, NATIONALISM, PAN-ASIANISM

17. Djajadiningrat, 3.
18. Djajadiningrat, 12–13.
19. "Motie Congres C.S.I. Madioen, 18 Pebruari 1923," *Bintang Islam*, March 1923; "Sayf al-Islam wa mujaddid al-Khilafa," *Bintang Islam*, April 1923.
20. Henri Lauzière, "Walking a Tightrope: Egyptian Reformers in Mecca, 1928–29," in *On the Ground: New Directions in Middle East and North African Studies*, ed. Brian T. Edwards (Doha: Northwestern University in Qatar, 2013), 65–71.
21. "Muhawalat ightiyal mudir al-Wifaq," and "Aydan muhawalat ightiyal mudir al-Wifaq," *al-Wifaq*, October 29, 1925.
22. "al-Wifaq," *Burubudur*, July 5, 1924.
23. These included Mustafa al-Babi al-Halabi, whose son established a branch in Surabaya in 1920 and soon advertised with Hachemi, as did the the Nabahan brothers, who were already resident there. See "Dar Ihyaʾ al-Kutub al-ʿArabiyya," and "al-Maktaba al-Nabahaniyya," *al-Salam*, 11 Shaʿban 1338 / April 29, 1920. While the Nabahan brothers were suspected for their links to Surkati, al-Halabi was at pains to point out to the consulate that he was neutral. Index, "El Halaby, Abdul Aziz," and "Nabahan, Achmad bin Saäd bin and Salim," R/20/A/1409, India Office Records and Private Papers (IOR), British Library (BL). ʿAbd al-ʿAziz was back in Cairo by 1924 and met Hachemi's children at Suez that year. See Kussaï Elmekki, *Évocations: écrits autobiographiques mémoires, letters, poésies* (Carthage: Cartaginoiseries, [2011]), 21.
24. "Lajnat taʿlim al-sharq al-islami bi-Misr," *al-Wifaq*, April 30, 1925; see also my "'Another Andalusia': Images of Colonial Southeast Asia in Arabic Newspapers," *Journal of Asian Studies* 66, no. 3 (2007): 689–722, 710–12.
25. "al-Salat bi-rikhsa," *al-Wifaq*, August 20 and 27, 1925; "al-Wishaya ladayy hukumat Hulandah didd al-Wifaq," *al-Wifaq*, October 29, 1925; Laffan, "Another Andalusia," 712.
26. "Balagh," *al-Wifaq*, October 29, 1925.
27. Martin Kramer, *Islam Assembled: The Advent of the Muslim Congresses* (New York: Columbia University Press, 1986), 95–96, 109–10. See also Hamka (Haji Abdul Malik Karim Amrullah), *Ajahku: Riwayat hidup Dr. H. Abd. Karim Amrullah dan perdjuangan kaum agama di Sumatera*, 3rd ed. (Djakarta: Widjaja, 1958), 91–101; and Daniël van der Meulen, *Hoort Gij de Donder Niet? Begin van het Einde Onzer Gezagvoering in Indië: Een persoonlijke terugblik* (Franeker: T. Wever, 1977), 114–15.
28. Bin Naji returned to Java to replace ʿAli Harhara as secretary to the sayyid organization in late 1927. Crosby to political resident at Aden, Batavia, December 9, 1927, R/20/A/1412, 424, IOR, BL.
29. Van der Meulen, *Hoort Gij de Donder Niet?*, 106–8.
30. Mohammad Rezuan Othman, "Conflicting Political Loyalties of the Arabs in Malaya Before World War II," in *Transcending Borders: Arabs, Politics, Trade, and Islam in Southeast Asia*, ed. H. de Jonge and N. Kaptein (Leiden: KITLV, 2002), 37–52, 48.
31. Engseng Ho, *The Graves of Tarim: Genealogy and Mobility Across the Indian Ocean* (Berkeley: University of California Press, 2006), 277.
32. Crosby to Austen Chamberlain, Batavia, April 11, 1928 and enclosure, R/20/A/1412, IOR, BL.

11. PAN-ISLAMISM, NATIONALISM, PAN-ASIANISM

33. Muhammad Rashid Rida, *al-Khilafa aw al-imama al-ʿuzma* (Cairo: al-Manar, 1934).
34. Crosby to political resident at Aden, Batavia, December 9, 1927.
35. Van der Meulen, *Hoort Gij de Donder Niet?*, 109, 114–16. For the lineage and ideological confusions of the uprisings, which merged Islamic and Marxist concerns but had little direction from Moscow, see Harper, *Underground Asia*, 568–76.
36. Crosby to political resident at Aden, Batavia, March 10, 1928, R/20/A/1412, IOR, BL.
37. El Mekky, *De Schoolfoto (Een tijdsbeeld)* (Beek: n.p., 1988), 20; Elmekki, *Évocations*, 18–19.
38. El Mekky, 22.
39. Crosby to political resident at Aden, March 10, 1928.
40. Crosby to Chamberlain, Batavia, April 11, 1928, R/20/A/1412, IOR, BL.
41. I had my own experience of this in a secondhand way in Jakarta when his son Tawfik entertained me and Nabiha Shahab for lunch in the early 2000s, organizing a goat stew for us while eschewing it as "Arab" food.
42. Elmekki, *Évocations*, 61–65.
43. According to Kussaï, who never understood why Hachemi brought his younger family to Tunis, the series on scouts appeared in the daily *al-Nahda* and inspired ideas of setting up a similar movement there. Elmekki, 57.
44. Elmekki, 57, referring to the daily *al-Muqattam*.
45. For but one permutation, see Michele L. Louro, " 'Where National Revolutionary Ends and Communist Begins': The League Against Imperialism and the Meerut Conspiracy Case," *Comparative Studies of South Asia, Africa, and the Middle East* 33, no. 3 (2013): 331–44. See also Harper, *Underground Asia*, 617ff.
46. For numerous sightings of Tan Malaka, see Harper, *Underground Asia*.
47. The twenty-year-old Sukarno had married Oetari Tjokroaminoto in 1921, but they were divorced in 1923.
48. Sukarno, *Di Bawah Bendera Revolusi*, 3rd ed., 2 vols. (Jakarta: Panitya Penerbit Dibawah Bendera Revolusi, 1964), 1:109–14. See also Deliar Noer, *The Modernist Muslim Movement in Indonesia, 1900–1942* (Kuala Lumpur: Oxford University Press, 1973), 254–56.
49. Sukarno, *Indonesia Accuses! Soekarno's Defence Oration in the Political Trial of 1930*, ed. and trans. Roger K. Paget (Kuala Lumpur: Oxford University Press, 1978).
50. Sukarno, *Indonesia Accuses!*, 47, 48, 54, 79. Stoddard's work was widely read in Muslim circles after its Arabic translation by ʿAjjaj Nuwayhid and annotation by Shakib Arslan in 1924.
51. It is not clear to me when Sukarno first used this formulation, though he would backdate it in 1955. See Sukarno, *Indonesia Accuses!*, 15; and *Selected Documents of the Bandung Conference: Texts of Selected Speeches and Final Communique of the Asian-African Conference, Bandung, Indonesia, April 13–24, 1955* (New York: Institute of Pacific Relations, 1955), 2.
52. Sukarno, *Indonesia Accuses!*, 6–7.
53. Sukarno, *Indonesia Menggugat: Pidato Pembelaan Bung Karno Dimuka Hakim Kolonial* (Jakarta: Penerbitan S. K. Seno. 1956), 16–17. Note that I have adapted the gendered translation of Paget. Compare to Sukarno, *Indonesia Accuses!*, 17.

11. PAN-ISLAMISM, NATIONALISM, PAN-ASIANISM

54. Laffan, "Another Andalusia," 703.
55. Ethan Mark, *Japan's Occupation of Java in the Second World War: A Transnational History* (London: Bloomsbury, 2019), 40–51; for hints of Japanese addresses to a Malay Muslim South, see also Ono Ryosuke, "Southeast Asian Muslims in the Dai-Nihon Kaikyo Kyokai's Photography Collection," in *Islam and Multiculturalism: Exploring Islamic Studies within a Symbiotic Framework*, ed. Kazuaki Sawai, Yukari Sai, and Hirofumi Oka (Tokyo: Organization for Islamic Area Studies, Waseda University, 2015), 127–28.
56. See, for instance, the collected addresses of 1926–28 in Sukarno, *Di Bawah Bendera Revolusi*, 1:1–77.
57. Compare A. J. Wensinck, ed., *Verspreide geschriften van C. Snouck Hurgronje*, 6 vols. (Leiden: Brill, 1923–1924), vol. 4, pt. 2, 424; and *Indonesia Menggugat*, 76. See also *Indonesia Accuses!*, 47.
58. Another Shaykh Arshad had meanwhile been sent to Sulawesi, where he died in 1934. See Michael Francis Laffan, *The Makings of Indonesian Islam: Orientalism and the Narration of a Sufi Past* (Princeton, NJ: Princeton University Press, 2011), 226–27.
59. See James R. Rush, "Sukarno: Anticipating an Asian Century," in *Makers of Modern Asia*, ed. Ramachandra Guha (Cambridge, MA: Belknap Press of Harvard University Press, 2014), 172–98, 183.
60. For Sukarno's self-depiction on the cover of *Fikiran Ra'jat*, see his cartoons drawn under the pseudonym Soemini. Sukarno, *Di Bawah Bendera Revolusi*, 1:215.
61. Sukarno, "Surat-Surat Islam dari Ende," in *Di Bawah Bendera Revolusi*, 1:332–47; Ahmad Hassan, *Islam dan Kebangsaan* (Pasuruan: Lajnah Penerbitan Pesantren Persis Bangil, 1984), 131–32. See also Formichi, "Mustafa Kemal's Abrogation," 104–10.
62. Sukarno, "Minta Hukum Jang Pasti Dalam Soal 'Tabir,' " *Di Bawah Bendera Revolusi*, 1:353–55.
63. See Formichi, "Mustafa Kemal's Abrogation," 110–13.
64. See Rémy Madinier, *Islam and Politics in Indonesia: The Masyumi Party Between Democracy and Integralism* (Singapore: NUS Press, 2015).
65. On Baswedan, see Natalie Mobini-Kesheh, "The Arab Periodicals of the Netherlands East Indies, 1914–1942," *BKI* 152, no. 2 (1996): 236–56, 243; and Huub de Jonge, "Abdul Rahman Baswedan and the Emancipation of the Hadramis in Indonesia," *Asian Journal of Social Science* 32, no. 3 (2004): 373–400.
66. "Pranakan Arab dan Totoknja," *Mata-Hari*, August 1, 1934.
67. De Jonge, "Abdul Rahman Baswedan," 382–83.
68. Hassan, *Islam dan Kebangsaan*, 132.
69. Adnan El-Mecky, *Vergeten Namen* (Rotterdam: n.p., n.d.). An ironic exception seems to have been the local captain of the Arabs, "Ridha bin Akhal." See 72.
70. In this regard he repeated his choices from Batavia, where he had sent his eldest sons and daughters to a mixed Catholic school. Elmekki, *Évocations*, 39–41.
71. It is also reproduced in Elmekki, 50.
72. Elmekki, 63–64; Adnan El-Mecky, personal communication, Utrecht, July 19, 2017.

11. PAN-ISLAMISM, NATIONALISM, PAN-ASIANISM

73. See Laffan, "Another Andalusia," 714n40.
74. Basyuni's question appeared in the correspondence pages of 1930 and was the basis of Arslan's book. See "Limadha ta'akhkhara al-Muslimun wa taqaddamu ghayruhum?," *al-Manar*, December 20, 1930.
75. Laffan, "Another Andalusia," 712–16.
76. A copy of the photo of the gathering is now in the Rida family collection in Cairo. With thanks to Amr Ryad. Concerning Hayashi and his role in Manchuria, see Kelly Hammond, *China's Muslims and Japan's Empire: Centering Islam in World War II* (Chapel Hill: University of North Carolina Press, 2020). For an earlier encounter between Okawa, Mitsuru, and Rash Behari Bose in 1915, see Harper, *Underground Asia*, 295.
77. For Mansur's address of 1935, given at the twenty-fifth anniversary of Muhammadiyah, see Wirjosukarto, ed., *Rangkaian Mutu-Manikam*, 80–81.
78. Madinier, *Islam and Politics*, 44.
79. On the delegation, see Harry J. Benda, *The Crescent and Rising Sun: Indonesian Islam Under the Japanese Occupation 1942-1945* (The Hague: Van Hoeve, 1958), 104.
80. Benda, *Crescent and Rising Sun*, 231n9; Yasuko Kobayashi, "Islam During the Japanese Occupation," in *The Encyclopedia of Indonesia in the Pacific War*, ed. Peter Post, William H. Frederick, Iris Heidebrink, Shigeru Satō, William Bradley Horton, and Didi Kwartanada (Leiden: Brill, 2010), 300–11.

12. Forgotten Jihad

1. Unless otherwise noted, information on Adnan El-Mecky is derived from interviews in Utrecht in July 2017 and his engaging writings. His late brother in Tunis also offered an absorbing biography of their father in his own memoir of 2011. See Adnan El-Mecky, *Vergeten Namen: Verhalen uit Solo, een stad in de Vorstenlanden op Midden-Java* (Rotterdam: n.p., n.d.); Adnan El-Mecky, *De Schoolfoto (Een tijdsbeeld)* (Beek: n.p., 1988); and Kussaï Elmekki, *Évocations: écrits autobiographiques mémoires, letters, poésies* (Carthage, Tunisie: Cartaginoiseries, [2011]).
2. El-Mecky, *Vergeten Namen*, 67–72.
3. El-Mecky, *Schoolfoto*, 27.
4. El-Mecky, 22–23.
5. El-Mecky, 24, citing *Asia Raya*, July 27, 2602.
6. For images of Inada and Surkati together at ʿId al-Fitr prayers on October 11, 1942, see *The Encyclopedia of Indonesia in the Pacific War*, ed. Peter Post, William H. Frederick, Iris Heidebrink, Shigeru Satō, William Bradley Horton, and Didi Kwartanada (Leiden: Brill, 2010), 304; hereafter *IPW*.
7. *IPW*, 345. This was more probably his brother Muhammad Nur Surkati.
8. Ethan Mark, *Japan's Occupation of Java in the Second World War: A Transnational History* (London: Bloomsbury, 2019), 39–40, 47.
9. Harry J. Benda, *The Crescent and the Rising Sun: Indonesian Islam Under the Japanese Occupation 1942-1945* (The Hague: Van Hoeve, 1958), 102.

12. FORGOTTEN JIHAD

10. Martin van Bruinessen, "Muslims of the Dutch East Indies and the Caliphate Question," *Studia Islamika* 2, no. 3 (1995): 115–40. It had also been galling to the Dutch that the regent of Bandung, Wiranatakusuma, was there. See Jan Schmidt, *Through the Legation Window: Four Essays on Dutch, Dutch-Indian, and Ottoman History* (Istanbul: Nederlands Historisch-Archaologisch Instituut, 1992), 69 n96.
11. The sources suggest that it was either Charles O. Van der Plas, Salim's former supervisor as Jeddah consul and then governor of East Java, or else Pijper, the Leiden-trained philologist. See, for instance, Sutrisno Kutoyo, *Kyai Haji Mas Mansur* (Jakarta: Proyek Inventarisasi dan Dokumentasi Sejarah Nasional Indonesia, 1981), 68. The offer of the judgeship is mentioned in Benda (*Crescent and Rising Sun*, 225n80), *Asia Raya*, December 26, 1942.
12. Soebagijo I.N., *K. H. Mas Mansur: Pembaharu Islam di Indonesia* (Jakarta: Gunung Agung, 1982), 12–13.
13. K. H. M. Mansoer, "Tanggal 9 Maret," *Djawa Baroe*, February 15, 2603.
14. Anti-Semitic roundups commenced after the visits of the German consuls of Mukden and Shanghai in mid-July 1943. In Benda's case, this led to his fortuitous association with the sociologist Wim Wertheim (1907–1988), who encouraged him to pursue an academic career.
15. For its foundation in April 1942 in line with immediate concerns to control the media, see Mark, *Japan's Occupation*, 145–46. I suspect that the press may even have been that once used by Hachemi. Incidentally, Benda's own company had done its best to advertise its shoes in the pages of *Asia Raya* and to conform to Japanese notion of Pan-Asianism. See Mark, 340n132.
16. Nakano Satoshi, *Japan's Colonial Moment in Southeast Asia, 1942–1945: The Occupiers' Experience* (Abingdon: Routledge, 2018), 26–107. See also *IPW*, 306–7.
17. Jeremy Yellen, *The Greater East Asia Co-Prosperity Sphere: When Total Empire Met Total War* (Ithaca, NY: Cornell University Press, 2019).
18. Yellen, *Greater East Asia*, 155.
19. Benda, *Crescent and Rising Sun*, 115.
20. See *Soeara Madjlis Islam Aʿlaa Indonesia*, January 1, 2603.
21. See, for example, R. H. M. Adnan, "Sabar dan Sjoekoer," *Soeara MIAI*, January 1, 2603; and Sitti Noerdjannah, "Kedoedoekan Perempuan dalam Islam," *Soeara MIAI*, February 15, 2603. The same issue also presented photos of the "mothers" of Japan. There is little written on Noerdjannah, a teacher from West Sumatra who had her formation in al-Irshad schools in Jakarta, though she featured in an album of prominent Indonesians published by the Japanese administration and was noted as head of the Gaboengan Tabligh Akbar Islam Istri Djakarta. See *Orang Indonesia jang Terkemoeka di Djawa* (Jakarta: Gunseikanbu, 2604), 476; and Aiko Kurasawa, "Propaganda Media on Java Under the Japanese, 1942–1945, *Indonesia* 44 (1987): 59–116, 63.
22. Baswedan became the first minister for information for the republic; see Huub de Jonge, "Abdul Rahman Baswedan and the Emancipation of the Hadramis in Indonesia," *Asian Journal of Social Science* 32, no. 3 (2004): 373–400.
23. "Toeban" and "Pemoeda Arab," *Asia Raya*, September 29, 2603.
24. "Bantoehan Golongan Arab untuk Barisan PETA," *Asia Raya*, November 20, 2603; "Seroean kepada Pendoedoek Arab," *Asia Raya*, November 30, 2603.

25. H.Tj., "Sekeliling Bahaja Jahoedi," and Oemar Said, "Jahoedi dan Kejahoedian," *Soeara MIAI* 1, May 1, 2603; M. H. Alhabsji, "Palestina Delipoeti Sendja," *Soeara MIAI* 1, October 15, 2603.
26. Asa Bafagih, "Kemenangan Dai Nippon atas Roesia," *Soeara MIAI*, June 1, 2603.
27. Benda, *Crescent and Rising Sun*, 233n22; Soebagijo, *K. H. Mas Mansur*, 84; *IPW*, 305.
28. Mark, *Japan's Occupation*, 59, with details on 318.
29. T. M. Moesa Machfoeld, "Marilah dengan Soekarela, Madjoe kedepan Garis Perang!," *Asia Raya*, September 9, 2603. Machfoeld was a regular writer for the *Soeara MIAI* (see, for instance, his "Kembali Mengenal Diri dan Agama Manoesia dan Islam," January 15, 2603), and, as Benda notes, he supplied a similar mix of nationalist, martial, and Islamic sentiment for the soldier's journal *Pradjoerit*. Benda, *Crescent and Rising Sun*, 279n21. It is likewise worth noting the juxtaposition of pictures of Heiho recruits and an article on the impending fasting month: "Semangat dan Kemaoan Oentoek Membela Tanah Air," and "Memasoeki Bulan Poeasa," *Djawa Baroe*, September 15, 2603.
30. Benda, *Crescent and the Rising Sun*, 137ff.
31. "Kaoem Moeslimin Indonesia Toeroet Meminta Berdirinja Barisan Pendjaga Poelau Djawa," *Asia Raya*, September 13, 2603.
32. See "Samboetan Seorang Islam"; and "Solo-ko dan Mangkoenegaran-ko." According to veterans, Salim had played an important role in the recruitment process in the Heiho too. *Buku Kumpulan Kenang Kenangan Heiho Indonesia 1942-1945* (Jakarta: Yayasan Kesejahteraan Persatuan Keluarga Besar Bekas Heiho Indonesia, 1980).
33. "Membela Poelau Djawa," *Asia Raya*, September 15, 2603.
34. "Oemat Islam Sendiri Haroes Menjerboe di Medan Perang," *Asia Raya*, September 16, 2603.
35. "Samboetan Pengandjoer-pengandjoer Nahdatoel Oelama," *Asia Raya*, September 16, 2603.
36. On Mansur's elevation in Shumubu, see Benda, *Crescent and the Rising Sun*, 262n2.
37. "Tentara Pembela Tanah Air Lahir," *Asia Raya*, October 4, 2603.
38. "Hidoeplah dalam Kemoeliaan atau Matilah dalam Perdjuangan," *Asia Raya*, October 13, 2603.
39. *Asia Raya*, October 14, 2603. Two elite volunteer sisters were named as S .M. Hanani (aged twenty) and S. S. Kamariah Aminah (fifteen).
40. "Sekoetoe adalah Doerna, dan Mesti Lenjap! Ber-tjakap2 dengan Kiai Ageng Soerjomentaram," *Asia Raya*, October 16, 2603.
41. "Pekan Pembelaan Tanah Air: Rapat Besar Foedjin Kai," *Asia Raya*, November 12, 2603. Also noted as giving speeches were Tjoea Hin Hoei, the Chinese wife of Ali Alatas, and a Ms. Santakoer, wife of the representative for India.
42. "Pengharapan Pemerintah terhadap para Kijahi," *Soeara MIAI*, February 15, 2603.
43. "Darah Ksatria Tetap Mengalir dalam Toeboeh Pemoeda Indonesia," *Asia Raya*, October 15, 2603.
44. For instance, "Tentara Pembela Tanah Air," *Asia Raya*, October 21, 2603; and "Bertjakap-tjakap Dengan Tjalon Perdjoerit Indonesia," October 30, 2603.

45. "Memperdalam Tjinta pada Tanah Air dan Agama: Latihan Tjalon Opsir Tentara PETA," *Asia Raya*, November 11, 2603
46. Technically this amounted to a force of around thirty-seven thousand men (and some women) on Java and twenty thousand on Sumatra. Yet they only had some twenty thousand rifles between them in 1945.
47. Benda, *Crescent and the Rising Sun*, 150.
48. For recent treatment of this event, see Yellen, *Greater East Asia*, 141–57.
49. Aqsha mentions such figures as Anwar Risyad, M. Arsyad Al-Donggalawy, Abdul Mu'in Ampanany, A. Karim D.P., HAMKA, Amjad, Farid Ma'ruf, and Ibrahim Assanusi as being the collective behind his works. See Darul Aqsha, *K. H. Mas Mansur*, 96.
50. "Angkat Tjangkalmu!," *Soeara MIAI*, November 1, 2604.
51. "Tjara Mendjalankan Roekoen Islam," *Soeara Muslimin Indonesia*, January 15, 2604.
52. Rapy, "Tanah Air" and Mas Mansoer, "Bimbingan," in *Soeara Muslimin Indonesia*, February 1, 2604.
53. See "Bimbingan," as reproduced in Amir Hamzah Wirjosukarto, ed., *Rangkaian Mutu-Manikam: Kumpulan Buah Pikiran Budiman Kjahi Hadji Mas Mansur, 1896-1946* (Surabaja: Al-Ichsan, [1968]).
54. Benda, *Crescent and the Rising Sun*, 178–79.
55. Soebagio, *K. H. Mas Mansur*, 101.
56. His was a notable absence among the nine leaders who drafted the Jakarta Charter.
57. As noted above, Baswedan had also been a propagandist for Arab contributions to PETA, along with A. S. Shahab. "Seroean Kepada Pendoedoek Arab," *Asia Raya*, November 30, 2603.
58. Poetera Negara, "Doenia Internasional Tjoeriga?," *Soeara Moeslimin Indonesia*, December 6, 1945.
59. Sutrisno, *Kyai Haji Mas Mansur*, 162–65.
60. Lathiful Khuluq, "K. H. Hasyim Asy'ari's Contribution to Indonesian Independence," *Studia Islamika* 5 no. 1 (2014): 41–67.
61. Soebagijo, *K. H. Mas Mansur*, 124–24.
62. Kevin Fogg, "Islam in Indonesia's Foreign Policy, 1945–1949," *Al-Jāmi'ah: Journal of Islamic Studies* 53, no. 2 (2015): 303–35.
63. For an instructive history of the triangular struggle, see Chiara Formichi, *Islam and the Making of the Nation: Kartosuwiryo and Political Islam in Twentieth-Century Indonesia* (Leiden: KITLV, 2012).
64. Fogg, "Islam in Indonesia's Foreign Policy."

Epilogue

Epigraph: Selected Documents of the Bandung Conference: Texts of Selected Speeches and Final Communique of the Asian-African Conference, Bandung, Indonesia, April 13–24, 1955 (New York: Institute of Pacific Relations, 1955), 1.

EPILOGUE

1. For the background to the meeting, see Cindy Ewing, "The Colombo Powers: Crafting Diplomacy in the Third World and Launching Afro-Asia at Bandung," *Cold War History* 19, no. 1 (2019): 1–19.
2. Richard Wright, *The Color Curtain: A Report on the Bandung Conference* (New York: World, 1956).
3. *Selected Documents*, 2.
4. *Selected Documents*, 4.
5. Chiara Formichi, *Islam and the Making of the Nation: Kartosuwiryo and Political Islam in Twentieth-Century Indonesia* (Leiden: KITLV, 2012), esp. 145–201, for the fate of the Darul Islam movement.
6. On worldmaking as a concept, see Adom Getachew, *Worldmaking After Empire: The Rise and Fall of Self-Determination* (Princeton, NJ: Princeton University Press, 2019).
7. I was made aware of this quote from *O Jornal* in an unpublished paper by Sergio Infante, now a graduate student at Yale, to whom I express my thanks for offering some of his notes from the Indian National Archives.
8. Naoko Shimazu, "Diplomacy as Theatre: Staging the Bandung Conference of 1955," *Modern Asian Studies* 48, no. 1 (2013): 225–52.
9. Yoav Di-Capua, *Gatekeepers of the Arab Past: Historians and History Writing in Twentieth-Century Egypt* (Berkeley, CA: University of California Press, 2009), 174.

Bibliography

Abbreviations

AA	E. Gobée and C. Adriaanse, eds., *Ambtelijke adviezen van C. Snouck Hurgronje 1889-1936*, 3 vols. The Hague: Nijhoff, 1957–1965
Add	Additional Manuscripts, British Library
BKI	*Bijdragen tot de Taal-, Land- en Volkenkunde*
BL	British Library
EAP	Endangered Archives Programme, British Library
CO	Colonial Office Files, National Archives, Kew
FO	Foreign Office Files, National Archives, Kew
FW	Fitzwilliam Museum, Cambridge
IOR	India Office Records and Private Papers, British Library
IPW	Peter Post et al., *The Encyclopedia of Indonesia in the Pacific War*, 2 vols. Leiden: Brill, 2010
NA	Nationaal Archief, The Hague
NLSA	National Library of South Africa
Or.	Asian-language manuscript or file
OSEAR	İsmail Hakkı Kadı and A. C. S. Peacock, eds., *Ottoman-Southeast Asian Relations: Sources from the Ottoman Archives*, 2 vols. (Leiden: Brill, 2020)
PNRI	Perpustakaan Nasional Republik Indonesia, Jakarta
SLNA	Sri Lankan National Archives, Colombo
TNA	National Archives, Kew
TBG	*Tijdschrift van het Bataviaasch Genootschap*
VS	A. J. Wensinck, ed., *Verspreide geschriften van C. Snouck Hurgronje*, 6 vols. (Leiden: Brill, 1923–1924)
WCARS	Western Cape Archives and Records Service, Cape Town

BIBLIOGRAPHY

Archival Sources

Great Britain

BRITISH LIBRARY

Additional Manuscripts   44,110; 48,619; and 7936
Endangered Archives Program   212/2/6; 205/3/2; 609/10/1; 609/24; 609/3/1; 609/9/1
India Office Records and Private Papers   E/4/840; E/4/888; E/4/889; F/4/9; F/4/9/715; F/4/277; F/4/616; F/4/663; F/4/1309; G/34/193; L/PS/1/4; L/PS/1/5; L/PS/10/630; L/PS/10/629; L/PS/10/630, L/PS/19/14; R/20/A/508; R/20/A/1409; R/20/A/1411; R/20/A/1412; R/20/A/1414
Or. 15646

NATIONAL ARCHIVES, KEW

CO 414/1; CO 48/101; CO 48/121; CO 48/160; CO 54/61; FO 78/5176; FO 633/49; FO 633/61; 78/3615; FO 78/4267; FO 78/4268; FO 78/4589; FO 78/5176; FO 926/9; WO 12/10853; WO 43/492

FITZWILLIAM MUSEUM, CAMBRIDGE

Blunt Papers
MSS 1–1975; 21–1975; 48–1975; 313–1975; 325–1975

ROYAL COLLECTION TRUST

RCIN 450804
MS 12225

India

NATIONAL ARCHIVES OF INDIA

Simla 5, Foreign Department, Secret

BIBLIOGRAPHY

Indonesia

PERPUSTAKAAN NASIONAL REPUBLIK INDONESIA

Or. A 101

The Netherlands

LEIDEN UNIVERSITY LIBRARY

Or. 2241
Or. 7111
KITLV3, D H 797-290
KITLV3, D H 1083-132
V4518

NATIONAAL ARCHIEF

1.04.02; ;1.04.17; 2.05.03

NATIONAAL MUSEUM VAN WERELDCULTUREN

TM-60003143

RIJKSMUSEUM

NG-1985-7-1-43

South Africa

ASIYA ABDEROOF COLLECTION, WOODSTOCK

Manuscripts of Tuan Guru, photographed by Shafiq Morton

CAPE TOWN DEEDS OFFICE

Erven (plots) 2839, 3464, and 7840 (formerly 5021)

BIBLIOGRAPHY

CASTLE OF GOOD HOPE

William Fehr Collection, CD57

NATIONAL LIBRARY OF SOUTH AFRICA

N. E. Rakiep Collection, MSB 683, seen by way of copies held by Rakiep family, Cape Town

SIMONS TOWN HERITAGE MUSEUM

Papers of N. E. Rakiep and uncataloged Jawi manuscripts of local community

WESTERN CAPE ARCHIVES AND RECORDS SERVICE

ACC 602; AG 2324; AG 3845; BO 154; BO 155; BR 9; BR 59; BR 348; C 134; C 143; C 159; C 549; CJ 2568; CJ 3188; CJ 546; CJ 805; CJ 3189; CO 3905; CO 3984; CO 3996; CO 4069; CO 4087; CO 4096; CO 4129; CSC 2/1/1/156; GH 1/291; GH 1/366; GH 23/30; MOOC 6/9/31; MOOC 6/9/41; MOOC 6/9/166; MOOC 6/9/212; MOOC 7/1/41; MOOC 7/1/53; MOOC 7/1/251; MOOC 8/9.6; MOOC 8/10.76; NCD 1/27; NCD 1/41; RDG 2; SO 7/34

Sri Lanka

SRI LANKAN NATIONAL ARCHIVES, COLOMBO

1/87; 1/88; 1/191; 1/193; 1/200; 1/203; 1/204; 1/208; 1/219; 1/232; 1/4613; 1/4696; 1/4697; 1/4722; 1/4745; 1/4758; 2/2; 4/1; 4/157; 4/158; 4/82; 4/86; 4/158; 5/1; 5/2; 5/5; 5/6; 5/7; 5/8; 5/9; 5/10; 5/51; 5/75; 5/76; 5/78; 5/79; 5/80; 5/81; 5/82; 5/102; 6/1376; 6/1438; 6/2828; 6/7784; 6/8856; 7/44; 19/66; X/1/7; X/3/20

Republic of Turkey

NATIONAL ARCHIVES

BOA HR SFR 3 136/28
Y.A. HUS 232/66

BIBLIOGRAPHY

Newspapers and Periodicals

Academy, 1883
African Court Calendar, 1823–1826
Argus, 1980
Asia Raya, 2603
Azzachierah al-Islamijah, 1924
al-Bashir, 1914–15
Bintang Islam, 1923–24
Burubudur, 1921–24
Cape Argus, 1870, 1873, 2000, 2001, 2005
Cape of Good Hope Almanack, 1835
Cape of Good Hope Annual Register, 1838
Ceylon Observer, 1885, 1890–1891, 1899
Ceylon Times, 1887
Daily Sabah, 2017
Examiner, 1841
Gentleman's Magazine, 1817
al-Imam, 1906–1908
al-Iqbal, 1918–1919
Madras Mail, 1882
al-Manar, 1910, 1930
Manchester Guardian, 1860, 1887
Mata-Hari, 1934
Mecmua-yı Fünun 1863, 1864
Missionary Register, 1823
al-Munir, 1912–1913
New Annual Register, 1781
New York Times, 1883–1884
Nineteenth Century, 1885
Overland Ceylon Observer, 1889, 1890
Pall Mall Gazette, 1892
Pioneer, 1881
Prince of Wales Island Gazette, 1819, 1820
Quarterly Review, 1815
al-Salam, 1920
Scotsman, 1841
Singapore Free Press and Mercantile Advertiser, 1901
Soeara Madjlis Islam A'laa Indonesia, 2603
Soeara Muslimin Indonesia, 2604
South African Almanack and Directory, 1827–1828, 1834
South African Commercial Advertizer, 1828, 1836
Straits Times, 1901, 1903
Sunday Times, 1867, 1897

Times of India, 1882, 1883, 1887, 1893, 1901
Times, 1876
Wajah Selong, 1895–1897
Washington Post, 1882
Wazir India, 1878
Weekly Ceylon Observer, 1882
al-Wifaq, 1925

Unpublished Works, Theses, and Dissertations

Gençoğlu, Halim. "Abu Bakr Effendi: A Report on the Activities and Challenges of an Ottoman Muslim Theologian in the Cape of Good Hope." Master's thesis, University of Cape Town, 2013.
Hendricks, Seraj. "Taṣawwuf (Ṣūfism): Its Role and Impact on the Culture of Cape Islām." Master's thesis, University of South Africa, 2005.
Jappie, Saarah. "Between Macassars: Site, Story, and the Transoceanic Afterlives of Shaykh Yusuf of Makassar." PhD diss., Princeton University, January 2018.
Kooriadathodi, Mahmood. "Cosmopolis of Law: Islamic Legal Ideas and Texts Across the Indian Ocean and Eastern Mediterranean Worlds." PhD diss., Leiden University, 2016.
Laffan, Judith Cecily. "Negotiating Empires: 'British' Dragomans and Changing Identity in the 19th Century Levant." PhD diss., University of Queensland, 2011.
Raben, Remco. "Batavia and Colombo: The Ethnic and Spatial Order of Two Colonial Cities, 1600–1800." PhD diss., Leiden University, 1996.
Rafudeen, Auwais. "The Compendium of Tuan Guru: Translation and Contextualisation (A Research File)." Lodged with Universities of the Western Cape and Cape Town, 2004.
Rakiep, Al-Haj Nur-el-Erefaan,. "Tuan Guru (Prince Abdullah bin Qadi Abdus-Salam): Qadi of the Cape, ca. 1770s—1807(?)." Typescript held at Simon's Town Heritage Museum, 1993.
Shell, Rob. Hudson's "Essay on Slaves at the Cape." In *Out of Livery: The Papers of Samuel Eusebius Hudson, 1764–1828*. Edited by Rob Shell, Edward Hudson, and Raymond Hudson. On CD-ROM.
Shell, Rob. "Prosopography of Cape Imams." Excel spreadsheet kept by Sandy Shell.
Somasunderum, Ramesh. "British Infiltration of Ceylon (Sri Lanka) in the Nineteenth Century: A Study of the D'Oyly Papers Between 1805 and 1818." PhD diss., University of Western Australia, 2008.
Visser, Rogier. "Identities in Early Arabic Journalism: The Case of Louis Ṣabunji." PhD diss., University of Amsterdam, 2014.

Published Works

ʿAbd al-Rahman b. ʿUbayd Allah al-Saqqaf. *Muʿjam buldan Hadramawt al-musamma Idam al-qawt fi dhikr buldan Hadramawt*. Sanʿaʾ: Maktabat al-Irshad, 2002.

BIBLIOGRAPHY

ʿAli Mustafa Mistrati. *Combat d'un journaliste: Abouguécha à Tripoli / Kifah sahafi: ʿarid wa dirasa tahliliyya li-jaridat Abi Qisha sanat 1908-1911*. Beirut: Dar al-Ghandur, 1961.

A Collection of Legislative Acts of the Ceylon Government from 1796. 2 vols. Colombo: William Skeen, 1853.

Abdul Sheriff. *Dhow Cultures of the Indian Ocean: Cosmopolitanism, Commerce, and Islam*. New York: Columbia University Press, 2010.

Abdullah Munshi. *Kisah pĕlayaran Abdullah ka-Kĕlantan dan ka-Judah*. Edited and with an introduction by Kassim Ahmad. 5th ed. Kuala Lumpur: Oxford University Press, 1968.

Abu-Lughod, Janet L. *Before European Hegemony: The World System A.D. 1250-1350*. New York: Oxford University Press, 1989.

Ahmad ʿAbd al-Majid al-Fiqi. *Qissat Ahmad ʿUrabi*. Cairo: al-Dar al-Qawmiyya, 1966.

Ahmad ʿUrabi. *Mudhakkirat al-zaʿim Ahmad ʿUrabi*. Cairo: Dar al-Maʿarif, 1983.

Ahmad b. Zayni Dahlan. *al-Futuhat al-Islamiyya baʿda mudiyy al-futuhat al-nabawiyya*. 2 vols. Cairo: al-Halabi, 1968.

Ahmad Hassan. *Islam dan Kebangsaan*. Pasuruan: Lajnah Penerbitan Pesantren Persis Bangil, 1984.

Ahmat Adam. *The Vernacular Press and the Emergence of Modern Indonesian Consciousness*. Ithaca, NY: Cornell University Press, 1995.

Ahmed Ibrahim Abu Shouk. "An Arabic Manuscript on the Life and Career of Ahmad Muhammad Sûrkatî and His Irshâdî Disciples in Java." In *Transcending Borders: Arabs, Politics, Trade, and Islam in Southeast Asia*, edited by Huub de Jonge and Nico Kaptein, 203-17. Leiden: KITLV, 2002.

Aiyer, Sana. "Revolutionaries, Maulvis, Swamis, and Monks: Burma's Khilafat Moment." In *Oceanic Islam: Muslim Universalism and European Imperialism*, edited by Sugata Bose and Ayesha Jalal, 143-93. New Delhi: Bloomsbury India, 2020.

Alavi, Seema. *Muslim Cosmopolitanism in the Age of Empire*. Cambridge, MA: Harvard University Press, 2015.

Aldrich, Robert. *Banished Potentates: Dethroning and Exiling Indigenous Monarchs Under British and French Colonial Rule, 1815-1955*. Manchester: Manchester University Press, 2018.

———. "Out of Ceylon: The Exile of the Last King of Kandy." In *Exile in Colonial Asia: Kings, Convicts, Commemoration*, edited by Ronit Ricci, 48-70. Honolulu: University of Hawai'i Press, 2016.

Amrith, Sunil S. "Islam's Eastern Frontiers: Tamil, Chinese, and Malay Worlds." In *Oceanic Islam: Muslim Universalism and European Imperialism*, edited by Sugata Bose and Ayesha Jalal, 55-76. New Delhi: Bloomsbury India, 2020.

———. "Tamil Diasporas Across the Bay of Bengal." *American Historical Review* 114, no. 3 (2009): 547-72.

Andaya, Barbara. "From Rūm to Tokyo: The Search for Anticolonial Allies by the Rulers of Riau, 1899-1914." *Indonesia* 24 (1977): 123-56.

Andaya, Leonard. *Leaves of the Same Tree: Trade and Ethnicity in the Straits of Melaka*. Singapore: NUS Press, 2010.

———. *The World of Maluku: Eastern Indonesia in the Early Modern Period*. Honolulu: University of Hawai'i Press, 1993.

BIBLIOGRAPHY

Anderson, Clare. "History in and of a Penal Colony in the Bay of Bengal: Two Convict Mazars in the Andaman Islands." In *Belonging Across the Bay of Bengal: Religious Rites, Colonial Migrations, National Rights*, edited by Michael Francis Laffan, 193–206. New York: Bloomsbury Academic Press, 2017.
Aqsha, Darul. *K. H. Mas Mansur (1896-1946): Perjuangan dan Pemikiran.* Jakarta: Erlangga, 2005.
Archer, Rosemary, and James Fleming, eds. *Lady Anne Blunt: Journals and Correspondence, 1878-1917.* Cheltenham: Alexander Heriot, 1986.
Armstrong, James. "A Footnote on Shaykh Yusuf." *Bulletin of the National Library of South Africa* 74, no. 1 (2020): 9–14.
Arnold, David. "Islam, the Mappilas, and Peasant Revolt in Malabar." *Journal of Peasant Studies* 9, no. 4 (1982): 255–65.
[Aspeling, Eric]. *The Cape Malays: An Essay by a Cape Colonist.* Cape Town: W. A. Richards & Sons, 1883.
ʿAwda, Muhammad. *Sabʿat bashawat wa suwar ukhra.* Cairo: Ruz al-Yusuf, 1971.
Aydin, Cemil. *The Idea of the Muslim World: A Global Intellectual History.* Cambridge, MA: Harvard University Press, 2017.
Azra, Azyumardi. *The Origins of Islamic Reformism in Southeast Asia: Networks of Malay-Indonesian and Middle Eastern ʿUlamaʾ in the Seventeenth and Eighteenth Centuries.* Leiden: KITLV, 2004.
Bang, Anne K. *Islamic Sufi Networks in the Western Indian Ocean (c. 1880-1940): Ripples of Reform.* Leiden: Brill, 2014.
Barnard, Anne Lindsay. *Lady Anne Barnard's Watercolours and Sketches: Glimpses of the Cape of Good Hope.* Simon's Town: Fernwood, 2009.
Barrow, John. *An Account of Travels into the Interior of Southern Africa, in the Years 1797 and 1798.* 2 vols. London: Johnson, [1801–1804] 1968.
Bayly, Christopher. *The Birth of the Modern World, 1780-1914.* Oxford: Blackwell, 2004.
——. *Imperial Meridian.* London: Longman, 1993.
Benda, Harry J. *The Crescent and Rising Sun: Indonesian Islam Under the Japanese Occupation 1942-1945.* The Hague: Van Hoeve, 1958.
Benton, Lauren, Adam Clulow, and Bain Attwood, eds. *Protection and Empire: A Global History.* Cambridge: Cambridge University Press, 2017.
Berdine, Michael. *The Accidental Tourist, Wilfrid Scawen Blunt and the British Invasion of Egypt in 1882.* New York: Routledge, 2005.
Berg, Lodewijk Willem Christiaan van den. *Le Hadhramout et les colonies arabes dans l'archipel Indien.* Batavia: Impr. du gouvernement, 1886.
Bird, W. W. *State of the Cape of Good Hope in 1822.* Cape Town: C. Struik, [1823] 1966.
Bishara, Fahad. *A Sea of Debt: Law and Economic Life in the Western Indian Ocean, 1780-1950.* Cambridge: Cambridge University Press, 2017.
Blunt, Wilfred Scawen, *The Future of Islam.* Edited by Riad Nourallah. London: RoutledgeCurzon, 2002.
——. *Gordon at Khartoum: Being a Personal Narrative of Events, in Continuation of "A Secret History of the English Occupation of Egypt."* London: S. Swift, 1911.
——. *India Under Ripon: A Private Diary.* London: T. Fisher, 1909.
——. *My Diaries: Being a Personal Narrative of Events, 1888-1914.* 2 vols. New York: Knopf, 1923.

———. *Secret History of the English Occupation of Egypt: Being a Personal Narrative of Events.* 2nd ed. London: T. Fisher Unwin, 1907.
Bonney, R. *Kedah, 1771-1821: The Search for Security and Independence.* Kuala Lumpur: Oxford University Press, 1971.
Bose, Sugata. *A Hundred Horizons: The Indian Ocean in the Age of Global Empire.* Cambridge, MA: Harvard University Press, 2006.
Bose, Sugata, and Ayesha Jalal, eds. *Oceanic Islam: Muslim Universalism and European Imperialism.* New Delhi: Bloomsbury India, 2020.
Boxberger, Linda. *On the Edge of Empire: Hadhramawt, Emigration, and the Indian Ocean, 1880s-1930s.* Albany: State University of New York Press, 2002.
Bradley, Francis R. *Forging Islamic Power and Place: The Legacy of Shaykh Dā'ūd bin 'Abd Allāh al-Faṭānī in Mecca and Southeast Asia.* Honolulu: University of Hawai'i Press, 2016.
Bradlow, Edna. "Mental Illness or a Form of Resistance? The Case of Soera Brotto." *African Historical Review* 23, no. 1 (1991): 4-16.
Bradlow, Frank R., and Margaret Cairns. *The Early Cape Muslims: A Study of their Mosques, Genealogy, and Origins.* Cape Town: Balkema, 1978.
Braginsky, Vladimir. *The Turkic-Turkish Theme in Traditional Malay Literature: Imagining the Other to Empower the Self.* Leiden: Brill, 2015.
Brandenburg, U. "Imagining an Islamic Japan: Pan-Asianism's Encounter with Muslim Mission." *Japan Forum* 32, no. 2 (2020): 161-84.
Briefwisseling van Hendrik Swellengrebel Jr oor Kaapse Sake, 1778-1792. Cape Town: Van Riebeeck-Vereeniging, 1982.
Broadley, A. M. *How We Defended Arábi and His Friends: A Story of Egypt and the Egyptians.* London: Chapman & Hall, 1884.
Brohier, Richard Leslie. "The Boer Prisoner-of-War in Ceylon (1900-1902)." *Journal of the Dutch Burgher Union of Ceylon* 36, no. 8 (1946): 68-92.
Brooke, Thomas Henry. *A History of the Island of St. Helena, from Its Discovery by the Portuguese to the Year 1806.* London: Black, Parbury & Allen, 1808.
Brug, P. H. van der. "Malaria in Batavia in the 18th Century." *Tropical Medicine and International Health* 2, no. 9 (1997): 892-902.
Bruijn, J. R., F. S. Gaastra, I. Schöffer, and E.S. van Eyck van Heslinga. *Dutch-Asiatic Shipping in the 17th and 18th Centuries.* 3 vols. The Hague: Nijhoff, 1979.
Bruinessen, Martin van. "Muslims of the Dutch East Indies and the Caliphate Question." *Studia Islamika* 2, no. 3 (1995): 115-40.
———. "A Nineteenth-Century Ottoman Kurdish Scholar in South Africa: Abu Bakr Efendi." In *Mullas, Sufis, and Heretics: The Role of Religion in Kurdish Society*, edited by Martin van Bruinessen, 133-41. Istanbul: Isis, 2000.
Buku Kumpulan Kenang Kenangan Heiho Indonesia, 1942-1945. Jakarta: Yayasan Kesejahteraan Persatuan Keluarga Besar Bekas Heiho Indonesia, 1980.
Bussche, L. de. *Letters on Ceylon: Particularly Relative to the Kingdom of Kandy.* London: J. J. Stockdale, 1817.
Buzpinar, S. Tufan. "Abdülhamid II and Sayyid Fadl Pasha of Hadramawt: An Arab Dignitary's Ambitions (1876-1900)." *Journal of Ottoman Studies* 13 (1993): 227-39.
Byl, Julia, Raja Halid, Raja Iskandar, David Lunn, and Jenny McCallum. "The Syair Tabut of Encik Ali: A Malay Account of Muharram at Singapore, 1864." *Indonesia and the Malay World* 45, no. 133 (2017): 421-38.

BIBLIOGRAPHY

Caldwell, Robert. *A Political and General History of the District of Tinnevelly, in the Presidency of Madras, from the Earliest Period to Its Cession to the English Government in A.D. 1801.* Tirunelveli: Government Press, 1881.

Campbell, Gwynn. *David Griffiths and the Missionary "History of Madagascar."* Leiden: Brill, 2012.

Campbell, John. *Travels in South Africa: Undertaken at the Request of the Missionary Society.* London: Black & Parry, 1815.

———. *Voyages to and from the Cape of Good Hope: With an Account of a Journey into the Interior of South Africa.* Philadelphia: Presbyterian Board of Publication, 1840.

Carey, Daniel. "The Political Economy of Poison: The Kingdom of Makassar and the Early Royal Society." *Renaissance Studies* 17, no. 3 (2003): 517–43.

Carey, Peter. *The Power of Prophecy: Prince Dipanagara and the End of an Old Order in Java, 1785-1855.* Leiden: KITLV, 2008.

Champion, G. *Journal of an American Missionary in the Cape Colony: 1835.* Edited by Alan R. Booth. Cape Town: South African Library, 1968.

Charbonneau, Oliver. *Civilizational Imperatives: Americans, Moros, and the Colonial World.* Ithaca, NY: Cornell University Press, 2020.

Chauduri, K. N. *Trade and Civilisation in the Indian Ocean: An Economic History from the Rise of Islam to 1750.* Cambridge: Cambridge University Press, 1985.

———. *The Trading World of Asia and the English East India Company: 1660-1760.* Cambridge: Cambridge University Press, 1978.

Chijs, J. A. van der, ed., *Nederlandsch-Indisch Plakaatboek: 1602-1811.* 17 vols. Batavia: Landsdrukkerij, 1885–1900.

Coates, Peter Ralph. "P. E. De Roubaix's Delusions." *Quarterly Bulletin of the National Library of South Africa* 64, no. 1 (2010): 31–48; and no. 2 (2010) 86–104.

Codrington, H. W., intro. and ed. "Diary of Mr. John D'Oyly." *Journal of the Ceylon Branch of the Royal Asiatic Society* 25, no. 69 (1917): iii–xvi, 1–269.

Cole, Alfred W. *The Cape and Kafirs: Notes of Five Years' Residence in South Africa.* London: Richard Bentley, 1852.

Cole, Juan. *Colonialism and Revolution in the Middle East: Social and Cultural Origins of Egypt's 'Urabi Movement.* Princeton, NJ: Princeton University Press, 1993.

The Colebrooke-Cameron Papers (Documents on British Colonial Policy in Ceylon, 1796-1833). 2 vols. Edited by G. C. Mendis. Oxford: Oxford University Press, 1956.

Cordiner, James. *A Description of Ceylon: Containing an Account of the Country, Inhabitants, and Natural Productions with Narratives of a Tour Round the Island in 1800, the Campaign in Candy in 1803, and a Journey to Ramisseram in 1804.* 2 vols. London: Longman, 1807.

Corfield, Justin. *Historical Dictionary of Ho Chi Minh City.* London: Anthem, 2014.

Correspondence Respecting the Egyptian Exiles in Ceylon, Egypt. No. 8 (1883). London: Harrison & Sons, 1883.

Crawfurd, John. *History of the Indian Archipelago: Containing an Account of the Manners, Arts, Languages, Religions, Institutions, and Commerce of Its Inhabitants.* 3 vols. Edinburgh: Constable, 1820.

Cromer, The Earl of (Evelyn Baring). *Modern Egypt.* 2 vols. London: Macmillan, 1908.

Da Costa, Yusuf, and Achmat Davids, eds. *Pages from Cape Muslim History.* 2nd ed. Gatesville: Naqshbandi-Muhammadi South Africa, 2005.

BIBLIOGRAPHY

Dale, Stephen Frederic. *Islamic Society on the South Asian Frontier: The Mappilas of Malabar, 1498-1922*. Oxford: Clarendon, 1980.
Das Gupta, Ashin. *Indian Merchants and the Decline of Surat: c. 1700-1750*. Wiesbaden: Franz Steiner Verlag, 1979.
Davids, Achmat. *The History of the Tana Baru: The Case for the Preservation of the Muslim Cemetery at the Top of Longmarket Street*. Cape Town: Committee for the Preservation of the Tana Baru, 1985.
———. *The Mosques of Bo-Kaap: A Social History of Islam at the Cape*. Athlone: South African Institute of Arabic and Islamic Research, 1980.
Dep, Arthur C. *The Egyptian Exiles in Ceylon (Sri Lanka), 1883-1901*. Colombo: Arabi Pasha Centenary Celebrations Committee of the All Ceylon Muslim League, 1983.
———. *A History of Ceylon Police: Volume II (1866-1913)*. Colombo: Police Amenities Fund, 1969.
Deringil, Selim. "The Ottoman Response to the Egyptian Crisis of 1881-82." *Middle Eastern Studies* 24, no. 1 (1988): 3-24.
DeYoung, Terri. *Mahmud Sami al-Barudi: Reconfiguring Society and the Self*. Syracuse, NY: Syracuse University Press, 2015.
Di-Capua, Yoav. *Gatekeepers of the Arab Past: Historians and History Writing in Twentieth-Century Egypt*. Berkeley, CA: University of California Press, 2009.
Diemont, Marius and Joy. *The Brenthurst Baines: A Selection of the Works of Thomas Baines in the Oppenheimer Collection, Johannesburg, etc.* Johannesburg: Brenthurst, 1975.
Dijk, Kees van. *The Netherlands Indies and the Great War, 1914-1918*. Leiden: KITLV, 2007.
Drewes, G. W. J. "Further Data Concerning 'Abd al-Samad al-Palimbani." *BKI* 132, nos. 2-3 (1976): 267-92.
Dunn, Ross. *The Adventures of Ibn Battuta: A Muslim Traveler of the Fourteenth Century*. 3rd ed. Berkeley: University of California Press, 2012.
Ebrahim, Mogamat Hoosain. *The Cape Hajj Tradition: Past and Present*. Cape Town: Mogamat Hoosain Ibrahim & International Peace University, South Africa, 2009.
El-Mecky, Adnan. *De Schoolfoto (Een tijdsbeeld)*. Beek: n.p., 1988.
———. *Vergeten Namen: Verhalen uit Solo, een stad in de Vorstenlanden op Midden-Java*. Rotterdam: n.p., n.d.
Elmekki, Kussaï. *Évocations: Écrits Autobiographiques, Mémoires, Lettres, Poésies; Établis et Présentés par Rabâa ben Achour*. Carthage: Cartaginoiseries, 2011.
Emery, Frank. " 'South Africa's Best Friend': Sir Bartle Frere at the Cape, 1877-80." *Theoria* 63 (1984): 25-35.
Ewing, Cindy. "The Colombo Powers: Crafting Diplomacy in the Third World and Launching Afro-Asia at Bandung." *Cold War History* 19, no. 1 (2019): 1-19.
"An Exposition Concerning the Malays." In *Modernist Islam; A Sourcebook*, edited by Charles Kurzman, 339-43. Oxford: Oxford University Press, 2002.
Fadl b. ʿAlawi Mawla al-Dawila Ba ʿAlawi. *Majmuʿ thalath rasaʾil ʿilmiyya*. Edited by Anwar b. ʿAbdallah Salim Ba ʿUmar. Kuwayt: Dar al-Diyaʾ, 2018.
Famy, Khaled. *All the Pasha's Men: Mehmed Ali, His Army, and the Making of Modern Egypt*. Cambridge: Cambridge University Press, 1997.
Farouque, H. M. Z. "Muslim Law in Ceylon: An Historical Outline." *Muslim Marriage and Divorce Law Reports* 4 (1972): 1-28.
Feener, Roy Michael. "Tabut: Muharram Observances in the History of Bengkulu." *Studia Islamika* 6, no. 2 (1999): 87-130.

BIBLIOGRAPHY

Ferguson, John. *Ceylon in the "Jubilee Year."* Colombo: J. Haddon, 1887.
———. *Mohammedanism in Ceylon: Moormen, Malay, Afghan, and Bengali Mohammedans.* Colombo: Observer, 1897.
Fogg, Kevin. "Islam in Indonesia's Foreign Policy, 1945–1949." *Al-Jāmi'ah: Journal of Islamic Studies* 53, no. 2 (2015): 303–35.
Formichi, Chiara. "Indonesian Readings of Turkish History." In *From Anatolia to Aceh: Ottomans, Turks and Southeast Asia*, edited by A. C. S. Peacock and Annabel Teh Gallop, 241–59. Oxford: British Academy, 2015.
———. *Islam and the Making of the Nation: Kartosuwiryo and Political Islam in Twentieth-Century Indonesia.* Leiden: KITLV, 2012.
Formichi, Chiara. "Mustafa Kemal's Abrogation of the Ottoman Caliphate and Its Impact on the Indonesian Nationalist Movement." In *Demystifying the Caliphate: Historical Memory and Contemporary Contexts*, edited by Madawi al-Rasheed, Carool Kersten, and Marat Shterin, 95–116. London: Hurst, 2013.
Forrest, Thomas. *A Voyage to New Guinea and the Moluccas, from Balambangan: Including an Account of Magindano, Sooloo, and Other Islands . . . Performed in the Tartar Galley, Belonging to the Honourable East India Company, During the Years 1774, 1775, and 1776.* London: G. Scott, 1779.
Freitag, Ulrike. *A History of Jeddah: The Gate to Mecca in the Nineteenth and Twentieth Centuries.* Cambridge: Cambridge University Press, 2020.
———. *Indian Ocean Migrants and State Formation in Hadhramaut: Reforming the Homeland.* Leiden: Brill, 2003.
Freitag, Ulrike, and Hanne Schönig. "Wise Men Control Wasteful Women: Documents on Customs and Traditions in the Kathīrī State Archives, Say'ūn." *New Arabian Studies* 5 (2000): 67–96.
Further Correspondence Respecting the Affairs of Egypt: Egypt. No. 1 (1883). London: Harrison & Sons, 1883.
Gaastra, Femme. "Soldiers and Merchants: Aspects of Migration from Europe to Asia in the Dutch East India Company in the Eighteenth Century." In *Migration, Trade, and Slavery in an Expanding World: Essays in Honour of Pieter Emmer*, edited by Wim Kloster, 99–118. Leiden: Brill, 2009.
Galbraith, John S. "The Trial of Arabi Pasha." *Journal of Imperial and Commonwealth History* 7, no. 3 (1979): 274–92.
Gallop, Annabel Teh. "A Golden Sword for a Diamond Sword: Two Malay Letters from Raffles to Aceh, 1811." In *Qasidah tinta: sebuah festschrift untuk Prof. Emeritus Dr. Ahmat Adam*, edited by Lai Yew Meng, 27–60. Kinabalu: Pusat Penataran Ilmu dan Bahasa, Universiti Malaysia Sabah, 2013.
Gamieldien, Fahmi. *The History of the Claremont Main Road Mosque, Its People, and Their Contribution to Islam in South Africa.* Cape Town: Claremont Main Road Mosque, 2004.
Gelvin, James L., and Nile Green, eds. *Global Muslims in the Age of Steam and Print.* Berkeley: University of California Press, 2013.
George Viscount Valentia. *Voyages and Travels to India, Ceylon, the Red Sea, Abyssinia, and Egypt in the Years 1802–1806.* 4 vols. London: Rivington, 1811.
Getachew, Adom. *Worldmaking After Empire: The Rise and Fall of Self-Determination.* Princeton, NJ: Princeton University Press, 2019.

BIBLIOGRAPHY

Gleanings in Africa: Exhibiting a Faithful and Correct View of the Manners and Customs of the Inhabitants of the Cape of Good Hope. London: Albion, 1806.
Gleaves, Albert. *The Admiral: The Memoirs of Albert Gleaves, Admiral, USN.* Pasadena: Hope, 1985.
Göksoy, İsmail Hakkı. "Acehnese Appeals for Ottoman Protection in the Late Nineteenth Century." In *From Anatolia to Aceh: Ottomans, Turks, and Southeast Asia*, edited by A. C. S. Peacock and Annabel Teh Gallop, 175–97. Oxford: British Academy, 2015.
Gommans, Jos J. L., and Jacques Leider, eds. *The Maritime Frontier of Burma: Exploring Political, Cultural, and Commercial Interaction in the Indian Ocean World, 1200–1800.* Leiden: KITLV, 2002.
Gosselink, Martine, Maria Holtrop, and Robert Ross, eds. *Goede Hoop: Zuid-Afrika en Nederland vanaf 1600.* Amsterdam: Rijksmuseum/Van Tilt, 2017.
Green, Arnold H. *The Tunisian Ulama, 1873–1915.* Leiden: Brill, 1978.
Green, Nile. *Bombay Islam: The Religious Economy of the West Indian Ocean, 1840–1915.* Cambridge: Cambridge University Press, 2011.
Gregory, Anne. *Arabi and His Household.* London: Kegan Paul, Trench, 1882.
Gregory, William. *Egypt in 1855 and 1856; Tunis in 1857 and 1858.* 2 vols. London: John Russell Smith, 1859.
———. *Sir William Gregory, K.C.M.G., Formerly Member of Parliament and Sometime Governor of Ceylon: An Autobiography.* Edited by Augusta Gregory. London: John Murray, 1894.
Hall, Stuart. "Negotiating Caribbean Identities," *New Left Review*, no. 209 (1995): 3–14.
Hamka (Haji Abdul Malik Karim Amrullah). *Ajahku: Riwayat hidup Dr. H. Abd. Karim Amrullah dan perdjuangan kaum agama di Sumatera.* 3rd ed. Jakarta: Widjaja, 1958.
Hammond, Kelly. *China's Muslims and Japan's Empire: Centering Islam in World War II.* Chapel Hill: University of North Carolina Press, 2020.
Harper, Tim. "Singapore, 1915, and the Birth of the Asian Underground." *Modern Asian Studies* 47, no. 6 (2013): 1782–811.
———. *Underground Asia: Global Revolutionaries and the Assault on Empire.* Cambridge, MA: Belknap Press of Harvard University Press, 2021.
Harries, Patrick. "Middle Passages of the Southwest Indian Ocean: A Century of Forced Migration from Africa to the Cape of Good Hope." *Journal of African History* 55, no. 2 (2014): 173–90.
Ho Engseng. *The Graves of Tarim: Genealogy and Mobility Across the Indian Ocean.* Berkeley: University of California Press, 2006.
Hofmeyr, Isabel. *Gandhi's Printing Press: Experiments in Slow Reading.* Cambridge, MA: Harvard University Press, 2013.
———. "South Africa's Indian Ocean: Boer Prisoners of War in India." *Social Dynamics: A Journal of African Studies* 38, no. 3 (2012): 363–80.
Holman, James. *A Voyage Around the World.* 4 vols. London: Smith, Elder & Cornhill, 1834–1835.
Hopper, Matthew S. *Slaves of One Master: Globalization and Slavery in Arabia in the Age of Empire.* New Haven, CT: Yale University Press, 2015.
Hussainmiya, B. A. "Baba Ounus Saldin: An Account of a Malay Literary Savant of Sri Lanka (b. 1832–d. 1906)." *JMBRAS* 64, no. 2 (1991): 103–34.
———. *Lost Cousins: The Malays of Sri Lanka.* Bangi: Universitas Kebangsaan Malaysia, 1987.

BIBLIOGRAPHY

———. *Orang Rejimen: The Malays of the Ceylon Rifle Regiment.* Bangi: Penerbit University Kebangsaan Malaysia, 1990.

Huysers, Ariën. *Beknopte beschryving der Oostindische etablissementen verzeld van eenige bylagen, uit egte berigten te zaamen gesteld.* 2nd ed. Amsterdam: Jan Roos, 1792.

Iza Hussin. "Textual Trajectories: Re-reading the Constitution and Majalah in 1890s Johor." *Indonesia and the Malay World* 41, no. 120 (2013): 255–72.

Jacob, Wilson Jacko. *For God or Empire: Sayyid Fadl and the Indian Ocean World.* Stanford, CA: Stanford University Press, 2019.

Jasanoff, Maya. *Liberty's Exiles: American Loyalists in a Revolutionary World.* New York: Vintage, 2012.

Jubilee Book of the Colombo Malay Cricket Club. Colombo: Malay Cricket Club of Colombo, 1924.

Jeffreys, K. M. "The Malay Tombs of the Holy Circle: The Kramat at Zandvliet, Faure." *Cape Naturalist* 1, no. 6 (1939): 195–99.

———. "The Malay Tombs of the Holy Circle: The Tombs of Signal Hill Ridge." *Cape Naturalist* 1, no. 1 (1934): 15–17.

———. "The Malay Tombs of the Holy Circle: The Tombs of Signal Hill Cemetery." *Cape Naturalist* 1, no. 2 (1935): 40–43.

Jeffreys, Kathleen M., ed. *Kaapse Archiefstukken.* 7 vols. Cape Town: Cape Times, 1926–1938.

Jeppie, Shamil. "Leadership and Loyalties: The Imams of Nineteenth-Century Colonial Cape Town, South Africa." *Journal of Religion in Africa* 26, no. 2 (1996): 139–62.

———. "Re-classifications: Coloured, Malay, Muslim." In *Coloured by History, Shaped by Place: New Perspectives on Coloured Identities in Cape Town*, edited by Zimitri Erasmus, 80–96. Cape Town: Kwela, 2001.

Johnston, Alexander. "A Cufic Inscription Found in Ceylon," and "A Letter to the Secretary Relating to the Preceding Inscription." *Transactions of the Royal Asiatic Society*, 1 (1827): 545–48, 537†–48†.

Johnston, Arthur. *Narrative of the Operations of a Detachment in an Expedition to Candy, in the Island of Ceylon, in the Year 1804.* London: C. & R. Baldwin, 1810.

Jonge, Huub de. "Abdul Rahman Baswedan and the Emancipation of the Hadramis in Indonesia." *Asian Journal of Social Science* 32, no. 3 (2004): 373–400.

———. "Dutch Colonial Policy Pertaining to Hadhrami Immigrants." In *Hadhrami Traders, Scholars and Statesmen in the Indian Ocean, 1750s–1960s*, edited by Ulrike Freitag and William G. Clarence-Smith, 94–111. Leiden: Brill, 1997.

Jonge, Johan Karel Jakob de, Marinus Lodewijk van Deventer, Leonard Wilhelm Gijsbert de Roo, Pieter Anton Tiele, Jan Ernst Heeres, eds. *De Opkomst van het Nederlandsch Gezag in Oost Indie.* 18 vols. The Hague: Nijhoff, 1862–1909.

Kadı, İsmail Hakkı. "The Ottomans and Southeast Asia Prior to the Hamidian Era: A Critique of Colonial Perceptions of Ottoman-Southeast Asian Interaction." In *From Anatolia to Aceh: Ottomans, Turks, and Southeast Asia*, edited by A. C. S. Peacock and Annabel Teh Gallop, 149–74. Oxford: British Academy, 2015.

Kadı, İsmail Hakkı, and A.C. S. Peacock, eds. *Ottoman-Southeast Asian Relations: Sources from the Ottoman Archives.* 2 vols. Leiden: Brill, 2020.

Kahn, Joel. *Other Malays: Nationalism and Cosmopolitanism in the Modern Malay World.* Singapore: NUS Press, 2006.

Kannangara, A. P. "The Riots of 1915 in Sri Lanka: A Study." *Past and Present* 102 (1984): 130–65.
Kaptein, Nico. *Islam, Colonialism, and the Modern Age in the Netherlands East Indies: A Biography of Sayyid ʿUthman (1822-1914)*. Brill's Southeast Asian Library, Vol. 4. Leiden: Brill, 2014.
Kawashima Midori. "The 'White Man's Burden' and the Islamic Movement in the Philippines." In *OSEAR*, 2:877–929.
Kazeni, Arash. *The City and the Wilderness: Indo-Persian Encounters in Southeast Asia*. Oakland: University of California Press, 2020.
Khan, Syed Ahmed. *The Causes of the Indian Revolt*. Introduction by Francis Robinson. New York: Oxford University Press, 2000.
Kollisch, Maximilien. *The Mussulman Population at the Cape of Good Hope*. Constantinople: Levant Herald, 1867.
Kop, G. G. van der. *Batavia, Queen City of the East*. Batavia: Kolff, 1925.
Kramer, Martin. "Pen and Purse: Ṣābūnjī and Blunt." In *The Islamic World: From Classical to Modern Times*, edited by C. E. Bosworth, Charles Issawi, Roger Savory, and A. L. Udovitch, 771–80. Princeton, NJ: Darwin, 1989.
Kramer, Martin. *Islam Assembled: The Advent of the Muslim Congresses*. New York: Columbia University Press, 1986.
Kurasawa Aiko. "Propaganda Media on Java under the Japanese 1942–1945." *Indonesia* 44 (1987): 59–116.
Laffan, Michael Francis. "Another Andalusia: Images of Colonial Southeast Asia in Arabic Newspapers." *Journal of Asian Studies* 66, no. 3 (2007): 689–722.
———. "From Javanese Court to African Grave: How Noriman became Tuan Skapie, 1717–1806." *Journal of Indian Ocean World History* 1 (2017): 38–59.
———. *The Makings of Indonesian Islam: Orientalism and the Narration of a Sufi Past*. Princeton, NJ: Princeton University Press, 2011.
———. "The Sayyid in the Slippers: An Indian Ocean Itinerary and Visions of Arab Sainthood, 1737–1929." *Archipel* (2013): 191–227.
———. "'A Watchful Eye': The Meccan Plot of 1881 and Changing Dutch Perceptions of Islam in Indonesia." *Archipel* (2002): 79–108.
Lambourn, Elizabeth. *Abraham's Luggage: A Social Life of Things in the Medieval Indian Ocean World*. Cambridge: Cambridge University Press, 2018.
Latifa Muhammad Salim. ʿUrabi wa rifaquhu fi jannat Adam, 1883-1901. Cairo: Maktabat al-Anjalu al-Misriyya, 1987.
Lauzière, Henri. "Walking a Tightrope: Egyptian Reformers in Mecca, 1928–29." In *On the Ground: New Directions in Middle East and North African Studies*, edited by Brian T. Edwards, 65–71. Doha: Northwestern University in Qatar, 2013.
Lawrence, Kelvin. "Greed, Guns, and Gore: Historicising Early British Colonial Singapore Through Recent Developments in the Historiography of Munsyi Abdullah." *Journal of Southeast Asian Studies* 50, no .4 (2020): 507–20.
Leibbrandt, H. C. V., ed. *Precis of the Archives of the Cape of Good Hope: Letters Received, 1695-1708*. Cape Town: W. A. Richards & Sons, 1896.
———. *Precis of the Archives of the Cape of Good Hope: Requesten (Memorials) 1715-1806*. 5 vols. Cape Town: Cape Times, 1905–1989.
Leupe, P. A. "Raden Mas Kareta in 1778," *BKI* 5 (1856): 441–48.

Liaw Yock Fang. *A History of Classical Malay Literature*. Translated by Razif Bahari and Harry Aveling. Singapore: ISEAS/Yayasan Obor Indonesia, 2013.
Lima, J. S. de. *The Califa Question: Documents Connected with this Matter*. Cape Town: Van de Sandt de Villiers, 1857.
Linder, Adolphe. *The Swiss at the Cape of Good Hope*. Basel: Basler Afrika Bibliographien, 1997.
Loos, Jackie. *Echoes of Slavery: Voices from South Africa's Past*. Cape Town: David Phillips, 2004.
Louro, Michele L. " 'Where National Revolutionary Ends and Communist Begins': The League Against Imperialism and the Meerut Conspiracy Case." *Comparative Studies of South Asia, Africa, and the Middle East* 33, no. 3 (2013): 331–44.
Low, Michael Christopher. *Imperial Mecca: Ottoman Arabia and the Indian Ocean Hajj*. New York: Columbia University Press, 2020.
Lunn, David, and Julia Byl. " 'One Story Ends and Another Begins': Reading the Syair Tabut of Encik Ali." *Indonesia and the Malay World* 45, no. 133 (2017): 391–420.
Lutfi Effendi, Omer. *A Travelogue of My Journey to the Cape of Good Hope*. Cape Town: El-Khaleel, 1991.
Luttikhuis, Bart, and Arnout van der Meer. "1913 in Indonesian History: Demanding Equality, Changing Mentality." *TRaNS: Trans-Regional and -National Studies of Southeast Asia* 8, no. 2 (2020): 115–33.
Mackay, James. *Sir Thomas Lipton: The Man Who Invented Himself*. New York: Random House, 2012.
Mackenzie, Kirsten. *Imperial Underworld: An Escaped Convict and the Transformation of the British Colonial Order*. Cambridge: Cambridge University Press, 2015.
Madinier, Rémy. *Islam and Politics in Indonesia: The Masyumi Party Between Democracy and Integralism*. Singapore: NUS Press, 2015.
Mahathir Bin Mohamad. *The Malay Dilemma*. Singapore: Donald Moore for Asia Pacific, 1970.
Mahmud Fahmi. *al-Bahr al-zakhir fi tarikh al-ʿalam wa akhbar al-awaʾil wa al-awakhir*. 4 vols. Cairo: al-Matbaʿa al-Amiriyya, 1312.
———. *Mudhakkirat Mahmud Basha Fahmi: Wazir ashghal al-thawra al-ʿUrabiyya al-munaffi wa-l-mutawaffi bi-Saylan*. Cairo: al-Shinnawi, 1976.
Mandal, Sumit K., *Becoming Arab: Creole Histories and Modern Identity in the Malay World*. Cambridge: Cambridge University Press, 2018.
———. "Forging a Modern Arab Identity in Java in the Early Twentieth Century." In *Transcending Borders: Arabs, Politics, Trade, and Islam in Southeast Asia*, edited by Huub de Jonge and Nico Kaptein, 163–84. Leiden: KITLV, 2002.
Marasebessy, Bunyamin, and Moh. Amin Faroek. *Tuan Guru Imam Abdullah bin Qadhi Abdussalam: Perlawanan Terhadap Imperialisme Belanda dan Pengasingan di Cape Town*. Jakarta: Abdi Karyatama, 2005.
Mark, Ethan. *Japan's Occupation of Java in the Second World War: A Transnational History*. London: Bloomsbury, 2019.
Marsden, William. *The History of Sumatra: Containing an Account of the Government, Laws, Customs and Manners of the Native Inhabitants*. London: Thomas Payne & Son, [1783] 1784.

BIBLIOGRAPHY

Marshall, Henry. *Ceylon: A General Description of the Island and Its Inhabitants.* London: William Allen, 1847.
Mayson, John Schofield. *The Malays of Capetown.* Manchester: Galt, 1861.
McGilvray, Dennis B. "Arabs, Moors, and Muslims: Sri Lankan Muslim Ethnicity in Regional Perspective." *Contributions to Indian Sociology* 32, no. 2 (1998): 433–83.
McKenzie, Kirsten. *Imperial Underworld: An Escaped Convict and the Transformation of the British Colonial Order.* Cambridge: Cambridge University Press, 2015.
Meer, Arnout van der. *Performing Power: Cultural Hegemony, Race, and Resistance in Colonial Indonesia.* Ithaca, NY: Cornell University Press, 2021.
Memoirs of a Malayan Family, Written by Themselves, Translated from the Original. Translated by William Marsden. London: Murray, 1830.
Memoirs of Ryckloff van Goens Delivered to His Successors Jacob Hustaart on December 26, 1663 and Ryckloff van Goens the Younger on April 12, 1675. Translated by E. Reimers. Colombo: Ceylon Government Press, 1932.
Mendis, G. C., ed. *The Colebrooke-Cameron Papers (Documents on British Colonial Policy in Ceylon, 1796-1833).* 2 vols. Oxford: Oxford University Press, 1956.
Mestyan, Adam. *Arab Patriotism: The Ideology and Culture of Power in Late Ottoman Egypt.* Princeton, NJ: Princeton University Press, 2020.
Metcalf, Thomas. *Imperial Connections: India in the Indian Ocean Arena, 1860-1920.* Berkeley: University of California Press, 2007.
Methley, V. M. "The Ceylon Expedition of 1803." *Transactions of the Royal Society* 1 (1918): 92–118.
———. "Greeving's Diary." *Journal of the Ceylon Branch of the Royal Asiatic Society* 26, no. 71 (1918): 166–80.
Meulen, Daniël van der. *Hoort Gij de Donder Niet? Begin van het Einde Onzer Gezagvoering in Indië: Een persoonlijke terugblik.* Franeker: T. Wever, 1977.
Millie, Julian, ed. *Hasan Mustapa: Ethnicity and Islam in Indonesia.* Clayton: Monash University Press, 2017.
Minault, Gail. *The Khilafat Movement: Religious Symbolism and Political Mobilization in India.* New York: Columbia University Press, 1982.
Mirza Abu Taleb. *Westward Bound: Travels of Mirza Abu Taleb.* Edited with an introduction by Mushirul Hasan. Translated by Charles Stewart. New Delhi: Oxford University Press, 2005.
Mobini-Kesheh, Natalie. "The Arab Periodicals of the Netherlands East Indies, 1914-1942." *BKI* 152, no. 2 (1996): 236–56.
———. *The Hadrami Awakening: Community and Identity in the Netherlands East Indies, 1900-1942.* Ithaca, NY: Southeast Asia Program, 1999.
Mohammad Rezuan Othman. "Conflicting Political Loyalties of the Arabs in Malaya before World War II." In *Transcending Borders: Arabs, Politics, Trade, and Islam in Southeast Asia,* edited by H. de Jonge and N. Kaptein, 37–52. Leiden: KITLV, 2002.
———. "The Ottoman's [sic] War with the Europeans: A Paradigm Shift in the Development of Malay Political Thought." *Jebat* (1995): 89–96.
Morton, Shafiq. *From the Spice Islands to Cape Town: The Life and Times of Tuan Guru.* Cape Town: Awqaf SA, 2019.

BIBLIOGRAPHY

Mosse, A. H. E. *An Account of the Arab Tribes in the Vicinity of Aden*. Bombay: Government Central Press, 1909.

Mountain, Alan. *An Unsung Heritage: Perspectives on Slavery*. Cape Town: David Philip, 2004.

Muhammad Abdul Sathar, K. K. *Mappila Leader in Exile: A Political Biography of Syed Fażl Pookoya Tangal*. Calicut: Other Books, 2012.

Muhammad Hajji Salih, ed. *Early History of Penang*. Pulau Pinang: Penerbit Universiti Sains Malaysia, 2015.

Muhammad Rashid Rida. *al-Khilafa aw al-imama al-ʿuzma*. Cairo: al-Manar, 1934.

——. *Tarikh al-ustadh al-imam al-shaykh Muhammad ʿAbduh*. Cairo: al-Dar al-Fadila, 2007.

Naam-boek van de wel edele heeren van de hoge Indiasche regering zoo tot, als buiten, Batavia: mitsgaders van de politique bedienden... zoo als dezelve onder ultimo december... alhier in weezen zyn bevonden. Vol. 4. Batavia: Pieter van van Geemen, 1791.

Nadaraja, Tambyah. *The Legal System of Ceylon in Its Historical Setting*. Leiden: Brill, 1972.

Nakano Satoshi. *Japan's Colonial Moment in Southeast Asia, 1942-1945: The Occupiers' Experience*. Abingdon: Routledge, 2018.

Neethling, E. M., and L. C. P. *Die Neethlings in Suid-Afrika*. Pretoria: Raad vir Geesteswetenskaplike Navorsing, 1979.

Noer, Deliar. *The Modernist Muslim Movement in Indonesia, 1900-1942*. Kuala Lumpur: Oxford University Press, 1973.

Norton-Kyshe, J. W. *Cases Heard and Determined, 1808-90*. 4 vols. Singapore: Singapore & Straits Printing Office, 1885-1890.

Obeyesekere, Gananath. *The Doomed King: A Requiem for Sri Vikrama Rajasinha*. Colombo: Sailfish, 2017.

Ochsenwald, William. *Religion, Society, and the State in Arabia: The Hijaz Under Ottoman Control, 1840-1908*. Columbus: Ohio State University Press, 1984.

Oddie, Geoffey. "The Western-Educated Elites and Popular Religion: The Debate over the Hook-Swinging Issue in Bengal and Madras, c. 1830–1894." In *Society and Ideology: Essays in South Asian History Presented to Professor K. A. Ballhatchet*, edited by Peter Robb, K. N. Chaudhuri, and Avril Powell, 177–95. New York: Oxford University Press, 1993.

Ono Ryosuke. "Southeast Asian Muslims in the Dai-Nihon Kaikyo Kyokai's Photography Collection." In *Islam and Multiculturalism: Exploring Islamic Studies Within a Symbiotic Framework*, edited by Kazuaki Sawai, Yukari Sai, and Hirofumi Oka, 127–28. Tokyo: Organization for Islamic Area Studies, Waseda University, 2015.

Orang Indonesia jang Terkemoeka di Djawa. Jakarta: Gunseikanbu, 2604.

Özcan, Azmi. *Pan-Islamism: Indian Muslims, the Ottomans, and Britain, 1877-1924*. Leiden: Brill, 1997.

——. "The Press and Anglo-Ottoman Relations, 1876–1909." *Middle Eastern Studies*, 29, no. 1 (1993): 111–17.

Papers Relative to the Condition and Treatment of the Native Inhabitants of Southern Africa, Within the Colony of the Cape of the Good Hope. London: House of Parliament, 1835.

Pearson, Michael. *The Portuguese in India*. Cambridge: Cambridge University Press, 1987.

Peires, J. B. *The Dead Will Arise: Nongqawuse and the Great Xhosa Cattle-Killing Movement of 1856-57*. Bloomington: Indiana University Press, 1989.

BIBLIOGRAPHY

Penn, Nigel. "Mapping the Cape: John Barrow and the First British Occupation of the Colony, 1795–1803." *Pretexts* 4, no. 2 (1993): 20–43.

Percival, Robert. *An Account of the Cape of Good Hope: Containing an Historical View of Its Original Settlement by the Dutch, Its Capture by the British in 1795, and the Different Policy Pursued There by the Dutch and British Governments*. London: C. & R. Baldwin, 1804.

———. *An Account of the Island of Ceylon, Containing Its History, Geography, Natural History, with the Manners and Customs of Its Various Inhabitants: to Which Is Added, the Journal of an Embassy to the Court of Candy*. London: C. & R. Baldwin, 1803.

Pieres, Anoma. *Architecture and Nationalism in Sri Lanka: The Trouser Under the Cloth*. London: Routledge, 2017.

Plessis, I. D. du. *The Cape Malays*. Cape Town: Maskew Miller, [1944].

Poeze, Harry. "Early Indonesian Emancipation: Abdul Rivai, Van Heutsz, and the Bintang Hindia." *BKI* 145, no. 1 (1989): 87–106.

Poivre, Pierre Le. *Travels of a Philosopher: or, Observations on the Manners and Arts of Various Nations in Africa and Asia*. Glasgow: Robert Urie, 1770.

Post, Peter, William H. Frederick, Iris Heidebrink, Shigeru Satō, William Bradley Horton, and Didi Kwartanada, ed. *The Encyclopedia of Indonesia in the Pacific War*. Leiden: Brill, 2010.

Powell, Michael. "Fragile Identities: The Colonial Consequences of CJR Le Mesurier in Ceylon." *Journal of Colonialism & Colonial History* 11, no. 1 (Spring 2010): https://oneira.com.au/the-colonial-consequences-of-cjr-le-mesurier-in-ceylon/ (accessed February 9, 2022).

Prange, Sebastian. *Monsoon Islam: Trade and Faith on the Medieval Malabar Coast*. Cambridge: Cambridge University Press, 2018.

Prestholdt, Jeremy. "From Zanzibar to Beirut: Sayyide Salme and the Tensions of Cosmopolitanism." In *Global Muslims in the Age of Steam and Print*, edited by James Gelvin and Nile Green, 204–26. Berkeley: University of California Press, 2014.

Raffles, Thomas Stamford. *The History of Java*. 2 vols. London: Black, Parbury & Allen, 1817.

———. *Malay Annals: Translated from the Malay Language, by John Leyden*. London: Longman, 1821.

———. "On the Maláyu Nation, with a Translation of its Maritime Institutions." *Asiatick Researches* 12 (1818): 102–58.

Rafudeen, Auwais. *The ʿAqidah of Tuan Guru*. Cape Town: Samandar, 2004.

Rasheed, Madawi al-, Carool Kersten, and Marat Shterin. "The Caliphate: Nostalgic Memory and Contemporary Visions." In *Demystifying the Caliphate: Historical Memory and Contemporary Contexts*, edited by Madawi al-Rasheed, Carool Kersten, and Marat Shterin, 1–30. London: Hurst, 2013.

Realia: Register op de Generale resolutiën van het kasteel Batavia, 1632–1805. 3 vols. Leiden: G. Kolff, 1882–16.

Reese, Scott. *Imperial Muslims: Islam, Community, and Authority in the Indian Ocean, 1839–1937*. Edinburgh: Edinburgh University Press, 2018.

Reid, Anthony. *The Blood of the People: Revolution and the End of Traditional Rule in Northern Sumatra*. Singapore: NUS Press, 2014.

———. "Habib Abdur-Rahman az-Zahir (1833–1896)." *Indonesia* 13 (1972): 36–59.

———. *An Indonesian Frontier: Acehnese and Other Histories of Sumatra*. Leiden: KITLV, 2005.

BIBLIOGRAPHY

———. *The Ottomans in Southeast Asia.* Asia Research Institute Working Paper Series, no. 36. Singapore: ARI, 2005.
Reputations Live On: An Early Malay Autobiography. Edited by Amin Sweeney. Berkeley: University of California Press, 1980.
Ricci, Ronit. *Banishment and Belonging: Exile and Diaspora in Sarandib, Lanka, and Ceylon.* Cambridge: Cambridge University Press, 2019.
———. "The Malay World, Expanded, the World's First Malay Newspaper, Colombo, 1869." *Indonesia and the Malay World* 41, no. 120 (2013): 168–82.
Ricklefs, M. C. *Jogjakarta under Sultan Mangkubumi, 1749–1792: A History of the Division of Java.* London: Oxford University Press, 1974.
———. *Polarising Javanese Society: Islamic and Other Visions, c. 1830–1930.* Singapore: NUS Press, 2007.
———. *Soul Catcher: Java's Fiery Prince Mangkunagara I, 1726–95.* Honolulu: University of Hawai'i Press, 2018.
Rinn, Louis. *Marabouts et Khouan: étude sur l'Islam en Algérie.* Algiers: A. Jourdan, 1884.
Ritchie, John. *Lachlan Macquarie: A Biography.* Melbourne: Melbourne University Press, 1986.
Rocher, Rosane, and Ludo Rocher. *The Making of Western Indology: Henry Thomas Colebrooke and the East India Company.* London: Royal Asiatic Society Books/Routledge, 2011.
Rodionov, Mikhail, and Hanne Schönig. *The Hadramawt Documents, 1904–51: Family Life and Social Customs Under the Last Sultans.* Beirut: Ergon/Orient-Institute, 2011.
Roff, William R. *Bibliography of Malay and Arabic Periodicals.* London: Oxford University Press, 1972.
———. "Sanitation and Security: The Imperial Powers and the Nineteenth-Century Hajj." *Arabian Studies* 6 (1982): 143–60.
Rogers, John. "Colonial Perceptions of Ethnicity and Culture in Early Nineteenth-Century Sri Lanka." In *Society and Ideology: Essays in South Asian History Presented to Professor K.A. Ballhatchet,* edited by Peter Robb, K. N. Chaudhuri, and Avril Powell, 97–109. New York: Oxford University Press, 1993.
Rohmana, Jajang A. *Informan Sunda Masa Kolonial: Surat-Surat Haji Hasan Mustapa untuk C. Snouck Hurgronje dalam Kurun 1894–1923.* Yogyakarta: Octopus, 2018.
Roolvink, R. "The Variant Versions of the Malay Annals." In *Sějarah Mělayu or Malay Annals,* edited by C. C. Brown, xv–xxxv. Kuala Lumpur: Oxford University Press, 1970.
Ross, Robert. *Status and Respectability in the Cape Colony, 1750–1870: A Tragedy of Manners.* Cambridge: Cambridge University Press, 2004.
Rothman, Natalie. *Brokering Empire: Trans-Imperial Subjects Between Venice and Istanbul.* Ithaca, NY: Cornell University Press, 2012.
[Roubaix, Petrus. E. de.] *Correspondence Passed between His Highness Aali Pacha, Minister of Foreign Affairs, of the Sublime Porte, and the Honorable P. E. De Roubaix, Esq., Consul General of the Sublime Porte, Cape of Good Hope.* Cape Town: J. H. Hofmeijr, 1871.
Ruete, Emily, E. van Donzel, ed. *An Arabian Princess Between Two Worlds: Memoirs, Letters Home, Sequels to the Memoirs, Syrian Customs, and Usages.* Leiden: Brill, 1993.

BIBLIOGRAPHY

Rush, James R. "Sukarno: Anticipating an Asian Century." In *Makers of Modern Asia*, edited by Ramachandra Guha, 172–98. Cambridge, MA: Belknap Press of Harvard University Press, 2014.

Russell, William Howard. *The Prince of Wales' Tour: A Diary in India: With Some Account of the Visits of His Royal Highness to the Courts of Greece, Egypt, Spain, and Portugal.* New York: R. Worthington, 1878.

Saldin, B. D. K. *Orang Melayu Sri Lanka dan Bahasanya*. Colombo: Sridevi, 1996.

Saldin, Baba Ounous. *Syair Fayd al-abad: Artinya kediamannya berbagai pengetahuan*. Colombo: Alamat Langkapuri, AH 1322.

Samaweera, Viyaya. "Arabi Pasha in Ceylon, 1883–1901." *Islamic Culture* 50, no. 4 (1976): 219–27.

Samir Muhammad Taha. *Mahmud Fahmi Pasha: Raʾis ʿumum arkan harb al-jaysh al-Misri qabil al-ihtilal al-Baritani sanat 1882*. Cairo: Maktabat Saʿid Raʿfat, 1984.

Samuelson, Meg. "Orienting the Cape: A 'White' Woman Writing Islam in South Africa." *Social Dynamics* 37, no. 3 (2011): 363–78.

———. "Re-imagining South Africa via a Passage to India: M. K. Jeffreys's Archive of the Indian Ocean World." *Social Dynamics* 33, no. 2 (2007): 61–85.

Schmidt, Jan. *Through the Legation Window: Four Essays on Dutch, Dutch-Indian, and Ottoman History*. Istanbul: Nederlands Historisch-Archaologisch Instituut, 1992.

Schofield, G. "Notes and Communications." *Bulletin of the School of Oriental and African Studies, University of London* 24, no. 1 (1961): 139–41.

Schrieke, B. "Bijdrage tot de bibliographie van de huidige godsdienstige beweging ter Sumatra's Westkust." *TBG* 59 (1919–21): 249–325.

Schrikker, Alicia. "Caught Between Empires: VOC Families in Sri Lanka After the British Take-over, 1806–1808." *Annales de démographie historique* 122 no. 2 (2011): 127–47.

———. *Dutch and British Colonial Intervention in Sri Lanka, 1780–1815: Expansion and Reform*. Leiden: Brill, 2007.

Seben, H. Taner. *The First Turkish Representatives in Singapore and Consul General Ahmed Ataullah Efendi*. Singapore: Republic of Turkey Embassy, 2015.

Selms, Adrianus van. *Abu Bakar se 'Uiteensetting van die godsdiens:' 'n Arabie-Afrikaanse Teks uit die Jaar 1869*. Amsterdam: North-Holland, 1979.

———. "Introduction." In *The Religious Duties of Islam as Taught and Explained by Abu Bakr Effendi*, edited by Mia Brandel Syrier, x–xxxvii. Leiden: Brill, 1960.

Semple, Robert. *Walks and Sketches at the Cape of Good Hope*. Edited by F. R. Bradlow. Cape Town: Balkema, [1803] 1968.

Sevea, Teren. "Keramats Running Amuck: Islamic Parahistories of Travel, Belonging, Crimes, and Madness." In *Belonging Across the Bay of Bengal: Religious Rites, Colonial Migrations, National Rights*, edited by Michael Francis Laffan, 57–71. New York: Bloomsbury Academic, 2017.

Sharkey, Heather J. "Aḥmad Zaynī Daḥlān's *al-Futuḥāt al-Islāmiyya*: A Contemporary View of the Sudanese Mahdi." *Sudanic Africa* 5 (1994): 67–75.

Shell, R. C. H. "The March of the Mardijkers: The Toleration of Islam in the Cape Colony." *Kronos* 22 (1995): 3–20.

Shimazu Naoko. "Diplomacy as Theatre: Staging the Bandung Conference of 1955." *Modern Asian Studies* 48, no. 1 (2013): 225–52.

Shiraishi Takashi. *An Age in Motion: Popular Radicalism in Java, 1912-1926*. Ithaca, NY: Cornell University Press, 1990.
Silva, R. K. de. *19th-Century Newspaper Engravings of Ceylon—Sri Lanka: Accompanied by Original Texts with Notes and Comments*. London: Serendib, 1998.
Sivasundaram, Sujit. *Waves Across the South: A New History of Revolution and Empire*. London: William Collins, 2020.
Skinner, Cyril, ed. *The Battle for Junk Ceylon: The Syair Sultan Maulana*. Dordrecht: Foris, 1985.
Skinner, Thomas. *Fifty Years in Ceylon: An Autobiography, 1818-1868*. Edited by Annie Skinner. London: W. H. Allen, 1891.
Slight, John. *The British Empire and the Hajj, 1865-1956*. Cambridge, MA: Harvard University Press, 2015.
Smith, G. Rex. "'Ingrams Peace,' Ḥaḍramawt, 1937-40: Some Contemporary Documents." *Journal of the Royal Asiatic Society* 12, no. 1 (2002): 1-30.
Snouck Hurgronje, C. *Mekka in the Latter Part of the 19th Century: Daily Life, Customs, and Learning of the Moslems of the East Indian Archipelago*. Translated by J. H. Monahan. Leiden: Brill, 1931.
Snouck Hurgronje, C. "Jâwah Ulama in Mekka in the Late Nineteenth Century." In *Readings on Islam in Southeast Asia*, compiled and edited by Ahmad Ibrahim, Sharon Siddique, and Yasmin Hussain, 70-79. Singapore: Institute of Southeast Asian Studies, 1985.
Soebagijo I. N. *K. H. Mas Mansur: Pembaharu Islam di Indonesia*. Jakarta: Gunung Agung, 1982.
[Solomon, S.] *The Progress of His Royal Highness, Prince Alfred Ernest Albert, Through the Cape Colony, British Kaffraria, the Orange Free State, and Port Natal, in the Year 1860*. Cape Town: Saul Solomon, 1861.
Sparrman, Andrew. *A Voyage to the Cape of Good Hope Towards the Antarctic Polar Circle and Round the World: But Chiefly into the Country of the Hottentots and Caffres, from the Year 1772, to 1776*. 2 vols. London: Johnson, 1971.
Stapel F. W., ed. *Corpus Diplomaticum Neerlando-Indicum*. The Hague: Martinus Nijhoff, 1955.
Stavorinus, Johan Splinter. *Reize van Zeeland over de Kaap de Goede Hoop, naar Batavia, Bantam, Bengalen enz. gedaan in de jaaren MDCCLXVIII tot MDCCLXXI*. 2 vols. Leiden: A. & J. Honkoop, 1793.
———. *Reize van Zeeland over de Kaap de Goede Hoop, en Batavia, naar Semarang, Macasser, Amboina, Suratte, enz. gedaan in de jaaren MDCCLXXIV tot MDCCLXXVIII, enz*. 2 vols. Leiden: A. & J. Honkoop, 1797-98.
———. *Voyages to the East Indies*. 3 vols. Translated by Samuel Hull Wilcocke. London: G.G. & J. Robinson, 1798.
Stockdale, J. J. *Sketches, Civil and Military, of the Island of Java and Its Immediate Dependencies*. 2nd ed. London: J. J. Stockdale, [1811] 1812.
Streets-Salter, Heather. *World War One in Southeast Asia: Colonialism and Anticolonialism in an Era of Global Conflict*. Cambridge: Cambridge University Press, 2021.
Subrahmanyam, Sanjay. "Connected Histories: Notes towards a Reconfiguration of Early Modern Eurasia." *Modern Asian Studies* 31, no .3 (1997): 735-62.
———. *Explorations in Connected History*. 2 vols. New Delhi: Oxford University Press, 2005.

———. *The Political Economy of Commerce: Southern India, 1500–1650.* Cambridge: Cambridge University Press, 1990.
———. *The Portuguese Empire in Asia, 1500–1700.* London: Longman, 1992.
Sukarno. *Di Bawah Bendera Revolusi.* 3rd ed. 2 vols. Jakarta: Panitya Penerbit Di Bawah Bendera Revolusi, 1964.
———. *Indonesia Accuses! Soekarno's Defence Oration in the Political Trial of 1930.* Edited and translated by Roger K. Paget. Kuala Lumpur: Oxford University Press, 1978.
———. *Indonesia Menggugat: Pidato Pembelaan Bung Karno Dimuka Hakim Kolonial.* Jakarta: Penerbitan S. K. Seno. 1956.
Suryadi. "Sepucuk Surat dari Seorang Bangsawan Gowa di Tanah Pembuangan (Ceylon)." *Wacana* 10, no. 2 (2008): 213–44.
Sutrisno Kutoyo. *Kyai Haji Mas Mansur.* Jakarta: Proyek Inventarisasi dan Dokumentasi Sejarah Nasional Indonesia, 1981.
Symes, Michael. *An Account of an Embassy to the Kingdom of Ava, Sent by the Governor-General of India, in the Year 1795.* London: W. Bulmer, 1800.
Tagliacozzo, Eric. *The Longest Journey: Southeast Asians and the Pilgrimage to Mecca.* Oxford: Oxford University Press, 2013.
Taylor, Jean Gelman. "Belongings and Belonging: Indonesian Histories of Inventories from the Cape of Good Hope." In *Exile in Colonial Asia: Kings, Convicts, Commemoration,* edited by Ronit Ricci, 165–92. Honolulu: University of Hawai'i Press, 2016.
Temple, Richard. *Oriental Experience: A Selection of Essays and Addresses Delivered on Various Occasions.* London: J. Murray, 1883.
The Voyage of John Huyghen Van Linschoten to the East Indies: From the Old English Translation of 1598. 2 vols. Edited by Arthur Coke Burnell. Abingdon: Routledge, 2016.
Theal, George McCall. *Records of the Cape Colony.* 36 vols. Cape Town: n.p., 1897–1905.
Thomas, Paul. "Oodeen, a Malay Interpreter on Australia's Frontier Lands." *Indonesia and the Malay World* 40, no. 117 (2012): 122–42.
Thunberg, Carl Peter. *Travels at the Cape of Good Hope, 1772–1775: Based on the English Edition London, 1793–1795.* Cape Town: Van Riebeeck Society, 1986.
Travers, Robert. "The Connected Worlds of Haji Mustapha (c. 1730–91): A Eurasian Cosmopolitan in Eighteenth-Century Bengal." *Indian Economic & Social History Review* 52, no. 2 (2015): 297–333.
Trumbull, George R. "French Colonial Knowledge of Maraboutism." In *Islam and the European Empires,* edited by David Motadel, 269–86. Oxford: Oxford University Press, 2014.
Tschacher, Torsten. "Circulating Islam: Understanding Convergence and Divergence in the Islamic Traditions of Maʿbar and Nusantara." In *Islamic Connections: Studies of South and Southeast Asia,* edited by R. Michael Feener and Terenjit Sevea, 48–67. Singapore: Institute of Southeast Asian Studies, 2009.
———. "'Walls of Illusion': Information Generation in Colonial Singapore and the Reporting of the Mahdi-Rebellion in Sudan, 1887–1890." In *Singapore in Global History,* edited by Derek Heng and Muhd Khairudin Aljunied, 67–88. Amsterdam: Amsterdam University Press, 2011.
Toulba, Ali Foad. *Ceylon: The Land of Eternal Charm.* London: Hutchinson, 1926.
Um, Nancy. *The Merchant Houses of Mocha: Trade and Architecture in an Indian Ocean Port.* Seattle: University of Washington Press, 2009.

Valentijn, François. *Oud en Nieuw Oost-Indiën*, 8 vols. Dordrecht: J. van Braam, 1724–1726.

VOC-Glossarium: Verklaringen van termen, verzameld uit de Rijks Geschiedkundige Publicatiën die betrekking hebben op de Verenigde Oost-indische Compagnie. The Hague: Instituut voor Nederlandse Geschiedenis, 2000.

Wal S. L., van der, ed. *De Opkomst van de Nationalistische Beweging in Nederlands-Indie: Een Bronnenpublikatie*. Groningen: J. B. Wolters, 1967.

Wallace, Alfred Russell. *The Malay Archipelago: The Land of the Orang-Utan, and the Bird of Paradise*. London: Macmillan, 1869.

Ward, Kerry. *Networks of Empire: Forced Migration in the Dutch East India Company*. Cambridge: Cambridge University Press, 2009.

Wasti, Syed Tanvir. "Sir Syed Ahmad Khan and the Turks." *Middle Eastern Studies* 46, no. 4 (2010): 529–42.

Wazir Jahan Karim. "The 'Discovery' of Penang Island at Tanjong Tokong Before 1785: Bapu Alaidin Meera Hussein Lebai and Captain Francis Light." *Journal of the Malaysian Branch of the Royal Asiatic Society* 86, no. 1 (2013): 1–29.

Wettenhall, R. L. "Gregory, John (1795–1853)." In *Australian Dictionary of Biography*, National Centre of Biography, Australian National University.

Wickramasinghe, Nira. *Slave in a Palanquin: Colonial Servitude and Resistance in Sri Lanka*. New York: Columbia University Press, 2020.

Widjojo, Muridan. *The Revolt of Prince Nuku: Cross-Cultural Alliance-Making in Maluku, c. 1780–1810*. Leiden: Brill, 2009.

Wiggers, F. *Toerki dan Joenani (Griekenland)*. Batavia: Albrecht, 1897.

Wirjosukarto, Amir Hamzah, ed. *Rangkaian Mutu-Manikam: Kumpulan Buah Pikiran Budiman Kjahi Hadji Mas Mansur, 1896–1946*. Surabaya: Al-Ichsan, [1968].

Worden, Nigel, and Gerald Groenewald, eds. *Trials of Slavery: Selected Documents Concerning Slaves from the Criminal Records of the Council of Justice at the Cape of Good Hope, 1705–1794*. Series 2, no. 36. Cape Town: Van Riebeeck Society for the Publication of South African Historical Documents, 2005.

Wright, Arnold. *Twentieth Century Impressions of Ceylon: Its History, People, Commerce, Industries, and Resources*. London: Lloyd's Greater Britain Publishing, 1907.

Wright, Richard. *The Color Curtain: A Report on the Bandung Conference*. New York: World, 1956.

Yahaya, Nurfadzilah. *Fluid Jurisdictions: Colonial Law and Arabs in Southeast Asia*. Ithaca, NY: Cornell University Press, 2020.

Yellen, Jeremy. *The Greater East Asia Co-Prosperity Sphere: When Total Empire Met Total War*. Ithaca, NY: Cornell University Press, 2019.

Zolondek, L. "Sabunji in England 1876–91: His Role in Arabic Journalism." *Middle Eastern Studies* 14, no. 1 (1978): 102–15.

Index

Abas b. Muhammad Taha, 269–71, 276
ʿAbbas Hilmi, Khedive, 227–28, 235, 252, 280, 298, 299, 302
ʿAbbasid caliphs, 197
ʿAbd al-ʿAl Hilmi, 210, 214, 218, 223, 227
Abd al-Alim (Dul Alim), 63, 354n36
ʿAbd al-ʿAziz al-Halabi, 307
Abd al-Bahhar, Khatib at Colombo 175, 176
Abd al-Bari (Abdolbarick), 110, 112, 275
Abd al-Basir (Abdolbazier), 110, 114
Abd al-Hamid, Capetonian imam. *See* Abdol Gamiedt
ʿAbdallah, Shaykh and trader at Cape, 104
ʿAbdallah, Sidi, 298
ʿAbdallah al-Ahdal, 168–69
Abdallah bin Abd al-Salam (Tuan Guru): background of, 27–28, 55–56, 67; burial place of, 28, 193; in Cape Town, 55–72, 74; daughter of, 65–66; death of, 89; exiling of, 25, 37–38; father of, 55–56; handwriting of, 71; Javanese identity of, 67–68; legacy and followers of, 28–29, 31–34, 59–64, 66, 71–72, 74–75, 102–3, 108–14, 118, 184, 188; letters of, 44, 46, 56–57, *58*, 65–67; *Maʿrifat al-Islam wa-l-iman*

(The knowledge of Islam and belief), 33–34, 49, 51–52, 57; marriage of, 57; Qurʾan owned by, *49*; religious activities of, 34, 43, 48–52, 55–56, 62, 71–72, 87; on Robben Island, 27, 33–34, 40–47, 53, 55, 57, 65; as slave holder, 64, 69–70, 102; sons of, 40, 45, 46, 52, 53, 64, 65, 68, 118, 352n14; and Sufism, 63; will made by, 65–66, 68–69, 112
ʿAbdallah al-ʿAttas, 253, 268, 270, 276, 284–85
ʿAbdallah Ba Dhib, 175
ʿAbdallah Badjerei, 290
ʿAbdallah al-Haddad, 168
ʿAbdallah al-Junayd, 241–42, 244–45, 247, 249
ʿAbdallah Ba Kathir, 264
Abdallah Mukarram Shah, Sultan of Kedah 128–29, 132
ʿAbdallah II of Anjouan, 101, 103
ʿAbdallah b. ʿUmar al-Quʿayti, 250
ʿAbdallah Zawawi, 261
Abd al-Malik (Abdol Malik Betawi), 63, 65, 68, 69, 104, 356n68
ʿAbd al-Muttalib, Sharif of Mecca, 199–200

[443]

INDEX

ʿAbd al-Qadir, Amir, 203
ʿAbd al-Qadir Jilani, 184, 231
ʿAbd al-Rahman Ba Junayd, 249, 253
ʿAbd al-Rahman al-Misri, 195
ʿAbd al-Rahman Naqid, 192
ʿAbd al-Rahman b. Saqqaf, 272
Abd al-Rahman Khan, Amir of Afghanistan, 269
ʿAbd al-Rahman al-Zahir al-Saqqaf, Habib, 195–96, 246–48, 251–52, 400n73
Abd al-Rakib (son of Abdallah), 59, 65, 68–69, 105, 108
Abd al-Rakib (grandson of Abdallah), 181, 186–87, 189
Abd al-Rauf, qadi of Tidore, 32, 38, 40–42, 44–47, 65
Abd al-Rauf (son of Abdallah), 64, 65, 68–69, 105, 110, 115, 118, 181–83, 187
ʿAbd al-Raʾuf Sabban, Shaykh, 297–98
Abd al-Salam (qadi and father of Abdallah), 28, 55–56
ʿAbd al-Samad of Palembang, 125, 128, 175, 195; *Sayr al-salikin*, 125
Abd al-Shukur, 61, 65, 355n49
Abd al-Wahab (Abdol Wahab), 114–15, 118–19, 182–83
Abd al-Wahhab Deli, Haji, 408n127
ʿAbd al-Wahhab, Muhammad b., 290
Abd al-Wahid Tapanuli, 298
Abd al-Wasi (Abdol Wassie, Galant van Balie), 63, 68, 105, 109–10, 111–12
Abdol Gamiedt (Abd al-Hamid), 74, 89, 104
Abdol Garies (Abd al-Haris), 96
Abdolrapiek (Rafiek?), 104
Abdol Zaghie, 95–96, 117, 121
ʿAbduh, Muhammad, 15–16, 196, 202, 204–5, 207–8, 233, 235, 237, 252, 264, 271, 283, 290, 291
Abdulaziz, Ottoman Sultan, 13, 15, 126, 171, 172, 177, 178–79, 182, 185, 194, 233
Abdul Hamid, Mas. *See* Anang, K. H.
Abdulhamid II, Ottoman Sultan, 14–15, 19, 126, 190, 193, 198–201, 203, 205, 209–10, 215, 225, 233–34, 248–49, 251, 254, 254–59, 261–62, 269, 298
Abdul Jappar (Abd al-Jabbar), 104
Abdullah, Capetonian Hajji, 178, 188–89, 385n50
Abdullah (son of Samoudien), 116
Abdullah bin Abd al-Qadir, Munshi, 92, 161
Abdullah Ahmad, 270
Abdullah, Sultan of Perak, 196
Abdul Malek (Abd al-Malik Betawi), 104
Abdulmecid, Ottoman Sultan, 13, 121, 165, 167, 169, 180
Abdul Rahman Ijahad, 216
Abdul Rakib, 65
Abdul Wahab Hasbullah, 299, 301, 303, 318, 326, 327
Abdurahman, Abdullah, 291
Abdurresid Ibrahim, 314
Abi l-Siddiq Muhammad Sadiq, 30
Abcarius, Negib, 214
Abu al-Huda al-Sayyadi, 199
Abu Bakar of Johor, 15, 196, 233–34, 244, 246, 252, 259, 269, 303
Abu Bakr (first caliph), 93, 117, 174
Abu Bakr al-ʿAttas, 270, 274, 276, 284–85, 303
Abu Bakr b. Sunkar, 253
Abu Bakr Effendi, 113, 178, 180–95, 249, 260, 280; *Bayan al-din*, 187, 190
Abu Fadl al-Ansari, Muhammad, 305
Abu Qisha (newspaper), 284
Abyssinia, 194, 211
Abyssinia (ship), 190
Aceh, 14, 36, 170, 189–90, 195–96, 216, 234, 243, 245–48, 250–52, 255–56, 260, 263, 269
Achmat Sadick (son of Achmat van Bengalen), 115, 117–18, 187–89
Achmat van Bengalen, 59–60, 63–64, 66, 69, 71, 72, 74, 97, 103–5, 107–12, 114–15, 117, 180–81, 183, 186, 356n64
Achmet of Arabia, 104
Achtardeen, 110
Aden, 18, 168, 192, 287–88

[444]

INDEX

Adnan, R. H. M., 322
Advertiser and Mail (newspaper), 120
African Court Calendar (newspaper), 104, 105, 114
Agie, Raden Tumenggong, 59
Agung, Sultan, 328
Ahagé. *See* Hagi
Ahelepola Nilame, 156–58
Ahl al-Watan (People of the Homeland), 299
Ahmad, Kapitan Laut of Ternate, 40, 47–48, 55–58, 63, 65, 68, 70
Ahmad Ba Junayd, 262–63
Ahmad b. Sumayt, 264
Ahmad b. Uthman al-Sumbawi, 171
Ahmad Effendi, 257
Ahmad Emin Aali Pasha, 189
Ahmad Fauzi Imran, 271, 298, 403n18
Ahmad Hassan, 311, 313, 319
Ahmad Khatib al-Minangkabawi, 257
Ahmad Lampung, 297
Ahmad Marzuqi, 297, 298
Ahmad Muhtar Pasha, 252
Ahmad Najm al-Din, 128
Ahmad Ratib Pasha, 205, 209
Ahmad Taj al-Din, 129–31, 169
Aisa, Sitti, 135
ʿAʾisha (wife of Muhammad), 326, 327
Afghani, Jamal al-Din al-, 202, 215, 252, 310
Alamat Langkapuri (journal), 172, 174–77, 194
ʿAlawi (Tuan Said), 12, 28–29, 31, 34, 41, 48, 50–51, 55, 63, 65, 68, 71, 136, 192
ʿAlawi al-Saqqaf, 168
ʿAlawi Bond (al-Rabita al-ʿAlawiyya), 304
ʿAlawiyya, 63
Albert, Prince Consort, 165
Albert Edward, Prince of Wales, 127, 165, 229, 230
Aldrich, Robert, 196
Alexander II, Tsar, 14
Alfred, Prince, 9, 119–21, 182, 224
Algemeene Studieclub, 308
ʿAli, fourth caliph, 231

Ali Haji, Raja, 171
ʿAli b. ʿAlwi al-Jifri, 171
ʿAli al-ʿAttas, brother-in-law of Hachemi, 305, 316, 320, 407n94, 416n41
Ali brothers (Khilafat Movement), 275, 300
ʿAli b. Ahmad b. Shahab (Habib ʿAli Menteng), 4–5, 273, 279–81, 287, 302, 312, 405n69, 407n109
ʿAli b. Sahl, 262
ʿAli al-Shibli, 277
ʿAli Junayd, 246
Al-Islam Conferences. *See* Indies Islam Congress
All-Ceylon Malay Association, 291–92
alliances, 36–37
Alsagoff, Mohamed (Sayyid Muhammad al-Saqqaf), 242, 244, 397n3
Alting, Willem Arnold, 135
Amangkurat III, 41
Amanullah Khan, 309
amok, 54, 78, 81–83, 85–86, 88, 91, 100, 143, 160, 161, 231, 234
Amsterdam van de Kaap. *See* Wirakusuma, Raden Tumenggong
Anang, K. H. (Mas Abdul Hamid), 270, 276, 293–94, 301
Anatolia, 277
Andaman Islands, 300
Angas, George, *Carel Pelgrim and Nazea*, 113, *114*
anti-Semitism, 323
Arabic language, 271–72
Arabi Pasha. *See* ʿUrabi, Ahmad
Arab League, 332–33
Arabs: in the Indies, 3–4, 244–49, 268–89, 293–94, 312–14, 323; and Indonesian nationalism, 312–14, 323; Malays' ancestry traced to, 21, 232; Malays compared to, 271; Moors' ancestry traced to, 21, 92, 95, 138, 197, 215, 266
Ariapen Panular, Raden, 138
Arifin, Teuku Muhammad, 247
Armenians, 234, 242

[445]

INDEX

Arsalna, Khatib, 42, 44
Arslan, Amir Shakib, 314; *New World of Islam*, 323
Arun Shah, 47
Asian Relations Conference (Delhi, 1947), 333
Asia Raya (newspaper), 317, 320, 323, 325, 327–29
Asnawi, Kyai, 301
Assana, 152, 155–59, 165
Asyʿari, Hasyim, 303, 318, 321–22, 324, 326, 329–30, 332
Attaoullah, Ahmad, 192, 260–62, 269
Australia, 331
Auwal Masjid (First Mosque), Dorp Street, Cape Town, 32, 62–63, 72, 74–75, 97–98, 103, 108, 112
Ava, 129, 133, 158, 167
ʿAwad bin Sunkar, 288, 407n110
Awaladien, 96–97
ʿAwda, Muhammad, 236
ʿAwn al-Rafiq, Sharif, 254
ʿAydarus al-Mashhur, 302
Aydin, Cemil, 12, 13, 17
Aydroos Lebbe (Sayyid Musa Ngidrus, Musa ʿAydarus), 136
ʿAynifar, 220–21
al-Azhar, 165, 192, 195, 203–4, 260, 269, 271, 292, 307, 388n99
Azor, 96
Azra, Azyumardi, 30
Azzachirah al-Islamijah (journal), 290–91, 302
ʿAzzam, ʿAbd al-Rahman Hasan, 333

Bacchante, HMS, 222–23, 228, 231, 393n60
Badan Pembantoe Pradjoerit (Soldiers' Aid Body), 323
Badr al-Din of Tidore, 38, 40–42, 44–47, 52
Bafagih, Asa, 323
Bagus Nassar of Banten, 48
Bagus Oedien of Banten, 48
Bahadur Shah II, 167
Baines, Thomas, 115, 119

Baird, David, 73
Bajasut brothers, 323
Balai Muslimin, Jakarta, 331
Balkans, 270, 299
Ba Maw, 322
Bandaranaike, Sirimavo, 336
Bandaranaike, S. W. R. D., 336
Bangkok, 1, 5, 125, 128–30, 158
Banks, Joseph, 79
Baraja, Muhammad b. Salim, 276–77
Barghash, Sultan, 15, 199–200, 341n28
Barnard, Andrew, 60, 62
Barnard, Anne, 60
Barnes, Edward, 161
Barrow, John, 55, 60, 91, 99, 129; *Account of Travels into the Interior of Southern Africa*, 86–87, 89
Barudi, Mahmud Sami al-, 204, 209–10, 214, 217–18, 223, 230, 235, 237
al-Bashir (newspaper), 271–74, 277, 302
Baswedan, ʿAbd al-Rahman, 312–13, 323, 328, 331, 336
Basyuni, Muhammad, 314
Batavia: alignment of, with Arabs, 268–75; Arabs in, 258; description of, 284–85; as Dutch Asian capital, 10, 25, 150–51, 244; exile to and from, 37, 40–43, 54–59, 138; Muslims in, 95; population of, 77–78; punishment regime in, 55, 82
Batavia (ship), 135
Batavia Castle, 25, 39, 53
Batavian Republic, 10, 35, 139, 150
Battle of Surabaya (1945), 332
Bayly, Christopher, 17
Been, 20
Bencoolen (Bengkulu), 76, 79, 82, 91, 132, 141, 161, 230, 247, 311
Benda, Harry, 315, 318, 320, 322, 330
Bengal, 76–77
Berg, L. W. C. van den, 244
Bergh, Adriaan Vincent, 64
Bergh, Oloff M., Jr., 62
Bergh, Olof Martini, 64
Biccard, F. L. C., 117
Biccard, Ludwig Godlieb, 96

INDEX

Bigge, John Thomas, 101–2, 107–8, 162
Bilal, 70
Bin ʿAqil, Muhammad, 4, 269, 275, 279–80, 289, 303
Bin Hashim, Muhammad, 271–74, 276–77, 282, 302, 303, 304, 312
Bin Shahab, Hasan b. ʿAlwi, 269, 287
Bintang Hindia (journal), 270
Birch, James, 196
Bird, William Wilberforce, 94, 98–100, 102, 105, 363n21; *State of the Cape of Good Hope*, 98
Bishara, Fahad, 18
Blair, Charles, 98
Blair, William, 102
Blunt, Anne Isabella King, 198–99, 206, 217–18, 227
Blunt, Wilfrid Scawen, 198–210, 217–20, 226–28, 230, 235, 237, 248, 252, 279, 387n93, 391n31, 391n32; *Bayan-nama li-ummat al-Sharq*, 200; *Future of Islam*, 203, 210
Boediman, 139
Boers, 66, 86, 87, 190
Bo-Kaap, Cape Town, 33, 113, 238, 337
Bolsheviks, 280, 293
Bonkus, 139
Bose, Subhas Chandra, 325
Bose, Sugata, 17
Bosnia, 254
Bourguiba, Habib, 333
Braginsky, Vladimir, 257
Brandes, Jan, View of Cape Town, 54, 55
Brazil, 336
British East India Company (EIC), 34, 101; imperial growth furthered by, 11–13, 166–67, 243; and imperial politics, 6, 36–37; military forces of, 140–42; VOC vs., 8, 10, 43, 76–77
British Empire: bases and acquisitions in eighteenth and nineteenth centuries, 90; character of governance in, 82–83, 85, 232–33; and Crimean War, 166; Dutch vs., 305; Egypt and, 3, 14, 200–10, 254; in Great War, 16, 274–77; growth of, 11–15; Indies under rule of, 305; Malay behavior under rule of, 82–83, 133, 143; Malays in employment of, 82–83, 140–44, 153, 155, 162, 166–67, 230; Muslim attitudes toward, between the wars, 275–95; Muslim loyalty to, 6, 12, 15–16, 115–16, 118–21, 144–46, 160, 165–66, 186, 196, 217–18, 233, 275, 300; Netherlands vs., 34–38, 43–48, 150, 268; Ottoman relations with, 4, 13–14, 116, 118, 127, 166, 167–68, 178–79, 182, 248, 260, 266, 268, 275; and postwar Middle East, 277; rule of Cape Town, 10–11, 59–65; sayyids' relationship with, 4, 260, 279–80, 285
Broadley, Alexander, 209–10
Brownrigg, Robert, 156–60
Buchanan, James, 138
Buddhists, 36, 125–26, 129, 133, 147, 158, 167, 232, 288, 294, 324, 336
Buitengracht Mosque, Cape Town, 112, 118, 181, 187
Bukumbu Mosque, Kandy, 175
Bulgaria, 198, 199–200, 254
Burma, 36, 125, 129, 158–59, 167, 210, 322, 324, 329, 334, 336
Burney Treaty (1826), 132
Burubudur (journal), 288–90
Bushido, 328
Bussche, Louis de, 155–57, 159–60

caffers (guards), 48, 54, 63, 136
Cakraningrat IV, 39
Califa (*ratib*), 9, 95–97, 116–21, 184, 198, 230, 337
caliphate: Indian Ocean Muslim identities and, 9; origins of modern ideal of, 6; Ottoman Empire and, 21, 121, 127, 131, 200, 225, 243, 254, 258, 289; postwar controversy over, 279, 293, 300–4, 318; Turkey and, 4
Callaga Berboe (Kalaga Prabhu), 47–48, 153
Calvinism, 25
Campbell, George, 220–21, 223

INDEX

Campbell, John, 97–98, 101
Camphuys, Joannes, 30
Cape Argus (newspaper), 118, 119, 192
Cape Town: British rule in, 10–11, 59–65, 89; commission of inquiry in, 101–7; Dutch rule in, 10, 87–88; exile to, 38–40; Islam and Muslims in, 60–64, 73–75, 102–21, 178, 180–93, *181*; law and justice in, 100, 183–84, 187–89; Malays in, 94, 100–21; Muslims exiled to, 25–34, 38–40; Ottoman Empire and, 126, 178–93
Cardo, M. T., 216
Carel Pelgrim (Hajji Gazanodien [Hasan al-Din] Abdallah), 101, 103–4, 113–14, *114*, 118
Cassiem (Qasim, son of Samoudien), 116
Castle of Good Hope, 43, 44, 53, 55, 115
Castlereagh, Lord, 154
Catharina "Trijn" van de Kaap, 58–59, 70, 105
Cathcart (general), 116
Ceylon: British rule in, 10–11, 160; Buddhist majority in, 132; commission of inquiry in, 162–63; Dutch rule in, 133; and Indonesia, 333; Islam and Muslims in, 132–40, 197, 212–30; law and justice in, 127, 130, 147–49, 151, 153–54, 163; Malays in, 20, 83–84, 94, 132–40, 161–62, 230–38, 291; Moors in, 66, 133, 135–39, 147–48, 151, 153, 161–63, 165, 197, 212–32, 232; Muslims exiled to, 29–31, 38–39, 47, 51, 197, 211–38, *213*; post–World War II, 336, 337
Ceylon Government Gazette (newspaper), 160
Ceylon Observer (newspaper), 223–24, 231
Ceylon Rifle Regiment, 162, 167, 174, 230
Ceylon Standard (newspaper), 261
Champion, George, 116–17
Chauduri, K. N., 17
Chiang Kai-shek, 278
China, 278
Chiri, 96

cholera, 242
Christianity, 13–14, 85, 208, 209, 285, 289. *See also* missionaries
Clive, Robert, 76
Cloete, Gerhard L., 62
Cloete, Hendrik, 45
Cloete, Hendrik, Jr., 96, 97
clothing, 3, 193, 262, 267–68, 271, 272, 285, 312
Coates, Peter, 180
Coen, Jan, 313
Cole, Alfred, 115, 117
Cole, Juan, 203, 208
Colebrooke, Henry Thomas, 98–99, 101–2, 153
Colebrooke, William MacBean George, 101–2
Colebrooke-Cameron Commission, 162–63
Colombo, 133–40, 172–77, 197, 211–38
Colombo Castle, 66, 73, 133–34, 139
Colombo Powers, 334, 336
colonialism. *See* imperialism
Colvin, Auckland, 203
Commission of Eastern Inquiry, 100
commissions of inquiry, 11, 101–8, 162–63
Committee for the Education of the East, 307
Committee for Union and Progress, 16, 259, 276, 296, 298
Communism, 290, 300, 304, 307, 309
conversion, to Islam, 35, 69, 70, 79, 100, 102, 105–6, 157, 253
convicts, 10, 25, 40, 41, 43
Cook, A. G., 175
Cook, James, 78, 79, 83
Coomeraswamy, Ananda, 291
Copts, 208
Cordiner, James, 143, 145–47, 158, 159
Coridon of Bengal, 58
Cormie Didin, 142
Corradoe Berboe (Koradu Prabhu), 47–48, 58, 153
corvée labor, 134, 162, 205

[448]

INDEX

Craig, James Henry, 59–60, 105
Crawfurd, John, 292; *History of the Indian Archipelago*, 93
cricket, 193, 196, 230
Crimean War (1853–1856), 166, 170, 247
Cromer, Evelyn Baring, Lord, 220, 226–28
Crosby, Josiah, 1, 4–5, 286–88, 305–6
crustaceans, 189
Curtis, Rogert, 61

Dahlan, Ahmad b. Zayni, 168, 196, 253–55, 263, 265, 290, 299; *Futuhat al-islamiyya*, 254
Dai-Nippon Kaikyo Kyokai (Greater Japan Muslim League), 315, 318, 326
Dalrymple, Alexander, 34–35, 46, 60, 79
Damon van Bugis, 69, 105
Dar al-ʿUlum, Cairo, 283, 302
Das, C. R., 308
Davids, Achmat, 33–34, 59, 114, 189
Davie, Adam, 144–46, 149, 152, 155, 156–57
De Lima, Josephus Suasso, 117, 189, 367n84
Denyssen, Daniel, 99, 104, 105, 188, 363n21
Denyssen, Petrus Johannes, 188–89
Deringil, Selim, 209
Dessin, Joachim Nicolaus van, 39
Dewantara, Ki Hadjar, 320, *321*
dietary laws, 189
Digna, ʿUthman (general), 254
Dipanagara, Prince, 11, 38, 40, 132, 162, 169, 346n45
Disraeli, Benjamin, 14
Djajadiningrat, Abu Bakar, 253
Djajadiningrat, Ahmad, 274
Djajadiningrat, Hoesein, 319, 326
Djawa Baroe (magazine), 320, 327–28
Dole Samat (Abd al-Samad), 83
Dolie van de Kaap (Mansoer, Manzur), 105, 109, 111
Dorp Street, Cape Town, 32–33, 58–60, 62–64, 67, 69–70, 72, 74–75, 97, 100, 103–4, 108, 112, 115

Douglas, John, 212, 214, 215
D'Oyly, John, 156, 157–58
Driberg, Diederich Carel von, 139
Driberg, Frederik Wilhelm von, 139, 142
Dufferin, Lord, 209–10, 211, 217
Dul Alim, 48. *See also* Abd al-Alim
Dundas, Francis, 60
Dundas, Henry, 141
Du Plessis, Izak David, 33
D'Urban, Benjamin, 108, 110, 112, 183
Dusain (lieutenant), 157–58
Dutch East India Company (Vereenigde Oostindische Compagnie, VOC): in Ceylon, 133; decline of, 10, 25, 77; EIC vs., 8, 10, 43, 76–77; and imperial politics, 6, 38, 42; map of possessions of, *26*; military forces of, 59, 76, 78, 83, 126, 139–40; religious restrictions of, 49–50, 60
Dutch East Indies. *See* Indies

East India Company. *See* British East India Company; Dutch East India Company
East Indies. *See* Indies
Edries, 96
education: of enslaved people, 105, 106; in Mecca, 266; of Muslims, 3–4, 42–43, 136, 148, 152, 175, 193, 259, 265–66, 268, 276–77, 285; of women, 193. *See also* al-Azhar
Edward VII, 228
Egypt: Blunt and, 198–210; Britain and, 3, 14, 200–210, 254; exiles from, 211–38; France and, 141, 201, 204; importance of, in Muslim world, 194–95; Indonesia and, 336; international prominence of, 197–98; modernization of, 194–95; Muslims and, 3, 6, 212; nationalism in, 299; Ottoman Empire and, 8, 12, 15, 200–210; political struggles in, 201–11
EIC. *See* British East India Company
El-Mecky, Adnan, 305–7, 313, 316–17, 333, 406n82, 407n94

INDEX

Elmekki, Kussaï, 283, 306–7
SMS *Emden*, 275
Emin Bey, 262
Empat Serangkai (Four-Leafed Clover), 320, 324
Enci' Abu Salih bin al-Wahid, 233
Encik Pantasih, 172
Endeavour (ship), 78
enslaved people: Abdallah's comfort for, 29, 31; conversion to Islam, 69, 70, 100, 102, 105–6; education of, 105, 106; fear of, 11, 44, 55; living conditions of, 41, 47; manumission of, 20, 39, 50, 58, 60, 69, 70, 104, 356n65. *See also* slavery
Ertugrul (ship), 225, 251–52, 258, 261
Eugénie, Empress, 177
Eugenius Manoppo, 41–42, 59
Euralyus (ship), 119
Eve, Richard, 209
exile: in Batavia, 211–38; in Cape Town, 25–34, 38–40; in Ceylon, 29–31, 38–39, 47, 51, 197, 211–38
Exter, Gabriel, 54, 112

Fadjar Asia (journal), 308
Fadloellah, Mohamed, 271, 298, 410n15
Fadl b. ʿAlawi, Sayyid, 12, 18, 167–68, 195, 199, 215, 216, 242, 248, 264
Fahmi, ʿAli, 201, 214, 221–25, 228
Fahmi, Mahmud, 214, 218–19, 221–24, 226, 227; *al-Bahr al-zakhir*, 221, 235–36
Fahmy, Khalid, 208
Fakhr al-Din (Raja Oesman), 134, 142, 144, 145, 161
Falck, Willem, Jr., 147, 153
Farquhar, William (resident), 161
Faruʿ al-Watan (Branches of the Homeland), 299
Faruq, Umar, 42
Faruq, King, 302
Fatah, R. Wali Al, 326
Fatima Ba Mahmush (wife of Hachemi), 20, 285, 306–7, 313
Fattah al-Makki, Muhammad al-, 302–3, 305

Faysal, Prince, 336
Ferguson, John, 224–25
Finley, John, 280
FitzPatrick, James Coleman, 188
Fleck, Abraham, 62
Fluyt, Abitum van, 139
Fogg, Kevin, 332
Foreign Orientals, 1, 249, 268, 278, 279
Forrest, Thomas, 35–37, 44, 46, 56, 79, 82
Fortnightly Review (journal), 203
Fourth Anglo-Dutch War, 44–46, 77
France: alliance with Dutch and Spanish, 44; and Batavian uprising, 10; Britain vs., 87, 150, 155; and Crimean War, 166, 170; Egypt and, 141, 201, 204; Ottoman relations with, 168; and postwar Middle East, 277; and Tunis, 14, 203, 254
Frans van Bengalen, 60–64, 67–69, 73–74, 88–89, 105, 111–12, 114
Freijer Compendium/Freijer Code, 147, 153, 163
Freitag, Ulrike, 18, 254
Frere, Henry Bartle, 15, 190, 198, 199, 341n28
Friday Mosque, Kuta Raja, 251
Fuʾad, King, 237

Galle, 29, 43, 133, 139–40, 152, 163–65, 194
Gamal al-Din, Sultan, 35–38, 46–47, 56
Gamiem a.k.a. Hamim or Ammie (son of Achmat van Bengalen), 117–18, 187
Gandhi, Mohandas, 17, 293, 300, 309, 311, 325
Gençoğlu, Halim, 180
George III, 160
Germany, 16, 268, 273–74, 280, 296
Ghalib b. ʿAwad al-Quʿayti, 3, 16, 280, 287–88
Ghalib Bey (Ottoman consul), 249–52
al-Ghazali, *Bidayat al-hidaya*, 125
Gifford, William, 158
G. Kolff, 302
Gladstone, William, 200, 202–4, 206–10
Gleaves, Albert, 222

INDEX

Gobée, Emile, 290, 408n127
Golden Jubilee celebrations, 223, 224, 230, 257
Gonavajoyah (Gunawijaya), 83
Gordon, Arthur Hamilton-, 216, 219, 221-22
Grand Mosque, Zaytuna, 283
Granville, Lord, 206-7, 217
Graphic (journal), 230
Greater East Asia Conference (Tokyo, 1943), 322, 329
Greater East Asian Co-Prosperity Sphere, 321
Greater Japan Muslim League (Dai-Nippon Kaikyo Kyokai), 315, 318, 326
Great Game, 202, 207
Great Revolt (India, 1857), 12, 15, 118, 167, 190, 195, 300
Great War, 4, 16, 21, 273-77, 291, 296
Greece, 13, 132, 164, 198, 241, 257, 260
Green, Nile, 17
Greeving (Dutch surgeon), 144-46
Gregory, Anne, 211
Gregory, Augusta, 198, 221
Gregory, John, 102-5, 112, 162, 203
Gregory, William Henry, 198, 214-15, 219, 221-22, 226, 231
Greig, George, 107, 368n105
Greig, William, 384n34
Grey, George, 117, 118, 119, 121
Griep of Mozambique, 95-97, 111, 121
Groot Constantia, 96, 97
Guest, Montague, 210

Habib ʿAbd al-Rahman Zahir. *See* ʿAbd al-Rahman al-Zahir al-Saqqaf
Habibullah, Sharif, 29, 31, 138
Alhabsji, M. H., 323
Hachemi, Mohamed (Muhammad b. ʿUthman al-Hashimi), 21, 268, 282-95, 301-2, 304-7, 313, *314*, 316-17, 333
Hadi, Sayyid Shaykh al-, 269
Hadith, 328
Hadje (Hatje) van de Kaap, 104

Hadramawt, 1, 3-4, 28, 127, 244, 249, 268, 272, 277, 280-81, 286-87, 304, 306, 312
Hadramawt (newspaper), 302
Hadramis: and Arabs' future prospects, 277; diaspora of, 18; of Hijaz, 168, 245; in the Indies, 195, 241, 244-45, 249-51, 256, 263-64, 276, 279, 281-82, 304; Ottoman relations with, 249-50; in Zanzibar, 116, 190
Hafiz Ibrahim, 277
Hagi (Ahagé, Imam Hajji), 110, 114
al-Halabi, Mustafa al-Babi, 411n23
Hall, Stuart, 7
Hall, Sydney Prior, the Prince of Wales arriving in Colombo, Sri Lanka, December 1, 1875, *229*, 230
Hamid Effendi, 261
Hamilton, Edward, 200, 206, 210
Hamka (son of Haji Rasul), 324, 326
Hammat van Macassar, 95-97, 105
Hanafi juridical school, 127, 184, 187-89, 192, 203, 254, 388n99
Hapipa, Sitti, 134, 146, 150
Hardy (colonel), 156
Haron, Hajji, 182
Hasan al-ʿAttas, 303
Hasan Mustafa, 253, 255, 265, 270, 274
Hasib Pasha, 170
Hasyim, Wahid, 326, 329, 331
Hatice Hanım, 252, 259
Hatta, Mohamed, 320, *321*, 328, 329
Hazeu, G. A. J., 264, 269-70, 408n127
Heaphy, Thomas, 89
Heiho, 325
Hendricks, Shaykh Seraj, 34
Hidayat al-Watan (Guidance of the Homeland), 299
Hijaz: British intervention in, 279, 294, 296; control of resources in, 242; Egypt and, 104, 194; Hidramis in, 168, 245; migrants from, 244, 255; migration to, 167, 248, 304, 307; Muslim-led violence in, 168; Ottoman control of, 14, 18, 165-68, 184, 194-95; pilgrims stranded

[451]

Hijaz (continued)
  during Great War, 275, 296; political struggles in, 298, 302, 304; Sharif Husayn and, 279, 282, 293, 298; uncertain conditions in, 12, 74. See also Mecca
Hindus, 133
Hizb al-Watan, 332
al-Hizb al-Watani (Egyptian National Party), 205, 228, 235
Hizboellah, 325, 328, 330, 332
Ho, Engseng, 18, 19
Hobart, Lord, 143
Hofmeyr, Isabel, 17
Hollandsch-Arabisch School, 284
homeland. See watan
Hopper, Matthew, 18
Horie Yozo, 320, 322–23
Hottentots (Khoisan), 66, 86, 97
Hudson, Samuel, 61–62, 68, 69, 88–89
Hughes (admiral), 46
Husayn, Sharif, 16, 276, 279, 282, 286, 288, 293, 296, 298, 301–2, 304
Hussainmiya, B. A., 160, 172, 174
Hussein Lebbe Markar, 171, 177, 216
Huysers, Ary, 38, 47, 77, 83, 95, 135
Hyder Ali, 12, 44, 48

Ibn Battuta, 197
Ibn Khaldun, 283
Ibn Saʿud, 302–4
Ibn Taymiyya, 277
Ibrahim (heir to Abu Bakar), 233
Ibrahim Asmara, 136
Ibrahim Bey, 234
Ibrahim Pasha, 163–64, 194
ʿId al-Fitr, 175
Idenberg, A. W. F., 270, 275
identities: Arab, 21; imperial determinations of, 6; Indonesian, 4, 7, 21, 305; Islamic, 5, 7; Malay, 6, 7, 8, 20, 21, 34, 73, 77–79, 86, 92
Idris, Sayyid, 333
Idris, Tengku, 129
Idrisi Sufi order, 270
Ihagama, 159

Illustrated London News (journal), 222
al-Imam (journal), 259, 269–70, 280, 284, 291–92
Imamura Hitoshi, 324
imperialism, critiques of, 309–11, 319, 334–35
Inada, Abdul Muniam (Hosokawa Susumu), 317–18, 323
Indian Ocean, map of, 191
Indies: Arabs in, 3–4, 244–49, 268–89, 293–94, 312–14, 323; British rule in, 305; Dutch rule in, 1, 10–11, 43, 127, 133, 169, 243–44, 249–53, 264–65, 267–68, 279, 290; Hadramis in, 195, 241, 244–45, 249–51, 256, 263–64, 276, 279, 281–82, 304; law and justice in, 244; nationalism in, 305; Ottoman Empire and, 245–63, 274; political struggles in, 169; products of, 243–44; sayyids in, 14, 242, 246, 256–57, 265–66, 272, 276, 279–80, 286, 299, 303–4; transition of, to Indonesia, 243
Indies Islam Congress, 300–1, 318–19, 410n15
Indonesia: Egypt and, 336; formation of, 243, 305, 307; identities associated with, 4, 7, 21, 243, 305; independence for, 307, 318, 319, 328–31; international support for, 333; Japanese occupation of, 316–32; nationalism in, 235, 268, 307–15, 319, 322–24, 331–33; and Saudi Arabia, 302; in World War II, 316–32
Indonesia Merdeka (newspaper), 330
"Indonesia Raya" (anthem), 308, 315
Ingaby. See Nabe
Ingrams Peace (1937), 337
inheritance, 19, 147
Iqbal, Muhammad, 17
al-Iqbal (newspaper), 276–79, 288
Ireland, 198
al-Irshad, 265, 273, 276–81, 286–88, 293, 299, 301. See also Irshad School, Batavia
al-Irshad (journal), 287–88, 305

INDEX

Irshad School, Batavia, 3–5, 273, 276, 322. *See also* al-Irshad
Isaak Jukkie, 119
Iskandar, Sultan, 135
Islam and Muslims: Blunt and, 198–210; in Cape Town, 25–34, 60–64, 73–75, 102–21, 178, 180–93, *181*; in Ceylon, 29–31, 38–39, 47, 51, 132–40, 197, 212–30; clothing, 193; commission of inquiry on, 103–7; conversion to, 35, 69, 70, 79, 100, 102, 105–6, 157, 253; Dutch rule and, 243, 253–59; education of, 3–4, 42–43, 136, 148, 152, 175, 193, 259, 265–66, 268, 276–77, 285; egalitarianism in, 3, 16, 264–65, 268, 277–79; and Egypt, 3, 6; global status of, 6; growth of, 98; identities associated with, 5, 7; Japan and, 225, 233, 270, 294–95, 310, 314–32; and law, 19, 70, 74, 100, 106, 127, 130, 147–49, 151, 153–54, 163, 183–84, 187–89, 244, 374n107; leadership in, 108–15, 182–86, 194; loyalty to British Empire, 6, 11, 12, 15–16, 115–16, 118–21, 144–46, 160, 165–66, 186, 196, 217–18, 233, 275, 300; Malays and, 80–81, 85, 92, 101; mid-nineteenth-century British suspicions of, 12; military service in Dutch empire, 66; modern, 6, 9, 15–16; mortification rituals of, 9, 93, 95–97, 116–21; and nationalism, 9, 197, 297; reformism in, 15–17, 117, 195, 202, 214, 233, 237–38, 264–70, 273, 283–84, 290, 298, 304, 311; on Robben Island, 55; and slavery, 69–70, 104–5, 130, 162, 168, 241; VOC ban on, 49–50
al-Islam (journal), 284
Islam Bergerak (newspaper), 291, 293–94
Isma'il, Khedive, 177, 179, 194, 198–99, 204–5, 211
Ismail, Tuan Hajji, 35
Isma'il al-'Attas, 276, 278–79, 281, 314
Ismail b. Abdullah al-Khalidi, Shaykh (Ismail Simabur), 170–71, 194, 255

Ismail Marcair, 163
Israel, 336
Italy, 270, 274, 284, 299
al-Ittihad (journal), 271, 274, 298
al-Ittihad al-Arabi (journal), 200

Jacob, Wilson Chacko, 18
Jakarta, 316
Jalal al-Din, Sultan of Ternate, 47
Jam'iyyat Khayr, 259, 265, 270, 273, 284
Jam'iyyat Khayr School, Batavia, 265, 273
Janssens, Jan Willem, 60, 65–67, 73, 89, 110–13
Jan van Bugis (Muhammad bin Fadl), 64–66, 69, 73–75, 89, 100, 102–5, 108–12, 114, 181, 184
Japan: in Great War, 274; imperialism of, 310; Indonesia and, 316–32, *317*; late nineteenth-century and early twentieth-century rise of, 194, 271; Muslims and, 225, 233, 270, 294–95, 310, 314–32; in World War II, 316–32
Jappie, Saarah, 31
Jasanoff, Maya, 9
Java: Abdallah's connections to, 28, 42–43, 67, 74–75; Arabs in, 278–95; character of residents of, 250; Communism in, 304, 307; Dutch rule of, 161, 169, 243, 245, 249–53; exile from, 38–40; nationalism in, 6; political struggles in, 267–68; Raffles and, 10, 91; rebellion on (1825–1830), 11, 132, 162, 169; return to, 39, 50, 57, 74, 89, 136; and World War II, 5–6, 325–26, 328
Java War (1825–1830), 11, 91, 132
Jawa: alignment of, with Arabs, 268–75; alignment of, with Ottoman Empire, 263–64, 268–75; British suspicion of, 16; in Mecca, 255; and postwar caliphate controversy, 303–4; Southeast Asians as, 3, 63, 84–85, 131, 155–56, 170, 174–75, 233, 242–43, 292
Jawa Nippo (newspaper), 294

[453]

INDEX

Jawa Shimbun (newspaper), 320
Jawi Hisworo (newspaper), 278
Jawi Peranakan (journal), 234–35, 257
Jayah, T. B., 291
Jeddah, SS, 397n3
Jeddah, 12, 168, 199–200, 241, 244, 248, 302
Jeffreys, Kathleen, 31–32, 33
Jeppie, Shamil, 75, 113
Jeptha of the Cape, 50
jihad, 12, 16, 128, 167, 169, 248, 255, 273, 275, 327–29, 332
Jihad Resolution, 332
Johnston, Alexander, 153–54, 156, 161, 165
Johnstone, George, 44–45, 101
Jonas van Batavia, 53
Jonge, Huub de, 312
Jong Islamieten Bond, 312
Judson, Pieter, 9
Junayd al-Junayd, 245, 247
Jurang Pati (Joerang Patty), 126, 139
Juru, Raden Ayu, 136

Kadı, İsmail Hakkı, 126, 131
Kahar, 54
Kalaga Prabhu. *See* Callaga Berboe
Kalatura, 140
Kamal al-Din, Raja Muda of Tidore, 37–38
Kamil, Mustafa, 19, 235, 236, 237–38, 256–60, 263, 269–70, 273, 297, 299, 309, 310; *Rising Sun*, 323
Kamil al-Din, 46
Kamil Bey, Mehmet, 253, 262, 279
Kampong Melaka Mosque, Singapore, 241
Kampung Kertel. *See* Slave Island
Kampung Pejagalan, Batavia, 57
Kandy, 126, 129–30, 133, 143–47, 149, 151, 153–60, 167, 174, 175, 224, 226, 231
Kareta, Raden Mas (Bagus Kareta), 39, 50, 50–51, 128, 134, 151
Kartadiredja, Raden B., 270
kaum muda (new generation), 271
Kautsky, Karl, 309

Kedah, 36, 125, 128–32, 162, 167, 169, 234, 247
Keijda van der Kaap (Lady Qaʿida), 20, 57, 59, 64, 65, 68
Kemal, Mustafa, 289–90, 300–1, 311, 313
Kepping, 139
Khalduniyya, 283
Khalil Bangkalan, 297
Khilafat movement (Ali brothers), 270, 275, 293, 300–1, 404n36
Khitab al-Watan (Speeches of the Homeland), 299
Kimberley, Lord, 211
Kimberly, 260–61
Kipling, Rudyard, 294
KIZ. *See* Office for Native Affairs
Klerck, Reinier de, 38, 65
Kobe Mosque, Japan, 315
Kollisch, Maximilien, 118, 180, 184, 186, 189, 382n7
Koradu Prabhu. *See* Corradoe Berboe
kora-kora (rowed vessels), 35–36
Kostaki Musurus Pasha (Konstantinos Mousouros), 171
Kotelawala, John, 336
Ksatria, 328
Kuchler (major), 110–11
Kudin, Tunku, 132
Kuniaki Koiso, 318
Kuppen, 157

Lambert, J., 216
Lambourn, Elizabeth, 17
Lamidin, Tengku, 128
Lanka. *See* Ceylon
Latifa (wife of Hachemi), 306–7, 317
Laurel, Jose P., 322
law: in Cape Town, 100, 183–84, 187–89; in Ceylon, 127, 130, 147–49, 151, 153–54; in the Indies, 244
Lebbies, 147–48
Lee Warner, W.H., 263, 279–82, 287, 302
Lens, Frans, 39
Libya, 270, 284, 298, 333
Liem Koen Hian, 313

INDEX

Light, Francis, 36, 128
Linschoten, Jan Huyghen van, 77, 80, 358n10
Lipton, Thomas, 226
al-Lisaan (journal), 319
literacy, 64
al-Liwaʾ (newspaper), 235, 274
Loethfie, Moechtar, 331
London Missionary Society, 97
Longden, James, 212, 215–17, 219
Long Street, Cape Town, 74–75, 89, 100, 111–12, 115
Low, Chris, 14, 19
Loyal Fifth, 275
loyalty, of Muslims to British Empire, 6, 8–9, 11, 12, 15–16, 115–16, 118–21, 144–46, 160, 165–66, 186, 196, 217–18, 233, 275, 300
Lughod, Janet Abu, 10, 17

al-Maʿarif (journal), 305
Macartney, Lord George, 60, 87
Macdowall (general), 143
Macedonian and Cretan War, 258
Machfoeld, T. M. Moesa, 325, 416n29
Machmet (priest, Machmut), 59, 353n24
Macquarie, Lachlan, 101, 364n32
madhhabs, 127, 189
Madras, 12, 46, 101, 141–42
Madras Mail (newspaper), 231
Madura, 59, 78, 126, 136, 138, 139, 152
Magmoud, 113
Mahathir Mohamed, 7
Mahbub Ali Khan, 15
Mahdi. *See* Muhammad Ahmad
Mahmud II, Ottoman Sultan, 132, 163, 194
Mahomed Nur al-Din, 216
Mahomet Sangerang, 139
Maitland, Thomas, 149–55
Malabar, 12, 18, 48, 195, 248, 300
Malacca, 12, 77, 79–80, 84, 92, 130, 132, 161
Malay Archipelago. *See* Indies
Malay Cricket Club, 230
Malay Dramatic Club, 218, 230

Malay Peninsula (Malaya), 6, 11, 151, 196, 238
Malay Regiment, 140, 142, 144, 146, 149–50, 154, 172, 231
Malays: alignment of, with Ottoman Empire, 238, 248, 252–53, 257; amok associated with, 81–83, 85–86, 88, 91, 100, 143, 160, 231; Arab ancestry of, 21, 232; Arabs compared to, 271; British conception of, 6, 7, 8, 20, 21, 34, 73, 77–79, 86, 92, 292; British employment of, 82–83, 140–44, 153, 155, 162, 166–67, 230; and Califa, 93; in Cape Town, 94, 100–21; in Ceylon, 20, 83–84, 94, 132–40, 161–62, 230–38, 291; characteristics of, 76, 78–81, 84, 86, 88, 94, 99, 107, 115–16, 147, 158–60, 167, 291–92, 358n10; diverse peoples considered as, 35, 73, 77, 83, 86; Dutch conception of, 77–78, 136; effect of British rule on, 82–83, 133, 143; and Islam, 80–81, 85, 92, 101; islanders' conception of, 80; language of, 80; martial character and employment of, 78, 84–85, 125–26, 140–44, 147, 149–51, 152–55, 157–58, 160, 162, 166–67, 231, 237–38; Moors' relations with, 161; in South Africa, 337; status of, 75–76
Malet, Edward, 204, 206, 209–10
Maʿlumat (newspaper), 259
Mamat van de Kaap, 73–74, 184
al-Manar (journal), 237
Manchester Guardian (newspaper), 119
Mandal, Sumit, 271
Mangkunegara, 128
Mangkupraja, Raden Gatot, 325
Manqush, ʿUmar, 3–5, 264–65, 272, 281, 287–88, 304
Mansur, Mas, 296–301, 303, 311, 312, 315, 318–33, *321*
Mansur al-Junayd, 248
Mansur b. Ghalib, Sultan of Sayʾun, 250
Mansur Shah, 170, 245–47
Maphilindo, 337
marabouts, 283–84

[455]

INDEX

Maradana Mosque, Colombo, 197, 215, 220
Mareotis (ship), 211–14, 228
marriage, 19, 103, 153. *See also* bigamy; polygamy
Marsden, William, 79–87, 91–93, 143, 175, 243, 292; *History of Sumatra*, 79–85, 79, 89, 92, 158
Martabat, 42, 44
Masjoemi, 329–30, 332
Mata-Hari (newspaper), 312–13
Matale rebellion (1848), 166, 183
Mawaa van Ternate, 64, 69–70, 356n68
Mayson, John Schofield, 101, 113, 115–19
McLoughlin, Patrick, 260
McLoughlin Academy, Cape Town, 260
Mecca: education in, 266; Egyptian protection of, 163; exile to, 248; Ottoman protection of, 127, 169, 193–96, 268; pilgrimages to, 14, 113, 117–18, 126, 169, 184, 188, 241–42, 244, 258, 296–98, 304; Saudi protection of, 302, 304; uprising of 1855, 12. *See also* Hijaz
Mecidiye medal, 15, 170, 171, 178, 180, 184, 247, 249, 252–53, 261, 263, 387n81, 399n36
Mecmua-yı fünun (journal), 182, 184
Medan Moeslimin (journal), 291, 293–94
Medina, 132, 163, 167, 196, 208, 216, 268–69, 279, 302–3
Meer, Arnout van der, 267
Mehmed Hasib Pasha, 169, 184
Mehmed II, Ottoman Sultan, 175, 177
Mehmed V, Ottoman Sultan, 268, 276, 298
Merdeka (newspaper), 293
Mestyan, Adam, 194
MIAI. *See* Supreme Council of Indonesian Islam
millenarianism, 244, 248, 255, 310
Mindon, King, 167
Minstrel (ship), 101, 129
Minte of Ternate, 41, 48, 59
Minto, Lord, 132, 151, 156
Mir Jaʿfar, 76

missionaries, 97–98, 100–1, 116–17, 161, 199
Mitsui Bishen Kaisha, 294
Mochadien, 42, 45
Mochamat Achmat (son of Achmat van Bengalen), 117–18, 121, 182
Moendoe, 139
Moluccas, 28, 35, 65, 76, 142
Moors: Arab ancestry of, 21, 92, 95, 138, 197, 215, 266; in Ceylon, 66, 133, 135–39, 147–48, 151, 153, 161–63, 165, 197, 212–32; on the islands, 156; Malays' relations with, 161; Muslim faith of, 80
Moplah revolt (1921–1922), 300
Morton, Shafiq, 33, 34
Mozambique, 59, 88, 147, 150, 154, 162, 190
mucks. *See* amok
Mudaffar Sjah of Ternate, 33
Muding (Meeding, Hadjee Medien, Hadjee Mogadien), 102–4, 107, 111, 113, 117–18
Muhammad (Prophet): aphorism of, 272; celebration of birth of, 39–40, 93, 259, 301, 323; claimed descent from, 4, 21, 28, 29, 178, 231, 242, 244; satire about, 278
Muhammad ʿAbduh. *See* ʿAbduh, Muhammad
Muhammad Agha ibn Nal Band, 192
Muhammad Ahmad (Mahdi), 219, 221, 234, 254
Muhammad al-ʿAbbasi, 203
Muhammad ʿAli of Zanzibar, 184, 192
Muhammad ʿAli (Nawab of Arcot), 11, 138
Muhammad ʿAli Pasha (Wali of Egypt), 12, 132, 163–66, 194
Muhammad al-Saqqaf, 244, 252–53, 260–61
Muhammad Arshad b. Alwan, 253, 255, 310
Muhammad b. ʿAbdallah (ʿAbd al-Sharif), 138
Muhammad bin ʿAqil. *See* Bin ʿAqil, Muhammad.

INDEX

Muhammad Ba Busayl, 263
Muhammad b. Ahmad, Shaykh, 245
Muhammad Balangkaya, 161
Muhammad Basyuni, 298
Muhammad b. Hashim. *See* Bin Hashim, Muhammad
Muhammad bin Fadl, 64–65
Muhammad Ghawth, 170, 247
Muhammadiyah movement, 265, 290–93, 299, 301, 303, 311, 312, 318–19, 326, 329
Muhammad Khalil, 202
Muhammad Salih b. ʿAli Batawi, 169, 170, 184, 189, 194
Muhammad Salim al-Kalali, Shaykh, 269
Muhammad Shamwili, 248
Muhammad Tahir Jalal al-Din al-Azhari, 269
Muhammad Wajih al-Kilani, 280
Muhammad Zafir, Shaykh, 205, 209
Muhammad Zayn al-Abidin of Tidore, 134, 135, 142
Mukalla, 1, 3, 15, 242, 250, 305
Mukhbir al-Islam (newspaper), 315
al-Munir (journal), 270–71, 297
al-Muqattam (newspaper), 236
Murad, Crown Prince, 13
Muslim Chronicle (newspaper), 232
Muslim Educational Society, 227
Muslim Journal, 261
Muslim League, 275, 300
Muslim Nesan (newspaper), 214, 217, 232, 234
Muslims. *See* Islam and Muslims
Mustahak, 42
Musurus Pasha, 178, 180, 199–200, 245
Rakiep, Muttaqin,TK 34, 49
Muwallad, 3, 323. *See also* Peranakan
Muzakkar, Abdulkahar, 331

Nabahan brothers, 411n23
Nabe (Ingabeij van Cheribon), 55, 64, 96, 111, 112, 119, 362n2
Nadlatul Ulama (NU), 321–22, 326, 329
Nahdat al-Watan (Rise of the Homeland), 299

Nahdlatul Ulama, 318
al-Nahla (journal), 199, 219
Naʿim al-Din, Gagugu of Bacan 135
Nakano Satoshi, 321
Napier, George, 112
Napier, Mark, 209
Napoleon, 141, 283
Napoleonic Wars, 10, 167
Napoleon III, 177
Naqshbandiyya Sufi fraternity, 170
Nassar, Raden Bagus, 42, 48, 57
Nasser, Gamal Abdel, 9, 229, 336–37
nationalism, 237–38; anticolonialism linked to, 309–11, 313; Egyptian, 204–8, 227, 235, 299; Indonesian, 236, 268, 307–15, 319, 322–24, 331–33; in Java, 6; Muslims and, 9, 197, 297; South African, 337; Turkish, 5
National Party of Egypt, 204–5
Natsir, Mohammad, 311
Nawab of Arcot. *See* Muhammad ʿAli
Nawab of Bengal, 76
Nazea, 114
Neethling, Christian Ludolph, 45, 50, 65, 75
Neethling, H. L., 66
Neethling, J. H., 65–66, 95, 96, 111–12
Nehru, Jawaharlal, 325, 333
Neracha (newspaper), 270–71, 276
Netherlands: Batavian uprising in, 10; Britain vs., 34–38, 43–48, 150, 268, 305; and Great War, 16, 276; Indies under rule of, 1, 10–11, 43, 127, 133, 169, 243–44, 249–53, 264–65, 267–68, 279, 290; Ottoman relations with, 127, 245, 249, 253–60, 268–69; reconstituted, 243
Newcastle, Duke of, 171, 180
new generation (*kaum muda*), 271
Ne Win, 336
ngabehi, title of, 42
Nieuwe Rotterdamsche Courant (newspaper), 279
Nilofer, 20
Nizam of Hyderabad, 12
Noerdjannah, Sitti, 20, 322

[457]

Nolland Noya, 139
Non-Aligned Movement, 9, 336
non-cooperation movement, 293, 300, 311
Noriman. *See* Nur Iman
North, Frederick, 83, 140–44, 146–49, 151, 152, 163, 165
NU. *See* Nadlatul Ulama
Nuku, Kaicili, 34–35, 37, 46, 134, 349n92
Nur al-Din, 144–46, 158
Nur al-Din al-Raniri, *Bustan al-salatin*, 62
Nur Iman (imam, Noriman, Norman), 42, 48, 53, 55, 59, 64, 68, 88, 113, 114, 193
Nur Iman (Tidorese secretary), 38, 40, 44, 45
Nuthall, T. J., 167

Obeyesekere, Gananath, 156
O'Brien, Terence, 171
Odin (Uddin), 157–58
Oedien, Raden Bagus, 42, 48, 57
Oesman, Raja, 142, 144, 161
Office for Native Affairs (Het Kantoor voor Inlandsche Zaken; KIZ), 244, 256, 265, 276, 280, 288, 290, 296, 313, 315, 320. *See also* Shumubu
Okawa Shumei, 315
Omar (Imam Haji), 113–14
Omer Lutfi, 178, 180
Ono Nobuji (Abdul Hamid Ono), 324
Oosterlingen, 25, 77, 77–78, 82
opium, 81–83, 143, 147, 160, 231
Order of Oranje Nassau, 288
Osman Nuri Pasha, governor, 254–55
Osman Pasha, captain, 251–52
Othman Belgacem Elmekki, 283
Ottoman Empire: British enemies of, 198–210; British relations with, 4, 13–14, 116, 118, 127, 166, 167–68, 178–79, 182, 248, 260, 266, 268, 275; caliphal authority of, 21, 121, 127, 131, 200, 225, 243, 254, 258, 289; and Cape Town, 178–93; control of Arabian provinces, 4, 12–14; decline of, 270, 300–1; Dutch relations with, 127, 245, 249, 253–60, 268–69; Egypt and, 8, 12, 15, 200–10; in Great War, 16, 273–77; and Hanafi practices, 127; and the Indies, 245–63, 274; Jawa alignment with, 263–64, 268–75; Malays alignment with, 238, 248, 252–53, 257; Mecca and Medina under protection of, 127, 169, 193–96, 268; protection of Hijaz by, 14, 18, 165–68, 184, 194–95; Russia and, 13, 14, 166, 179, 190, 199, 201, 248, 254, 257, 274, 275. *See also* Sublime Porte
Oudtshoorn, William van, 70

Padri wars, 170
Pakir Bawa Latif, 176
Pakubuwana II, 39, 50
Pakubuwana III, 50
Pal, Bipin Chandra, 308
Palestine, 323, 333
Palmer, Edward, 206, 209
Palmerston, Lord, 165
Pan-Asianism, 243, 310, 313, 315
Pancaran Warta (newspaper), 273
Pandan Bali, 138
Panenga, 138
Pangeran Arya Mangkunegara, 39, 41, 135, 137
Pangeran Mas Adipati Mangkurat, 150
Pangeran Pali, 126
Pangkor Treaty (1874), 196
Pan-Islamism, 14, 126, 179, 205, 208, 212, 248, 254, 261, 264–65, 297, 300, 315
Pan-Slavism, 14
Partai Nasional Indonesia (PNI), 307–9, 318
Partai Sarekat Islam Indonesia (PSII), 319, 320, 322
Patra Alam, 37, 134
Pattani, 125, 128–29, 169, 196
Patti Malaijo, 134
Peace of Amiens (1802), 10, 86, 142, 150
Peacock, Andrew, 126
Pembela Tanah Air (PETA), 325, 327–28, 330, 332

INDEX

Penang, 11, 12, 36, 76, 101, 125, 128–30, 142, 161, 162, 166, 234
Peranakan, 7, 92, 161, 172, 232, 260, 312. See also Muwallad
Percival, Robert, 60, 81, 84–87, 91, 133, 140, 143, 146; Account of the Cape of Good Hope, 85; Account of the Island of Ceylon, 84–85, 143, 158
Persatuan Islam, 311
PETA. See Pembela Tanah Air
Philippines, 322, 324, 329
Phillida, 104
Pijper, G. F., 290, 315, 415n11
pilgrimages, 14, 113, 117–18, 126, 169, 184, 188, 241–42, 244, 258, 296–98, 304
Pilimatalava (Pilima Talawa), 155, 156, 159
plantations, 243
Plettenberg, Joachim van, 39
PNI. See Partai Nasional Indonesia
Poespajaya. See Surood, Yahya Dane
Poetera movement, 320
Poivre, Pierre, 80
Poligar Wars, 11, 84, 142
polygamy, 103, 107, 219
Popham, Home, 73
Portugal, 133
Prange, Sebastian, 17
Prawiradinata, 267
Prince of Wales Island, 129
Prince of Wales Island Gazette (journal), 129
PSII. See Partai Sarekat Islam Indonesia

Qadis, 28, 38, 40, 44–46, 55–56, 74, 148, 192, 283
Qadiri Sufism, 63
Qaʿida, Lady. See Keijda van der Kaap
al-Qibla (newspaper), 288, 304
Qurʾan, 27, 32, 33, 49, 49, 149, 175, 253, 258, 260, 283, 310, 324, 325, 328

Raban (son of Omar [Imam Haji]), 118
Rachbat of Mozambique, 69
Radio Australia, 331

Raffles, Thomas Stamford, 7, 10, 91–94, 101–2, 115, 161, 243, 292; The History of Java, 91; "On the Maláyu Nation," 92
Raffles Institution, Singapore, 276
Rafiek, 95–97, 362n2
Rafudin, Auwais, 34
Rahim, Haji, 276
Rahmatullah Kairanawi, 195
Rajab, 48, 63, 68, 354n36, 362n6
Rakea Maker, 182, 186, 192
Rakiep, Muttaqin, 34, 49
Rakiep, Nurul Erefaan, 33–34
Rama, 328
Rama Varma VIII of Cochin, 43, 47
Rangoon, 167
Rasul, Haji, 324, 303
ratib. See Califa
Rato Bagoes, 135
Rawlinson, Henry, 206
Rawothan, Packier Pulle, 162
Rawson, Rawson W., 116
Red Crescent, 270, 272–76, 282, 301, 323
Reese, Scott, 18
Reʾfat Bey (Ottoman consul), 274, 276, 289
reformism, 15–17, 117, 195, 202, 214, 233, 237–38, 264–70, 273, 283–84, 290, 298, 304, 311
Rennell Rodd, James, 236–37
Reuters, 273
Rheenen, Jacob G. van, 62
Rheenen, Jacobus Arnoldus van, 69
Ricci, Ronit, 19, 84, 136, 145, 172, 174–75
Richard the Lionheart, 326
Rida, Muhammad Rashid, 237, 264–65, 271, 280, 290, 294, 298, 304, 314
Ridgeway, West, 227
Rifaʿiyya Sufi order, 93, 184, 362n6
Rifki Bey (Ottoman consul), 251
Rinkes, D. A., 269, 274–75
Rinn, Louis, 284
Riyad Pasha, 201
Robben Island, 27–28, 33–34, 40–44, 53, 55, 57, 65, 96, 337
Robinson, Hercules, 174

[459]

INDEX

Roda Island, 298
Rothman, Natalie, 9
Rothman, Sebastiaan, 53
Roubaix, Petrus Emanuel de, 115, 117–18, 121, 171, 178, 180–81, 184–86, 190, 280
Royal Asiatic Society, 98, 102, 153, 206, 214, 292
Royal Commission of Eastern Inquiry, 162
Rum, Sultan, 257
Russell, Earl, 245
Russia: and Crimean War, 13, 116; freedoms in, 14; in Great War, 274; Japan and, 270–71; Ottoman Empire and, 13, 166, 179, 190, 199, 201, 248, 254, 257, 274, 275
Russo-Japanese War (1904–1905), 270–71
Russo-Turkish War (1877–1878), 190, 199, 201, 248, 257

Saartjie, 58–59, 64, 69, 70, 356n64
Saboo Latiff, 138
Sabunji, John Louis, 199–200, 203, 206–8, 217–19, 279, 391n31, 391n32; al-Khilafa, 200; Bayan-nama li-ummat al-Sharq, 200
Sadar Alam, 135
Saddaku, 156–57
Sadiq Baligh Effendi, 262, 264
Saʿdiya (sister-in-law of Hachemi), 305, 407n94
Sah al-Din, Muhammad (Sultan of Bacan) 35, 47, 135
Saʿid, Wali of Egypt, 194
Said, Oemar, 323
Saʿid Ba Junayd, 262–63
Saikeirei, 324
Sakandu, 156–57
Sakkur van Java (Abd al-Shukur), 63
Salahakan Din, 44
Salahudin, 172
al-Salam (journal), 282, 286–87
Salawati, Raja, 36, 82, 345n34

Saldin, Baba Ounus, 84, 156, 166, 172, 173, 174–77, 231–35, 291; Syair Fayd al-Abad, 172, 233
Saldin, M. K., 291
Salea van Makassar, 64
Salih b. Salim b. ʿAbdat, 1, 2, 3–6, 16, 21, 278, 287–88, 337
Salih b. ʿUbayd b. ʿAbdat, 5
Saliha, Nyai, 66
Salim, Agus, 299–301, 304, 308, 311, 312–13, 319–20, 323, 326, 333, 336
Salim b. ʿAbdat, 278
Salim b. Sumayr, 170–71
Salimudin, 166
Salmoen, M. A., 326
Salomon Manoppo, 41
Samarqandi, Abu al-Layth al-, 49, 51, 62–63
Sameda van de Kaap, 75, 89
Samin, Mohammed, 293–94
Samoudien (Sami al-Din), 113–14, 116, 118
Sangalen, 157
Sangha, 158
Sangkilan (Karaeng Sangunglo), 145
Sanusi, Yusuf al-, Umm al-barahin, 49, 52, 62
Sanusi Pané, 318
Sanusi Sufi order, 270
Sanusiyya, 298, 333
Sarah van Boegis (Sara van Batavia), 20, 39, 50–51
Sarekat Islam, 265, 268, 272, 274–75, 278–79, 290–94, 299–301, 303
Sasranegara, Tumenggong, 137, 147
Sasrawijaya (Sassaro Widjojo), 137, 138
Saudi Arabia, 302
Sawers, Simon, 152, 164–65, 280
Sayf al-Din, 144–45, 158
sayyids: betrayal of Ottoman Empire by, 323; British relations with, 4, 260, 279–80, 285; criticisms of, 289; customs of, 16, 264–65, 277; and Egyptians, 195, 218; in the Indies, 14, 242, 246, 256–57, 265–66, 272, 276,

[460]

INDEX

279–80, 286, 299, 303–4; and postwar caliphate controversy, 302–3; threats perceived by, 4, 16
Sayyida Zaynab, 236
Schrieke, B. J. O., 279
Secour, 104
Sejarah Melayu. See *Sulalat al-Salatin*
Sekolah Tinggi Islam, Jakarta, 331
Sellia, 137
Semple, Robert, 64, 76, 87–88, 91; *Walks and Sketches*, 129
Senjuro Hayashi, 315
sepoys, 139, 143, 149, 154, 156, 160–61, 167, 230
Seychelles, 196
Shafiʿi, Imam, 176, 184, 187–88
Shafiʿi juridical school, 56, 71–72, 74, 127, 161, 184, 187–90, 250, 253
Shafiʿi Mosque, Cape Town, 181, 187
Shamaʾil al-Huda, Pekalongan, 277
Shams al-Din al-Imbabi, 203, 207
Sharif Pasha, 203–4
Shaukat Ali, 293, 310
Shawashi, Salih, 278, 282–83
Shaykh al-Islam, Ottoman, 273; for the Philippines, 280; for Indonesia, 301
Shee, George, 151
Sherrif, Abdul, 10
Shumubu, 320, 323–24, 326, 330–31
Siam, 36, 125, 128–30, 132, 133
Siddi Lebbai (Mukammatu Kacim Cittilevvai), 214–15, 217, 220, 227
Sinar Hindia (journal), 291
Singai Nesan (newspaper), 234, 257
Singa Joeda, 139
Singapore, 10, 92, 161, 162, 170, 245, 247–48, 251, 260–61, 279
Singa Troena, 139
Sin Po (newspaper), 278
Sin Tit Po (newspaper), 313
Sitia Isa. *See* Aisa, Sitti
Sitti Hapipa. *See* Hapipa, Sitti
Sixth Buddhist Council (Rangoon, 1955), 336

Sjahab, A. S., 323
Skeen, William, 172
Skinner, Thomas, 160, 162, 166, 169, 230
Slave Island (Kampung Kertel), 135–36, 160, 161, 174, 218, 220, 230, 232
Slave Lodge, Cape Town, 47–49, 52, 66, 68, 353n25
slavery: British opposition to, 12, 75; commentary on effects of, 86–88; commission of inquiry on, 102, 104–7; local support of, 11, 12, 32; Muslim slave holders, 69–70, 104–5, 130, 162, 168, 241; opposition to and persistence of, in Cape Town, 66, 75; Zanzibar's opposition to, 199. *See also* enslaved people
Slight, John, 126
Sneyd, Richard Malone, 163
Snouck Hurgronje, Christiaan, 244, 253–62, 264–65, 269–70, 274, 309–10; *Mekka*, 255
Soeara MIAI (The Voice of the MIAI; journal), 320, 322–23, 327–29
Soeara Moehammadijah (journal), 291
Soeara Muslimin Indonesia (journal), 329, 331
Soeara Raʿjat (journal), 291
Soebagijo, 330
Soeloeh Hindia (newspaper), 288
Soerjomentaram, Kiai Ageng, 327
Soetomo, Raden, 318
Soewardi Soerjaningrat (Ki Hadjar Dewantara), 267
Solomon, Saul, 119–20
Somerset, Charles, 98
Somerville, William, 87
Sourdeen (Salomon), 69, 91, 103, 105
South African Commercial Advertiser (newspaper), 107, 108, 337
South African Malay Association, 291
Southeast Asians. *See* Jawa
South Yemen, 337
Spain, 44
Spakler (Dutch consul general), 269

INDEX

Sparrman, Anders, 50
St. Aloysius School, Cape Town, 260
Stanley, Lord, 245
Star of India, 179
Stavorinus, Jan Splinter, 78, 82–83, 89
Stockdale, John, 89, 91
Stoddard, Lothrop, *New World of Islam*, 309, 314, 412n50
Straits Settlements, 92, 161, 166, 172, 230, 232, 244, 245, 257, 292
Straits Times (newspaper), 261
Sublime Porte, 171, 185–86, 209, 245–47, 249, 251, 259
Subrahmanyam, Sanjay, 17
Sudan, 194, 206, 219, 234, 254, 298
Sudirman, 332
Suez Canal, 126, 127, 174, 197–98, 242, 247, 310, 336
Suffren, Pierre André de, 44
Sufism: criticisms of, 270, 284; Idrisi, 270; mortification rituals in, 9, 93; Naqshbandi, 170; Qadiri, 63; reform critics of, 15; Sanusi, 270; ʿUrabi and, 219
Suhaymi, Muhammad, 298
Sukarno, 9, 295, 299, 307–13, 320, 323, 328–29, 331–37, 412n47
Sulabesi, 42
Sulalat al-Salatin (*Sejarah Melayu*, or *Malay Annals*), 77, 79
Suluh Indonesia Muda (newspaper), 310
Sumatra, 76, 79–82, 91–92, 196, 244, 245, 246, 255, 275, 290, 293–95, 298, 304, 307, 328
Sun Yat-sen, 309
Supreme Council of Indonesian Islam (Majlisul Islamil A'laa Indonesia; MIAI), 315, 318–20, 322, 329
Surabaya, 259, 265, 274–77, 282, 287, 297, 299, 302–3, 322, 331–33
Surabrata, 48, 54–55
Surakarta, 50, 151, 258, 265
Surkati al-Ansari, Ahmad, 3–4, 265–66, 273, 276–77, 281–82, 284, 287, 288, 290–92, 294, 301, 302, 304, 305, 312, 314–15, 317–18, 408n127

Surood, Yahya Dane (Poespajaya), 291–92
Swellengrebel, Hendrik, Jr., 66
Swettenham, Frank, 292
Syafi'i, R. Moh., 326
Sydney, HMAS, 275
Syed Ahmad Khan, 12, 14, 17; *Asbab-e-Baghawat-e-Hind* (*The Causes of the Indian Revolt*), 12–13, 179, 193, 214
Syria, 277

tabut (parading of coffins), 230
Tagliacozzo, Eric, 19
Tagore, Rabindranath, 17, 335
Taha Sayf al-Din, 171
Tahora Saban, 192, 193
Taïeb ben Aïssa, 284
Taleb, Mirza Abu, 70, 104
Talip, 139
Tamby, 156, 157
Tan Malaka, 309, 337
Tantawi Jawhari, 302–3, 307
Tartar (ship), 35
Taswir al-Afkar, 299, 301
Tata Layar, 61
Tawfiq, Khedive, 15, 193, 198, 201–3, 207, 209–10, 216, 234, 252
Tayyib al-Sasi, 304
Tayyiban, 176
Temple, Richard, 14
Tentara Kanjeng Nabi Muhammad (Army of Lord Prophet Muhammad), 278
Ternate, 27, 37, 47
Thai-Burma Railway, 325
Thoen, Jan Albertus, 157
Thomas, George Housman, 179
Thomas, Julian, 231
Thunberg, Carl Peter, 40, 50, 62
Tidore, 27, 35–38, 42
Tilak, Bal Gangadhar, 325
Tilimsani, Muhammad b. ʿUmar al-, 52, 70
Times (London; newspaper), 203, 208, 217
Tipu Sultan, 12, 73, 87, 349n100, 361n57
Tjiremai (ship), 305

INDEX

Tjokroaminoto, Harsono, 323
Tjokroaminoto, Oetari, 412n47
Tjokroaminoto, R. A., 265, 274–75, 291, 293–94, 296, 299, 301, 303, 304, 308, 313, 318
Tojo Hideki, 322, 329
Tokyo Mosque, Japan, 323
Tombe, Charles François, 89, 91
Toulba, Ali Foad 228
Toyama Mitsuru, 315
Tranchell (major), 214, 221–23, 230
Treaty of Amiens (1802), 10, 86, 142, 150
Treaty of London (1824), 132
Treaty of London (1840), 165
Treaty of Paris (1856), 166
Treaty of Sevres (1920), 300
Truter, H. A., 62
Truter, Johannes A., 96, 99, 111–12
Truter, Petrus Johannes, 87, 96
Tsuyoshi, Muhammad Suzuki, 323
Tuan Guru. *See* Abdallah bin Abd al-Salam
Tuan Said. *See* ʿAlawi
Tulbagh, Rijk, 39
Tulba ʿIsmat, 210, 214, 217–21, 223, 227, 236, 237
Tunas Melayu (newspaper), 276
Tunis, 14, 203, 207, 254, 284, 306–7
Turkey, 4, 5, 301, 311
Tusun Pasha, 163

ʿUkasha, 70–71
ʿUmar al-Junayd, 241, 245
ʿUmar al-Saqqaf, 275
ʿUmar b. Abi Bakr Ba Junayd, 263–64
ʿUmar b. Sulayman Naji, 303
ʿUmar b. ʿUbayd Bin ʿAbdat, 5
ʿUmar Nasif, 200
ʿUmar Sumbawa, 298
United Arab Republic, 337
United Nations (UN), 333
United States, 280
U Nu, 336
ʿUrabi, Ahmad, 8, 177, 196, 202–12, 214–15, 217–23, 225–29, 231, 233–37, 248–49, 254, 260–61, 309, 336

U.S. Civil War, 194, 198
Usuf, Encik Hajji, 37, 56–57
ʿUthman, Caliph, 151
ʿUthman, Sayyid of Southern India, 131–32
ʿUthman b. ʿAqil b. Yahya, Sayyid of Batavia, 195, 244, 249, 255–58, 263, 265, 269, 271
Uva Rebellion (1817–1818), 160

Valentia, Viscount, 148
Valentijn, François, 31, 77
Van Dort, John, illustrations of Egyptian exiles arriving in Colombo, *213*, 214
Vellore mutiny (1806), 151
Vera Bengala (Wira Manggala), 83
Vera Wangxa (Wira Wangsa), 83
Victoria, Queen, 12–14, 94, 118, 165–66, 179, 180, 186, 196, 197, 210, 212, 223–25, 227, 230, 233, 252, 257
Victoria and Albert (ship), 178, 190, 194
Victoria Mosque, Cape Town, 115, 185–86
Vietnam, 309
Vikrama Rajasimha of Kandy, 143–44, 152
VOC. *See* Dutch East India Company
Vorm, Petrus van der, 77

Wahhabis, 12, 163, 194, 198, 241, 254, 302, 304
Wajah Selong (journal), 151, 231–32, 234, 257, 266, 267
Wallace, Alfred Russel, 243
Wapche Marikar, 214, 216, 220, 227
Ward, Kerry, 39
War of the Axe, 115, 119, 140, 187
Washington, George, 288, 289–90
watan (homeland), 3, 6, 7, 179, 197, 236–38, 273, 286, 294, 299, 305, 309, 312
Wazir India (newspaper), 257
Wekanda Mosque, Colombo, 138, 161, 163, 172, 175–76
West Sumatra, 11

INDEX

Wickramasinghe, Nira, 18, 162
Wiera Mongolo, 139
al-Wifaq (journal), 302
Wiggers, Ferdinand, 258
Wilcocke, Samuel, 82–83
Wilhelmina, Queen, 258–59, 263, 275, 279
William V, Prince, 10, 60
Wilson, Charles, 209
Wilson, John, 154–55, 260
Wirakusuma, Raden Tumenggong (Amsterdam van de Kaap), 50–51, 151
Wira Wangsa, 139
Wirjopranoto, Soekardjo, 328
Wodehouse, P. E., 181, 183
Wolseley, Garnet, 206
women: education of, 193, 271; household responsibilities of, 64, 221; military contributions of, 160, 162, 172, 327–28; petitions from, 139–40, 221, 227; status and roles of, 301, 311, 323, 324; wives of Egyptian exiles in Ceylon, 221; worship by, 72
Wondoamiseno, 320, 322
World War I. *See* Great War
World War II, 316–32
Wright, Richard, 334
Writer, Sannadi, 157

Xhosa, 86, 97, 114, 190

Yahaya, Nurfadzilah, 19
Yahya, Imam, 304
Yaʿqub Sami, 214, 220–24, 226, 228
Yasin, Sayyid, 161
Yellen, Jeremy, 321
Yogyakarta, 91, 332–33
Yonge, George, 60, 61–62, 105
Young Turks, 263
Youth Congress (Batavia, 1928), 308
Yusr, Faraj, 242
Yusuf (son of Raja Oesman), 142
Yusuf al-Maqassari, Shaykh, 29–32, 34, 42, 51, 62, 63, 67, 70, 112, 134, 136, 183; *al-Nafha al-saylaniyya fi al-manha al-rahmaniyya* (*The Ceylonese Scent Concerning the Merciful Gift*), 30, 34

Zahira College, Ceylon, 229–30, 232, 291
Zanzibar, 100, 116, 127, 184–85, 192, 199
Zawahiri, Muhammad al-, 303
Zaynab, 192
Zayn al-Abidin, 37
Zayn al-Din al-Malaybari, 74
Zeepart (ship), 25
Zhou Enlai, 334
Zohrab, James, 248
Zorn, Johannes, 96–97
Zulu, 114, 190
Zulu Wars (1879), 199

COLUMBIA STUDIES IN INTERNATIONAL AND GLOBAL HISTORY
Cemil Aydin, Timothy Nunan, and Dominic Sachsenmaier, Series Editors

Cemil Aydin, *The Politics of Anti-Westernism in Asia: Visions of World Order in Pan-Islamic and Pan-Asian Thought*

Adam M. McKeown, *Melancholy Order: Asian Migration and the Globalization of Borders*

Patrick Manning, *The African Diaspora: A History Through Culture*

James Rodger Fleming, *Fixing the Sky: The Checkered History of Weather and Climate Control*

Steven Bryan, *The Gold Standard at the Turn of the Twentieth Century: Rising Powers, Global Money, and the Age of Empire*

Heonik Kwon, *The Other Cold War*

Samuel Moyn and Andrew Sartori, eds., *Global Intellectual History*

Alison Bashford, *Global Population: History, Geopolitics, and Life on Earth*

Adam Clulow, *The Company and the Shogun: The Dutch Encounter with Tokugawa Japan*

Richard W. Bulliet, *The Wheel: Inventions and Reinventions*

Simone M. Müller, *Wiring the World: The Social and Cultural Creation of Global Telegraph Networks*

Will Hanley, *Identifying with Nationality: Europeans, Ottomans, and Egyptians in Alexandria*

Perin E. Gürel, *The Limits of Westernization: A Cultural History of America in Turkey*

Dominic Sachsenmaier, *Global Entanglements of a Man Who Never Traveled: A Seventeenth-Century Chinese Christian and His Conflicted Worlds*

Perrin Selcer, *The UN and the Postwar Origins of the Global Environment: From World Community to Spaceship Earth*

Ulbe Bosma, *The Making of a Periphery: How Island Southeast Asia Became a Mass Exporter of Labor*

Raja Adal, *Beauty in the Age of Empire: Japan, Egypt, and the Global History of Aesthetic Education*

Mona L. Siegel, *Peace on Our Terms: The Global Battle for Women's Rights After the First World War*

Nicole CuUnjieng Aboitiz, *Asian Place, Filipino Nation: A Global Intellectual History of the Philippine Revolution, 1887-1912*

Michael Christopher Low, *Imperial Mecca: Ottoman Arabia and the Indian Ocean Hajj*

Jessica Namakkal, *Unsettling Utopia: The Making and Unmaking of French India*

Eva-Maria Muschik, *Building States: The United Nations, Development, and Decolonization, 1945-1965*

GPSR Authorized Representative: Easy Access System Europe, Mustamäe tee
50, 10621 Tallinn, Estonia, gpsr.requests@easproject.com

www.ingramcontent.com/pod-product-compliance
Lightning Source LLC
Chambersburg PA
CBHW031227290426
44109CB00012B/194